www.wadsworth.com

wadsworth.com is the World Wide Web site for Wadsworth and is your direct source to dozens of online resources.

At *wadsworth.com* you can find out about supplements, demonstration software, and student resources. You can also send email to many of our authors and preview new publications and exciting new technologies.

wadsworth.com
Changing the way the world learns®

EXPERIENCING MUSIC TECHNOLOGY

EXPERIENCING MUSIC TECHNOLOGY

3RD EDITION

David Brian Williams
Illinois State University

Peter Richard Webster
Northwestern University

THOMSON
SCHIRMER

Australia • Canada • Mexico • Singapore • Spain
United Kingdom • United States

THOMSON

SCHIRMER

Experiencing Music Technology, Third Edition
David Brian Williams, Peter Richard Webster

Publisher: Clark Baxter
Development Editor: Beth Hoeppner
Assistant Editor: Julie Yardley
Editorial Assistant: Emily Perkins
Technology Project Manager: Matt Dorsey
Marketing Manager: Diane Wenckebach
Marketing Assistant: Rachel Bairstow
Marketing Communications Manager: Patrick Rooney
Project Manager, Editorial Production: Paul Wells
Art Director: Maria Epes
Print Buyer: Doreen Suruki

Permissions Editor: Stephanie Lee
Production Service: Stratford Publishing Services, Inc.
Text Designer: Roy Neuhaus
Photo Researcher: Cheri Throop
Copy Editor: Frank Words
Illustrator: Stratford Publishing Services, Inc.
Cover Designer: Cuttriss & Hambleton
Cover Images: Photodisc Collection/Getty Images, Digital Vision/Getty Images, Steve Cole/Getty Images, Anthony Saint James/Getty Images
Compositor: Stratford Publishing Services, Inc.
Printer: Edwards Brothers, Incorporated

Printed in the United States of America
1 2 3 4 5 6 7 09 08 07 06 05

For more information about our products, contact us at:
Thomson Learning Academic Resource Center
1-800-423-0563
For permission to use material from this text or product, submit a request online at http://www.thomsonrights.com. Any additional questions about permissions can be submitted by email to thomsonrights@thomson.com

Library of Congress Control Number: 2004116285

ISBN 0-534-17672-0

Thomson Higher Education
10 Davis Drive
Belmont, CA 94002-3098
USA

Asia (including India)
Thomson Learning
5 Shenton Way
#01-01 UIC Building
Singapore 068808

Australia/New Zealand
Thomson Learning Australia
102 Dodds Street
Southbank, Victoria 3006
Australia

Canada
Thomson Nelson
1120 Birchmount Road
Toronto, Ontario M1K 5G4
Canada

UK/Europe/Middle East/Africa
Thomson Learning
High Holborn House
50–51 Bedford Row
London WC1R 4LR
United Kingdom

Latin America
Thomson Learning
Seneca, 53
Colonia Polanco
11560 Mexico
D.F. Mexico

Spain (including Portugal)
Thomson Paraninfo
Calle Magallanes, 25
28015 Madrid, Spain

To Kay and Connie

Brief Contents

Contents

VIEWPORT VI Doing More with MIDI and Beyond 269

Module 17 Adventures in Sound Shaping and Synthesis 272

Module 18 Extending MIDI: Controllers, SoundFonts, and Timing 311

VIEWPORT VII   Music Notation   331

Module 19   Coding Systems for Music Notation and Performance   335

Preface

"By looking for the structure in signals, how they were generated, we go beyond the surface appearance of bits and discover the building blocks out of which image, sound, or text came. This is one of the most important facts of digital life."

—*Nicholas Negroponte*, Being Digital (1995)

Welcome to the third edition of *Experiencing Music Technology*! If you are familiar with the earlier versions of this textbook, we hope you will appreciate the changes herein and find this version as useful as the last. If you are a new reader, we hope you will enjoy this introduction to music technology and its role in the contemporary music scene.

Writing about this field is exciting. Many times since the last edition, we have stopped the process of reviewing and testing new software and hardware, remarking to each other how truly amazing the field's achievements have been since our last edition. In 1993, when we first decided to create this textbook, we were motivated in large part by the power of music technology to enhance the experience of musicians of all ages and experience levels. As researchers, educators, and musicians, we saw the role of music technology as a major force in teaching the technical aspects of music and, perhaps most importantly, encouraging the creative experience of music composition, improvisation, performance, and music listening. More than 12 years later as we conclude this edition, we believe this more than ever before.

Of course, updating such a book presents us with one obvious challenge: the persistence of change. Developments in hardware, software, and even the very culture of music technology itself seem to escalate exponentially. Since 1999, we have seen: (1) major operating-system changes in both PC and Macintosh computers, (2) a tripling of the power of personal computers accompanied by major drops in cost, (3) literally hundreds of new music-software titles in every major category produced by companies in the United States and abroad, (4) new hardware devices for a variety of music needs at all price points, and (5) major shifts in the way music is acquired and enjoyed by us all. Just a few of the new technologies we have seen emerge include mobile computing, wireless, DVD and surround sound, soft synths and effects, and the prevailing dominance of digital audio, with a bias toward software rather than hardware solutions. All of this has an obvious effect on our ability to do a credible job of accounting for the field, for those both inside and outside academe.

The task is made a little easier because of the approach we have taken since the start. In each edition, we concentrate less on the specifics of each software program or piece of hardware and devote most of our space to what to expect in, for example, a good MIDI-keyboard or sequencing program. We do refer to specific products that are as current as possible, but we do so with the idea that the specifics are of less importance than an overall understanding of how the products function and the future direction of the technology. This approach continues in the third edition.

What also keeps the book current is our attention to the future. In the second edition, for example, we anticipated the growth of the Internet as a resource for teaching and for music productivity. Our design for categorizing computer-aided instruction continues to be valid and useful for bringing order to this important part of music technology. Certainly the tendency for digital audio to be used more pervasively as part of sequencing and notation software has been carried to levels beyond our expectations. Predicted advances in DVD, computer connectivity, and other hardware and conceptual content have come to pass in the last four years. In this edition, we continue to chronicle what is clearly on the horizon for the near term, including such developments as Internet 2 for musicians, wireless and mobile computing, surround sound and MPEG, miniaturization, and software emulation of hardware.

Readers will note that we have also retained our accent on people and how they put technology to use (procedures) as the most important elements of music technology. Based on our continued experience as teachers, consultants, and workshop leaders, we continue to believe in the critical importance of understanding the underlying concepts and data structures for how music software and hardware function to help us be more musical and use the technology to full advantage. We also have continued to organize topic material into larger sections called *Viewports*. For us, Viewports are "portals" for "viewing" and organizing major topics that reflect people's common use of music technology, such as digital audio, notation, and computer-aided instruction. We have created revised modules in each larger section to reflect the concepts of data structures, software, and hardware. The accompanying DVD-ROM contains newly crafted projects for each major section of the book.

So, What's New?

Since our last writing, we have been pleased to hear from many students and instructors who have used the book. Our research shows that the book is the most widely used one in introductory college and university courses and this positive response has been most gratifying. We also find the book used in many other settings such as public schools and community colleges and for self-study. We are deeply indebted to the reviewers of the last edition, some known to us and others who remain anonymous. Many have offered extensive and detailed suggestions for change and we have included as many of those suggestions as possible.

This has led to two major changes. First, sections on graphics and stand-alone multimedia have been removed in order to focus attention on music issues. This has made the book leaner and more focused on the material most requested by our readers. Secondly, we have re-ordered the viewports. After the opening sections on musicians and their use of technology and on computer and Internet concepts, we present two completely reorganized sections on digital audio. This reflects the amazing growth of digital audio as part of the music-technology scene. We continue with a newly crafted viewport on sequencing with MIDI and digital audio and a new software module on advanced MIDI sequencing, together with sound shaping and synthesis. Newly designed viewports on music notation and computer-aided instruction conclude the book.

Introductions are briefer and include more attention to content objectives for the coming viewport. A more-comprehensive approach to software comparisons and hardware-equipment models is presented throughout the book.

Finally, the book contains all new sections on important leading-edge topics in technology, including: MPEG-4, streaming, surround sound, DVD, plug-ins, soft synths and samplers, virtual studios, web-based notation, wireless technology, and USB and Firewire.

Book Content and Goals

Experiencing Music Technology, 3rd Edition, covers the essential topics a musician should consider when exploring the use of computers and technology in the many aspects of the music experience: listening, performing, composing, teaching, and managing. The book is designed as an introductory resource for a wide audience both inside and outside the academic setting. Although it is introductory in scope, it still provides considerable depth of coverage on critical music-technology topics.

Modular in design, the book's resources can be used in many ways. Although intended as the text for a complete undergraduate or graduate course of study devoted to music technology, it can also serve as a supplemental resource for other courses in the curriculum: general musicianship, piano pedagogy, theory and aural skills, arranging and orchestration, music composition and improvisation, instructional design, and other contemporary topics.

In addition, the book can be easily read and used for self-study by people who are simply curious about and intrigued by the use of computers for music making. Professional musicians, parents, children, computer aficionados, and lay musicians of all kinds may find the book helpful in increasing their understanding of music technology.

Experiencing Music Technology is designed to meet the following goals:

- Provide a conceptual overview of music and technology by combining tutorial material on the DVD-ROM with essential study and reference material
- Give a broad perspective of the many ways people can use technology in music applications
- Offer modular organization of the material to provide flexibility for the reader and the instructor
- Note historic milestones in music computing and technology
- Promote a systems approach to computer understanding, planning, and implementation by stressing five components: people, procedures, data, software, and hardware
- Emphasize hardware and software unique to music applications
- Focus on the conceptual and cross-application features that define current commercial hardware and software
- Avoid featuring industry-specific products for their own sake, instead emphasizing features in common or contrast with other products to illustrate their general application to music experiences.

Experiencing Music Technology Companion DVD-ROM and Support Website

A companion DVD-ROM disc included with this text is designed to run on both Macintosh and PC computers. While the textbook illustrates concepts of music technology with a broad range of software examples, the DVD-ROM provides hands-on activities focused on specific commercial software to parallel the major topics in the book. All of the materials on the DVD-ROM have been designed as web pages that can be easily viewed through a web browser.

Each DVD-ROM software activity is a tutorial that features step-by-step directions for using a specific software application. A generous number of screen shots are provided to illustrate the steps in the tutorials. Links are included to related materials, including worksheets that students can use to track their progress and teachers can use to evaluate work completed. These worksheets can be viewed and printed right from the web browser or from any word processor. In addition, selected study materials have been placed on the DVD-ROM.

The website for the book is www.emtbook.net. Be sure to check this site frequently for added project tutorials and other helpful resources.

DVD-ROM
Watch for the DVD-ROM icon throughout the book for hands-on software experiences on the DVD-ROM enclosed with this textbook.

Icons in the Margin of the Book

To help you as you progress through each chapter, we have created several icons that will alert you to different levels of help. Watch for these icons:

- LINKS to helpful information related to this topic elsewhere in the book

- TIPS that are especially helpful to those just starting to use computers and music technology

- ASIDES that are interesting notes for reading enjoyment and mind expansion

- DVD-ROM tutorial materials: training on the DVD-ROM that accompanies this textbook and provides hands-on experience with software noted in the textbook

Definitions

In addition to the term *viewport,* a few other terms are critical in this book. We need to be sure that you understand what terms like *musician, music experience, computer,* and *technology* mean for us.

Musician

The term *musician* refers to anyone, at any level of sophistication, engaged in music experiences. This definition of musician includes the parent, child, student, teacher, administrator, performer, and composer. We realize that the usual use of this term refers to individuals with advanced skills in music, particularly in performance. However, in the interest of promoting a view of music computing accessible to the widest-possible audience, we have chosen this more-relaxed definition.

Music Experience

Music experience refers to the fundamental ways people interact with music cognitively, emotionally, and aesthetically. Included in this are the processes of listening to, performing, and composing music, which are the hallmarks of music as art. Throughout this book, we are interested in ways that technology can enhance these fundamental aspects of experiencing music. In addition, we are concerned with how technology can help with teaching and studying music and managing music activities. Although these activities are not primary music experiences, they are vital to music as practiced in our society.

Computer

The term *computer,* as used in this book, refers to small computer systems commonly known as personal computers. In creating our illustrations, we have chosen to focus on the two primary icon-based computing environments used today by musicians: (1) IBM PCs and their compatibles, commonly referred to as either "Windows" or "PC" machines, and (2) Macintosh, sometimes called "Mac," computers. Throughout the book, we refer to these as either "Macintosh" or "PC" machines, or "Macintosh" or "Windows" operating systems, regardless of whether the versions are OS 8, OS 9, OS X, Windows 2000, Windows NT, Windows XP, or any future versions of these. By *icon-based,* we mean operating systems that use graphic images or *icons* for common operations with the computer.

Technology

The term *technology* refers to computers and all of the music and nonmusic peripherals needed to perform music tasks with computers. These peripheral devices include such hardware as electronic-music keyboards, MIDI controllers, printers, scanners, CD players, and so on.

Acknowledgments

First, we'd like to renew our thanks to everyone recognized in the two previous editions for their generous help, insights, and guidance in bringing this book project to fruition. For this third edition, we extend our sincere thanks to James Frankel (Teachers College, Columbia University), Sara Hagen (Valley City State University), Evelyn K. Orman (Louisiana State University), several anonymous reviewers who offered insightful critiques of the second edition, and a number of colleagues across the country who have read portions of the new edition and offered comment, factual accuracy, and revised wording. These include a select group of people who provided technical reviews of our written materials: Frank Clark (Georgia Institute of Technology), Don Byrd (Indiana University), Chris Douglas (Edirol), Scott Genung (Illinois State University), Ken Johnson (M-Audio), Virgil Moorefield and Scott Lipscomb (Northwestern University), and Ken Pohlmann (University of Miami). Then there were those who came through with critical information and support materials at just the right time: James Bohn; John Dunn (Indiana University); David Dvorin (eMagic); Ben Flin, Peter Maund, and Greg Smith (Sibelius); Bill Hanson (Apple Computer); Billee Kraut (AABACA); Tom Lykins (Sound Marketing); Tom Johnson (MakeMusic!); Henry Panion (University of Alabama-Birmingham); Sam Reese (University of Illinois); Perry Roland (University of Virginia); Eleanor Selfridge-Field (Center for Computer Assisted Research in the Humanities), Tom White (MIDI Manufacturers Association); Lee and Laura Whitmore (SoundTree/Korg); Larry Worster (The Metropolitan State College of Denver); and Bobbie Thornton (SoundTree); and numerous industry contacts who came through with photos and information for us. These professionals have added enormously to the reliability and validity of the material herein. Of course, any errors remain solely our responsibility.

Thanks go to the many students who have taken our courses and to colleagues in our workshops and conference sessions who have offered much help with their thoughtful questions and suggestions over these last three years. A special thanks to Marc Jacoby, Jay Dorfman, and Maria Horvath, who helped with certain DVD-ROM projects.

To the administrators at our respective universities, Illinois State and Northwestern, we offer our appreciation for the support given over the past 12 years for our book research and those scholarly activities that work in tandem with this activity.

Our final acknowledgments go to Linda DeMasi, Clark Baxter, and Beth Hoeppner. Linda at Stratford Publishing wonderfully navigated the pressures of the final publication process with exceptional finesse. Clark and Beth, our editors at Wadsworth, helped us over several speed bumps in the transition from Schirmer Books to Wadsworth Publishing. Clark and Beth showed remarkable patience and perseverance with two authors who attempted to interweave writing and research time with many other administrative and teaching responsibilities and they have our thanks!

David Brian Williams, Normal, Illinois
Peter Richard Webster, Winnetka, Illinois

About the Authors

David Brian Williams and Peter Richard Webster have partnered for more than 15 years to provide leadership to the music profession in technology applications; workshops on the application of technology to music and music education; and presentations for state, national, and international conferences, including MENC, CMS, ATMI, and NASM.

David Brian Williams is Professor of Music and Arts Technology at Illinois State University. Dr. Williams founded one of the first nationally recognized integrated arts technology programs and has recently completed a four-year appointment as Associate Vice President for Information Technology on his campus. In the late 1970s, he cofounded Micro Music, Inc., and developed numerous music-education titles for the Apple II and the MMI DAC sound card. He has written extensively in the areas of music education, music psychology, music and arts technology, and instructional development. He has served on the boards of MENC, CMS, Illinois Music Educators Association, and ATMI. He chaired the MENC task force for developing Opportunity-to-Learn Standards for Music Technology and, in 2001, received the Illinois Music Educators Association Distinguished Service Award for his work in music technology.

Peter Richard Webster is the John Beattie Professor of Music Education and Technology at Northwestern University's School of Music, where he also serves as the Associate Dean for Academic Affairs and Research, directs doctoral research in music education, and serves on the music technology, cognition, and music-education faculties. He is the author of Measures of Creative Thinking in Music, an assessment tool designed for children aged 6–10. He has published in numerous professional publications, such as *Music Educators Journal*, *Journal of Research in Music Education*, *CRME Bulletin*, *Contributions to Music Education*, *Arts Education and Policy Review*, *Research Studies in Music Education*, *Music Education Research*, and *Psychomusicology*. He has authored chapters in several books, including chapters on creative thinking in music and music technology research in the first and second editions of the *Handbook of Research on Music Teaching and Learning*. He has served on the board of CMS and is the immediate past president of ATMI.

Musicians and Their Use of Technology

"Computing is not about computers anymore. It is about living."

—*Nicholas Negroponte*, Being Digital (*1995*)

"Technology is easy; people are hard."

—*John Gage of Sun Microsystems*, CAUSE Computer Conference, *Orlando, FL* (*1997*)

Overview

The overarching design of this course of study in music technology is based on a systems model. This model, applied to music technology, emphasizes five components: people, procedures, data, software, and hardware. Our first Viewport focuses on the most important component of a computer music system: the *people* or musicians who are involved in *using* and *making* music technology.

Objectives

In Module 1, we provide background on *people making technology* and highlight some of the most important historical developments. Contrary to some beliefs, the field has a long history and is not a new phenomenon. We briefly summarize five periods of development and provide a listing of some of the most important people in the field. Module 2 focuses on *people using technology* in music, noting some shortcomings and strengths of technology. We introduce you to a number of real-life individuals who regularly use technology in music. Module 3 provides some thoughts on *people questioning technology*. We address commonly held misconceptions in the hope of improving general attitudes about this subject. Module 4 concludes this introductory Viewport with *people helping with technology*. Here we point you toward important resources you can turn to when you need expertise in computing and music technology.

At the end of this Viewport, you should understand:

- The importance of people in music technology
- Historical periods in music technology development, including the names of key individuals
- Common misconceptions
- How people use technology

DVD-ROM
As with all software modules in this text, the accompanying DVD contains hands-on software projects to help you to practice your skills.

- How best to pace yourself in learning
- Where to get help with technology

DVD-ROM Software Projects

For Viewport I, as you learn about the importance of people in music technology, you should be able to:

- Interview a professional who routinely uses technology (Project 1)
- Find help for your computing and music technology needs (Project 2)

M o d u l e   1

People Making Technology

LINK
Be sure to consult the Selected Readings section at the end of this text for much more information on the fascinating history of music technology.

It's difficult to imagine any aspect of music today that is not touched by technology. As listeners, we hear recorded music that has been produced by advanced digital techniques. As performers, we use instruments and perform in spaces that have benefited from countless technological advances in materials and design. As composers and arrangers, we no longer rely on pencil and paper alone to represent our music; powerful computers, printers, and electronic sound devices provide additional resources for our creative thinking. As educators and scholars engaged in thinking, writing, and talking about music, we use many advanced tools to support our analyses and illustrations. Certainly, the way we experience music today is far different from the way the previous generation did when they were young. This book helps to explain why this is so.

Ballet of Technology and Music

Where did all these technology advances come from? People, of course—people making technology. There is a long history of people looking for new tools to feed our enjoyment of listening, performing, and creating music. This can be viewed as a fascinating ballet played out over the centuries between the demand for new tools for creative expression and people using the technological innovations of the time to meet the demand. Devices for reproducing music performance are a case in point. Consider the evolution of the music box to the player piano, to the vinyl recording, to the personal music players we now carry in our pockets as we walk or jog for exercise.

Music technology development required the help of physicists, engineers, inventors, scientists, and mathematicians interested in music. As these people collaborated, an avenue of technological development was built. Often, these inventive minds kept coming back to the same problems, each time with a new level of sophistication. You will see that the pursuit of both better music and better number machines (computers) helped improve both technologies.

Throughout this book, you will find references to both music and computer technology from five historical periods.

Five Periods of Technology History

Period I (1600s–mid-1800s)

During this period, number and music machines depended on imaginative applications of mechanical gears, cogs, cams, and levers. Here we see music machines such as music boxes, calliopes, mechanical organs, player pianos, and mechanical phonograph recorders and jukeboxes—machines that you have to wind up and crank. Number machines included the Calculating Clock, the Pascaline, and the Babbage Difference Engine. Charles Babbage set the stage for the evolution of computers some 200 years later.

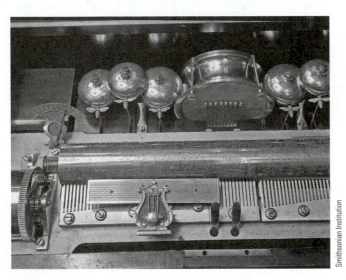

FIGURE 1.1 Swiss music box with music coded as pins on a cylinder

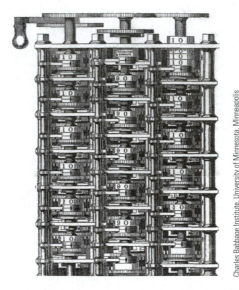

FIGURE 1.2 Woodcut impression of Babbage's Difference Engine No. 1

Period II (mid-1800s–early 1900s)

During this period, number and music machines took advantage of the invention of electricity and electric motors to automate the mechanical solutions of Period I, thanks to Thomas Edison and others. Here we see music machines such as the Singing Arc, the Telharmonium, and the Hammond organ. For number machines, we have the Arithmometer, the early calculators of Moore and Burroughs, and the early analog computers of Bush and Zuse.

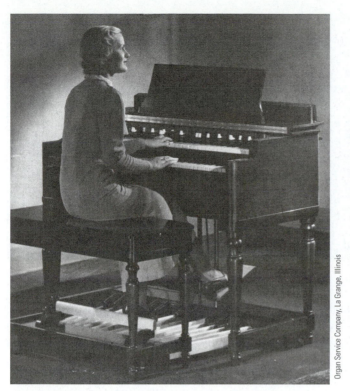

FIGURE 1.3   Early Hammond organ; sound produced with motorized spinning disks

FIGURE 1.4   One of the dynamos from Cahill's Telharmonium

Period III (early 1900s–mid-1900s)

During this period, number and music machines benefited from the unique technology that vacuum tubes and electromagnetic relay switches provided. Lee de Forest's invention of oscillators and amplifiers from vacuum tubes had a revolutionary impact on music and computer technology.

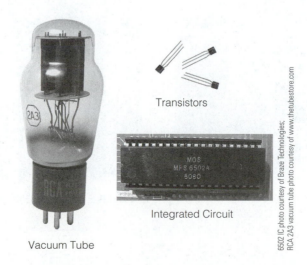

Transistors

Integrated Circuit

FIGURE 1.5   Migration from tubes to transistors to integrated circuits

Vacuum Tube

FIGURE 1.6 Harry Olson at the keyboard and Herbert Belar with the 1955 Columbia–Princeton Mark I Music Synthesizer

David Sarnoff Research Center

FIGURE 1.7 Alexandra Stepanoff playing the RCA Theremin, 1930

Smithsonian Institution

The vacuum-tube oscillator was an incredible boon to music machines. Not only did it lead to the design of amplifiers, phonographs, tape recorders, jukeboxes, and even early electric guitars but it also provided the earliest attempts at electronic performing instruments. Products of this generation include the Theremin, Trautonium, Ondes Martenot, and the early synthesizers of Givelet

FIGURE 1.8 Staff showing off circuit boards from early computers, including the ENIAC, EDVAC, ORDVAC, and BRLESC-I.

U.S. Army

FIGURE 1.9 ARP 2600 transistor-based synthesizer

Kevin Lightner and www.synthfool.com

FIGURE 1.10   Popular transistor-based portable Buchla music synthesizer

FIGURE 1.11   DEC transistor-based PDP-8 minicomputer

and Coupleux. Even today, some musicians prefer the soft and smooth sound of tube technology. For number machines, vacuum tubes led to the construction of "tube-monster" computers like the ENIAC, EDVAC, UNIVAC, ABC, and, for music, the Columbia–Princeton Mark I Music Synthesizer. Many were as big as city blocks.

Period IV (mid-1900s–1970s)

During the fourth period, number and music machines were completely transformed by the transistor and semiconductors. With the invention of the transistor—thanks to the engineers at Bell Labs—came modularity, smallness, and electronic flexibility. Robert Moog's design of voltage-controlled circuits and Donald Buchla's electronic sequencers led to the first portable commercial music synthesizers. Almost any school or musician could purchase an ARP or a Putney and begin exploring electronic music and the world of sound and acoustics. The same trend transformed number machines. Not only did the "big iron" get bigger (computers like the IBM 360 series and the CDC 6000s and Cybers), but computers became portable, commercial, and common. The DEC PDP-8 ushered in the era of minicomputers.

Period V (1970s–present)

In the current period of technology, number and music machines became exponentially smaller and more powerful, thanks to the inventions of Jack Kilby and Robert Noyce, which led to mass production of integrated circuits (ICs). The transistor was soon followed by the first Intel microprocessor chip. With ICs and chips, music and number machines became ever smaller and cheaper. Music and number machines joined forces and out came music synthesizers with computing power rivaling the minicomputers of the last decade. MIDI and FM, digital, and physical modeling synthesis all emerged in small portable boxes: keyboards, controllers, drum machines, sound modules, and more. For number machines, the personal computer or PC put more CPU power and memory into every home, desktop, lap, and palm than the designers of the city-blockwide ENIAC ever dreamed of. The Apple II, IBM PC, Macintosh, Dell Latitude, Palm Pilot, iPod, and many other computer devices were born.

FIGURE 1.12 M-Audio Ozone USB keyboard with digital audio, MIDI, and MIDI controllers

M-Audio

FIGURE 1.13 Dell Latitude laptop

Dell Computer, Inc.

Important People in Music Technology's Development

The following is a brief list of some key personalities who have contributed to the evolution of music technology and the use of technology for music instruction.

1646–1716	Leibniz, Gottfried	Studied binary system of numbers and proposed binary calculator
1653–1716	Sauveau, Joseph	Discovered overtone series
1768–1830	Fourier, Jean	Developed Fourier synthesis, basis for systems of music synthesis
1791–1871	Babbage, Charles	Designed earliest calculating machines that would automate computing of navigation tables and solve mathematical problems
1815–1864	Boole, George	Founder of Boolean algebra or logic, pivotal concept in internal logic operations of computers
1821–1894	von Helmholtz, Hermann	Pioneering work on physics and acoustics of sound, *On the Sensations of Tone*
1847–1931	Edison, Thomas	Founder of phonograph and many other inventions that figured critically in development of music technology
1867–1934	Cahill, Thaddeus	Inventor of Telharmonium; explored synthesis of complex tones
1873–1961	de Forest, Lee	Credited with designing first electrical oscillator and first valve amplifier with vacuum tubes
1882–1961	Grainger, Percy	With Burnett Cross, built early music synthesizer with eight oscillators that could be synchronized
1883–1965	Varèse, Edgard	Wide use of various electronic composition techniques; *Equatorial* used Theremins, *Déserts* used tape techniques
1889–1963	Givelet, Armand	With Coupleux, developed one of first analog synthesizers, with four oscillators controlled by punched paper rolls
1895–1973	Hammond, Laurens	Designed and produced Hammond organ in 1928
1896–1993	Theremin, Leon	Inventor of Theremin, early popular electronic performing instrument
1900–1996	Luening, Otto	Produced some of first taped composition in United States; cofounded Columbia–Princeton Electronic Music Center with Ussachevsky
1901–1982	Olson, Harry	With Herbert Belar, constructed RCA Mark I and II music synthesizers used at Columbia–Princeton
1903–1995	Atanasoff, John	With Clifford Berry, invented ABC, first computer
1903–1957	von Neumann, John	Designed EDVAC, first electronic computer with stored computer program
1907–1980	Mauchly, John	With Brainerd and Eckert, built ENIAC, one of first general-purpose electronic digital computers, which used 17,468 vacuum tubes!
1910–1989	Shockley, William	One of inventors of transistor at Bell Labs; his California company started Silicon Valley
1914–2003	Kuhn, Wolfgang	With Reynold Allvin, developed early computer-based instruction with mainframe computer connected to electronic organ
1916–	Babbitt, Milton	Composed *Ensembles for Synthesizer and Philomel* on RCA Mark II synthesizer; worked with Luening and Ussachevsky
1916–	Shannon, Claude	Applied symbolic logic to relay circuits; information can be quantified and manipulated by machine

(continued)

important people in music technology's development (continued)

1918–	Forrester, Jay	Developed magnetic-core memory as alternative to vacuum-tube technology; used in MIT Whirlwind computer system
1923–	Kilby, Jack	Invented first working integrated circuit
1924–1994	Hiller, Lejaren	With Isaacson at University of Illinois, created first computer-composed musical work, *Illiac Suite* (1957)
1925–	Boulez, Pierre	Prominent contemporary electronic composer and founder of Institut de Recherche et Coordination Acoustique/Musique (IRCAM)
1925–	Smith, Leland	Wrote SCORE notation program, among first powerful notation programs for minicomputer; later translated to IBM PC
1926–	Mathews, Max	Considered father of digital sound synthesis; created first software at Bell Labs to control parameters of music through computer
1927–	Carlsen, James	Created one of first commercially successful programmed instruction tape series for melodic dictation, published by McGraw-Hill
1928–	Stockhausen, Karlheinz	First to explore additive synthesis and to carefully score his electronic works; composed *Studies I and II* in 1953
1932–	Oliveros, Pauline	First woman to be known primarily for her electronic music work; helped found San Francisco Tape Center in 1961
1934–	Bitzer, Don	Inventor of Control Data PLATO computer-assisted instruction system at University of Illinois
1934–	Chowning, John	Inventor of FM synthesis; established Center for Computer Research in Music and Acoustics (CCRMA)
1934–	Moog, Robert	Name synonymous with synthesizers due to popularity of his instruments; built first synthesizer using voltage-controlled oscillators, amplifiers, and semiconductors
1937–	Buchla, Donald	Designed popular voltage-controlled modular synthesizer installations of 1970s; collaborated with composer Morton Subotnick
1937–	Hoff, Marcian, Jr.	Invented first microprocessor chip, Intel 4004/8008
1938–	Risset, Jean-Claude	Bell Labs; worked with Mathews; pioneering work with analysis of complex tones and waveshaping synthesis
1939–	Appleton, John	Composer and collaborator in development of Synclavier synthesizer and ABEL computer

1942–	Peters, G. David	Developed early CAI applications for PLATO system and founded Electronic Courseware Systems
1943–	Williams, David Brian	With David Shrader, founded Micro Music, Inc., and developed some of first commercial CAI music programs for personal computers
1945–	Moorer, James	Produced some of first 3-D analyses of music waveforms at Stanford University
1945–	Winter, Robert	Authored first commercial music HyperCard stack to use interactive audio CD
1946–	Speigel, Laurie	Composer and codeveloper of GROOVE music system at Bell Labs; designer of music software and hardware devices, such as Music Mouse
1948–	Kurzweil, Ray	With Robert Moog, created Kurzweil Music System, which produced authentic grand piano sound for portable music keyboard
1949–	Hofstetter, Fred	Author of GUIDO music curriculum developed initially for PLATO system, and producer of Delaware Videodisc Music Series
1950–	Wozniak, Steve ("Woz")	With Steve Jobs, built 6502-based microcomputer with BASIC, Apple I, and founded Apple Computer, Inc. in 1975
1953–	Machover, Todd	Composer of numerous contemporary works and designer of new technology for music; his *Brain Opera* invites audience to use his "hyperinstruments" to participate in music live or over Internet
1955–	Gates, William "Bill"	With Paul Allen, wrote BASIC interpreter for Altair 8800 microcomputer and founded Microsoft Corporation
1955–	Berners-Lee, Tim	Created concept of World Wide Web and first web client and server; he defined URL, HTTP, and HTML in 1990 at CERN, the European Particle Physics Laboratory
1958–	Gannon, Peter	Canadian physician and amateur musician who created first computer-aided accompaniment software, Band-in-a-Box, and founded PG Music Inc. in 1988
1971–	Andreesen, Marc	Designed first graphical browser for World Wide Web, NCSA Mosaic, and cofounded Netscape Communications with James Clark, founder of Silicon Graphics
19–	Scarletti, Carla	Designer of Kyma, visual language for specifying and manipulating digital audio signals; composer and computer scientist, founder of Symbolic Sound Corporation, and researcher at University of Illinois CERL Sound Group

Module 2

People Using Technology

Before we go further in our study of computers and music technology, it's important to understand that *people using technology* is the most important component of a computer music system. Whatever great achievements flow from the process of using technology in music making, it is not the machines that should earn the credit. Rather, the human mind and creative spirit are responsible. Likewise, artistic failures are not attributable to the medium alone. Despite our society's constant attempt to blame the computer for this or that, ultimately it is a "people problem." We are the artists forming art, not the machines.

The Unexpected Turn

We will address some of the common misconceptions that lead to questionable attitudes about technology in the next module, but one needs to be mentioned immediately. This is the myth that machines, like computers or electronic music keyboards, are somehow smarter than people.

There is little doubt that a digital computer can accomplish amazing things. For some time now, computers have been able to do routine (and sometimes not-so-routine) mathematical calculations, item sorting, and data transformations—often at remarkable speeds. Computers can make informed decisions, communicate at a basic and even a not-so-basic level with other computers, and—most importantly for musicians and artists—display, sound, and print a wide variety of information. More recently, there have been major advances in the ability of computers to record and play back music, control external sound devices, and recognize speech and the printed word.

In all of this, three important points must be remembered. First, programmers and engineers have created these abilities; the computer is entirely at the mercy of the software that controls it. Actually, computers are somewhat ignorant. You will see in the next Viewport that all a computer understands inherently is whether a switch is on or off. Granted, it knows about millions of these switches and it can accomplish this switching with extreme speed, but it has no more ability than this. It takes human intelligence, sensitivity, and creativity to make the computer offer its power to others.

Second, central to this creativity is the human ability to think with the added complexity of feeling—or what is commonly referred to as the affect or aesthetic dimension. Yes, we can imagine programming a machine to respond to us in subtle ways that simulate the simplistic surface indications of affect. Remember Hal—the computer in Arthur Clarke's *2001: A Space Odyssey*? We can imagine code being written to do just what Hal did—perhaps even more impressively. But no amount of programming imaginable today can simulate the deep emotional feeling in Yo Yo Ma's mind during the closing moments of a live performance as he shapes a musical phrase in one of Bach's unaccompanied cello suites. It is quite doubtful that any machine can replicate the complex web of thought and feeling that must have occurred in the mind of Igor Stravinsky as he conceived the "Sacrificial Dance" in *Rite of Spring*, Charlie Parker as he improvised classic solos that so influenced the jazz world, or Nadia Boulanger as she thought of new and subtle ways to teach students like Aaron Copland, Darius Milhaud, and Elliott Carter.

Third, and maybe most important, it is inconceivable at this point in history that people can create hardware and software systems that come close to the human ability to think, feel, and understand in a way that can approximate the creation of music as art. We freely admit that advances in artificial intelligence research have given computers and connected devices some extraordinary capabilities, as we shall see in the coming modules on music notation and composition. But the ability of humans to make intuitive leaps and links as they store and process information is vastly superior to even the most advanced computer system today and in the foreseeable future. Consider this, as well: Even if it were possible for a machine to come reasonably close to the complexity of thought and feeling in human cognition, what about the machine's ability to communicate these subtleties to other machines in ways that parallel our ability as humans to exchange ideas, create art, and pass on culture—in short, to contribute to society?

So what's the point? Simply this: Because of the genuinely human attribute of affect, musicians as creative artists are acutely aware of that unexpected turn in the creative process that is inspired by the complex commingling of rational thought with intuition, feeling, and imagination. It is this fascinatingly human mixture that makes people far more important in the creative process than the technology itself. Hardware and software will constantly improve and will continue to be tremendous aids to the creative musician, but such technology stands quite apart from the capacity of humans to conceive and execute great art or to understand and convey its import.

Given all this, it seems far more meaningful to consider the role of technology in the hands of musicians who have demonstrated their ability to use it in a creative way. Such people will serve as inspirational guides for us as we set our course through the maze of computers and music technology in the sections that follow.

Innovation and Creativity

Artists and musicians find that technology can open new and exciting doors to empower their creative needs. Oftentimes, innovation in technology and creative expression go hand in hand. Many of these creative products come from using technology to manipulate sound and graphics and from interactive uses of music devices controlled through the Music Instrument Digital Interface, or MIDI.

Your imagination, be it visual or aural, can be expressed in a neutral, unbiased form—binary numbers in the computer. As binary numbers—a topic to be discussed in more detail in subsequent modules—all sound, text, and graphics are

TABLE 2.1
To Be or Not to Be

	Binary	Decimal
T	01010100	84
O	01001111	79
	00100000	32
B	01000010	66
E	01000101	69
	00100000	32
O	01001111	79
R	01010010	82
	00100000	32
N	01001110	78
O	01001111	79
T	01010100	84

stored in the computer as alternating sequences of ones and zeros. Table 2.1 shows Hamlet's well-known phrase transformed first to the decimal numbers (ASCII codes) used to represent letters by all computers and then to the binary values the machine understands.

As a tantalizing aside, think of some interesting possibilities. A computer image of Andy Warhol could be heard by playing the image back through MIDI sounds. Or, the computer codes for the sounds of the Grateful Dead could be seen by displaying the music as graphics. Pretty far-out stuff, but certainly possible. Visual artists like Joan Truckenbrod and musicians like Charles Ames provide some of the early artistic efforts for using fractals, artificial intelligence, expert rule systems, and other techniques to transform mathematical structures into music and art. Figure 2.1 shows a sample of Truckenbrod's computer-generated art, which she calls a "diagrammatic dialogue," and Ames's computer-generated music, "Concurrence." Ames's diagram for his solo violin piece represents a relational network or knowledge base used to guide closeness or distance between rhythmic patterns.

FIGURE 2.1A
Computer-generated art and music: "Differential Morphology" by Joan Truckenbrod

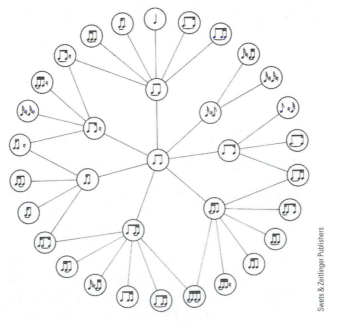

FIGURE 2.1B
"Concurrence" by Charles Ames (*Interface: Journal of New Music Research,* 17, n.1, 1988)

Pacing

The many ways people use technology provide you with a wonderful repertoire of ideas for putting computers to use in your work as a musician. We can use computers to:

- Organize music information and communicate with musicians
- Publish information about music
- Play games (preferably music ones!)
- Learn about music
- Conduct historic, analytic, and systematic research
- Perform music
- Chat with friends and colleagues over the Internet
- Compose and notate music
- Create music software and multimedia

However, with all these activities it must be remembered that using music technology takes practice. It is not realistic to think that you can understand a sophisticated digital audio program or a music sequencer and hardware synthesizer in an afternoon. Just like learning to play a musical instrument competently takes time, so too does learning music hardware and software. We suggest that you approach computers through a gradual process, gaining experience along the way that will generalize quickly to the next stages. For example, learning a beginning-level sequencing program as completely as you can helps enormously with more advanced software in the same family and in applying more advanced digital audio and music notation techniques.

A comparison to swimming pool psychology might be helpful. As you learn to swim, you wisely select the low end of the pool to start, then more boldly move to the middle of the pool, and then progress on to the deep end. Much satisfaction and real learning occur at all three depths. The last thing a new swimmer should do is to head for the diving board right away. This book will provide support for whatever level makes sense for you.

Music Technology in Practice

It takes little effort to find examples of people actively engaged in using music technology and music applications at all of these levels. Figure 2.2 shows college students using a multimedia lab for various applications and Figure 2.3 captures a moment with two middle school students learning to use a MIDI keyboard. Everywhere you look, you will find *people using technology* for music enjoyment, study, composition, and performance.

In each Viewport, check out the Music Technology in Practice area in the Introduction section. We have found examples for you of real people using technology for music in creative ways:

Viewport II: Chi Fan, a student using both Mac and Windows PCs for web searching, created her own website.

FIGURE 2.2 A computer lab used for music teaching at Northwestern University

FIGURE 2.3 Two middle-school students working with an iMac and a digital keyboard

DVD-ROM
Project 1 Interviewing Professionals Who Use Technology

Viewport III: Kevin Robbins, a church minister, who is a "taper," recording his favorite jazz and blues groups in live concert (where taping is permitted, of course); and Nate DeYoung, a student who has built a large collection of MP3 music files.

Viewport IV: John Shirley, a music professor, who built a laptop digital recording rig in a backpack and wandered Cambodia recording indigenous music; and Aaron Paolucci, a sound designer, who builds his own speakers and creates surround-sound recording on CD laser discs.

Viewport V: Jeff Shuter, a young freelance composer and arranger in Hollywood, who uses sequencing and digital audio software and some unusual hardware to create soundtracks for films.

Viewport VI: Henry Panion, a composer, conductor, and music professor, who uses Digital Performer and Sibelius for composing his own music and arranging music for top recording artists like Stevie Wonder and Aretha Franklin.

Viewport VII: Mike Wallace, a junior-high band director, who uses Finale to transpose parts for the school and community band he conducts, create experiences for his students, and restore very old arrangements for band; and Jouni Koskimäki, a Finnish composer/educator, who uses Sibelius to teach composition, study the music of the Beatles, and compose music.

Viewport VIII: Susan Young, a middle-school music teacher, who uses computer-aided instruction software to encourage her students to work cooperatively on composing soundtracks for movies.

Each profile tells you something about the person, how they use the technology, and what software and hardware they've chosen to meet their needs. You will notice that they come from all levels of mastery—all levels of the swimming pool.

Module 3

People Questioning Technology

Before moving to the heart of the textbook and issues related to data, software, and hardware, it is important to expose a few misguided ideas that might slow you down. We have already dealt with a major one in the last module: that *computers are somehow smarter than people*. There are a few others. Some of these misconceptions have a grain of truth. In general, though, they may lead to major attitude problems toward music technology. We have phrased them here as questions that people frequently raise concerning the use of technology in music.

Ten Misconceptions

No. 1. Does technology refer only to hardware?

The decision to purchase a computer or music keyboard is not where the story begins and ends. Hardware is part of a system in which there is much more to be considered. What are the needs (people and procedures), the information to be treated (data), and options to treat it (software)? Hardware is an important (and perhaps the most talked-about) part of all this, but hardly the only thing to think about. Think, instead, of the big picture.

No. 2. Is there intimidating hidden "knowledge" inside the hardware?

This misconception often scares the person using hardware (what some call cyberphobia). In Viewport II, we deal with how a computer works. This will help you grasp just what is or can be put inside a computer. Yes, there is a certain amount of "knowledge" built into a computer by the manufacturer, but only to get things going when you turn it on. Then the machine sits there, dumb and happy, waiting for you—the boss—to tell it what program to run, what data to treat, what tasks to do. This is generally true for music keyboards and other devices. Just knowing a little bit more about the inside workings and realizing that you are in charge will go a long way.

No. 3. Will the hardware break if something is done incorrectly?

Short of hitting a piece of hardware with a hammer (an urge that is certainly possible at times of frustration!), there is not much you can do to hurt a piece of equipment by using it normally. No computer or music device that we know of breaks because a button is pushed or a key depressed in error. Sometimes the software can cause the computer to crash and require restarting. However, the machine does not break, and it is likely that whatever happened can be corrected easily. Except for rare equipment failures that are usually out of your control, you cannot damage hardware by normal use.

No. 4. Isn't computer technology really reserved for the technical elite?

At one time, this was true. When computers were large and delicate and required trained systems operators, and when the first sound devices relied on complicated procedures to connect one element to another, you needed to know a good deal about technical things. This has all changed. Newer computers and music devices offer much easier interfaces. Mice, touch-sensitive screens, and microphones have made working with computers much easier. Computers are now portable and can be used just about anywhere. Liquid crystal displays, slider bars, and simple switches have made music devices easier to use. Software designers have become aware of the importance of user friendliness.

Of course, certain concepts and procedures need to be understood. And sometimes, regardless of your level of understanding, you must turn to more technically knowledgeable people. Yet it is far easier these days to use technology than at any point in our history. If you have learned to play a musical instrument or sing, you can use a computer or a MIDI keyboard quite effectively.

No. 5. Doesn't computer technology take too long to learn?

If you are impatient, computers and music technology may not be for you. However, if you have achieved any success in music, it is likely that you have learned how to live with small but important gains from practice. If you approach computers and music technology in the same way, rich rewards will follow. Some computer software programs take longer to learn than others, especially if you are learning basic computer operations at the same time. Try to do this work in stages. You set yourself up for failure when you try to accomplish a complex technology task, such as entering and printing a score and parts, with an unrealistic deadline. You may find that you are spending a lot of time at the beginning of your work, but you will quickly find the time very well spent.

No. 6. Isn't computer technology only for the young?

Thinking along these lines is like deciding not to listen to pop music composed after 1960 or refusing to drive a car with an automatic transmission. There is little evidence to suggest that people of all ages cannot learn to use technology productively. Perhaps this misconception has more to do with open-mindedness and willingness to change than with age and technology themselves.

No. 7. Doesn't technology remove the creative spirit, producing music that is antiseptic or sterile?

Sometimes this is true, especially if the musician lacks imagination or if the technology doesn't allow for subtlety. (If the latter is true, get better technology; if the former, don't blame the technology!) A good deal of poor music gets created with technology. From the "boom-chic-a-boom" sounds of trite preprogrammed drum tracks to the insipid melodic drivel that may pour out of Joe Cool's synthesizer, there's plenty of bad music created by people with machines. What's more, this is not restricted to any one genre; we've heard just as much uninspired and tiresome music from "serious" electronic music studios as we have from the popular scene. Bad music is bad music! Of course, this is true for traditional acoustic music as well—a point that seems to be lost on some of technology's harshest critics.

No. 8. Aren't computers, digital audio, MIDI, and DVDs, when used for teaching about music, just another expensive set of technological gimmicks that take time and money away from the real business of music education?

This complicated misconception probably has less to do with technology itself and more to do with beliefs about what teaching strategies and the real business of music education should be. To us, the focus should be on expressive sound and its role in music experiences. We believe that the technological tools described in this book provide powerful support to open up the world of music to as many people as possible. MIDI and digital audio devices provide effective ways to teach about timbre, melodic and rhythmic subtlety, dynamics, and articulation. They offer extraordinary ways to engage students in the creative process of sound shaping through improvisation and composition—experiences that, until now, have been rarely considered. DVD and CD-ROM players attached to computers provide elegant support for focused listening experiences, together with supportive visual information. For us, these tools are not fads, but major advances in teaching. The investment of time and money seems well worth it.

No. 9. Doesn't technology, not music, become the focus?

This can be true when technology is used poorly. If the most interesting aspect of a performance was the performer's ability to play both keyboard and wind controller while working the mouse on a computer, apparently the music itself didn't capture your interest. If you attend a talk about music in which the graphics displayed on the overhead projector were more interesting than the content, you should blame the speaker, not the technology. Musicians who spend inordinate time engaged in the frills of technology perpetuate this misconception. Again, place the blame where it belongs.

No. 10. Isn't it true that technology replaces musicians' jobs?

Yes and no. Certain employment opportunities are affected by music technology, but what is often not considered is the number of new jobs created because of technology—and the time saved for more creative work.

Resulting Attitudes

Each of these misconceptions, considered as a whole or in combination, leads to rather deeply held, negative attitudes about technology and the music experience. We meet many in the music enterprise who have great suspicions about technology. Some flatly refuse to consider its merits, citing technology's impersonality, technical complexity, and unmusical qualities. When pressed to say why they feel this way, we find that people often base their feelings on a number of bad experiences at concerts or in school. Most are uninformed about technology and unwilling to even consider its merits. Others can't seem to say why they hold these negative attitudes.

On the other hand, we also meet a number of musicians who have gone too far in the other direction—often relying so heavily on technology that they lose sight of the point of fine music making. They often buy the latest software or audio device merely to have the latest gimmick. They hold the potentially dangerous attitude that any new idea is a great development for the art, without much careful consideration.

We suggest a middle ground. There are legitimate concerns about the present role of technology in music and we must keep a careful eye on all new trends. Here are a few tips that might be useful in forming your attitudes:

- Work from a position of knowledge. Try to learn as much as you can about technology and how it is used in the aspect of music that most interests you. Do this by doing research and talking with others who use technology in music.
- Plunge right in! Start working with technology yourself by experimenting with a few projects.
- Be patient at first. Avoid focusing your first experience with technology on an unreasonable deadline.
- Try not to rush to judgment. Develop your opinions after as many experiences as possible. Be open-minded!
- Keep your focus on the artistic and pedagogical end product. Use technology to improve the music experience.

People Helping with Technology

DVD-ROM
Project 2 Tracking Down
Campus Computing
Resources

Returning to our swimming-pool analogy, when venturing out into the waters of music technology it's a good idea to know where the lifeguards are stationed. In general, we find that people who work around computers and technology are friendly and willing to share their expertise. Many computer scientists and engineers are fascinated with producing music on a computer and are often eager to get involved when they have a chance. Don't hesitate to seek them out for help.

You can look for help and support as you begin your study of computer and music technology from people with technical skills, computer facilities, published materials, and professional associations, including:

People with Technical Skills
- Computer technical support staff on campus or at work
- User groups
- Friends and fellow students with computer expertise
- People at local computer stores
- Online help from people on network services and the Internet

Computer Facilities
- Campus computer lab(s)
- Campus computer store or resource center
- Music computer lab(s)
- Electronic and/or MIDI music lab(s)
- Public and campus libraries
- Local computer stores

Published Print and Nonprint Materials
- Computer books and magazines
- Software and hardware manuals
- Video- and audiotape training materials
- This book

Professional Associations
- Association for Technology in Music Instruction (ATMI)
- The Technology Institute for Music Educators (TI:ME)

People with Technical Skills

Begin with those closest to you. If you are on campus, this means your instructor, fellow students or friends, teaching assistants, and technical computer staff. In the community, seek out friends who use computers and look for help from the computer store where you purchased your computer (this is one of the best reasons to buy your computer locally!). The next step is to seek out local or regional computer-user groups compatible with your interests. Usually they form around certain computer types (e.g., Macintosh, Windows, etc.) or application types (e.g., business, graphics, music, etc.). Then get connected to the Internet, where you will find an unlimited number of resources. We will talk more about the technical aspects of networking in Viewport II.

When looking for computer assistance, be sure to take a quick reading on the technical competence of your volunteer lifeguard. Make sure your resource is at least several yards ahead of you in the swimming pool and that your problem matches his or her repertoire of skills.

Computer Facilities

Again, find the physical resources closest to you. You never know when you may need a printer, scanner, faster computer, or MIDI and digital audio equipment.

If you are on campus, find out where the computer labs are located and what resources they have. Check what restrictions apply. Find out if your campus has a store or resource center where you can purchase computers and supplies, perhaps at reduced cost. Then do a survey of what your music department or school has available in the way of a computer lab, electronic music studio, MIDI studio, and so on.

If you are in the community, see if a local college or public school will let you use their facilities. It may be worth signing up for a computer class just to gain access to campus computing resources. The continuing or adult education program on a campus may be able to help you as well. See what facilities your local computer store will let you use gratis or on rental. Many copy shops provide computers and printers for use on an hourly basis. Computer resources are becoming standard offerings at public libraries, which may also provide computer books, software, and hardware. Many coffee houses and other businesses have free wireless connections to the Internet.

LINK
A comprehensive set of readings is available in the Selected Readings list provided at the end of the book.

Print and Nonprint Materials

There is an abundance of computer books, magazines, videos, and digital movies to choose from, including books for almost every major commercial software application. Take some time to scan through books before you buy them. Check that the technical level matches your own. Computer books are expensive, so ask for recommendations and read book reviews in computer magazines, or try to find them at the library. Several firms specialize in developing video training materials for computers and software that some libraries and video rental stores may stock.

Professional Associations

Finally, joining professional associations that focus on music technology may help. For example, the Association for Technology in Music Instruction (ATMI) (atmionline.org/) is designed to assist teachers of music technology, primarily in college and university settings. The group meets regularly for presentations on music technology, maintains an active listserv, and publishes a courseware directory.

The Technology Institute for Music Educators (TI:ME) (www.ti-me.org/) is dedicated to helping music educators at the primary and secondary levels apply technology to improve teaching and learning in music. It publishes materials to assist teachers and holds many conferences each year at various locations. The group also acts as a certification body for different levels of competence in music technology.

VIEWPORT II

Computer and Internet Concepts for Musicians

"It is now 2009. Individuals primarily use portable computers, which have become dramatically lighter and thinner than the notebook computers of ten years earlier. Personal computers are available in a wide range of sizes and shapes, and are commonly embedded in clothing and jewelry such as wristwatches, rings, earrings, and other body ornaments. . . . Computers routinely include wireless technology to plug into the ever-present worldwide network, providing reliable instantly available, very-high-bandwidth communication. Digital objects such as books, music albums, movies, and software are rapidly distributed as data files through the wireless network, and typically do not have a physical object associated with them."

—*Ray Kurzweil*, The Age of Spiritual Machines (*1999*)

ASIDE
Microsoft rolled out network services to "smart watches" made by Fossil, Abacus, and Suunto in 2004. News and other data are delivered to the computer watch wirelessly through FM radio signals.

Overview

Although Kurzweil's notions of embedded computers in clothing and jewelry are just starting to appear, his predictions in 1999 of portable computers, wireless technology, and digital objects are certainly here today. This Viewport presents information about operating systems and their support for music technology. We explain how computers work by focusing on important concepts, data structures, and hardware features that musicians must understand. We also deconstruct the world of the Internet by explaining how to get connected and how to use important software for music productivity. This information will help lay the foundation for topics to come.

Objectives

Module 5 is devoted to understanding features of computer operating systems and Internet software. Information presented here is likely to be useful when you begin working with a new computer and when you connect your machine to the Internet. Modules 6 and 7 round out the Viewport by explaining how computers represent and process data and how different components of computer hardware work.

At the end of Viewport II, you should understand:

- The role of operating systems (Mac, Windows, UNIX, and Linux) and why they are important
- How to set up your computer and deal with streams of data in and out

DVD-ROM
As with all the software modules in this text, the accompanying DVD contains hands-on projects for you to use to practice your skills.

- How to connect to the Internet and use common Internet software for web browsing, e-mail, chat, and music sharing
- Details for Internet connections via modem, DSL, cable, wireless, Bluetooth, and direct link
- Graphic user interface and hierarchical file structures
- Analog and digital data structures
- File formats and how these work with the Internet
- Serial and parallel data communication
- Data storage and disk formats, including fixed disks and CD and DVD discs
- Ways to deal with viruses and other threats to the integrity of your computer and how to maintain your operating system and the files it controls
- Types of Internet software, including those titles that use client-server and peer-to-peer modes
- Maintaining your computer for safe operation
- The IPOS Model, including hardware details for bus, USB, Firewire, keyboard, and mouse connections
- Issues of CPU function, memory, and clock speed

DVD-ROM Software Projects

For Viewport II, using computer operating systems and Internet software, you should be able to:

- Set up and understand your computer and its operating system (Project 3)
- Search and surf the Web using browsers (Project 4)

MUSIC TECHNOLOGY IN PRACTICE

Chi Fan
Music Teacher, Taiwan, China

Chi Fan working on personal website

Application

Chi became familiar with computers and the Internet late in life. Before attending graduate school in the United States, she used computers only to write papers and send e-mail. She has taken graduate classes in music education and technology at Northwestern University and these classes have introduced her to music applications and multimedia creation. Most recently she has learned to construct her own website, which features information for vocalists and for music teachers who teach general music and choir. Using books written in both English and Chinese, she has taught herself how to create music content in Macromedia Flash and Director. Following her graduate work, she returned to Taiwan to teach music with music technology support.

Hardware and Software

Chi uses a mid-range, PC laptop computer that runs the Windows operating system. She keeps this computer in her apartment and uses Microsoft Office and Internet Explorer for browsing and e-mail. For her multimedia work, she has become proficient with Macintosh computers in the university computer labs and uses Photoshop, Dreamweaver, Flash, and Director for Web development. She is an avid user of music notation and sequencing programs.

M o d u l e   5

Computer Operating Systems and Internet Software

This module presents information on the software that runs your personal computer and its connections to the outside world. We will explain what to expect in a typical operating system.

DVD-ROM
Projects 3–4 on the accompanying DVD are designed to give you hands-on experience with computer operating systems and Internet software.

ASIDE
The word "boot" comes from the very early days of computing when the idea of starting a computer was likened to the idea of "pulling yourself up by your bootstraps."

LINK
You can find more on the workings of a computer in Module 7.

The Desktop: Your Computer and Its Operating System

We assume that you have access to some kind of desktop or laptop computer with some music hardware. Take a moment to study the back of your computer and the connections that lead from it to your network, printer, audio gear, and MIDI equipment. Systems vary greatly in design, but Figure 7.2 (EMT-1: Basic Computer Workstation) will come close to representing what you have. You will learn more about this hardware and the types of connections in Module 7.

The Function of an Operating System

The operating system is a set of programs that act as a bridge between you and your application software (e.g., music printing, sequencing, audio processing) and between you and the hardware. Whatever you choose to do is sent through the operating system to the computer itself. The operating system is a kind of silent manager or conductor that is responsible for the smooth operation of the computing enterprise.

The operating system begins work the very moment you turn your computer on. In these initial seconds as the machine is "booting up," internal instructions are being carried out, including a check of the important circuitry inside the computer, the sending of initial messages to the screen and appropriate sounds to the speaker, and the loading of routines that control the work of the computer.

Streams of Information

The operating system must manage different streams of information going in and out of your computer. As a musician, during the course of daily work with the computer, you will work with all of these streams of data input and output. Most of these streams will be covered in subsequent modules. These streams include:

- Storage (Module 7)
- Internet (Modules 7 and 8)

- Digital Audio and Analog Audio (Modules 10 and 13)
- MIDI (Module 14)
- Printer/Mouse/Keyboard (Modules 7 and 21)

Storage

There are many options for local storage. One important device is the fixed hard drive within your computer that contains all of the operating system software and most of the software applications you will use. You may have a second disk that is external. It could be a CD or CD/DVD device that can be used for burning discs. This kind of storage might be used for backing up your internal hard drive or as an additional place to save your valuable work. Other external drives might include an additional hard drive, a flash card reader, or a removable, miniature "thumb" drive.

Internet

A second stream of data is provided by your network connection. If you are at home, this link might be through a DSL connection that uses your telephone line or a cable or satellite link. If you are in a computer lab or in a building that has a direct connection to the Internet, your link is a direct one managed by your host institution.

Digital Audio and Analog Audio

A very important data stream for musicians is audio. Analog audio, the actual waveforms that are captured by microphones or played back by speakers, are also processed by computers. Typically, computers have microphone "in" and audio "out" jacks for dealing with analog audio.

Digital audio, actual sound waves sampled into numbers that require special chips to encode and decode, is used by many music applications such as MP3, digital recording, and sequencing software. These data use either Universal Serial Bus (USB) or Firewire (IEEE 1394) connectors and usually require an additional hardware interface.

MIDI

MIDI data, a stream of digital information describing sound events that we will explain in much more detail in coming Viewports, may also flow in and out through a USB connector or dedicated MIDI cables. These data flow from MIDI data devices like music keyboards and (depending on the MIDI device) might require additional interface hardware.

Printer/Mouse/Keyboard

Finally, your local printer, mouse, and keyboard will likely be linked to your computer, usually with a USB or wireless interface. The operating system must control these input and output devices so that the streams of information can be kept organized.

LINK
Check Module 6 for more on the difference between the terms "digital" and "analog."

DVD-ROM
Project 3 Setting Up and
Understanding Your
Computer

Look and Feel: Graphic User Interface (GUI)

So what does an operating system look like? Figures 5.1a and b represent the two major operating systems that run personal computers, one using the (a) Macintosh operating system from Apple Computer, and the other using the (b) Windows operating system from Microsoft. Both screens use a desktop metaphor where small pictures (icons) represent data files, software applications, folders, local storage drives, remote servers, and links to the Internet. In the Macintosh example (a), three windows are open: One represents the contents of the "EMT3" folder, the second shows the connection status to the Internet, and the third shows the progress of a virus-scanning operation. In the Windows example (b), a music application is open and another program is about to be opened. These icons and windows are what the GUI (pronounced "gooey") is all about.

Staying Organized with Hierarchical File Structure

Learning to use the operating system includes learning how to manage resources. One problem that all musicians face is how to organize and manage the growing number of files that become part of your computer's environment. Your applications all generate files that you need to manage.

Volumes, Folders, Files

The GUI for Macintosh and PC machines uses volumes, folders (also called "directories" in Windows and UNIX operating systems), and files in similar ways. Figure 5.2 provides an example of the hierarchy created in the Windows operating

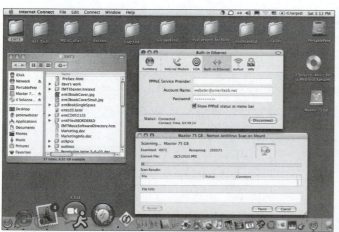

FIGURE 5.1A   Macintosh OS X Operating System

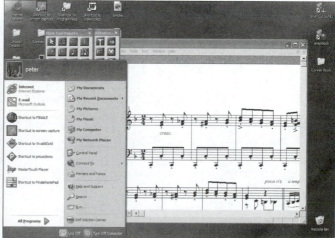

FIGURE 5.1B   Windows XP Operating System

TIP

The "Properties" (Windows) or "Get Info" (Mac) items in a contextual menu that is associated with a file icon can give you the location of a file.

systems to manage files. The Mac OS X is similar. Each operating system displays its organization of volumes, folders, and files moving from left to right. In Figure 5.2, the volume "Local Disk (C:)" contains folders or directories, one of which is called "Program Files." Here the folder is opened to reveal a subfolder called "Cakewalk Home Studio 2002." The contents of that folder are displayed to the right. Obviously, subfolders can be embedded into folders to create very extended hierarchies.

Importance of Volumes and Pathnames

Files and folders are located on local hard disks, on CD-R or DVD-R discs, and on remote servers. These storage areas are considered "volumes" by the operating system. As you save more and more files and folders to different locations, the operating system needs to keep track of where these are located. Volume names help with this; volumes can also be represented by icons on the computer's desktop.

Once a name has been given to a file, its folder, and its volume, the operating system keeps track of the location of files by assigning each file a specific "pathname." This is shown in Figure 5.2 in the top section after the word "Address." The pathname: "C:\Program Files\Cakewalk\Cakewalk Home Studio 2002" identifies the location of the files displayed. Notice the use of the slash mark to separate names.

Naming Files

You have reasonable freedom in naming files, folders, and volumes. However, a few conventions will make your work easier:

- Develop the habit of naming files with standardized extensions used to denote an application (characters to the right of a period "."). For instance, it's a good idea to name Microsoft Word files with a ".doc" extension or a standard MIDI file with a ".mid" extension. The Windows OS forces these naming extensions.
- Keep the names of volumes, folders, and files as short as possible: 10 characters or less if you intend to share these files across the Internet. For Internet use, the preference is for lowercase letters only.

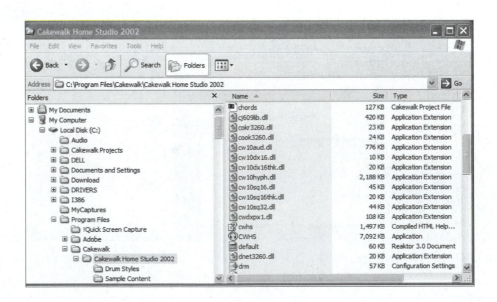

FIGURE 5.2 File Hierarchies in Windows

LINK
See Module 6 for technical information on formatting.

- Avoid using slash marks ("/" or "\") and a colon (":") in the titles of files or folders. These symbols interfere with the creation and readability of path-names. It's common to use the underscore if you need a space in a file name, e.g., my_music_files.

Important Work Habits

Now that you have a grasp of what the GUI is and how you can use it to organize your desktop, we will review important procedures for working with files and maintaining your computer's integrity.

Saving Files

We cannot stress enough the importance of developing good habits for saving files. In our years of experience working with hundreds of students and colleagues, nothing is so discouraging and frustrating as losing critical digital data, which almost always happens because of carelessness in saving and backing up. Please read this section carefully.

As you use computers to create data, this information is stored only temporarily; it is not generally stored on disk immediately. A dramatic interruption of the computer's work before you have saved to disk will result in the loss of this work. It is vital that you develop the habit of saving your work frequently. If a software application offers an option to auto-save at designated intervals, use this option. Forgetting where you have saved a file and saving a file in the wrong folder are common mistakes. Both operating systems provide a helpful search option to find files.

There are many ways to save your data to hard disks and other media. Applications that create data always offer a "Save . . ." option, usually under the File menu. The system presents a dialog box that asks for three important pieces of information:

- what you want to call your data file
- where you want to save it
- what file format to use

Figures 5.3a and b present two Save dialog boxes, one from a Macintosh and the other from a Windows operating system. In the Macintosh box (a), a file named "mod05.doc" is saved to a hard disk volume called "Peter's Work" using the file format "Microsoft Word document." In the Windows dialog box (b), a nota-tion file in Finale is saved in a folder named "Tutorials." Here, we have asked to see file details in the save box. In both systems, it is possible to save files with dif-ferent file formats, as seen in the drop-down menu.

Another option on the File menu is the "Save As" item. This allows you to save a new version of the file under a new name, in a new location, or perhaps in a different format. This option is very handy for making backup copies.

Knowing how and when to save is very important for successful computing. Software owners (licensees) should make copies of their legally obtained applica-tion software and files for use on their computers. But software owners do not have

FIGURE 5.3A Macintosh Save Box

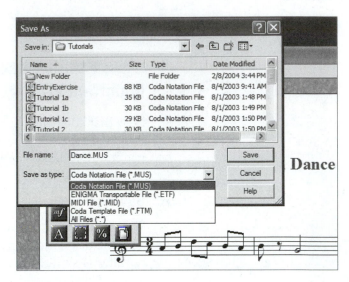

FIGURE 5.3B Windows Save Box

the right to duplicate commercial software applications or purchased files from a music service and give them away to friends! Although a number of gray areas do exist in the legalities of technology, this is not one of them. This is a clear violation of copyright law and is absolutely illegal. It is stealing!

Importance of Copyright

Copyright awareness is critical for music technology users! Because file compression without noticeable loss in quality has allowed more room for music in our digital world and because it has become so easy to create customized CDs of this music, it is tempting to distribute and accept music without regard for legal ownership. We want to stress the importance of not distributing your legally acquired music to others and not accepting from others any music that is clearly not owned by you. Doing so is a clear violation of copyright law.

Copyright restrictions also apply to using computer software to scan, recreate parts from a score, or producing a PDF image of copyrighted sheet music. Copyrighted music cannot be posted on the Internet in printed or recorded form without permission.

Copyright and "Fair Use"

Copyright law is not new. It has its roots in the British statutes of 1710 and the subsequent United States Copyright Act of 1790, which has been amended many times. Lawsuits related to music copyright appeared even in the 1880s, with disputes over player piano roll infringements on composers' and publishers' rights to protect their creative work from exploitation. In 1976, copyright was extended to unpublished works.

Eventually, the concept of "fair use" was established and library use of copyrighted materials was clarified. In 1990, the Copyright Act was changed to prohibit lending of computer software, establishing the ability to make "one archival copy." The Digital Millennium Copyright Act (DMCA) of 1998 defined the role of Internet service providers (ISP) in helping to control copyright infringement and establish restrictions on the copying of digital materials, especially those with security codes embedded.

Today libraries make materials available electronically to their patrons under the provisions of "fair use" or by paying annual licensing fees. Under current law, you are allowed to make a backup copy of your music files that you clearly own for a compilation CD or for a personal MP3 player. However, you cannot make your music files available for others, nor are you permitted to accept music files from others when you are unsure of their ownership.

Under fair use, educators have a separate set of rights to display and perform others' works in the classroom. These rights are explained in Section 110(1) of the current Copyright Act. In addition, the TEACH Act, which became law in 2002, has helped expand the scope of educators' rights to perform and display music for distance education; however, the TEACH Act specifies that the delivery of copyrighted content in distance education must be limited in scope.

Determining Copyright

How can you tell if music is copyrighted? Any music composed, recorded, and produced between 1923 and 1977 is protected for 95 years. Anything after 1977 is protected for 70 years beyond the death of the author or creator. Of course, some Internet sites distribute music files sanctioned by the copyright owner. Policies should be clearly indicated on the site. In general, if you are in doubt, do not accept or distribute.

Just as you have an obligation not to violate copyright law, the recording industry has an obligation to consider the lawful distribution of their artists' work electronically at a fair cost. One often-cited factor in illegal file exchanges aided by the Internet is the high cost of commercial CDs. Thankfully, we see changes in the recording industry directed toward using the Internet as a new method of distribution, accompanied by advancements in digital rights management (DRM) techniques.

Viruses Defined

ASIDE
You may hear terms like "Trojan Horses," "Worms," and "DOS Attacks" in addition to the term "virus."

Protecting your operating system, application, and data files against viruses is important for safe computing. Viruses are fragments of software designed to attach themselves to other applications or to files. They attack application software, data files, and system software, depending on their nature and intent. Viruses transfer from one computer to another by exposure to other pieces of software and by finding a host as a base of operations.

Possible ways to become infected are by using:

- other people's volumes that might contain a virus (such as shared CD-ROMs or flash memory cards)
- a public computer that supports software that has not been routinely monitored
- the Internet and network software that is not well controlled
- code attached to shared files, including shared MP3 music files from the Internet
- an attachment to an e-mail message or embedded in the codes of an e-mail message

This last way has become the most pervasive in recent years. Never open an attachment to an e-mail message if it is from a person you do not know. Even if you do know the individual, it is best to determine by phone or separate e-mail message that the attachment is legitimate.

Viruses are not funny. Some are designed to be humorous and not do much damage to files, presenting what may seem to be humorous remarks or events. Others are much more malicious, doing serious damage to critical data on your hard drive. Others use your e-mail addresses to spread the virus unwittingly to others. And, still others take over your computer and use it to mount attacks on web servers (known as "denial of service" [DOS] attacks).

Following the precautions above can help protect a computer from outside attack; however, virus protection software is also a good defense. This software accomplishes two tasks. First, it scans your volumes for any known viruses and attempts to repair the damage. Second, it may provide protection against the intrusion of viruses, either by providing a small operating system file that watches for suspicious activity or by actively scanning volumes detected by the operating system. In choosing which software to use, be sure there is a clear policy about updating the product when new viruses are defined in the computing community. Such software is only as good as the latest update.

Backing Up

If you maintain and operate computers correctly, they generally are quite reliable. Unfortunately, sometimes computers fail because of outside variables or fatigue. If a backup system is followed, losses will be minimal.

A safe system of backup requires a consistent approach to saving data. Perhaps the most economical approach is to save important data files on a second physical location such as a CD or DVD or external hard drive. This ensures that a copy exists on both the internal hard drive of your computer and an external volume. If you are working in a public site such as a library or school lab, or perhaps on another person's computer, keep two volumes of your work and do not rely on the computer you are using. Public computers are often "wiped clean" at the end of the day, with any foreign files deleted. Other backup approaches require a greater investment of time and money, but they may become important as valuable data become more extensive.

Software utility programs are available to automate the backup process. These programs allow you to specify which files are to be backed up (i.e., all your data files). If your backup volume is large enough, you can automate this process without even being around. All this backing up may seem time-consuming, but it will pay off in a big way the first time a major disaster (that lost final report or all-night project) has been averted because of your vigilant approach to data protection.

Additional Good Habits for Computer Maintenance

Frequent use of virus protection software, systematic backups, and care in opening attachments to e-mail are all excellent habits for safe computing. You should also:

- Run operating system updates from Apple and Microsoft. The operating systems are linked to the Apple or Microsoft, which enables home servers automatic updating of key resources. Checks for updates can be automated for a set time each week.

- Regularly run utilities such as "Error-checking" in the Properties option for Windows XP volumes and "First Aid" within the Disk Utility for Macintosh OS X volumes. Both these programs check for bad files and other operating system errors that might have been caused during a computer crash or other unexpected event.
- Use mail programs that have the capability to filter out spam. Advanced mail programs can automatically detect such junk mail or can be manually programmed with filter options to direct junk mail in to a separate folder.
- Install a software "firewall" to protect your computer while online. Such programs help prevent hackers from detecting your computer's network address and attempting to access your files.

Other Operating Systems

Although Macintosh and Windows represent the major operating systems for personal computers, two others are worth noting.

UNIX

The UNIX (pronounced "you-nicks") operating system was developed by AT&T's Bell Research Laboratories in the early 1970s. It was designed initially for powerful scientific workstations. With the increased power of today's computers, UNIX is used on a wider assortment of machines, and it continues to be used for high-end workstations. Macintosh's OS X operating system has the UNIX operating system at its core, with the GUI written on top of a UNIX base. The Terminal program in the applications set that comes with the operating system can be used to actually work in UNIX on the Mac.

UNIX's strength lies in its ease of use for those with advanced programming knowledge. It uses an object approach, where units of software create flexible building blocks for designing applications that run on the system. It also supports multiple users and advanced multitasking capabilities that permit the computer to work on more than one job at a time. However, it is difficult for the average computer user to learn and it has been plagued by multiple versions that compete with each other for general acceptance.

A few effective music applications for UNIX machines have been created by music researchers, theorists, and electronic music composers. These applications are generally designed for advanced technical work with sound.

Linux and the World of Open Source Code

A UNIX-related language called Linux has gained a fair amount of popularity in recent years. It was developed in large part by Linus Torvalds while working at the University of Helsinki. He created the "kernel" or main core of the operating system, the part that speaks to the main CPU of the computer. Torvalds wished to create an operating system that was free for others to develop and, in 1991, was able to work with a few similar-minded individuals in the United States to launch a first version. Linux has developed at a rapid rate with the aid of the Internet.

Today, different "distributors" provide users with a version of Linux that can be installed on different hardware platforms such as Macintosh and PC machines.

Applications for productive work both inside and outside the music field are written for Linux in the spirit of total collaboration, similar to the operating system itself. Both the finished applications and the code that created the programs are frequently distributed freely for others to have and to improve. This open approach to programming and sharing is an attractive way to build creative applications for different audiences. The downsides to working with Linux are the small number of music applications and the need to be savvy about computer hardware and the UNIX/Linux software environment. For some, however, the Linux solution is a pleasant way to accomplish work without significant financial investment in commercial products. The list of music applications for Linux and other UNIX-related systems is steadily growing.

Extending the Desktop: Connecting to the Internet

LINK
Many books, articles, and websites summarize the history and design of the Internet. More details about the Internet and networking can be found in Modules 6 and 7.

Musicians and their work are linked by cables, fiber optics, radio waves, and satellites. The basis for this information superhighway of connectivity for computers is the "Internet." The Internet is a collection of networked computers around the world that are linked to each other, forming a huge network of networks. Operating system software comes fully ready to take advantage of networking using an Internet connection. A new Macintosh or PC will come equipped with additional software for browsing the Internet and sending electronic mail.

Using the Internet is vital for musicians. Each of the topics in the Viewports to follow is supported vigorously by musicians using the Internet. Improving the way we teach, perform, create, and experience music is the primary reason for exploring music technology and the links to people and data that technology provides. This is all possible because of the network resources that are being created, the musicians that "serve up" the information, and the computers themselves.

Types of Internet Software

LINK
Read Module 7 for more information about client/server and peer-to-peer network modes.

Once you are connected to the Internet, you can use software that takes advantage of this connectedness. We end this module with an overview of these software options. Table 5.1 highlights the software services frequently used by musicians, typical software titles, and the mode of network activity used by the software, either client-server or peer-to-peer.

Client-server means that a server somewhere on the Internet supplies data that a client (usually software on your computer) requests. The server contains relatively large amounts of information to be distributed to clients that request it. Examples include web browsing, music sound files purchased from a store, e-mail serving, and news distribution.

Peer-to-peer means that two relatively equal programs running on different computers exchange information. Examples include text and video chatting and

TABLE 5.1   Internet Software

Internet Service	Browser-Based	Other Software	Mode of Activity
Web Surfing/ Searching	Safari (Mac); Microsoft Internet Explorer (Mac/Win); Netscape (Mac/Win); FireFox (Mac/Win)		Client/Server
Electronic Mail/ Listservs	Web mail	Outlook Express (Mac/Win); Eudora (Mac/Win); Apple Mail (Mac)	Client/Server
Digital Audio Purchase/Sharing	Lycos Music; Wal-Mart Music	iTunes (Mac/Win); Rhapsody (Win); Napster (Win)	Client/Server
		KaZaA (Win); LimeWire (Mac/Win); Acquisition (Mac)	Peer-to-Peer
Chat	Yahoo! Chat		Client/Server
		iChat (Mac); AOL Instant Messenger (Mac/Win); mIRC (Win)	Peer-to-Peer
Forums	MacMusic Forums; Music Banter; OS X Audio; Sound Blaster Alive		Client/Server
News Reading	Google; Yahoo Groups; Netscape	Multi-Threaded NewsWatcher (Mac); Thoth (Mac); Agent (Win)	Client/Server
File Transfer	WebDAV server	Fetch (Mac); FTP Voyager (Win)	Client/Server
		Operating System Features	Peer-to-Peer

DVD-ROM
Project 4 Surfing and Searching the Web for Music Resources

ASIDE
The idea of hypertext is not new. It was first considered by Vannevar Bush in 1945 and by Ted Nelson's Xanadu hypermedia project, first proposed in the 1960s.

file sharing. Some server activity may be needed at times to start up and maintain peer-to-peer activity, but the majority of work is done between two equally established peers.

Web Surfing and Searching

Using the Internet for web surfing and searching is perhaps the most popular Internet activity for musicians. Servers connected to the Internet that provide text information, graphics, animation, sound effects, music, and movies are called "web servers," and the clients that access the servers are called "browsers." Web servers support links among each other and can support links embedded within documents. You might be reading about Scott Joplin's ragtime music on a server in New Orleans and encounter a link that moves you to a server in Paris that has some digital pictures of Joplin as a youth. Still other buttons might play sound clips of early ragtime music, show a score, or perhaps play a short movie—all of which might be "served" from different locations in the world.

This concept first began with linking text information. From the first design concepts of Tim Berners-Lee in the early 1990s, the idea of a network-based hypertext system quickly caught the imaginations of computer scientists around the world. The concept was to have links within documents on one computer call into action documents on another computer using Hypertext Markup Language

(HTML). This expanded to include not only hypertext, but also graphics, sounds, and digital movie technology. Thus was born the concept of a World Wide Web (WWW) of computers connected by the Internet to share multimedia resources.

Web Page Appearance

Figure 5.4 provides a view of a typical page from a music-related site. This is the "home" page that has been constructed as the entrance to the site. The address of the home page is displayed in the center top as http://www.lyricopera.org/home.asp. This is the "uniform resource locator" (URL) that represents the address of the site and its home page on the Internet. The "hypertext transfer protocol" (http://) helps to identify the address as a web page resource on the Internet. The use of ".asp" in the URL is an example of the behind-the-scenes use of database software to create the web page.

Take a close look at the content on the page itself. A background graphic serves as a backdrop for the information provided. Across the top of the page to the left are a series of links that lead to other pages within the site. There are other links displayed as well, including a set at the bottom of the page and drop-down links under the menu items below the words "Lyric Opera of Chicago." We have revealed the items under the "Buy" menu. A selection of one of these items will lead to other pages or even to other sites on the Internet. To the left is a column that represents a series of upcoming events. Placing the cursor over these reveals the box of information at the center that has its own links. Pages like these have many ways to display information and to invite the user to interact with the information provided.

Pages often contain more information than can comfortably fit in one window on your computer screen. Browser software allows the screen to be resized accord-

FIGURE 5.4   Typical page displayed in Safari

ing to your particular monitor size and to scroll vertically and horizontally as needed. The web design format can be flexible in its approach to layout.

As you move through the links within a site, content is often replaced in the window. A second window might also appear that contains additional information. Browser software typically supports multiple windows so that you can have many windows within one open at one time. Multiple sites can be open at the same time as well.

Browser Features

Typical browsers feature flexible navigation, web searching, and saving/printing.

Navigation   Figure 5.5 displays a number of approaches to navigation. The Address bar can be used to type in a URL. Browsers are programmed to remember past addresses and, as you type, the software reveals a drop-down listing of complete links from which you might want to choose. Also, the file menu has an "open" item that leads to the Open dialog box displayed. In this box, you can type a full URL or simply type the name of a local HTML file that you wish to display. The Browse option reveals the navigation dialog at the bottom of the graphic.

Once you have visited a site that you wish the browser to remember, you can save the address in a "Favorites" or a "Bookmark" list for later use. A history list of recently visited sites is archived by many browsers. To the left in Figure 5.5, this software supplies sites visited weeks, days, and moments ago. Back and forward buttons are provided in the toolbar at the top to navigate to pages just displayed.

Searching   A large part of a browser's function is to search for needed information and services. Searches can occur: (1) within a site as an option of the site designers, (2) as a function within the structure of a company's web browser and the operating system itself, or (3) through an independent "search engine" site that specializes in comprehensive searches of the Internet.

Take another look at Figure 5.5. This site's option to "Search Northwestern"

FIGURE 5.5   Navigation options in Internet Explorer

Microsoft, Inc. [Win]

TIP

For more information about search engine sites, including their history and how they work, go to The Spider's Apprentice at www.monash.com/spidap4.html.

allows the user to look for specific content within the Northwestern University site. This can be handy if you are only interested in content there; however, wider-based searches are probably more useful. In the middle of the toolbar for the browser in Figure 5.5, notice the "Search" button. This Internet Explorer option provides a left-hand column containing questions to help guide your search, including the option to scan your local hard drive as well as the Internet. Choosing the Internet for a search provides "hits" first on Microsoft's own MSN network. Other options include a number of other search engine sites, such as Google, Yahoo!, Lycos, Excite, or Ask Jeeves.

The Google search engine site is a popular choice, based on its comprehensive listings and speed of operation. The designers of a service like Google create a system that compiles lists of site content across the Internet on a regular basis and provide these lists as a match to the keywords you enter. In Figure 5.5, you will notice a separate toolbar for Google below the address line. We have typed in "classical mp3" to search for sites that feature gateways to music files of this type. In Figure 5.6, we opened the Google site directly and completed a search for "garageband." The Google site provides many options for advanced searches and for databases other than general ones. For example, choosing "Images" provides a set of graphics that best match the keywords. Notice that for each "hit" you receive a small selection of text from the site, as well as an option for similar pages. The "cached" option supplies a limited view of the home page without actually going to it. A search engine site first displays the most prominent matches for your keywords and then lists links in groups on separate pages. The search yielded 482,000 hits in .11 seconds.

Saving/Printing When searching or browsing the Web, you might find a graphic or sound file that you wish to use in your own work. Saving such a file to your own machine can often be accomplished as easily as using the right-click (Windows) or Ctrl-click (Mac) techniques. In Figure 5.7, we have done this on an interesting image. Notice the options for saving the graphic. This same technique may work for a sound file as well, but much depends on how the website is designed.

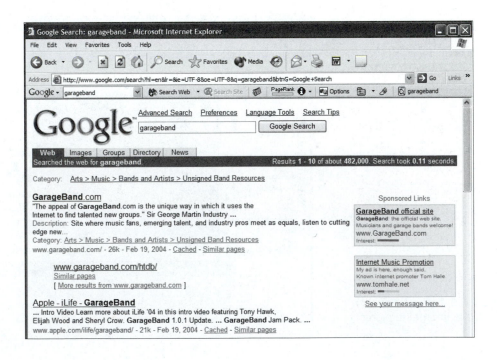

FIGURE 5.6 Google search using Internet Explorer

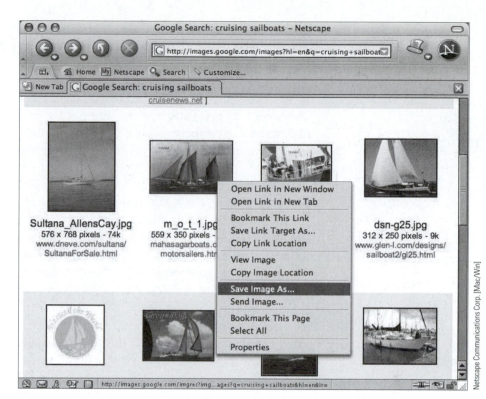

FIGURE 5.7   Saving an image in Netscape

ASIDE
Important!! Saving and printing content raises many issues of copyright and plagiarism. Reuse of media and text must be done responsibly. Using the intellectual content of any site without attribution or permission may be unlawful and/or unethical and could have grave consequences.

LINK
See Module 6 for more information on e-mail addressing.

Saving is not limited to single media types. Text can also be copied and saved if it is not part of a graphic. Browsers also enable you to save entire pages and even entire sites, including the media files associated with the web page. For example, Netscape's "Save As" option under the File menu will let you save either just the HTML file or all of the elements of the entire page. A page can be saved with or without the source code containing the HTML tags. The "Edit Page" option in Netscape will even move the browser into its "Composer" mode, which enables you to edit the elements of that page on your own computer. The edited version will reside on your computer, however, and you will not be able to mount the changes back to a server without an account and password.

Printing is easy with browser software. Most software programs provide print preview windows so you can make sure you have chosen the right material. Some Internet sites even provide their own buttons for printing, which ensures that the material is formatted for the printed page.

Browsing Software Support for Other Internet Services

Table 5.1 shows how browsing software supports many other network services in addition to browsing and surfing the Web. In the examples that follow, we will blend the use of browsers with other client and peer-to-peer software that may be useful for producing music.

Electronic Mail/Listservs

Electronic mail (e-mail) programs and web browsers are the most used Internet software for musicians. Such programs provide individual, asynchronous (different time) communication with text and attached files. E-mail is a client-server service because mail is maintained on a server and then read by client software on an individual's computer. A listserv is based on a server that maintains a list of subscribers who send and receive e-mail messages on a specified topic.

Digital Audio Purchasing/Sharing

LINK
Streaming audio, Internet radio, CD burning, and the MP3 file format will be explained more in Viewport III.

Another very popular use of the Internet for musicians is to purchase or share digital audio files, either by using a central server for distribution or by peer-to-peer arrangements. Software can either be a separate application or the browser itself.

Client-Server

Figure 5.8 shows the Lycos Music site, where music can be heard with streaming techniques or actually downloaded to a client's computer. Some of this music is freely available. In this example, we have searched on the term "Miles" in hopes of finding some classic jazz by Miles Davis. We found an interesting file and chose to listen to it with the browser's selected helper application for playing MP3 files, Winamp. The Lycos service provides a kind of "portal" for other sites that offer MP3 files to share.

LINK
More information is provided about iTunes in Module 9, Viewport III.

Music Subscription   Notice the link on the left for "Music Subscription." This leads to information about Rhapsody, a music subscription service. Lycos and other organizations such as Sprint and Verizon Online use the service as part of their commercial offerings. Rhapsody distributes a free client software program that, when opened, links your computer to a database containing thousands of music titles. For a monthly fee, the service streams audio to your computer. You can build a personal set of regularly audited files in your account and log on from any computer that has the software installed in order to listen to selected music. Rhapsody also creates custom-designed Internet radio stations and sells individual files as tracks that can be compiled on custom CDs.

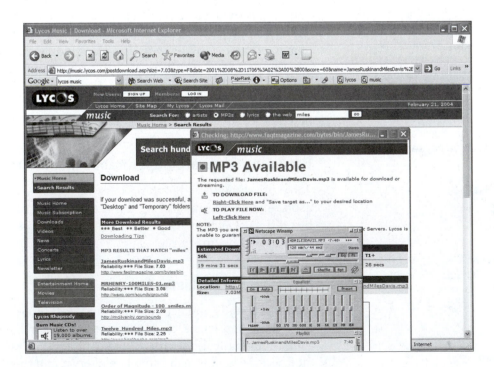

FIGURE 5.8 Lycos music download page in Internet Explorer

Music Store   Another example of an online music store is Apple's iTunes Music Store. The iTunes software (Mac/Win) is distributed freely to computer users and has a built-in link to the company's online music store, which features more than one million music files in several genres. Although there is no subscription service fee, you pay for each track, partial album, or complete album downloaded. In Figure 5.9, we are listening to an offering on the music store site while adjusting the balance. Note the listing on the left of the music categories already cataloged.

Peer-to-Peer

Table 5.1 lists examples of popular peer-to-peer software programs designed to allow individuals to share music files, often MP3, over the Internet. The software turns a computer into a server, connecting to a network that shares the same software. Figure 5.10 is a view of the KaZaA software designed for this purpose. A search for "bach fugue" received 18 hits on locations for various titles. The third item is highlighted, the famous Toccata and Fugue in D minor, and a pop-up window supplies the file's characteristics. Clicking on the "Download" button begins the process. More than one site offers this file, which may speed the process. A click on the "Traffic" button on the toolbar provides a progress report on the downloading process. The software can also be used to search web-server resources; incentives are added to use licensed digital rights managed (DRM) files produced by a variety of professional content providers. KaZaA runs primarily on PCs, but similar file-sharing programs are also available for Macintosh.

Chat

Another form of Internet software supports synchronous (real-time) interactive chatting. This can be in the form of text exchanges or audio/video interaction. The Yahoo! website offers chat rooms on a number of topics, including several on music. You can join a chat room in progress or create one of your own. You can also send a private instant message to any member of the chat session.

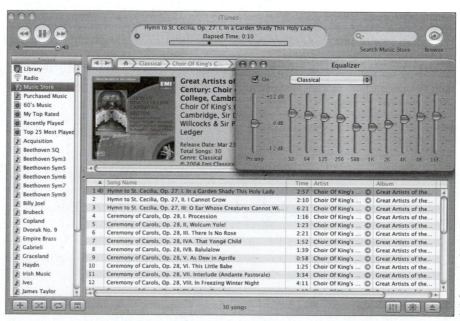

FIGURE 5.9   iTunes

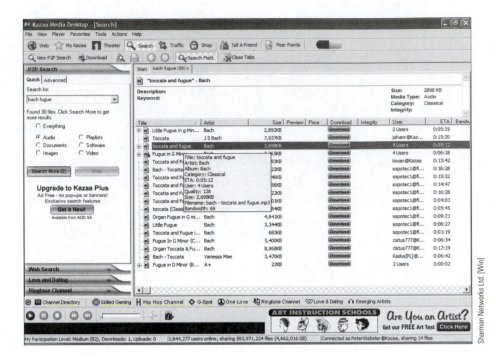

FIGURE 5.10   KaZaA
Media Desktop

Video and audio chatting is possible over the Internet with software like iChat and others. Once the software is installed on your computer, you can interact with other users who have the same software installed. Figure 5.11 shows a videoconference in progress. The "Buddy List" on the upper-right-hand side displays a list of people available for chatting and the window to the left shows a chat session in the embedded window. At any time during the chat session, text messages and files can be exchanged via instant messaging. All that is needed is a digital camera attached to each computer. Such personal videoconferencing is possible over the Internet without expensive hardware and software on private networks.

Forums, News Reading, and File Transfers

Forums and news reading are important ways of staying informed about topics of interest. Most forums are web based and are delivered from a central server. Many groups are devoted to music topics that include genres and performers. Forums and newsgroups differ from listservs in that they do not use e-mail and you can visit them whenever you wish.

Finally, you may wish to transfer files from your personal computer to other locations, such as web servers or a friend's computer. Software is available to aid this process using the file transfer protocol (FTP) approach common on the Internet. If you are maintaining a personal website, you may need to move files that you create from your personal computer to a commercial server using FTP software. FTP service might be built directly into your web page editing software as well. If you want to simply share files with individuals on the Internet, you can take advantage of your operating system's file-sharing capabilities. Public folders can be shared with or without password protection, but your friends will need to know your Internet address to find you online.

Apple Computer, Inc. |Mac

FIGURE 5.11   Videoconferencing on the Internet using iChat

Additional Uses of the Internet with Music Software

Many more specialized types of music software that we review in coming Viewports make frequent use of the Internet. For example, the music notation software described in Viewport VII uses the Internet to distribute files and certain computer-assisted instruction software described in Viewport VIII works from servers. It is difficult to imagine any group of musicians today who do not need some kind of connection to the Internet in order to do their work.

Module 6

Computer and Networking Concepts

Now that you know how to navigate around the desktop of a GUI operating system and surf the Internet, it's time to look under the hood. In this module, we present four concepts that will be important throughout the textbook:

- Analog and digital
- Serial and parallel
- Internet protocols
- File formats and compression

Understanding these concepts will increase your confidence in using computer and music technology.

Analog to Digital: Computers and the Analog World

Let's examine two important notions associated with computers and computer music: *analog* and *digital* representation of events and *binary numbers*. To understand how a digital computer works and how it interacts with music instruments and events in the real world, you need to be aware of the difference between *analog* events and *digital* ones. In the simplest terms, *analog* represents events that are recorded as continuous, as opposed to events that are recorded as discrete steps or numbers.

Our timepieces provide a good illustration. A traditional analog watch measures time by visually circling the dial in a smooth, continuous motion. Time is relative and infinite in the analog dimension and we describe it accordingly: "half past four"; "10 till the hour"; "almost 11." Digital watches, on the other hand, dramatically shift our perception of time and the symbols we use. Time is measured in precise increments, commonly down to the unit of a second. We now say: "*4:31*", "*9:50:02*", "*2:15*", "*10:59 and 32 seconds*." Time is no longer continuous revolutions around a circle but a precise, numeric point within a 12- or 24-hour frame.

Computers perform in digital; that's why they are called digital computers. People perform in analog. How a computer translates analog events to digital and, in turn, translates digital events back to analog influences our understanding of everything we do in computer music and technology.

Figure 6.1 illustrates the difference between the two dimensions. Notice how the drawing of a simple sound vibration is represented by a smooth curve on the

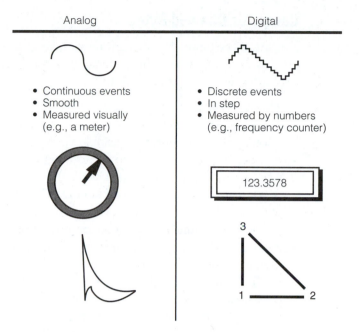

FIGURE 6.1 Comparisons of analog and digital events

analog side and by stair steps on the digital side. Here the computer has translated analog sound into numeric values, each representing a step in time or samples of time. The analog and digital meters illustrate analog and digital clocks. The bottom of the figure shows the path of a baton while conducting a 3/4-meter pattern. On the left is pictured the smooth analog path of the baton; on the right is a digital representation of the meter pattern: 1–2–3.

Counting and Thinking with 1 and 0

We made the point that computers are digital machines. When a computer translates analog information into digital, those data are represented in a simple numeric form. Back in 1666, philosopher-scientist Gottfried Leibniz came up with a system for representing numbers and performing logic decisions that required only two values, 1 and 0. This system is referred to as the *binary* or *base-2* number system. The system we are most familiar with is the *decimal* or *base-10* number system we inherited from India and Arabia around AD 700.

The figure in the margin shows you how you would count from 0 to 15 using both the decimal (base-10) and the binary (base-2) system. Counting in base 2 is very tedious for humans, but machines—especially computers—revel in it. Why? For two reasons. First, the beauty of the binary system is that 1 and 0 can be represented mechanically in many ways: holes punched in paper or metal (1= hole and 0 = no hole), switches turned on or off, light reflections (1= light and 0 = no light), gears in or out of position, pins inserted or not in a board, and so on. All of these possibilities have been used over the past 300 years for number-calculating machines and even for some music machines. The present-day computer uses millions of microscopic semiconductors for binary switches that are either on or off. Compact audio discs and DVD discs of video and audio use light reflected off a laser beam for creating their 1s and 0s. Floppy and hard disks use the position of magnetic particles to define binary numbers.

TABLE 6.1

Binary	Decimal
0000	0
0001	1
0010	2
0011	3
0100	4
0101	5
0110	6
0111	7
1000	8
1001	9
1010	10
1011	11
1100	12
1101	13
1110	14
1111	15

TIP
Base 16 or hexadecimal comes in handy when working later with MIDI. "11111111" in binary is "FF" in hexadecimal, where each of 16 digits (0-F) equals four bits.

TIP
Knowing the word size of a computer is important when it comes to filling it with memory.

Computer Bits and Bytes

You should be familiar with a few terms related to the binary nature of a computer: bits, bytes, and words. These elements form the basic building blocks of how a computer represents information:

- The terms *bit* and *byte* are based on binary numbers. A bit (Binary digIT) is the most fundamental unit in a computer. It is one electronic switch that can be on or off and is represented by a single binary digit, 1 or 0.
- A group of bits is referred to as a *byte*. A byte is a group of eight bits, with the smallest byte value being $(00000000)_2$ (represented as $(0)_{10}$ in decimal), and the largest byte value being $(11111111)_2$ (or $(255)_{10}$ in decimal). (The subscript 2 tells you it is a base-2 or binary number; the subscript 10 tells you it is a base-10 or decimal number.) In computer lingo, eight bits make a byte.
- As the number of bits a computer uses increases beyond eight, the term *word* is used to generally refer to a group of bits. The early Apple II personal computer, manufactured in the late 1970s, was an 8-bit machine. This means that the largest word it could computationally represent was eight bits long. When the IBM PC was released in the 1980s, its word size was 16 bits. Many present-day computers have 32- and 64-bit word sizes.

Serial and Parallel: Computers and Their Peripherals

Computers are always talking with the external, analog world, translating analog information into digital form and then back to analog. Here we look at the data structures a computer uses to communicate with its own devices, such as disk drives, keyboards, printers, scanners, modems, and even MIDI music keyboards. On an elementary level, all devices that connect to a computer do so through a serial or a parallel connection.

Expressing Data in Parallel Form

Figure 6.2 illustrates a *parallel* connection between a computer and an external device. It is called parallel because the binary bits in the computer are connected with the bits in the external device on a one-to-one basis. You might say that physically a wire connects each bit of the computer with the parallel bit of the device. This is a fast and direct way to connect devices.

If a computer uses 32-bit words, then every parallel connection requires a bundle of 32 wires going from the computer to the device. This is what happens when a disk drive is connected to a computer. The older SCSI interface used for disk drives and printers is a parallel interface. However, the cables for a parallel connection get cumbersome, especially for a long-distance connection.

Expressing Data in Serial Form

Figure 6.2 also shows the *serial* alternative to parallel data. Here only one wire is used between the computer and an external device. Serial exchange of data presents a classic problem, however. How do you take data stored in a computer and transmit them to another computer or device at a distant location? The answer is

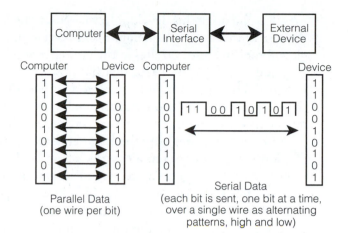

FIGURE 6.2 Serial and parallel forms for transmitting data

to convert the data into a serial stream of information, which can then be translated back into parallel information by the receiver.

For sending computer data over telephone wires or through direct wiring, the serial form is a stream of binary (on and off) electrical voltages in specific patterns to represent numerals, punctuation, and letters of the alphabet. The first communication of this type used a standard code for computer text data called ASCII. The original ASCII code had seven possibilities or seven binary bits in its code to work with; that gave 128 possible combinations of characters and punctuation, both upper- and lowercase.

Therefore, when you deal with any form of computer networking and communications, the data in your computer must be packaged and sent as a stream of binary 1s and 0s to be transferred over the network to another machine. At the other end, the data must be unpackaged from its serial form and translated back into parallel bits of data for use by the receiving computer. Typical devices that communicate through serial interfaces are printers (some printers also use parallel connections), modems, scanners, mice or joysticks, keyboards, other computers, and all MIDI music instruments.

Distance and single-wire simplicity are the advantages of serial connections. USB and Firewire are standard serial connections now commonly used in place of the more cumbersome parallel cables for computer peripheral devices.

ASIDE
Ethernet is one of those marvelous inventions that came out of the Xerox PARC "think tank" in the early 1970s. It is called Ethernet because its networking environment is passive, or "ether," and it is by far the most prevalent networking data structure in use today. It uses what is known as a contention network strategy because the network has to deal with collisions between data packets traveling both ways over a one-lane road. More on this in Module 7.

Internet Protocols: Computers Connecting to the Internet

Using a modem or a direct connection like Ethernet, a computer can communicate with other computers over the Internet through an online service, a school or college campus, or a local ISP. The Internet, or the "commodity Internet," as it is sometimes described, is a worldwide consortium of networks connecting government, university, commercial, and other computers. It truly is a network of networks!

The Internet also has a special data structure used so that all computers talking over its network can understand each other. This data structure is known as TCP/IP, or Transmission Control Protocol/Internet Protocol. Your computer speaks the TCP/IP language in order to use the Web, e-mail, or news groups or transfer files over the Internet.

LINK
Internet software that uses TCP/IP is discussed in Module 5, and hardware issues are addressed in Module 7.

How did all of this develop? In the 1950s, the RAND Corporation was given the task of inventing a communications system that would connect all the strategic military and research sites in the United States. The solution was a network of four nodes built in the 1970s that has now expanded into what we know as the Internet. The Internet's design makes it virtually indestructible. No one manages the Internet; the operation is distributed with no central authority controlling or managing or censoring data. It is a democracy, with all nodes created equal.

How is data shared over the Internet? Data is broken down into small packets of information. The packets are broadcast out on the Internet to find their own best route to a computer or network server. Packets take flight from node to node on the network, much like carrier pigeons. Should one node be out of operation, another will suffice. A packet of data couldn't care less what path it takes through the maze of networks that make up the Internet; it only cares that it gets to its destination. At the receiving end, all the packets are assembled back together to create the original message or file that was sent. It is a simple, robust, and elegant system.

Internet Addressing

Internet addresses have a fixed format and exist in both a numeric form (IP addresses) and a labeled form (domain names). Names are much easier for people to read and remember. Every node and every activity on the Internet has a unique address. We will examine personal Internet addresses, addresses for Internet websites or URLs, and addresses for various servers, such as e-mail, Web, news, and so on.

Server Internet Addresses

Here is the structure for an Internet server address:

> machine.subdomain.organization.domain

Here is a domain name and IP address, for example, of a music mail server on a campus (a completely fictional address for illustration, of course):

- Domain name = mozart.arts.ecsa.edu
- IP address = 196.55.200.2

ASIDE
A special type of IP address called private IP addressing is used within a local Internet network only. Typically, the IP number is something like 10.1.200.4 or some combination of 10.n.n.n.

Most domain name addresses are written lowercase even though case is not important. (Case is important, however, for passwords!) A dash can be used in the address as well as the digits 0 to 9, but no other punctuation is allowed.

The IP address (the one that computers use) is in reverse order from the domain name address (the one that people use). Thankfully, most people rarely encounter the IP address; a software program called a Domain Name Server (DNS) translates the domain names into IP addresses so that the computer can understand them.

The domain portion of the address categorizes network users into distinctive categories: universities (.edu), commercial users (.com), government users (.gov), nonprofit organizations (.org), and networking organizations (.net). International codes include such domains as Australia (.au), Canada (.ca), United Kingdom (.uk), and so on. The organization name, coupled with the domain, is the unique identifier for a site on the Internet, that is to say, ecsa.edu or 196.55. A newer set of alternative domain name extensions have been added: .biz, .tv, .ws (website), .pro, and several more.

TIP
If you know the IP number, you can use this in any Internet address. An e-mail address of "baudtalk@ 196.55.6.2" would work just fine, especially if the software that resolves DNS names at your site is not working.

LINK
URLs from web browsers are also discussed in Module 5.

Addresses for computer workstations and servers have a common numbering scheme. Further, common services like mail, news, and Web have a common naming scheme. The fictional East Chicago School of the Arts (esca.edu) campus is no exception. The IP numbers all start with 196.55 to match the domain names that end with esca.edu and the names of Internet services follow common practice.

E-Mail Internet Addresses

E-mail addresses on the Internet are formed by taking the domain name of your e-mail server and generating an ID unique to that mail server. Here is the structure for a personal Internet address: userid@machine.subdomain.organization.domain.

The ID for our "baudtalk" example only has to be unique to the e-mail server running on "mozart.music.ecsa.edu." A person can often use the abbreviated form of the address (e.g., esca.edu) for some activities, such as e-mail, because the campus server knows the full address locally.

Web Internet Addresses or URLs

Web browsers use a variant of the domain name address called URLs, or Uniform Resource Locators. Table 6.2 illustrates the variations of this addressing. The prefix "http://" is added in front of a server's domain name to tell the web browser that this server is a web server. If the URL is an FTP server for downloading files, then the prefix to the domain name would be "ftp://" and so on. A prefix of "https://" is a special, secure form of web URL.

The Internet 2 Fast Lane

The TCP/IP protocol and Internet addressing scheme discussed above is also known as IPv4, for IP version 4. It was developed as the commodity Internet grew and expanded. Internet 2 (I2) is a different network set aside to support a consortium of universities partnering with industry and government to research and deploy advanced Internet network technologies.

Separate fiber channels for Internet connectivity have been established among I2 members. One of the largest of the channels is the Abilene I2 backbone. When packets of data are sent out from one I2 site to another I2 site, the data will automatically be routed over an I2 channel such as Abilene through various "gigaPOP" network nodes.

What are the advantages of I2? Massively greater bandwidth and transmission speed approaching 10 gbits/sec is one advantage. Synchronous data transmissions are another advantage: Given our analogy above, pigeons traveling over I2 can be

TABLE 6.2

Baudtalk's address	baudtalk@mozart.music.ecsa.edu
His full domain name	mozart.music.ecsa.edu
Abbreviated domain name	esca.edu
Baudtalk's alternative address	baudtalk@esca.edu
IP address	196.55.1.2
Baudtalk's address with IP	baudtalk@196.55.1.2

LINK
Network connectivity options and transmission speeds are discussed in Module 7 under network hardware.

choreographed to arrive at their location on the same path and at the same time. These two improvements alone will make it possible to carry out live music performance with audio and video from remote sites over I2.

The IPv4 TCP/IP protocol is also being enhanced to IPv6. IPv6 will provide better security, quality of service, and, most importantly, expanded Internet addressing possibilities. Instead of 32 bits per address, 128 bits per address will provide enormously expanded new IP numbers for registering devices on the Internet.

File Formats: Sharing Files over the Internet

Return to the serial nature of data over networks and the Internet. In all forms of networking, we are moving a large volume of bits across great distances and we want to move them as fast as possible. One technique for increasing speed is to increase the bit rate of the transmission. The range of modem transmission can start with 56 kbits/sec for POTS modems, and increase up to 100 mbits/sec or faster for gigabit Ethernet. Only with Fast Ethernet or Internet 2 do we approach the speed necessary to directly deliver audio and video data over networks and the Internet.

There are other ways, fortunately, to increase transmission speed by using *file compression* and *optimized methods* for file transfers. When you access FTP servers abundant with freeware and shareware files on the Internet, most of these files will be stored in a compressed format. When your web browser downloads graphics, sounds, and movie clips needed to create the multimedia web pages on your browser's desktop, the files will also be optimized and compressed.

Packaging and Compressing Files

Table 6.3 provides a list of some of the more common schemes you will find on the Internet for packaging and exchanging files. Some provide compression to reduce file size. The column on the left indicates the file extension that will be appended as a suffix or *extension* to the file name (e.g., myfile.exe or myapp.zip, or muscode.sea). The second column indicates the computer that can originate or receive each file type. The remaining column briefly describes the packaging or compression scheme.

Shrinking File Sizes

In its simplest form, file compression works by replacing patterns of redundant information in a file with more efficient coding. There are many different software algorithms for accomplishing this. Error checking is also built into the process. When a file is uncompressed, a validity check is done to see if any data were lost in the exchange.

Extensions like .sit and .zip are for compression schemes developed around early software utilities that have become pervasive through common use: Stuffit (Aladdin Software), PKZIP (PKWARE), and WinZip (WinZip Computing) are examples. Self-extracting compression files (.sea and .exe) are frequently .sit or .zip files with extra code added so the file will uncompress itself when downloaded to a computer, without the need for special software.

TABLE 6.3	File Formats and Extensions for Exchanging Files over the Internet	
File Extension	**Computer**	**Description**
.sit	Mac/Win	Created with StuffIt
.zip	Mac/Win	Created with StuffIt, WinZip, or other similar software
.sea	Mac	Self-extracting version of StuffIt format
.exe	Win	Self-extracting DOS/Windows compressed-file format
.bin	Mac	Binary format that includes Mac file with desktop information
.z, .Z, .gz, .tar	Unix	Common UNIX file-compression formats
.hqx	Mac	Binhex format that converts Mac binary files to a text form
.uu or .uue	Unix	UUcoded format that converts binary files to a text form

MacBinary is unique to the Macintosh world. MacBinary with the .bin extension is a file-compression format that includes all binary data from the file plus key Mac resource and Finder information. This added information ensures that the file, when uncompressed, appears on your Mac desktop with the correct icon. Most Mac programs, Fetch for example, decode MacBinary automatically.

Files with extensions like .z, .Z, .gz, and .tar are compressed files that originated on a UNIX system. A "tar" file is actually a collection or library of several files that are compressed into one package for file transfer.

An early method of sending binary files over the Internet was the conversion of binary codes to ASCII text; no compression took place, just a conversion into text to facilitate transmission. Two formats are used: *binhex* (.hqx) conversion, popular for Macintosh files, and *Uucoded* (.uu or .uue) for UNIX files.

Exchanging Documents with Universal File Formats

General file compression is one important issue when transferring files over networks and the Internet. Another is cross-platform independence once the files have been uncompressed: the ability to exchange application files across any computer or software platform. This need for universal exchange of files has become especially critical with the growth of the World Wide Web. Media files such as sounds, video clips, and graphics are automatically downloaded to a person's web browser with the server having no knowledge of the browser's computer platform. Table 6.4 notes a few of the universal file formats used for exchanging media.

Exchanging Text Documents

The first set of files shown in Table 6.4 includes ASCII text and Postscript. One common denominator among all computer software and machines is the ASCII text file. When in doubt, send an ASCII text document; most word processors will

TABLE 6.4	Some Common Universal File Formats and Their Extensions	
File Extension	**Types**	**Description**
.txt	Text	Universal ASCII text file format
.ps	Postscript	Postscript file format
.pdf	Document	Portable document format for electronic publishing
.html or .htm	Text	HTML document format for the World Wide Web
.wav or .aif	Sound	Sampled sound and music files
.rm, .wma, .mp3	Sound	Compressed sound and music files
.aac, .m4a, .m4p	Sound	MPEG 4 compression for AAC and Apple iTunes audio
.mid	MIDI	MIDI music files
.gif	Graphic	8-bit compressed graphic format
.jpg or .png	Graphic	High-resolution compressed graphic formats
.mpg, .mp4, .avi, .divx	Video	Digital video formats
.mov, .rm, .wmv, .asf	Video	Streaming web video formats

TIP
Rich Text Format (.rtf) is an alternative file format to ASCII text files that can be used when you need to exchange formatting information as well. Many word processors can read .rtf files.

provide the option of saving or creating documents in this form as "text only" documents. The drawback to using ASCII files, of course, is that all style and formatting information is lost (e.g., bold, underline, fonts, font sizes, paragraphs, margins). Moreover, if word spaces or space runs (a series of spaces) were used to create tables or formatting effects, alignment can be easily destroyed if margins and fonts do not match at the receiving end.

Because Postscript is used on most printers, many documents are being exchanged as Postscript files noted with the .ps (Postscript). Using the Postscript format ensures that the printed copy at the receiving end is a good replica of the original fonts, styles, document formatting, and graphics. Postscript files are text files containing the codes or instructions used to generate desktop-published documents. After downloading one of these files, you can use a Postscript utility to print the file.

Adobe's Portable Document Format (.pdf) is a special document type that encapsulates the Postscript data from an electronic document along with graphics, hyperlinks, and other elements, and creates a portable file for exchanging the document with computers that have the Adobe Acrobat Reader, a free software program, installed. It will display the original word-processed or desktop-published document just as it appeared on the screen or printer of the computer that created it. The file may then be printed and, again, it will look the same as it did on the original computer. A good deal of printed documentation from class notes to journal articles to software manuals is distributed online in PDF format.

To create PDF files, your application must be able to save in that format or you can use any of the family of Acrobat products to convert files to PDF. Mac OS X has the ability to create PDF files built into its operating system. A special application from Adobe is required to create the PDF file.

ASIDE
There are two forms of the HTML extension for web documents: htm and html. Web browsers and servers usually accept both forms.

LINK
We will return to HTML in Viewport VII, where we look at web based music notation.

LINK
Audio and MPEG file formats are discussed in depth in Modules 8 and 11; more details on MIDI files can be found in Module 14.

ASIDE
Don't confuse the older AU audio format with Apple's Audio Unit (AU) plug-in protocol under OS X!

LINK
MIDI file types are discussed in Module 14—see Table 14.5.

Exchanging Web Documents

The HTML (HyperText Markup Language) document uses a special file-formatting language developed from an earlier markup language called SGML. It is used to exchange complex documents with styles, graphics, and even data links over the Internet through World Wide Web document servers. HTML files are web files that can be read by any web browser regardless of the computer platform. HTML files are simply text files, but imbedded within the text are HTML tags enclosed in brackets, such as < A HREF > or < IMAGE > or < P >. The web browser uses these tags as instructions for formatting the web page, displaying the graphics and other media, and creating links to other HTML documents on or off the Internet.

Exchanging Digital Audio and MIDI

Two rows in Table 6.4 describe universal file formats for digital audio and MIDI music. WAV and AIF files, for Windows and Mac, respectively, are the primary uncompressed digital audio file formats.

The earliest audio compression format on the Internet was the AU file (not shown here). This is seldom used because of its poor audio quality. Several widely used formats provide excellent *compressed* digital audio: RealAudio (.rm), Windows Media Audio (.wma), MP3 (.mp3), and the newer AAC MPEG (.aac). MP3, the most prevalent, is being replaced with WMA and AAC because software offers better support for these formats. Apple iTunes uses .m4a for AAC-coded audio and .m4p for AAC with their proprietary digital rights management coding sold from the iTunes store.

MIDI files (.mid) provide a standardized way for transferring MIDI performance codes across computer platforms. Most MIDI applications will read the standard, Type-0 format, MIDI file. Many web browsers provide support for playing Type-0 MIDI files without special software. Given their small size compared to digital audio files, MIDI files are a good choice for low-bandwidth, web-page music clips.

Exchanging Graphics and Video

A summary of graphic and video file formats is presented in the remaining rows of Table 6.4. These are the most common file formats, but many other options and variations are available.

Graphics

GIF (Graphic Interchange Files or .gif), JPEG (Joint Photographic Experts Group or .jpg), and PNG (Portable Network Graphics or .png) are universal formats for graphic files. GIF provides compression for 8-bit or 256-color graphics and is one of the most prevalent graphic file types on the Internet. It works best for line-drawn color images. JPG or JPEG format, which provides high-resolution graphic compression and up to 32-bit color, is especially suitable for photographic images. PNG graphics (pronounced "ping") also handles compression of complex color images up to 48-bit resolution.

Graphics and multimedia applications and most web browsers read all three formats. If you need to transfer a photographic image, choose JPEG or PNG. For any other graphic image, try GIF if the reduction to 256 colors doesn't affect the quality of the image. A more recent JPEG 2000 standard will provide better-quality photographic images at the same file size, or greatly reduced file sizes at the same quality of image as JPEG.

Video

As the last two rows of Table 6.4 show, there are several competing formats for digital video. Formats such as MPEG-1 (.mpg), MPEG-4 (.mp4), Microsoft's first video format (.avi), and DivX (.divx), are best used for applications other than the Web. For any substantial video, these formats, while offering compression, still generate very large files. They are best used for video created for CD, VideoCD, or DVD file exchange.

Video compression formats optimized for web applications include Apple's QuickTime (.mov), RealNetworks' RealVideo (.rm), and Microsoft's Windows Media Player video formats (.wmv and .asf). For the most part, these formats can be used across Windows, Macintosh, UNIX, and Linux applications.

Most websites offering digital video clips provide MOV, WMV, and RM options. Besides compression, these formats also offer streaming and instant-on features. Streaming technology delivers the video (or audio for that matter) in a constant stream from the server to the client, thus removing the need to download and store very large video files. Instant-on refers to streaming video playback starting immediately, without the need to wait for initial buffering of a portion of the video file.

Module 7

The Mechanics of Computers and Networking

Module 6 acquainted you with the concepts of the binary logic of computing machines and the protocols used for networking. We will use these concepts to gain insight into computer hardware and networking operations.

Computer Hardware Operations and the IPOS Model

There are four stages to the mechanics of any computer system, as illustrated in Figure 7.1: input, process, output, and storage (IPOS):

- The *input* stage represents devices for getting data into the computer
- The *process* stage stores and transforms the data
- The *output* stage represents devices for getting data out of the computer
- The *storage* stage represents devices for saving and transporting data

Between each of these stages are *interfaces* that translate the signals coming from the input, output, and storage devices to the process part of the computer, often performing analog-to-digital and digital-to-analog conversion. We will examine interfaces first, that walk through the process, input, output, and storage stages.

Interfaces

Interfaces that apply to all computer processes include bus, parallel and serial, USB and Firewire, and video. Network interfaces will be addressed later in this module.

Computer Bus

Inside a computer, all components are connected to each other through an internal *bus* on the motherboard. This pathway of microscopic wires connects the various circuits within the computer. Computers provide slots or connections that enable external devices to access data, controls, and timing signals on the bus. The PCI (Peripheral Component Interconnect) bus is commonly used by the industry across all computer platforms. Following the PCI standard makes it easy to purchase a new device for a computer, like a hard drive or music or video board, for example, without worrying whether it is a Macintosh or a Windows PC.

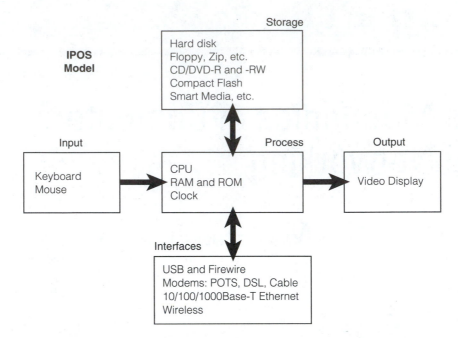

FIGURE 7.1 The Input-Process-Output-Storage (IPOS) model of a computer

ASIDE
The numbering system in the EMT-workstation charts is used as a system of reference numbers for various hardware options. The reference number will be consistently used for any given device throughout the text. A complete list of hardware from the EMT workstations is provided in the Appendix.

Figure 7.2 illustrates a basic computer workstation with a laptop; the same principles apply to a desktop computer system. The bus in the EMT-1 connects the internal components, including the digital audio (DA) sound card (4), hard disk (2), CD- or DVD-R drive (3), and internal network circuitry (7) shown in the diagram.

Another standard that functions like a bus, especially among laptops, is the

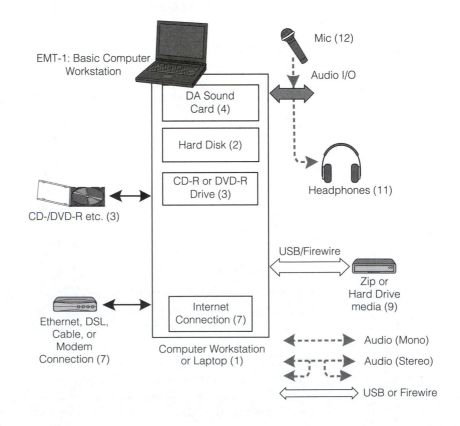

FIGURE 7.2 The EMT-1 basic computer workstation

LINK
The concept of serial and parallel communication is covered in Module 6.

LINK
Audio interfaces are covered in depth in Module 10 and there is much more to come on MIDI interfaces in Module 16.

ASIDE
"B" when paired with KB, MB, or GB represents "bytes" while "b" represents "bits." Hence "Mbps" used here is megabits per second and "MB" or "GB" used elsewhere, is megabytes or gigabytes.

PCMCIA (Personal Computer Memory Card International Association) card interface. PCMCIA is a standard for small, credit-card-sized devices, called PC Cards and the PC CardBus. From a laptop, PC Cards can be popped in and out for modems, Ethernet networking, fax, storage devices, digital audio and video, and more.

Serial and Parallel Interfaces

Over the years, computers have had various serial and parallel standards for connecting hardware. The older interfaces for printers and storage devices, Centronics and SCSI, respectively, are two classic systems for parallel connectivity. Serial interfaces have been used in the past for modems, external keyboards, and computer mice. MIDI is a unique serial interface just for connecting music devices. Each type of parallel or serial interface has a distinctive connector to ensure that the correct cable is used for the appropriate device.

USB and Firewire

Like the PCI and PCMCIA computer bus architecture, USB (Universal Serial Bus) and Firewire (IEEE 1394) are standard solutions for interfacing almost any external device with a computer. The EMT-1 workstation in Figure 7.2 has both USB and Firewire interfaces.

USB and Firewire were part of an industrywide effort to simplify the number of connectors on a computer device. At the same time, the improved design would give the interface fast bandwidth to support audio and video, thus making it possible for audio and video processing to be remote from the computer workstation. The design also eliminates the need for powering down the computer to swap devices. This is known as "hot swapping" USB or Firewire devices.

For Firewire, transfer rates of 100 to 400 megabits per second (Mbps) are possible. Real-time audio can be transported over the same serial bus as data moving to and from hard drives, laser disc recorders, and digital video and audio devices. Firewire serves professional-level audio and video interface needs, as well as high-speed computer storage devices.

It takes about 1.4 mbits/sec (Mbps) to move CD-quality audio data being captured in stereo. The 1.4-Mbps speed hardly puts a dent in the 400-Mbps transfer rate of the Firewire interface. The newer Firewire 800 specification provides twice the transfer rate, up to 800 Mbps. Firewire is truly designed for high-speed, daisy-chaining of hardware.

The design of the USB interface was driven by a need to eliminate the complexity of connections on the back of a computer, to replace various serial and parallel connectivity solutions, and to continue to improve the plug-and-play features of consumer computers. Keyboards, mice, printers, scanners, consumer audio, and the like almost universally use USB across all computer platforms. USB's transfer rate is 12 Mbps compared to Firewire's 400-Mbps range. Devices on a USB bus can be hot swapped up to 127 devices in a single daisy chain. A newer USB 2.0 standard provides transfer rates as high as 480 Mbps, making it competitive with the Firewire 400 standard.

With USB and Firewire, connecting and sharing external computer devices has reached a new level of simplicity. With all of your devices plugged into a USB or Firewire hub (a connector box for multiple devices), it is possible to plug in one cable to a laptop, and instantly have all of your external devices successfully communicating with your computer.

ASIDE
A "pixel" is a picture element or one dot of color on a video screen.

Video Interfaces

Connecting computer video to a computer has always had its own unique connector, the VGA (Video Graphics Array) analog interface. VGA computer displays (640x480 pixels) use the same cathode ray tube (CRT) technology as TV sets. As computer resolution increased, variations on the VGA theme included SVGA (800x600 pixels), XGA (1024x768), and SXGA (1280x1024). Flatscreen computer displays do not use CRT technology, but rather a Liquid Crystal Display (LCD), and function entirely as digital technology, not analog. Flatscreen monitors may use a Digital Video Interface (DVI) connector in place of the traditional VGA interface. The EMT-1 Workstation (Figure 7.2) uses a built-in LCD flatscreen in the laptop computer.

Process

Let's now turn our attention to the deeper internal workings of a computer system. The *process stage* is what some call the "brains" of the computer. It is here that computers do what they are designed to do: transform or change data. Numbers are added, text is manipulated, music codes are arranged and modified, and machine-level decisions are made. The IPOS diagram in Figure 7.1 shows three important components of the process stage: the central processing unit (CPU), memory, and a clock.

ASIDE
The Pentium 4 CPU chip contains about 42 million transistors connected by wires a fraction of a micron apart; by comparison, a human hair is 100 microns thick.

Central Processing Unit (CPU)

The CPU is an electronic circuit called the microprocessor integrated circuit or *chip*. The CPU is the "brain" of a computer and coordinates the flow of data in and out of the machine. AMD's Athlon, Intel's Pentium and Celeron, and IBM and Motorola's PowerPC are names commonly associated with CPUs used in personal computers.

Memory

In the simplest terms, there are two kinds of *memory* in a personal computer: *Random-access* memory (or RAM) and *read-only memory* (or ROM).

ASIDE
If your computer has battery power to support RAM, as do many laptops, you will not lose your data in memory.

More appropriate names for RAM are *read-and-write memory* or *changeable memory*. A computer can retrieve data stored in RAM and it can write data back to RAM memory. RAM memory is what you use the most in a computer; it's your best friend. Your best friend, however, has one bad character trait: As soon as you turn off the power to the computer, all the RAM data are lost! This is why we have disk storage.

In an 8-bit computer like the vintage Apple II, it would take eight 1-Kb chips to give you 1,000 bytes of RAM. Memory sizes of chips are now commonly referred to in bytes with total memory installations on laptops and desktops from 256 or 500 megabytes (MB) to more than 2 GB (gigabytes) of RAM.

ROM or *read-only memory*, as the name suggests, can only be read. You cannot change the contents of ROM. When you turn on the computer, the information stored in ROM is always there. The main kernel of the operating system is placed in ROM by the manufacturer to ensure that your computer has some intelligence when you first turn it on. Programs stored in ROM are called *firmware* rather than software because they cannot be erased.

LINK
Module 6 discusses bits and bytes if you need to review.

Historical Perspective on Computers

More than 350 years have passed since William Schickard designed his Calculating Clock. Except during the period from 1940 to 1970, most calculating machines have been small desktop units. With the appearance of the first personal computers and microprocessor chips in the 1970s, the small, personal calculating machine returned, with power for logic and computation that far surpassed the designs of any of the "big iron" mainframe computers from the middle of this century.

With Charles Babbage's design of his Analytical Engine in 1834, certain critical components of the computer were born. Babbage's mechanical computer had a "store" for numbers, a "mill" to perform calculations with those numbers, a "barrel" to control the flow of numbers, and punched cards to program the machine's mechanical gears—an idea Babbage borrowed from the Jacquard weaving loom that used punched cards to remember patterns.

The ENIAC (Electronic Numerical Integrator and Computer) realized Babbage's design on a huge scale. Completed in 1946, the machine was the first all-electronic computer. It used 19,000 vacuum tubes, covered a city block, and consumed so much electricity that the lights in its section of Philadelphia dimmed when it was turned on. In addition to the drawback of its size, the ENIAC lacked the ability to store or remember instructions.

Working with the designers of the ENIAC, the mathematician John von Neumann conceived of the computer as we know it today. The design concept of the EDVAC, built in 1951, is used in present-day personal and desktop comput-

ers and is known as the *von Neumann machine. Input* devices (corresponding to Babbage's punched cards) bring information into the machine. The *process* (Babbage's "mill") carries out the computations and controls the information flow ("barrel"). The *storage* component (Babbage's "store") holds the results of the computation or data waiting to be processed, and *output* devices display the results of the computer's calculations. (Von Neumann's IPOS model is reinforced throughout this textbook.) The unique element that von Neumann added to this design was the idea of a stored program. Just as data are stored in the computer, so is the program, or instructions for processing those data. Programs can be changed just as easily as data.

Around the same time as the EDVAC, Forrester and Everett built the first real-time computer, the Whirlwind, at MIT (see the 1951 photo). This later became the SAGE computer used for the nation's air defense and early warning system. Several of its innovations were precursors of features in today's computers. The Whirlwind used the first *magnetic core* memory (an ancestor of today's random-access memory) for storage. Because of its interactive nature (e.g., monitoring aircraft flight patterns), techniques were developed for controlling external devices and visualizing the results. We see this today in any computer controlling a MIDI music system and visualizing music notation on a screen. The Whirlwind was the first computer to use CRT video display monitors and light guns for pointing to enter commands.

One of the first computer installations at an academic institution was the ILLIAC computer at the University of Illinois. Lejaren Hiller used this computer for electronic music generation. His *ILLIAC Suite for String Quartet* is recognized as the first music composition created with a computer. A photo of the Musicwriter typewriter interfaced to the ILLIAC for music output is in Module 19.

Several important developments led to computer miniaturization: the inventions of the transistor at Bell Labs in 1947; the integrated circuit (or *chip*) at Texas Instruments in 1952; the first RAM chips in 1968; and the first microcomputer on a chip at Intel in 1972.

Other developments led to the look and feel of the personal computers we use today: The first personal computers with sound and graphics as standard features (the Apple II and Commodore PET, among others) were introduced in the late 1970s. The Xerox Star computer developed at the Palo Alto Research Center (PARC) was the precursor to graphic-based systems, with windows, icons, pull-down menus, and a mouse. This design first appeared commercially in the Apple Lisa computer, followed by the Apple Macintosh and then the OS/2 and Windows operating systems for PC computers.

MIT Museum

Dodd, Forrester, Everett, and Ferenz with the Whirlwind I Computer at MIT

Clock

The third component of the process stage is the *system clock*. For musicians, this is a simple concept. Every computer has the equivalent of a metronome, a clock that synchronizes all events that take place within its various stages. The tempo of the metronome is the computer's *clock speed*. Clock speed is measured in *Hertz (Hz)*, or cycles per second; the abbreviation mHz indicates *MegaHertz*, or millions of cycles per second. Clock speeds have increased from 1 mHz, to 500 mHz, to 3 gigahertz (gHz) in the 20 years since the first personal computers were introduced. Laptops, because of battery consumption and heat issues, typically run at slower clock speeds than their sibling desktop computers.

Input

In order for the CPU to process information, data must be entered into the computer. Input techniques used at one time or another include punched cards and paper tape, magnetic tape, typewriter-like keyboards, music keyboards, musical instrument controllers, and a host of pointing devices. Pointing devices include light guns, light pens, touch panels, graphics tablets, joysticks, and the one most commonly used with graphic operating systems today, the mouse.

Keyboard

The keyboard has a long association with communications and computers dating back to the early teletype machine. The impetus for the ASCII system came from the need to standardize the codes for each key so that teletypewriters and computers could communicate. Many of the names for ASCII keys stem from their teletype heritage. For example, the return key is known as the carriage return from older typewriter technology where the carriage physically moved across the page when a new line started. Each computer manufacturer maintains the standard QWERTY layout and then adds special keys: escape (esc), control (ctrl), enter, cursor movement keys, and function keys (F1, F2, . . . F15). Windows PC keyboards have certain idiosyncratic keys like the ALT, INS, and function keys. Macintosh extended keyboards also have function keys and "enter" as well as "return." The one unique Macintosh key is the Command key, also known as the Open Apple or Flower ⌘ key.

Most keyboards have what is called *n-key rollover*. This means that the keyboard will let you press another key before your finger has released the previous key—a must for fast typists.

Mouse

The *mouse* gets its name because it looks like a little creature with a tail. It was invented as a *point-and-click device* by Douglas Engelbart at the Stanford Research Institute in 1964, and was made popular by the Macintosh computer.

There are two mouse designs: mechanical and optical. The *mechanical* mouse uses a rubber-coated ball that rotates within the mouse case as you roll it over a flat surface. The *optical* mouse uses optical sensors within the case to track the movement of the ball.

The traditional Macintosh mouse has only one button for selecting options from pull-down menus, check boxes, and the like; the traditional Windows mouse has two buttons. The left button behaves like the Macintosh button. The right button, when clicked, usually brings up a pop-up menu with various options that can be selected from the object chosen.

Output

After data have been manipulated by the computer, the results must be translated back into human-readable form. Output devices include color and monochrome video displays, and different kinds of printers, including black-and-white, and color, laser, and inkjet. Video displays go by many names, including CRTs (cathode ray tubes), monitors, screens, displays, and terminals. As noted earlier, flatscreen monitors are favored over the older CRT technology due to their compact size, light weight, energy-saving characteristics, cost, and, for some, lower level of eye fatigue.

Storage

The remaining stage of the IPOS model is storage of applications and data on a variety of devices. On each type of storage device, binary information is recorded in a permanent form external to CPU and memory. We will examine four storage solutions, each one of which has a number of alternatives: flexible, fixed, memory, and laser storage.

Table 7.1 provides an overview of disk performance specifications based on performance data available in 2003. Why is this important? When working with large amounts of digital audio, the data is most likely captured directly to disk and streamed from disk for playback, with very large file sizes involved. Understanding storage performance is critical to ensuring flawless capture or performance of your music. The key attributes that determine the performance and capacity of a storage device are:

- *Access or seek time:* This is how long it takes a storage device to find the correct location in order to read or write data. For hard disks or floppy drives, this is the time it takes to position the read-and-write head over the correct track and sector. As shown in Table 7.1, internal fixed-disk storage (hard drives) has a seek time around 8.5 milliseconds (ms). Faster is better.

TABLE 7.1 Approximate Specifications for Various Forms of Disk Storage (shown by decreasing performance based on 2003 data)

Storage Form	Access/Seek Time	RPM	Transfer Rate
Internal hard disk	~8.5 ms at 7200 rpm	3,600—7,200	100 Mbps[1] at 7,200 rpm
External Firewire hard disk	~8.5 ms	4,200—7,200	~34 Mbps
PC Card hard drive	12~15 ms	3,600—4,500	5—60 Mbps
Compact Flash	~10 ms	NA[2]	1.5—16 Mbps[3]
SD and Mini-SD	~10 ms	NA[2]	2—20 Mbps[3]
Memory Stick	~10 ms	NA[2]	1.5—20 Mbps[3]
Smart Media	~10 ms	NA[2]	.8 write/1.8 read Mbps
Zip 250 flexible disk	29—40 ms	2,941—3,676	.9—2.3 Mbps[4]
3.5-inch floppy	100 ms	300—360	.5 Mbps

[1]Megabits/sec.
[2]Memory disks are solid-state electronics with no moving platter or read/write heads.
[3]Transfer rates vary as a function of the memory disk's size in megabytes (bigger is faster) and whether data are being read or written to the disk (read is faster).
[4]Zip disk speed varies as a function of the connectivity form (e.g., USB, USB 2.0, Firewire, internal, etc.), with USB the slowest at .9 Mbps.

TIP

When you get a "disk full" message from your computer, the computer is telling you that there are no empty sectors remaining on the storage device. Different computer operating systems and disk formats vary in terms of the number of tracks available on a storage medium and the number of sectors on those tracks.

- *Disk revolution speed:* This is the speed at which a disk platter spins, applicable to flexible and fixed-disk solutions. Memory disks are static storage with no moving parts. This attribute is measured in revolutions per minute (RPM) and more is better. Hard disks can have RPM in the range of 3,600 to 7,200 (Table 7.1); Zip disks 2941 or 3676 RPM depending on drive technology; and floppy drives 300 to 360 RPM.

- *Data transfer rate:* This is how long it takes to get data from the computer to the storage device and back again. This rate is difficult to assess because it depends on many design factors. Table 7.1 shows approximate speeds from .5 Mbps for floppy disks up to 100 Mbps for internal hard-drive storage.

- *Storage capacity:* This refers to how many bytes of data can be stored on the storage device. Storage starts with 1.4 MB for a floppy disk, jumps to 250 or 750 MB for a Zip disk, and then moves up into the gigabyte range for fixed- and memory-disk storage.

- *Interface:* This is how the storage device connects to the computer. Options include an internal computer bus interface or external Firewire 400 or 800, or USB 1.0 or 2.0 interfaces. PC Card, USB, or custom interface designs are used for memory-disk storage.

- *Disk formats.* In addition to the attributes described above, all storage media are formatted with a prescribed pattern of sectors and tracks and with a directory or index that tells the operating system the name of a file or directory and where its data are stored on the disk. The tracks and sectors are laid down in a series of concentric circles from the inside to the outside of a disk. Each file is allocated a series of sectors taken from any empty sectors available on the disk. When a file is deleted, the sectors used are freed up and made available for the next time a new file is created and saved to the disk.

  File formatting standards include Windows/DOS formats (FAT-16 and FAT-32), Macintosh formats (HFS and HFS+), and the newer Universal Disk Format (UDF) that can be used on any operating system. The legacy formats like FAT-16 and FAT-32 can only access up to 2 or 4 GBs of storage (hardly usable for a 500-GB hard drive). UDF, on the other hand, will accommodate up to 1 TB (terabyte) of data storage—that's a trillion bytes of data!

Flexible Disk Storage

The original flexible disk storage is the floppy disk, a storage medium that has been around for more than 30 years. Inside an outer protective shell is a circular disk coated with the same magnetic material as audio recording tape. The inner disk is thin and flexible, hence the name "floppy." The older 5.25-inch floppy disks were formatted to hold as little as 160 KB, but the current 3.5-inch floppy disks hold 1.4 to 2.8 MB of data.

A number of super-floppy disk technologies have been tried. The Iomega Zip disk is the dominant flexible-disk solution and is an installed option on many personal computers. The original Zip disk held 100 MB of data; 250 and 750 MB storage formats are now available. The size of the Zip is 3.5 inches, just like floppy disks, but the Zip disk is just a little thicker. An Iomega Zip 750MB USB disk media and drive are shown in Figure 7.3a.

Fixed-Disk Storage

Floppy and Zip disks are great for transporting small amounts of data; a 3.5-inch floppy fits nicely into your shirt pocket and is reasonably safe from damage. But the demands of digital audio and graphics require massive storage and faster access than flexible storage can provide.

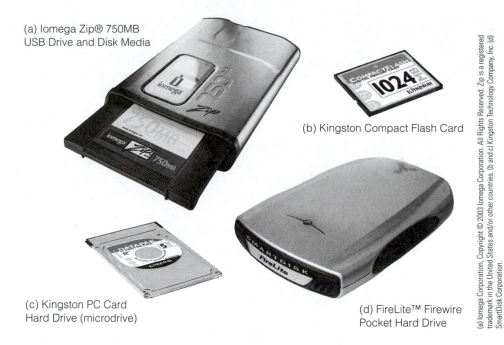

(a) Iomega Zip® 750MB
USB Drive and Disk Media

(b) Kingston Compact Flash Card

(c) Kingston PC Card
Hard Drive (microdrive)

(d) FireLite™ Firewire
Pocket Hard Drive

FIGURE 7.3   Four examples of storage devices

(a) Iomega Corporation, Copyright © 2003 Iomega Corporation. All Rights Reserved. Zip is a registered trademark in the United States and/or other countries. (b and c) Kingston Technology Company, Inc. (d) SmartDisk Corporation.

ASIDE
The original Winchester hard-disk concept using a magnetic platter and a floating read-and-write head was developed by IBM in 1973. It first appeared for personal computers as the Shugart drive in 1978.

TIP
Use *disc* for laser discs, including CDs and DVDs; use *disk* for all other disks.

A fixed or hard disk uses an inflexible, rapidly spinning platter. The platter is coated with magnetic material and the disk uses a read-and-write head that floats on a cushion of air. The read-and-write head never touches the platter and the entire mechanism is sealed from the environment. Its storage capacity is typically somewhere in the 1–500 GB range, with terabytes of storage bytes available. As with floppy disks, the hard-drive platter must be formatted before any computer data can be stored on the disk.

Fixed-disk solutions are internal components installed inside workstations or laptops, or self-contained, external devices connected to the computer with USB or Firewire. Figure 7.3d shows a Firewire pocket hard drive that is 3x5x7 inches in size. Removable versions of fixed-disk technology are also available to provide portability and flexibility for storage. The Kingston PC-Card hard drive shown in Figure 7.3c is an example of innovative miniaturizing technology; a 5-GB fixed drive is installed inside the case of a PC Card and can be plugged into a laptop, handheld, MP3 player, or any device with a PC Card slot. The device weighs less than two ounces!

Memory-disk storage

Memory-disk storage relies on nonvolatile, flash memory that requires no power or moving parts to store data. This type of memory first appeared with digital cameras. It is now used for portable storage among cameras, handhelds, laptops, printers, and more. All of the disks are the size of postage stamps and very light. Memory-disk devices cost more per megabyte of storage when compared to flexible or fixed-drive storage, and accommodate less storage capacity and slower access speeds. The trade-off is their small size and portability.

There are several alternative technologies for memory-disk storage. Several of these solutions can be formatted with a Windows DOS format, typically FAT-12 or FAT-16, that can be read by both Mac and PC operating systems:

- *Compact Flash (CF)*: a widely used format that comes in storage sizes up to 4 GB and is used for cameras, laptops, handhelds, and MP3 players. Figure 7.3b shows a 1 GB Kingston compact flash memory disk.

ASIDE
Third-generation flash memory is forecast to handle storage capacities in the 16-GB range.

- *Smart Media (SM):* comes in storage sizes up to 256 MB and is smaller than the CF disk; this format is used in older cameras and MP3 players and some MIDI keyboard workstations like the Korg Triton LE.
- *Secure Digital (SD):* another popular format with storage sizes up to 1 GB; widely used with many handhelds, cameras, and MP3 players. SDs are thinner and narrower than CF disks. An even smaller one, the "miniSD," provides 32–128 MB of storage for very small devices like cell phones.
- *Memory Stick:* unique design developed for Sony products; newer Pro version stores up to 2 GB.
- *xD-Picture Card:* designed by Fuji and Olympus for their cameras offering 16 MB to potentially 8 GB of "eXtreme-Digital" media storage in a ultra-compact form.
- *Portable* USB Flash (also known as USB Key Drive or Thumb Drive): Flash memory affixed to a USB connector for very portable storage from a key chain.

CD and DVD Storage

TIP
Data are formatted on CD and DVD drives using the universal ISO 9660 or UDF formats, or formats unique to Windows or Macintosh. Laser discs can also be in a hybrid format that makes them mountable on Windows or Macintosh computers. More on this in Module 11.

Optical disc drives, a reliable and primary means of computer storage, use a different principle for recording information than flexible or fixed storage. CDs and DVDs use laser technology to record data to 7.5-inch optical platters. Instead of magnetic particles arranged on a spinning surface, optical devices use light reflected off minute crystalline particles. Consumer CD and DVD laser discs, or CD- and DVD-ROM discs, can only be read. CD-ROM and DVD-ROM drives for computers offer the ability to read commercially produced CD or DVD discs, including CD audio recordings, CD-ROMs with software to be installed, DVD movies, or DVD-ROMs with prerecorded digital graphics, audio, or video files.

A CD can hold up to 640 MB of data, 600 times more than a floppy disk. A DVD (Digital Versatile Disc) offers far greater storage capacity, up to seven times the capacity of a CD-ROM, or 4.7 GB per disc, with enough space to put a digital copy of a full-length feature film on one disc. The latest generation of DVD drives offer fast 200-ms or greater access times. More notable, though, is the fact that this generation of DVD drives supports the playback of a wide variety of backwards-compatible laser formats, including CD audio, CD-ROM, laser disc with recorded MP3 files, DVD, and CD and DVD recordable formats.

LINK
Viewport IV includes more extensive coverage of CD and DVD applications and formats.

CD and DVD Recordables

Optical drives write as well as read data. To write binary codes to an optical disc, a laser beam heats or changes a spot on the disc from a random or amorphous spot (binary 0) to a crystalline or ordered spot (1). To read the data back, the laser beam looks for reflections from the crystalline particles. These disc formats are known as CD- or DVD-Recordable (CD- or DVD-R) or CD- or DVD-ReWritable (CD- and DVD-RW) discs. The -R and -RW drives are CD or DVD drives that let you record or "burn" data directly from your computer to a blank CD or DVD disc. The -R technology allows you to burn once to a blank laser disc. The -RW format offers the option of recording to the blank disc several times (hence the RW for ReWrite). Other recording formats for DVD include DVD+R, DVD+RW, and DVD-RAM.

TIP
Be sure to match the recordable format carefully to the drive. DVD-RAM discs, for example, are not the same as DVD-Rs.

Your computer may likely include a DVD drive, or even a DVD-RW drive. External CD and DVD drives (as well as their recordable variations) can be connected to a computer with USB, USB 2.0, or Firewire 400 or 800. Blank CD-R and DVD-R recordable discs are the most economical; CD- and DVD-RWs are more expensive. No matter which CD or DVD recordable format you choose, laser technology is an excellent choice for storing and archiving large amounts of data, including various multimedia files like digital video, graphics, and digital audio.

Networking: Routes to Connectivity

Let's turn our attention from the mechanics of computers and storage devices to networking computers. Network hardware enables our computers to expand beyond the desktop with worldwide access to other computers and servers, both wired and wireless.

Getting Access

We will consider several elements necessary for Internet or Internet 2 access. These include getting connecting to a local area network (LAN) and finding an Internet Service Provider (ISP).

LANs and WANs

Groups of computers can be networked to each other through a LAN. A LAN can be defined as a network that provides connectivity between computers and network servers in a local workgroup for file exchange, printer sharing, network maintenance, and software updates. In a campus or corporate setting, multiple LANs are interconnected through a network *backbone*. Computer users in this environment (Wide Area Network, or WAN) gain access to the Internet through one or more ISPs.

Internet Service Providers (ISPs)

The "on ramps" to the Internet are ISPs. You need a relationship with an ISP in order to use the Internet. Schools, universities, statewide networks, and local or commercial services all provide access to the Internet.

Talking among Computers

Peer-to-peer and *client-server* networking are terms used to describe relationships among computers over a network. Peer-to-peer network activity takes place directly between two computers. File exchange, contacts and memo exchange, interactive gaming, electronic chatting, and text, audio, or videoconferencing can take place. The clients all have equal status on the LAN, with the workload distributed among them; thus the term peer-to-peer networking. Any of the computer workstations or laptops in Figure 7.4 could engage in peer-to-peer communications within the LAN or between computers on the LAN and workstations on the Internet.

The other mode of network activity is *client-server*. Notice the "campus host" on the LAN in Figure 7.4. This computer might maintain a variety of databases for the campus information system: student records, course offerings and syllabi, a campus phone book, e-mail, web pages, downloadable applications, and the like.

LINK
The importance of having an ISP for the Internet software you use is explained in Module 5.

LINK
Peer-to-peer and client-server, terms applied to the Internet software you use, are described in Module 5.

LINK
Web, e-mail, FTP, and news clients are used to perform many Internet client-server activities. Check these out in Module 5.

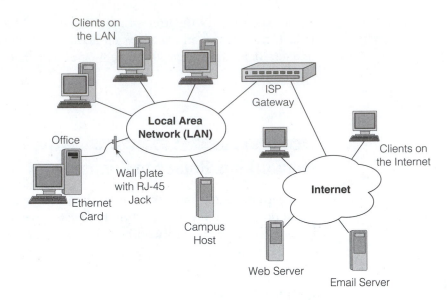

FIGURE 7.4   Peer-to-peer and client-server networking activities on a simple local-area network (LAN) with connectivity to the Internet.

It is called a "server" since its function is to "serve up" data to "client" computers on request. Any of the other clients on the campus LAN can carry out client-server activities with the campus host by accessing the servers on this machine.

Through the campus LAN and its role as an ISP, client-server connectivity can also be established with other web, news, and e-mail servers throughout the world. Note the e-mail and web servers on the Internet in Figure 7.4.

Creating servers on networks can be as simple as setting up server software on a PC, UNIX, Linux, or Macintosh computer workstation; in fact, this option is built into most personal computer operating systems. However, computers that act as servers for a large number of users, especially with Internet access, are typically machines with faster and more sophisticated processors, memory, and storage, and higher-speed network access.

Network Topologies

Connecting a series of computer devices requires consideration of the most appropriate layout, or "topology," for the network of devices. Understanding network topology is helpful whether you are planning to connect peripherals to your desktop computer, a series of MIDI electronic music devices, a network of Firewire digital audio devices (e.g., using an mLAN network), or your computer to a local area network or the Internet. We will review three topologies for constructing networks: daisy chain, bus, and star topologies, which are illustrated in Figure 7.5.

Daisy Chain

The *daisy chain* topology is the simplest network to implement. Just connect network wiring from one device to the next. One device hands off the data to the next device in the chain. This topology is recommended for small LANs with a few workstations on the network or a network of MIDI devices in close proximity to each other. However, daisy chains are only as good as the next client in the chain; if a device is disabled, the chain stops there. Firewire and USB may be deployed as daisy-chain topologies.

LINK
Figure 14.2 illustrates a MIDI daisy-chain topology.

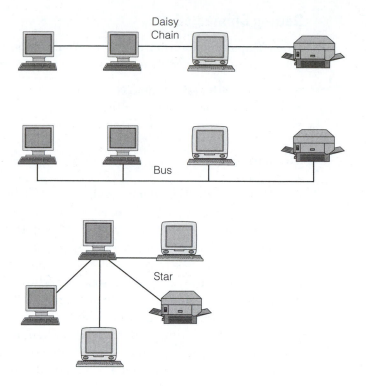

FIGURE 7.5 Three network topologies

TIP

Consider these same topologies and issues when configuring a MIDI network. As you will see in Module 16, a good MIDI network is one that uses a star topology with the MIDI interface or patch bay as the central hub.

Bus

As you start to expand a network, you can improve upon a daisy chain by using a *bus* topology (see Figure 7.5), which is simple to implement and maintain. A bus topology lays down a primary wiring pathway that all of the devices on the network tap into. Each message is sent out on the bus in search of its destination address.

Networks built with a bus topology use a minimum of wiring and are easy to implement. Their major advantage over daisy-chain topologies is that any node on the network can be taken out of operation, or a new node added, without disabling the rest of the network. The disadvantages are traffic jams, network security, and maintenance.

Star

In the *star* topology (also known as hub-and-spoke), all the devices on the network radiate out from a hub or central workstation (see Figure 7.5). This configuration provides a highly controlled network environment. Each device has its own private wiring to the central hub for fast and reliable data transfer. New clients can be added easily. Maintenance and security are excellent, because data can be traced to each specific node. Disadvantages include the need for considerably more wiring and, more importantly, the fact that the device that serves as the main hub has a lot of work to perform.

Ethernet networks can be implemented with a star topology. Stand-alone hubs or network servers can be the central hub on the star. USB and Firewire devices may use a star topology. A USB hub can connect multiple devices such as a printer, a scanner, an MP3 player, and a MIDI controller to a computer workstation.

Stars can be combined to form *tree* topologies. The Internet is undoubtedly the biggest, most extensive *tree* of *star* networks built!

TIP

The term "modem" originally comes from MOdulate and DEModulate, where digital data is converted to analog tones (modulate) and sent over the phone and then back to digital data (demodulate) at the other end.

TIP

Your campus or ISP may offer additional security for connecting remotely to the local LAN using a technology called Virtual Private Networking, or VPN. VPN is created by installing software on your computer that encrypts all of the data between your computer, laptop, or handheld, for example, and the servers your ISP maintains. Use this feature if you are connecting remotely to your e-mail and other critical data.

Getting Connected

To participate in Internet or LAN activities you need to get connected. Three alternatives with several variations for network connectivity include:

- modems with phone, cable, and DSL
- direct-wire connection over the Ethernet
- wireless with infrared, WiFi, and Bluetooth

Modems

POTS (Plain Old Telephone Service)   A POTS modem is the most ubiquitous and economical way to get connected. The telephone modem has been around for more than 40 years as a way to send computer data in digital form over analog, copper-wire phone lines. The speed has slowly increased from around 100 Mbps to the present 56 Kbps (a speed limit set by the Federal Communications Commission). This modem speed works well for text-based communications like e-mail, but is only marginally useful for web browsing and large file transfers. POTS modems are only connected while the phone connection is in place (while your computer is talking to the network); you must reconnect every time the computer needs to connect to the network. The network topology for POTS is a star topology, with the central phone switchboard as the hub for each phone line dialing in.

Phone modems are built into most computers or may be provided with a PCI or PC Card. The jack for the phone modem is a standard RJ-11 phone jack.

DSL (Digital Subscriber Line)   Different solutions are required to overcome the 56 Kbps barrier of POTS modems. DSL technology enables sending data entirely in digital form over standard-telephone copper wire. With DSL, speeds range from 512 Kbps to multimegabit speeds for downloading, and 128 Kbps to multi-megabit speeds for uploading. The actual speed is limited by loop distance, line quality, and the type of service you've ordered from your local phone company. For web browsing, downloading speed is most important.

DSL modems are plugged directly into a standard RJ-11 phone jack just like a telephone; your computer then connects to the DSL modem as if it were an

FIGURE 7.6   Three connectivity solutions: (a) 3COM 10/100Base-T Ethernet PC card; (b) 3COM Wireless Wi-Fi PC card; and (c) 3COM Bluetooth USB device.

LINK
A variety of network protocols is discussed in Module 6. Many good books and information on the Internet are available should you wish to delve deeper into this topic.

ASIDE
In 1941, Actress Hedy Lamarr and the early 20th-century American composer George Antheil patented the concept of "frequency hopping" that is used in today's wireless computer networking.

TIP
What do you need for infrared networking? Two devices with infrared built in and aimed at each other across the room.

Ethernet connection (see below) with an RJ-45 cable. To prevent interference with voice calls over the same phone line, filters are provided for each phone headset connected to the same line. DSL connections are always-on connections and, like your phone, the data connection to the Internet is a dedicated circuit directly to the main DSL service hub. This conforms to the star network topology mentioned earlier.

Cable Another alternative to always-on connectivity to the Internet is using cable TV service. Cable by its very nature works on one-way TV channels; for two-way Internet service, two cable channels are used. The optimal network bandwidth from cable is about 30 Mbps for downloading and 10 Mbps for uploading. Where DSL uses a star network topology, cable uses a daisy-chain topology. All subscribers within a given cable LAN segment share the bandwidth. The more who use it simultaneously, the slower network performance becomes. Using a typical number of subscribers per segment, the average bandwidth per user is about .5 to 1.5 Mbps, a potential improvement over DSL.

The cable modem uses coax to connect to your cable service (just like the cable that connects to your TV or set-top box); it then connects to your computer using a standard Ethernet RJ-45 cable, USB cable, or PCI or PC Card for internal installation on your computer.

Direct Connection with Ethernet

No modem is required to communicate directly through a LAN, but networking hardware is. The office computer shown in Figure 7.4 is connected to an Ethernet LAN. The computer is using an Ethernet interface card. Ethernet is the most common protocol used for network connectivity within a LAN; its transmission speeds can run from 10 Mbps up to 1 Gbps. These speeds are 10Base-T, 100Base-T, and 1000Base-T.

Many PCs come with Ethernet already built in, so there is no need for an additional card. Figure 7.6a shows a 3Com PC Card for a laptop that provides a 10/100Base-T Ethernet connection. Like modems, Ethernet network cards are available as internal cards, external devices that can connect to a USB port, and PC Card versions. Most networking cards can be used interchangeably on Macintosh and PC computers.

Wireless: Freedom from Wires

Exciting things are happening to free us from the tyranny of wires, cables, plugs, and jacks. Wireless technologies offer both an attractive cost and a physical alternative to drilling holes and pulling wire. We will review four wireless solutions: infrared, Bluetooth, cellular, and WiFi. Table 7.2 gives you an overview of their capabilities.

Infrared When you need very short-range wireless, with two devices in sight of each other, *infrared* will work for simple tasks like printing from your handheld computer or exchanging a small file between two handheld PCs. Infrared is provided with many computer workstations, laptops, printers, and handhelds. Devices that can "talk" infrared are known as IRDA devices. Using the same technology as TV and VCR remote controllers, infrared signals can broadcast data throughout a room with speeds from 9.6 Kbps up to 4 Mbps. The IRDA ports on both devices must be pointed at each other.

TABLE 7.2 Comparison of Wireless Network Performance Ordered by Range of Coverage (based on 2003 data)

Type	Speed	Distance	Penetration	Use
Infrared	230 Kbps	Within a room	Line of sight	Short-range device control, print, file transfer
Bluetooth 1.0	1 Mbps	30 feet	1 or 2 walls within range	Short-range file transfer, printing, text messaging, printing, MIDI control; no video and graphics
Bluetooth 2.0	12 Mbps	30 feet	1 or 2 walls within range	Above plus sending video and audio to sound system or projector
1G Cellular	14.4 Kbps data	Several miles within range of subscriber cell tower	Most walls except for steel and concrete	Remote voice, text messaging, and e-mail
3G Cellular	2 Mbps data	Several miles within range of subscriber cell tower	Most walls except for steel and concrete	Remote web services with graphics; streaming video and music (limited)
Wi-Fi 802.11b	Up to 11 Mbps	300 feet from base station	A few walls from base station	All Internet activities; streaming video and music (limited)
Wi-Fi 802.11g	54 Mbps	A little farther than 802.11b	A few walls from base station	Above plus streaming video and music, as well as faster data rates

TIP
What do you need for Bluetooth networking? Two Bluetooth-enabled devices. Figure 7.6c shows a Bluetooth device using the USB port of your computer.

TIP
What do you need for cellular networking? In most cases, a cell phone, cell phone service, and a custom USB cable from your handheld or laptop to your cell phone.

Bluetooth Bluetooth wireless improves on infrared by being able to penetrate walls within its 30-foot range. Bluetooth is ideal for electronic chatting and exchanging files between other laptops and handhelds, peer-to-peer, within a room; beaming a document to a Bluetooth-enabled printer; or beaming photos from a Bluetooth-enabled digital camera to a laptop. Bluetooth MIDI devices may offer a solution for eliminating all MIDI wires for a music setup. If your cell phone has Bluetooth, your laptop could use it as a wireless modem as the phone sits in a briefcase or your pocket. Bluetooth 2.0 promises to increase the bandwidth from 1 Mbps to 12 Mbps (10Base-T Ethernet speed), with the potential of beaming streaming digital audio to a Bluetooth 2.0-enabled speaker system or video to a Bluetooth 2.0-enabled computer projector.

Cellular Cellular wireless breaks away from the restrictions of short-range infrared and Bluetooth technologies. The cell phone can be used as a modem for data transmission, as well as for voice calls. With data transmission rates for first-generation (1G) cellular at 14.4 Kbps, a cell phone provides global wireless networking, although with slow connectivity. The only requirement is that you be in range of a tower that provides your cell phone service.

That's first-generation (1G) cellular networking. Handhelds, PDAs, cell phones, and color flat displays, and the need for web browsing from these devices, are all converging to produce a single device that offers ubiquitous, anywhere web services. For this, so-called 3G or "third-generation" cellular technology provides

ASIDE
Network security is a serious issue with wireless, especially Wi-Fi and Bluetooth. If poorly managed, both technologies can create wide-open doors to your personal computer and to the Internet. If you create your own Wi-Fi network in your office or home, be sure to turn on security features provided in the software to prevent an interloper from borrowing your network access. Remember, wireless travels through walls!

TIP
What do you need for Wi-Fi networking? Wi-Fi built into your laptop or handheld or a Wi-Fi PC Card like the one shown in Figure 7.6b. Then, find the nearest access to a Wi-Fi service.

ASIDE
Open, free wireless access can be commonly found in public meeting areas, coffee shops, restaurants, and the like, encouraging laptop surfing as a social activity—bringing new meaning to the menu item "surf and turf."

network speeds that rival DSL and cable modem network solutions with bandwidth speeds of up to 2 Mbps. From the color screen of your cell phone, you can place voice calls, check e-mail, browse the Web, or use the phone as a modem for your laptop.

Wi-Fi   None of the wireless solutions discussed provide direct Ethernet speeds for connectivity through walls beyond the 30-foot range of Bluetooth 2.0. Enter what is commonly referred to as "Wi-Fi" for "wireless fidelity." Wi-Fi complements Ethernet networking by creating nodes of wireless communities (within its 300-foot range) for untethered Internet activities. Wi-Fi zones that are either free or pay-as-you-go can be found in libraries, airports, cafés, hotel and meeting rooms, and other public areas.

Multiple broadband wireless standards continue to emerge, most of them defined under what are known as the IEEE 802.11 Wi-Fi standards. The first of these to gain wide acceptance is IEEE 802.11b, which offers speeds ranging from 1 Mbps to 11 Mbps of bandwidth depending on signal strength and quality. Using the same spectrum and offering compatibility with 802.11b clients or base stations, 802.11g has emerged to offer speeds that range up to 54 Mbps. Each node in a Wi-Fi environment shares the bandwidth of the Ethernet connection; with 20 users in an 802.11g node, for example, each user has an estimated 2.7 Mbps of bandwidth to use.

Wireless Convergence   Bluetooth, Wi-Fi, and cellular wireless are, in a sense, all competing for the same demand for peer-to-peer and client-server access. Any one of these solutions could end up being the dominant service. As the cost of its hardware decreases, Wi-Fi could obviate the need for Bluetooth. As Wi-Fi becomes ubiquitous, with more and more access points available to the public, using a cell phone to access the Internet will become less attractive. Cellular and Wi-Fi could, in the near future, merge at some point. Keep your wireless options open.

Digital Audio Basics

"No one else has any of these sounds on their hard drives or in their samples, anywhere in the world . . . That's what we really go for. We just take a basic wave form and build on it and build on it until it's our own."

—*A musician describing laptop jamming in a New York City bar from "Clash, Then Synthesis: Joys of a Laptop Jam" by Johanna Jainchill, The New York Times, (July 10, 2003)*

"Technology is 'technology' only for people who are born before it was invented."

—*Alan Kay, Futurist*

The Big Picture

It's all going digital! That is the most important message for this Viewport and those that follow. Viewports III through VI focus on digital audio and MIDI production used in home and studio settings to create and represent music. Below is a topic grouping that categorizes music production for this textbook:

- Basic capturing, encoding, and editing of digital audio (Viewport III)
- More advanced digital audio, including multiple track and channel recording (Viewport IV)
- Music sequencing with MIDI and digital audio (Viewport V)
- More advanced music sequencing, including sound design and virtual studios (Viewport VI)

An additional kind of music software should be noted. Known as "plug-ins," these programs offer everything from special effects for digital audio and MIDI to instrument sounds for sequencing programs. These software resources either work in partnership with other software or stand alone as separate programs. We present plug-ins throughout the modules that follow.

Table VPIII.1 lists music production software titles representative of digital audio and MIDI work. We have organized these by the Viewports that follow and by typical tasks you might want to accomplish. Although there is some overlap among software features in these categories, these represent the major divisions. A well-designed software set will contain titles from each category, but you might get by with fewer resources if you choose wisely for the tasks you have in mind.

Viewport III centers on data, hardware, and software used for basic capture, encoding, and editing of digital audio. The popular practices of extracting ("ripping") digital audio from CDs and other sound sources and storing these files on CDs or MP3 portable players are reviewed. The use of streaming media is noted.

TABLE VPIII.1 The BIG Picture: MIDI and Digital Audio Software in 2004

Overall Topic	III: Capturing, Editing, and Storing Digital Audio	IV: Software for Multiple Tracks and Channels of Digital Audio	V: Software Techniques for MIDI Sequencing with Digital Audio	VI: Adventures in Sound Shaping and Synthesis
Software Task	MP3/AAC Players • Download and listen to MP3/AAC • Create playlists • Encode MP3/ACC • Create and use streaming media Audio Editing • Record and edit live sound and CD excerpts • Advanced editing and special effects with stereo sound	Multitrack Audio • Record multiple tracks of digital audio • Use built-effects processing Effects Processing • Use separate effects plug-ins • Mix and master, including surround sound Looping • Design music with loop-based software	MIDI Sequencing • Record multiple tracks with MIDI • Edit MIDI files and use built-in MIDI plug-ins • Use built-in virtual instruments • Add digital audio • Mix MIDI and digital audio and convert to digital audio product for distribution	DAW Sequencers • Record, edit, and master with advanced sequencing features Virtual Instruments • Add separate plug-ins for virtual instruments, synthesizers, and samplers Virtual Studios • Create music with virtual studio environments Sound Programming • Create sounds with graphics and command-line interfaces
Exemplar Software	Winamp, Musicmatch Jukebox, iTunes, Audion, Windows Media Player, QuickTime, RealPlayer, Audacity, PeakLE, Sound Forge, WaveLab	Audition, DeckLE, Pro Tools, Samplitude, xpansion, Ina-GRM Tools, Restoration Bundle, Altiverb, ACID Music Studio, Soundtrack, Garage Band, Toast with Jam, SurCode	PowerTracks Pro, HomeStudio, Logic Express, Metro, Cubase SE	Digital Performer, Sonar, Logic Pro, Cubase SX, Battery, Attack, Pluggo, Tassman, EXP24, Reaktor, HALion, Reason, Max/MSP, Csound, SuperColider

Editing of single or stereo tracks of digital audio is covered, including the addition of special effects with features built into the software or by way of plug-ins.

If your interests include recording a live concert or using software to produce your ensemble's CDs, the multiple track and channel topics in Viewport IV are for you. Here is where we cover software titles for looping that can be used to create interesting grooves. Information about MPEG and surround sound are key topics in this Viewport.

Viewport V contains information about MIDI sequencing. It summarizes software that uses MIDI and digital audio tracks in combination. Understanding MIDI and MIDI keyboard hardware is an important part of this section.

Viewport VI continues the presentation of MIDI sequencers, but with more advanced programs that are commonly called digital audio workstations (DAW). We cover software-based synthesizers and samplers (virtual instruments) and sound construction with programming tools, and end with coverage of virtual studio environments. SoundFonts and SMPTE and MIDI Time Codes are covered in this Viewport, as well as a wide variety of MIDI controller devices.

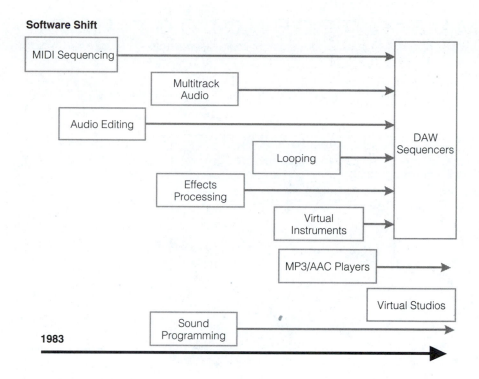

FIGURE VPIII.1
Software shift

The order in which we present these software categories is not necessarily the way they developed over time. To help understand the chronology of the development of digital audio and MIDI, we provide Figure VPIII.1. This chart shows MIDI sequencing as starting it all in 1983, concurrent with the establishment of MIDI as a data structure. Digital audio editing began shortly thereafter with multiple-track digital audio, effects processing and sound programming following. Within the last 10 years, looping software, virtual instruments and studios, popular MP3/AAC formats, and the powerful DAW titles dominate the landscape. As the chart demonstrates, the advanced DAW sequencers represent a natural evolution that merges these categories into one.

Viewport III Overview

Digital audio is the most pervasive method used today to represent sound and music. The term "digital audio" refers to sound represented by a series of numbers. Certainly CDs and DVDs come to mind as an obvious use of digital audio, but there is much more. The sound effects you hear at the basketball game and sound bites on the radio are all digitally recorded, shaped, and played back. The sounds that come from your multimedia software are all digitally recorded and edited. Even broadcast television is using digital resources more and more. Soon, all televised sound and visual images will come to our homes in digital form. Perhaps the most obvious examples of digital audio for musicians are commercially purchased discs or Internet files. Full-length music albums in all styles of music are recorded digitally, either directly to hard-disk systems or to digital tape. These recordings are edited and processed digitally and then finally transferred to CD and DVD in

MUSIC TECHNOLOGY IN PRACTICE

Nate DeYoung
Undergraduate Student at the School of Communication, Northwestern University, Evanston, Illinois

Nate DeYoung and MP3 collection

Peter R. Webster

Application

Nate has been interested in the Internet and digital audio since his high school days in Corvallis, Oregon. He has downloaded thousands of MP3 and other compressed audio files and has burned hundreds of CDs. He stores many recent files on his hard drive and uses his computer to send audio through his sound card to the large sound system that he and his roommate share. His favorite music genre is hip hop and his major sources of digital audio are legal copies from peer-to-peer downloads and Internet sites for the bands he's interested in. Majoring in media studies within the Radio, Television, and Film Department, Nate intends to work as a developer and editor in multimedia when he graduates. He has taken the Introduction to Music Technology class at Northwestern with Professor Scott Lipscomb and has used this text in that class.

Hardware and Software

Nate uses a custom-built PC with Windows XP that runs on a Pentium III chip. His machine has 128 mg of RAM, a 40-GB hard drive, a Sound Blaster Live audio card, and a CD-RW drive. His software includes Winamp (his first MP3 player, which he continues to use), ACID for basic editing tasks, Nero for CD-ROM burning, and Soulseek as his current peer-to-peer client for downloading. He uses the Windows Media Player, RealOne, and QuickTime as he needs to. He enjoys the Flash movies with accompanying audio found on his favorite bands' Internet sites.

DVD-ROM
As with all the software modules in this text, the accompanying DVD contains projects for you to use to practice your skills.

digital form or made available for Internet download. It's quite likely that the disc or file you purchase is entirely produced with digital audio techniques.

Objectives

In the opening module for Viewport III, we explore common ideas about acoustics and digital sound creation that will set the stage for many of the topics to follow. Digital audio file types will be explained. In Module 9, we will explore some of the common software applications available for capturing, editing, and storing digital audio with a desktop or laptop computer. We will end the Viewport with a description of hardware that will provide a basis for many of the common musical tasks with digital audio.

At the end of Viewport III, you should understand:

- Categories of digital audio software
- Features of basic and advanced digital audio editors
- Varieties of MP3 and AAC software
- The role of digital audio software drivers such as DirectX, ASIO, and Core Audio
- Basic acoustical and perceptual properties of sound
- Concepts of digital sampling and its relationship to analog synthesis
- Types of sound synthesis
- Digital audio file types and approaches to sound compression

Kevin Robbins
Minister of the Christian Church
(Disciples of Christ), Mackinaw, Illinois

Kevin Robbins with portable recording gear

Close-up of microphones, Mini-Me digital interface, and Sony DAT recorder

Application

As a hobby, Pastor Robbins enjoys capturing digital recordings from folk, jazz, and pop music concerts in the tradition of bluegrass and Grateful Dead concerts. These groups permit taping of concerts for nonprofit sharing of recordings. Kevin has taped Bela Fleck, Ekoostik Hookah, OM Trio, and many others. Using a portable set of equipment, he captures the live performance with a laptop computer, edits the recording with his WaveLab software, and then mixes the final result down to burn on a CD audio disc. He then shares and exchanges recordings with other "tapers." According to Kevin, about 10% of the big-name artists are "pro taping," including Pearl Jam, U2, and Metallica. He stresses the many challenges to public taping: the weather for outdoor concerts, highly inebriated patrons for club concerts (including the person who wanted to scream into his mics), uncooperative security guards and recording managers, and, of course, the unknown challenges of acoustics in old buildings.

Hardware and Software

The heart of Kevin's portable setup is a Fujitsu C-Series 1.1 mHz Windows laptop with 500 mb of RAM and a 40-GB hard drive. He has an Apogee Mini-Me ADC box that provides two channels of 24-bit/96 mHz digital audio from his MP2 preamp and pair of AKG-C480 microphones. From the Apogee, he connects to his laptop via the USB interface, at the same time connecting Sony TCD-D8 DAT recorder via the S/PDIF interface. The DAT recorder provides just-in-case backup recording. His software is Steinberg's WaveLab, running on Windows XP. He prefers to capture his digital audio at 24-bit/48 mHz stereo sampling rates.

- Digital audio streaming from the Internet
- Setting up a basic digital audio workstation with software and hardware
- Digital-to-analog and analog-to-digital hardware operations
- Features of audio jacks and plugs, mixers, and microphones
- Hardware storage options for digital audio, including MP3 players

DVD-ROM Software Projects

For Viewport III, using MP3/AAC, streaming, and basic digital audio editing software, you should be able to:

- Work with MP3 software titles for listening, creating playlists, encoding files, producing CDs, and connecting with portable digital music players (Project 5)
- Record and edit a live and a CD segment of digital audio (Project 6)
- Experiment with applying effects in digital audio (Project 7)

Module 8

Acoustics, Digital Audio, and Music Synthesis

Viewport III provides your "initial plunge" into capturing, manipulating, and creating music and sound with a computer. Before covering software (Module 9) and hardware (Module 10) for accomplishing these digital audio tasks, this module presents some fundamental concepts related to both analog and digital audio, including:

- acoustical and perceptual dimensions of sound
- concepts of digital sound and sampling
- optimizing the quality of digital audio
- formats and compression for storing digital audio
- forms of music synthesis

LINK
The distinction between analog and digital events is covered in Module 6.

ASIDE
Viewport I provides photographs of vintage hardware synthesizers, the Arp 2600 and a portable Buchla synthesizer.

Acoustical and Perceptual Dimensions of Sound

The study of sound and music generation starts with the physics of sound or "acoustics." Why does a musician need to know about acoustics? Sound and music as we live with them every day exist as vibrations transmitted through a variety of physical media, including the air you breathe, your eardrums, the wires that connect televisions and telephones, and speakers and headphones. Generating music with any machine, computer or otherwise, requires manipulating, editing, mixing, and controlling these vibrations or the acoustical properties of sound.

Before computers had sufficient processing power to create sounds through digital techniques, composers depended on music synthesizers that were analog hardware devices. They directly manipulated hardware oscillators, envelope generators, filters, amplifiers, and other devices to produce the sounds of their electronic musical compositions. Many of the analog synthesizers have reappeared as software synthesizers or "soft synths," simulating the same physical controls of sound. The Native Instruments' Pro-53 soft synth shown in Figure 8.1 is a virtual recreation in software of the Sequential Circuits Prophet-5 synthesizer built in the late 1970s. Notice the array of knobs and switches for controlling sound waveforms, oscillators, filters, and the like.

To begin to understand what these various analog terms mean and the element of control they provide for creating music, we need to look "under the hood" of music synthesis.

FIGURE 8.1 Pro-53 software recreation of Sequential Circuits Prophet-5 hardware synthesizer

Recreate in your mind for a moment a favorite piece of music. Perhaps you hear the opening movement to Beethoven's Eroica symphony, or the Beach Boys singing "Surfin U.S.A.," Victor Wooten playing "Amazing Grace" on his electric bass, or Alison Krause singing "Forget About It." Can you hear the music in your mind? Freeze a moment of that music in your mind. That brief moment holds the complex array of all its physical properties. This is like taking a drop of water from a pond and examining the contents under a high-powered microscope to see more than you see with the naked eye.

Figure 8.2 shows two computer-generated views of single musical instrument tones, a clarinet and a violin. Figure 8.2a is an example of one of the early graphs generated by James Moorer at Stanford University in the 1970s, using a computer to perform a "spectrum analysis" of the acoustical complexity of instrument tones. Figure 8.2b is a similar spectrum analysis of a violin tone generated with one of the more common audio editing software packages, Sound Forge. You can see that graphically there is a lot going on in both of these analyses. Can you imagine what a single moment in time from a full symphony orchestra might look like when displayed in this form?

We can study the *acoustical* properties of sound to determine its physical characteristics independently of how we hear it. We can also examine the music in terms of its *perceptual* properties: what we hear. Table 8.1 shows the four basic acoustical properties of sound and their parallel perceptual properties.

TABLE 8.1	Comparison of Acoustical and Perceptual Properties of Sound
Acoustical	**Perceptual**
Frequency	Pitch
Amplitude	Loudness
Envelope	Articulation
Harmonic spectrum	Timbre

It is important to keep a clear distinction between these two ways of examining sound. When we use terms like *pitch*, *loudness*, *articulation*, and *timbre*, we are describing how we hear and perceive the sound. We can describe sound as getting higher or lower, louder or softer, brighter or duller, and so on, with an infinite variety of adjectives. These properties are not physically quantifiable by measuring devices like frequency counters, sound-pressure level meters, oscilloscopes, and computer analysis. Observing the distinction between acoustics and perception, a computer or an analog synthesizer does not generate pitch, loudness, and timbre. Rather, these devices generate frequency, amplitude, envelope, and harmonic spectrum: the physical properties of sound. We will discuss each of these four properties in turn.

FIGURE 8.2A Two different 3-dimensional views of single instrument tones: (a) a clarinet tone from James Moorer's early research at Stanford University (1975) showing the amplitude envelope (y) over time (x) for each harmonic (z); (b) a violin tone analyzed with Sound Forge (Sony Pictures Digital, Inc. [Win]) software showing frequencies (x) and their amplitudes (y) for a series of time slices (x) from the onset of the tone.

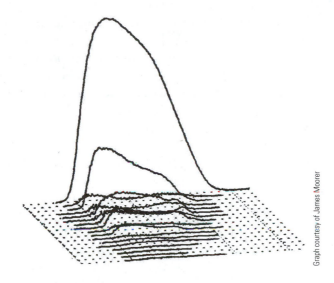

Graph courtesy of James Moorer

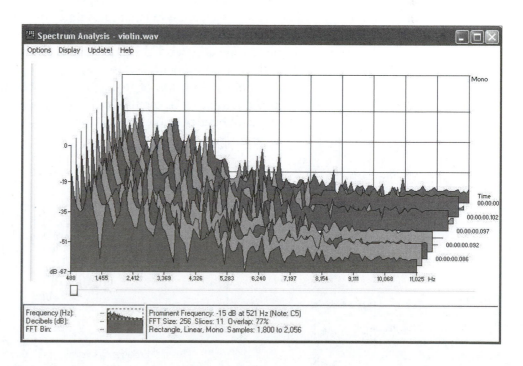

FIGURE 8.2B

Vibrations, Frequency, and Amplitude

Figure 8.3 illustrates the vibrations in a single moment of sound. Sound is produced when something vibrates or oscillates. There must be a vibrating source of energy, or *oscillator,* to create sound: think of striking a metal pipe, blowing across the top of a soda pop bottle, plucking a string, buzzing your lips, or moving your vocal cords by speaking or singing. Electronic devices like the Prophet-5 analog synthesizer provide electronic oscillators to create sound vibrations.

When anything vibrates, it sets the molecules around it in motion, starting a chain reaction through whatever media surround it. When you hear a sound, its oscillation has passed through air, a vibrating membrane (your eardrum), vibrating bones (your middle ear), fluid motion, and vibrating hair cells or cilia (your inner ear or cochlea).

Vibrations produce alternating patterns of change in molecules as they are pulled apart and pushed together—an increase and decrease in energy or pressure—graphically represented in Figure 8.3 by a curve that is shown repeatedly going above and below the center line. The curve above the line represents an increase in pressure, below the line, a decrease in pressure. Each pattern of increase and decrease is one *cycle* of the vibration. The graph of the pattern is called the sound's *waveform,* and, because the waveform contains similar patterns that repeat over and over, it is called a *periodic* waveform.

Frequency

Frequency is a measure of the rate of an oscillation: how many cycles occur in a certain frame of time. The standard orchestral tuning note A is a vibration at 440 cycles per second (cps). We can indicate this as 440 cps or 440 Hz. (Hz represents Hertz, the international standard unit for cycles per second.) Just as we use the letters *k* and *m* to mean thousand or million bytes in the size of memory chips, we use them to abbreviate *kiloHertz* and *megaHertz.* For example, we could say 2 kHz or 5.5 kHz instead of 2,000 Hz or 5,500 Hz. Figure 8.4 shows a graphical analysis of a single violin tone as displayed in Sound Forge. Can you identify the same elements apparent in Figure 8.3? Look for the individual cycles of the sound's vibrations over time and the overall waveform or shape of the sound over time. This flute tone is about 523 Hz or vibrating 523 cycles per second, equivalent to C5 on the piano keyboard.

It is helpful to think of frequencies for sound vibrations in familiar terms. When the frequency of oscillation increases, you hear the pitch getting higher. When the frequency of oscillation decreases, the pitch you hear gets lower. Fig-

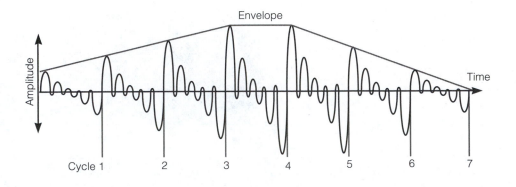

FIGURE 8.3

A wave sample showing the acoustical properties of amplitude, frequency, and envelope

Frequency = cycles per second

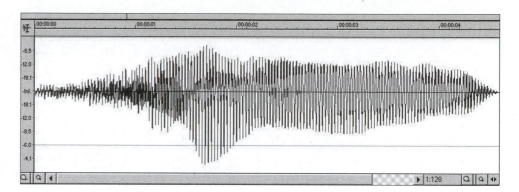

FIGURE 8.4 The waveform of a single violin tone displayed in Sound Forge digital audio software

LINK
Frequencies and MIDI values will be useful when working with MIDI software for sequencing and other tasks in Viewport V.

ure 8.5 shows the assignment of frequencies to the 88 keys on a piano keyboard. Next to each white key, the figure also indicates the MIDI music codes associated with that frequency. The human ear is responsive to frequencies from 20 Hz to about 20 kHz, depending on how acute one's hearing is.

Amplitude

Amplitude is a measure of the magnitude of the oscillation—how great an increase and decrease in air pressure is produced by a vibration. When the amplitude of a sound increases, we hear it get louder. When the amplitude decreases, we say that the sound gets softer. The distance of the curve's rise and fall above and below the middle line in Figure 8.3 represents the amplitude of the sound.

Amplitude can be measured in many ways, depending on the vibrating medium. Most commonly, we measure amplitude using a relative scale of *decibels*, or dB. The difference in amplitude between two sounds is commonly expressed as a logarithmic value called a "decibel." Decibel scales are always relative to some standard amplitude or reference point.

One common decibel scale—the SPL or "sound pressure level" scale—begins at 0 dB SPL, the *minimum* point at which the human ear can just perceive a 1,000-Hz tone. This is its reference point. The dB SPL scale then extends to the amplitude of sound that causes pain to the human ear, roughly 130 dB SPL. Figure 8.6a shows a dB SPL scale correlated with various environmental sounds from 0 to 130 dB SPL.

Another common decibel scale is the dB VU or "volume unit" scale found on analog recording equipment meters. A typical VU meter is shown in Figure 8.6b. The reference point of 0 dB VU on the meter is the *maximum* amplitude recommended for recording on that equipment. Beyond 0 db VU, distortion occurs and is noted in red. Decibel readings below this maximum point are then shown as negative values: –2, –4, –8, and so on.

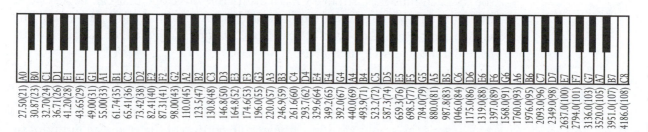

FIGURE 8.5   Frequencies of notes on the piano keyboard (MIDI note values in parentheses)

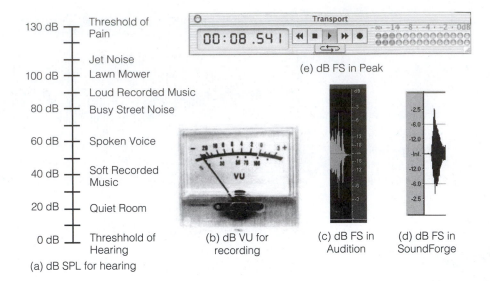

FIGURE 8.6 Various relative scales using a decibel measurement for human hearing (dB SPL), recording (dB VU), and digital audio (dB FS)

Figure 8.6c shows the dB scale used in the digital audio software, Audition (Adobe, Inc. [Win]). For digital audio, a dB FS or "full scale" measurement is used. Like the VU scale, 0 dB FS is the *maximum* level at which a digital audio sound can be captured (the maximum "digital amplitude" so to speak). Beyond this level, "clipping" occurs—digital audio's version of distortion. A value of 0 dB FS also represents the largest number possible that can be used to represent a digital sample value: For 16-bit digital audio, that value is +/– 32767. The decibel values of –6 and –12 represent amplitude values down from 0 dB FS until that level reaches infinity. Infinity represents very small audio sample values that are at the noise level and imperceptible. In Sound Forge audio editing software (Figure 8.6d), the dB FS scale is expressed in steps 0, –2.5, –6.0, –12.0, and infinity. Peak (Bias, Inc. [Mac]) software's transport bar (Figure 8.6e) uses steps 0, –2, –4, –8, –14, and infinity dB FS.

To summarize, all decibel scales are relative to some standard. The three examples given here are the dB SPL scale for measuring the range of human hearing, the dB VU scale for measuring the recording range with analog sound equipment, and the dB FS scale for measuring the digital values for sampling ("digital amplitude") in digital audio recording.

Envelopes

Notice in Figures 8.3 and 8.4 that the amplitude of each cycle is not the same: It gradually increases, then stays constant, and then decreases toward the end of the sound sample. This pattern of amplitude change over time is the *envelope* of the sound. Each musical instrument has a distinctive envelope that can be described by a number of time points from the sound's start until its end. The simplest envelope can be described by its *attack, decay, sustain,* and *release,* or ADSR as illustrated in the margin figure:

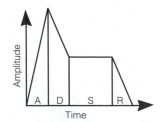

- *Attack* is the initial onset of the tone when the oscillator or instrument begins to vibrate.
- *Decay* is the brief decrease in amplitude immediately after the attack.
- *Sustain* is the amplitude during the middle portion of the envelope just prior to its release.

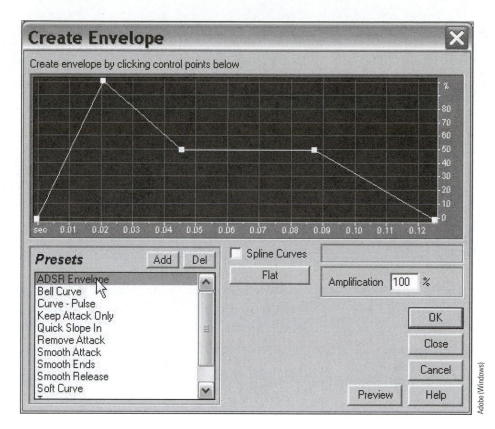

FIGURE 8.7 Envelope tool in Audition digital wave editing software illustrating a classic ADSR envelope shape

- *Release* is when the instrument stops producing a sound—the time it takes the instrument to stop vibrating or come to a state of rest.

ADSR describes the simplest four points of an envelope shape. The more points in the envelope that can be defined, the more accurate the description. To accurately recreate the envelope of the clarinet or violin tones in Figure 8.2 would take hundreds of amplitude points. Envelopes can be generalized into a few common shapes, as shown in the margin illustration.

- Rectangular envelopes are typical of mechanical devices, like organ pipes opening and closing.
- Trapezoidal envelopes are typical of instruments in which air is blown through a pipe, for example, wind and brass instruments.
- Triangular envelopes are typical of plucked or struck instruments like pianos, guitars, and dulcimers.

What we perceive as timbre is due, in part, to the shape of the envelope. Most of the information that we use in identifying a unique timbre comes from the attack phase of the envelope. Later we will see how this property is used in the design of computer music samplers. We also perceptually describe the envelope of a sound by its articulation, using such terms as staccato, legato, and marcato.

Harmonic Spectrum

Envelope accounts for only part of what we perceive as timbre. We also need to analyze the amplitude of each of the frequencies that make up the sound. This is called the *harmonic spectrum* of the sound. Where the envelope represents changes

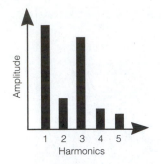

Amplitude

1 2 3 4 5
Harmonics

ASIDE

In the early 1700s, Joseph Sauveur discovered the *overtone series:* the phenomenon that complex sounds contain frequencies following a common pattern of ratios.

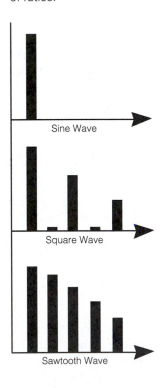

Sine Wave

Square Wave

Sawtooth Wave

in amplitude over time, the harmonic spectrum represents the amplitude of each frequency at a given point in time.

To understand the principle of the harmonic spectrum, we will examine the concepts advanced by three important scientists: Sauveur, Fourier, and Helmholtz.

Overtones

Figure 8.8 shows Sauveur's overtone series for a pitch sounding on A. The initial frequency in the series is called the *fundamental*, in this case 110 Hz, or A. All periodic vibrations contain frequencies or overtones above the fundamental, with the same intervallic relationships. A sound with no overtones, only the fundamental, is known as a *sine* wave.

If you know the frequency of the fundamental, you can always calculate the overtones above the fundamental using this standard set of ratios. When blowing through a brass instrument like a bugle or trumpet, you can produce many of the notes in the overtone series simply by changing the rate of vibration of your lips and the air pressure. The closest natural sound to a sine wave—a sound with no overtones—is a human whistle; a pure sine wave can only be produced with an electronic oscillator.

Overtones are also called *harmonics*, with the first harmonic being the fundamental. You will also encounter the term *partial*, a synonym for *harmonic*. The first overtone is the *second harmonic* or *second partial*, the second overtone is the third harmonic and partial, and so on.

Harmonic Spectrum and Fourier's Theorem

Fourier's theorem states that any periodic vibration can be expressed as a series of sine waves. We can add sine waves to make increasingly complex sounds (additive synthesis); we can take a complex sound and subtract sine waves to make simpler sounds (subtractive synthesis); and we can analyze any sound by identifying the amplitude of every sine wave in the overtone series present in that sound (spectrum or harmonic analysis).

Figure 8.9 shows two views of how you can analyze the harmonic spectrum of a complex sound. On the left (a), you see a graph indicating the amplitude of each harmonic in the overtone series up to the fifth harmonic. On the right (b), you see the sequential addition of five sine waves, one for each harmonic, that add up to the complex wave at the bottom (the "sum" of the sine waves). The graph on the left can be produced with a spectrum analyzer; the one on the right with an oscilloscope—devices that measure and represent physical phenomena.

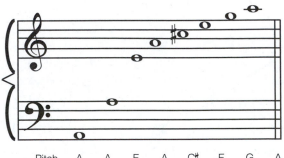

FIGURE 8.8 The overtone series starting on the pitch A or 110 Hz

Pitch	A	A	E	A	C#	E	G	A
Frequency	110	220	330	440	550	660	770	880
Harmonic	1	2	3	4	5	6	7	8

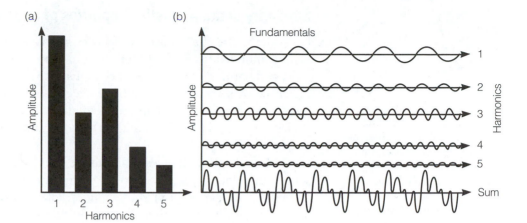

FIGURE 8.9
The construction of a complex wave

Electronic oscillators used in analog synthesizers are commonly sine, square, and sawtooth oscillators. The figure in the margin on page 88 shows the harmonic spectrum of each. Notice that the sine wave has no overtones, the square wave has only the odd harmonics, and the sawtooth generator contains the full spectrum of harmonics. Figure 8.10 illustrates how these sounds can be constructed by applying the concepts of harmonic analysis using Adobe's Audition wave editor. Figure 8.10a illustrates constructing the most basic sine wave with only one harmonic on A 440; Figure 8.10b illustrates constructing a square wave using only the odd harmonics.

Changes in the harmonic spectrum of a sound are perceived as changes in timbre. The timbre of each instrument has a unique, characteristic harmonic spectrum. Clarinet sounds favor the odd harmonics like the electronic square wave. Rich sounds like oboes have lots of harmonics at strong amplitudes. Flute sounds favor the octave harmonics.

Understanding the harmonic makeup of sounds is absolutely critical to working with digital sound synthesis. Altering harmonics is the key to techniques of synthesis, filtering, sampling, and many other notions related to computer music.

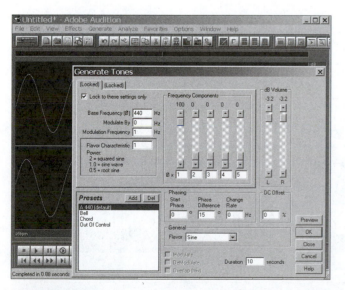
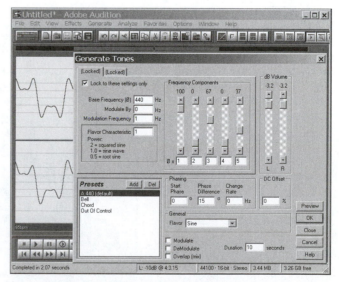

FIGURE 8.10   Using Audition wave editor and harmonic analysis concepts to build a (a) sine wave and a (b) square wave at A440 or 440 Hz

ASIDE

Try this experiment with a grand piano. First, hold the damper pedal down, lifting all the dampers off the strings. Then sing or play different instruments into the open piano. You should hear an echo of the same timbre you played. Each string in the piano *sympathetically vibrates* to match the amplitude of each sine wave in the spectrum of the instrument you are playing. The grand piano is a spectrum or harmonic analyzer.

ASIDE

In the mid-1800s, Hermann von Helmholtz, using hollow vibrating glass spheres, was able to demonstrate the first harmonic analysis of complex sounds following the Fourier theorem.

LINK

See Viewport VI, Module 17, for examples of how current soft synths and effect plug-ins use these acoustical concepts and the synthesis concepts that follow.

FIGURE 8.11 Harmonic analysis of the first eight partials of the violin tone portrayed in Figure 8.2b showing the frequency of each harmonic and the note in the overtone series

Summary of the Acoustic Properties of Sound

Let's summarize the acoustic properties we have discussed. Any complex sound can be analyzed in terms of four physical properties: frequency, amplitude, envelope, and harmonic spectrum. The graphs of the clarinet and violin tone in Figure 8.2 show these three dimensions. Frequency measures the rate of vibration and amplitude the amount or intensity of the vibration. Frequency is measured in cycles per second (cps) or Hertz (Hz), and amplitude is measured in dynes/cm2 or decibels (dB).

You can look at changes in amplitude over time to analyze the envelope of the sound. Envelopes typically follow a pattern of attack, decay, sustain, and release (ADSR). You can look at the amplitude of each sine wave present in a sound at a point in time to analyze its harmonic spectrum. This is the basis of Fourier's theorem.

You now have the basic concepts necessary to interpret the graphs in Figure 8.2. Figure 8.11 shows the harmonic spectrum of just one time slice for the violin tone in Figure 8.2b. Each spike in amplitude along the frequency axis of the graph represents one of the harmonics in the overtone series. They are each labeled starting with the fundamental of 521 Hz (C5). Use what you have learned about the overtone series and determine how the frequency of each partial and the pitches were assigned to each harmonic.

Concepts of Digital Audio and Sampling: Analog to Digital and Back

In the first part of Module 8, we introduced the concepts of analog sound and acoustics. To review, *analog* represents events that are recorded as continuous in nature, as opposed to *digital* events that are represented as discrete steps or numbers. Figure 8.12 represents sound vibrations being transformed by analog *transducers*.

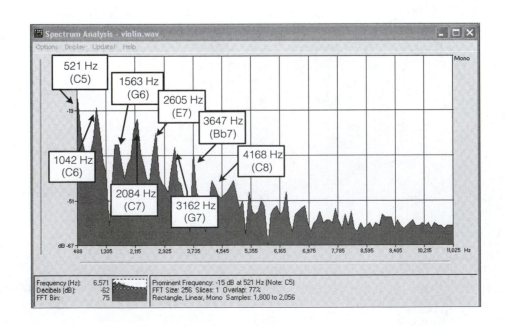

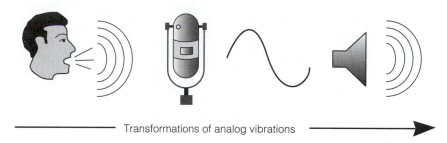

Transformations of analog vibrations →

FIGURE 8.12 Analog transformations of sound from voice, to air, to microphone, to speaker, and back to air

The analog vibrations begin as rapid movements of the singer's vocal cords, then are transformed into fluctuations in air pressure, then to changing electrical voltages by the microphone, then to rapid movements in the cone of a speaker, and then once again to fluctuations in air pressure. The vocal cord, air, microphone, and speaker cone are all analog *transducers* of sound. They convert acoustical vibrations and energy from one analog form to another.

How can we store or capture analog sound vibrations? An old-fashioned magnetic tape recorder is an example. Figure 8.13 adds a magnetic tape recorder to our chain of transducers. Now the electrical voltage oscillations from the microphone are transformed by the tape recorder's recording head into patterns of magnetic particles along the length of recording tape. For playback of the tape, the magnetic particles are converted back into voltage changes through the playback head of the recorder. Again, all of these transformations are analog representations of sound.

Figure 8.14 replaces the tape recorder with a computer, a digital device. The continuous changes in voltage from the microphone are now converted into a series of numbers that the computer stores. Analog-to-digital conversion has been performed. The box marked ADC represents a device that performs the analog-to-digital conversion. To change the number series back into analog data, a *digital-to-analog* converter (DAC) is used.

Let's convert a sound from its original analog form to digital and back again. Figures 8.14 and 8.15 represent this process. From left to right, the original analog vibration passes through the analog-to-digital converter (ADC) and produces a series of numbers. Each number is a discrete point or *sample* from the analog sound. Next, a digital-to-analog converter (DAC) converts the numbers back to analog form, enabling the speaker to produce the analog sound as shown at the right of the figures.

ASIDE

The term *sample* is used in two different ways. It may refer to a single point: one number in the ADC process. However, a series of samples that create a set or series of numbers is also referred to as a *sample*.

FIGURE 8.13 Adding analog recording to the chain of transformations

Recording with analog tape →

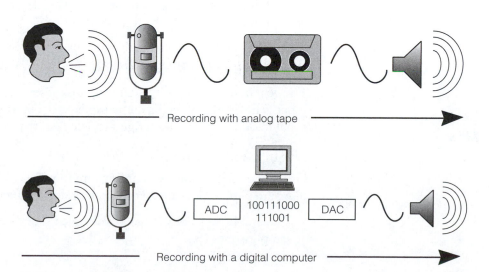

FIGURE 8.14 Converting analog sound to digital (ADC) and digital back to analog (DAC)

ADC 100111000 111001 DAC

Recording with a digital computer →

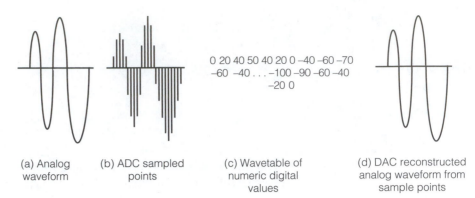

(a) Analog waveform

(b) ADC sampled points

0 20 40 50 40 20 0 −40 −60 −70
−60 −40 . . . −100 −90 −60 −40
−20 0

(c) Wavetable of numeric digital values

(d) DAC reconstructed analog waveform from sample points

FIGURE 8.15 The digital sampling process from an analog waveform, to a waveform table, then reconstructed again as an analog sound

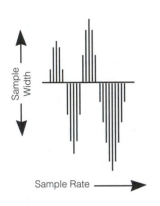

Sample Width

Sample Rate →

ASIDE
Quantizing as used here has a different meaning from the same term used with MIDI data in Viewport V. The term "bit depth" is also used to refer to sampling width or quantizing; they all mean the same thing.

TIP
Sample resolutions of 96 kHz with 24-bit sampling sizes are now commonplace for digital audio.

The extent to which digitized sound samples match the original sound depends on the accuracy with which the computer samples the analog sound data. This accuracy depends on two factors: sampling rate and sampling width (also known as *quantizing*). We will go into these concepts in greater detail later, but for now we offer a simple explanation.

Sampling Rates and Quantizing

The sampling rate is the speed at which the computer can convert analog changes to numbers: the number of samples per second. Ideally, we'd like a sampling rate that is as good as the upper limits of human hearing, or 20 kHz. A sampling rate of 44 kHz will give us an upper frequency limit of 22 kHz on playback. The frequency limit on playback is always half the sampling rate.

Sampling width or *quantizing* refers to the *resolution* of the sampling: how large a number is used to represent each data point or sample. Typical number sizes are 8-, 12-, 16-, or 24-bit numbers. With sampling rate and quantizing size, faster and bigger is better—if possible. Music can be digitized with reasonable quality with 8-bit resolution and 22-kHz sampling rates, comparable to AM and FM radio; the standard for CD audio quality, however, is 16-bit/44-kHz resolution.

Bear in mind, however, that when sampling on a computer system, there is a direct relationship between the sampling rate and width you use and the amount of storage space you need. With a bit-depth or width of 16 bits and a 44-kHz sampling rate, a one-minute sample of analog stereo sound will consume about 10 MB of hard disk space. Using an 8-bit width (bit-depth) and 22-kHz sampling rate, a one-minute sample uses about 2.5 MB of space—a dramatic difference.

Optimizing the Quality of Digital Audio

The goal in terms of quality digital audio and sound sampling is to match output to input. The quality of digital audio produced from a device like a computer must be equal to or better than the original analog audio that was digitized.

Nyquist and S/N Ratios

Given the relationship of sampling rate to width, two rules related to digital sampling are important in furthering your understanding of digital audio:

- The usable frequency range of a sampled sound (S) is from 0 up to one-half the sampling rate (S/2).

TIP

Width	S/N Ratio
1 bit	6 dB
8 bit	48 dB
12 bit	72 dB
16 bit	96 dB
24 bit	144 dB

- The dynamic range of a sampled sound or its signal-to-noise ratio (S/N) can be determined by multiplying the sampling width (W) times 6 decibels ($6 \times W$ decibels).

Frequency range. The Nyquist theorem helps to determine the effect of sampling rate on the quality of digital audio. Figure 8.16 shows a continuum of frequencies, beginning with the lowest sound the human ear can detect, 20 Hz. The highest note (C8) on the piano is shown at 4,200 Hz or 4.2 kHz. The upper limit of human hearing is 20 kHz. Bear in mind that even though the highest note on the piano at 4.2 kHz is a long way from the 20-kHz limit of the ear, we must take into account the frequencies of all the harmonics of an instrument's harmonic spectrum. The eighth harmonic of a 4.2-kHz tone would be 33.6 kHz (8×4.2 kHz), well beyond the range of the human ear.

Nyquist's theorem says that the rate we use for sampling audio must be twice as high as the usable frequency we need. So if we want a sample rate that will be at or above the upper range of the human ear, then the sampling rate needs to be twice as high, or 40 kHz (2 x 20 kHz). In practice, the frequency range is "up to a little less" than one-half the sampling rate. For this reason, a common sampling rate used in the industry is 44 kHz (technically, 44.1 kHz) with a usable Nyquist frequency of 22 kHz, 2 kHz above the upper limit of the human ear. This is what is shown in Figure 8.16.

The audio card or component built into most computer systems can sample a full range from 11 kHz to 48 kHz, with 96 kHz or higher possible. Using a sampling rate of 22 kHz, the Nyquist frequency will be only 11 kHz (S/2); the computer will not be able to reproduce the full range of frequencies that the human ear can detect. With a sampling rate of 44 kHz, however, the Nyquist frequency will be increased to 22 kHz. In terms of our goal of having the output of a digital audio system equal to or better than the input, you can see that sampling rates less than 44 kHz will give us less than the optimum quality we seek.

The dynamic range or signal-to-noise ratio. The second rule helps us determine the effect of *sampling width* (bit depth) on the quality of the digital audio process. This concept says that the usable dynamic range of the sampling process is a function of the sampling width; this is similar to what is known as the signal-to-noise (S/N) ratio. Common sense should tell you that the greater the number of digits you use in measuring something (i.e., the numeric width), the more accurate the measurement. With any measurement, you have to round off the value at some point, and, the greater the size or width of the value, the less likely that any errors due to rounding will have a noticeable effect. Thus, the larger the S/N ratio in digital sampling, the less likely that rounding errors will be detectable by the human ear when the digital sample is recreated.

FIGURE 8.16   A comparison of frequencies in relation to the Nyquist frequency

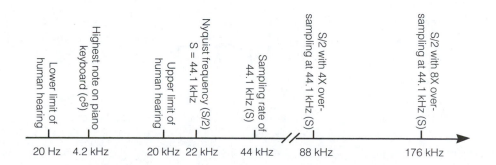

ASIDE

Have you noticed wagon wheels in old Western movies that go backward? That is visual aliasing. The camera, at 24 frames per second, is undersampling the wagon wheel because it is spinning faster than the sampling rate of the camera.

ASIDE

In modern audio systems, aliasing should not be audible; it is a conceptual issue, not a performance one.

LINK

Filters will come up several times in the text. In Module 9, they are discussed in terms of effect processing in digital audio.

The rule also says that, in calculating the signal-to-noise ratio, for each bit added to the value used for measuring a sample, the dynamic range is improved by 6 dB. As the Tip in the margin on page 93 shows, the S/N ratio increases as the size of the value representing each sample increases.

Aliasing, Filters, and Oversampling

In our quest for the best quality possible in reproducing an audio image from a digitized sound sample, there are a few more factors to consider besides sampling rate and width. In Figure 8.17, notice that we have added filters to the digitizing chain: one before the ADC and another after the DAC. The filters are added to eliminate distortion generated by the sampling process.

The resulting audio signal from the DAC (Figure 8.16d) prior to filtering is not equal to the initial audio signal (Figure 8.16a). The audio signal output from the DAC has *jaggies*. The jaggies are the result of unwanted harmonics added to the sample during digitization.

There is another issue with sampling known as audio *aliasing*. Aliasing refers to unwanted sounds that may be audible in the output from a DAC, sounds that are masquerading and add distortion. Aliasing is caused by sounds above the Nyquist frequency. Do you remember that the eighth harmonic for the piano tone of 4.2 kHz would be 33.6 kHz? Take another look at the chart in Figure 8.16 and you will see that with a 44-kHz sampling rate, the 33.6-kHz harmonic would be above the Nyquist frequency of 22 kHz. This sampling rate can't keep up with a 33.6-kHz sound. The data are undersampled and, systematically, samples are lost. With undersampling, the audio result that you hear will be frequencies below the Nyquist frequency of 22 kHz, dissonant and unwanted sounds that are aliases for sounds above the Nyquist point.

Different techniques are used for eliminating unwanted aliasing and to smooth the jaggies from digital audio. One alternative is the placement of what are known as low-pass or antialiasing *filters* before the ADC, and brickwall "anti-imaging" filters after the DAC, in the digital audio processing chain (see Figures 8.17b and 8.17d). A low-pass audio filter allows all frequencies below the threshold of the filter to pass; all frequencies above the filter's threshold are removed. A brickwall low-pass filter has a very sharp or rapid cutoff that allows very few frequencies beyond its threshold to pass. A brickwall filter set to 20 kHz (just below 22 kHz for a safe margin), for example, will stop any frequency beyond a 22-kHz

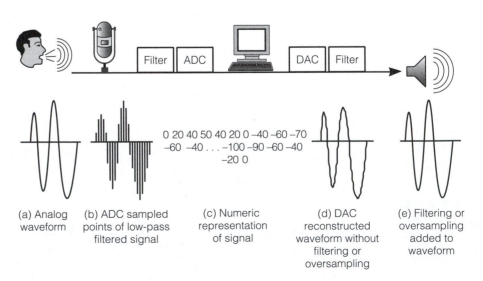

(a) Analog waveform   (b) ADC sampled points of low-pass filtered signal   (c) Numeric representation of signal   (d) DAC reconstructed waveform without filtering or oversampling   (e) Filtering or oversampling added to waveform

FIGURE 8.17 Adding filters to the digitizing process

Nyquist frequency from being passed along; the higher frequencies figuratively "run into a brick wall."

A second alternative for eliminating aliasing and jaggies is to oversample. It is common to see ads for MIDI devices, audio CD players, and hard-disc recorders that make claims, for example, such as "8x oversampling D/A converters." An oversampling filter increases the sampling rate by adding more samples between the ones obtained from the analog signal. In the case of 8x oversampling, seven interpolated samples are placed between each sample point by using a digital filter.

What advantage is this? Look back at the continuum in Figure 8.16. Notice that we have indicated where the Nyquist frequency will fall with 4x and 8x over-sampling. Oversampling electronically improves the sampling rate through digital signal processing. At 8x oversampling and a 176-kHz Nyquist frequency (22 kHz × 8), the high-frequency jaggies have been greatly reduced. So, instead of using brute force with a brickwall filter, over-sampling filters simply moves the Nyquist frequency way out of the range of human hearing to minimize distortion. Moreover, the remaining high frequencies can be easily removed with a simple filter.

Going Higher: 24 Bits at 96 kHz and Beyond

Sampling with 16 bits and 44.1 kHz seems like the ideal upper limit for CD-quality digital audio. However, if you examine specifications for high-end digital audio hardware and software, sampling rates are provided for 48 kHz, 96 kHz, and higher. DVD audio uses sampling rates up to 192 kHz. And, instead of 16 bits of sampling depth, you may find 20 and 24 bits.

Is there anything to gain by the increased sampling resolution? Consider our discussion above on aliasing and filters and oversampling. The higher the sampling rate, the further the Nyquist frequency is from the 22 kHz upper limit of hearing. This means aliasing and jaggies occur much further beyond the range of hearing as well. The filters required to remove these unwanted sounds can be much simpler in design. And, with 24 bits of precision, our S/N ratio greatly improves. Many musicians notice this subtle but perceptible gain in audio quality.

Formats and Compression for Storing Digital Audio Files

Digitally sampled music quickly consumes large amounts of computer storage space, with each minute of stereo music sampled at 44.1 kHz and 16-bit samples using up 10 megabytes of storage. The problem of size is greatly magnified when exchanging digital music files with others or playing digital music in real time over the Internet. Several solutions for storing digital audio files are currently available, including formats that offer compression to reduce file size. Table 8.2 shows the more common audio file types that you will encounter and the techniques used to encode and decode audio data (codecs).

The origin for digital audio formats begins with PCM, or Pulse Code Modulated, files or their equivalent used in laser audio formats, linear, or LPCM. PCM represents an uncompressed file where every byte in the file is a digital audio sample. The CD-DA format shown at the top of the table is the most prevalent PCM format designed for placing digital audio data on commercial compact audio discs. This format is part of the original Sony-Philips Red Book standards that

TABLE 8.2   Common File Formats for Storing Digital Audio Files

File Extension	Computer	Encode/Decode (codecs)	Description
CD-DA	N/A	PCM	Pulse Code Modulation (PCM) uncompressed format used on CD audio discs; based on CD Red Book format for audio
.aif	Mac	PCM	The default sampled-sound format for Macintosh, Audio Interchange File Format (AIFF); may be compressed or uncompressed at a variety of sampling rates and sample bit depths. AIFC is compressed format for AIF.
.wav	PC	PCM	The default sampled-sound file format for Windows since Win OS 3.1; uncompressed format for 8- or 16-bit audio files, mono and stereo, with a variety of sampling rates including 44.1 kHz.
.mp3	Mac or PC	MPEG-1 Audio Layer-3	Based on MPEG standards (International Standardization Organization ISO), perceptual coding compression format commonly used on the Internet and for MP3 music players (stereo) with sampling rates of 32, 44.1, and 48 kHz. Compression expressed as bit rate from 28.8 to 320 Kbps.
.ra or .rm	Mac or PC	RealNetworks Proprietary	RealAudio format with high compression ratio and fast encoding/decoding times; used on the Internet, especially for streaming audio
.aac or .m4a	Mac or PC	MPEG-2 AAC NBC	Advanced Audio Coding (AAC) extends the MP3 perceptual coding format with multiple channels and sample rates up to 96 kHz. AAC is Non-Backwards Compatible with MP3.
.wma	PC	Microsoft Proprietary	Windows Media Audio format is a newer Microsoft audio compression format that is competitive with MP3 and RA for audio files and streaming audio. WMA's 64 Kbps bit rate said to be comparable in quality to MP3 128 Kbps bit rate with one-half the file size.
.mov	Mac or PC	QT 6.0 using AAC and MPEG-2 for audio	QuickTime is a multimedia system for audio, MIDI, video, and animation that sets a number of different codecs, including MPEG-4 and, for audio, MPEG-2.
.ogg	Mac or PC	OGG	Freely distributed but unique compression
.flac, .shn	Mac or PC	Free Lossless Audio codec and Shorten codec	Used for free lossless compression on the Internet for swapping live concerts of trade-friendly bands
.au, .voc, .mod, .snd	Mac and PC	Various	Older file formats replaced in practice by newer formats above

defined formats for CD audio and other CD-ROM data coded onto compact laser discs. Other uncompressed file formats presented in Table 8.2 are the two audio formats for Windows and Mac operating systems, WAV and AIF, respectively. Each of these have a different structure or format for storing PCM data, but the sampled audio data remain uncompressed.

Sound Compression

To provide a convenient way to exchange digital audio files, some means of compression is necessary to reduce the file size. The challenge is to remove data without sacrificing sound quality! Increasingly sophisticated techniques are evolving to meet this challenge.

For both sound and graphic data compression, there are two approaches to reducing the amount of digital data stored: *lossy* and *lossless*. When a compression technique is said to be "lossy," data are lost in the compression or encoding process that will not be replaced when the file is decoded or decompressed. A "lossless" compressed file, on the other hand, when decompressed, restores all the data back to its original form. As we will see, sound files that are compressed almost always use some combination of a *lossy* or *lossless* technique. The "packed" PCM with Meridian Lossless Packing (MLP) used in DVD audio formats provides lossless compression—all the original information is there when uncompressed. Two other lossless compression formats shown in Table 8.2 include FLAC (Free Lossless Audio Codec) and SHN (Shorten) formats used on the Internet for swapping high-quality live concert recordings of "trade-friendly bands." Both compression formats are free and open source.

Increasing Compression While Fooling the Ear

Many different schemes are available for lossy compression. Information can be more selectively eliminated from an audio file through mathematical algorithms. The computer intelligently eliminates samples rather than just dropping samples or bits. ADPCM, or Adaptive Difference Pulse Code Modulation compression, as an example, converts the data into a more compact code by taking the difference between the values for each sample. This technique encodes only the audio information that has changed from the previous samples. ADPCM is used on a variety of proprietary file compression formats. The data that are intelligently removed from the digital samples are sounds the human ear is unable to hear (hence, the term perceptual encoding). The strategy is "if you are not going to hear it, then you don't need to save it!"

The common MP3 compression format noted in Table 8.2 uses perceptual encoding to reduce file size. What does this mean? In the most general terms, MP3 files take advantage of three techniques for reducing file size in the encoding process, two using lossy techniques and one using lossless:

- Threshold of hearing (lossy). Our hearing is more or less sensitive to sounds as they move across the range of hearing from 20 Hz to 20 kHz. To reduce data in the compressed format, sounds below the human threshold of hearing are eliminated.
- Masking (lossy). Louder sounds tend to mask out or cover up softer sounds; strong audio signals make weaker signals imperceptible. Algorithms in the compression scheme can look for sounds that are masked and eliminate them from the sampled audio data.
- Redundancy of information (lossless). Music contains a good deal of repetition. Repeated patterns of data can be summarized algorithmically into a small compressed space during encoding, and then expanded during the decoding process. MP3 encoding applies this algorithm to compression after the perceptual schemes above have been used. The "Huffman" encoding/decoding formula is one such technique.

Most current audio compression schemes use some combination of "perceptual encoding" algorithms and redundancy algorithms. This applies not only to MP3 files but also to others shown in Table 8.2, namely WMA, RM, AAC, and OGG.

LINK
Check Module 11 for more on DVD audio formats.

LINK
The distinction between acoustical and perceptual dimensions of audio and music is discussed earlier in this module.

ASIDE
MPEG (pronounced "M-Peg") is a suite of file standards approved by the Moving Picture Experts Group for audio, video, animation, and multimedia. MP3 audio is one of those standards, known as MPEG-1, Level 3. More on MPEG audio is presented in Module 9 on MP3 software, and again in Module 11. Stay tuned!

TIP
Streaming audio files are now "instant on" with playing happening "instantly" on downloading a music or video file.

LINK
You will encounter this array of digital audio file types, streaming media, and bit rates many times throughout the text. Module 9 discusses these file formats in relation to Internet audio and digital audio editing software.

LINK
Look ahead to Module 9 for more on streaming software.

Streaming Audio Files for the Internet

When you deal with sending files over the Internet, a new challenge presents itself. Not only do the files need to be compressed in size but also, in order to play the audio file in real time, the audio data have to be "streamed" from one computer to another. "Streaming" means that the audio file is not completely downloaded to a computer desktop before it starts playing. After a small portion of an audio file has been received, the computer begins to play the audio while it continues to download or stream more of the data from its source. When the music has stopped playing, typically none of the digital audio data remain or are stored on the computer.

With streaming audio, sound quality directly depends on the speed or bandwidth of the Internet connection. Six audio file formats in Table 8.2 may be streamed: RM, WMA, MOV, OGG, MP3, and AAC.

Streaming audio files are described in terms of their transmission speed, expressed in 1000s of bits per second or "Kbps." That is, how many bits of audio data are transmitted in one second, or the audio file's "bit rate." An MP3 file may have a bit rate from 28.8 Kbps to 360 Kbps. The higher the bit rate, the better the perceived audio quality of the sound. Table 8.3 shows a comparison of the "bit rates" for MP3 file compressions. Bit rates of 96 Kbps to 128 Kbps are common compression rates found for MP3 files on the Internet. The bit rate of a pure, uncompressed CD-DA audio file is 1.4 Mbps. Besides *constant bit rates* (CBR), compression alternatives also permit *variable bit rates* (VBR), where the encoding process varies the bit rate to fit the complexity of the audio content being compressed at any point in time.

Table 8.3 communicates a good deal about strategies for selecting appropriate compression for MP3 files. Again, it is a balance between physical issues (transmission speed) and perceptual issues (quality of the audio). First, remember that compressed audio files all originate as PCM files, typically sampled at 44.1 or 48 kHz, 16-bit stereo and saved as WAV or AIF files. From the table, you can select a bit rate appropriate for the transmission, view the compression ratio and

TABLE 8.3   Comparison of Various Bitrates for MP3 Audio Compression Illustrating the Trade-Off in Sound Quality for File Size and Transmission Rate

Bit rate	Compression Ratio	File size for MP3 compressed 60 secs from a 16-bit/44kHz stereo WAV file*	MPEG quality ratings (varies by style of music and instrumentation)	Parallel sound experiences
8 Kbps	1:96	.06 MB	Very annoying (1)	Analog telephone
32 Kbps	1:24	.24 MB	Annoying (2)	AM mono radio
96 Kbps	1:24	.72 MB	Slightly annoying (3)	FM stereo radio
128 Kbps	1:12	.96 MB	Perceptible, but not annoying (4)	Near CD audio
256 Kbps	1:6	1.92 MB	Transparent CD quality (5)	CD audio (can't tell the difference)
1400 Kbps	1:1	10.5 MB	Original, no compression	Pure PCM audio, no compression

* File size calculated as Kbps ÷ 8 bits x 60 secs.

LINK
Compare the bit rates of audio files with the transmission rates of Internet connectivity discussed in Viewport II. At the slow end with 56 Kbps modems, 28 Kbps bit rates are needed for streaming audio; at the high bandwidth end with DSL, cable, or direct Internet connectivity, 128 Kbps audio bit rates will work. Review a list of Internet radio stations and you will see that their transmission speeds run from 28 to 128 Kbps bit rates.

ASIDE
Streaming audio files may also include coding built in to ensure copyright protection. The Secure Digital Music Initiative (SDMI) is one such set of codes that can prevent copying of commercial, copyright-protected digital music files.

LINK
Module 9 discusses more about MP3 and software. MPEG formats are covered in depth in Viewport IV when DVD and surround sound are discussed.

resulting file size in comparison to an uncompressed PCM file, and then judge the quality against either the five-point scale used in MPEG testing or the comparison to real life, sonic experiences. Note that different musical styles (rock, folk, classical, jazz) and varying instrumentation (vocal, piano, jazz ensemble, full orchestra) are affected differently by the MP3 encoding algorithms. What works for one style and instrumentation may not be perceptually acceptable for another.

RealAudio (RA or RM), QuickTime (MOV), Windows Media Audio (WMA), and Advanced Audio Coding (AAC) audio file formats also offer streaming compression options. The RM (or RA) format is a proprietary scheme developed by RealNetworks and was one of the first streaming audio formats available on the Internet to provide very high compression ratios with acceptable quality for radio-like broadcasts. AAC is part of a set of multimedia standards known as MP4. AAC's sound format is defined under MPEG-2; MP3 audio format is defined under MPEG-1, Layer III. As of QuickTime release 6.0, MP4 and AAC is available as a compression format (technically called a "codec"). WMA is Microsoft's proprietary compression format. Both AAC and WMA are becoming as common as MP3 for Internet audio.

No one compression scheme works best for all audio recording environments and the competition to continue to improve the streaming algorithms translates into higher-quality audio at increasingly lower bit rates. For example, various listening tests have reported that AAC's 96 Kbps compression is superior to MP3's 128 Kbps and WMA's 64 Kbps compression comes close to MP3's 128 Kbps compression. RealNetworks claims a 25% improvement over MP3 bit rate quality. The freely distributed but unique Ogg Vorbis (OGG) format claims superior quality at lower bit rates than MP3. Regardless of the commercial claims or listening tests, in the end, your musician's ear will determine the most appropriate format given the style and instrumentation of the music you are encoding for Internet delivery.

Varieties of Music Synthesis Techniques

Any time you create sounds electronically in any form you are engaging in sound or music synthesis. In this Module, you have been introduced to a wide range of concepts related to both analog and digital audio. A summary of the various techniques for music synthesis will help bring together many of these concepts. With analog synthesizers appearing as virtual software synthesizers, the line between analog and digital sound synthesis is greatly blurred. We will briefly review the following forms of music synthesis:

- Analog synthesis: additive, subtractive, and distortive (frequency modulation)
- Physical modeling synthesis
- Digital wave synthesis
- Granular synthesis

Analog Synthesis: Additive, Subtractive, and Distortive

Additive synthesis combines oscillators to build up more complex sounds. Recall the Fourier theorem. By adding sine waves at varying amplitudes, you can create different harmonic spectra. So, by changing the amplitude of different electronic oscillators in various combinations, you can change the harmonic spectrum of a sound and therefore the timbre you perceive.

Historical examples of instruments that used additive synthesis include the Telharmonium (around 1900), which used immense electronic dynamos to create complex waveforms; the Hammond organ (1930s), which used mechanically controlled tone wheels to create complex sounds; and Max Mathews's (1957) first experiments, which created sounds on a digital computer at Bell Labs. With software synthesizers available to simulate vintage synthesizers on a computer, many opportunities exist for applying the techniques of additive synthesis. Figures 8.10a and 8.10b demonstrate how additive synthesis in Adobe's Audition can be used to construct a sine and square wave.

Subtractive synthesis starts with a complex sound, like that of a sawtooth electronic oscillator. It then uses electronic filters to subtract selected harmonics. Again, Fourier's theorem comes into play. Subtracting selected harmonics from the overtone series alters the harmonic spectrum. Subtractive synthesis was a common technique used by analog synthesizers such as the Moog, Buchla, and ARP synthesizers of the 1960s. Tools provided in Native Instruments Pro-53 software synthesizer (see Figure 8.1) or Propellerhead Reason's "SubTractor" analog soft synth instrument can be used to take a complex sawtooth wave, for example, and then apply various filters to remove or subtract frequencies to obtain the desired sound.

Distortive synthesis takes several forms; one of the more common is FM or frequency modulation synthesis. Distortion means that one physical property of sound is used to distort or modify the same or a different property of sound. (Some also use the term *multiply* synthesis because one sound may multiply properties of the other.) With FM synthesis, the sound generated by one oscillator (called the *carrier*) is distorted by another oscillator (called the *modulator*). The result produces a unique and harmonically rich spectrum of sounds. John Chowning at Stanford University refined this method of analog synthesis and licensed the techniques to Yamaha. Many of Yamaha's electronic synthesizers in the 1980s, among them the FB-01 and the DX-7, used this technique. Yamaha called the carriers and modulators operators. Native Instruments' "FM7" provides a software FM synthesizer usable in most sequencers that accept plug-ins.

Physical Modeling

A more recent technique for sound synthesis is *physical modeling*. Physical modeling simulates the acoustic properties of a sound and the physical movement of mechanical parts of musical instruments through mathematical formulas. No

LINK
Reason software is covered in depth in Module 17.

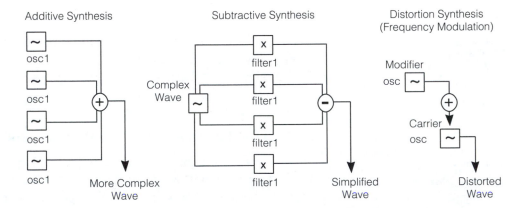

FIGURE 8.18 Three forms of analog music synthesis: additive, subtractive, and distortive

image of the sound is stored in the computer, only the model of its behavior. Applied Acoustic Systems' Lounge Lizard and Tassman software synthesizers are good illustrations. Lounge Lizard uses physical modeling (see Figure 8.19) to simulate the mechanics of a Rhodes electric piano by modeling the mallet, fork, pick-up, and other physical parameters. It is only with faster processor speeds and large amounts of memory that physical modeling as a means of sound synthesis is possible. Most high-end synthesizers and sound modules have physical modeling capabilities.

Digital Wave Synthesis

As we have seen in this module, a computer can be used for music synthesis by generating series of numbers to construct digital images of a wide variety of sonic events. As you work with digital audio synthesis in Module 9 and in other Viewports in this book, you will find four techniques for using digital synthesis: single-cycle waveform, single-tone sample, complete sample, and wave shaping.

Single-cycle waveform. A series of numbers are created that represent one cycle of a waveform. This series may be sampled from an analog source or computed mathematically. It contains only the harmonic information. To produce a tone in the computer, the series, or *wavetable* is repeatedly cycled through at the rate of the desired frequency, and the resulting numeric values are played back through a DAC. A computer or synthesizer using this technique is called a *digital synthesizer*— it uses *digital oscillators*. The wavetable in this case contains no envelope information to shape the attack and decay of the sound. The amplitude information for the envelope needs to be added from a separate DAC device and an *envelope table*. The single-cycle waveform data structure, which works best for situations where memory is critical, was used on several of the last-generation MIDI keyboards. With sufficient memory and processor speeds, keyboards and sample players are now more likely to use complete samples or wave shaping for creating realistic instrument sounds.

Single-tone sample. A digitized sample is made of one complete musical tone. The sample contains all the envelope and harmonic spectrum information needed to produce a real-sounding single tone of an instrument. For best realism, however,

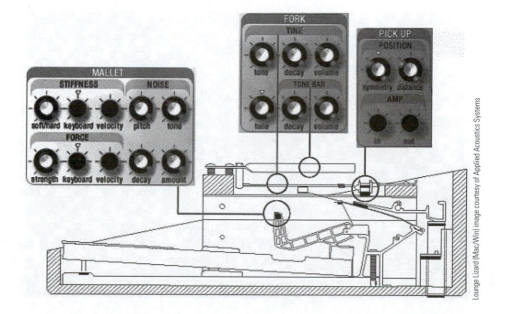

FIGURE 8.19 A diagram showing the relationship between the mechanics of a Rhodes electric piano and the physical modeling synthesis in the Lounge Lizard EP-1 software module

multiple samples, one for each pitch, need to be created to represent an instrument's full range of timbres. This technique works best where a degree of realism for various instrument timbres is needed. If you play on a digital or sampling keyboard, single-tone sampling (or its more sophisticated variant, wave shaping, discussed below) is the likely way it creates its sound.

Complete sample. A digitized sample is made of a complete segment of music. To reproduce the sample, the complete series of digitized, numeric values is played back through a DAC device or a digital oscillator. This offers the best computer realization of an analog sound sample, but consumes large amounts of memory and storage. Hardware and software that both record and play back complete samples are called *samplers*. Those that only play back prerecorded samples are called *sample players*. In Module 9, you will see how software such as Peak, Sound Forge, and Audition can be used for sampling and editing complete productions of music performance.

Wave shaping. Since digital audio first appeared in personal computers in the late 1970s, engineers have experimented with the first three forms of digital sampling to continue to improve the quality of the musical sounds that a computer can produce. What have emerged are increasingly complex techniques for capturing audio and sound sampling and producing the most realistic digital instrument sounds. Combining these forms can be termed *wave shaping*. Wave shaping refers to more complex digital sound generation where algorithms are used to *shape* the digital waveform through various combinations of digital oscillators, digital-controlled amplifiers, digital-controlled filters, and digital effects processors.

Several different wavetables can be combined to create the final instrument sound generated by the digital device. The attack portion of an instrument's sound envelope may be one wavetable, another may be used for the decay of a sound's envelope, and a third wavetable may be repeated many times or *looped* to create the sustained portion of the instrument's envelope. More complex shapes can be constructed when the envelope is described by many wavetables to create subtle nuances in the shape of an instrument's waveform. Sound loops and arpeggiation effects can also be added to an instrument's wave shape. This concept of looping will be illustrated in Module 9 when software for building sound loops is presented.

Digital synthesizer manufacturers have proprietary techniques for the hardware and algorithms used to shape a digital sound. Except for the very low-end MIDI keyboards and samplers, most use some form of wave shaping in creating their digital instrument sounds. In addition, many add analog and physical modeling synthesis features to round out the musician's repertoire of available synthesis techniques.

LINK
Module 16 presents a variety of synthesizers and reviews the unique synthesis engines developed by various manufacturers.

Granular Synthesis

The last sound synthesis technique we will make note of is termed *granular* synthesis. You might say that granular synthesis is "slicing and dicing" of sound samples. A sound sample is literally sliced into very small "grains" of 100 msecs or less. If these grains are played back in exactly the same order without any processing, the result will sound the same as the original sampled sound as in wavetable synthesis. Where granular synthesis comes into play is in the process of reordering the grains, changing the speed at which they are played back, looping subsets of grains, or processing subsets of grains with various effects. The list of synthesis options is extensive. The "Malstrom Graintable" soft synth packaged with Propellerhead's Reason software (see Module 17) provides a good environment to experiment with granular synthesis techniques.

M o d u l e   9

Software for Capturing, Editing, and Storing Digital Audio

DVD-ROM
Projects 5–7 on the accompanying DVD are designed to give you hands-on experience with the tasks in Table 9.1.

LINK
As noted in Module 8, the original popular MPEG audio format was MP3. The newer AAC and WMA formats offer improved quality and compression. Be sure to review the compression details for these audio files in Module 8 and the hardware possibilities in Module 10. When we refer to web audio or web music, we are referring to MP3, WMA, and AAC.

In the last module, you learned about acoustics and the distinction between digital and analog sound. We stressed the historic notions of sound synthesis and how these form the basis for modern sound design. You also learned the important sound file formats and became acquainted with compression techniques such as those found in MP3 and AAC files. In this module and in the many software modules to come, we describe how to apply many of these ideas to making and enjoying music.

Digital audio software is the fastest-growing category of music software today. Five years ago, perhaps 15 software titles were widely used for digital audio work, mostly in professional studios and labs. Now, the number is well over 100, with additional titles hitting the shelves monthly. Software has now replaced much of the hardware used to capture and process digital audio and many musicians are working with this generation of digital audio software in professional studios, home setups, and Internet settings.

As with each of the software modules to come in this book, we stress the importance of matching software to your desired task. Table 9.1 displays a set of tasks that are commonly done when capturing, editing, and storing digital audio. The table suggests a likely setting for each task and some typical software titles that can be used. In the remainder of the module, we present information for each task.

Working with Audio on the Web

One of the more popular uses of digital audio with computers involves MP3 software and streaming media. In this section, we focus on the use and production of MP3 files and the newer formats, AAC and WMA. The popularity of these audio file formats, especially MP3, has grown enormously, fueled by Internet sites that enable sharing thousands of these files in all genres of music and the development of free and inexpensive software that encodes MP3 files from sound sources such as commercial CDs. An entire generation of small, very portable hardware devices known as MP3 players has developed to host these files, directly supported by a personal computer. Custom-created CDs that are filled with these files are easy to create with today's software tools and such discs can often be played in the same player that hosts the more traditional audio CDs.

TABLE 9.1   Tasks for Basic Digital Audio

Setting	Task	Typical Software
Home	• Download and listen to MP3 files	Winamp (Win)
	• Create playlists and organize MP3 files	Musicmatch (Win)
	• Create custom CDs for your MP3 files	iTunes (Mac/Win)
	• Encode MP3 files from CDs and use ID3 tag data	Media Jukebox (Win), Audion (Mac)
	• Use and create streaming media	Windows Media Player (Mac/Win), QuickTime Pro (Mac/Win), RealOne Player (Mac/Win)
Home and Studio	• Prepare your computer for importing sound from CDs; live recording with simple microphones	Operating System Settings
	• Record and edit a live and a CD segment of digital audio	Audition (Win), Audacity (Mac/Win), Sound Studio (Mac)
	• Use basic editing, file management, effects-processing options	PeakLE (Mac), Sound Forge Audio Studio (Win)
	• Experiment with advanced editing, file management, and effects-processing options	Peak(Mac), Sound Forge (Win), WaveLab (Win)

LINK

See Viewport II, Module 5, for Internet software concepts, including information about legal downloads.

LINK

Peer-to-peer network computing, as well as client-server networking, is explained in Modules 5 and 7.

Obtaining Web Music Files

Large numbers of these audio files, especially MP3s, that are free and legally offered to the public can be found on the Internet and downloaded by using procedures defined by websites, FTP servers, and news groups. In using any of these sources, we stress that it is your responsibility as a user to verify that the content you download is, in fact, legally distributed. Locations such as these offer music CDs for purchase, but also provide MPEG audio files that can be auditioned or downloaded for use at a later time. Often, these sites have agreements with artists and recording companies that allow them to offer this music in the hopes that you might want to purchase a full CD.

Another popular source for free and legal web music files is the actual Internet site for the ensemble or artist you are interested in. For example, rock groups may actually encourage distribution of their music to increase concert attendance or CD sales.

Finally, another method of obtaining web music files is an approach that often is called "peer-to-peer" distribution. This was the technique used by the Napster site when it was launched in 1999. Music files are exchanged directly between personal computers with no central server needed; everyone shares. This approach was challenged in court by the recording industry as encouraging copyright infringement and the industry won cases that forced the Napster site to close in 2001. As we noted in Module 5, similar peer-to-peer software programs have emerged following Napster's demise. We strongly advise against using this method of obtaining MP3 files unless you are very sure that the material is intended to be free.

Some sites on the Internet that once were portals for free MP3 distribution have now developed a commercial approach that encourage you to purchase

ASIDE
Napster was reborn as a month-by-month, subscription-based web music service after its assets were purchased by Roxio, Inc. Roxio then changed its name to Napster, Inc. in December 2004.

MP3s for your collection. This form of marketing music is becoming increasingly popular as an alternative to purchasing CDs at a local store and has contributed greatly to the decline of CD sales worldwide. Online purchasing of music in this way may become the dominant approach to music distribution in the coming years.

Organizing and Playing Web Music Files

Software for organizing and playing music files is readily available for all types of computers. Two such programs are displayed in Figures 9.1a and b. Winamp is a classic program that has had a long history of supporting MP3s and other file formats such as CD audio, WAV, and MIDI. The software is free and does not produce any pop-up ads on your screen. Windows Media Player comes free with the Windows operating system and is Microsoft's all-purpose media player, supporting its proprietary WMA format as well as MP3, among others.

Take a moment to study the displays for both titles. For Winamp, we have captured this view as the software is playing back the second item in the playlist editor. A similar but more expanded playlist is displayed in Windows Media Player. A playlist is simply a collection of, in this case, MP3 files that make logical sense for you. For example, you may want to create a large playlist that has all the titles by the King Singers or you may want to create a playlist of various music titles that depict love or a favorite guitar player. Most MP3 software allows you to organize the music in any way you want. For Winamp, buttons on the bottom of the playlist window allow for this organization; Windows Media Player has similar controls.

One additional point about playlists relates to the information itself. The MP3 file format provides for what is known as "ID3" tag information to accompany data for the audio. This means that text for the artist, title, band name, genre, year, and other information can be included. The nature of the information allowed by the format is expanding all the time; additions may include song lyrics and even artwork, such as CD covers. Such information can be used by the software to enhance displays.

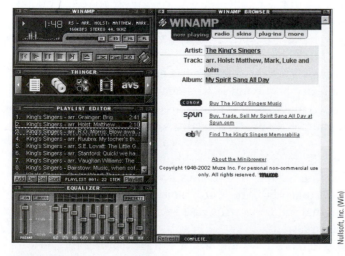

FIGURE 9.1A Winamp

FIGURE 9.1B Windows Media Player

LINK

For help understanding what 160 Kbps means, go back to Module 8.

ASIDE

The concept of "plug-ins" will return many times throughout the software modules in this text. Nearly all music software companies today make use of plug-ins as a way of extending the power and function of their titles.

DVD-ROM

Project 5 Using MP3 Jukebox Software

TIP

Portable digital audio players are called MP3 players, even though they now play other audio formats such as WAV, AIF, RM, and AAC.

The controls for playback in the upper left of Figure 9.1a are self-explanatory. They control the playback of not only MP3s but also inserted audio CDs and other digital audio files on the computer. The software shows the timing progress and also the attributes of the file playing (MP3 file encoded at 160 Kbps, stereo at 44.1 kHz). The equalizer (EQ) graphic at the bottom left is a common feature with MP3 players. Moving the slider buttons changes the filtering for frequencies in the various auditory ranges as described in Module 8. We will present more information about EQ later in this module.

The mini-browser window to the right, a special feature of MP3 players, is designed to seek information from the Internet to support the music playing locally, as well as provide commercial links. Notice the links to plug-ins. The company that distributes Winamp gives programmers enough code to customize extensions for the software. This allows expandability of components, such as special visualizations (changing graphic displays for visual interest), sound processing effects, or input/output controls.

Notice that in both the Windows Media Player and Winamp, reference is made to "radio" and "skins." Many MP3 software titles offer expandability by hosting Internet radio streams that turn the software into a kind of special software radio station for different kinds of music. These may not be real radio stations per se, but rather streams of audio organized to be heard through the software. "Skins" is a special name for visual representations of the software interface. Applying such skins allows you to customize the look of the software to suit your mood or personality, but has no effect on the music heard.

Creating and Storing Your Own Web Music Audio

If all you could do with web music audio software was play and organize other people's files, there would be far less interest in this digital audio category. Besides the clear advantages offered by file compression and high-quality sound, the ability to encode and store your own collections of digital music has contributed enormously to the MP3 craze.

Settings that show how to do the encoding are included within the software. Figure 9.2 gives a clear picture of how this is done in the iTunes software offered free for Macintosh and PC computers. In this graphic, we are importing music from the same Miles Davis CD. In the middle screen, we can see the MP3 encoding. The bit rate for stereo files is set at 160 Kbps which, as you can tell from Module 8, Table 8.3, is slightly better than near-quality CD sound. The software provides for a range from 8–320 Kbps.

Variable bit rate encoding allows the software to change the 160 setting "on the fly" based on the complexity of the music it is sampling, thus offering more sophisticated matches between music and bit rate. This option may actually make the file bigger with no great difference in sound quality, so use your ears to test this option.

The software also filters all inaudible sounds below 10 Hz for added efficiency in size. The Joint Stereo setting reduces redundancy across the two stereo tracks and is most useful for bit rates under 80. The Auto Sampling Rate option matches the software rate to the original source (in this case 44.1 kHz) and is the recommended choice in nearly all situations.

The iTunes graphic also demonstrates important storage features for software such as this. Notice that the Sketches of Spain CD is mounted while the encoding

LINK

Burning CDs is presented in more detail in Viewport IV, Module 12. Hardware for CD-R, DVD-R, and DVD-RWs is discussed in Modules 7 and 13.

ASIDE

CDDB, one of the most complete databases used by the industry, was begun in 1995 by two software developers who simply wanted a method for maintaining their own CD collection. It is now run by Gracenote, Inc. and serves a worldwide audience.

process is occurring; however, the original CD would be ejected and replaced by a blank CD-R or CD-RW if you wanted to save an MP3, AAC, or WMA file back to a removable medium. Notice the "Burning" button at the top of the software window. Clicking on this would cause iTunes to seek out a writeable CD-R or CD-RW drive and begin the process of copying a single or multiple file set to disc. The process is very simple and is integrated into nearly all jukebox MPEG audio software titles.

The other object on the desktop in Figure 9.2 is an icon that represents a portable MP3 player, in this instance an Apple iPod. iTunes works closely with hardware players like the iPod by polling the device to see if the library of MP3 files on the computer matches the portable device. Since the assumption is that you want to synchronize the portable device with the library, it automatically does so, in this case by way of the Firewire serial connection (IEEE 1394, as described in Viewport II, Module 7). Various web music audio software programs support a wide array of CD-burning drives and portable MP3 players, but you do need to check these matches when making purchase decisions.

One last point before leaving this activity of personal MPEG audio creation: online database management. When you first insert a commercial CD into a computer running this type of software, you might have noticed that, if your machine is connected to the net, there is a small pause and, as if by magic, the titles appear for each track together with album information. Is this information on the CD? No, actually the information resides in a remote database that maintains all this information on commercial CDs released by the major recording companies. A unique ID number is sent to the database by your software and the proper information is sent back to be stored with your digital audio data. This is how the MP3 files generate the ID3 tag information without you doing a thing. For this reason, it's always good to be connected to the net when ripping commercial CDs.

FIGURE 9.2   iTunes

Working with Streamed Media

In the previous section, we mentioned how many web music audio software titles can be used as Internet radio receivers. Digital audio (or video) that arrives at your desktop from remote sources in nearly "real time" is a common occurrence on the Internet. Some of these streams of information are, in fact, real radio stations using the Internet as an alternative to the local airwaves. But what is much more common are digital audio broadcasts from archive sources delivered to you on demand. Media content of all sorts is plentiful now on the Internet and will only grow as computers become more powerful and the delivery system more robust.

Streaming Audio in Action

Streaming audio works by sending a file to your desktop with enough data for you to begin to hear it before it all arrives to its destination. In fact, most streaming systems will not even leave the file on the listener's computer; instead they only provide enough data for the music to be heard at any one time. Streaming can serve many people at once at many different times. All this is made possible by the serving software and advances in compression you learned about in the last module.

Figure 9.3 provides a view of streaming in action. You may have encountered this already in high school or college courses that use technology support. In this case, a music-listening course is taught with the support of a web-based course management system called Blackboard. The teacher has created a page with a link to music by the composer Messiaen. The user has clicked on this link and is now listening to music being delivered from a streaming server located somewhere on campus. With more than 80 students in the course, it is likely that the server is sending this same music to many other students at the same time.

LINK
Return to the last module to review the technical way that streaming works. Pay particular attention to file types such as MOV, WMA, RM, MP3, and AAC.

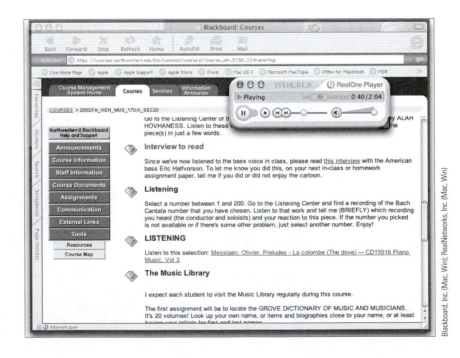

FIGURE 9.3 Course management software Blackboard serving as a trigger for the streaming software RealOne Player

Blackboard, Inc. (Mac, Win); RealNetworks, Inc. (Mac, Win)

Three Systems of Streaming

In addition to MP3, you are likely to encounter three dominant systems when working with streaming digital audio content:

- RealNetworks' RealOne
- Microsoft's Windows Media Series
- Apple's QuickTime

Each system has a player that works on both Macintosh and PC computers and each offers encoding options and server software. The RealNetworks and Microsoft systems generally require PCs as dedicated servers. Apple's solution runs from Macintosh computers. As a consumer, you need to be prepared for each of these systems by installing the free player application as part of the Internet software setup.

Listening to Streamed Media

Except for the MP3 players we reviewed in the previous section, you will encounter streaming audio most frequently as part of links in websites. The players that actually play the streamed media for each of three major systems of streaming may need to be installed separately after your Internet browser of choice is installed. These players can also run by themselves without the browser software.

Making Streamed Media

Each of the three systems provides encoding software to create media for its player. These encoding packages are designed to (1) compress the original file, (2) prepare the file for the desired delivery speed to the user, and (3) provide other options depending on the streaming system. When these steps are finished, the file is ready to be used on a server for hosting websites. The QuickTime Pro version of QuickTime software, for example, provides options for creating streamed media. The other systems do the same.

Preparing Your Computer for Digital Audio Recording

Take a look at Table 9.1 again. Up to this point, we have concerned ourselves with music listening or configuring audio and have done little with actual recording. In the next sections, we will describe basic recording and editing of single mono or stereo tracks and applying effects to the audio signal. We will also describe tasks that may likely be encountered in music studios. These are the tasks noted in the lower half of Table 9.1. Before you can do so, some simple preparations are necessary to make your computer ready to record.

PC Computers

To prepare your PC and its Windows operating system for sound input, you should check the settings for sound management for your sound card and CD. Settings in the Control Panel collection of resources for sounds will help you do this. You can control the volume levels for the CD, microphone, and Line In (if you were going to record into your computer from a tape recorder or another sound source). By the same token, you can control sound out with sliders. You can "pan" or move the sound from one speaker to another for each setting. These settings are very important for PCs, so be sure to check these before doing basic audio capture, even though your editing software of choice might also be used to make these settings.

Macintosh Computers

Similar settings for Macintosh computers can be found in System Preferences. If the Macintosh has a special audio card, it's likely that the software for that sound card has been installed and it would show up as a resource. A volume-level control is included so that you can check the level.

Using Digital Audio Editing Software

This might be a good time to return to the last Viewport and study the EMT-1 Basic Computer Workstation chart (Figure 7.2) and then glance ahead to the next module to find the EMT-2 No-Frills Digital Audio chart, which adds speakers, headphones, and an MP3 player. There is nothing fancy or terribly expensive here for making digital audio files. These setups are perfect for producing single-track mono or stereo projects for:

- creating files for the Internet
- editing music for a digital movie
- converting, cleaning, and archiving your old tape or LP albums
- making a CD for teaching or entertainment
- producing a professional portfolio for CD or DVD

These specific objectives relate to the kinds of tasks anticipated by Table 9.1 and can be completed at home or in a studio with the help of the software described next.

What Is Digital Audio Editing Software?

The vast majority of software described so far has not permitted actually changing the content of the music. The software titles noted below do exactly this. Here are some common capabilities of such software:

- supporting single mono or stereo track
- recording a number of sound sources, including live, analog recording with microphones; "line-in" feeds from cassette decks, LP record players, or other analog sources; and digital material transferred from CDs
- creating as a minimum 16-bit, 44- or 48-kHz, stereo sound saved in traditional formats such as AIF, WAV, and MP3 or AAC
- allowing digital signal processing (DSP) functions that alter such aspects as dynamics, pitch, tempo, and timbre
- providing protection against altering the original sound file with a system of "nondestructive editing" or multiple levels of "undos"

Note that this is NOT the software to use when you want to record multiple channels of audio in a concert setting, create a numbers of loops for popular music, combine MIDI data with digital audio, or create a digital sound from scratch. That software will be described later in this text.

Basic Capture and Display of Digital Audio Editing Software

Live Recording

Figure 9.4 provides an example of how this type of software manages to capture and display audio. Here, we are using Sound Studio. In capturing live audio, a microphone is used to record and the signal is displayed as a complex waveform in mono or stereo in the main window. Input levels are monitored in a separate window and can be adjusted if the signal is too loud or soft. Basic programs offer a wide variety of settings for bit depths and sampling rates up to 16-bit and 48-kHz stereo.

Microphone options for live recording are mentioned in Module 10. We cannot stress enough the importance of the best-quality original sound for all your work. It is tempting to settle for a cheap microphone, given the cost of computer hardware and software. This is a false economy in the long run. Knowledge of good recording techniques is a real plus and will make your work with software editors much more satisfying.

Other Ways to Import Audio

In Figure 9.4, we have just imported ("extracted" or "ripped") an audio track from an audio CD. The software is simply directed to the mounted CD and asked to import a track. Programs like QuickTime and iTunes can extract such audio, but digital audio editors will also provide you with a visual display and the tools to edit the audio to your liking.

Most digital audio software editors also allow you to capture audio directly from a "line in" source such as a cassette tape or older LP record. This type of software is an excellent choice for converting recorded audio from an analog source to digital form.

Of course, if digital audio files already exist, these can be opened directly by these programs. Typically, WAV, AIF, and MP3 formats are supported for import.

Typical Display

The central window display in Figure 9.4 can be changed to show greater resolution (smaller time units) and can be enlarged vertically to better show the amplitude. Selection of all or a portion of the waveform allows you to change the content (moving, cutting, or pasting), and by asking the program to "treat" the selected waveform in some way by applying effects, shown in coming sections. Most titles also display counters that show where you are in the file. The software also provides a top window that displays the waveform for the overall sound file.

There are a wide variety of digital audio editors to choose from. A few, like the Audacity software, are offered free or with a small shareware charge. Others, such as Sound Studio and the entry-level versions of Peak (Peak LE and Peak DV) and Sound Forge (Sound Forge Audio Studio) cost less than $100. Still others, such as WaveLab, Audition, and the full versions of Peak and Sound Forge, cost more. The expensive programs offer wider ranges of options, including more built-in effects processing, extensive plug-in and sound management options, and support for very large audio files. As with all the software profiled in our text, you need to match the software to your task. The more expensive programs may not be necessary for what you wish to do.

TIP

If you are importing sound from an older-style LP record player, be sure to invest in a small pre-amp designed for phono input to boost the signal strength as it comes into your computer.

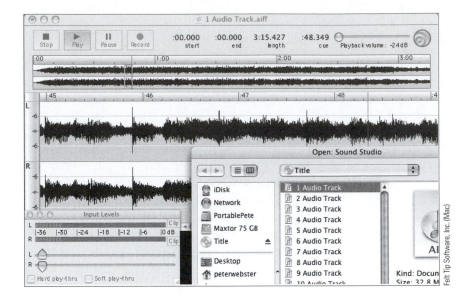

FIGURE 9.4
Sound Studio

DVD-ROM
Project 6 Basics of Digital
Audio Editors

To give a better sense of the many options beyond basic capturing and display, we have created a table to guide your study (see Table 9.2). Editing software accomplishes two types of tasks: (1) editing/file management and (2) effects processing. In the first instance, the work is about moving parts of sound files around and managing the results. For effects processing, the work involves changes that are often dramatic and most often associated with digital editors. In Table 9.2, we display these tasks in both basic and more advanced categories. The basic cells of the table contain features that you can expect in any software program of this type. The more advanced items can be expected in the more expensive titles, but there are plenty of variations that might surprise you as you review each program carefully.

Basic Editing and File Management

"Project" Folders and Nondestructive Editing

One additional point about importing and working with digital audio editors relates to the concept of a "project" file set. Some programs, such as Audacity, Peak, and Sound Forge, are optimized to leave the original sound file untouched and to create small editing files that actually record the changes you are making. Of course, in the end you need to save the finished file that "rewrites" the original data, but you can maintain this as a separate end product so that the original data is not altered. This "nondestructive" editing approach, also used in the multitrack recording programs described in Viewport IV, protects the original data and speeds the work process.

Cutting, Pasting, and Manipulating Sound

It is a joy to work with digital audio editing software when you are moving segments of audio around. Because you can "see" the actual waveform in some depth using "zoom in" features, you can find the exact points where an attack or release in the music exists. Selecting the portion to cut to the computer's clipboard for moving elsewhere or just removing the portion from the total mix is a snap to do. Of course, much more is possible.

TABLE 9.2   Comparison of Basic and More Advanced Tasks in Digital Audio Editing Software

	Editing/File Management	Effects Processing
Basic Tasks	• Importing sound (live, "in-line," CD) • Cutting, pasting, duplicating, slicing, splitting, realigning • Creating clips • Saving (standard formats) • Converting file formats • Other basic features such as mix, swap channels and invert, and resample	• Volume changes (overall gain and normalize) • Fade in, out (linear and custom) • Echo/delay, chorus, and flange • Reverberation (room simulation)
Advanced Tasks	• Support for more advanced sound management (e.g., WDM, ASIO, DirectSound, CoreAudio) • Loop-creation tools and links to hardware devices • Waveform editing down to the single-sample level • Markers and playlist creation for CD rendering • Automatic triggers • Menu customization • Batch processing of files • Analyses of waveforms (spectral analysis) • Support for files with high bit sizes and resolution (e.g., 32-bit samples and 192 kHz sampling) and larger file sizes (2–4 GB single files) • Saving in larger number of formats (including RealMedia)	• Noise reduction • Pitch and tempo shift • Cross-looping support • Pan • DC offset • Plug-in support for third-party (VST, DirectX, Audio Units) processing and effects (e.g., EQ, advanced reverb) • Unique effects by program (e.g., harmonization, acoustic mirror)

Figure 9.5 displays an approach that uses Audacity to duplicate and move digital audio in ways that create interesting results. We have selected a portion of a waveform and asked the computer to duplicate it in an accompanying track. Then, we highlighted this new clip of sound and "slid" it to the left so that it sounds a few moments earlier. This kind of fine adjustment in sound can be useful for special effects or for aligning music to exact points in a digital movie or animation. Many of the basic audio editors accept QuickTime or AVI movie file sound tracks for just this kind of task.

Saving and File Conversion

Audacity software includes saving options for standard file types. This program also offers options for the MP3 format. Note, too, the AIF format with track markers. This would be useful if you imagined using an audio track as a trigger for other events.

Digital audio editing programs are also excellent utilities to use for converting files to different formats. If you are developing sound files for the Web, for example, the same file can be saved in different formats for downloading or streaming options.

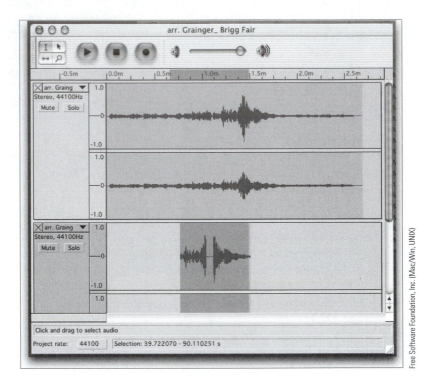

FIGURE 9.5 Copying and pasting in Audacity

Free Software Foundation, Inc. (Mac/Win, UNIX)

Other Basic Management Options

Depending on the software, a number of other options might be expected in basic packages. Here is a listing with brief explanations:

- *Mix.* A mix function takes the contents of the computer's clipboard memory and mixes it directly into a selected region of audio. It does not create a new track, but simply merges the audio information. This might be useful when adding sound tracks to digital movies or simply making the audio more complex.
- *Swap Channels and Invert.* Swapping channels in a stereo signal might be useful in creating a special effect when the channels have significantly different content. Inverting an audio waveform has no effect on sound but does provide a display that places the negative peaks on the top and positive on the bottom, or vice versa.
- *Resample.* Resampling allows for changing the bit size and sample rate. If you are working with 24-bit audio at 48 kHz and you wish to create a standard CD with the format common for conventional CDs, resampling allows you to lower the setting to 16-bit, 44-kHz sound, which is required. Resampling can also make stereo files into mono ones if necessary.

Advanced Editing and File Management

More Advanced Sound Management

When analog audio is recorded by the computer and then stored for playback, the application software, the operating system, and the hardware have to establish a way of working with each other to manage the flow. This all falls under the heading of sound management and Macintosh and PC systems each have ways to handle this. Developments in hardware and software design by Apple, Microsoft,

LINK
Lower latency is better! Latency is a measure of how fast information flows between a computer and external devices like digital audio hardware. See Module 10.

and others have improved the speed of information flow, allowing everything to move faster with very low latency.

This has resulted in the development of standards for sound management such as ASIO, DirectSound, and CoreAudio. In Module 10, we will cover these software "drivers" for hardware in some depth. Here, we need to stress that the more advanced digital audio editors support the faster technology.

Figure 9.6 demonstrates this with the Peak software. The Record Settings dialog box under the Audio menu is where you choose the sound management system and other settings for how the computer is to handle the incoming numbers. Because Macintosh OS X natively employs the newer CoreAudio sound management system, the dialog in the upper right comes up when we click on the "Device and Sample Format . . ." button. Here we can set the way we wish the CoreAudio routines to handle data, including sample rate, channels, and bit depth.

The "Hardware Settings" button displays the choices for what devices to use. In this case, we are using the built-in equipment, but if we were using a different audio hardware interface such as an external card or special USB or Firewire device, we would see these listed here. This is the place, too, where we can set the "buffer size" for the incoming data. The bigger the buffer, the higher the latency (which is best described as the lag between capturing the sound and realizing it through the computer's output back to us). The smaller the buffer, the more likely the system will miss important incoming information if the computer is processing other tasks. Similar settings are featured in a variety of PC products as well, using ASIO or DirectSound. The point of all of this is that the more advanced audio editors (and many of the more interesting digital audio programs described in coming modules) all work much better with audio when these sound management systems are used.

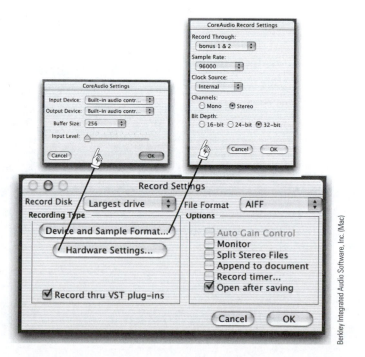

FIGURE 9.6 Advanced sound management in Peak

LINK

Wave shaping with sustained sound loops is first discussed in Module 8 in the context of digital wave synthesis techniques.

LINK

Check out Viewport V for more about MIDI.

LINK

We will present much more about digital audio loops in Viewport IV, Module 12, when we explain "sequential" loops in multitrack recording software.

"Sustained" and "Sequential" Loop Creation and Links to Hardware Samplers

Loops are simply recurring sections of digital audio, often with carefully crafted beginning and end points so that the loop sounds smooth when it is heard. There are basically two kinds of digital audio loops: sequential and sustaining.

Sequential loops are used extensively in music with repetitive structures and are often heard in popular music of many genres. Let's say you have created a drum track that you want to serve as the basis of a composition. This might be a five- or 10-second sequence of two to four measures' worth of recorded drum sounds that you want to repeat, over which you would layer a vocal or keyboard track. This kind of loop can be manipulated in many ways; the special software designed to handle this kind of multitrack recording is covered in Module 12. However, editing audio software of the kind described in this module can help fine-tune these tracks by adjusting tempo and beginning and end points for the loop.

Another type of looping is for a short section of digital audio, say a sample of an instrument timbre, that you would like to repeat for as long as a key on an instrument is depressed. Often, these loops last for only a second or less of time and contain envelope properties that sustain similar to that presented in Module 8. This sort of loop is sometimes called a "sustained loop" and can result in an "instrument sample" that can be used by hardware or software samplers. The creation of this sustained loop can be engineered using digital audio software.

Figure 9.7 shows this process using Sound Forge. We have selected a short section of a brass timbre and activated the edit sample window under the Special menu. Notice the ability to fine-tune the loop start and stop locations and the markers inserted into the main data window that mark the sustain and release portions. You can assign a MIDI value that establishes a pitch and fine-tune that value in the box below. The software lets you listen to the loop as you make these changes.

Once these loops are created, advanced software can send these digital files to hardware samplers. Both Peak and Sound Forge have links to allow transfer of data to hardware devices.

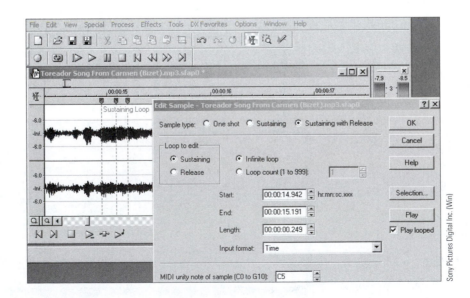

FIGURE 9.7 Sample editing with Sound Forge

Waveform Editing

In addition to being able to control the start and stop points of a loop, other detailed editing is possible in any waveform. Figure 9.8 shows the ability of advanced software to actually control the waveform down to the most basic level with a pencil tool. Such editing capability allows you to modify the crossover points of a loop and edit a waveform in general if, in doing so, you are interested in altering sound for a particular reason. This might occur, for instance, if there is an unusual disturbance in a live concert recording and such editing might eliminate the phenomenon from the waveform.

Markers and Playlists

Another interesting way to manage digital audio is to create regions in an audio file for the purpose of creating separate sections. Imagine that you are preparing a digital audio file for presentation in class and you want to be able to isolate sections of audio so you can highlight your presentation by playing each individual section. Sections can be named and a playlist created for a custom CD that can help with your presentation.

Additional Editing and File Management Features

The following lists other advanced editing and file management features of digital audio editing software. Taken as a group, these features might well justify the cost of a more advanced program:

- *Automatic triggers.* Software can be set to start recording when a certain sound level is reached, or stop or pause at other designated times. Also, the software can be triggered by the computer or MIDI keyboard.
- *Customized menus.* Menus can be easily changed to meet the needs of projects that require repetitive tasks.
- *Batch processing.* A large number of files that need to be treated similarly with a series of operations (such as changes in file type, resampling, filtering, or volume change) can all be changed at one time.
- *Spectrum analysis.* Waveforms can be viewed as a spectrum in order to study the properties of the audio for noise problems (see Figure 8.2b in Module 8).

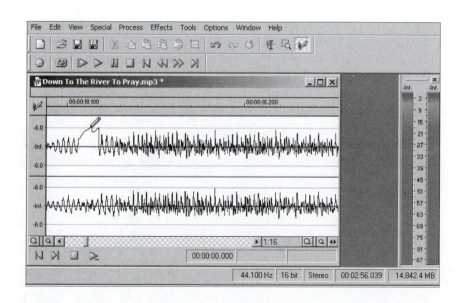

FIGURE 9.8 Editing a waveform with Sound Forge

- *File support*. Advanced programs can handle file resolutions equal to and in excess of 24 bits and handle sampling rates from 48 kHz to 96 kHz or higher. There are much higher limits to file size as well, often accommodating files as large as 4 gigabytes or close to six hours of CD-quality stereo sound.
- *File format*. Advanced editors can import and export far more types of file formats than basic software. Sound Forge, for example, supports some 15 file formats for import and 17 for export, including encoded compressed formats such as RealAudio, Windows Media, and MP3. This means that a program like Sound Forge can be used to master content for stand-alone or streamed formats without the need for additional encoding software.

Effects Processing

DVD-ROM
Project 7 Applying Effects
with Audio Editors

Up to now, we have focused on basic and advanced work that involves editing and file management. In these final two sections, we focus on changing the sound itself through effects processing. This was once only possible with specialized hardware devices or digital signal processing (DSP) chips on add-on cards. Such hardware solutions continue to be available for special requirements in high-end studios; however, most effects processing today can be handled completely within software such as the audio editors described in this module and in multiple track (Module 12) and sequencing (Module 17) software.

Study the common types of effects processing as described below. We have grouped these in five families with the first two (amplitude and time) being the most common and the others (frequency, timbre, and specialized) being more advanced. In the remaining pages of this module, we describe how some of these effects are used in basic and more advanced audio editing programs. In other modules to come, we will return to this topic in more detail.

- **Amplitude**: gain, tremolo, normalization, fading, cross-fading, compression, expansion, envelope or ADSR manipulation, panning
- **Time**: reverb, echo, delay, flanging, chorus, time shifting
- **Frequency**: various wah effects, phase shifting, pitch shifting
- **Timbre**: noise reduction/addition, distortion, clipping control, limiting, rectification, equalization, resonator
- **Specialized Effects**: harmonizing, vocalizing, ring modulation, Leslie speaker rotation

Amplitude

Perhaps the most used effect with digital audio files is amplitude change. Such activity takes the form of changes in the overall signal and changes based on fading. Amplitude changes, as most of the effects processing described here, are really accomplished by applying certain software-designed filters to the original sound. This is much like what was done in the early days of electronic music with hardware (see Module 8), but it is now accomplished with software.

Typically, a region of audio or the complete file is highlighted and an amplitude or "gain" change is executed for the selected region or file. The software displays a dialog box that contains the controls for raising or lowering the amount of gain. "Clipping" (exceeding the threshold of loudness, which creates distortion) is often controlled automatically by the software if you choose this.

A special kind of amplitude adjustment is called "normalization." Normalized sound has been boosted in amplitude only after the selected waveform is analyzed

LINK

See Module 8 for a full explanation of decibels and the scales that govern it.

to determine the highest peaks of sound. The waveform is adjusted to be as loud as it can be without the highest peaks being distorted. The entire waveform is adjusted accordingly.

Two other effects are "compressor" and "expander." These filters boost the lows and compress the highs in such a way as to alter the overall waveform. This may be useful when you want to have a very quiet section in a performance boosted or a loud section reduced to help create a better balance.

Figure 9.9 displays two applications of amplitude change. The highlighted section of the waveform to the right has been changed by the Amplify Volume dialog box below it. Notice that the volume is changed by about 5.1 dB, which is about an 80% increase (100% is the base figure of no gain in this software). It does not take much to make a significant gain in sound intensity. The Preview button allows you to hear what you are doing. The Blending option is really a kind of cross-fade function in this software that blends the volume change in and out with the material around it by a factor specified in milliseconds. The section of audio to the left has been normalized by just under 100%. Notice that the waveform fills the available bandwidth to the 83.2% level and that everything is adjusted in relation to the highest peaks. Normalization is treated separately for each channel.

Fading audio in and out is a typical adjustment in basic effects processing. There are countless uses for this in digital audio editing and it is accomplished in a similar way to changing volumes, described above. The section of audio on which the fading effect is to be applied is highlighted. You then tell the software if you want a linear adjustment (consistent rate of fade from start to finish) or if you want some kind of nonlinear shape such as a slow or fast rate. Figure 9.10 shows a custom,

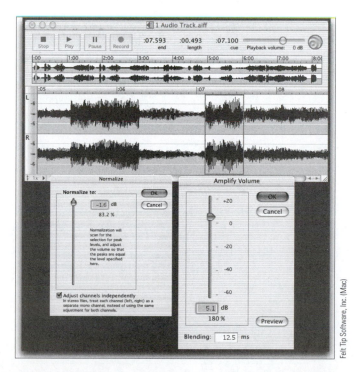

FIGURE 9.9   Amplitude adjustments in Sound Studio

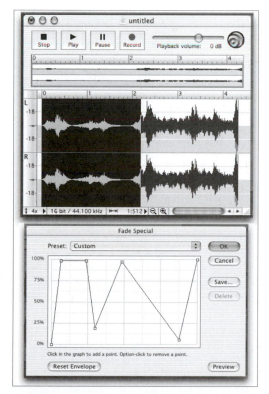

FIGURE 9.10   Custom fade in Sound Studio

LINK
These concepts have their roots in the early days of electronic music and the manipulation of analog sound with oscillators, filters, and patch cords. Be sure to link this with the material in Module 8.

TIP
LFO = low-frequency oscillator

nonlinear shape. The data window displays the final fading envelope and the box below it has the envelope as we defined it. The more elaborate fades that are possible in the context of loop construction are noted in the following section.

Panning, or moving the audio signal's intensity from one stereo channel to another to give the illusion of moving the sound in space, is very common in digital audio editors. This effect can be found in many audio applications, including sequencers. It takes on a new life in surround-sound work, when more than two audio channels are involved; this is covered in more detail in Module 12.

Time

Many of the effects in this family work much the same way but each has a distinctive sound, depending on the settings chosen. To understand them, you need to understand the concept of "wet" and "dry" sound. "Dry" sound is the original audio and "wet" sound is the same audio fed back into the signal at a different time and intensity. Actually, the intensity of both wet and dry sound can be controlled in all three of these effects.

Study Figures 9.11a and b carefully. Echo/Delay and Chorus are displayed in Figure 9.11a. For the Echo effect, a delay time is specified. You can have the delayed audio take output as its input (feedback), creating an echo effect. Without the feedback checked, the signal would just have a delay effect in which you hear only one repeat.

Chorusing is more complex. Here, the idea is to offset the signal a bit to create a fuller and perhaps slightly out-of-tune signal. The wet signal, which is slightly delayed, is controlled by the LFO waveform shape, with the sine wave being

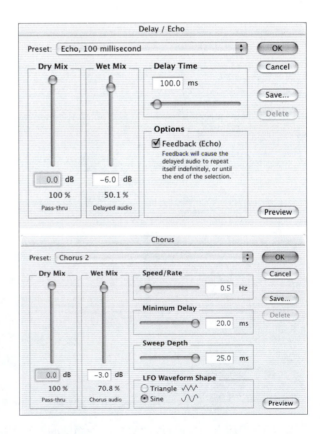

FIGURE 9.11A
Echo/Delay and Chorus in Sound Studio

TIP
Good sound-reproduction hardware in the form of quality headphones or loud speakers is necessary for this work, even with very basic EMT-1 and 2 setups.

smoother than the triangle wave. The Speed/Rate scale controls the magnitude of the LFO's effect on the wet sound. Minimum Delay and Sweep Depth also control the timing and out-of-tune quality. Describing these settings in words is difficult; they must be experienced musically with various dry sounds as original source material.

Figure 9.11b demonstrates the Flange effect. This is very much like the Chorus effect but has shorter delay times. A sweeping whooshing sound is created by this effect and the rate and depth settings control the effect. Again, the effect must be used with real music to get a sense of the sound. Not all of these effects are included in basic software and each program treats them differently.

Reverb is often confused with echo/delay, but it really is different. Rather than combining wet and dry sound in a delay state, reverb recreates the acoustical properties you experience as a listener in a closed space. The effect tries to simulate the properties of live audio as it is heard bouncing around a room from walls, ceiling, floor, and the source itself. When you record live audio into the computer or import sound from another source, it may lack a sense of "depth" or "warmth" that you have come to expect in a live concert. Reverb adds subtle touches to recreate this sense of reality.

Each software program provides its own way of creating these artifacts in the sound. Figure 9.12 shows Sound Forge's own reverb effect. To experiment with the settings, an MP3 file that seems to warrant a "warm space" is loaded in. Adjustments in reverb amount, room size, and liveliness relate to how filters work to adjust the highs and lows of the signal while adding small amounts of delay for different parts of the spectrum. Using these settings is not an exact science and, as with all of the human judgments about effects processing, much depends on your ear and the experience you have had with sounds.

Advanced Effects Processing

The more advanced digital audio editors often contain more powerful built-in effects. As we have noted before, not all of these effects are found in expensive

FIGURE 9.11B
Flange in Sound Forge

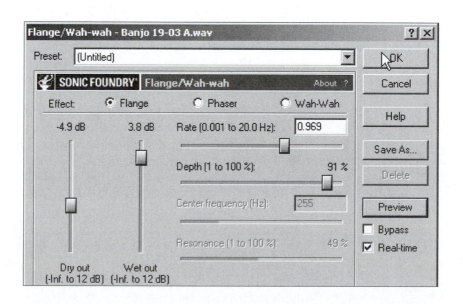

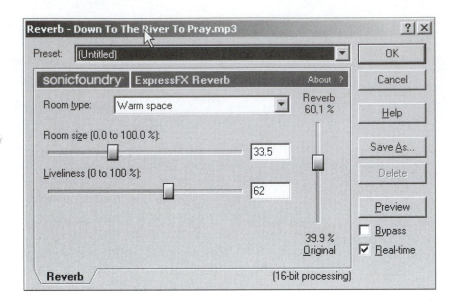

FIGURE 9.12 Reverb dialog box for Sound Forge

programs and not all effects are equally well engineered. Experimentation with your own ears is key.

Frequency and Time

A more advanced feature set involves shifting both pitch and tempo of selected regions in a waveform or entire files. There are many reasons why each of these procedures might be useful. For example, working with a sound track for a digital movie, you may be interested in stretching or constricting the time to fit the video image. If you are developing audio as an accompaniment for teaching, you may want to lower or raise the pitch to accommodate a voice range or an instrument's key.

Figure 9.13 provides an example of how this might be done. The example shows a dialog box for settings to stretch a region of audio. At the bottom of the dialog box, notice the options for stretching time but preserving the pitch and for shifting the pitch but preserving the time (tempo)! This notion of changing one dimension and keeping the other constant may seem trivial, but it is very powerful. This can be especially useful in working with digital audio. Pitch change is also possible.

Timbre: Noise and Silence

Both removing and adding noise and silence are important capabilities. One popular reason to invest in more advanced digital audio editing software is its ability to "clean up" a messy audio file. Many people own older recordings on cassette tape or even long-playing (LP) vinyl records. These sources often contain valuable, in some cases irreplaceable, data; however, the recording also contains background noise, tape hiss, and distracting crackles and pops.

Figure 9.14 shows a solution. The figure portrays noise removal for a selected region. This approach requires that you first "teach" the software what you mean by noise and then ask the program to filter a region based on that intelligence. Other advanced software programs use different techniques, including support for stand-alone programs such as plug-ins that use quite unusual and powerful algorithms to clean up sound. Many of these are quite expensive and are designed for highly skilled sound engineers.

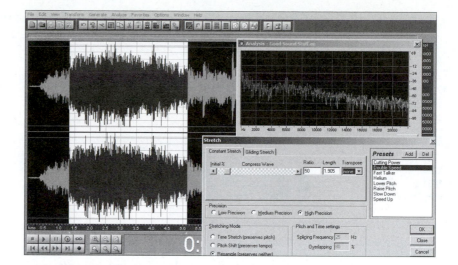

FIGURE 9.13   Tempo shift in Audition

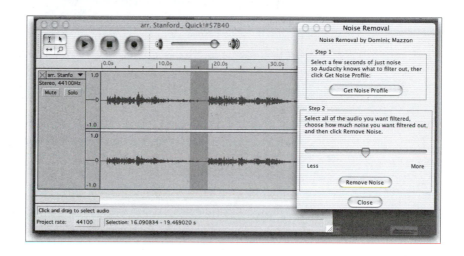

FIGURE 9.14   Noise removal in Audacity

Adding noise and portions of silence are two additional features possible with digital audio editors. Adding a touch of distortion may be useful in certain instances and inserting silence is often needed when dealing with sound tracks for film or television.

Timbre: Equalization

Another very important timbre effect is equalization (EQ). Equalization helps balance the frequencies within an audio spectrum by filtering out certain specified ranges of the spectrum. Figure 9.15 displays how this is done in Sound Studio with a 10-band EQ. More bands provide greater control over the frequency range; here we have chosen to cut the mid-range of a selected part of an audio clip. The sliders allow you to control the filtering level for the particular band. Module 17 has an example of a much more sophisticated EQ plug-in.

Advanced Amplitude: Crossfade Loop

A particular kind of fading effect useful in sustained loop construction is the cross-fade loop. This is an advanced technique tied to the creation of loop start and end points. The shape of the crossfade can be controlled and the time can be specified

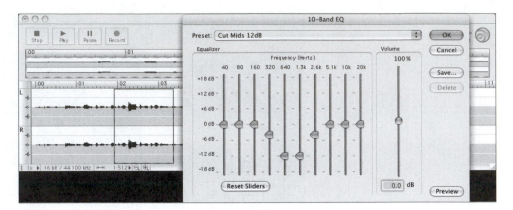

FIGURE 9.15 EQ adjustments in Sound Studio

as well. Most software lets you preview your choices so you can use your ear to test how the fading will sound in real time.

Specialized Effects

Certain advanced effects are peculiar to one program or another. For example, in WaveLab, a harmonization effect is included. This interesting effect creates an harmonic accompaniment when applied to a melodic line. You will see how music notation programs using MIDI can also create a harmonic context in Viewport VII, Module 20.

Another example of a rather unique effect is the Acoustic Mirror in Sound Forge. Related to the family of reverb effects, Acoustic Mirror uses real acoustical data from experiments within certain famous concert spaces. This information gets stored in a special formatted file with the .sfi extension. These files can be downloaded from the Sony Media Software website and found on the application

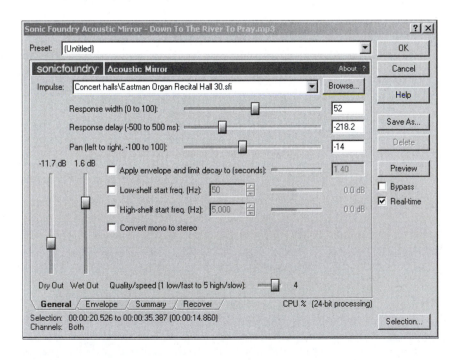

FIGURE 9.16 Acoustic Mirror in Sound Forge

SIDEBAR

Audio Utility Software

In addition to built-in and plug-in support for digital audio, a few audio utility programs are available as adjuncts to digital audio editing packages. These programs are distributed for minimal cost and offer special capabilities that might not be available elsewhere. Here are a few of these programs and a short description of what they do:

- Soundhack (Soundhack, Inc. [Mac]) Provides many processing and utility functions, such as time stretching, pitch shifting, and sonogram creation. Plays and converts many sound formats and records input from built-in Macintosh input. Changes values in the sound file header.
- SoundConverter (Steve Dekorte, *www.dekorte.com* [Mac]) A batch sound format conversion program that supports many input and output formats, including ringtone formats.
- SoundSoap (Bias, Inc. [Mac/Win]) Offered both as a stand-alone and as a plug-in, this software aids noise reduction by using two knobs to adjust for unwanted hiss, room noise, rumble hum, and other unwanted artifacts.
- Amazing Slow Downer (Roni Music, Inc. [Mac]) Slows down music from 50–400% without changing the pitch. Works from a CD and supports MP3, AAC, AIF, and WAV formats.
- Transcribe! (Seventh String, Inc. [Mac/Win]) Also slows down music without changing pitch. Supports AIF, MP3, and WAV files.

CD. When applied to a region of audio or an entire file, this effect can be used to simulate what the audio might sound like in that real environment. Figure 9.16 shows a dialog box that has a favorite concert hall featured.

Other effects specific to one program or another include:

- Ring modulator: multiplies two audio signals together, creating a somewhat "metallic" sound
- Phase Vocoder: allows you to alter the duration and/or pitch of an audio region
- Rappify: applies extreme dynamic filtering to a selection
- Reverse Boomerang: combines an original source with a version of itself played backwards

Plug-in Support for Digital Audio Editors

Plug-ins are small programs that work in tandem with larger "host" programs like Peak, Sound Forge, and WaveLab. They function in many ways, but most are designed to offer advanced versions of effects not available in the host program. We will provide much more detail on plug-ins and their formats in Modules 12 and 17.

Plug-in software for audio editors is typically placed in a folder in the same directory as the host program. Once there, the software becomes "available" to be used as part of the processing system of the audio editor.

Plug-ins can be used in combination. This allows the host software to use the processing power of two or more plug-ins (even from different vendors, if they conform to an accepted plug-in format such as DirectX or VST) together to make simultaneous changes in audio. For example, Figure 9.17 shows a reverb effect

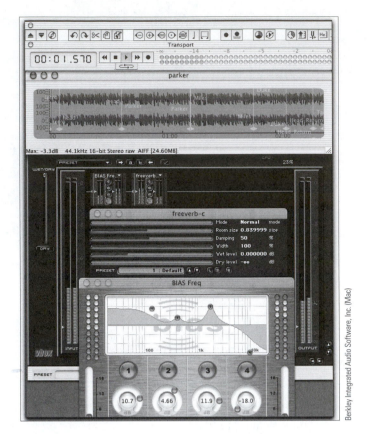

Berkley Integrated Audio Software, Inc. (Mac)

FIGURE 9.17   Multiple plug-ins in Peak

used together with an equalization (EQ) effect in the host program Peak. EQ is an effect that enables you to highlight frequencies across the spectrum. You probably use this option in stereo systems that use slider bars to adjust various levels of treble, mid-range, and bass. In the Peak example, notice the ability to change the amount of the effect "in play" in the small boxes in the center of the graphic. Many other features are offered by combining plug-in effects. Keep in mind that, as multiple plug-in effects are used, more powerful computer processing is necessary.

Building a No-Frills Digital Audio Workstation

In Module 10, we will explore the hardware required to transform a computer into a basic "no-frills" digital audio workstation in order to take advantage of the software presented in Module 9. We will attempt to do so with a minimal amount of extra equipment and cost beyond the EMT-1 Basic Computer Workstation presented in Viewport II.

LINK
In Viewport IV, we will continue to build on the EMT workstation model with additional professional gear and options.

IPOS Model

In the Viewport II discussions of computer hardware, the input-process-output-storage, or IPOS, model was introduced. The IPOS model shown in Figure 10.1 begins to categorize the different hardware possibilities for digital audio music applications.

For *input*, we include the use of analog electronic instruments (e.g., keyboards and guitars) and the use of analog-to-digital converters (ADCs) for changing analog sounds into digital files. On the *output* side of our IPOS model, we examine digital-to-analog converters (DACs) for transforming digital files back into analog signals for listening. The *output* box in Figure 10.1 also indicates the need for basic audio equipment. Stereo earphones or a set of powered speakers are the minimum requirement. A basic mixer may be needed to connect several audio devices to the computer's single-input ADC channel. The *process* stage in this chart represents a typical laptop or desktop computer system. For digital audio work, a fast processor (1 gHz or faster), plentiful RAM (500 MB or more) and hard-drive space (10 GB or more), networking, and a built-in digital audio sound card with ADC and DAC are needed.

The *storage* stage of the IPOS model illustrates the devices commonly used for storing digital audio data: CD/DVD-R discs; Zip disks; compact flash, and smart media cards for removable storage; and music players for digital audio music files. Figure 10.1 also contains a box designating hardware *interfaces*. Firewire and USB interfaces were discussed in Module 7 and are important options for connecting music peripherals to a computer. Analog audio refers to sounds transmitted electronically from any audio device, tape recorder, amplifier, electric bass, keyboard, or similar electronic device.

We will examine the various stages in the IPOS chart in more detail as we review the features of two EMT Digital Audio Workstations (EMT 2 and 3).

LINK
USB and Firewire interfaces are discussed in Module 7, as well as other computer terms used in the discussion ahead. Don't hestitate to review computer concepts like these.

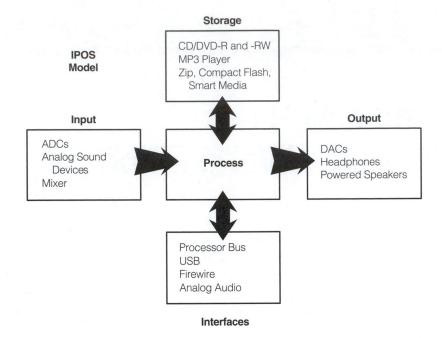

FIGURE 10.1 IPOS model for a computer workstation configured for entry-level, digital audio activities.

LINK
Look ahead to Module 13 for more about DSPs.

Basic Digital Audio Hardware: ADCs and DACs

Module 8 presented the concepts behind analog and digital audio. In the simplest form, analog vibrations are sampled or captured by an analog-to-digital converter (ADC) and stored in a computer as a series of numbers, a *sample*. To play a digital sound sample back, the series of numbers is sent to a digital-to-analog converter (DAC), which converts the numbers back into analog voltages. These voltages oscillate the cone in a speaker or set of earphones so you hear the reconstructed analog sound.

Digitizing hardware, ADCs and DACs, can be components of a computer, stand-alone music device, or synthesizer. When both ADC and DAC digital recording and playing capabilities are built into a computer or synthesizer, it is called a *sampler*. A device implementing only the DAC process that uses preexisting samples is properly called a *sample player*. Digital music players like those from Apple, Sony, Creative Labs, and Toshiba are sample players for MP3, WMA, AAC, WAV, AIF, and other digital file types. Soft synths, like their hardware equivalents, may also be sample players or samplers.

Digital Audio Interface

Built-In Digital Audio

Figure 10.2 shows a digital audio (DA) sound card (4) as part of the computer in the EMT No-Frills Digital Audio Workstation (EMT-2). This sound card contains both ADC and DAC capabilities in the form of integrated circuit chips. Special *digital signal processing* chips, or DSPs, are used to handle the demands of high-resolution digital audio.

Speed is of the essence in moving between analog and digital information. Hence, ADC and DAC devices are built directly into the computer's hardware or

LINK
Digital audio file formats are explained in Module 8.

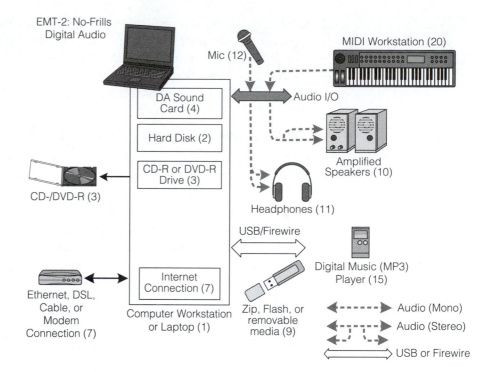

FIGURE 10.2   The EMT-2 No-Frills Digital Audio Workstation (DAW). Note: Numbers for the various components of the system are referenced in the text as they are discussed. A complete list of all equipment numbers is provided in the Appendix.

LINK
Check the end of Module 8 for a review of various music synthesis techniques.

mounted on a circuit card that connects the device to the computer's internal bus. Figure 10.3 illustrates these key components for audio in a computer workstation or laptop. The "SoundBlaster" *de-facto* standard for a computer sound card was set in the 1980s by Creative Labs. For this reason, sound circuitry that comes with a computer is usually "SoundBlaster compatible." Digital audio circuitry and DSPs for computers are manufactured by firms such as Creative Labs, ESS, Aureal, Turtle Beach, and others. Originally, SoundBlaster audio used FM synthesis extensively; sound cards now use wavetable sampling and wave-shaping synthesis techniques.

Bus-Extended or External Digital Audio

Should your computer not have digital audio built in, or if you want to purchase a different digital audio solution, bus-extended digital sound cards are available for both Macintosh and PC computers using the industry standard PCI bus for desktops or PC-Card bus architecture for laptops. USB and Firewire digital

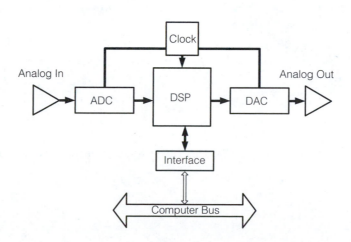

FIGURE 10.3   A diagram of the key components to a typical digital audio circuit in a computer workstation

ASIDE
The terms "PCMCIA Card," "PC Card," and "CardBus" all refer to the small, flat, 3.5x2-inch computer cards that can be inserted into the slots found on many laptops. These cards can provide memory storage, Internet access, wireless, or digital audio sound capabilities. PC Card readers can also be purchased for desktop computers.

TIP
The audio quality of the microphone input on most computers (and any microphone provided) is usually not professional level audio. Be sure to experiment with it before considering booking a major recording gig!

audio options are also available. Since USB and Firewire are industry-standard interfaces, these options for adding external audio are very flexible. You can move your digital audio among different computers, even between Macintosh and PC. Figure 10.4 shows two different, low-cost solutions for USB and PCI audio; Firewire and PC-Card solutions tend to be more feature laden and expensive.

Input and Output: Connecting to the Outside World

To digitize sounds with a computer, you need a means of connecting to the outside analog world. Two common methods for the *input* of sound to the computer are a microphone or a stereo audio input source. To digitize live music and sound (12), the PC workstation will typically have a microphone jack or, in the case of a laptop, the microphone may be built into the computer itself. For recording stereo audio, a jack similar to the inputs on any tape recorder may be provided or a stereo minijack that looks similar to a headphone jack. In the EMT-2 diagram (Figure 10.2) the analog sound from a MIDI workstation (20) is connected to the digital audio sound card (4) of the computer.

Output from the computer's sound device is typically provided as a stereo connector suitable for an audio amplifier or powered speakers (10) or stereo headphones (11). This output may be in the form of stereo phono jacks, stereo headphone minijacks, or both. (More on plugs and jacks in a moment.)

In our discussion of digital audio in Module 8, we noted two variables key to the quality of the captured sampled audio: *sampling rate* and *sampling width* (bit depth). Typical DA sound cards in Macintosh and PC laptops and workstations are of 48-hHz/16-bit stereo resolution, comparable to the quality of CD audio. Under software control, it is possible to select sampling rates in the 4–48-kHz range and sample widths from 8 to 16 bits. Figure 10.4 shows a bus-extended (PCI) and external DA sound solution (USB), the Terratec 128iPCI and the Edirol UA-1A. Both are comparable to the minimum built-in to computer systems (16-bit/44.1-kHz AD/DA), but with additional input and output options.

(a) (b)

FIGURE 10.4 Two digital audio solutions: (a) Terratec 128iPCI-card solution; (b) Edirol's UA-1A USB audio capture interface

LINK

In Viewport IV, more advanced digital audio capabilities through external or bus-extended solutions are presented.

LINK

For guidance on setting up your computer's operating system for digital audio and MIDI, see Modules 9 and 15.

Sound Drivers and Latency: Who's in Charge Here?

We need to take a moment and deal with the software "drivers" necessary for the proper functioning of digital audio sound cards with computers and computer operating systems. Drivers are that magic "glue" of computer code that lets your computer, sound card, and MIDI gear talk to each other. Table 10.1 provides a glimpse of a select number of sound drivers provided either by Apple and Microsoft or by third-party vendors like Steinberg/Yamaha, Mark of the Unicorn, and DigiDesign/Avid. At the top of the table are the two legacy drivers, WAV for Windows and SoundManager for Macintosh. These were developed at a time when 44.1-kHz/16-bit stereo was considered to be the ultimate in sound quality on a personal computer. All of the newer drivers provide 24-bit/96-kHz digital audio with six-channel surround sound or more.

Needless to say, a driver's operation speed is the real test of performance. In its simplest form, "latency" may be defined as the minimum time it takes to store a sample in memory from an ADC, and then copy that sample through the DAC back out to a sound source. The latency between a key press on a MIDI keyboard and a sound emanating from the computer needs to be perceptibly small enough that you do not hear the delay. For this to occur, a latency of 10 msec or less is required. How well a driver performs in terms of latency depends on many factors, including the operating system, the hard drive speed, the amount of RAM, the number of applications running at the same time, and, for external digital audio, whether USB or Firewire is used to communicate with the PC.

In Table 10.1, we have represented *latency* for these drivers in the most general terms, from very low to high. "High latency" represents almost one-second latency with MME running under Windows 95 or the original Apple SoundManager. "Very low" latency represents 2–3 milliseconds with CoreAudio under Mac OS X or with ASIO under Windows XP on a computer with a 1-gHz-or-faster processor.

The "Talks to" column in the Table indicates whether the driver communicates directly with the computer's hardware, or has to communicate through other drivers that, in turn, talk with the hardware. MME and DirectSound, for example, communicate through WDM to get to the hardware. Each layer of communication adds to the latency. The reason why third-party solutions like ASIO or EASI evolved was because the developers of pro-level sequencing and digital audio software needed to go around drivers like Apple's SoundManager to obtain better performance.

You should first decide on the software applications that best fit your needs and then investigate what drivers the software supports and what hardware options are available. Many applications support multiple drivers. You should study the performance specifications and pick the driver that offers the best latency performance for your digital audio workstation.

TABLE 10.1   A Comparison of Audio Sound Drivers for Macintosh and PC

Driver	OS	Talks to	Source	Rate	Width	Channels	Latency	Comments
Legacy Drivers for Microsoft and Apple								
WAV	Win3.0+	MME	Microsoft	44.1 kHz	16-bit	2	high	
SoundManager	Mac+	OS	Apple	44.1 kHz	16-bit	2	high	
Microsoft Drivers								
MME	Win3.0+	WDM	Microsoft	44.1 kHz	16-bit	2	Moderate to high, depending on OS	Microsoft Multimedia Extension
DirectX/ DirectSound	Win98+	WDM	Microsoft	48 kHz	24-bit	6	Moderate to high, depending on OS	
WDM	W2K or WinXP	Machine	Microsoft	96 kHz	24-bit	6+	Low, depending on OS	Windows Driver Model
Apple Drivers								
CoreAudio	Mac OSX	Machine	Apple	96 kHz	32- bit	6+	Very low	
Third-Party Drivers								
DAE	Mac+PC		DigiDesign	96 kHz	24-bit	6+	Low	Digidesign Audio Engine
MAS	Mac		Mark of the Unicorn	96 kHz	24-bit	40+	Low	MOTU Audio System
ASIO	Mac+PC	Machine	Steinberg	96 kHz	24-bit	6+	Low	Audio Stream Input Output
EASI	Mac	Machine	Emagic	96 kHz	24-bit	6+	Low	Enhanced Audio Stream Interface

Sorting Out Plugs and Jacks

Sound equipment—tape recorders, amplifiers, microphones, CD and DVD players—uses a variety of plugs and jacks for connectivity. Table 10.2 sorts the different options for audio connectors and Figure 10.6 provides visual identification.

The table and figure should be self explanatory. Discussion of a few terms will help your understanding:

- *Tip, Ring, and Sleeve.* Examine the various plugs in Figure 10.6, especially the phone plugs. You will notice a black band on one and a double black band on

TABLE 10.2   Comparison of Various Audio Jacks and Plugs and Their Application

Jack/Plug Type	Size	Metric Size	Function	Comments
Phone plug/jack	1/4"	6.35mm	Commonly used for pro-level microphones, mixers, electronic musical instruments, and patch bays. The TS version of the plug was used in the first telephone switchboards, hence the name "phone" plug.	2-conductor "mono" with Tip and Sleeve (TS and unbalanced) or 3-conductor "stereo" with Tip/Ring/Sleeve (TRS and balanced).
RCA phono plug/jack	NA		Commonly used on consumer audio and video recorders, amplifiers, and the like. Originally used on phonograph record players, hence the name "phono plug."	Audio uses Red and White connectors; video yellow. Rounded center pin with an outer shield.
XLR plug/jack (NB. "XLR" has no meaning other than the original part number assigned by Cannon, the manufacturer.)	NA		Pro-level audio connector of choice used for mics, amplifiers, and mixers. Safest, most reliable, and noise free. Also known as "microphone" or "balanced Low-Z" connector	Three pins provide two separate voltage lines and a grounding line, plus shielding ("balanced"), and the connector is typically used on low-impedance microphones ("Low-Z").
Mini plug/jack (NB. Also a submini 1/32" version)	1/8"	3.5mm	Consumer headphones, portable CD and MP3 players, and commonly used for built-in computer audio.	Most commonly 3-conductor Tip/Ring/Sleeve for stereo connections; 2-conductor mono also available
S/PDIF "Toslink" digital cable. (NB. "Toslink" is short for "Toshiba Link," since Toshiba is the company that developed this connector.)	NA		Fiber optic version of pro-level S/PDIF digital audio format used for DVD, MiniDisc recorders, hard-disk recorders, AV amplifiers, etc.	Fiber optical cable using laser light for transmission. S/PDIF is the Sony/Philips Digital Interface Format. The connector is a unique pentagonal "Toslink" design.
S/PDIF Coaxial digital cable	NA		Coaxial version of S/PDIF format for consumer digital audio using copper wire rather than optical connectivity.	Coaxial implementation of S/PDIF using copper wire; connector resembles RCA phono plug and jack. The data format is the same for both Toslink and Coaxial S/PDIF connectors, but the transmission medium is not. A device like the M-Audio C02 provides a coaxial-to-optical converter if needed.

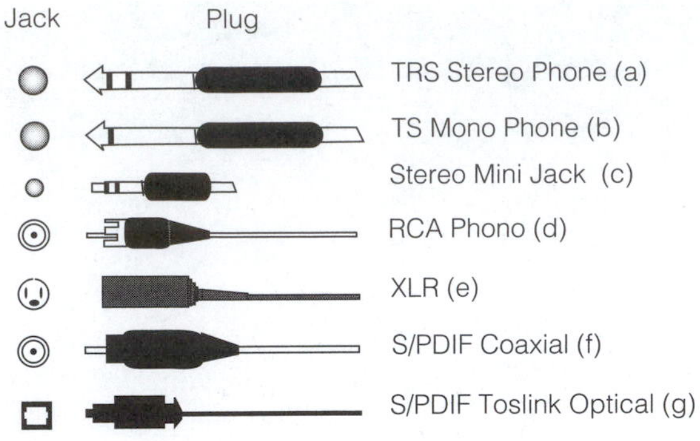

FIGURE 10.5 Seven varieties of audio cables

the other. These are the insulating bands that separate the contacts made at different places along the shaft of the phone plug. The first contact on the monophonic phone plug is the "tip" and the second contact is the "sleeve." The tip carries the signal and the sleeve carries the common wire or ground. The stereo plug also has a "tip" that carries one of the stereo audio signals, but the two insulating bands provide the second stereo channel through the "ring" (between the two black bands) and the common or ground through the "shield." The abbreviation "TS" represents tip and shield and "TRS" represents tip, ring, and shield.

- *Balanced and Unbalanced.* When an audio connector provides only one wire for a signal and the other for a common or ground it is referred to as an "unbalanced" audio line. The TS plug/jack provides unbalanced audio. When two discrete wires are provided for the signal, with a third wire for the common or ground, it is referred to as a "balanced" audio line. Balanced lines permit longer cables and are much more resistant to picking up noise and hum in the audio lines. The TRS phone plug/jack and the XLR plug/jack are two audio options for balanced audio, with the XLR preferred for pro-level audio operations.

- *Impedance.* Impedance is the resistance to flow of electrical current in a circuit. Different devices have different levels of impedance and you want to match impedance levels as much as possible when you are connecting audio devices. Impedance is measured in "ohms" (also shown as the Greek Omega symbol). Some devices are high impedance, referred to as "Hi-Z" devices. Examples include consumer electronics audio devices and less-expensive microphones with impedance levels of 600 ohms and higher. Others are low impedance or Low-Z devices. The best example is pro-level microphones with impedance levels of 50–600 ohms. Low-Z is preferred because it provides wider dynamic ranges, less susceptibility to hum and noise, and longer cable lengths. High-Z is cheaper but more susceptible to hum and noise and requires the use of shorter cable lengths. Even the wire that is used for connecting audio devices has an inherent impedance level. A good-quality audio wire has a 75-ohm impedance rating.

Adding a Mixer and Performance Options with EMT-3

In Figure 10.6, we've expanded on the EMT system to create EMT-3. The significant additions are a mixer, additional sound gear, and a recorder. What do you do when you want to:

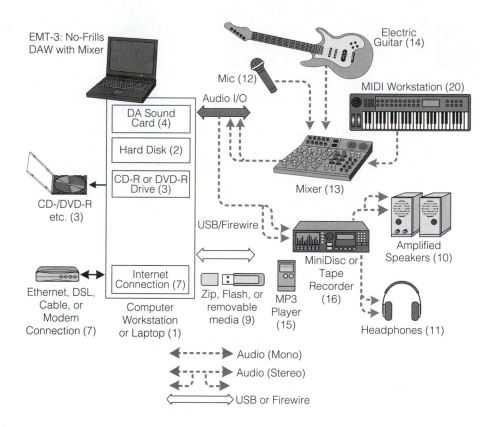

EMT-3: No-Frills DAW with Mixer

Electric Guitar (14)

Mic (12)

Audio I/O

MIDI Workstation (20)

DA Sound Card (4)

Hard Disk (2)

CD-R or DVD-R Drive (3)

CD-/DVD-R etc. (3)

Mixer (13)

Amplified Speakers (10)

USB/Firewire

MiniDisc or Tape Recorder (16)

Internet Connection (7)

Ethernet, DSL, Cable, or Modem Connection (7)

Zip, Flash, or removable media (9)

MP3 Player (15)

Computer Workstation or Laptop (1)

Headphones (11)

Audio (Mono)

Audio (Stereo)

USB or Firewire

FIGURE 10.6 EMT-3: No-Frills Digital Audio Workstation with Mixer

TIP

A poor person's solution to a mixer in this simple case may be to use audio Y-splitter cables to combine inputs without a mixer. However, this does not solve the impedance or electrical issues of connecting guitars and microphones and is an inflexible solution for future expansion.

- record more than two audio inputs into the left and right stereo inputs provided with your computer's digital audio sound card?
- record with professional-quality microphones or an electric guitar?
- adjust the volume of one sound source or channel so it is louder than another or adjust the balance between the stereo channels?

The solution is to add an audio mixer to your music system. A mixer gives you professional-level control over the audio signals or channels in your music-sequencing activity and it solves some of the issues related to microphones and guitars. Mixers span a range from very low-cost, simple devices, to very high-end, high-cost consoles like those found in professional recording studios. A low-cost mixer is illustrated for EMT-3.

In the EMT-3 music system (compare Figures 10.2 and 10.6), a 6x2 mixer has been added: 6 input and 2 output channels. The example is a Berhinger mixer; similar basic mixers are available from Mackie, M-Audio, and many others. The microphone (12) is connected to the mono Channel 1 of the mixer (13). A single audio channel from the electric guitar (14) is shown connected to the mono input Channel 2. Stereo audio channels from the MIDI workstation (20) are connected to Channels 3 and 4 (as stereo). This leaves one stereo channel open on the mixer, Channels 5 and 6. The stereo output (two channels) of the mixer is then connected to the stereo input of the computer's sound card (4). We now have three different sources of live performance routed to the one stereo input of the sound card. Mixers come in all sorts of configurations besides the 6x2 employed here: 12, 14, or 16x2; 24 or 32x4; 16x4x2, and so on with infinite variety. A configuration like 16x4x2 is one in which the mixer will let you output either a group of four channels (e.g., to a multitrack recorder) or a group of two channels.

ASIDE

A condenser microphone requiring phantom power can also be connected to the audio input of a PC sound card through the use of a microphone pre-amp; the pre-amp takes care of the phantom power and impedance issues.

The low-cost mixer chosen for the EMT-3 setup has two channels (in the upper right-hand corner) with balanced XLR connections typically found on microphones. These two channels are especially designed for electronic issues unique to guitars and mics. The voltage or signal coming from them is very different from the *line* voltage of audio gear such as CD players, electronic keyboards, stereo receivers, and the like. The balanced XLR connections are technically of low impedance and require power. Reflecting back on the discussion of low impedance, mics and guitars are low impedance and also may require phantom power (more on this in a moment). By using a basic mixer such as the one shown here, the mixer accommodates the special power and impedance needs for guitars and professional-level microphones and offers a solution for using them with the input normally provided with a computer's sound card. This solution permits the use of pro-level microphones with a personal computer.

Mixer Input Controls

Figure 10.7 shows the detailed controls available on the 6x2 mixer used in the EMT-3 configuration. Remember, each channel of sound in a mixer can be manipulated by a unique set of controls.

Three types of input connections are typically provided with a mixer: phone (balanced and unbalanced), RCA phono (unbalanced), and XLR (balanced) jacks. A combination of these connectors is provided for each channel of the mixer. Some mixers may provide phone and phono jacks for each input channel but XLR microphone connections for only a few of the channels. Remember from our discussion above that XLR connectors are superior because they provide the highest quality of electrical connectivity and grounding, thus minimizing the likelihood of hum and static due to poor connections.

Let us walk through the controls on the 6x2 mixer as shown in Figure 10.7, starting at the bottom of a single channel. At the bottom of the control panel, find the control knob or *pot* (short for *potentiometer*) labeled *level*. This pot lets you control the overall amplitude of the signal for this channel being added to the overall audio mix. Some mixers will provide a *fader* that slides up and down, rather than a pot. Mixers may also provide a peak-level indicator for each channel—a light comes on when the intensity of the input signal exceeds the *peak* level, the point at which audio distortion will occur.

TIP

Pots are the round control knobs, *faders* the sliding controls, and *switches* the on/off controls or buttons on a mixer.

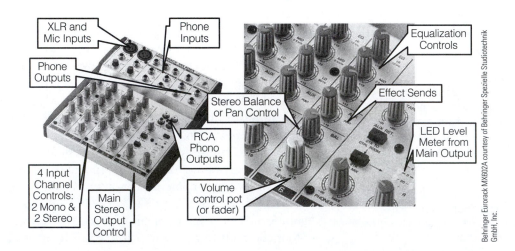

FIGURE 10.7   Details on the control surface of a simple 6x2 Behringer mixer

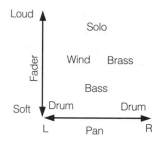

ASIDE

Many of the functions of hardware mixers described here will return when we discuss software mixers in Modules 12, 15, and 17.

TIP

When no effects have been mixed with an audio signal, it is a *dry* signal; the signal becomes *wet* as effects are added.

The next pot is labeled *balance*, or *bal*, for the stereo channels and *pan* for the mono channels. The *balance* pot lets you control the location of the audio signal within the left-to-right balance of the stereo input, or *pan* from front to back of the audio signal on a mono channel.

Study the diagram in the margin. The diagram shows the placement of six musicians in a recording studio. Part of the art of mixing involves the practiced placement of your music channels into audio space that matches the live recording environment. Each musician represents one channel: solo, wind, brass, bass, and two drum channels. Audio space is manipulated by faders that control the volume of each audio channel and pan pots that control the left-to-right proximity of each channel. The perceived location in recording each of these musicians is created by the interaction of the fader and pan controls.

To continue with the walking tour of the mixer in Figure 10.7, the next pot moving up the panel for the Channel 5–6 controls is labeled *Aux*. This pot lets you connect a device to the mixer to add effects such as reverb, echo, flanging, and other electronic processing to your audio signal. These devices are called "effects processors." The Aux pot gives you control over how much of a given effect is added to the signal on this channel. For example, if you have reverb programmed in an effects processor connected to the mixer, the more you rotate the Aux pot clockwise, the more reverb is added to the audio mix on this channel.

Next you see in Figure 10.7 three equalization or EQ pots. Equalization lets you boost, reduce, or eliminate certain frequencies of the audio signal by selective filtering. Our EMT-3 mixer uses a simple EQ setup, with a low, middle, and high filter similar to the bass (removing or adding low frequencies) and treble (removing or adding high frequencies) controls on a car radio, and then a control for the mid-range of frequencies. The EQ controls on mixers can get very complex with tunable filters that let you precisely control the range of frequencies filtered out of an audio signal.

Mixer Output Controls

Because this is a 6x2 mixer, it provides a pot to control the final stereo output signals from the mix of six channels for the two stereo left and right channels. You can see this pot in the lower left-hand corner of the mixer controls in Figure 10.6. To provide monitoring of the output signal, mixers provide either a VU *meter* or an *LED ladder* for each output channel. The VU meter is an analog dial that shows the strength of the output signal; the LED ladder gives you a row or ladder of small LED lights indicating the strength of the signal. In the Behringer mixer used in EMT-3, an LED ladder of lights serves as the master-level meter. Some mixers may also provide a headphone output and a control-room output with separate control pots for monitoring the final output mix.

Microphones

Capturing the human voice is just about the most natural thing anyone would want to do with a recording system. Digital audio recording with a computer is no exception. The EMT-1 and EMT-2 layouts show a basic microphone (12) that comes with most computer systems: an inexpensive, High-Z impedance, "cardioid dynamic" mic that is good for spoken voice and minimally acceptable for music recording. With the mixer added to the EMT-3 system, you can now take advantage of the wide variety of pro-level microphones available. What follows is a brief overview of the key characteristics of pro-level microphones and an explanation of the more common terms like "cardioid" and "dynamic": physical operation, pick-up pattern, impedance, and dynamic range and frequency response.

- *Physical Operation*. Microphones are designed to convert patterns of air-pressure changes into corresponding patterns of electrical current through a physical "transducer." Transducers may include carbon, crystals, magnets, capacitors, or moving coils. The two most common are "dynamic" (moving coil) and "condenser" (changing capacitor) microphones. Both of these mic designs have a diaphragm that vibrates sympathetically with air-pressure changes. The *dynamic mic* has a wire coil and a magnet attached to the diaphragm. The diaphragm moves, the coil moves, changes happen in the magnetic field, and varying electrical voltages are generated and passed through the microphone cable. The *condenser mic*, on the other hand, has two plates, one moving (the diaphragm so to speak) and one fixed. When air-pressure changes cause the movable plate to vibrate, changes in the voltage occur in the capacitor of the second plate, and the change in voltage is passed through the cable of the microphone. To create the electrical capacitance in a condenser mic, a small voltage must be supplied. Because of this, condenser mics require "phantom power" either through the cable or from batteries. In the mixer discussion, it was noted that XLR connections often provide phantom power to the microphone for this reason.
- *Dynamic mics* are versatile and rugged, do not easily distort the audio signal due to loud sounds, are reported to have a "warm sound," and require no outside power. *Condenser mics*, on the other hand, are less versatile but more sensitive in dynamic range. They more easily distort the audio signal when processing loud sounds and require power to operate. The trade-off, however, is that condenser microphones provide superior frequency response and dynamic range for very quiet sounds, and reportedly provide much "crisper" and "cleaner" sound signals.
- *Pick-up pattern*. When using a microphone, you may want it to record or pick up the sounds of everything around it (all the voices in a room, for example) or just pick up the sounds from one instrument or voice. A microphone that picks up sounds in any direction is called an "omnidirectional" mic; lavalier mics for speaking tend to be omnidirectional. When a mic needs to be more selective, a "cardioid" or directional mic is used (so called because its pick-up pattern resembles an inverted heart or cardioid shape). To narrow the reception range further, you can select a "hyper-cardioid," mic (typical of shotgun mics used for movies and sports events), or a "super-cardioid" where the mic must be pointed directly at the person speaking or performing. Camcorders use hyper- and super-cardioid microphones.
- *Impedance*. Impedance was presented earlier with the discussion of audio plugs and jacks. Low-Z mics with impedance levels under 600 ohms are typical of pro-level microphones. Condenser mics tend to be Low-Z and require a low-level of "phantom power" for operation. Hi-Z mics require no amplification, typically have an impedance level above 600 ohms (often around 1500 ohms), and are less costly.

- *Dynamic range and frequency response.* The specifications on every microphone should tell you something about the frequency range it responds to and the sensitivity of the mic to certain frequencies. A mic with a "flat response" is one that provides the same voltage output at any frequency. Mics designed particularly for vocal performance, on the other hand, may produce little voltage response to low frequencies, adequate response in the mid-range frequencies, and a boost to the response to high frequencies. Mics designed for percussion often boost the low frequencies and dramatically attenuate higher-frequency responses. As you can see, each mic is custom designed in its dynamic range and frequency response to fit a specific sound application

Given these choices, what's a musician to do? Recording engineers have their favorite mics for just about any situation. Names like AKG, Crown, Nady, Neuman, Sennheiser, Shure, and others are quite common. You might begin by purchasing a fairly standard, low-cost dynamic cardioid mic for instrumental recording (a Shure SM57 or 58, or equivalent). Since it is dynamic, you will not need a mixer with phantom power, and they are relatively inexpensive and extremely durable. Then for vocal recording you might look at purchasing an AKG or Neuman mic, depending on your budget. These are more expensive—typically condenser mics that require phantom power, but with a frequency response and dynamic range tuned for vocal recording. An AKG 414 condenser mic and the Neuman KMS 105 are two possibilities. The Neuman 105 is designed for vocalists and is a supercardioid condenser microphone. Then, find a mic good for percussion sounds. Here you want bass boost in the dynamic range with little to no higher-frequency response, a dynamic mic that will take lots of abuse when it comes to loud sounds. The AKG D112, for example, is a cardioid condenser mic with a frequency response down to 20 Hz and bass boost in the 50–200 Hz range, with an extra boost at 4000 Hz. It is designed for "clean kick drum and bass guitar performance with a powerful, punchy sound." Tom and snare drums require a different mic (e.g., the Shure PG56). There are so many choices that you will need to let your budget, your ear, and whatever advice you can find help you with your selection. One consolation to spending money on good microphones is that they can last for a lifetime of recording.

TIP

If you want to sound like you are in the know, be sure to pronounce Neuman microphones as "Noy-min."

ASIDE

CD and DVD rewriteable options have been grouped into a category of CD/DVD-R and -RW. CD-R and CD-RW are well standardized for recordable and rewriteable recording technologies. It will take time for a preferred, industry-standard format to emerge for DVD recordables (DVD-R and DVD+R) and DVD rewriteables (DVD-RAM, DVD-RW, and DVD+RW).

Storage Devices for Digital Audio Work

Digital audio sampling consumes an enormous volume of storage space, even with the use of various compression schemes like MP3 or AAC. For this reason alone, storage outside the hard disk of the computer workstation is necessary. The primary purpose for transforming your computer into a digital audio workstation is to create musical experiences that can be shared with others and used in a portable listening environment. For this reason, techniques are needed to transport digital audio events in other formats. To meet both of these needs, storage and music listening, the EMT-3 system provides CD/DVD-R storage and recording (3), Zip or other removable storage (9), interface to an MP3 player (15), and a MiniDisc (16) or equivalent recorder.

LINK

Several concepts mentioned in this section are covered earlier. Zip disk, hard disk, CD and DVD video, CD-ROM, and DVD/CD-RW are presented in Module 7 of Viewport II. File-compression formats for digital audio are featured in Module 8 of this Viewport.

LINK

Check Module 11 for a discussion of CD and DVD formats and how they work.

ASIDE

Initially, portable music players were called "MP3 players" for playing the popular MP3 music files; these devices are now flexible enough to play WAV, AIF, AAC, and other audio file options.

ASIDE

Personal digital assistants (PDAs) like the Palm and PocketPC devices can be used as MP3 music players as well.

CD/DVD-R and -RW Storage

At the time Sony developed the MiniDisc format, making a CD audio or CD-ROM disc was an expensive proposition and the notion of portable MP3 players didn't exist. In quick evolutionary succession, however, CD/DVD-R and -RW recordable devices—provided as standard equipment with a computer workstation—have made producing your own CD cheaper than buying any stand-alone recording system such as DAT or MiniDisc. The ingredients are very simple: a blank CD or DVD recordable disc, CD-burning software bundled with the computer, and a selection of digital audio or video files on your computer.

With these ingredients, you can quickly produce CD or DVD audio in one of several formats. The sound file can be formatted in such a way as to create a:

- CD audio or DVD audio or video disc playable on any commercial CD or DVD player
- CD disc formatted to store MP3, AAC, AIF, or WAV files playable on CD players that accommodate those formats
- CD/DVD-R or CD/DVD-RW disc formatted for storage of computer files readable on any computer system

The CD/DVD-R drive (3) shown in the EMT-3 system can be used for any of these three options and is one of the preferred methods of recording or storing digital audio work.

Digital Music Players

Digital audio is very versatile and portable. Devices abound for taking digital audio files with you wherever you go or exchanging copyright-free music over the Internet. The Apple iPod is one example of the many commercial digital music players currently available. An iPod, depending on the model, can hold 40 GB or more of music files; it can play MP3, AAC, WAV, and AIF files; and it can connect to a computer using Firewire for exchanging audio files. An MP3 player (15) is shown in the EMT-3 diagram. This player typically holds 64 MB or more of MP3- or WMA-formatted music and interfaces to the computer with USB.

Many digital music players offer removable storage options, including compact flash, Smart Media, Sony memory stick, and secure media. With a USB or Firewire connection, digital audio files can be saved to the music player's storage media, much like any other storage device from the computer's operating system.

Speakers and Recorders

You've finished sequencing your first computer-generated composition and now you're ready to record the final production. Our EMT-3 music system has some options for audio gear. First, a pair of amplified speakers (10) and headphones (11) are included. Then, take your choice of budget-minded recording devices: a cassette tape recorder, a portable MiniDisc recorder (16), a portable DAT recorder, or even a portable CD audio recorder. Shown in Figure 10.5 is a Sony MiniDisc (MD) recorder (16). Given the prevalence and declining costs of digital media storage, and the ease and low cost of producing CD and DVD discs, analog tape options and MiniDisc are not as attractive as they once were.

The MiniDisc recorder in our EMT system example is connected to the stereo line output of the digital audio sound card. The amplified speakers (10) or the headphones (11) would then be plugged into the stereo headphone jack of the sound card (4). If both the line-out and headphone jack are not provided, then the speakers and headphones could be connected directly through the recorder (16).

Doing More with Digital Audio

"From the creative perspective, the most important element in recording is to have an unwavering passion for what you do and a strong sense of integrity about the product you are making. Ultimately, mastering is not a software tool you can buy off the shelf or a class you can take, nor is it something that automatically rubs off on you just because you were in the same room with someone who was proficient at it. Rather, like all parts of the recording process, mastering is an art form that requires dedication, patience, and a keen ear, not to mention a highly developed sense of humor!"

—*Emily Lazar, chief mastering engineer at The Lodge,*
a Greenwich Village mastering facility in New York City;
adjunct professor in the music technology program at New York University,
Interview in Electronic Musician *(January 2003)*

ASIDE
We use "multiple-track" and "multitrack" interchangeably to mean the same thing; similarly, multiple-channel and multichannel.

Overview

We now focus on digital audio and its growth in recent years as a major force in music creation. In the last Viewport, we focused on the basics: acoustics; digital sampling and analog synthesis; sound file formats; software for MP3, streaming media, and digital audio editing; and hardware for analog-to-digital conversion, mixers and microphones, plugs and connectors, and file storage. In this Viewport, we examine a more complicated picture by considering MPEG standards (especially in terms of surround sound), laser disc formats, multiple-track recording software, and hardware for multiple-channel digital audio.

If you imagine creating an audio CD or DVD of your own, perhaps featuring your own band, or if you have a desire to arrange music for a movie or a play, information in this Viewport will be important to you. Until most recently, professional-sounding recordings were possible only by renting expensive studios. Today, music production from start to finish can be done in home studios with results that rival the professional world.

Objectives

In Module 11, we explain how MPEG standards have helped frame the structure for multiple-channel sound and how the various audio formats have developed, including options for DVD media. CD and DVD laser-disc formats are presented. Module 12 covers the major multiple-track recording software, including loop-based solutions. A brief introduction to mixing, mastering, and CD/DVD production is also included. Module 13 examines hardware for multiple-channel

MUSIC TECHNOLOGY IN PRACTICE

John Shirley

Professor of Sound Recording Technology at the University of Massachusetts, Lowell campus, and freelance sound and recording engineer

John Shirley recording with Cambodian musicians with laptop and M-Box in foreground

Portable recording studio in a backpack

Application

How do you pack when heading for Cambodia to record the traditional music of the country? As light as possible! Dr. John Shirley has recorded the Lyric Opera and the Chicago Symphony, but his most intriguing problem was how to achieve professional-level recording while wandering the Cambodian countryside. Some of the issues he faced included durability, power, recording quality, recording capacity, price, and backup of the recordings. His solution was to take advantage of software recording tools available for his five-pound Macintosh laptop. With the addition of a four-channel ADC box (24-bit sampling and mic preamp included) and some microphones, he had everything he needed to set up recording anywhere. He used DigiDesign's ProTools multichannel recording software and was able to burn CD-ROMs and CD audio discs directly from the Mac laptop. As John explained it: "I used ProTools software with the M-Box on the trip. I have a full-blown ProTools rig at my home studio, so it worked out well." Some things John didn't plan for were the erratic behavior of his hard drive when confronted with tropical humidity, the lack of any acoustical control for background noises, and how to fit an ensemble of musicians in his small hotel room for the recording session (all arriving on "motos" or scooters), instead of the anticipated solo musician!

Hardware and Software

John's final gear list included a Macintosh Titanium Powerbook G4 laptop (550 mHz, 512 MB RAM, DVD/CD-R, and 20-GB hard drive); DigiDesign M-Box; Audio Technica AT 825 stereo mic (balanced, AA battery powered, and bass roll-off) and stand; two pairs of headphones (AKG and Yamaha); various cables; two Powerbook batteries; and a power transformer (220 to 110) and surge protector. All of this was neatly packaged in a backpack designed just for laptops. The M-Box interfaced with the laptop through a USB connector.

Aaron Paolucci

Professional sound designer and member of the arts technology and theatre design faculty at Illinois State University. Also resident sound designer for the Illinois Shakespeare Festival.

Paolucci's home surround-sound studio with custom-built speakers

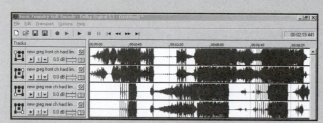

Paolucci encoding Dolby Digital with Soft Encode

Application

Mr. Paolucci specializes in sound design using digital audio tools built into a computer workstation. His work involves sound design for theatre productions, mastering and remastering music recordings and audio for video, and, of course, teaching and sharing his sound-design expertise with his students. He likes working in surround-sound mixes. As he puts it, "Theatre sound design is rapidly catching up to the multichannel audio experience movie-goers hear, so there is a push to design in surround for plays as well." The best way to illustrate how Aaron works in surround sound is the following experience he shared:

"I recently recomposed music for a combination bal-let/modern performance. The choreographer gave me four separate songs that he wanted blended to form a com-pletely new piece. I knew the performance space had surround-sound playback capabilities, so I decided to cre-ate the piece in four-channel surround to fully immerse the audience. The first thing I did was chop the music up into phrases and samples to use as building blocks. Most of these blocks were then filtered, FXed, and pitch-shifted into raw 'audio blobs,' some 50 separate sound bytes. I then went into the multitrack screen of Cool Edit Pro and assigned different tracks to front and rear outputs. I inserted a click track to keep rhythm and tempo. I put lots

Editing Paolucci's multitrack audio with Cool Edit Pro

of attention on the surround-sound field, playing with keeping the sound tight and focused front center, then opening up to the whole space, then back tight and small again, back and forth. I really wanted the audience to feel drawn in and pushed away, surrounded and then isolated systematically so that image and location were as much compositional elements as the actual sounds, rhythms, and melodies. I also experimented with sounds 'walking' around the audience rhythmically and sometimes different elements moving around the sound field at different rates and in different directions. The choreographer intuitively mirrored this 'locational' behavior with his choreography for the performance."

Hardware and Software

Mr. Paolucci has built a PC digital audio workstation around a 1.5-mHz Windows XP computer with "lots of RAM." For digital audio, he uses the Echo GINA24 sound card with 2-in/8-out ADC/DAC audio channels. Two things that he feels are critical for his sound design work are multiple large hard drives and dual video monitors. With multiple hard drives he is able to use a Windows XP feature called "software RAID" to give him very fast, sustained, read-write speeds of around 100 Mbps. The dual displays pro-vide the convenience of displaying toolbars and files on one screen and digital audio data tracks on the other.

Aaron uses Cool Edit Pro and Soft Encode (Sound Forge) almost exclusively. Cool Edit (now Audition) does all the editing, multitracking, recording, native effects (FX) pro-cessing, and video integration. When his work is done in Cool Edit, he mixes all the tracks down to surround-sound assignments, from four-channel to the typical Dolby-Digital 5.1-channel mixdown. Then he drops the tracks into Soft Encode to create the AC3, Dolby Digital stream. (Professor Paolucci notes that Soft Encode is no longer available from Sound Forge; comparable applications are available to do the same thing.) At this point, Aaron either burns the AC3 audio to a DVD as a DVD-Video (with one photo filler as video) or encodes it as an AC3.wav file (AC3 "camouflaged to act like a WAV file") and then burns it to a CD. This AC3 CD audio disc can be played on any CD or DVD player with S/PDIF digital audio out to an amplifier/receiver with Dolby Digital decoding built in.

Aaron believes that a digital designer must consider all components in the design of a DAW studio and that includes the surround amplification system and speaker array. Ever budget minded, he specializes in building his own speakers from scratch and buying used electronic components from online auctions. All of his audio sources are tied into the surround-sound system and speakers, which means they are also tied into the computer: DVD, CD, cassette, MiniDisc, mixer, and TV.

realization, both as a producer and as a consumer. Stand-alone digital recorders are described. At the end of this Viewport you should understand:

- Basic recording and editing of multiple-track digital audio software
- Loop-based software sequencers
- Mixing, mastering, and distributing digital audio recordings
- MPEG standards and their importance in understanding multiple-track digital audio
- Distinctions between DVD-Video and DVD-Audio
- CD and DVD laser-disc formats, including how recording options work with this technology
- The use of DAT, ADAT, and stand-alone recorders
- Digital communication over S/PDIF and AES/EBU connections
- How to expand a computer system to a surround-sound environment

DVD-ROM
As with all the software modules in this text, the accompanying DVD contains projects for you to use to practice your skills.

DVD-ROM Software Projects

In terms of hands-on tasks for multiple-track software, you should be able to:

- Record and edit multiple-track digital audio (Project 8)
- Create a loop-based composition (Project 9)
- Mix, master, and burn a CD (Project 10)

Sonic Realism: MPEG, Surround Sound, and Laser Discs

ASIDE
3-D movies were also introduced in the 1950s with red and green polarized cardboard glasses to heighten the sense of realism. Anything to pull the 1950s viewer away from that other new invention, the TV set!

LINK
Module 8 is the place to review sampling rates and width (bit depth), and, especially, the notion of sampling bit rates as they apply to sending digital audio LPCM codes in serial fashion, one bit at a time. MP3 and AAC audio are introduced in Module 8 and software applications in Module 9.

Sonic realism! Engineers and inventors have experimented with innovations for improving the reproduction of sound and music for more than 100 years. Long-play (LP) vinyl recordings introduced in the 1950s with a "stereo" format achieved a new level of sonic realism with only two channels of audio recorded on both sides of the record's vinyl groove. At the same time, movies were also attempting to push the edge of the sonic experience. Cinemascope, introduced with *The Robe,* and Todd-AO, introduced with *Oklahoma,* employed four and six channels of audio, respectively, to titillate the movie audience. Since then, new surround-sound techniques have accompanied blockbuster movie releases such as *Apocalypse Now* (Dolby Surround Sound), *Return of the Jedi* (THX), *Batman Returns* (Dolby Digital 5.1), *Jurassic Park* (DTS), and *Last Action Hero* (SDDS) with four to six or more channels of sound enveloping the moviegoer.

The trend in realism migrated to home movies in 1997 with the introduction of DVD-Video and DVD-Audio, providing six channels of digital surround sound through an array of equipment supporting multiple speakers throughout the room. The ability to access this sonic capability from the computer desktop soon followed. Technical information once reserved for movie sound engineers has entered the repertoire of the musician. Terms like DVD-Video, DVD-Audio, multichannel recording, MPEG, MP3 and AAC, DTS, Dolby Digital 5.1, and the like are associated with techniques now readily available from the hardware and software of the desktop or laptop computer. And, the de facto recording medium for surround-sound experience, be it video or audio, is the CD and DVD laser disc.

Viewport IV covers digital audio multitrack, multichannel, and surround-sound recording. In Module 8, you were introduced to a wide range of basic concepts necessary to your understanding of digital audio and music synthesis. This module extends this introduction to:

- MPEG and other surround-sound standards and their application to audio
- Audio formats for laser disc players and recorders, CD, and DVD

Multichannel Digital Audio Formats

There are two broad categories for the representation of multichannel audio in digital form. The first category (represented in Table 11.1) includes those standards that have emerged under the efforts of the Moving Picture Experts Group

(MPEG), a working group of the International Standards Organization (ISO). The second category (represented in Table 11.2) involves those multichannel audio formats that have developed around movie and DVD formats. This discussion will emphasize those features most useful to the musician and audio attributes and applications from this array of formats and standards.

LINK
DSP chips are first discussed in Module 8 and again in Module 13.

MPEG

MPEG formats are international standards for coding both audio and video. In the past, MPEG required special hardware for encoding and decoding the audio and video data. With the present-day speed of computer processors, software-only solutions enhanced by DSP chips for coding MPEG make tools and media based on MPEG formats accessible from most desktop and laptop computers.

The various MPEG standards have considerable depth and complexity. Table 11.1 attempts to reduce this complexity. MPEG standards are classified in terms of "phases" and "layers." The "phases" are MPEG-1, MPEG-2, MPEG-3, MPEG-4, MPEG-7, and MPEG-21. The "layers" are defined in Table 11.1 for MPEG-1 and MPEG-2. As can be seen, each layer contains a different set of specifications for audio applied to different applications.

T A B L E 1 1 . 1 MPEG Phases and Levels for Audio

Phase	Audio Layer	Channels	Sampling Rate	Bit Rate Range (typical rate)	Comments
MPEG-1 (1992)	Designed for coding progressive video with a transmission rate near the 1.41 Mbps of CD-ROMs. Used for VideoCDs and computer games. Perceptual lossy compression, 352x240 video at 20 fps. MP3 Internet music format grew out of MPEG-1/Layer III.				
	I	Mono or Stereo	32, 44.1, 48 kHz LPCM	32–448 Kbps (192 Kbps per channel)	
	II	Mono or Stereo	32, 44.1, 48 kHz LPCM	32–384 Kbps (96–128 Kbps per channel)	Used for VideoCD (White Book) and satellite broadcasts
	III	Mono or Stereo	32, 44.1, 48 kHz LPC	32–320 Kbps (64 Kbps per channel, 128 Kbps stereo)	Popular MP3 audio format used for sharing music on the Internet
MPEG-2 BC (1994)	Designed for coding interlaced video and the 4.7 Mbps transmission needed for DVD-Video. Backward compatible (BC) with MPEG-1. Added support for 5.1 surround audio, including low-frequency effects, lower bit and sampling rates, and several compression alternatives. 720x480 video at 60 fps.				
	I-III	5.1 channels	16, 22.05, 24, 32, 44.1, 48 kHz LPCM	384–640 Kbps for 5.1 channels (64 Kbps per channel)	Video MPEG-2 used on DVD movie discs, but audio standard for movies is DD 5.1 and LPCM

TABLE 11.1 *(continued)*

Phase	Audio Layer	Channels	Sampling Rate	Bit Rate Range (typical rate)	Comments
MPEG-2 AAC NBC (1997)	Non-Backwards Compatible (NBC) audio format designed for multichannel, high-quality compressed audio with low bit rates. Now used as the AAC audio standard and integrated into the MPEG-4 standards				
		Mono, stereo, 5.1, and multichannel up to 48	44.1/88.2/ 176.4 or 48/96/192 kHz	8–160 Kbps per channel (384 Kbps for 5.1 or 64 Kbps per channel)	AAC audio standard successor to MP3; significantly more efficient lossy compression to MP3. Three levels of compression: main, low-complexity (LC), and scalable sampling rate (SSR) in declining degrees of resolution quality
MPEG-3	Merged with MPEG-2 standards/not used				
MPEG-4 (1998)	Multimedia format standards designed for integrating media objects (video, still graphics, music, spoken voice, etc.) into low-bit-rate, streaming media packages for Internet and network delivery. Uses MPEG-2 AAC for audio standards and compression. Not compatabile with MPEG-1 or MPEG-2 BC files or applications.				
MPEG-4 SA	MPEG Structured Audio is a set of tools in the tradition of Music V, Max, Csound, and others for producing and synthesizing sound by defining the interaction of various sound objects. SOAL (pronounced "sail") is the software synthesis language used for MPEG-4 SA.				
MPEG-7	Multimedia "description" standards for content management and for database search on audio/visual content descriptors				
MPEG-21	Multimedia "framework" standards for creating, packaging, and delivering multimedia, including intellectual property management and protection				

Notes:
BC = Backwards Compatible; NBC = Non-Backwards Compatible
AAC = Advanced Audio Coding
LPCM = Linear Pulse Code Modulation
DD 5.1 = Dolby Digital 5.1 surround sound
Kbps or Mbps = transmission rate of bits of information (audio or video) in series; refer to Module 8 for explanation.

LINK
See similar settings in Figure 9.4 and a discussion of how to use MP3 encoding software in Module 9.

MPEG-1 and MP3

MPEG-1 was used in the first CD-ROM games, videoCD movies, and MP3 compressed music files. Table 11.1 shows that the standards for all three audio layers for MPEG-1 provide mono or stereo channels, uncompressed digital LPCM audio sampled either at 32, 44.1, or 48 kHz, and varying sampled bit rates in a range of 32 to 448 Kbps (Kbits/s). Layer III is most important. This is the well-used MP3 audio format presented in Table 8.3 of Module 8. Even though Layer III offers a range of 32 to 320 Kbps sampling rates, 64 Kbps for a single channel, or 128 Kbps for stereo, delivers good-quality compressed music audio ("near CD quality").

Figure 11.1a illustrates typical software for extracting files from CD audio discs

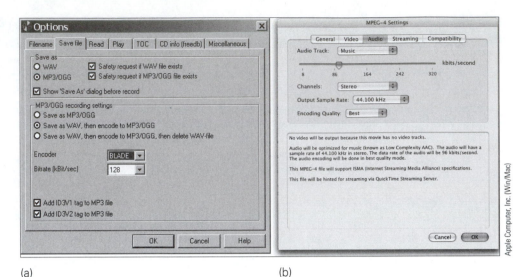

FIGURE 11.1 Views of (a) MP3 settings from Xactrator CD Ripping Software (S. Schulz/ MarvinTec [Win]); and (b) AAC settings from QuickTime

(a)   (b)

and converting them to MP3 compressed audio files. The options panel shown displays the recording setup. MP3 conversion is set using the "Blade" encoder with a bit rate of 128 Kbps. Other examples of MP3 encoders are Lame, Xing, and the original, Fraunhofer.

Layer II of MPEG-1 is of interest to those who create VideoCDs. This format provides compression for movies with sound tracks, especially applications that seek to fit feature-length films on CDs.

Two Flavors of MPEG-2: BC and AAC

MPEG-2 BC (approved in 1994), is an update or an expansion of previous work with MPEG-1. How did MPEG-2 improve on MPEG-1? It added 5.1 surround sound and AAC audio, the successor to MP3 audio. As Table 11.1 shows—BC meaning Backwards Compatible—MPEG-2 BC expanded MP3 (Phase 1/Layer III) to support multichannel and full-screen video. There are six channels of audio with the sixth channel (the .1 in the 5.1), a restricted-frequency channel reserved for special super-bass sound effects (also known as the low-frequency-effects or LFE channel).

MPEG-2 AAC (NBC or Non-Backwards Compatible) was a new audio standard aimed at improving on MP3. Notice that this portion of the MPEG-2 phase was finalized three years later than MPEG-2 BC, in 1997. MPEG-2 AAC is now referred to as AAC audio and, as will be seen below, is a key component to the MPEG-4 multimedia standards.

Examining Table 11.1 for MPEG-2 AAC, this format accommodates 5.1 surround-sound audio and is extensible to any other multichannel format up to 48 channels. Sampling rates offer doubling or tripling above either the 44.1-kHz CD audio standard or the 48-kHz rate up to 176.4 or 192 kHz, respectively. The sampling bit rates, however, reinforce a move to lower rates, but with more efficient lossy compression. Superior-quality digital audio can be realized from 128 Kbps per channel when compared to MP3 audio compressed at the same rate. In some instances, AAC may provide the same quality as MP3 at 70% of the bit rate.

Note that the table indicates three levels of compression for MPEG-2/AAC audio, starting with the highest-quality compression entitled "Main," to "low complexity," or LC, and then "scalable sampling rate," or SSR. AAC takes advan-

ASIDE
As we will soon see, commercial DVD-Video uses a different audio configuration than specified in the MPEG-2 standard

LINK
To understand the advantages of using the most appropriate sampling rates, consult the discussion in Module 8.

Apple Computer, Inc. (Win/Mac)

TIP
Versions of QuickTime from
6.0 on support AAC audio; the
default level is "low
complexity," or LC,
compression.

ASIDE
Apple Computer was the first
to introduce AAC to the
consumer market with its
iTunes software and online
music service in April 2003.

tage of several compression tools not used in MP3. These tools are referred to as "temporal noise shaping," "backward adaptive linear prediction," "gain control," and enhanced "joint stereo coding." Figure 11.1b shows the MPEG-4 Settings window for AAC Audio in QuickTime with low-complexity AAC at 96 kbits/sec.

MPEG-4 and MPEG-4 SA

MPEG phases prior to MPEG-4 were primarily concerned with video and audio compression. The MPEG-4 phase provides standards for the larger issues involved in the delivery of multimedia content—text, speech, sound effects, music, video, music notation, and other media objects—in an increasingly variegated network world. MPEG-4 addresses such issues as defining:

- How media objects relate and interact with each other
- How multimedia content can be flexibly reformatted and rescaled for delivery that ranges from high-speed Internet connectivity to low-bit-rate mobile connectivity for cell phones and handheld computers
- How media objects can be flexibly manipulated in real time for the Web, computer gaming, and training materials
- How intellectual property rights for multimedia content can be managed and protected (digital rights management)

This "toolbox" of MPEG-4 support provides a multimedia author with tools for designing applications that can be flexibly scaled for different delivery methods without reprogramming and tools that offer the assurance that copyright and ownership will be properly documented and protected.

For audio or digital music, MPEG-4 uses the MPEG-2 AAC format and provides very low sampling bit rates for delivering music to narrow bandwidth applications like cell phones and handhelds. Stereo audio can be scaled to as low as 40 Kbps (mono to 24 Kbps) and still offer reasonable FM and near-CD quality. Video created with the MPEG-4 standards is referred to as MP4 video and uses the .mp4 extension for its audio and video files.

Apple Computer uses the extension .m4a for nonprotected AAC files encoded with its iTunes software; it uses the extension .m4p for protected AAC files purchased from its online music service. QuickTime uses MPEG-4 extensively. Figure 11.1b shows the MPEG-4 settings dialog in QuickTime with a bit rate set to 96 Kbps stereo with AAC LC compression.

MPEG-4 Structured Audio (SA) is a very interesting addition to the media-object toolbox of this phase of MPEG standards. The lineage for this set of sound-synthesis tools can be traced back to Max Mathews and the Music I through Music V and GROOVE music programming tools, and forward to Barry Vercoe's Csound and NetSound languages. The MIT Media Lab was involved in coordinating the efforts of developing and finalizing the MPEG-4 SA standards.

MPEG-7 and MPEG-21

The next two MPEG phases provide standards for the search and retrieval of MPEG-4 databases of multimedia content and developing a framework for packaging and delivering these multimedia products. Issues of content management and metadata structures, coding and keywords for search and retrieval of media objects, and tools for managing intellectual property rights, copyright, and protection are part of these two MPEG phases.

The core of MPEG features for digital audio is in MPEG-1, MPEG-2, and

LINK

Modules 12 and 17 address multitrack digital audio software that provides the tools for producing music and sound productions that can be mixed down to surround-sound and multichannel formats.

MPEG-4. MPEG-7 and MPEG-21 deal with larger, meta-issues associated with building, distributing, and protecting the intellectual property rights of multimedia applications.

Surround-Sound Audio Formats

Many proprietary surround-sound formats were engineered to enhance the realism of the movie theater experience. What began as technology for motion pictures has migrated to consumer video through DVD-Video discs and home-theater systems. This same technology has expanded the possibilities for music recordings. Surround-sound music recordings are evolving from stereo CD audio to surround-sound DVD-Audio using the formats of DVD-Video, DD 5.1/AC-3, DTS, and DVD-Audio. Table 11.2 provides a sample of multichannel audio formats, including AAC, discussed above.

TABLE 11.2 Comparison of Multichannel Audio Formats

Format		Channels	Owner	Comments
Generic		5.1, 6.1, 7.1, 10.1		Typical options in digital audio sequencers as discrete channels without compression
Dolby ProLogic	Dolby Surround ProLogic	4 (LCR/S)	Dolby Labs	Hi-Fi VHS format and film; consumer equivalent to Dolby Surround Sound
DD 5.1 (AC-3)	Dolby Digital 5.1 (Audio Coding 3)	5.1 (LCR/LsRs) + LFE	Dolby Labs	Used on DVD-Video, HDTV, and DIRECTV
Dolby EX 6.1	Dolby Digital EX	6.1 (LCR/LsCsRs) + LFE	Dolby Labs and LucasFilms with THX versions	Movie format first used in *Star Wars: Episode 1—Phantom Menace*
DTS and DTS-ES Discrete	Digital Theatre Systems Surround Sound and Extended Surround	5.1 (LCR/LsRs + LFE) or 6.1 DTS-ES (LCR/ LsCsRs+LFE)	Digital Theatre Systems. Requires DTS decoder for Coherent Acoustics Coding (CAC)	First used in *Jurassic Park* movie and the ES Discrete on *The Haunting;* alternative audio on some DVDs and also on CDs
SDDS	Sony Dynamic Digital Sound	7.1 channels (LCl/C/CrR/ LsRs+LFE)	Sony	Movie format used in *Pearl Harbor* and others
MPEG-2 AAC	Advanced Audio Coding or MP4 audio	5.1 (LCR/LsRs + LFE) and up to 48 channels	Dolby AAC decoder	Could replace MP3 as Internet coding of choice with AAC
MLP	Meridian Lossless Packing	6 (LCR/ LsCsRs) or (LCR/LsRs + LFE)	Meridian Audio, licensed by Dolby Laboratories	Compression standard on DVD-Audio, used on DVD or CD
DSD	Direct Stream Digital	5, 5.1, or 6	Sony/Philips	Used for SACD audio discs

Notes:
LFE = low-frequency effects for the .1 channel, a reduced-frequency channel for low-frequency, deep-bass effects.
Channel designations are L(Left), R(Right), C(Center), S(single rear surround), Ls (back left surround), Rs (back right surround), Cs (back center surround), and LFE (.1 deep bass). Cl and Cr are Center Left and Center Right used in SDDS environment.

LINK
Software tools for multiple-channel mixing will be covered in detail in Module 12.

The first two columns in Table 11.2 show the abbreviated and full names of the surround-sound formats. At the top of the table are the generic options available in software such as DigiDesign ProTools, MOTU Digital Performer, BIAS Deck, and Cakewalk Sonar. Without applying any compression standards, audio software can mix down a production of music or combinations of music, speech, and sound effects to an array of channels that simulate a complete surround-sound performance environment. The .1 designation refers to an additional channel—a sixth channel in the case of 5.1, for example—that provides a limited low-frequency range (LFE) of super-bass effects. You can see how Digital Performer can be set up for a 5.1-channel mix, as well as Quad, LCRS, 6.1, 7.1, and 10.2, in Figure 11.2.

The uniqueness in any of the proprietary surround-sound formats is:

- the spatial arrangement of the speakers in the theater or room
- the compression techniques used for encoding the audio signals onto a distribution medium (from 70-mm file for the cinema to laser disc for home DVD movies)
- decoding the compressed signals for the theater, home, or personal performance

Spatial Arrangement

Figure 11.3 illustrates the basic 5.1-channel placement with left (L), center (C), and right (R) channels at the front of the room; left-surround (Ls) and right-surround (Rs) at the back side of the room; and a low-frequency-effects (LFE) channel. This arrangement is used for DD 5.1/AC-3, DTS, MPEG-2/AAC, MLP, and DSD. Refer to Table 11.2 for more information. It is the standard for surround-sound audio using DVD-Video with DD 5.1/AC-3 or DTS or DVD-Audio using MLP.

The earlier Dolby ProLogic Surround Sound was a four-channel configuration with only a single surround-sound (S) channel at the back of the room. The 6.1 configurations for Dolby EX and DTS-ES add a rear center channel as well, and

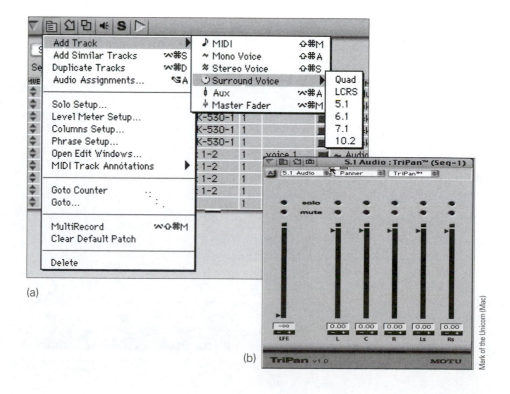

FIGURE 11.2 Digital Performer (a) menu for setting up various surround-sound mixes and (b) mixer showing a 5.1-channel mix with the LFE super-bass channel

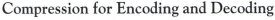
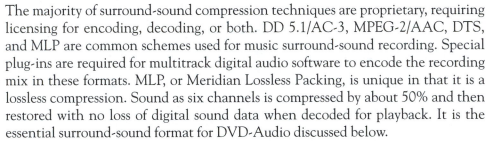

FIGURE 11.3 The 5.1 (six) channels of surround-sound audio in a home theater system.

ASIDE
The more surround-sound formats a DVD player, receiver/amplifier, or disc accommodates, the more likely it will cost more. Each proprietary encoding standard is associated with licensing fees.

the SDDS 7.1 channel configuration is front center left (Cl) and center right (Cr) channels.

Compression for Encoding and Decoding

The majority of surround-sound compression techniques are proprietary, requiring licensing for encoding, decoding, or both. DD 5.1/AC-3, MPEG-2/AAC, DTS, and MLP are common schemes used for music surround-sound recording. Special plug-ins are required for multitrack digital audio software to encode the recording mix in these formats. MLP, or Meridian Lossless Packing, is unique in that it is a lossless compression. Sound as six channels is compressed by about 50% and then restored with no loss of digital sound data when decoded for playback. It is the essential surround-sound format for DVD-Audio discussed below.

Figure 11.4 illustrates the plug-in software required to encode a multichannel mix from multitrack software. Kind of Loud Technologies produces both a Dolby Digital encoder and a DTS encoder that can be used to create CD or DVD music discs from the Macintosh version of ProTools. Minnetonka's SurCode software for the Windows operating system comes in many flavors to meet most surround-sound coding needs from CD- and DVD-DTS to DD 5.1 AC-3 and even to MLP compression for DVD-Audio discs.

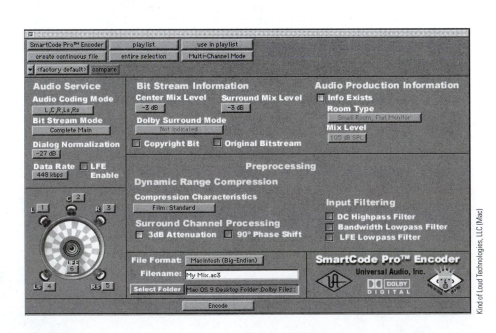

FIGURE 11.4 The SmartCode Pro plug-in for encoding a surround-sound mix into a Dolby 5.1 Digital file

LINK

Laser disc hardware issues for CDs and DVDs related to both internal and external installation were discussed in Module 7.

CD and DVD Laser Disc Formats

Surround-sound audio and video require enormous quantities of storage space. All of the media are represented by billions of binary codes that need to be stored, exchanged, and transported. The 4.7-inch CD and DVD laser technologies help to satiate the appetite for ever-increasing storage needs in a durable, long-lasting, optical form. The emergence of more expansive DVD laser storage coincides nicely, and not accidentally, with the demand for multichannel audio tools for personal computers.

Laser discs come in two basic flavors, CD or DVD, with several variations. Playable and recordable CDs and DVDs are ideally suited to music recording, provide an excellent storage medium for large volumes of data like digital images and MP3 and AAC music files, and offer a vast resource for interactive multimedia applications where large amounts of storage are required for high-resolution sound and imagery. With the introduction of the first CD audio discs in the 1980s, musicians and music listeners were rewarded with a truly magical technology.

Laser discs can be pressed through a manufacturing process or created with a CD or DVD recording device. Blank CD or DVD discs that can be recorded only once are CD and DVD Recordable discs (CD-R or DVD-R). Blank discs that can be erased and rerecorded are ReWritable discs (CD-RW or DVD-RW, DVD-RAM, or DVD+RW).

General Characteristics of CD and DVD Laser Discs

How does a laser disc work? All forms of DVD and CD discs work in essentially the same way. The key to a laser disc's operation is light emitted from a laser beam and an optical sensor or pickup to detect light from the reflective surface of the disc. This light is projected onto a spinning disc. A change in reflected intensity signifies a 1; otherwise it is a 0.

Manufactured or Pressed Discs

For commercial CD audio discs or DVD movies that are pressed by a manufacturer in quantity, data are encoded in patterns of flat areas (lands) and pits arranged in a spiral from the inside of the disc outward (Figure 11.5a). When the laser beam hits the edge of a pit in the spinning disc, the light is reflected away from the optical sensor. Figure 11.5c illustrates a sample coding of binary 1s and 0s determined by a pattern of lands and pits.

CDs use only one side and one layer of the disc. On a typical CD disc that is 4.75 inches in diameter, there are some two billion data pits across more than three miles, or 22,000 revolutions, of spiraling tracks. DVDs contain significantly more data by using a more tightly wound spiral (track pitch) and by positioning the pits more closely together (see Figure 11.5d). Figure 11.5e shows how two layers of pits are recorded on each side of a DVD disc using alternating reflective metals so the laser beam can distinguish between the two layers of data. With two layers on both sides of a 4.75-inch DVD disc, the spirals of data total almost 30 miles in length. Table 11.3 gives you some idea of the comparison of storage capacity between CD and DVD discs with multiple layers and sides.

ASIDE

How long will CDs and DVDs last? Five, 30, or 100 years? That's difficult to say. The longevity of a laser disc depends on many factors, including how it was created and subsequently handled and stored. For recordable laser discs, the most important factor is the dye used. The laser beam heats and melts the dye to create the data patterns on the disc. The better the quality of the organic dye, the longer the CD-R or DVD-R will last. The real question, of course, is whether computers will still read the same media 100 years from now!

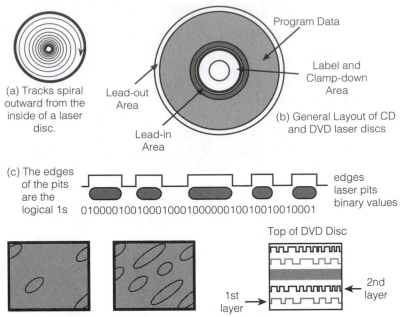

FIGURE 11.5 The layout and format of a laser disc showing (a) the outward pattern of spiral tracks, (b) disc content areas, (c) binary patterns of pits, (d) difference in pit density between CD and DVD, and (e) the layers and sides possible with DVD discs.

(a) Tracks spiral outward from the inside of a laser disc.

(b) General Layout of CD and DVD laser discs

(c) The edges of the pits are the logical 1s

0100001001000100010000001001001001001

edges laser pits binary values

(d) Pits and lands for CD (left) and DVD (right) laser patterns

(e) Cross sections of a double-sided, double-layer DVD disc

TABLE 11.3 CD-ROM and DVD-ROM Storage Capacity

Data	CD-ROM or CD-R	Maximum Audio Bit Rate for Disc	Copy Protection	DVD Single-Sided Single-Layer	DVD Single-Sided Double-Layer	DVD Double-Sided Double-Layer
Computer storage	.65 GB (650 MB)		No	4.7 GB	8.5 GB	17 GB
CD audio (16-bit/44.1-kHz)	1.25 hrs (75 mins)	1.4 Mbps	No	7.5 hrs	15 hrs	30 hrs
VideoCD or DVD-Video	74 mins (VideoCD)	4.3 Mbps	May be copy and region protected	2.2 hrs	4.4 hrs	8.8 hrs
DVD-Audio (MLP 6ch 24-bit/96-kHz)		9.6 Mbps	Yes	74 mins	2.2 hrs	4.4 hrs
DVD-Audio (DTS 6ch 24-bit/48-kHz)		9.6 Mbps	Yes	7 hrs	14 hrs	28 hrs
Music recording guesstimate (using CD audio 16-bit/44-kHz stereo LPCM)	Beethoven's 9th Symphony			All nine Beethoven symphonies	Recording of the Wagner Ring Cycle	Beatles and Grateful Dead complete anthologies

ASIDE

Self-destructing DVD? Dyes are available that begin to change chemically when exposed to air—intended for movie rentals where the DVD "expires" after a period of time. Disney was the first to try this with its EZ-D DVD movie discs that play for only 48 hours.

Recordable Discs

Recordable CDs and DVDs written from a personal computer onto a CD or DVD recordable drive are basically similar to manufactured or pressed laser discs. Binary 1s and 0s are written onto the disc in some fashion to create a spiral of reflective patterns from a laser beam during playback. However, three unique features make recordable discs possible and earn this process the unique name of "burning" a disc:

- A spiral pattern is pregrooved into the blank laser disc to ensure that the laser beam tracks the correct spiral path.
- There is a separate "write" laser beam for recording onto the disc, a laser beam of much greater intensity than the "read" laser.
- Different chemicals are embedded in the disc to enable an active physical change in the disc medium to create binary patterns of data.

A different technology is required to facilitate recording data directly to a disc from a computer, or to be able to erase and rewrite data to a CD-RW or DVD-RW disc. When blank recordable discs are manufactured, a metallic or reflective layer (e.g., silver or gold) and a layer of heat-absorptive organic dye have been embedded in the disc. On a blank disc, the dye is translucent. The laser light beam shines directly through onto the metallic layer and reflects back onto the optical pickup. When the dye is heated by a special high-intensity write laser, it creates opaque spots (like pits) that prevent the light from passing through to the reflective layer. Hence the term "burning" a laser disc by heating spots in the dye. There are many different dyes with different colors, many of them with proprietary chemical ingredients. Different brands reflect different colors and different quality.

Rewritable or erasable discs do not use a dye. Instead, they use a special chemical layer that changes its reflective characteristics (called "phase change") when heated to a specific temperature by the write laser beam and then cooled. The heating and cooling cycle changes its reflective state.

In its original state, the chemical layer is translucent or crystalline, allowing reflected light. The burning process entails heating the crystalline layer to its melting point with the write laser. This changes it into an amorphous, nonreflective state. To erase this state, an erase laser heats the chemical layer back to its crystalline condition, thus restoring its translucent character. The amazing property of an erasable laser disc is its ability to retain the "phase changes" permanently, or until erased and rewritten.

Disc Data Format

As noted above, data on a laser disc are laid down starting at the inside of the disc and move outward in a continuous spiral of tracks (see Figure 11.5a). The first data placed on the disc constitute the *lead-in* area. Then the actual program data (e.g., music, graphics, or video) follow in a wide variety of formats. The space left on the outer edge is the lead-out area. The lead-in and lead-out areas are used as cues by laser players to identify the beginning and end of a disc and to determine key settings for the operation of the player itself.

CD and DVD discs use a technique known as constant linear velocity, or CLV, to record the spirals of data. With CLV discs, the speed at which the disc spins varies inversely with the location of data being read on the disc. As you can see by studying the pattern of spiral tracks in Figure 11.5a, more data can be stored on the outer tracks than on the inner tracks. So, in order to read all data at the same speed, the disc spins faster when the inner tracks are being read than when the outer tracks are being read.

ASIDE

Data can also be stored on a disc surface using constant angular velocity, or CAV. Phonograph records use the CAV technique: The record always spins at a fixed speed, 33 1/3 or 45 revolutions per minute. Some DVD+R, DVD+RW, and DVD+RAM operations use the CAV technique mixed with CLV.

ASIDE
Rumor has it that 74 minutes was picked as the length of a compact audio disc because the well-known conductor of the Berlin Philharmonic, Herbert von Karajan, wanted to record Beethoven's Symphony No. 9 on one disc. Another version of this story is that the wife of Akio Morita, one of the founders of Sony, wanted her favorite piece of music, Beethoven's Ninth Symphony, recorded on the first compact disc.

Now that you've been introduced to the general characteristics of laser technology, the sections that follow explain the difference in format and application for various types of CD and DVD discs.

Compact Laser Disc Playables and Recordables

Standards for CD discs are denoted by a series of *book colors* first defined by Sony and Philips when the two companies created the digital audio disc back in the 1980s. CD audio is the *Red Book* standard, for example, and CD-ROM follows the *Yellow Book* standard, and so on. Table 11.4 gives an overview of the more common CD laser-disc formats, all of which evolved from the Sony-Philips Red Book standard.

Compact Disc-Digital Audio: Musician's Miracle Media

CD audio discs were revolutionary in the way they dramatically changed consumer music and provided the musician with the first effective drop-the-needle, random-access tool for music recordings. They truly were seen as "miracle media" by many musicians and their fans! First introduced in 1982 in Europe (1983 in the U.S.), the Compact Disc-Digital Audio (CD-DA) format is the basis for most compact disc data structures. The format, though initially used for commercial audio production, was flexible enough to allow the medium to be extended and adapted for other applications.

The CD audio format permits 74 minutes of recording on one side of the 4.75-inch laser disc. Audio on a CD-DA disc is digitally sampled in LPCM form at

---

TABLE 11.4 Common CD Laser Disc Formats (Sony/Philips Books)

Name	Code	Standards Books	Capacity	Comments
Compact Disc Digital Audio	CD-DA	Red	74 mins	CD audio music recordings
Compact Disc Read-Only Memory	CD-ROM	Yellow: ISO 9660 or HFS	650 MB	Computer data formatted for ISO standard format or Mac (HFS) or Hybrid
Compact Disc Recordable	CD-R	Orange II: ISO 9660, HFS, or UDF	63 mins/550 MB, 74 mins/650 MB, or 80 mins/700 MB	Create CD-DA, CD-ROM, or mixed formats. CD-Rs are one-time-only records. Can be used for MP3 music files playable on some CD players. Hybrids contain ISO 9660 + HFS
Compact Disc ReWriteable	CD-RW	Orange III: ISO 9660, HFS, or UDF	650 MB	Create CD-DA, CD-ROM, or mixed formats. CD-RW can be erased and reused
Video Compact Disc	VideoCD	White	74 mins	MPEG-1 movie on CD
Super Audio CD	SACD	Scarlet: ISO 9660 +UDF	110 mins stereo per layer	Sony/Philips format using Direct Stream Digital (DSD) 1-bit sampling techniques; hybrid format with CD and DVD layers

a typical sampling rate of 44.1 kHz, 16 bits per sample. Music can be accessed by track numbers (0 to 99) or by relative times within a track.

The data structure designed by Philips and Sony is very robust. The CD player uses these data to produce a flawless playback performance, regardless of fingerprints and scratches that may have accumulated on a disc. The Red Book audio format serves as a point of reference for all other CD formats; they are all variations on the CD audio theme.

Compact Disc Read-Only Memory: Music Education Bonanza

The CD-ROM was a bonanza for music education in that it enabled mixing of computer and digital audio media to create never-before-seen interactive music instruction. CD-ROM discs were designed for just such storage of large amounts of data from text, numbers, and digital graphics, video clips, and sound. The data structure for CD-ROM is defined by the Sony-Philips Yellow Book documentation (Table 11.4). Data on CD-ROM discs can be formatted to conform to common computer operating systems like DOS, Windows, and Mac OS, or to an industry-standard file structure like the ISO 9660 format. "Hybrid discs" can also be created both in the ISO 9660 format on PCs and in the HFS format for Macintosh. This makes it possible to read CD-ROM data on most computer systems.

A newer standard for recording computer files and folders or directories onto a CD-ROM disc is the ISO 13346 UDF or Universal Disc Format standard. The UDF file structure allows for the drag and drop of files from the computer desktop to the laser recording medium, and maintains and updates the directory structure or table of contents on the laser much more efficiently.

Those areas that are used for audio data on CD-DA are used by the CD-ROM disc for computer data. The basic frame structure remains the same. Data are accessed in terms of minutes, seconds, and blocks, with a total data capacity of 650 MB of storage.

"Burning" Compact Recordable and ReWriteable Discs: Music Lover's Storage

With CD recording technology built into most computer workstations and laptops, you have the power to produce your own laser discs. The technology once reserved for an expensive manufacturing enterprise is now accessible to anyone from a computer desktop. For music lovers, artists, or performing groups of any genre, this provides easy access to building albums of music tracks as CD audio discs or as data files onto CD-R discs of MP3 and AAC files.

CD-R (Compact Disc Recordable) and CD-RW (Compact Disc ReWritable) formats are defined in the Orange Book II and III standards (refer to Table 11.4). Both disc formats are recordable, but CD-R can only be recorded one time (originally called CD-WO for Write Once). CD-RW can be erased and rewritten many times.

For the content or program areas of the disc, the format may follow CD-DA if the content is audio, CD-ROM if the content is computer data, or a "mixed session" where CD-ROM data is stored at the beginning with CD-audio to follow. Based on the initial Red Book standards, CD-Rs and CD-RWs hold either 74 minutes of audio or 650 MB of data. There are 63-min/550-MB versions (usually data storage with CD-RWs), and, by winding the spiral tracks tighter, nonstandard 80-min/700-MB and even 99-minute discs are available. Remember that the spiral is pregrooved into a CD recordable disc when it is manufactured.

ASIDE

The first successful multimedia application using a mix of audio and graphics media on a CD-ROM was Robert Winter's instructional disc on Beethoven's Symphony No. 5 produced by Voyager, Inc.

ASIDE

When you use software like Toast (Roxio/Sonic Solutions) to burn a CD-ROM, the software will likely default to the standard disc format for your computer's operating system. For archiving your own files, that's fine. It's only when you want to share files with others that you need to investigate something like the ISO 9660 standard.

TIP

Compatibility problems do exist between CD recorders and various CD players. The problems typically result from either the reflectivity of the laser pickup (CD-Rs may have more intense laser beams than CD players), the calibration of the laser tracking, or the accuracy or winding of the spiral groove.

LINK

You will see TAO and DAO again in Module 12 when burning a CD is discussed.

LINK

So-called MP3 Audio Discs are CD-Rs with MP3 files recorded to the disc in a CD-ROM or data format and not in a CD-DA audio file format. ID3v1 or ID3v2 tags may also be added to the MP3 files to code title, artist, album, year, comments, and genre information with the music. These discs can be played back on CD/MP3 players specially designed for this purpose. See Module 9 for using these tags in MP3 software.

Much of the difference in formatting for recordables lies in the creation of the table of contents (TOC). The TOC in the lead-in area of a CD disc (see Figure 11.5b) provides an index of timings for audio recording or a directory of locations for blocks of computer data. CD-R and CD-RW discs have to build up this TOC as various recording sessions add data to the original blank discs. The following describes the recording options:

- *Single session.* All of the data are written from the computer workstation to the CD-R or CD-RW disc at one time, or in one session. Data can be written to the laser disc as a Disk-at-once (DAO) or Track-at-once (TAO) operation. For DAO, all of the data are written to the disc in one pass, including the TOC. This is the preferred option for recording CD audio discs as it ensures the best compatibility with various CD players and clean transitions between audio tracks.
- *Multisession recording.* The data on the CD-R or CD-RW disc is added over time over many sessions. Each recorded session contains its own TOC with a link to the next session recorded on the disc. Because of the overhead needed for this chain of TOC information from session to session, multisession discs consume considerable overhead space and are best used only for storage of computer data.
- *Packet recording.* The data are written to a CD-RW (CD-R is also possible) disc in small increments of data, a file at a time, much like data are stored on a computer disc drive. Packet recording uses the Universal Disc Format (UDF).

Important Note: When a CD-R or CD-RW session is completed, it can be kept "open" for more data to be added at another time or recording or it can be "closed" or "finalized." When closing a CD recording session, the TOCs and their links are updated and the final format may be altered for greater compatibility with different CD players. For example, a UDF multisession recording could be converted to an ISO 9660 format when finalizing the recording, or vice versa.

CD-RW discs are different only in the way data can be erased and rerecorded and the physical makeup of the disc. In all other ways, they resemble CD-R multisession media. The primary reason to use CD-RW is when there is a need to store and change computer data on laser media, typically for archival file copies and for computer backup. This format is not very suitable for audio recording.

Video Compact Disc: Feature Film on One Disc Short

Feature films are around two hours in length. With 74 minutes possible on one CD, Beethoven's Symphony No. 9 may fit on it but it comes up one disc short for feature films. Nonetheless, full-motion video is possible on two CD laser discs with the VideoCD (VCD) format, which has had some success as an alternative to VHS tape in Asia. Using CD-R discs, the VCD format provides a way for 74 minutes of home video with audio to be recorded onto a CD with the appropriate software tools. A questionable use for it is for distributing pirated copies of feature-length movies.

The audio and video on VCD take advantage of MPEG-1 compression (Table 11.1) to fit 74 minutes of movie time onto a CD. The video resolution is 352x240 pixels compared to 700x480 for DVD. The audio is 44.1-kHz/16-bit sampling. The format for videoCDs follows the Sony-Philips White Book standards, which also includes karaoke and interactive video discs (Table 11.4). VideoCDs can be played on most personal computers and DVD players, as well as dedicated videoCD players.

Super Audio CD (SACD): CD Audio on Steroids

In 1999 Sony/Philips introduced a successor to CD audio that increased the amount of music stored on a 4.7-inch laser disc, as well as the sound fidelity. The standards for SACD are defined in the Scarlet Book (see Table 11.4). The Super Audio disc now competes directly with DVD-Audio (see discussion to follow) with a multichannel, high-resolution digital audio format, Digital Stream Digital or DSD (discussed earlier in reference to Table 11.2). DSD is a 2.8-mHz/1-bit sampling technique.

SACD music discs requires an SACD player; the player will also play CD audio discs. Up to two layers can be placed on a one-sided laser disc similar to that noted in Figure 11.5e. Two different "read" lasers focus on each layer at different wavelengths. The initial layer is always multichannel DSD audio content with up to six channels and 110 minutes of audio. The second layer typically contains a standard Red Book 44.1-kHz/1-bit version of the music that can be played on any CD audio player. The DSD content consists of a table of contents, a two-channel recording, a multichannel version, and optional text and graphics.

Digital Versatile Discs (DVDs)

DVD and the technology that makes it work represent a merger of many of the advanced concepts discussed so far in this Module: compression, MPEG formats, surround sound, and continued advancement in the engineering of the 4.7-inch laser disc format. The impetus for these advancements comes from the movie industry; the challenge was to find a way to deliver a full-length feature film in a single-disc format.

A trail of 4.7-inch laser disc formats, with names like "MMCD," "SD disc," and "Taz" (named after the Looney Tunes "Tasmanian Devil"), and collaborations among movie studios and consumer electronics companies, led to the first consumer release of DVD movies and players in 1997. The DVD Forum became the official organization for overseeing the "Book" standards for three applications: DVD-ROM, DVD-Video, and DVD-Audio. DVD-R, DVD-RAM, and DVD-RW recording options were also eventually approved. Table 11.5 provides an overview of the DVD Forum Book formats from Book A for DVD-ROM through Book F for DVD-RW.

How did the DVD Forum's format manage to almost quadruple the storage capacity of the existing 4.7-inch CD disc? A combination of technologies redefined the engineering of this laser space:

- Tighter winding of the spiral of bits on the disc
- Multiple layers of data on both sides of the disc
- More efficient storage of data using the Universal Disc Format
- New compression schemes for video (MPEG-2), multichannel audio (e.g., Dolby 5.1 Digital), and higher-resolution audio (e.g., Meridian Lossless Packing at 96-kHz/24-bit sampling)

The formats that emerged enabled DVD to provide a compact medium for home video, but more importantly, provided the composer, arranger, home and small-studio recording engineer, remix artist, and music audiophile with the following, all accessible from a desktop or laptop computer:

- DVD-Audio formats with much higher resolution than CD audio (e.g., 96-kHz/24-bit sampling)

TIP
Originally the DVD acronym stood for "Digital Video Disc." Since the format that emerged was expansive enough for multimedia applications, it was renamed the "Digital Versatile Disc."

TIP
To hear the full effect of DD 5.1, DTS, or DVD-Audio, you will need a DVD player with the necessary decoder for each of these formats and an amplifier or receiver that permits the input of six unique audio channels from the player and a set of six surround-sound speakers (Figure 11.3). DVD players, however, do come equipped with common stereo left and right channels for playing DVD-Video on standard high-fidelity audio systems.

TABLE 11.5 Common DVD Laser Disc Formats (DVD Forum Books)

Name	Code	Books	Capacity	Comments
Digital Versatile Disc Read-Only Memory	DVD-ROM	A:UDF Bridge w/ISO 9660	4.7, 8.5, or 9.4 GB[1]	Computer games, multimedia, and large quantities of computer data storage
DVD Video Discs	DVD-Video	B: UDF	133 mins per layer with average bit rate of 4.7 Mbps	DVD movies using MPEG-2 video, LPCM, & AC-3 5.1 surround audio
DVD-Audio	DVD-Audio	C: UDF	79 mins per layer with two channels LPCM stereo, and MLP 5.1 with data rate of 9.6 Mbps and 24-bit/96-kHz sampling[2]	High-resolution commercial music recordings with LPCM stereo 5.1 MLP audio. Wide variety of sampling rates (44.1/88.2/176.4, or 48/96/192) and sample sizes (16, 20, 24 bit) possible, as well as optional encoding with DTS and others.
DVD minus R	DVD-R General & Authoring	D: UDF	4.7 or 8.5 GB (DL)	Recording DVD-Video, DVD-Audio, or storing computer data
DVD minus RAM	DVD-RAM	E: UDF	4.7 or 8.5 GB (DL)	Recording, erasing, and re-recording computer data, including audio and video encased in cartridge
DVD minus RW	DVD-RW	F: UDF	4.7 or 8.5 GB (DL)	Recording, erasing, and re-recording computer data, including audio and video

[1]DVDs can be single-sided/single-layer (DVD-5 spec), single-sided/dual-layer (DVD-9 spec), double-sided/single-layer (DVD-10 spec), or, possibly, double-sided/double-layer (DVD-18). Double-sided are avoided due to the necessity of flipping the disc over ("flippers").
[2]A wide variety of audio formats, sampling rates, and sample sizes can be used, just so long as the final bit rate of the disc output is 9.6 Mbps.

- Greatly improved audio compression, such as AAC, DTS, DD 5.1/AC-3, and Meridian Lossless Packing (MLP)
- DD 5.1/AC-3, AAC, or DTS encoded music through DVD-Video disc format
- MLP, DD 5.1/AC-3, and DTS encoded music through the Digital-Audio disc format
- Massive laser disc storage for data, music files, and multimedia

Table 11.3 compares the storage capacity of a CD disc with DVD taking into consideration the number of sides and layers used in the formatting. A DVD disc holds seven times more data than a CD; that's going from 650 MB of data to 4.7 GB of data, or 75 minutes of music to more than seven hours of CD-quality music, or 70 minutes of small-screen digital video to 2.2 hours (133 minutes) of full-screen, full-motion digital video of commercial quality.

It gets even better! DVD is designed so that two layers can be created on one side of the disc to double its capacity. You can have single-sided, single-layer discs (known as DVD-5) or single-sided, double-layer discs (DVD-9). And there's more. The flip side can be recorded on to give you a single-layer, double-sided disc (DVD-10) or a double-layer, double-sided disc (DVD-18) that, once again, doubles the capacity.

DVD Book Formats

Unlike CD formats, the DVD disc was designed to be a computer-compatible standard from the outset. Hence, DVD disc formatting is much easier to understand in all its variations. There is one simple rule to follow: There is only one DVD disc format. At the heart of the DVD format is the Universal Disc Format discussed earlier under CD recording formats. UDF is an alternative to the ISO 9660 standard that uses a random-access file structure that can be supported by most computer operating systems. This means that all DVD media of any type will mount on a computer desktop, just as other disc storage media will mount on the desktop, whether you are using Macintosh, Windows, UNIX, or some other operating system.

There are five DVD Books, all formats using UDF: DVD-ROM, video, audio, and recordable and rewriteable formats (DVD-R, DVD-RAM, and DVD-RW). Table 11.5 provides an overview of the five books.

DVD-ROM and DVD-R Discs: Super-Sized Music Storage

The DVD-ROM architecture follows the UDF disc structure, just like computer files on a hard disc. Data is stored on the disc in *directories*, with *files* stored within directories, and those *files* contain various *data streams* of audio, video, text, graphic images, and the like. Three basic "zones" of content are defined on a DVD-ROM: video zone (VIDEO_TS directory), audio zone (AUDIO_TS) directory, and the "Others Zone," with directories and files of any name and designation. The zones can be viewed in Figure 11.6.

In its simplest form, a DVD-Video disc player expects to find a directory labeled VIDEO_TS on the disc with all of the necessary files for playing a movie inside this directory; a DVD-Audio disc player expects to find an AUDIO_TS directory with all of the files needed to play music inside this directory; and a computer with a DVD-ROM drive has no expectations as to what to find. The UDF directories may contain computer software or application data files for Windows (e.g., "win"), Macintosh ("mac"), or UNIX. Table 11.5 notes that DVD-ROMs are formatted to read the ISO 9660 disc format or the recommended UDF format to ensure compatibility with older computer operating systems.

The DVD-R format (Book D) is the recordable or write-once version of DVD-ROM. It works like a CD-R disc, using a write laser to alter the reflective state of a layer of organic dye embedded in the blank DVD. For a musician, the most desirable application of DVD-R discs is for storing and archiving large digital music files. The capacity of a DVD-R can extend beyond 4.7 GB for single-layer, single-sided, to 9.4 GB for single-layer, double-sided.

DVD-Video Discs: Not Just for Movies

DVD-Video standards are specified in Book B of the DVD Forum. Examine Figure 11.6a. Following the structure described earlier, there is a VIDEO_TS directory, an AUDIO_TS directory that is empty, and miscellaneous files in the "Other Zone" of the disc. Everything needed to play the movie from a DVD-Video player is in the VIDEO_TS directory; this includes files with their data streams for the video, audio, subpictures or subtitles, and menu navigation. This DVD movie, however, also has special features that can be accessed only through a personal computer. In the "Other Zone" are files typical for a Windows OS: win directory, AUTORUN.INS, README.TXT, etc. The "win" directory has setup and installation files for installing software on the computer.

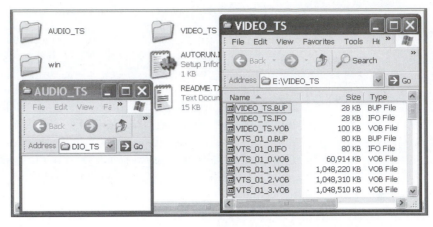

(a)

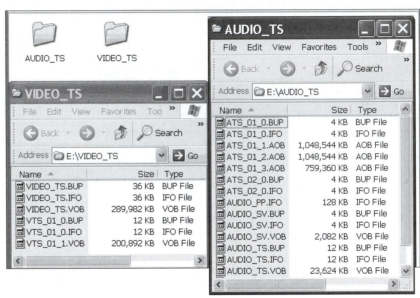

(b)

FIGURE 11.6 Two views of the UDF directory contents of a DVD disc: (a) DVD-Video disc with a feature-length movie and (b) DVD-Audio disc with a music recording

TIP
Each laser format has a maximum bit rate that it cannot exceed due to engineering constraints. These rates are shown in Table 11.5. DVD-Video's maximum bit rate is 4.3 Mbps. The sum of the bit rates of all data streams on a disc cannot exceed this maximum level.

The VOB, or Video Object, files shown in Figure 11.6a are the data streams with the movie contents. The figure shows several VOB files that are more than one gigabyte in size. These files contain the primary digital video and audio content.

The real power in the DVD-Video format is its ability to deliver professional-quality digital video and audio. The video format uses the MPEG-2 standard (Table 11.1), which provides 60-frame-per-second video (commercial-quality delivery speed) and full-screen resolution of 780x480 pixels of 24-bit color. A DVD disc can hold 133 minutes of MPEG-2 video on a single layer, enough time for most feature-length films; two layers provide up to four hours of movie time, enough for those long, director-cut movies like *Lawrence of Arabia*.

DVD Book B specifications provide stereo LPCM digital audio (typically 48-kHz/16-bit sampling), multichannel DD 5.1 audio, and up to eight language sound tracks. Eight independent audio channels are available to accompany video in the Book B standards.

Looking beyond movies and video applications, DVD-Video provides a format for musicians to produce surround-sound digital audio with significantly higher sampling resolution than CD-Audio. The only minimum video content required in the standard is one graphic image. With appropriate DVD recording software, a DVD-Video disc can be dedicated to digital audio without a movie.

At a bit rate of 448 Kbps for DD 5.1 surround sound, more than 24 hours of music could be recorded on a single layer of a DVD with nothing else on the disc but the minimal requirement of a single graphic image. With CD-quality (48-kHz/16-bit), uncompressed LPCM stereo recorded in DVD-Video format, some seven hours of music could be placed on a disc. Increasing the resolution of uncompressed PCM stereo to 96-kHz/24-bit, two hours of music could be recorded. All of these options far exceed the capacity of a CD-audio disc and produce a digital audio disc playable on any DVD-Video disc player without the need for a special decoder.

DVD-Audio or DVD-A Discs:
Testing New Levels of Laser Audio Quality

The DVD-Audio disc (DVD Forum Book C) is a uniquely new format and, in order to achieve the full sonic realism of the data stream coded on the disc, may require a DVD player that can read and decode one of the surround-sound formats: multichannel LPCM, MPEG-2/AAC, MLP, DTS, DSD, or SDDS (refer to Table 11.2). The only requirement of "DVD-Audio" is that the disc have an LPCM data stream of the recording events, either stereo or multichannel, and that the performance be present in a six-channel mix of the highest possible sound quality. All DVD players with the "DVD-Audio" logo must also decode MLP data streams.

The mix of the six channels of surround sound for DVD-Audio is different from the DD 5.1 six-channel sound mix for movies. All of the surround-sound speakers (refer to Figure 11.3) can be treated equally. This means that the rear speakers are used much more intensively than for sound-track effects in a movie, and the super-bass, LFE channel may not be used at all. The .1, in other words, gets dropped in favor of five or six fully used audio channels. The sonic realism of the music performance may be further enhanced by use of Meridian Lossless Packing (MLP) compression sampled at 96-kHz/24-bit, DTS 48-kHz/20-bit, or uncompressed LPCM at 96-kHz/24-bit sampling.

Figure 11.6b shows an example of the UDF directories and files from a typical DVD-Audio disc. The AUDIO_TS directory is the important aspect. VOB files from DVD-Video are now replaced by AOB, or Audio Object, files; you can see that there are three very large AOB files at 1.048 GB, 1.048 GB, and .75 GB.

DVD-A specifications require that the disc have as a minimum an LPCM version of the music, stereo or multichannel LPCM. The audio material may have up to six channels at sample rates of 48, 96, or 192 kHz (also 44.1, 88.2, or 176.4 kHz) and sample sizes of 16, 20, or 24 bits. The disc shown in Figure 11.6b has LPCM stereo versions of the music, a DD 5.1 mix of the music playable on any basic DVD-Video player, and an MLP six-channel mix playable only on a DVD player with "DVD-Audio" decoding.

DVD Recordabes and Rewritables: Many Options

DVD technology wouldn't be very enjoyable or useful if it didn't offer recordable formats that make it easy to exploit the technology from a personal computer desktop or laptop. You can extrapolate from the technical discussion earlier in this module on CD recordable and rewritable format and techniques to DVD. DVD-Rs physically operate using a dye-change technology to create the binary patterns of data; DVD-RWs use a phase-change technology to create the binary

ASIDE

As you've no doubt noted, there are a number of competing laser-disc formats for audio. The question is which format is likely to be the successor to the popular CD-A format for mass-market, consumer use: SACD, DVD-Video with DD 5.1 or DTS, DVD-Audio with MLP or DTS? Only time will tell!

TIP

Caution: When purchasing DVD-Audio discs it is important to note the surround-sound compression options on the disc. A disc of Handel's Messiah produced as a multichannel recording may only be playable in two-channel stereo on your DVD system if you do not have a DTS or DVD-Audio decoder for the surround-sound formats.

LINK
You will find a number of creative, music education applications for CDs and DVDs in Viewport VIII.

TIP
When selecting a DVD player or recorder, check out what formats it will read, for both DVD and CD. Don't assume it reads all formats. And, for the recorders, you'll have to match the blank media with the drive, e.g., a DVD+R blank for a DVD+R recorder is not the same as a DVD-R blank.

patterns. Multisession recording is permissible and a choice may be made between UDF or ISO 9660 disc formats. DVD-R, DVD-RW, and DVD-RAM specifications are officially sanctioned by the DVD Forum. There are a few unique issues with DVD recordables:

- One side of the DVD disc can be recorded, offering 4.7 GB of data on one layer, or 8.5 GB on two layers (the extension of "DL" to the format, e.g., DVD+R DL, denotes the "Double Layer" format.
- DVD recordables have an "authoring" mode and a "general" mode. The general mode is designed for consumer use and, among its differences from the authoring mode, is the lack of copy protection, no data written in the lead-in area of the disc, and some physical differences in laser wavelength, pit addressing, error correction, and the like. The authoring mode is designed for creating masters and test titles for large-production pressed DVD-ROMs.
- DVD-RAM uses a very precise, close-track pitch and, for that reason, requires a cartridge or caddy to enclose and protect the disc from impurities introduced in its handling.

So what are DVD+Rs and DVD+RWs? Sony, Philips, and HP, with many other manufacturers joining in, were looking for a recordable format that was highly compatible with any DVD-Video player or computer DVD-ROM drive. Their solution—not an official standard of the DVD Forum—was DVD+R and DVD+RW. The discs hold 4.7 GB of data on one layer on one side and, since the format is DVD-ROM, computer data, video, or audio should be writeable to the discs. The newer DL format uses double layers on one side for 8.5 GB of storage.

What's Next? New DVD Alternatives

There would certainly seem to be enough options for DVD and the consumer audio, video, and computer market to tap into for some time to come. Nevertheless, the tendency is to always push the engineering edge. To continue to increase the storage space in a single layer, efforts are focused on even more precise systems for recording data with ever decreasing track pitch and pit length. At the same time, low-bit rate MPEG-4 strategies will increase the compression ratio while maintaining the perceived quality of the music and audio.

Blu-Ray format is one example of this effort. It uses blue-violet lasers rather than the red read lasers of current DVDs. This technology would increase the storage capacity of the 4.7-inch disc by some six times. With MPEG-2 compression and the precision of blue-violet lasers, more than 27 GB of computer data could be written on a single layer, or more than two hours of high-definition, HDTV video. BD-ROM and BR-R recordable formats are also planned.

Another area ripe for development is the interactive media potential of DVD. DVD is a standard format for some computer game devices. The ability to embed interactive web links in the materials opens the door for a blending of online and on-disc content constructed not only for computer applications but also for TV and gaming applications. Performing artists could produce albums for on-disc listening enjoyment mixed with online, contemporaneous interactions with the artists, real-time concerts, demos of the newest hit tunes, and the like.

Module 12

Software for Multiple Tracks and Channels

DVD-ROM

Projects 8–10 on the accompanying DVD are designed to give you hands-on experience with the tasks in Table 12.1.

ASIDE

The Musical Instrument Digital Interface (MIDI) format will be described in Viewports V and VI. MIDI is a data structure that describes parameters of sound (pitch on and off, which pitch to play, and how loud to play it); it is up to the connected device or software resource to create the sounds. Digital audio, on the other hand, is a data structure that is the sampled sound itself. DSP chips help record and play back the sounds, as described in Module 6. MIDI files are small and digital audio files are large. The software described in Viewports IV, V, and VI can support both data structures at the same time.

In Viewport III, Module 9, we worked with MP3 audio and with digital-audio editors; this involved a single or dual track of monophonic or stereo audio. The purpose was to collect, organize, and enjoy digital audio and to edit the waveforms. We now take a more creative turn by considering software that:

- records and edits multiple tracks of digital audio
- provides special plug-in effects to treat the audio
- creates multiple tracks of looping sequences
- provides special support for mastering
- creates custom audio CDs or DVDs

As we will soon see, a number of software programs can accomplish these tasks; choosing which one to use depends on your resources and desired end product. Table 12.1 provides a set of tasks that will guide our study.

In this module, we present features that relate strictly to digital audio. Some of the programs described in Viewport V and VI such as Cakewalk Home Studio, SONAR, Cubase SX, Logic Pro, and Digital Performer include multiple tracks of digital audio. Unlike the software described here, those programs began primarily as MIDI programs with digital audio added later.

Important Terms

As we describe multiple-track programs in this module and in software modules to come, it might help to clarify a few commonly used terms and concepts.

Types of Multiple-Track Software

The simple truth is that the categories of multiple-track music software today have no standard nomenclature. When we first began writing our text in 1996, and even its first revision in 1999, there were two major types of multiple-track programs: MIDI and digital audio. As digital audio and MIDI have merged into single programs and as looping software and specialized plug-ins have emerged, the landscape has become much more complex. Here is one approach to organizing these programs.

TABLE 12.1 Tasks for Multiple Tracks and Channels

Setting	Task	Typical Software
Studio or Live Concert Setting	• Record multiple tracks of digital audio from microphones, line sources, and CDs	Audition, Deck, Pro Tools, Samplitude
Studio with or without Live Performers	• Create multiple "takes" of live performances and perform basic editing and built-in effects	Audition, Deck, Pro Tools, Samplitude
Studio	• Apply special plug-in software before final mixing and mastering	GRM Tools, mda, Fxpansion, MixPack, and many more
Studio with Performers or Studio Only	• Create multiple tracks of looping sequences from live or previously recorded digital audio (typically for popular or dance music styles)	Recycle, ACID, GarageBand, Live, FL Studio
Studio	• Mix and master multiple tracks	All software from the first four tasks
Studio	• Prepare multitrack stereo and surround-sound files for distribution	Toast with Jam, SurCode Surround Plug-In Pack, A.Pack with DVD Studio Pro

LINK
Review Table VPIII.1 and the figure showing the evolution of sequencers and the like in the introduction to Viewport III.

Multiple-Track Recorder/Editors

This is software that is designed primarily to record, edit, and store multiple tracks of digital audio mostly for live performance venues, much like a hard-disk recorder or a multiple-track tape recorder. Examples of this kind of software include Audition, Samplitude, Deck, and ProTools. You use this type of software to record a composition with live musicians in a studio or a live concert. This type of software is featured in this module.

Loop-Based Software

This software functions very much like multiple-track titles, but the digital content of the majority of tracks comprises patterns that are meant to loop continuously. The data structures of the loops are also designed to be easily altered to match rhythms and pitch. Examples of this kind of software include GarageBand, ACID, and Live. This software is used to produce dance music or works that might be appropriate for backgrounds to multimedia or film experiences. This type of software is also featured in this module.

Beginning-Level Sequencers

In the past, the term "sequencing" was used to describe multiple-track MIDI software and it continues to be useful in that context. However, most beginning-level sequencing programs like Power Tracks Pro Audio, Cakewalk Home Studio, and Logic Express include some digital audio capabilities as well. The affordability of this software makes it a wise choice for work in a home studio and you could use these titles to record live musicians producing digital audio *together* with MIDI instruments producing MIDI data. This software is featured in Viewport V, Module 15.

Digital Audio Workstation (DAW) Sequencers

This is advanced sequencing software that includes many powerful features you might find in multiple-track editor/recorders. Such advanced software includes more plug-in and effects possibilities, more flexible views for editing and mixing, audio features like pitch shifting and stretching, advanced MIDI editing capabilities, support for multiple sound cards, multiple-track MIDI recording, higher audio resolutions, more varied hardware support, advanced mixing and mastering options, and many other features. DAW software, which is often the most expensive multiple-track software, is used in professional settings. Examples of such software include Logic Pro, Sonar4 Producer Edition, Cubase SX, and Digital Performer. This software is featured in Viewport VI, Module 17.

Virtual Studios

This type of software is only now emerging as an alternative to the major DAW titles noted above. These titles combine software-based synthesizers, samplers, and drum machines with looping, sequencer, and multiple-track recording capabilities for both MIDI and digital audio tracks. Examples of this software include Reason, Storm, FL Studio, and Project5. We describe some of this software in Viewport VI, Module 17, along with virtual instruments and sound programming.

Tracks and Channels

You should have a good understanding of editing "tracks" of audio from the work in Module 9. The tasks were focused on recording and working with mono or stereo sound. In the first module in this Viewport, you learned about surround sound and the many "channels" of audio possible with today's equipment. Confused about the difference between a track and a channel?

Think of tracks as a software idea that represents simultaneous patterns of sound (digital audio or MIDI) from any number of sound sources. These tracks might be recorded all at the same time with separate microphones or "line-in" feeds from instruments, or might be layered one on top of the other in several "takes" during a recording session. In either manner, you wind up with layers of digital audio waveforms or MIDI data that can be edited. Tracks are software representations of recorded sounds in vertical layers.

Channels relate more to the hardware input and output side. For example, you might use a digital audio interface box such as the ones described in Table 13.1 in the next module to help control analog and digital audio coming into and out of your computer. These streams of data are often referred to as channels of sound.

Often, an input and output channel will correspond to a software track, but not always. For example, when you are mixing and creating the final version of your music, you might choose to have a series of tracks "mixed down" to create a stereo mix (two tracks) that will be routed to two channels of output.

Effects, Inserts, and Buses

In Module 9, we described effects processing as an important part of what digital audio editors do. This is true for multiple-track digital audio software as well. Nearly all of the applications described in this module support effects processing, as do many of the software programs highlighted in Viewports V and VI. Special effects can be added with the capability of the host program itself or, most often, with the use of a special plug-in supplied by another company. Since the software described in this module involves many more tracks of sound and because these tracks can be merged, mixed, and treated in complex ways, the special effects possibilities are more complicated. To help keep this straight, consider the following:

LINK
See Module 13 for more detailed information about "channels" and mixers in the hardware context.

TIP
If you skipped the previous Viewport, please turn back to the section at the end of Module 9 that describes basic and advanced effects processing, since many of the concepts we described there apply directly to software in this module!

ASIDE
The term "insert" comes from hardware-based effects devices that are physically inserted into the audio production system. For example, the M-Box described in Table 13.1 in the next module contains ports for hardware inserts.

Insert

Each track can be assigned its own special effect *before* being sent for mixing with other tracks. An effect applied to one track in this manner is often called an "insert." Common inserts include filtering for compressor effects, EQ, and distortion.

Bus

Tracks can be routed together to form a group of tracks that form a "bus." This bus can be assigned a set of inserts before being mixed. This is useful when, for example, a set of vocal tracks needs some reverb or delay effects as a group. This saves you from having to treat each track separately in the same manner. Bus routing also saves valuable computer processing time.

Preparing Your Computer for Digital Audio and MIDI Input and Output

Software in this module (and all of the remaining software modules that use digital audio, MIDI, or both) will profit greatly from special interface hardware such as the devices we describe in Module 13. Your application and operating system software should be informed about what hardware will be used for channel input and output. We begin with the assumption that you have installed the proper "driver" software for the interface hardware. Websites of the particular hardware vendor are almost always the best places to search for the latest drivers.

PC Computers

Figure 12.1 shows how checking the hardware setup might be accomplished for PC computers. The Sound and Audio Devices control panel in Windows has a properties option for audio. In Figure 12.1, we display the options for the Tascam US-428 that we discuss in Module 18, Viewport V. The Tascam provides multiple channels of digital audio in, stereo audio out, and two sets of in/out MIDI ports. Notice that we have set this device to work with both the digital audio in and out (channels A:B) and as the MIDI interface on Port 1. If your audio device is not listed in this control panel, this is a good sign that there may be a problem with installing the driver software for your device or that there is a physical problem with the connections.

Do not assume that an application will automatically figure out what channels you want. Each PC application that uses digital audio and MIDI will have a set of options for you to check within the software that will refer to the hardware you have for MIDI and digital audio. You should routinely look for these settings when using this type of software.

Macintosh Computers

For the Macintosh OS X operating system, it is important to open a utility program called "Audio MIDI Setup" to check both digital audio and MIDI settings. Figure 12.2 shows both the audio (top) and MIDI connections (bottom). The Tascam US-428 is set for audio input and output devices and other settings are offered

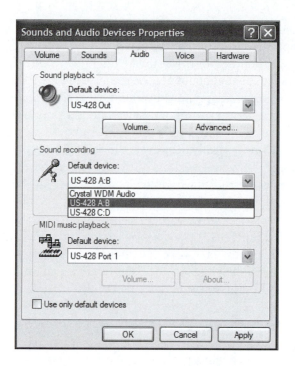

FIGURE 12.1 Windows control panel settings for Tascam US-428

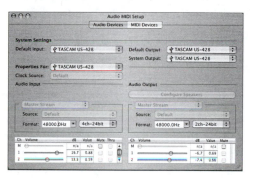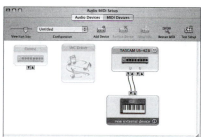

FIGURE 12.2 Audio MIDI setup for OS X

LINK
Module 13 will help you see how these connections are physically made using common hardware interfaces.

to control volume for each track together with resolution and sample rate. The MIDI Devices view shows the various installed software drivers. The Tascam is shown with a MIDI device declared. It is to your advantage to "define" your studio as completely as you can. Under System Preferences in OS X, choose the "Sound" preference and set Output and Input in a similar way to what you would with the PC computer. As with PC software, it is a good idea to confirm these settings in Macintosh applications.

Recording, Editing, and Using Built-In Effects

The first two tasks noted in Table 12.1 involve recording audio from multiple sources, including microphones, CDs, and other "line-in" devices such as tape and DAT recorders. The venue for the first task might be a live concert where microphones are arranged in strategic places and the computer and its software serve as a live recording setup. Although hard-disk recording devices and direct-to-CD

DVD-ROM
Project 8 Recording and Basic Editing with Multiple-Track Sequencers

TIP
Most experts agree that sampling at the highest bit rate you can creates better audio quality, even if you need to return to 16-bit audio for CD creation.

LINK
We described nondestructive editing in Module 9, Viewport III.

TIP
Most multiple-track software supports multiple levels of the "undo," so that even if you do destructive editing, you can back up after several actions.

recorders can do this, computers with the kind of software reviewed here can also capture live performances in concert.

Other uses for this software might be to extract audio from a CD, import a previously created audio file, or record from a MIDI device or from a tape recorder. For example, suppose your friend has recorded a wonderful piano accompaniment on tape. You can import that piano performance to a track and then add a live vocal and/or percussion track to the mix.

More typically, however, the second task in Table 12.1 reveals the power of multiple-track recording software. Here, the software is used to record performances in studios where live performers create tracks several times to form a collection of "takes." The engineer records these takes and then, after the performers are finished, works with the various tracks to create the final mixdown for the recording. This is the approach to recording used by the majority of artists in all music genres. The work flow includes recording sessions, basic and advanced editing (including effects processing), mixing and mastering, and then burning to CD or DVD. The software described in this module can do all of this.

Starting a Project

When you begin a project with multiple-track software, you need several pieces of information. Figure 12.3 displays a typical screen for setting up a project or "session." The figure shows a dialog box from Samplitude. Here we have indicated a 5.1 surround-sound setup that automatically creates six tracks. We have specified a sample rate of 48 kHz, a probable length of 10 minutes for our recording, and have specified bars and beats as our unit of measure.

File Management—Nondestructive and Destructive Editing

The name you give the session in these initial dialog boxes will actually be assigned to a folder that will contain many support files for your project. For example, if you created a project using Deck software and called it "supermix," this folder would contain all of the separate digital audio files imported or created directly through recording for the project, a set of support files for defining effects such as fading, and a small separate file called "supermix."

Most of the changes made to the project, such as assigning the audio to tracks, mixing the tracks, treating the audio with plug-in effects, and many other edits, are all recorded in the small file called "supermix" and *do not affect the original digital audio*. Called "nondestructive editing," this system preserves the original audio files and allows the computer to work more efficiently. Of course, certain tasks found in multiple-track software directly affect and change the content of the digital audio files. This "destructive editing" is identified by the software so that you know what's happening.

The project folder adds more files to this collection as your editing continues and as you do more extensive tasks. Other programs such as Pro Tools, Audition, and Samplitude work the same way. When you are finally ready to save the final multiple-track composition, mixed and mastered, to CD/DVD, the software creates a large, single file with all the pieces combined.

Setting Up Tracks for Recording and Imported Sound

One of the most useful next steps is preparing the tracks for recording and imported sound. Figure 12.4 shows the opening display for Samplitude. We have asked the software to create a project with four tracks. The region to the left shows

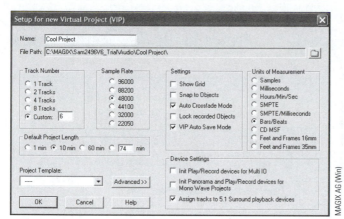

FIGURE 12.3   Samplitude Producer 2496

FIGURE 12.4   Samplitude track information

the track headers with adjustments for volume and pan, as well as meters to monitor the tracks' input levels. More about these controls shortly. Notice that no waveforms are shown in the track data windows since audio has not been recorded or imported. The window in the right foreground is the Track Info dialog that is activated when clicking on the track header. Here we specify: (1) the sources that will be used for input and output of data, (2) the kind of data for the track (Audio or MIDI), and (3) the name of the track (in this case "lead vocal"), along with links to other functions. This information, which must be set for all tracks, allows you to specify the source of the incoming and outgoing data, such as microphones or "line-in" devices attached to a hardware input/output (I/O) device. Outgoing sound can be rerouted with the mixer controls as well, as you will soon see, but these settings can get you started with your project.

Notice the buttons in the track header labeled "Rec," "Solo," and "Mute." The Solo and Mute buttons control playback options, but the Rec button empowers the recording process. Simply click this button to "arm" the track for recording and then click the Record button in the Transport window on the lower left. Perform some music and digital audio is recorded! The Mute button can be used to quiet an unwanted track during recording or playback and the Solo button can turn a track on and all the others off.

Each program follows a different procedure for importing CD audio directly from a CD or simply using a previously created audio file for a track. For example, Deck first requires that you add audio to a working library of sounds that can be used for the tracks. Audition allows you to extract a CD track into its Edit view and uses the Insert menu to offer a way to import a WAV file. ProTools and Samplitude have similar features.

Editing

If you were recording a live concert, you would record all the tracks of audio at once, with each included in the final mix after editing. If you were in a studio working on a recording with live musicians, you would likely record several tracks of audio for your project with the hope of saving the best tracks and deleting others. In either case, you will want to perform some basic editing using the flexible features of this software.

FIGURE 12.5 Project overview in Audition

FIGURE 12.6 Project overview in Pro Tools

ASIDE

Punching in and out allows for adding new material to replace what was originally recorded. The in and out points provide references for where new material should go when you are performing. This will be described again with MIDI sequencing software in Module 15, Viewport V.

Basic Operations

To gain a sense of the basic editing operations of multiple-track software, we begin with a careful look at major editing screens from two programs. Figure 12.5 displays a small project in Audition and Figure 12.6 is a more sophisticated example in Pro Tools.

In the Audition graphic, we have arranged several important windows. This is the "multitrack view" of this software and four tracks are shown in the center. Notice that the tracks have the digital audio starting at different times. Each of these audio regions in the tracks can be moved around as objects. A timeline at the bottom of the tracks shows the recording unfolding in time (other units of measurement are also possible, such as beats/measures) and the vertical line running through the tracks in the playhead is for playback.

To the right is the mixer window, which controls the volume of each track and of the master recording. The mixer window is also a place to add special effects and to route output in different ways. The mixer window in multiple-track software functions much like a hardware mixer.

To the left of the tracks is the track header information, which is similar to that in other software. Notice the buttons for Record, Solo, and Mute, as well as the volume and pan settings. Still further to the left is the list of separate audio files that make up each track. Double-clicking on any of these files moves Audition into the "Edit Waveform" view, which allows the user to make destructive edits with these original files. The MIDI, WAV, and video files that can be added to the project would be listed here as well.

Along the bottom are the controls for playback in Audition. The buttons with the magnifying glasses control the view size of the tracks. The usual counter is displayed, with a level meter displaying overall volume. There are also settings for beginning and end points for looping and for punching in and out. Settings for tempo, key, and meter are provided as reference points for editing.

In the Pro Tools graphic, many of the same window functions apply. The list of audio files on the right represent the many "takes" that have occurred during the session. Notice that not all of these are used in the waveform window in the center. The track header options are similar to those in Audition, but are minimized to make room for all the tracks. Track names appear to the extreme left; you can control the visibility of the tracks here. Buttons along the top allow you to grab objects, select regions, and change the size of views. The pencil tool allows you to redraw the waveforms at a micro level and the speaker icon represents a "scrubbing" tool that allows you to audit specific parts of the track by moving the cursor over the represented audio. Transport and Mixer windows although not shown, do exist. In each of these programs and in nearly all multiple-track software, menu items control opening and saving options, as well as access to built-in effects.

Specific Options

Take another look at Figures 12.5 and 12.6. We have noted that the objects or blocks of sound that get recorded in each of the tracks can be moved around. As a complete unit, they can be cut, copied, and pasted just like words in a word-processing program. It is possible to shift the blocks in time and then lock them in place. Blocks can also be grouped so that a shifting operation can be done on units across tracks. Blocks can be duplicated one after the other to create a loop, although the software described in the next section is better for extensive looping.

Figure 12.7 displays a pop-up window in Audition for editing a block of sound. To make this window appear, you right-click on any block of audio. Note the many options for just this one small block of audio, the one in the very first track. Among the many options, you can adjust volume, panning, loop options, muting, and even removal. These edits can be made for just one block of sound in one track.

If you choose to edit the waveform of the block, you can do so by double-clicking on the block or choosing the first option on the menu in Figure 12.7. In Figure 12.8, we show the options for deleting or trimming a section of the block by using markers to indicate a selection area. The software can even help you find a zero-crossing point in the waveform so you can have a very clean edit with no clicks or pops. Using typical characteristics of the waveform, the software can also attempt to find a rhythmic beat to aid in editing. At this level of editing, you can insert or delete silence or mix sounds using the clipboard.

FIGURE 12.7 Menu for sound block editing of effects in Audition

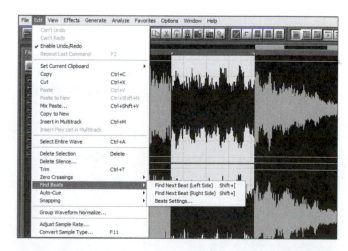

FIGURE 12.8 Working with waveforms in Audition

LINK

Be sure to review the effects processing description in Module 9.

Built-In Effects

Just like audio editing software, this software category includes a large number of built-in effects. In general terms, built-in effects are either applied to (1) a single block of sound destructively or (2) multiple tracks nondestructively. If you apply effects to single blocks, the software may alter the original waveform; for this reason, it is a good idea to make a backup of your project if you intend to do a great deal of editing on individual blocks of sound. The application of destructive effects is also cumulative. If you add a reverb first and then EQ, the EQ gets applied to the reverb-treated sound. The order you apply these effects in is important.

For effects that are applied to larger amounts of sound found in a single track or groups of tracks, the result may not affect the original waveforms and could be easily removed or reapplied in different ways. Such effects are often applied concurrently in sets, or "racks," of effects. The more of these effect combinations that are applied, the more processing power is required by the computer. Be cautious about how much effects processing you use in this way so that you avoid performance problems. Plug-in effects described in another section of this module are often used in this multiple-track, nondestructive manner.

Each software program uses the families of built-in effects described in Module 9 in different ways and experimentation with one program or another will lead you to conclude which is most comfortable. The family groupings described in Module 9 were: amplitude, time, frequency, timbre, and specialized. We do not have space to describe all of the built-in effects in multiple-track software, but we have included a few examples below. We start with effects applied to waveforms in sound blocks and move to effects applied to larger units.

Block-Level Effects

In "edit-view," Audition provides a number of block-level effects. These include examples from all the classic families. In terms of filters from the timbre family, Audition offers a few special examples. Figure 12.9 demonstrates a notch filter that is very useful for removing artifacts. The filter removes precisely defined frequencies while leaving others alone. We have shown the preset for removing vocal sibi-

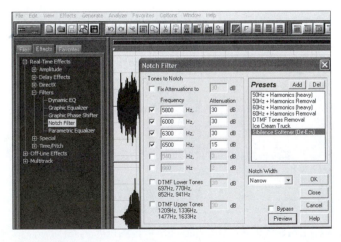

FIGURE 12.9 Notch filter in Audition

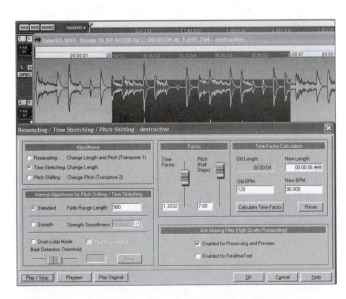

FIGURE 12.10 Resampling/time stretching/pitch shifting in Samplitude

lance that might be useful when working with speech and/or choral music. This type of effect is similar to noise reduction that treats clicks, hisses, and noise.

Another block example comes from the time and frequency family in Samplitude (Figure 12.10), the Resampling/Time Stretching/Pitch Shifting effect. This destructive effect is excellent for fixing a problem with an instrument or voice sound that might be slightly out of tune or enters/leaves the mix at the wrong point rhythmically. Notice the powerful options for changing both length and pitch or each separately. Precise controls allow you to select just the right part of a waveform and make carefully crafted adjustments.

Track-Level Effects

Figure 12.11 shows Audition in "Multitrack View." Right-clicking on an empty track creates this pop-up menu with many options for that track. The "Insert" menu item allows insertion of WAV files, MIDI data, and even video. "Mix Down to Track" can be used to merge many selected waveforms down to a single track. We will address this capability when we deal with mixing and mastering as important last steps in creating a finished recording. Other items in this menu deal with effects that can be applied directly to the entire track. We have revealed two windows in the lower left that are called into action by this menu: Track Equalizers and Track Properties. The equalization settings offer basic control over low, mid, and upper frequencies. More exact filtering is possible with other tools in the software. The track properties window leads to control of effects that might be assigned to the track.

Applying Built-In Effects Singularly and in Groups

How do you assign these effects to a track or set of tracks? In Audition, one way is to select the regions within a track or tracks and then choose one of the highlighted effects in the list to the left in Figure 12.11. This leads to a dialog box similar to the one in the upper right of Figure 12.12, which we have called "big sound." In this setup, we have added two effects together to apply to many track regions at once (note the selected areas in the multiple tracks in the background).

FIGURE 12.11 Menu for track editing of effects in Audition

FIGURE 12.12 Rack set of built-in effects in Audition

Racks   These two effects (Dynamic Processing and Stereo Field Rotate) are used together in a "rack" of sounds defined by the box in the lower center of the figure. The small mixer tab in the "big sound" dialog controls how much of each effect to add to the mix, as well as whether the effects are applied in parallel or serially. You can apply even more effects to the rack if your computer's processing power will allow it. This creates a great deal of possibilities for sound experimentation.

Buses   An additional option is to define a rack arrangement such as the one depicted in Figure 12.13 but rather than assigning it to a region, apply it to a whole track through "bus" routing. In this figure, we have created a rack set that is assigned to Bus "A." This bus is called "voice processing" and can be assigned to vocal tracks in the mix. This is done in the section of the track header that is just to the left of the waveforms. The beauty of this arrangement is that the vocal tracks that need to be treated in a similar way can be assigned to one rack set for efficiency.

Other Approaches

All of these procedures are relevant for Audition, but other programs use different approaches to track-level effects. Figure 12.14 displays a very common kind of track editing in Deck: envelope shaping with a kind of "rubber band" interface. In this case, the volume of a track is being changed, but basic panning can also be controlled this way. You simply click once to create a point and move the cursor in a particular direction to create a linear slope. This approach is used in many of the software titles in this module and is a form of automated editing that we will see again in other sections of the text.

Deck also allows you to add track-level effects in combination by using the major mixer window. In Figure 12.15, we show the addition of a Delay and a Gain effect in Track 1 as part of the Mixer window in the center foreground. To the right is the Effect window that displays the slider controls for the characteristics of the Delay: length, feedback, cutoff, and wet control. The Gain has one simple slider control.

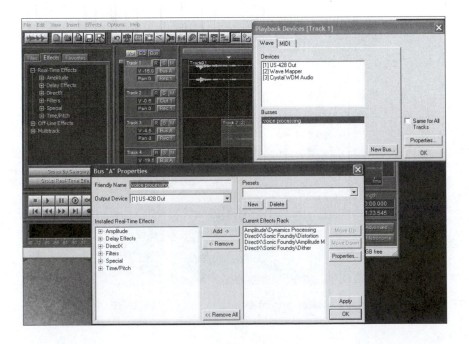

FIGURE 12.13   Bus arrangement for built-in effects in Audition

FIGURE 12.14   Rubber band envelope editing in Deck

FIGURE 12.15   Mixer control for effects in Deck

Effects Plug-Ins

We now move to the third task in Table 12.1, the application of plug-in software for special effects. Plug-in effects were first presented in Module 9 in terms of their use with audio editors. With multiple-track software, plug-in effects are even more important. They are used extensively with this software and the software described in Modules 15 and 17.

Categories of Plug-Ins

The plug-ins we noted in Module 9 and those reviewed here are all designed to alter a previously recorded digital track or track portion in meaningful ways. We call these "effects plug-ins." A second major category is "instrument plug-ins," which are designed to create sounds that emulate instruments such as classic synthesizers and drums. Some of these can be fully functional synthesizers and samplers in their own right. A third, somewhat less popular, category is "MIDI plug-ins," which are designed to alter MIDI data. We will present these latter two groups in Modules 15 and 17 when we work with beginning-level sequencing and more advanced DAW software.

How Plug-Ins Are Called into Action

Plug-ins are often manufactured by companies other than the ones that make host software and can only work in cooperation with a host. The ones that are engineered to also run as stand-alone applications are becoming more common. Figure 12.16 shows how plug-ins are often used in multiple-track software. Notice how Pro Tools refers to these plug-ins from the Mixer window on the right, much like the approach used in Deck in Figure 12.15. You simply click on one of the "slots" for a track in the mixer display—in this case, a black dot in the middle of a rectangular box. Plug-ins installed in the plug-in folder for the host software are displayed as options. Here, we are adding a plug-in for Track 1. Track 2 already has

LINK
Review our introduction to effects plug-ins in Module 9.

TIP
All the plug-ins that we describe in this book can be used effectively with editors (Module 9), multiple-track programs and loop-based software (Module 12), sequencers and DAW software (Module 15), and virtual studios (Module 17).

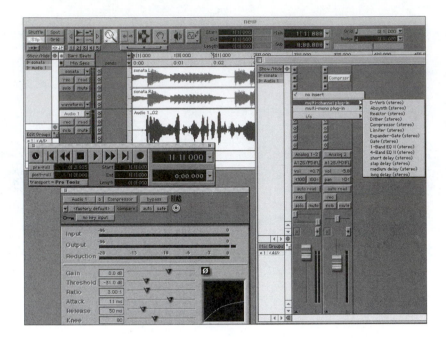

FIGURE 12.16 Adding plug-ins in ProTools

TIP
Companies that create effects plug-ins such as the ones described here frequently change their products, so check carefully.

ASIDE
If a certain platform cannot host a format, companies have written special "wrapper" utilities that solve this problem. For example, Fxpansion sells a VST to AudioUnits utility that lets OS X users take advantage of the VST plug-in.

the "compressor" effect chosen and is listed as such. Notice the open window at the lower left that displays controls for the compressor plug-in.

Some software refers to these locations in mixer windows as "inserts." Just as with the built-in effects described above, these inserts can be organized into rack sets (see Figure 12.13) and routed with special buses (see Figure 12.14). We will deal with this again when we get to mixing and mastering at the end of this module. This may all sound complicated, but it really is much easier to use than it sounds. A little experience with how a particular program uses these routing options with built-in effects and effects plug-ins will help clarify things.

Overview of Effects Plug-Ins

Table 12.2 provides a listing of effects plug-ins that can be added to the multiple-track software described in this module. Some of these products are bundled sets and others are single-function sets. There are more than 100 such products on the market today; we display a cross-section representing various contents, formats, host platforms, and costs.

Format and the Platform

Not all host programs support the same format. With the greater processing power of today's computers, "native" solutions that do not require expensive special gear are much more common.

The most common native formats for plug-ins are: (1) VST (Virtual Studio Technology), originally designed by the Steinberg software company; (2) DirectX, designed by Microsoft for the Windows operating system; (3) AudioSuite and RTAS (Real Time Audio Suite), developed by Digidesign to work with ProTools; and (4) MAS (MOTU Audio System), designed by Mark of the Unicorn to work with its popular Digital Performer program for the Macintosh. VST formats work in many host applications on both Macintosh and Windows computers, whereas the DirectX format works with host programs only on the PC platform. The AudioSuite and RTAS formats work only with ProTools on both Macintosh and PC computers.

TABLE 12.2	Examples of Effects Plug-Ins			
Plug-In	**Type and Content**	**Format**	**Host Platform**	**Approx. Cost**
mda-vst (Paul Kellet)	**Bundle:** Combo, Delay, Detune, Dub Delay, Leslie Simulator, Round Panner, Stereo Simulator, Dynamics, De-esser, Limiter, and many more	AU, VST	Mac/Win	Free
MixPack (PSPaudiowave)	**Bundle:** MixBass, MixSaturator, MixPressor, MixTreble	VST	Mac/Win	$100
Ultrafunk Sonitus:fx Plug-In Pack (Ultrafunk)	**Bundle:** Compressor, Six-Band Parametric Equalizer, Modulator, Phase Adjust, Reverb, Surround Panner, Wah-Wah	VST, DirectX	Win	$200
Ina-GRM Tools (distributed by Electronic Music Foundation)	**Bundle:** Delays, Doppler, Freezing, Reson (special filtering)	VST, RTAS, TDM	Mac/Win	$349
Native Bundle (TC Works)	**Bundle:** EQ, Dynamic Processing, Reverb, Limiting, Maximizing	VST, MAS	Mac/Win	$499
Restoration Bundle (Waves)	**Bundle:** X-Click, X-Noise, X-Crackle, and X-Hum	RTAS, AudioSuite, VST, MAS, DirectX	Mac/Win	$1,200
SuperFreq (Bias)	**Single Purpose:** Equalization	VST	Mac	$70
Vintage Warmer (PSPaudiowave)	**Single Purpose:** Analog Multiband Compressor	VST, DirectX, MAS	Mac/Win	$149
Spektral Delay (Native Instruments)	**Single Purpose:** Delay	Stand-alone, VST, AU	Mac/Win	$300
Altiverb (AutoEase)	**Single Purpose:** Reverb	HTDM, RTAS, AU, VST and MAS	Mac	$500

One other format is important for software running on Macintosh computers. With the creation of Apple's Core Audio strategy for its OS X operating system, the AU (AudioUnits) format for plug-ins is very popular. It is built directly into the code for OS X and, for that reason, creates a very fast (low-latency) response time for working in real time.

Real-Time Response Real-time response is very important in working with these formats. When you are experimenting with effects, you want to immediately hear what the effect does for the track and be able to compare different parameter settings. All of the major formats (VST, RTAS, MAS, AU, DirectX) support real time, but you should check on how this will work with your own computer before you buy.

Plug-In Automation Another aspect of plug-in formats is their ability to automate during a recording. Automation is a topic we describe later in our section on mixing and mastering. In the context of plug-ins, automation involves manipulating parameters in real time during performance and recording changes so they are recreated automatically on playback. For example, if you are working with an echo effect that fades into a transition from one melody to another, you want your plug-in to record this action automatically so that when you play it back again it will be retained. All of the major formats support automation in their most recent versions, but you should check this carefully to be sure.

LINK
Refer back to Table 10.2 for information on DirectX, CoreAudio, and latency.

ASIDE
Advanced work with effects processing is a complex topic that we cannot treat with the justice it deserves. See the Selected Readings section at the back of this text for sources on this topic. Check the Internet, too, for online tutorials with specific plug-ins and for effects processing in general.

Cost

Powerful plug-ins for professional work can be some of the most expensive software in music technology. As your needs develop, you may find that paying for more expensive effects plug-ins is a natural and important part of your work, but you will not need to spend a great deal as you get started. Note from our examples in Table 12.2 that there are a number of free or inexpensive products. Free plug-ins are often made available on the Internet by generous programmers who have the altruistic desire to aid the creative process and music making.

Type and Content

We will examine a few of these native effects plug-ins. A review of the content for each of the examples offered in Table 12.2 shows that each of the effects families in Module 9 is well represented.

Single Purpose   Various single-purpose plug-ins might offer a level of sophistication that simple built-in effects do not. Figure 12.17 is an example from the amplitude family. Vintage Warmer is a compressor effect that is especially good for emulating older analog tape recorders and the special effects possible with those devices. Its appearance in the editing window has a neat retro look. Compressors can use filters to limit defined frequencies in such a way as to make certain tracks more or less pronounced. Notice that this software supports single- and multiband modes. In single-band mode, the entire signal is treated, and in multiband mode the signal is split into regions that are separately controlled. Meters for monitoring are provided and a number of presets that come with the software are useful for premixing work and for the final mastering (which is likely where you will use this the most).

Figure 12.18 displays a powerful reverb plug-in called Altiverb. Similar to the Acoustic Mirror feature in Sound Forge, this plug-in allows you to treat a signal

FIGURE 12.17   Vintage Warmer

FIGURE 12.18   Altiverb

based on reverberation algorithms from famous concert halls. You can create custom settings as well.

SuperFreq (Bias, Inc. [Mac]) is an advanced equalization plug-in that offers parametric control over 10 bands of frequencies. Parametric equalization allows more detailed control over the gain (db), resonance (Q), and frequency range (Hz) in the 10 bands. Different kinds of filters can be applied (peak, notch, high-shelf, low-shelf, high-cut, and low-cut) and individual bands can be bypassed completely. Parametric EQ is more precise than graphic EQ, which is offered in built-in effects.

Bundles   The families of effects represented in the bundle sets we feature here cannot be easily placed in one group or another. For example, the Ultrafunk bundle includes amplitude and frequency-alteration effects, whereas the MixPack set provides support for the final stages of mixing and mastering and the Restoration Bundle is designed to treat noise-filled tracks. The Ina-GRM, Native, and mda bundles are excellent all-purpose sets that provide advanced options for a variety of effects processing.

DVD-ROM
Project 9 Creating a Loop-Based Composition

Loop-Based Software

Before moving to the final stages of mixing, mastering, and creating a CD or DVD, it's important to review one final category of multiple-track recording: loop-based software. In Module 9, we introduced the idea of loops (both sustained and sequential) and how digital editors can help to edit and create them. Here, we focus on the sequential loop and its use in multiple-track software.

As we have noted, sequential loops are found in many popular genres of music, including techno, soul, dance, rap, and the many forms of rock. Music for motion pictures and television might also use sequential loops as a basis for scoring. In this section of the module, we focus on multiple-track recording software that specializes in using loops as a basis for composition.

Sequential loops comprise music structures that are 1–10 measures in length and that have crafted beginning and end points that allow the loop to repeat without an anomaly like a pause or "hiccup" in the sound. In the early days of using loops without special software, it was difficult to get the loops to work together in multiple tracks. There would be problems with each loop "locking" together and, over time, they would drift apart. It was also very hard to easily change tempo and key.

Slicing Digital Audio

To solve the problem of loop synchronization and to allow users to have flexibility in changing a composition's tempo and key without affecting synchronization, a system was developed for "slicing" the individual notes, drum hits, or other segments into marked areas. The individual sounds of the instruments are not changed, but an edit list or playlist of markers is created that can help alter tempo and key and aid in synchronization. This is a more efficient way of handling changes than using the complicated digital signal processing (DSP) techniques described earlier. Audio files with this marking system in place can be purchased as special loop libraries from any number of commercial vendors that sell them on CDs for any style of music. These prepared loops can be audited and then added to a composing project. You can also import a digital audio file from a regular CD or other source into a loop-based software program that uses a process called "transient detection" to add markers based on the peaks in the audio file.

The first software program to offer a slicing function was ReCycle (Propellerhead Software, Inc. [Mac/Win]). ReCycle is not a multiple-track program, but a utility that creates the slicing markers for an imported digital audio file and then saves the file in the REX-2 format for use with sequencing programs like Reason, Logic, and Cubase, which are described in Module 17. Recycle can be used to create loop beginning and end points and help with other editing tasks in preparing loops for hardware sequencers or for other software.

The ACID Scene and Looping Software

No, this has nothing to do with drugs, but with a software program that is perhaps the most popular for multitrack, loop-based work. The ACID software comes in many versions, but here we concentrate on ACID Pro, the most capable of them. Other versions include ACID Xpress and ACID Music Studio. A special version for children, Super Duper Music Looper, is featured in Viewport VIII, Module 23. We will use ACID Pro software to explain the basic functions of looping software and end this section by highlighting other well-known programs for looping work.

Composition Construction

Figure 12.19 provides a good overview of the multiple-track environment for ACID. There are two working areas: the Timeline on the top and the Docking area on the bottom. The Timeline contains the basic menu icons, the multiple tracks in a timeline arrangement, and the strip at the bottom that reveals the tempo, key, and controls for playback and recording. The Docking area includes any windows in the program that can be "docked" or displayed as part of this bottom section. In this case, we show two traditional windows: the Explorer window that displays how files are organized on the hard drive and the Mixer window. Like much music software, all the windows are resizable.

Take a moment to study the layout. The top of the timeline has markers that indicate important changes in tempo, time signature, and key. These changes affect the entire score. Waveforms for each loop are included in each track. Notice that the loops are not in every "measure" of the score; this means that they only sound in the composition as the entire timeline is played from left to right. The composer simply chooses the loop file from the list of files in the Explorer window and then "paints" them into the track where needed. Each track contains a loop file ready to play based on where the painting occurs—one loop per track. Notice

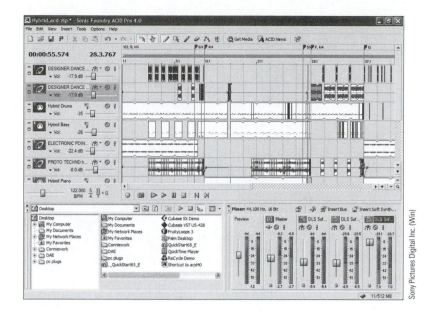

FIGURE 12.19 Overall view of ACID's workspace

that in our example, the "Designer Dance" loop is used in both the first and second tracks because the composer wanted to treat this loop differently in the composition. Envelope controls for panning, volume, and special effects are also displayed on each track. To the left of each track is the header information, which contains information about the kind of media (digital audio, video, or MIDI files) and other track properties, such as volume and special effects.

The Explorer window allows the composer to locate loops that may be added to the project and also allows pre-auditing of the loops so that you can hear just what you are adding. The Mixer window provides ways to master the whole output, allowing for organization of plug-ins and bus routing similar to what we described for other multiple-track software.

Editing

Figure 12.20 displays an example of editing techniques. You can see some editing options for a single track. Notice the little notch in the waveform graphic just below the measure indicator for 9.1. This notch is the indicator for the end point for a loop and the beginning of the next loop. If needed, the composer can use the eraser tool to eliminate the material right after the end of the loop. The menu options also can be used to cut, copy, and delete selected areas and split and join loops in different ways. Sections can also be raised and lowered in pitch without changing tempos. A Chopper window is also available that allows fine-tuning of a loop. A loop can be shifted one way or the other and a "fade" can be added as a subtle adjustment.

Just as with multiple-track programs such as Deck and Audition, built-in and DirectX plug-ins are easily added to ACID for single tracks or for groups of tracks with routing techniques. These effects can be added in chains and audited in real time so that you can hear the changes.

Adding Loop Material from Independent Sources

Up to this point, we have been working with loops that already come from ACID either as part of the program's library of loops or as loops found on commercial loop CDs. How about creating new loop material from other sources? ACID allows you to import any digital audio source as the basis for loops. Just as ReCycle

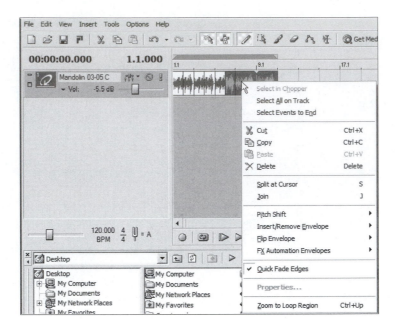

FIGURE 12.20 Editing options in ACID

and digital audio editing programs can create sequential loops, so can ACID by recording live audio or importing audio from a CD or other source.

Also, each track can contain nonlooping material as well! For example, you can import a vocal line from a CD or record an oboe solo as a track of audio just as with other multiple-track recording programs and treat that audio as a single line of nonlooping material. Under that track, you can add drum or keyboard loops or whatever you want as accompaniment as you construct your composition.

Whenever ACID imports sound of this sort, it assumes that you want to "beat-map" or add markers to provide flexibility. Figure 12.21 displays the Beatmapper Wizard from ACID that comes up automatically when it senses that beatmapping might be necessary. This procedure scans the digital audio and makes its best guess as to where the markers might go. The grid markings in Figure 12.21 show this

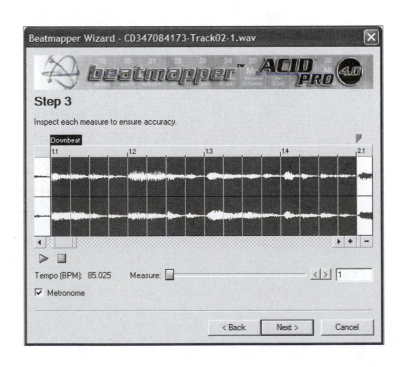

FIGURE 12.21
Beatmapper Wizard in ACID

with a new line of imported digital audio; it allows you to listen to determine if any changes are necessary. Remember that this system does not literally segment the audio; it just places markers that might be helpful in guiding the alteration of pitch or tempo. After adding additional loop material in other tracks, these markers also ensure synchronization.

Of course, all the original sound clips and loops used in a project are never touched because all the steps for creating a composition are nondestructive. After a composition has been edited, effects have been added, and the final mix has been completed, ACID can save the entire set of tracks into a single final data file as MP3, WAV, AIF, MOV, RM, and many other final formats. Rendering in surround-sound format will be presented in the final section of this module.

Other Looping Software

GarageBand

ACID and its product family are not the only loop-based multiple-track programs available. GarageBand, a part of the iLife series of software products freely distributed with new Macintosh computers, offers looping capabilities, as well as live digital audio recording and basic MIDI sequencing. Figure 12.22 shows the basic interface for GarageBand. The top graphic displays the tracks, controls, and loop window list. Clicking on the "plus" button adds a track and you can choose either a "real instrument" or a "software instrument." If a real instrument is chosen, a track is created in the list and the software is ready to accept live digital audio recorded from an acoustic instrument or voice. If a software instrument is chosen, a timbre is provided by the software and you can use a connected MIDI device to record content.

Previously designed loops can be used for software instruments; you can find these on the list at the bottom of the top graphic in Figure 12.22. Notice that they

LINK
Some of the MIDI sequencing capabilities of GarageBand will be clearer after reading Viewport V, Module 15.

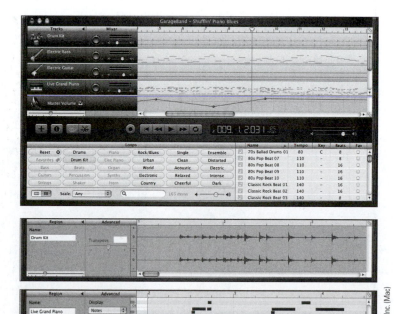

FIGURE 12.22
GarageBand

Apple Computer, Inc. (Mac)

are organized into categories on the left. "Drums" has been selected and the list of separate loops for drums is provided on the right. Clicking on the individual loops will play the loop. Once you have found a loop that you like, you can drag it into the track for the software instrument you want and adjust the loop's length, much like you can do with ACID. The software allows you to control the loudness of each track and of the overall file. Both the digital audio and MIDI data in Garage-Band can be edited. The bottom two graphics in Figure 12.22 display the windows that replace the loop list when you double-click on a track's data. Notice that both the MIDI data and the digital audio can be transposed to different keys and MIDI data can be adjusted or "quantized" to a specific timing grid.

Finally, GarageBand allows you to assign effects processing for both real and software instruments. Figure 12.23 shows this capability. Double-clicking on the track instrument's name in the track window reveals this dialog. Here, we have chosen the Hollywood Strings instrument and have chosen the Treble Reduction effect as one effect and the brightness level (equalization) as another.

A nice feature of GarageBand is its ability to save a final composition mix into a two-track, 16-bit, 44-kHz AIF file that can be exported to iTunes for CD burning. It can be compressed in iTunes to MP3 or AAC and can then be exported to your iPod, used on the Web, or burned to CD.

Live

Figure 12.24 shows an overview of Live. This software has many of the same characteristics as ACID. In the center of the screen, the Arrange view of a composition with several tracks is displayed. Three tracks are revealed here with the names and waveforms of each. As in ACID, you can drag the loops into the track area and fill up the measures. You can also add multiple loop files of different bit rates and resolutions in the same track space.

Track header information in this program is to the right, with the usual controls for soloing, muting, and recording. Above the track area are the indicators for measures and a place for entering markers. Above that is the overview graphic, which displays a representation of the entire composition. To the far left is a

LINK

Live works interactively with programs like Reason (see Viewport VI, Module 17) using a linking system called "ReWire." This allows Live to use even more sound sources. ReWire will be explained in more depth in Module 17.

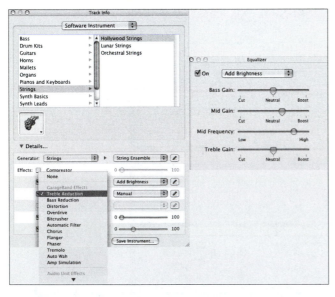

FIGURE 12.23   Effects processing in GarageBand

FIGURE 12.24   Live

Ableton, Inc. (Mac/Win)

browser-like window that contains listings for samples on the hard disk, available plug-ins, and built-in effects.

Below the track area are windows for describing what the mouse cursor is positioned over, including information about the highlighted loop and tools for possible changes to the loop. If plug-ins and special effects are applied to the loops, control boxes for these are displayed in this space as well. An entirely different view of the action in Live can be chosen that shows the mixer controls and the layout of the loops in section order from beginning to end.

One of the powerful features of Live is its ability to support the live performing musician with flexible sound routing. Loops can be preaudited to a set of headphones by routing the sounds to separate channels of a multiple-channel output device such as a four-channel sound card. This allows the musician to hear what is coming next before the sound can be routed to the main speakers. Live also allows you to record a performance with an onboard sequencer.

FL Studio

FL Studio (formally Fruityloops) is yet another software program best placed in the looping family. Although it could be compared to a virtual environment such as those described in Module 17 because of its many sound sources, such as soft synths, and its support for MIDI, it really is a loop-based program with a strong accent on pattern design.

Take a close look at Figure 12.25. You might begin composing with some choices about timbres displayed in the browser window to the far left. Choices to be made from the TS404 soft-synth presets in the middle of the list are revealed, but speech sounds, installed "SoundFonts," and many other built-in sounds are also possible. The Playlist window is the place where you organize the longer composition. Each pattern track is a set of patterns that are assigned timbres from the browser. In this example, we have dragged the "bass'n'drum" into Pattern Track 1, the "Bee" sound into Pattern Track 2, and so on.

To the far right is the step-sequencer, a set of 16 buttons (corresponding to a sixteenth note) that can be activated to play a repeated pattern (much like an older-style, hardware drum machine). We have entered a pattern for the "bass n'drum" line and then have returned to the playlist to draw in the places in the timeline where this pattern will play. Pitched pattern information for the

LINK
See Viewport VI, Module 18, for more on SoundFonts.

FIGURE 12.25
Overview of FL Studio

GrandPiano#2 timbre in Pattern Track 7 has been added in the Piano Roll editor in the lower center of the screen. The Channel Settings window in the lower right allows you to alter the timbre.

FL Studio can work as a stand-alone program or as a VST instrument plug-in with a host application. The software is best used for looping patterns that are quite rhythmic and it offers a number of complex options for loop work.

DVD-ROM
Project 10 Mixing, Mastering, and Burning a CD

TIP
Learning to mix and master as we describe here is an important part of using modern music technology to develop your own recordings. These very complex topics tax your aural skills and your understanding of sound design, hardware, and software. Much can be learned by experimenting as a novice, but getting professional advice for mixing and mastering your music production is highly recommended.

LINK
Be sure to read Module 13 for information on mixing hardware.

Mixing, Mastering, and Distributing

In this last major section of the module, we turn our attention to the final phases of music preparation with multiple-track software. Take one more look at Table 12.1 and the last two tasks: mixing/mastering the multiple tracks into a final audio file for distribution and then preparing a file for distribution on the Internet, as some kind of tape or MiniDisc recording, or as a CD or DVD. All of this work is done in the studio well after the performers have left.

Mixing and Mastering: Really the Same Thing?

No. They both may use similar effects and plug-ins but they really are two very different steps. Mixing is the process of working with individual tracks in a multiple-track recording to achieve a sense of balance in space: left, right (panning) and backwards, forwards (volume). In the case of stereo mixing, you work with panning and volume with two speakers. In the case of more than two speakers, such as with surround sound, you work with panning and volume in more complex arrangements. Mixing also includes working with special effects such as those discussed in this module and in Module 9.

For example, suppose you are working with a multiple-track recording of a country band with backup vocalists, a vocal soloist, guitars, drums, and violin. Each instrument is recorded on separate tracks. In addition to placing the tracks in the left to right panning zones to simulate the way the band is heard in live concert, and working carefully with the software mixer faders to be sure the balance is correct throughout the song, you might also apply a little reverb to the backup vocalists to enhance their role. Just a touch of amplitude modulation (vibrato) is nice for the violin line in spots and the drums need some compression to make the sound even.

All these adjustments are done as fine-tuning before the final "mixdown." A mixdown occurs when you ask the multiple-track software to "bounce" to disc or to merge the tracks down to one stereo file (or multichannel file in the case of a surround mix) after you are happy with all of the mixing.

Mastering, on the other hand, involves working with the final audio file to make sure that the music is ready to be distributed. During the mastering process, you might do overall compression to boost the volume of the entire song, add touches of EQ here and there to accentuate a section, or perhaps apply a noise-reduction program to eliminate some slight hiss or background sound from the overall mix.

Mastering also is the place where decisions are made about how to deal with the order of songs on a CD, how much time should be placed between the songs, and how the beginnings and endings of each song are to be engineered (e.g., fade-ins or fade-outs). Mastering is where the sound levels of each song on a CD are matched so that there are no inconsistencies in volume from track to track.

Working with Mixing and Mastering

Throughout this module, we have been addressing aspects of mixing and mastering each time we mentioned built-in effects, plug-in effects, and software mixing windows. Figure 12.26 shows a detailed view of a mixing window in Samplitude. This demonstrates quite well how the mixer can be used to help work with individual tracks and with the "master" output. Mixer faders in the center of the figure work with the tracks separately and the two faders in the stereo master area to the left control the two output channels. Note the controls in all of the columns for EQ, delay, reverb, and plug-in effects.

Most mastering work can be done with the multiple-track software described here or with the more advanced editing software described in Module 9, such as Sound Forge or Peak. In addition, excellent software programs are available that specialize in mastering.

Tips for Mixing and Mastering

Here are a few tips that can help you learn to mix and master your own music:

- **Equipment.** Use a good pair of studio speakers equidistant from you and each other. Try out your mastering solutions on different-sized speakers. Avoid using headphones for mixing and mastering. Plan on plenty of hard-disk space and have a system for archiving digital audio projects, including original takes, in case you need to recreate your mixing decisions. (Mastering cannot save a bad mix, so you may need to turn to a different mixing solution.) Of course, a CD or DVD burner is necessary for creating laser discs. Be sure to check Module 13 for information about surround-sound hardware.

LINK
Be sure to read Module 13 for more detailed information on hardware used in the mastering process.

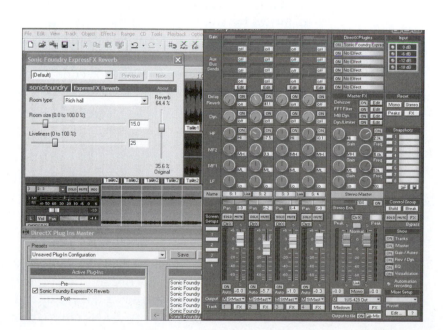

FIGURE 12.26   Mixer in Samplitude

- **Comparison to Commercial CDs.** Find five or 10 commercial CDs you like in the music genre you're working in and listen carefully to how they sound. Compare especially good tracks to the work you are doing and try to match the quality.
- **Study Structure.** The more you know about the structure of the music you are mixing and mastering the better. Understand the formal design of the music and the parts that need to catch the listener's ear. Consider mixing to one track in the music so that you are constantly aware of what is the most important line.
- **Volume and Hearing.** Humans hear high and low frequencies differently at different dynamic levels. For example, pay close attention to the quality of music passages that have a lower volume.
- **Equalization (EQ).** Use parametric EQ carefully. Certain instruments occupy specified ranges (e.g., bass drum 30 Hz–400 Hz; keyboards/guitar 100 Hz–8 kHz), so look for these as areas of most concern.
- **Compressor.** Practice with various thresholds of increased and decreased volume with the compressor settings. Dynamic range (difference between the lowest and highest points of volume) varies widely across music styles. Popular music tends to have limited dynamic range, whereas more classically oriented styles tend to have wide dynamic range.
- **Panning.** Place tracks that represent instruments and vocalists in left, center, and right positions corresponding to how listeners might expect to hear them in a live concert. Be careful not to exceed a 30% pan setting in either direction, since doing so may risk an artificial or experimental feel to the music.
- **Sampling Rate and Resolution.** Keep the sample rate and bit resolution higher than 44 kHz and 16 bit, until you are ready to do the final mixdown to burn. Then reduce as the last step.
- **Less Is More.** A small adjustment is best. Most professionals suggest that you use minimum effects, if possible.

LINK

In addition to Module 11, Module 13 provides detail on how to set up your studio hardware for surround sound. Options are explained in the text and illustrated in Figure 13.4, EMT-4A and 4B.

Mixing with Surround Sound

This would be a good time to review the descriptions of surround sound in Module 11. It is important that you understand the way surround sound supports more than two stereo speakers and the many file formats to consider, most of which have compression schemes that allow you to handle larger sample bit size and resolution.

Many multiple-track programs described in this module now support surround-sound mixing as part of their complete package (e.g., ACID, Deck, Samplitude, Pro Tools). In fact, much of the software described in Viewports V and VI support surround as well.

Refer again to Table 11.2 in Module 11. Notice that the very first format described is "generic," with no compression. This is what is offered in most mixing environments with the software in this module. Usually, six tracks of audio that correspond to the six channels in the DD 5.1 or DTS 5.1 format are offered: front right and left, rear right and left, a center channel and a special low-frequency-effects (LFE) channel for very low bass sounds. (It is important to remember that the multiple-track software titles like Audition, ACID, and ProTools do not actually create the final compressed files for CD or DVD. That requires special encoding software that we will describe shortly.) When you first begin a project in these programs, you indicate whether or not you intend to use surround sound or not. If you indicate that you do, six tracks are often created for you that correspond to the

LINK

Be sure to read Module 13, paying close attention to the options you have with tape, MiniDisc, and other hardware options for recording. You also need to be aware of the many hardware connection types (e.g., S/PDIF, AES/EBU) in play.

six channels in DD 5.1/AC-3 or DTS 5.1. As you record live sounds or add imported sounds, they can be assigned in any way you wish to the tracks.

If you are recording in a studio with surround sound as your project choice, software like Pro Tools can be configured so that certain performers use microphones assigned to one or more of the tracks. This way, you can engineer recording sessions so that material you know will be prominently heard in one speaker or another will be recorded properly. Of course, all of this can be changed and new material added.

Not all recorded material needs to stay linked to one track. In the case of the ACID example in Figure 12.27, the results of some automated, real-time panning across the speakers are shown. Here you can assign a track region to move from one place to another in the surround field in order to create a special effect. This type of panning is heard in modern movie theaters as score creators use this capability to create a sense of motion, depth, and realism. In the case of the music in the figure, the music in Track 1 is assigned to move to different locations and the surround panner box indicates this movement. The diamonds under the regions in Track 1 help show the marker points for directional change. Notice the volume controls in each track in the mixer to the lower right of the figure. The front and rear stereo speakers are controlled with the first two faders and the center and LFE have their own faders.

Distribution

Now that your music has been mixed and mastered, what do you want to do with it? It can simply reside on your computer and be played in your basement studio, but that is hardly a way for others to appreciate your hard work. We conclude this module with a review of the best ways to distribute your music.

Internet

One way to get your music out there is to distribute it on the Internet. This approach is gaining great popularity and the creation of Internet-friendly formats has never been easier than with the software in this module. Most of the software titles mentioned allow you to save your mastered stereo file in MP3 or AAC format, and some support RealAudio as well. QuickTime format is also well supported, as is the Windows Media Player. For even more flexibility, any AIF or WAV file that is

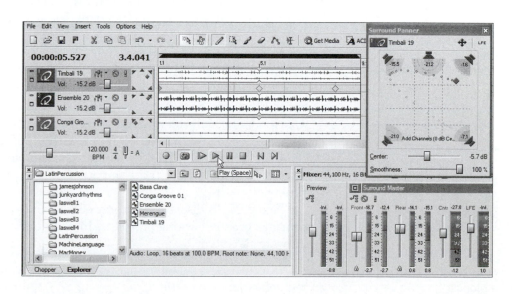

FIGURE 12.27
Surround-sound settings with automated panning in ACID

created by the multiple-track software reviewed here can be loaded into programs like iTunes or Sound Forge and treated in flexible ways for Internet distribution. Of course, Internet distribution typically supports monophonic and stereo sound and not surround sound. Also, you may want to have your music in a much more portable and high-quality format that you can give to others.

DAT, MiniDisc, or Analog Tape

Another approach is to record your music to tape or MiniDisc. This is, by far, the simplest approach and may only require a device linked to the stereo analog output of your digital interface. Unfortunately, tape players offer poor quality playback and much of your subtle mixing and mastering will be lost to the vagaries of analog tape. DAT and MiniDisc are better, but these formats do not enjoy the popularity they once did and few people have invested in DAT players.

CD/DVD Burning

By far, the most popular and highest-quality distribution method for your music is laser-disc technology. Nearly all music lovers have CD or DVD drives in their sound systems, cars, and computers, so burning a laser disc is a great choice. As we noted in Module 11, home sound systems are being influenced, too, by the reproduction of digital video/audio with more than two speakers and a DVD player in the center of the action (home theater systems). These setups are ideal for surround sound for music only. There are many options for doing this.

Straight from the Software   Many of the multiple-track software titles described in this module provide options for making an audio CD (CD-DA format) right from the program itself. Such approaches are fine for saving one or a series of music works on a CD-R or CD-RW disc, keeping the disc "open," and returning later to add tracks full of different music (you can include more than one composition in a track). This approach is called "track-at-once" (TAO) and it does work; however, very little production control, such as mastering the volume from track to track, exists with this approach.

A much more professional way to work with digital audio is to record all your tracks at once with a single pass. To do this, you need to create a master image of the entire CD contents on your hard drive and ask the software to burn everything at once (usually on a CD-R disc). This is called "disc-at-once" (DAO) and it is the best way to deal with creating CDs with digital audio because you can control volume levels among tracks, time between tracks, cross fading, and a host of other techniques that make for a stunning CD (see Module 11 for more details on CD formats, TAO, and DAO).

Special Burning Software   Enter special burning software. Special burning software for digital audio allows for more control over the recording process. Examples include Easy Media Creator for Windows (Roxio/Sonic Solutions) and the same company's Toast with Jam for Macintosh. Jam works in tandem with the Toast part of the company's software to burn a CD on a variety of CD-R recorders at a variety of speeds.

Figure 12.28 displays a portion of the Jam software that allows much more control over the burning processes. In addition to the points noted above, such software can often:

LINK
Review CD and DVD formats in Module 11.

- Print track data useful for mastering houses if you send your disc away for mass duplication.

FIGURE 12.28 Toast with Jam

- Provide for moving from 24-bit digital audio down to the required 16 bits while offering a "dithering" function to make the final sound file sound better.
- Offer mastering techniques like normalization, trimming, and fading.
- Support all the Red Book options for CD Audio (see Module 11).

Surround Sound Encoding   Creating CDs that hold your stereo mixes is one thing, but saving those surround-sound mixes is quite another. Until most recently, creating media (CDs or DVDs) that contained surround-sound files required expensive hardware. Today, a few software-based solutions are available for saving your surround mixes created in programs like ACID and ProTools.

In Module 11, you learned about two basic standards for surround-sound creation: DVD-Audio and DVD-Video. In Module 13, you will learn that these standards need to be hosted by hardware (CD players and DVD players) that can decode surround-sound files out to speakers or amplifiers by way of hardware devices that understand how to decode the surround-sound files. Module 13 will walk you through the methods for doing this.

The DVD-Video standard is very popular today because of the home theater market. As a result, DVD players are plentiful and offer the best opportunity for musicians to distribute music in surround sound. The options for software-based encoding of your surround mixes for the DVD-Video standard are the most affordable.

The DVD-Video standard (which will work on almost all DVD hardware) supports two principal file formats: Dolby Digital (DD) 5.1/AC3 and Digital Theater Systems (DTS) 5.1 or 6.1. These DVD-Video file formats use sound compression techniques recognized by the hardware as the music is decompressed and played back. The software for DD or DTS encoding uses the file-compression routines in creating the single file that contains all the sound information for the multiple channels.

Does it matter if you use CDs or DVDs for your recording media? Yes! Blank CD media are cheaper, but the CD players available to play your surround mixes may not be available. Of course, DVD players in home theater systems will support

CDs, but perhaps not the surround-sound mix that has been burnt on your particular CD. CDs also may not support coding of multiple approaches, such as DVD-Video and DVD-Audio, on one disc. In general, you are probably better off choosing DVD media for your final distribution.

Software for encoding your music for distribution continues to develop and much of it is not affordable for most musicians. Module 11 describes some options for you to consider. We anticipate that the standards and tools for encoding DVD surround sound will continue to become more accessible in future years.

We now turn our attention to hardware issues for multiple-track software before we address the world of MIDI. Remember that digital audio will also play a role in Viewports V and VI.

Module 13

Hardware for Multichannel Digital Audio

LINK
Hardware for the beginning design of a digital audio workstation is introduced in Module 10. Many of the concepts underlying those discussed in this Module are covered in Modules 5, 8, and 11. And, the software needed to put this hardware to good use is covered in Modules 12 and 17.

ASIDE
Multitrack and multichannel? When to use? Multitrack (or multiple-track) is used in this text to refer to the "tracks" in digital audio editing and sequencing software. Multichannel (or multiple-channel) is used to refer to external audio "channels," either as input to the computer or digital audio system, or mixed to output as stereo or surround-sound formats.

You have a good understanding of surround-sound and laser-disc formats. You have studied the software needed to capture and edit multiple tracks of digital audio. Now it's time to gather some hardware and start building your own digital audio workstation! This module will help you accomplish that task by examining various hardware configurations that will accommodate:

- multiple channels of input for recording
- mixing to stereo and surround-sound formats for recording
- surround-sound playback
- production of CD and DVD discs with stereo or multichannel commercial formats such as CD audio, AC-3/Dolby Digital (DD) 5.1, DTS, DVD-Audio, or DVD-Video.

The thought of what such a system might cost could easily cause you to hesitate before jumping in. Fortunately, the industry is moving in favor of low-cost solutions. Consumer emphasis is on multimedia workstations that will easily handle up to six channels of surround-sound audio with sampling up to and beyond 24-bit/96-kHz resolutions. DVD, home-theater surround sound, and computer gaming environments are driving this. Digital Signal Processing (DSP) chips embedded at the heart of these systems boost the computer's power for processing digital sound and music. To assist you in planning to build such a system, the following hardware topics will be discussed:

- DSP processing chips
- S/PDIF, AES/EBU, ADAT, Firewire, and USB digital interfaces
- Multichannel or surround-sound digital audio hardware
- MiniDisc and DAT recorders
- Portable digital recording studios
- Surround-sound amplification and speaker systems

IPOS Model for Multichannel Digital Audio

Figure 13.1 brings back the familiar IPOS systems model. Featured in this version are the critical components needed for multitrack recording, playback of surround-sound music, and the creation or "burning" of CD and DVD laser discs. On the *input* side, multichannel analog-to-digital converters (ADCs), MiniDisc (MD)

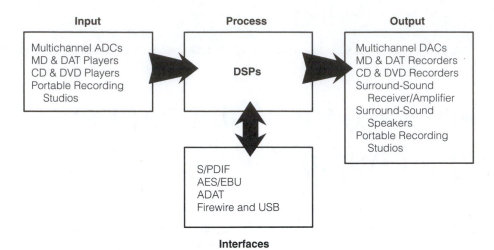

Input	Process	Output

Multichannel ADCs
MD & DAT Players
CD & DVD Players
Portable Recording
  Studios
	DSPs	Multichannel DACs
		MD & DAT Recorders
		CD & DVD Recorders
		Surround-Sound
		  Receiver/Amplifier
		Surround-Sound
		  Speakers
		Portable Recording
		  Studios

S/PDIF
AES/EBU
ADAT
Firewire and USB

Interfaces

FIGURE 13.1 IPOS model for multichannel digital audio

TIP
Remember, IPOS stands for Input, Process, Output, and Storage, with various interfaces needed to facilitate the flow of data among these elements.

and Digital Audio Tape (DAT) players, and portable digital recording studios will be examined. CD and DVD laser-disc players shown in the IPOS chart will only be briefly mentioned since they are covered in Modules 5 and 10.

For the *process* stage, the important component is the DSP, or digital-signal-processing chip. DSP technology is what makes professional quality digital audio possible on a personal computer. On the *output* side of the IPOS, multichannel, digital-to-analog converters (DACs) will be emphasized. DAT, MD, and CD or DVD appear on the output side of the chart as well as the input side. These devices are often players and recorders, permitting both reading and writing of sound data. CD and DVD recordables (both R and RW) are discussed in Module 10, but are noted here as well; laser recording is the method of choice for playback distribution of the massive files of data required to produce digital audio and video. For an all-in-one, stand-alone solution, portable digital studio recorders are added to the IPOS array of choices.

What enables the fast transfer of data among the stages of this IPOS model? Interface protocols especially developed for digital media applications. Digital I/O interfaces (S/PDIF, AES/EBU, and ADAT) are topics specific to audio applications; Firewire and USB are common interfaces for digital audio and video, as well as for general computer applications.

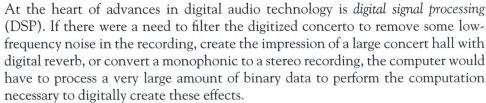

Superheroes: The DSP Chips

LINK
Many of the software synthesizer plug-in options discussed in Module 12 use DSP programming techniques.

At the heart of advances in digital audio technology is *digital signal processing* (DSP). If there were a need to filter the digitized concerto to remove some low-frequency noise in the recording, create the impression of a large concert hall with digital reverb, or convert a monophonic to a stereo recording, the computer would have to process a very large amount of binary data to perform the computation necessary to digitally create these effects.

Performing any of these operations on sound is *DSP*, based on an algorithm that someone has programmed to instruct the computer on how to carry out these tasks. The reverb effect to simulate a concert hall is just one example of a DSP algorithm. DSP algorithms may be performed entirely in software on very fast personal computers, or embedded in hardware as integrated circuits known as DSP chips.

Signal processing has been around for a while, but signal processing using large amounts of sound data in a personal computer has not. Only recently, through a combination of specially designed chips to carry out DSP algorithms and very fast processors, have computers and digital audio peripherals been able to perform DSP tasks quickly and cost-effectively. DSP chips are likely to be found in your computer, in digital audio cards, MIDI keyboard workstations, digital recorders, and just about any digital music device you can think of.

A DSP chip may contain a fixed program (e.g., an algorithm for digital reverb or for physically modeling a musical instrument) or may be programmable so that it can perform several tasks. DSPs are used in fax, voice, graphic imaging, audio, and many other applications. The power behind the newest generation of video games making use of exceptional-quality 3-D animation and surround sound is the DSP chip; the multifaceted power in palmtop, personal digital assistant computers, and cell phones is the DSP chip. It is truly the superhero of computing power!

One-on-One with Digital: S/PDIF, AES/EBU, ADAT, Firewire, and USB

Many times data need to be transferred among digital devices. One-on-one exchanges of data can occur between digital audio systems in computer workstations and many other digital audio devices, such as CD and DVD recorders, DAT and MiniDisc recorders, disk drives, digital hard-disk recorders, samplers, and effects processors. The last thing a musician wants to do with digital samples is to convert them back to analog audio just to send them to another digital device for processing. Each time a sample reenters the analog world, the sound is degraded. Going digital-to-digital all the way, even to the speakers (EMT item 10 in Figure 13.2), if possible, is the best way to go.

In general terms, how does digital-to-digital work? Digital data from the sending device (e.g., a computer) first gets translated into serial electrical signals that represent the binary codes of the audio sample. Then these data are sent via a cable to the other receiving device (e.g., a MiniDisc tape recorder (16), as shown in Figure 13.2). The receiving device then translates the codes into the digital format required for its hardware. Throughout the exchange, data remain in a digital form.

There are several ways to transmit digital audio data among devices: Firewire, USB, AES/EBU, S/PDIF, and ADAT formats. These are common interfaces found on many external digital audio devices, digital recorders, surround-sound systems, and digital speakers. USB and Firewire are covered in Module 6 under general computer interface issues.

S/PDIF and AES/EBU: Close Cousins

The S/PDIF interface is most commonly found on consumer digital products, and the AES/EBU interface is most commonly found on professional-level digital audio devices. S/PDIF stands for the *Sony/Philips Digital Interface Format*. About

TIP
Some digital audio devices can be installed directly in a laptop or desktop computer using the PC-Card slot in the laptop or the PCI-bus slot in the computer.

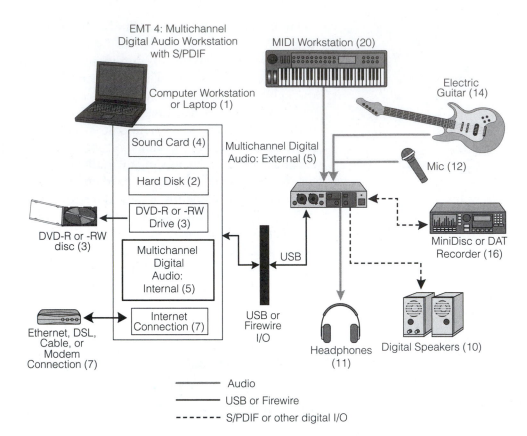

FIGURE 13.2 EMT-4 Multichannel Digital Audio Workstation with S/PDIF

TIP
If two devices are connected with S/PDIF, it is important that both devices be capable of exchanging compressed, multichannel data. Surround-sound speakers may only recognize a stereo audio stream, for example, if the sending device is not capable of sending an encoded AC-3 or DTS audio signal with 5.1 channels of sound.

LINK
See Figure 10.5's reference to S/PDIF, along with a discussion of various cable connectors like Toslink.

the same time that Sony and Philips drew up the specifications for the first compact audio discs and CD-ROMs, they also agreed on a way of exchanging digital data among audio devices. Originally, the S/PDIF standard was only two-channel stereo; a 1998 update to the standard established a protocol for transmitting multichannel data such as DD 5.1/AC-3 or DTS surround-sound formats.

Data exchanged through an S/PDIF interface are transmitted in a high-speed serial format in either 20- or 24-bit formats. The presence of an S/PDIF interface is distinguishable by the use of RCA-phono connectors and cables for sending and receiving stereo data over a coax connection. The fiber-optic Toslink cable is also a common option for connecting S/PDIF interfaces. The connectors are the same for two-channel and multichannel S/PDIF; coding in the digital data stream informs the receiving device as to what format is being sent.

AES/EBU stands for *Audio Engineering Society/European Broadcast Union* digital interface; it is also referred to as the AES3 format. Basically, AES/EBU is the professional version of S/PDIF and uses a 24-bit data format. The cables and connectors used are three-pin XLR connectors typical in professional-quality audio equipment.

ADAT

The ADAT digital audio format derives from its progeny, the Alesis Digital Audio Tape recorder first introduced in 1991. It was the first of its kind and set the initial standard for exchanging data between digital audio devices. The ADAT interface provides a minimum of eight channels of 24-bit, 48-kHz digital data between ADAT-compatible devices. The connection is optical, uses the same Toslink connector as S/PDIF, and is often referred to as the "lightpipe" ADAT optical interface.

EMT Digital Audio Workstation Goes Multichannel

Let's revisit the EMT-2 and EMT-3 systems presented in Module 10 (Figures 10.2 and 10.6) and expand the digital audio options. The most significant addition will be the increase in digital audio "power" beyond what typically comes with a laptop or desktop computer system. EMT-4, as shown in Figure 13.2, becomes a multichannel digital audio workstation, or DAW. The components added include:

- Digital audio system (5) capable of digitizing from two to eight channels or more of analog (input) or digital (output) audio with 16-bit/44.1-kHz to 24-bit/96-kHz sampling resolutions, and S/PDIF digital I/O; the system may be installed in the computer or externally through a Firewire or USB connection. Shown in Figure 13.2 with a USB connection external to the computer.
- DVD-R or -RW drive (3) for reading and writing CD or DVD laser discs (or DVD+R or DVD+RW).
- Multitrack digital tape recorder (16) with digital I/O—DAT, ADAT, or MD deck. Shown in Figure 13.2 with S/PDIF connection to the digital audio device (5).
- An array of analog sound devices connected to the digital audio device (5). Figure 13.2 shows input connections to the analog out from a MIDI keyboard (20), an electric guitar (14), and a professional-level mic (12).
- Amplification and speakers for monitoring the digital audio editing process. Figure 13.2 shows a pair of digital speakers (10) connected to the digital audio device (5) through the S/PDIF connector and a pair of headphones connected to the analog stereo headphone jack.

Items in the digital audio EMT system like the MiniDisc or DAT recorder (16), MIDI workstation (20), electric guitar (14), or microphone (12) are just a few of many options. They illustrate the variety of devices that can be attached. The MD or DAT recorder represents a portable means for distributing music productions beyond laser-disc solutions.

Look again at Figure 13.2, paying particular attention to the routing of the audio and digital channels. With this system, you have the ability to intermix live and digital audio in a number of creative combinations. Everything stays in the digital domain. All analog sound is routed to the digital I/O devices, where it is converted to high-resolution digital audio. From the diagram, this includes keyboard, guitar, and any live performance captured by microphone. Everything that is already in digital form stays that way: digital audio input either from the MiniDisc tape deck or digital audio from CD or DVD disc, for example. The audio sent to the speakers is even digital using S/PDIF. USB and S/PDIF are used to route digital signals around the EMT-4 configuration.

Two options are available for recording. The music can be recorded to some form of digital recorder such as DAT, ADAT, or MiniDisc (16), using either an S/PDIF, AES/BEU, or ADAT lightpipe connection. Or, the finished production can be recorded directly onto a blank CD or DVD-R or -RW disc (3) to create a CD audio, DVD-Audio, or DVD-Video disc.

Take note. There is no hardware mixer in the EMT-4 system; there are no external effects processors. As presented in Module 12, software like Deck, Pro Tools, and Audition use software to create virtual mixers and effects generators in concert with the multichannel digital audio system (5) and its array of DSP features and extremely fast audio conversion hardware.

LINK
Module 12 looks at Audition, Deck, ProTools, and other digital audio software where multiple tracks of digital audio can be captured, manipulated, and mixed in various multichannel formats for playback and recording.

ASIDE
The term "digital audio workstation," or DAW, is used to refer to two different things in today's music technology scene. Here DAW refers to a hardware computer or studio setup. In Module 17, we will also use the term to refer to advanced sequencing software.

Expanding to Multichannel Digital Sound

The heart of the EMT-4 configuration is the multichannel digital audio device (5). Analog audio streams enter this device; the data are digitized for computer storage, editing, mixdown, and playback; and digital or analog audio streams leave from this device. Table 13.1 provides a comparison of nine multichannel digital audio devices. Critical factors are noted in the left-hand column of the table. Let's review each of these in turn:

- *Analog input/output.* The range of analog inputs and outputs goes from two to eight. Two inputs are typical of the lower-cost devices. Two of the less expensive devices have no analog inputs; the Gigaport AG and the M-Audio Sonica are primarily designed for surround-sound playback. Units like the Edirol UA-5 or the Digidesign M-Box provide a typical combination of two-channel ADC and DACs (stereo in/out) as featured in the EMT-4 setup in Figure 13.2 (with the option of analog in/out or S/PDIF digital in/out). When there is a need for more channels, the Edirol DA-2496 or the MOTU 828mkII provide eight ADC/DACs, but for a higher cost.
- *Digital input/output and connectors.* All of these devices have S/PDIF. This means that at least a stereo digital input/output stream is available, except for the Sonica and Gigaport devices, which are audio output only. Some devices will pass multitrack digital audio through S/PDIF. This is not six discrete channels of digital audio; a single audio stream is passed between devices with multiple channels of digital audio encoded in some form such as AC-3, DTS, or DVD-Audio. The receiving S/PDIF device will need to decode the audio stream back into separate audio channels. The UA-5 and M-Box provide either stereo analog audio or an S/PDIF digital audio stream. Two devices in the chart also provide ADAT lightpipe eight-channel audio for use with other ADAT devices: the Gina24 and the Mark of the Unicorn (MOTU) 828mkII (the Edirol UA-1000 also provides ADAT).
- *Sampling resolution.* All of the devices can handle 16- to 24-bit resolution. The sampling rates vary between 48 kHz and 96 kHz; for playback of surround-sound music at 96 kHz, the Sonica and Gigaport AG provide very low-cost solutions; at the upper end, the Gina24 or DA-2496 provide multichannel capability at 96 kHz.
- *MIDI.* Three of the digital audio devices offer a MIDI interface: the Edirol UA-5 and 2496 and the MOTU 828mkII.
- *Speakers/headphones.* All but the Sonica provide a jack for monitoring with stereo headphones; the Emagic emi 2/6 and Edirol DA-2496 provide jacks for stereo monitor speakers as well.
- *Interface and operating system.* Most of the devices compared will operate on Mac or PC computers. This means that they offer drivers and software on the Mac and Windows OS. USB interface is the most prevalent; the more complex systems that handle more AD/DA channels use PCI-bus or Firewire to accommodate the greater bandwidth demands of handling eight independent channels of digital audio simultaneously. The VX Pocket is an example of one solution for a laptop with a PC-Card interface.
- *Other.* Microphones and guitars have special impedance needs. In the less expensive range, the UA-5 and M-Box provide the phantom power needed for condenser mics and the Hi-Z impedance for electric guitars. The DA-2496 and 828 are higher-priced solutions with eight channels. Note that the Sonica and the Gigaport are designed for playback of surround-sound data streams. The

ASIDE

A greater use of both Firewire 400 and 800 will be seen as this interface bus and mLAN audio networking (see Module 18), expand in the professional audio world. The faster bandwidth of USB 2.0 also provides improved performance over the slower USB 1.0 interface. The Edirol UA-1000 noted in the chart is a USB 2.0 device.

LINK

Refer to Module 10 for a discussion of impedance issues with mics and guitars.

TABLE 13.1	A Comparison of Representative Examples of Multichannel Digital Audio								
Specs	**M-Audio Sonica**	**Gigaport AG**	**Emagic A26**	**Edirol UA-5**	**Digidesign M-Box**	**Gina24**	**Edirol DA-2496**[4]	**MOTU 828mkII**	**Digigram VX Pocket**
Analog Out	2	8	6	2	2	8	8	8	4
Analog In	0	0	2	2	2	2	8	8	4
Digital Out	2	2	2	2	2	2/8[1]	2	2/8	2
Digital In	0	0	2	2	2	2/8	2	2/8	2
Digital Connectors	SPDIF	SPDIF	SPDIF	SPDIF	SPDIF	SPDIF/ ADAT[3]	SPDIF	SPDIF/ ADAT	SPDIF
Sample Resolution	To 24bit/ 96 kHz[2]	To 24bit/ 96 kHz	To 24bit/ 48 kHz	To 24bit/ 96 kHz	To 24bit/ 48 kHz	To 24bit/ 96 kHz	To 24bit/ 96 kHz	To 24bit/ 48 kHz	To 24bit/ 48 kHz
MIDI	No	No	No	No	No	No	Yes	Yes	None
Speaker/ Headphone Connection	None	Phone	Stereo monitor/ Phones	Phones	Phones	Phones	Stereo monitor/ Phones	Phones	Phones
Interface	USB	USB	USB	USB	USB	PCI-bus card	PCI-bus card (UA-1000 model provides USB 2.0)	Firewire	PC Card (PCMCIA)
System	PC/Mac	PC/Mac	PC/Mac	PC/Mac	PC/Mac	PC/Mac	PC/Mac	PC/Mac	PC/Mac
Other	Designed for 6-channel playback only	Playback only		Mic phantom power; Guitar Hi-Z	Mic phantom power; Guitar Hi-Z;		Mic phantom power; Guitar Hi-Z Breakout box	Pedal punch input; 2 mic preamps	Breakout cable from PC Card
Cost	Very Low	Very Low	Low	Low	Middle	Middle	High	High	High

Notes:
[1]2 or 4 or 2 or 8 designates reduced channels at 24-bit sample size, e.g., two at 24-bit and four at 16-bit.
[2]To 24 bit/96 kHz, for example, denotes a range of options up to this resolution, e.g., 16 bit/44 kHz, 16 bit/48 kHz, up to 24 bit/96 kHz.
[3]SPDIF/ADAT denotes stereo 2-channel S/PDIF and 8-channel ADAT.
[4]A newer Edirol UA-1000 10x10 multichannel digital audio device has similar features to the DA-2496, but with ADAT and a USB 2.0 interface.

Sonica, with its S/PDIF output, will handle six channels of output encoded in such formats as AC-3, DTS, or DVD-Audio. The Gigaport provides both S/PDIF and eight individual channels of audio output. The VX Pocket has a break cable extending from the PC-Card, while the DA 2498 has a breakout box that connects to the PCI card inserted in the computer.

• *Cost.* Relative pricing is provided for comparison: Very low is in the $100 range, middle is in the $300 range, and high is in the $800 range.

Now that the features of several digital audio devices have been reviewed, the EMT-4 solution in Figure 13.2 can be revisited. A key component is the multichannel digital audio device (5). For a basic system, two channels provide a budget-minded solution for production requiring nothing more than a final stereo mix but offering options for surround-sound mixes. Given the comparisons in Table 13.1, a device like the Edirol UA-5 or Digidesign M-Box works well. Two channels of input and output are available—either analog or S/PDIF, special provisions for mic and guitar are built into the devices, and 24-bit/48-kHz or 24-bit/96-kHz sampling resolutions are supported. Furthermore, S/PDIF output from these two devices offers options for encoding mixdowns from multitrack software into surround-sound audio streams for AC-3 or DTS, among others, to surround-sound devices for recording or playback. They both connect to a laptop or desktop with a USB cable.

If more analog inputs are needed, a basic mixer as described for the EMT-3 system (Figure 10.6 in Module 10) can be used. For those situations where more than two discrete digital channels are needed, for an all-digital recording session, for surround-sound recording or playback, or for multitrack playback without using audio encoding formats, you should probably select something comparable to the MOTU 828mkII or Edirol DA-2496 (or UA-1000).

To aid in understanding the hardware features of devices featured in Table 13.1, an examination of one of the eight-channel units is instructive. Figure 13.3 shows the front and back of the Edirol DA-2496. The DA-2496 connects to a computer with a PCI Card; note the DA-PCI connector on the back of the unit. (Other units may have USB or Firewire connectors and do not require a PCI Card; the UA-1000 uses USB 2.0 and the MOTU 828 uses Firewire.) The DA-2496 also provides MIDI IN and OUT as can be seen on the back of the unit just to the left of the AC IN receptacle.

This is an eight-channel IN/OUT device with eight analog-to-digital and eight digital-to-analog converters with 24-bit/96-kHz sampling resolution. For the eight analog IN channels, channels 1 and 2 are on the front and can be used for standard phone jacks or for microphones needing phantom power—note the phantom power ON/OFF buttons. These two jacks are uniquely designed for either phone or XLR connectors from microphones. Channels 3 and 4 have phone jacks on the front panel for Hi-Z devices like guitars and TRS jacks on the back for balanced analog IN with individual preamps. S/PDIF digital IN is provided on the back in either Toslink Optical or Coax IN (channels 7/8). Peak-level adjustment for amplitude is available for all eight channel inputs—channels 1–4 have individual preamps, channels 5–8 are stereo pairs. The thing to remember is that there are no more than eight inputs on the device, and the musician has to plan how to effectively use each channel, for example, mic, guitar, analog, optical, etc.

Likewise, there are no more than eight outputs, all of which can be accessed through the eight phone jacks on the lower left-hand side of the back panel.

FIGURE 13.3 The front and back panel of the Edirol DA-2496, 8-channel digital audio system

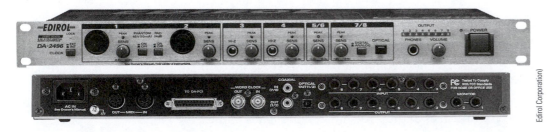

Edirol Corporation)

Channels 1 and 2 can be used for optical output either through coax or Toslink connections. Notice that 1–2 can be used to provide stereo monitoring to a set of speakers, as well as the stereo phone jack and volume control on the front panel. The Word Clock connector? Word Clock is a timing protocol for keeping digital audio devices synchronized—more on this topic in Viewport V.

Moving Up to Surround Sound

What do you need to add to the EMT-4 setup to do surround sound? The only hardware you need is that required to listen to surround-sound music in different encodings: DD 5.1/AC-3, DTS, DVD-Audio with MLP 5.1, etc. Surround-sound music is created in software with multitrack capture, editing, and sound processing, which can be accomplished with the hardware configuration of Figure 13.2. Some additional input channels may be needed for a live-performance recording session with surround-sound mic placement.

Surround-sound mixes can be mastered directly from multitrack digital audio software onto DVD or CD recordable discs without additional hardware. A software encoder will be needed for proprietary formats like those from Dolby Labs or DTS. SACD and DVD-Audio MLP encoding would also be desirable.

This leaves the hardware for playing back surround-sound recordings. Essentially, the computer needs to become a home theater system. Figure 13.4 shows two different solutions. For both solutions, the computer must have a DVD-ROM drive and DVD-Video player software that will minimally recognize DD 5.1/AC-3

LINK
Software issues for encoding and decoding surround sound are covered in Modules 11 and 12 of this Viewport.

EMT-4: Surround Sound
Multichannel Output Options

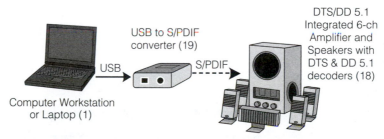

EMT 4A. USB to S/PDIF conversion for multichannel surround sound.
DTS or DD 5.1/AC-3 is passed through for decoding in the amplifier/speakers.

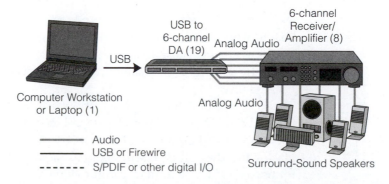

FIGURE 13.4 Two surround-sound options for the EMT-4 workstation

EMT 4B. USB to multichannel DACs for conversion to six analog audio streams.
DTS or DD 5.1/AC-3 decoding is done by the DA interface (19) to create six channels
of analog audio to the amplifier.

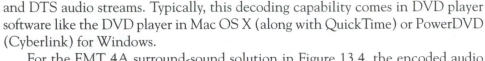

and DTS audio streams. Typically, this decoding capability comes in DVD player software like the DVD player in Mac OS X (along with QuickTime) or PowerDVD (Cyberlink) for Windows.

For the EMT 4A surround-sound solution in Figure 13.4, the encoded audio stream is passed directly to an amplifier and set of surround-sound speakers. The amplifier has the necessary decoders to translate the compressed and encoded audio streams into six analog channels directed to the array of speakers: left-right front, center, left-right surround, and LFE or subwoofer speakers. All that is needed between the computer and the amplifier is a device to convert the USB audio to S/PDIF and send the encoded audio on to the S/PDIF input of a surround-sound amplifier. For the illustration in Figure 13.4a, the M-Audio Sonica (see Table 13.1) fills this purpose. The amplifier in the illustration with S/PDIF input and DTS/DD 5.1 decoders is integrated into the surround speaker array. The advantage of this scenario is its simplicity—only a Firewire or USB-to-S/PDIF converter is needed.

For the EMT-4B solution, the DD 5.1/AC-3 or DTS encoded data stream is decoded by the digital audio interface (19) in Figure 13.4b, providing six channels of analog (not digital) audio to the amplifier. The only amplifier requirement is that it be surround-sound enabled with six separate analog inputs. In Figure 13.4b, the Apple A26 (Emagic) is used for this operation; the compressed six channels of digital sound delivered through the USB interface are converted to six analog channels through the Emagic device. The array of six analog audio streams is then connected to the amplifier, which in turn powers the array of six surround-sound speakers. The advantage of this scenario is its flexibility: Software decoders can be easily changed to provide a variety of compression formats and the six audio channels to the amplifier require no change in the external hardware. The disadvantage is the complexity: A six-channel digital audio interface is required, as well as six individual analog audio cables to the amplifier.

Both of the solutions illustrated in Figure 13.4 can be added to the EMT-4 setup of Figure 13.2, keeping the current digital audio device (5) for analog and digital inputs and additional S/PDIF outputs.

TIP
Surround-sound integrated speaker systems reduce the wires for six channels of analog audio with three mini-stereo jacks: (1) front left-right, (2) center-subwoofer, and (3) surround left-right.

ASIDE
The industry was afraid that digital recorders might be used to make illegal copies of CDs, DVDs, and digital tapes. Serial Copy Management System (SCMS) codes added to recordings are but one mechanism used to prevent making more than one copy of a digital-to-digital duplication from consumer recorders.

Recording and Playback in the Digital Realm

The digital music production is finished. How do you record it? You could always use analog recording with a cassette tape—boring indeed! But why return to the analog world when many digital recording options are available? By delaying a return to analog audio right up to the moment the recording is ready to be played back, the smallest loss of audio information occurs—so much the better for playback quality.

A variety of digital recording options are discussed later in the module: DAT, MD, CD and DVD, and portable digital recorders. Realize that whether the digital codes are stored on a CD, DVD, DAT or ADAT tape, MiniDisc, or a Compact Flash card, they all represent audio as digital samples to the computer; only the formats vary. These formats can provide basic two-track, stereo recording (DAT, MD, CD, and DVD), or multichannel recording with three or more channels, or DD 5.1/AC-3 or DTS channel recordings with CDs or DVDs. Interfacing the recorders to a computer can be accomplished with the usual options of USB, Firewire, S/PDIF, AES/EBU, or ADAT.

LINK
CD-R and DVD-R, as well as CD-RW and DVD-RW (and DVD-RAM and DVD+RW), are discussed in Module 6 in terms of hardware options and in Module 11 in terms of file formats and recording options.

CD and DVD Recordable Drives

Recording productions from a digital audio workstation to some form of laser-disc recorder is the likely first option to consider. The computer workstation in Figure 13.2 has a DVD-R/RW recorder (3) that can easily be used to burn a music mix down to laser disc. Recordable laser drives come installed in a desktop or laptop computer or can be added externally to a computer with either a Firewire or USB interface. DVD and CD recorders can also be purchased as stand-alone units designed for home entertainment centers or for professional fieldwork (Panasonic, Philips, Pioneer, Sony, and Toshiba all make consumer DVD recorders). Audio tracks and videos can be copied to the 40-GB or larger hard drives built into these recorders and then CDs or DVDs can be "burned" to blank CDs and DVDs without computer intervention. The consumer laser recorders, however, have limited interface resources for directly controlling the devices from a computer. S/PDIF I/O does allow for transfer of audio in digital form between these stand-alone recorders and a computer system.

DAT and ADAT Recorders

The first digital recording medium to surface in the 1990s was the *digital audio tape*, or DAT, recorder. Although CD discs have offered digital playback since the early 1980s, consumer digital recording appeared at a later date. A DAT recorder is basically a two-track tape recorder that records digital codes rather than analog patterns. DAT recorders are mechanically similar to analog cassette and videotape decks. The DAT tape cassette is a little larger than an audio cassette and may record up to 90 or 120 minutes. Recording is only on one side of the tape.

In 1991, Alesis introduced an eight-channel, multitrack DAT system (ADAT) that became an instant success for small recording studio needs. The ADAT recorder uses a videotape cassette (S-VHS) for recording 8–24 tracks of digital audio at sampling resolutions of 16-bit/44.1-kHz up to 24-bit/96-kHz. Other professional audio companies soon followed with other high-end models of DAT recorders. The Tascam DA-88 uses the Hi-8 video-cassette cartridge for a different digital audiotape format.

The DAT tape-recording mechanism has also been integrated into small mixing consoles to produce various portable studio configurations. The proprietary ADAT digital I/O format has become a common interface used on mixers, MIDI workstations, effects processors, digital audio cards, and other music devices.

MiniDisc (MD) Recorders

Sony released the MiniDisc format commercially in 1992. While others chose to stay with tape in their pursuit of low cost and flexible technology for consumer digital audio, Sony opted for laser-optic technology and a miniaturized CD disc. Three immediate advantages of MiniDiscs are the power of a random-access audio environment, the ability to record the equivalent of a full-length 75-minute CD on a writeable laser medium, and the reliability of a laser-recording mechanism. To get the same 75 minutes of playing time that a standard CD offers onto an MD, Sony created an audio perceptual compression called ATRAC.

There are two types of MD disc formats: a two-track audio playback or recordable MD and a MiniDisc Data, or MDD, for computer data applications. The professional multitrack MiniDisc recorders use the computer MDD discs. The two-track audio MD is most commonly used in consumer players and recorders. A

LINK
Perceptual audio compression and ATRAC (Adaptive TRansform Acoustical Coding) are discussed in Module 8.

ASIDE
Sony MiniDisc Walkman recorder/players are packaged as extremely small and thin portable units that can be easily used to play back many hours of MP3 files while walking, jogging, or working. With the NetMD feature and USB port connected to a computer, music files can be dragged and dropped to the MD Walkman.

professional-level MiniDisc recorder (16), for example, a Tascam MD-801, is shown in the EMT-4 system in Figure 13.2.

The two-track MD recorders, especially the consumer portable MDs, provide a good, low-budget solution for random-access digital recording for modest computer music workstations. With the use of MP3 compression, up to five hours of recording is possible from a single MD disc.

Stand-Alone Digital Recorders

What do you have when you cross a large hard drive, a mixer, multichannel AD-DA samplers, and multitrack sampling software? Throw in a computer processor and some DSP chips? A portable digital studio recorder.

When a musician needs to go portable with a completely self-contained digital recording system, a portable digital recorder provides an ideal solution. All features of the digital audio system and the hard drive are self-contained in one unit and operate much as with any multitrack recorder.

Table 13.2 describes the capabilities of these portable studio units by selectively comparing four of them: the least expensive, Zoom MRS-4; the very portable Tascam PocketStudio5; the entry-level professional Fostex VF80; and the full-featured Korg D1200. These units range from $200 to $1,000 in price.

Reviewing Table 13.2, some of the features that all four studios have in common are:

- Multiple input channels for instruments, microphones, and electric guitars, including MIDI input/output.
- Fader controls for adjusting amplitude of the input channels.
- Built-in DSP to provide a basic set of digital effects processing.
- LCD display of the amplitude levels of the input channels, the master stereo output mix, and location in the sampling sequence.
- Physical controls equivalent to the playback-and-record transport on a tape recorder, buttons for navigation and effects controls, and a jog wheel for quickly moving through time in a sampled sequence.
- Sampling rate of at least 16-bit/44-kHz resolution.
- Mix down to stereo output (with line and phone output).

Where do the four portable recording units differ?

LINK
Terms such as physical and virtual tracks, bouncing tracks, punch in/out, and markers that are common to audio mixing are discussed in Module 12.

- *Number of tracks, channels, and faders.* As the units get more expensive, they have more physical and virtual tracks, and a greater number of tracks that can be recorded or played back simultaneously. The more comprehensive solutions have additional channels and faders for controlling a greater number of tracks. For example, compare the four physical tracks (and no virtual tracks) of the Tascam with four audio faders with the 12 physical tracks and 96 virtual tracks of the Korg D1200's six monophonic and three stereo fader controls.
- *Effects.* The more sophisticated portable studios have a large library of effect algorithms and the ability to remember and automate mixer "scenes" of all the fader, control, and effect settings for any given recording setup. The Fostex and Korg studios provide scene memory.
- *Storage.* The low-end studios (Zoom and Tascam) use Smart Media and Compact Flash cards; the more advanced have an internal hard drive of 20 GB or more and the added ability to record directly to CD-R/RW discs (Fostex and Korg).

TABLE 13.2 A Comparison of Four Portable Digital Recording Studios

Specs	Zoom MRS-4 Digital Recorder	Tascam PocketStudio5	Fostex VF80	Korg D1200
Analog IN/OUT	2-line, 2-aux/2-line, phones	2-line or 1-guitar & 1-mic, 1-mic/2-line, phones	2-line, 2-mic XLR (phantom)/ 2-line, phones	4-line with 2-mic (phantom) & 1-guitar/2-line, 1-aux, 2-monitor, phones
Physical/Virtual Tracks	4/32	4/0	8/16	12/96
Simultaneous Record/Playback Tracks	2/4	4/2	2/8	12/4
Faders/Channels	4/4 ch	4-mono, 1-MIDI-tonegen, 1-masterLR/4 ch	7-mono, 1-masterLR/8 ch	6-mono, 3-stereo, 1-masterLR/16 ch
Effects Processors	Basic dynamic, send, and mixdown effects	100 effects with DSP	44 channel, 10 master, and 36 EQ presets with DSP and scene memory	96 different effect algorithms and presets with DSP and scene memory
Storage	Smart Media Cards as WAV files	Compact Flash as MP3 files	20-GB hard drive as WAV files	40-GB hard drive as WAV files
Record Device	Smart Media Cards	Compact Flash	CD-R/RW	CD-R/RW drive
Display	LCD of track, in- and out-levels	LCD of track, in- and out-levels	LCD of track, in- and out-levels & waveform display	LCD of track, in- and out-levels & waveform display
Digital IN/OUT	None	USB	S/PDIF	S/PDIF
Sample Resolution	20 bit/32 kHz	16 bit/44.1 kHz	16 bit/44.1 kHz	16 or 24 bit/ 44.1 kHz
MIDI	MIDI OUT	MIDI IN w/internal MIDI tone generator	MIDI IN/OUT	MIDI IN/OUT
Other Connectors			Foot Switch for punch in/out	Pedal Controller and Foot Switch for punch in/out
Other		Jog wheel, preprogrammed MIDI sequences	Jog wheel	Jog wheel
Computer Interface	None	USB	None	USB
Cost	Low	Medium	Medium	High

LINK
Review mixing terminology
in Module 10, where terms
like "pan," "balance," and
"pot" are discussed, and
Module 12, where they are
discussed in the context of
multiple-track software
mixing.

- *Display.* The more sophisticated studios will display the waveform of the digital audio recording to visually aid in editing points within the sample. Both the Fostex and the Korg provide this feature.
- *Digital IN/OUT.* The Fostex and Korg units have S/PDIF, which makes it possible to add prerecorded audio from a digital source (e.g., CD audio or MD) and to record the mixdown from the digital studio to another digital device (e.g., MD or computer workstation). The Tascam PocketStudio and Korg D1200 also have a USB port for an interactive connection to a computer.
- *Foot switch and pedal controller.* A foot switch is extremely handy for punch-down recording; the pedal controller permits expressive control for MIDI effects or for gradually increasing or decreasing amplitude.

To show these features applied to one portable studio, Figure 13.5 displays the desktop of the Korg D1200. Note the array of faders in the lower left-hand side of the desktop: six single-track faders (channels 1–6), three stereo faders (channels 7–12), and the master L-R or stereo fader for output control. Above each fader is a Pan or Balance knob ("pot") to adjust the spatial position of the sound (left-right or front-back), and above the pots are track status buttons indicating whether the track is in Play, Input, Record, or Mute mode.

The input channels are in the upper left-hand quadrant of the Korg desktop. Four inputs match Inputs 1–2 (phone-line inputs or XLR with phantom power for microphones) and Inputs 3–4 (phone-line inputs). Next to those can be found the Footswitch and Expressive Pedal control inputs, and below those, an Aux Out for sending signals to an external effects processor.

The LCD display occupies the upper right-hand quadrant of the Korg desktop. All of the navigation and control options are framed by the LCD display at the top and the transport controls along the bottom of the right-hand side. The transport controls are the typical Stop, Play, Forward, Rewind, and Record.

Directly below the LCD display are three knobs (black area) that are used to alter the complex DSP effects algorithms built into the D1200, called "modeling" in D1200 parlance. The column on the left under the modeling (black) area contains mixdown options (Insert, EQ, and Master Effects), and mastering options (Final Effect, Bounce, and CD). The far right-hand side of this column provides a

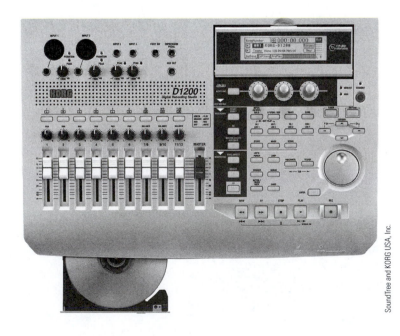

FIGURE 13.5 Desktop of the Korg D1200 digital recording studio

SoundTree and KORG USA, Inc.

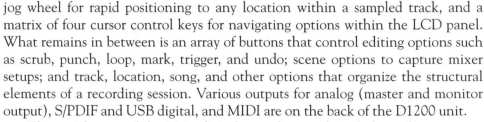

jog wheel for rapid positioning to any location within a sampled track, and a matrix of four cursor control keys for navigating options within the LCD panel. What remains in between is an array of buttons that control editing options such as scrub, punch, loop, mark, trigger, and undo; scene options to capture mixer setups; and track, location, song, and other options that organize the structural elements of a recording session. Various outputs for analog (master and monitor output), S/PDIF and USB digital, and MIDI are on the back of the D1200 unit.

This quick tour of the Korg digital recording studio's desktop demonstrates that an immense number of functions and controls is compactly organized into a small, portable 10x14-inch space. When a musician needs such portability and an all-in-one solution, the power of the digital recording studio is a "magic genie in a bottle," so to speak. The downside is the need to master the "secret codes" to unlock the genie's magic. Learning to effectively use any of the four studios in this comparison entails a good deal of study and practice in navigating the many settings and controls hidden within the LCD display window and accessed from combinations of buttons on the desktop. Each manufacturer—Fostex, Tascam, Zoom, and Korg—has a unique solution for learning the studio's mode of operation.

The PocketStudio5, the VF80, or the D1200 could be added to the multichannel EMT-4. The VF80 or D1200 with the S/PDIF interface could replace the MiniDisc or DAT recorder (16) as a hard-disk recorder or a CD-R/RW burner. The PocketStudio or Korg could connect as a USB device and WAV (Korg) or MP3 (Tascam) files could be easily moved between the computer (1) and the digital recording studio (16). The Fostex or Korg could be used for a live recording session and then coupled with the computer back in the studio for more complex digital audio editing tasks. Using software like Deck or Pro Audio from a full computer screen would be a distinct advantage for the final editing tasks.

Surround-Sound Amplifiers and Speakers

Brief mention needs to be made of speakers and amplifiers, especially as they relate to surround-sound solutions. For any recording studio, the minimum is a pair of monitor speakers. Monitors (10), as shown in Figure 13.2, have amplification built into their cabinet so that the stereo audio signals can come directly from the computer digital audio device, mixer, or recorder. They range greatly in price and recording engineers can argue at length over quality issues with various makes and models. Monitor speakers are also available as digital units with S/PDIF connections. Digital-to-analog conversion circuitry is built into the speaker cabinet. Analog and digital monitors are available from Mackie, Yamaha, Roland, Fostex, and many other manufacturers.

The speaker arrangement in Figure 13.4a is an example of expanding digital stereo monitors to multichannel surround-sound speaker environments. For example, Logitech, Creative Labs, Harmon/Kardon, and Klipsch, produce various surround-sound monitor configurations with amplification included. A few of those units have S/PDIF digital options with DTS and DD 5.1/AC-3 decoding included.

The tried-and-true solution, of course, is to use a separate amplifier and select a set of speakers that contain nothing else but the speaker hardware and circuitry. This is often a more expensive solution, but it does provide the greatest flexibility. Figure 13.4b shows a surround-sound amplifier and complete set of six speakers, including a subwoofer for the LFE sub-bass effects. Instead of S/PDIF digital to the amplifier, six discrete analog audio streams are connected to the amplifier from the USB to six-channel DA converter (19).

ASIDE
You must balance the portability advantages of a unit like the Korg D1200 against the flexibility of the software solutions featured in Modules 12 and 17.

Music Sequencing and MIDI Basics

"The first time that two MIDI-equipped instruments built by different companies were hooked up and played together was at the January 1983 National Association of Music Merchants (NAMM) show. . . . For sure, I was a lot more upbeat about the future of MIDI than a lot of then-active synth builders. But no way did I foresee all the directions in which MIDI would grow, or the amazing variety of music software that it would spawn! And it *still* blows my mind that hundreds of manufacturers around the world conform (or almost conform) *voluntarily* to the MIDI specification."

—*Robert Moog, Foreword from Lehrman and Tully's* MIDI for the Professional

Overview

In this Viewport, we turn our attention to the basics of the MIDI (Music Instrument Digital Interface) protocol. We begin with a description of MIDI as a data structure and end with hardware additions to a computer workstation that accommodate MIDI. Using illustrations from a variety of software products and platforms, we review the common features of sequencers, including some powerful ways to enhance MIDI sequencing with effects plug-ins, instrument plug-ins, and digital audio.

In times past, when computers where less powerful, sending MIDI messages to hardware devices like keyboard controllers and expansion boxes was the best way to create rich musical content. Today, MIDI combines with digital audio to provide an even more exciting mixture of options for the electronic musician. The MIDI specification has grown to include more functionality and more timbre options, and hardware interfaces now accommodate both MIDI data streams and digital audio. This Viewport will provide an introduction to MIDI and prepare you for the next section on advanced MIDI and digital audio environments.

Objectives

In Module 14, we cover what MIDI is and how it works. We provide detailed tables on General MIDI timbres and help you figure out how to connect your computer to a MIDI interface. Module 15 reviews basic-level MIDI sequencing software, including a section on how this software supports digital audio and special instrument plug-ins. We end the Viewport with Module 16's treatment of MIDI

MUSIC TECHNOLOGY IN PRACTICE

Jeff Shuter

Jeff Shuter works as a freelance producer and film/media composer. A recent graduate of Northwestern University, Shuter has designed his studio "bedroom" in West Hollywood, CA. Shuter has scored several highly acclaimed short films, theatrical works, and commercials. His debut LP "metaphysic" (Optik Records - Chicago) received strong reviews and an appearance at select Virgin Megastores, which led to radio-play for his single "How Does It Feel (Act2 Records - New York/Chicago). In addition, the music video for "How Does It Feel" received a student Emmy from the Academy of Television Arts and Sciences.

Kevin Weinstein, used by permission

Jeff Shuter working in his home studio creating hip-hop and dance music

Application

Jeff's interest in music began when he started playing cello, studying with a former principal cellist of the Milwaukee Symphony Orchestra. He became interested in piano and polyphonic textures, as well as his friend's drum machine. He started his first band in high school, playing presets on an older electronic keyboard. In college, Jeff didn't major in music but studied screenwriting. In his junior year, he discovered an interesting relationship between the structure of dramatic action in story writing and music composition. He began using an AKAI-MPC 2000 to do sequencing and this led to many music compositions based on developing plot lines and characters as metaphors for music forms and music elements. More sophisticated hardware and software followed.

Hardware and Software

Jeff's studio has grown quite a bit since the days of his first keyboard and drum machine. "After learning how to make any kind of decent-sounding grooves on a drum grid, I'm just about ready to take on anything. Pro Tools is so much easier!! This is my basic setup. It goes from the typical to the absolutely obscure:

- Mac G4 Titanium running Pro Tools 002 with Pro-Control
- Wavestation, Digital Performer, Logic, Koblo
- Gigasampler with Vienna Symphony Orchestra library
- Korg Karma w/expandable keyboard cards
- Novation Supernova (2nd silver edition)
- EMU Proteus (rackmount)
- Quasimidi 309
- Quasimidi Sirius
- Akai MPC-2000
- Akai DPS-12
- Emu-2000 (sampler)
- Evolution MIDI keyboard
- Joe Meek mic-pre
- Fostex burner
- Varied Roland reverb gear/fx processors
- Cello
- Varied percussion instruments
- Very cool-sounding trash cans (for interesting drum samples)
- Studiophile monitors
- 2 Roland 500 keyboard amps
- My "dictaphone" from junior year in high school
- A "Speak 'n' Spell" (yes, I am completely serious)"

Jeff still does about 90% of his sequencing on the MPC. He uses Pro Tools ". . . to expand the depth, breadth, and fluidity of my work. I also use Pro Tools for vocals, as well as most audio sweetening. In terms of stuff like trash cans, Speak 'n' Spells, and cellos ... these things make for some incredible soundscapes and wonderfully obscure drum sounds. For example, I'll sample consonants from my 'Speak 'n' Spell,' and layer them on top of a groove I've played on my trash cans. Then I'll have my digital drum kits on top alongside fragments of cello. So, instead of immersing myself in audio technicalities, I try to find the most obscure and fascinating fragments of rhythm from the world outside and only use my electronic gear to heighten the sound and really bring it to life."

hardware with special MIDI keyboard workstations and sound modules. At the end of this Viewport, you should understand:

- Differences between the MIDI and digital audio data structures
- MIDI codes and the MIDI performance language
- The General MIDI standard and its importance to computer music activities
- Storing and exchanging standard MIDI files
- How to record multiple tracks of MIDI data from a MIDI device
- Editing MIDI files, including the application of special effects and MIDI plug-ins
- How to apply special plug-in software for virtual instruments
- Adding digital audio to basic-level MIDI sequencers
- Mixing and saving MIDI data, as well as converting MIDI data to digital audio
- How to build MIDI networks with the many available hardware options
- The features of MIDI keyboards, workstations, and sound modules
- Sound synthesis approaches through hardware

DVD-ROM Software Projects

In terms of hands-on tasks, you should be able to:

- Create and edit MIDI tracks (Project 11)
- Combine audio and MIDI tracks as well as add plug-ins, virtual instruments, and mix, master, convert, and save MIDI files (Project 12)

DVD-ROM

As with all the software modules in this text, the accompanying DVD contains projects for you to use to practice your skills.

Module 14

How MIDI Works

We turn our attention now from digital audio and audio sampling to what is known as MIDI (rhymes with "city"), or the Musical Instrument Digital Interface. Viewports III and IV were devoted extensively to digital audio: data structures, software, and hardware for manipulating the binary codes that represent a computer's rendering of sonic experiences. In contrast, MIDI is based on data structures that represent music performance data, or machine-coded instructions for playing music.

As we probe the topic of MIDI, you will see that musicians need both digital audio and MIDI music representation systems in a computer music workstation. You need MIDI's ability to capture performance event data and the sonic realism of digital audio. In the past, musicians may have thought in terms of working with MIDI or working with digital audio as two separate environments. That is no longer valid. MIDI is part of the same all-digital world that can be used to manipulate and control the sonic realism of digital audio. Table 14.1 compares the attributes of MIDI and digital audio data structures to emphasize their unique characteristics.

ASIDE
As you saw earlier in the digital audio discussions, hardware devices may provide both digital audio and MIDI capture and playback in an integrated package. Edirol's UA-20, SD-90, UA-1000, and DA-2496 hardware are cases in point.

LINK
MIDI concepts will be covered in this module. Sequencing and other MIDI software such as Cakewalk Home Studio is the topic of Module 15. And, MIDI hardware such as the Triton LE and Tascam 428 is discussed in Module 16.

TABLE 14.1	A Comparison of MIDI and Digital Audio Data Structures
MIDI	**Digital Audio**
Performance or event data	Sampled-sound data
Sound quality depends on external sources	Sound quality inherent in sampled data
Flexible data structure	Inflexible data structure
Music parts can be separated from the whole	Music parts not easily separated from the whole
Small storage demands	Large storage demands
Reproduction depends on independent sound source	Reproduction depends on sampling hardware
Less-than-perfect reproduction of performance nuance	Perfect reproduction of performance nuance
Best suited for extended music performance with minimum storage needs	Best suited for performance where storage is not an issue (e.g., on CD- or DVD-R)

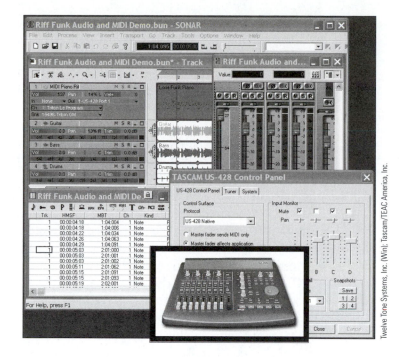

FIGURE 14.1 An overview of Cakewalk Sonar sequencing software showing a variety of features for MIDI and digital audio; the overlay shows a Tascam 428 hardware controller working in tandem with the Sonar software

The synthesizers and sound modules that MIDI needs for sound generation are digital devices. Because of this integration, sequencing and editing software has created environments where the two data structures not only coexist, but depend on each other. More importantly, these integrated environments provide the ability to synchronize data from both structures to produce music that makes the best use of MIDI's event structures and digital audio's sonic structures.

Figure 14.1 offers a sample of MIDI features to be discussed throughout this Viewport and illustrates the integration of MIDI and digital audio. This is a scene in the Cakewalk Sonar sequencer (software featured in Viewport VI). The "Lone Funk Piano" track consists of MIDI performance codes being sent out to a Korg Triton LE keyboard synthesizer. The Guitar, Bass, and Drum tracks are all digital audio. The software mixer in the upper left-hand corner is controlled with MIDI codes by the Tascam 428 hardware mixer shown in the overlay window; the Tascam Control Panel window is shown directly behind it. To the left of the Tascam photo is Sonar's MIDI event window, which shows the performance codes for all of the piano notes being sent out to the Triton synthesizer.

MIDI 20th Anniversary Logo

MIDI Sound Structures

How do MIDI performance codes work? By performance codes we mean, for example, the numbers generated by a MIDI keyboard when keys are pressed while playing some music. These numbers, sent to a computer and captured by MIDI sequencing software, communicate the number of the key played, the intensity with which the key was pressed, and the amount of time that each key was held down. Only these performance data are stored in the computer, not the actual sounds of the music itself. The performance data can then be sent to other MIDI music instruments that recreate the sound using the digital or analog sound generators available in that particular MIDI instrument. This structure, or way of describing and exchanging music performance data, is at the heart of MIDI.

MIDI is an industry standard for communicating music performance data among music devices such as computers, synthesizers, drum machines, instrument controllers, tape recorders, mixers, effects generators, and, as we will see in Module 18, a wide array of customized music-control devices. The MIDI standard includes both the performance language for communicating among MIDI devices (data structures) and the specifications for how MIDI devices are electronically connected (hardware).

Figure 14.2 illustrates two MIDI networks. Figure 14.2a shows two MIDI devices, a keyboard and a computer, communicating with one another. A minimum of two MIDI devices is needed to create a network: two synthesizer keyboards, a computer and a keyboard, a keyboard and a drum machine, and so on. Most MIDI devices can send MIDI data (OUT), receive MIDI data (IN), and pass MIDI data on through the network (THRU). A very basic MIDI system, with a computer connected to an electronic keyboard, looks like the one in Figure 14.2a.

Figure 14.2b shows an expanded MIDI network in which a series of MIDI devices are connected in a daisy chain. This diagram helps illustrate the notion of *channels*. The MIDI language can transmit performance data over 16 discrete MIDI channels that are similar to TV channels. Any MIDI device can tune in to one or more of these channels to receive the performance commands being broadcast over them.

Potentially, 16 MIDI devices can receive data over a MIDI network. Most MIDI devices default to Channel 1 as the base channel, but can be retuned to any of the 16 channels. Notice that the first MIDI device is the *master* unit and all of the others are *slave* devices. Each slave passes the network MIDI data on to the next device with its MIDI THRU connection. You would consider this type of network if you needed to add more MIDI devices: perhaps a sound module, a drum machine, or another keyboard.

MIDI Performance Language

MIDI performance codes are a simple computer language with commands and data. Combinations of commands and data are referred to as MIDI *messages*. MIDI messages allow considerable control over performance on any MIDI devices.

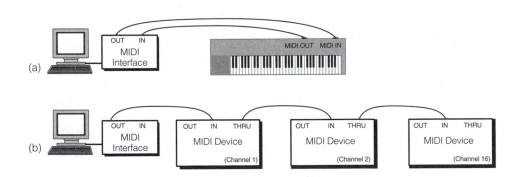

FIGURE 14.2 Two MIDI networks: (a) simple, two-device network, and (b) daisy-chain network

ASIDE

Other options for adding multiple MIDI devices exist if you have a more advanced MIDI interface. More on this in Module 16.

The two primary sets of MIDI messages are:

- *Channel messages*, which are commands broadcast to a MIDI device on any one of the 16 available channels
- *System messages*, which are commands broadcast to *all* devices on *all* MIDI channels

Channel Messages

Channel messages are commands broadcast on a specific MIDI channel. These commands include playing notes, expressive properties, and monophonic versus polyphonic performing modes. The two types of channel messages are *voice* and *mode*.

Channel voice messages. Most channel messages are voice messages. These commands are the "fingers" that do the playing, and they require certain data. Because they are channel messages, they require a channel number (1 to 16) to identify the unique channel for broadcasting the data.

The most used MIDI channel voice messages include:

- Note On
- Program Change
- Control Change

Note On produces the notes to be played on a MIDI device connected to the system. It is the most often used command in the MIDI language. This message requires data that specify which note is to be turned on or off. The notes are numbered on a continuum from 0 to 127; the 88 keys on the piano keyboard span from the values 21 to 108, with middle C being number 60.

The Note On command also requires a *velocity* value that controls the volume or dynamics of the note, including turning the note off. On a MIDI device without velocity sensing (e.g., a keyboard with no velocity-sensing keys), no matter how hard you strike the keys, the loudness or volume will not change. These devices produce only two values, 0 (off) and 64 (on). When the MIDI device has velocity sensing, the data values can range between 0 (off) and 127, with 1 being pianissimo (pp) and 127 being fortissimo (ff). Figure 14.3 analyzes a stream of MIDI note on-and-off data being sent to a keyboard from a computer to help illustrate how the MIDI syntax works.

The *Program Change* message sets the instrument or *patch* to be used on devices tuned into a channel. The message is accompanied by data indicating the channel and instrument numbers. Originally, instrument numbers were not standardized. You had to know the unique number for a given timbre for each MIDI

FIGURE 14.3 The flow of MIDI channel voice messages from a computer to a keyboard: the Note On and Note Off commands

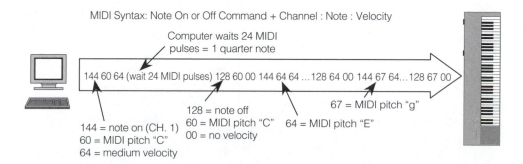

TIP

Most MIDI instruments have a General MIDI sound bank. Many have several other banks of instrument sounds (128 patches per bank). These nonstandardized banks are unique to each manufacturer and model.

device; a clarinet sound did not necessarily have the same number on two different synthesizers. Later, the *General MIDI* format (1991) introduced a standardized numbering system for MIDI instruments so that piano timbres, string timbres, wind timbres, and so on. would have the same patch or program number regardless of the MIDI synthesizer being used. The actual sounds, however, may still vary from device to device; one device's clarinet sample, for example, may not sound the same as another's (depending on the quality of the sample, the original sampled instrument, etc.).

The *Control Change* message provides performance control over a variety of expressive properties. These include vibrato, sustain or release time, overall volume on a channel, and so on. Like the other messages, the Control Change command is accompanied by a data value to set the degree of control.

Channel Mode messages. Mode messages control how many channels a MIDI device receives (Omni On or Omni Off) and how many voices it plays or transmits (Monophonic or Polyphonic; in MIDI, the term "voices" refers to the number of notes you can play simultaneously on any one channel). There are four combinations of Omni On or Off and Monophonic or Polyphonic; these combinations are known as Modes 1 through 4. Figure 14.4 illustrates the various mode combinations.

Mode 3 (Omni Off/Polyphonic), the Poly mode, is the most frequently used mode for music instruction, sequencing programs, and the like. Many MIDI devices have a default setting of Mode 3. In this mode, each MIDI channel contains specific, polyphonic performance data.

An additional handy Channel Mode command is All Notes Off. MIDI devices sometimes get stuck in play mode, and this command will turn off all sound. Some MIDI devices identify a specific "panic" button for this function.

System Messages

System messages do not contain channel codes. These commands affect *all* devices in the MIDI network, and broadcast over *all* channels. There are three types of system messages: Common, Real Time, and Exclusive. These commands control the timing events, sequences of performance data, and special effects unique to MIDI devices.

For most simple MIDI applications, channel messages are of primary concern and system messages are rarely needed. On the other hand, system messages take on greater importance for more advanced composing and performing techniques as a musician seeks to use more of the sophisticated MIDI techniques unique to a given music synthesizer or controller.

System Common messages provide indexing control over sequences of MIDI performance data. The common commands enable you to select various sequences,

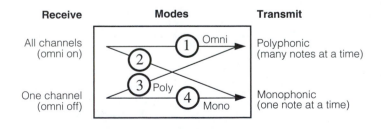

FIGURE 14.4 Four combinations of MIDI channel mode messages

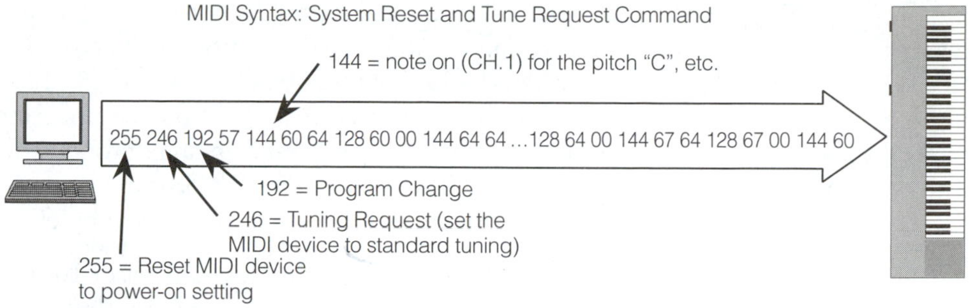

MIDI Syntax: System Reset and Tune Request Command

144 = note on (CH.1) for the pitch "C", etc.

255 246 192 57 144 60 64 128 60 00 144 64 64 ...128 64 00 144 67 64 128 67 00 144 60

192 = Program Change

246 = Tuning Request (set the
MIDI device to standard tuning)

255 = Reset MIDI device
to power-on setting

FIGURE 14.5 The flow of MIDI system messages from a computer to a keyboard

index specific locations within a sequence (song pointers), and carry out real-time indexing of sequences with MIDI time codes. MIDI devices generate a timing code of 24 pulses per quarter-note that all devices on the MIDI network can use to synchronize performance and performance effects. Also, System Common messages include a command that turns the General MIDI format on and off.

The System Messages serve the same function as controls on a tape deck. They provide commands for starting, stopping, pausing, and continuing the performance of MIDI sequences. Figure 14.5 illustrates how two system real-time messages, System Reset and Tune Request, can be embedded in a stream of MIDI data sent to a keyboard synthesizer.

System Exclusive messages offer each MIDI manufacturer exclusive codes or patches for its device. These are termed SysEx messages (pronounced "siss-ex"). A unique identification number is assigned to a given manufacturer's device and only that device will acknowledge SysEx messages addressed to it. There are now more than 150 different manufacturer codes on an ever-expanding list.

ASIDE
General MIDI is important to MIDI sounds used in multimedia and gaming environments, as well as to the dissemination of MIDI sequences across the Internet.

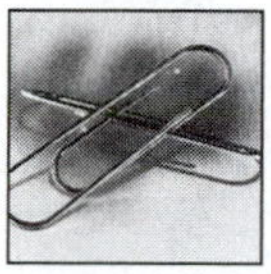

LINK
More on XG, GS, and other extensions to MIDI instrument patches in Module 18. Module 15 discusses using these extensions from software.

General MIDI

Consider the chaos that surfaced as manufacturers of the first MIDI instruments assigned different values to MIDI codes to suit the idiosyncrasies of their instruments. The values for Program Change codes representing instrument patches were different. Percussion sounds were assigned to different keyboard keys. Controllers for modulation, breath control, and portamento were assigned different values. The Timing Codes varied from 24 pulses per quarter-note to 96 or more. The instruments defaulted to different settings, some to Mode 3 and others to Mode 1. It made it very difficult to prepare a MIDI score with one MIDI network configuration and expect it to work on another. With the rapidly expanding consumer market using MIDI instruments, it was critical to have plug-and-play capability regardless of the instrument manufacturer.

Enter the General MIDI standard or GM. The MIDI Manufacturers Association (MMA) approved the GM standard in 1991. General MIDI defines a set of minimum standards among MIDI devices; instruments complying with these standards display the distinctive "General MIDI" logo.

In 1999, the General MIDI 2 standards were approved as an expansion of the original specifications. The original GM specifications are referred to as GM1. The MMA designed GM2 in response to initiatives like the Yamaha XG and

Roland GS extensions to General MIDI. These extensions added a richer array of instrument patches using additional "banks" of sounds, new banks of percussion sets, and additional controller options to enhance the sound quality of General MIDI music productions. MIDI devices meeting the GM2 specification have a "General MIDI 2" logo and include products from Roland, Yamaha, Korg, and others. A GM1 or GM2 MIDI instrument should provide as a minimum the following attributes (GM2 specifications in brackets):

- *Sound set.* Provides the standard set of 16 instrument groups defined with 128 patches or program changes within those groups, and the defined key set for percussion instruments [GM2 provides 256 standardized instrument patches and eight additional percussion patches by using bank switching to overlay additional instrument sounds to the original 128; the original 128 patches remain the same.]
- *Voices.* Perform 24 notes simultaneously, or 16 notes and eight percussion sounds. [GM2 provides 32 simultaneous notes.]
- *Channels.* Provide the full 16 channels, with Channel 10 reserved for percussion sounds. [GM2 recommends the use of Channel 11 to provide two channels for Rhythm.]
- *Channel messages.* Provide for velocity sensitivity, channel and polyphonic key pressure, and pitch bend with at least a ± 2 semitone range.
- *Controllers.* Provide codes (cc) for modulation (cc=1), volume (cc=7), pan (cc=10), expression (cc=11), sustain (cc=64), reset all controllers (cc=121), and all notes off (cc=123). [GM2 provides a greater array of controller standards, including bank select (cc=32), portamento (cc=5 and 65), vibrato (cc=76–78), attack-decay-release (cc=72, 73, 75), and reverb and chorus effects (cc=91 and 93).] Table 14.2 lists the more commonly used controller messages.
- *Universal System-Exclusive messages (SysEx).* The primary code is the one used to turn GM settings on or off. [GM2 added additional universal System Exclusive Messages (SysEx) codes for tuning, master volume control, reverb and chorus effect controls, and turning GM2 on and off.]

Table 14.3 shows the suggested channel assignments, with the critical Channel 10 reserved for percussion or rhythm and the GM2 alternative Channel 11 for two rhythm channels. Table 14.5 shows the 16 instrument groups established for General MIDI. Within each group are eight patches or instruments for program changes, providing a total set of 128 instruments. Table 14.5 also shows new instrument patches added for GM2. The method used for accessing the new sounds may seem strange, but the design ensures that GM2 is backward compatible with sounds on a GM1 device. The new instrument sounds were added to the current 128 instrument patches by placing the patches in different "banks" of sounds. To play a Mandolin sound with GM2, the patch would be 26 (Acoustic Steel Guitar), bank 2 (Mandolin). Likewise, to program a "Jazz Man" electric guitar timbre, the patch would be 29 (Muted Electric Guitar) and bank 3, Jazz Man. Playing these program settings on a GM1 synthesizer would default to Steel Guitar and Muted Electric Guitar; on a GM2 synth, the performance would render Mandolin and Jazz Man.

GM1 only provided one Standard percussion set; the percussion sounds were mapped onto the keys of the keyboard (MIDI notes 24–88). GM2 has seen a dramatic increase in percussion options; the range of the Standard set has been expanded from Notes 35–81 to Notes 27–88. Most significantly, there are nine

TIP

CAUTION! The GM and GM2 charts provided in this textbook use labels for instrument patches provided by MMA. Be aware that manufacturers of MIDI gear create their own "flavors" of instrument patch sounds and labels within the MMA standards. So don't be surprised when you read the instrument patch names on your Edirol SD-90, for example, to discover that they vary somewhat from the labels in our chart—especially for the GM2 patch names.

LINK

Trying to figure out how to choose the correct patch number and bank number to get the desired General MIDI 2 instrument patch may seem a daunting task. Take comfort in the knowledge that Module 15 will show you how sequencing software makes this task easy by letting the software do the MIDI coding required to select patches and banks.

T A B L E   1 4 . 2   Commonly Used Continuous, Switch, and Sound Controller Codes

Number	Resolution	Function	Comments
0, 32	MSB+LSB[2]	Bank switch	Selects among banks of instrument patches
1, 33	Coarse or Fine[1]	Modulation wheel	Adds vibrato to tone
2, 34	Coarse or Fine[1]	Breath control	Simulates breath control as on a single wind-instrument tone, may be used like after-touch
65	On or Off	Portamento switch	Glides between notes, on or off
5, 37	Coarse or Fine[1]	Portamento time	Rate of glide between two notes
7, 39	Coarse or Fine[1]	Volume	Overall amplitude of sound or all notes (def. value = 100)
11, 43	Coarse or Fine[1]	Expression	Dynamic change independent of volume to effect crescendos and diminuendos (def. value = 127)
10, 42	Coarse or Fine[1]	Pan	Spatial placement of sound, left-to-right or front-to-back
64	On or Off	Hold or sustain switch	When turned on, holds or sustains all notes played until turned off
66	On or Off	Sostenuto switch	When turned on, sustains any notes already on, but not any new notes; like the middle pedal on a piano
67	On or Off	Soft-pedal switch	Softens sound volume; like the left pedal on a piano
71	MSB -64 <0> +64	Filter resonance	When combined with cc 74, adjusts the harmonic resonance at the filter cutoff, thus changing the timbre of the sound
72	MSB -64 <0> +64	Release time (R)	Release part of ADR envelope
73	MSB -64 <0> +64	Attack time (A)	Attach part of ADR envelope
74	MSB -64 <0> +64	Filter cutoff or brightness	When combined with cc 71, controls the frequency setting of the filter, higher is brighter
75	MSB -64 <0> +64	Decay time (D)	Decay part of ADR envelope
76	MSB -64 <0> +64	Vibrato depth	Finer control of vibrato than cc=1, cc 76–77 provide three parameters for adjusting vibrato effects
77	MSB -64 <0> +64	Vibrato rate	Combined with cc 76–77
78	MSB -64 <0> +64	Vibrato delay	Combined with cc 76–77
91	MSB 0–127	Reverb effect	Adjusts send level for reverb effect (def. value = 0)
93	MSB 0–127	Chorus effect	Adjusts send level for chorus effect (def. value = 0)

Notes:
[1]Using one or two bytes of data for coarse (0–127) or fine (0–16,683) values for these controllers is optional.
[2]MSB indicates the use of a single byte of 7-bit data (0–127), or MSB+LSB, the combination of two bytes to create 14-bit data (0–16,683) for a controller's value setting.

percussion sets to choose from through the appropriate MIDI bank: Standard, Room, Power, Electronic, Analog, Jazz, Brush, Orchestra, and SFX. Concert Snare and Bass Drum sounds, as well as an octave of Tympani patches, are provided in the Orchestra set. The other seven new sets provide an array of specialty drum sounds with a number of Tom-Tom and Conga drums and a separate SFX set for special effects.

TABLE 14.3 General MIDI Channel Assignments				
Channel	**Part**	**Channel**	**Part**
1	Piano	6	Sub Melody
2	Bass	7	Lower Part
3	Chord	8	Harmony Part
4	Melody	9	Melodic Part
5	Sub Chord	10	Rhythm (Drum)
		11	Rhythm (Drum) added for GM2

Note: Assignment of the first 9 channels (16 available with GM standard) may vary to some degree, but Channel 10's use for percussion is inviolate in GM. GM2 added a second percussion channel with Channel 11, but its use is optional.

LINK
Exporting and importing music files for sequencing software is a key topic in Module 15 and again in Module 20 for notation software.

ASIDE
Even cell phones use MIDI files for their ring tones—MIDI SMF Format 0 files are used for this application.

LINK
The issue of display and performance codes for notation and MIDI is discussed in depth in Module 18.

Storing and Exchanging MIDI Files

The MIDI Manufacturers Association adopted a set of Standard MIDI File, or SMF, formats in 1988. SMF MIDI files contain performance events that happen over time: MIDI events like note on, note off, velocity, control codes, and so on. These files have the extension .MID (e.g., mysong.mid). Most music sequencing and notation programs allow you to import and save SMF files. Table 14.4 contrasts the differences among the three formats (also referred to as "types") of SMF files: Formats 0, 1, and 2. A quick study of this table conveys the essential point that Formats 0 and 1 are the most-used SMF file types: Format 0 for exchanging MIDI files in their simplest form, especially over the Internet; Format 1 for editing MIDI files between multitrack sequencing software where it is important to maintain track distinctions for MIDI data.

SMF files do not contain notation display information that may have been entered in a sequencer or notation software; they also do not contain audio tracks from a sequencer. Because SMF is a performance data structure designed to serve MIDI applications, SMF files contain only MIDI codes and related data. Text may be coded as SMF "meta events" and used for specifying track names, instrument names, lyrics, copyright notices, and the like.

Why have SMF files? Three reasons come immediately to mind. First, SMF files work fine when going from performance environment to performance environment, as with sequencers or with MIDI music players, for example. SMF Format 0 works well for sharing files over the Internet; Format 1 for exchanging multitrack music between different sequencing software and some GM hardware. Second, SMF in a notation environment can be used similarly to ASCII text files in a word processor. If a musician needs to go between notation programs, at least the basic content can be imported and exported: pitch and, with some limitations, meter and rhythm. Third, most music software and hardware seem to support the MIDI SMF standard, even given its deficiencies.

Do you have to use SMF files? No. Most music software has its own proprietary file format that retains all of the features and nuances added in the composing or arranging process. This should be the format of choice; only use SMF when you need to share files with other musicians using software that will not import these proprietary formats.

TABLE 14.4   Three Types of Standard MIDI Files Format Structure

Format Structure

0	Single track: all MIDI data from all 16 channels combined into one track; greatest compatibility with all sequencers due to its simplicity.
1	Simultaneous multitrack: MIDI data intended to be performed simultaneously, coded in multiple tracks; tempo and time signature in first track only; best used for exchanging multitrack data between sequencing software for editing.
2	Independent multitrack: MIDI data intended to be performed independently, coded in unique tracks; tempo and time signature coded separately in each track; least-used format.

Experiencing MIDI Software and Hardware

You now have an introduction to the basics of MIDI data structures. Capturing unique sound samples of traditional or new musical instruments with digital audio techniques and using MIDI codes to create music performances using those sound samples is a powerful combination. The sampled-sound data of digital audio and the music-event data of MIDI have achieved a common ground where musicians can work interactively and simultaneously within both structures. The next module will give you the opportunity to experience the software tools that make this synergy happen; Module 16 will then introduce you to the options for MIDI controllers and other MIDI hardware.

TABLE 14.5   General MIDI (GM1/GM2) Instrument Patch Map[1]

P#	Instrument Group	Instrument	GM2 Extensions[2]	P#	Instrument Group	Instrument	GM2 Extensions[2]
1	Piano	Acoustic Grand	[01]AG Piano (wide); [02]AG Piano (dark)	5		Electric Piano 1	[01]Detuned EP1; [02]EP1; (velocity mix); [03]60s E Piano
2		Bright Acoustic	[01]BA Piano (wide)	6		Electric Piano 2	[01]Detuned EP2; [02]EP2 (velocity mix); [3]EP Legend; [4]EP Phase
3		Electric Grand	[01]EG Piano (wide)				
4		Honky-Tonk	[01]HT Piano (wide)				

Note 1: Some abbreviations were used for naming GM2 extensions; every attempt was made to use the instrument names provided by the MMA GM2 specifications. Manufacturer labels vary from MMA labels.
Note 2: GM2 instrument extensions require a MIDI bank switch in parallel to the MIDI patch code. The codes in brackets, e.g., [01], [02], . . . [05] represent the MIDI bank assignment for that instrument extension. The advantage of this system is that music arranged for GM2 extensions is still backwards compatible with GM1, i.e., something close to the GM2 instrument will still play, since the patch number is the same.

(continued)

TABLE 14.5 General MIDI(GM1/GM2) Instrument Patch Map[1] *(continued)*

P#	Instrument Group	Instrument	GM2 Extensions[2]	P#	Instrument Group	Instrument	GM2 Extensions[2]
7		Harpsichord	[01]Harpsi (octave mix); [02]Harpsi (wide); [03]Harpsi (key off)	29		Electric Guitar (muted)	[01]EG (funky cutting); [02]EG (muted velo-sw); [03]Jazz Man
8		Clavi	[01]Pulse Clavi	30		Overdriven Guitar	[01]Guitar Pinch
9	Chromatic Percussion	Celesta		31		Distortion Guitar	[01]DG (w/feed back); [02]DG Rhythm
10		Glocken-spiel		32		Guitar Harmonics	[01]Guitar Feedback
11		Music Box		33	Bass	Acoustic Bass	
12		Vibraphone	[01]Vibe (wide)	34		Electric Bass (fingered)	[01]Finger Slap Bass
13		Marimba	[01]Marimba (wide)	35		Electric Bass (pick)	
14		Xylophone		36		Fretless Bass	
15		Tubular Bells	[01]Church Bell; [02]Carillon	37		Slap Bass 1	
16		Dulcimer		38		Slap Bass 2	
17	Organ	Drawbar Organ	[01]Detuned DO; [02]Italian 60s Organ; [03]DO2	39		Synth Bass 1	[01]SB (warm); [02]SB3 (resonance); [03]Clavi Bass; [04]Hammer
18		Percussive Organ	[01]Detuned PO, [02]PO2	40		Synth Bass 2	[01]SB4 (attack); [02]SB (rubber); [03]Attack Pulse
19		Rock Organ					
20		Church Organ	[01]CO (Octave Mix); [02]Detuned CO	41	Strings	Violin	[01]Violin (slow attack)
21		Reed Organ	[01]Puff Organ	42		Viola	
22		Accordion	Accordion 2	43		Cello	
23		Harmonica		44		Contrabass	
24		Tango Accordion		45		Tremolo Strings	
25	Guitar	Acoustic Guitar (nylon)	[01]Ukulele; [02]AG (nylon+key off); [03]AG (nylon2)	46		Pizzicato Strings	
26		Acoustic Guitar (steel)	[01]12-Strings; [02]Mandolin; [03]Steel w/body sound	47		Orchestral Harp	[01]Yang Chin
27		Electric Guitar (jazz)	[01]EG (pedal steel)	48		Timpani	
28		Electric Guitar (clean)	[01]EG (detuned clean); [02]EG (mid tone)	49	Ensemble	String En-sembles 1	[01]Strings & Brass; [02]60s Strings

TABLE 14.5 *(continued)*

P#	Instrument Group	Instrument	GM2 Extensions[2]	P#	Instrument Group	Instrument	GM2 Extensions[2]
50		String Ensembles 2		79		Whistle	
51		Synth-Strings 1	[01]Synth-Strings 3	80		Ocarina	
52		Synth-Strings 2		81	Synth Lead	Lead 1 (square)	[01]Lead1a (square 2); [02]Lead1b (sine);
53		Choir Aahs	[01]Choir Aahs 2	82		Lead 2 (sawtooth)	[01]Lead2a (saw 2); [02]Lead2b (saw+pulse); [03]Lead2c (double saw); [04]Lead2d (sequenced analog)
54		Voice Oohs	[01]Humming				
55		Synth Voice	[01]Analog Voice				
56		Orchestra Hit	[01]Brass Hit Plus; [02]6th Hit; [03]Euro Hit				
				83		Lead 3 (calliope)	
57	Brass	Trumpet	[01]Dark Trumpet Soft	84		Lead 4 (chiff)	
58		Trombone	[01]Tromb2; [02]Bright Tromb	85		Lead 5 (charang)	[01]Lead5a (wire)
59		Tuba		86		Lead 6 (air voice)	
60		Muted Trumpet	[01]MTrmpt2	87		Lead 7 (fifths)	
61		French Horn	[01]FH2 (warm)	88		Lead 8 (bass+lead)	[01]Lead8a (soft wrl)
62		Brass Section	[01]BS2 (octave mix)				
63		Synth-Brass 1	[01]SB3; [02]Analog SB1; [03]Jump Brass	89	Synth Pad	Pad 1 (new age)	
64		Synth-Brass 2	[01]SB4; [02]Analog SB2	90		Pad 2 (warm)	[01]Pad2a (sine pad)
				91		Pad 3 (polysynth)	
65	Reed	Soprano Sax		92		Pad 4 (choir)	[01]Pad4a (itopia)
66		Alto Sax		93		Pad 5 (bowed)	
67		Tenor Sax		94		Pad 6 (metallic)	
68		Baritone Sax		95		Pad 7 (halo)	
69		Oboe		96		Pad 8 (sweep)	
70		English Horn					
71		Bassoon		97	Synth SFX	FX1 (rain)	
72		Clarinet		98		FX2 (sound track)	
				99		FX3 (crystal)	[01]FX3A Synth Mallet
73	Pipe	Piccolo		100		FX4 (atmosphere)	
74		Flute		101		FX5 (brightness)	
75		Recorder					
76		Pan Flute					
77		Blown Bottle					
78		Shakuhachi					

(continued)

TABLE 14.5 General MIDI(GM1/GM2) Instrument Patch Map[1] *(continued)*

P#	Instrument Group	Instrument	GM2 Extensions[2]	P#	Instrument Group	Instrument	GM2 Extensions[2]
102		FX6 (goblins)		121	Sound Effects (SFX)	FX1 (guitar fret noise)	[01]Guitar Cutting Noise; [02]Bass String Slap
103		FX7 (echos)	[01]FX7a (echo bell); [02]FX7b (echo pan)	122		FX2 (breath noise)	[01]Flute Key Click
104		FX8 (sci-fi)		123		FX3 (seashore)	[01]Rain; [02]Thunder; [03]Wind; [04]Stream; [05]Bubble
105	Ethnic	Sitar	[01]Sitar2 (bend)				
106		Banjo		124		FX4 (bird tweet)	[01]Dog; [02]Horse Gallop; [03]Bird Tweet2
107		Shamisen					
108		Koto	[01]Taisho Koto				
109		Kalimba		125		FX5 (telephone ring)	[01]TeleRing2; [02]Door Creaking; [03]Door; [04]Scratch; [05]Wind Chime
110		Bag Pipe					
111		Fiddle					
112		Shanai					
113	Percussive	Tinkle Bell		126		FX6 (helicopter)	[01]Car Engine; [02]Car Stop; [03]Car Pass; [04]Car Crash; [05]Siren
114		Agogo					
115		Steel Drums					
116		Woodblock	[01]Castanets				
117		Taiko Drum	[01]Concert Bass Drum	127		FX7 (applause)	[01]Laughing; [02]Screaming; [03]Punch; [04]Heartbeat; [05]Footsteps
118		Melodic Tom	[01]Melodic Tom2 (power)				
119		Synth Drum	[01]Rhythm Box Tom; [02]Electric Drum				
120		Reverse Cymbal		128		FX8 (gunshot)	[01]Machine Gun; [02]Laser Gun; [03]Explosion

Module 15

Software Techniques for MIDI Sequencing

DVD-ROM
Projects 11–12 on the accompanying DVD are designed to give you hands-on experience with the tasks in Table 15.1.

With the basic understanding of MIDI supplied in the last module, we now turn to software for MIDI sequencing. Actually, you are unlikely to find a popular, music sequencer featuring MIDI that does not also support tracks for digital audio. As we noted in Viewport IV, many multitrack recorder programs like ProTools and Audition include MIDI. However, in this module we will stress MIDI recording and editing in software that is primarily known for MIDI support; we use the term "sequencer" to characterize these titles.

We begin with some concepts that will help you understand MIDI-based sequencing, including some important terminology. Basic-level sequencers are then featured, including sections on preparing for and doing the recording. Next, we move to editing techniques, including the use of built-in effects and MIDI effects plug-ins. We include an introduction to virtual-instrument plug-ins, present a section on adding digital audio to MIDI, and end the module with information on saving MIDI data files. As with tables in other modules, Table 15.1 provides a set of tasks that will guide your study.

TABLE 15.1 Tasks for Music Sequencing and MIDI Basics		
Setting	**Task**	**Typical Software**
Studio or Live Concert Setting	• Record multiple tracks of MIDI data from a MIDI device, edit MIDI files	PowerTracks Pro Audio, Home Studio, Metro SE, Logic Express, Tracktion, Cubase SE
Studio	• Apply virtual instruments and MIDI effects	Home Studio, VSC, VeloMaster Lite
Studio with and without Live Performers	• Add digital audio tracks to basic-level MIDI sequencers	PowerTracks Pro Audio, Home Studio, Metro SE, Logic Express, Tracktion, Cubase SE
Studio	• Mix and save MIDI data, as well as convert it to digital audio	PowerTracks Pro Audio, Home Studio, Metro SE, Logic Express, Tracktion, Cubase SE

Basic Design of Sequencing Software

Have you ever watched an old-time player piano work? If so, you probably noticed a paper piano roll with holes that moved across a tracker bar. The holes are triggers that control which notes are played and how loudly they're played. Even the keys and the pedals of the piano move appropriately, controlled by the paper roll. The player piano and the principle that makes it work date back some 150 years and provide an example of an early music sequencer.

What Does Sequencing Software Do?

One answer is "record and process music data." A more precise answer is "record and process MIDI and digital audio data." As you learned in the last module, MIDI is a kind of digital language that describes music performance. It uses numerical codes to tell some *other device* to turn on a sound, play it at a certain loudness level and with certain effects, and then turn it off.

Sequencing software acts as a tool for capturing and working with MIDI and

Historical Perspective on Sequencing

Music-sequencing machines are actually quite old. One clear beginning would be the eighteenth century, early music boxes and music composed by Mozart for barrel organ. The paper piano rolls that followed were created by artists who understood patterns in music and their complexity in time. In 1804, an instrument called the Panharmonium was designed by Maelzel. It was driven by air pressure and was intended to reproduce the timbres of traditional instruments. Beethoven wrote the Battle of Vittoria for this device, but it was never performed because of technical problems. The calliope was developed by Boch and Wacher in 1895 using a metal disk with punched holes to represent music.

The beginning of the twentieth century saw the creation of a number of early electronic instruments played by sequences of some kind. In the 1920s, Givelet and Coupleux's Pipeless Organ was one of the first programmable analog music synthesizers. At the same time, Seeburg, Wurlitzer, and others were building the first electronic jukeboxes.

The 1950s saw experiments with some of the first computer systems, like the ILLIAC and the RCA Mark 11 Synthesizer. Music was created on these devices with the help of codes punched on cards or paper tape.

In the next decade, the invention of the transistor helped Buchla create a transistor-based analog synthesizer with the first built-in electronic sequencer. Moog created a synthesizer that became a popular hit. This growth in small keyboard systems continued into the 1970s with the classic Prophet analog synthesizer and the Fairlight and Synclavier devices, which featured real-time sequencing. The first drum

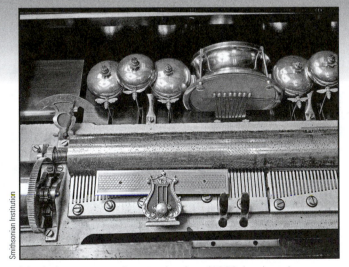

Smithsonian Institution

Music-box sequencing mechanism (1890s) using pins on a cylinder

machine was created by the Linn company, and Roland produced the first digital sequencing device controlled by a microprocessor.

Of course, the real boon for sequencing came in the 1980s with implementation of the MIDI protocol together with the growth of personal computers. Keyboards like the Roland Jupiter 6 and the Yamaha DX7 were among the first instruments to include MIDI. Hundreds of keyboard models

LINK

Look ahead to Module 16 regarding hardware setups that involve MIDI.

digital audio data, usually for the purposes of composing or arranging. This software lets you record multiple layers of information, much as you might record multiple layers of digital audio sound as described in Viewport IV.

Imagine you are working with a computer that has sequencing software installed and a MIDI keyboard coupled with your MIDI interface. You also have a microphone connected, similar to the setup you had in Viewport IV. You tell the software to "record" and then move to the keyboard to play a passage using the bassoon timbre. You begin the passage softly in the low register and then end in a long crescendo with several notes played in a higher register. You play a ritard at the end for a special effect. Returning to your computer, you stop the recording process, "rewind," and listen to what you played. The MIDI software plays back the passage exactly the way you played it, with all the subtleties of phrasing and dynamics.

Next, you ask your software to record on a different track. You return to your keyboard and add another track of percussion sounds while listening to your first passage played back to you by the same MIDI workstation. When finished, you "rewind" again and listen to the whole piece. You also ask your software to add a touch of rubato in the middle of the passage, together with some dynamic changes. You don't like the percussion sounds that your MIDI keyboard is producing, so you ask your software to use an instrument plug-in that simulates percussion sounds.

Now you rewind and add a third track by singing into the microphone. You

Paper-tape sequencing (1950s) with the RCA Electronic Music Synthesizer

have since followed suit, many with sequencers built into the hardware much like the Buchla.

On the computer side, the 1980s saw a growth in both PC and Macintosh music-related products. IBM produced its Music Feature Card, which allowed some software control of sound. Mark of the Unicorn's Performer software for the Macintosh became the first professional software-based sequencing package on a computer. Today, such software, the focus of this module, is plentiful.

The MIDI protocol began as the basic data structure for sequencing; however, the combination of digital audio with MIDI is now quite common. In fact, multitrack recording software that uses only digital audio or uses MIDI just as a triggering or control mechanism rather than for sound generation is emerging as a standard. Such technology is pervasive in all phases of the music enterprise, particularly in the popular music recording and concert scenes. Sound tracks for movies and for many multimedia products rely heavily on sequencing. Composers and conductors such as Pierre Boulez are experimenting with interesting combinations in live performance using analog instruments with MIDI sequencers driving digital equipment. Sequencing will continue to play a role in music development in the future, just as it has in the past.

sing a passage that goes along with your percussion and bassoon sounds. After listening to your voice, you decide to add a little reverb effect and maybe a plug-in effect, much as you did in Module 9 in Viewport III with digital audio editors.

When you're finished, you have two tracks of MIDI data and one track of digital audio. In a nutshell, this is what sequencing software accomplishes.

Better Than a Tape Deck!

Sequencing programs resemble the function of analog tape decks, but with powerful differences. The MIDI instructions and audio data can be flexibly altered in an instant. You edit both the MIDI and audio data for musical ends. You might ask the software to play back the data in a different key and in a different tempo. You can edit errors by simply changing values in a list, with piano-roll or traditional notation. All this flexibility is possible because the MIDI and audio data are just a set of numbers that describe a performance.

Timing

LINK

MIDI and sequencer timing is covered in more depth in Module 18.

Software sequencers constantly run a clock in the background during recording and playback of data. This clock keeps track of measures, beats, and fractions of beats, often referred to as *ticks*. The number of ticks per defined beat varies depending on the software, ranging from 96 to a resolution as high as 1,024. As data arrive at the software sequencer, rhythm is coded against an invisible time grid represented by the tick resolution. This allows the sequencer to be extremely sensitive to nuances in performance tempo. Generally, the higher the resolution, the more accurate the sequencer is in coding rhythmic performance.

The concept of "quantization" is also critical for understanding how sequencers work. Sequencers can be asked to adjust time values to make notes conform to standard grid alignments, such as an eighth- or sixteenth-note. This can be useful if you intend to export the file to a notation package for printing, or to fine-tune a section to make it sound rhythmically tighter.

Other Important Terminology

You need to understand three additional concepts specific to sequencing software: track, patch (sometimes called program or instrument), and channel.

Figure 15.1 displays an overview of a typical basic-level software sequencer. Notice the windows to the right that contain notation and lists of MIDI data. There is also a mixer window and an audio edit window, much like the software reviewed in Module 12. More on these later, but right now, study the Tracks window to the upper left.

LINK

Be sure to reread the basic description of MIDI in Module 14 and the discussion of channel messages.

Here you see three tracks, much as described above: two MIDI tracks (1 and 2) and one audio track (3). The concept of "track" in a sequencing program is really quite similar to how we defined a track in multiple-track recording: a convenient way for the software to visually and internally represent a location for an entered line of music. Software tracks can contain a large amount of information. Polyphonic textures created by a pianist, for example, can all be recorded on one track if desired. Sequencing software provides windows that let you edit these tracks. Portions of a single track can be moved around and defined in different ways by sequencing programs.

The notion of a "channel" in terms of MIDI is somewhat different from that in the hardware context that we described in the last Viewport, although both are related to routing. In MIDI terms, a channel is like an address to which a stream of data is sent. The MIDI language codes every note with a channel number, a kind

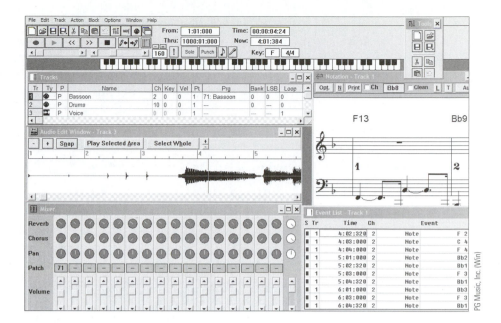

FIGURE 15.1
PowerTracks Pro Audio

LINK
Expanding MIDI channels is discussed in Module 18.

ASIDE
Additional patches can be accessed from various *banks* of sounds, 128 sounds per bank. This is particularly true with the expanded choices in the GM2 specification described in the previous module. See the listing of GM2 banks in Table 14.5.

DVD-ROM
Project 11 Editing MIDI Tracks with Basic Sequencing Software

of destination label like a TV channel. MIDI devices can be "tuned" to listen for notes on a specified channel. In this way, the sequencing software can send streams of notes to particular synthesizers or sound modules. In Figure 15.1, we have assigned the bassoon line to channel 2 and the drums to channel 10. It is quite common, in fact often required, that each separate timbre have its own channel number. You're allowed up to 16 channels on one MIDI cable. If you require more than 16 discrete timbres to sound at once, you'll need MIDI hardware and software that allow this.

Most often, you'll want to place a single channel on a single track with its own respective timbre; however, in some sequencing programs, multiple channels and their respective timbres can be included on a *single* track. For example, you might want to add a flute part to the bassoon melody by doubling an octave higher. Rather than create another track for the flute, it might be more sensible to add the flute line to the first track because it is playing the same music.

A "patch" or "program" is the sequencing term for an individual timbre. Most MIDI devices have a wide assortment of preset patches or timbres that can be addressed by MIDI. We used the bassoon and drum patches in the example above. MIDI software sends the MIDI patch code to the hardware device and the correct timbre is played for the music. The first General MIDI specification identified up to 128 different programs or patches and the newer GM2 specification adds more, as we described in the previous module. Many MIDI sound devices have hundreds of other patch sounds not standardized under General MIDI; they also can be accessed directly in sequencing software.

Basics of Using Sequencers with MIDI Data

First, a few words about the practical aspects of setting up your computer for MIDI work. In Module 12, Viewport IV, we described how to check your operating-system settings to be sure the computer knows about the digital audio and MIDI hardware you are using and how to route the digital audio and MIDI data. We recommend that you review that information now so that you are clear about how MIDI is handled by PC and Macintosh computers. Module 16 will describe many of the options for adding MIDI hardware to your computer. You will find useful information there about virtual routing, including the use of helpful utilities like MIDI-OX for PCs and MIDI Patchbay for Macintosh computers to support more extensive MIDI setups.

Entering MIDI Data

We will cover the basics of using sequencers by first entering data with a MIDI device such as a keyboard controller and then editing that data with typical techniques (see Table 15.1). Figure 15.2 reveals another basic layout of a sequencing program in Logic Express that is concerned primarily with MIDI. The upper window lists the tracks and gives a small graphic overview of the contents of each track. Clicking on any of the track overviews brings up a graphic editor with "piano-roll" notation.

As the project develops, the mixer is very useful and serves many of the same functions that a mixer did in the multiple-track digital audio software reviewed in Module 12. Finally, the Transport panel at the top left of the graphic contains the buttons necessary to play the project, rewind, stop, and so forth. Number displays show where the music is in terms of beats and measures and SMPTE timecode, a system useful when working with video.

Setting Up Recording

Of course, Figure 15.2 is of an already-completed composition. Figure 15.3a shows a project in its very beginning stages. Here, we have selected channel 1 in the Instruments column by choosing X5D-1. The program number is 73 for piccolo (the patch number used in the General MIDI bank for this instrument) and we have named the track accordingly. Notice we have "armed" the track for recording by clicking in the "R" column on the extreme left. The little dot indicates this. The recording process will start when you click on the larger dot in the Transport

LINK
SMPTE and other time codes are covered in Module 18.

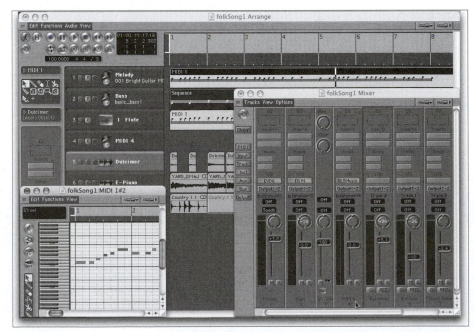

FIGURE 15.2 Overview of windows in Logic Express

Apple Computer, Inc. (Mac)

bar below. The "M" column is used to mute the track if needed, and the "S" solos the track and turns all the other tracks off.

You are just about ready to record. Next comes a series of options to control the recording. Nearly all sequencing software offers these options as standard features, although they are implemented in different ways. Refer to Figures 15.3a–d as we work through the setup.

Tempo, Meter, and Key   You'll want to think of a comfortable tempo for recording your music. You can choose a slower tempo than you plan to use for the final performance, because the tempo can be changed instantly without altering other

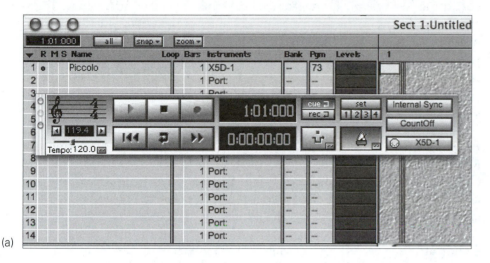

(a)

(b)

(c)

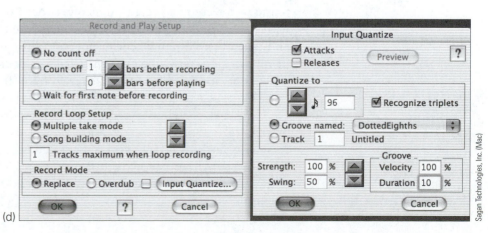

FIGURE 15.3   Recording setup options for Metro SE (a) Overview, (b) Metronome Dialog, (c) Recording Filter, (d) Metronome Setup and Input Quantize Dialogs

(d)

Sagan Technologies, Inc. (Mac)

variables. Tempo is initially set on the left of the Transport panel in Figure 15.3a. We have chosen a quarter-note equal to 119.4 beats per minute in this example.

Initial decisions about meter and key are set with menu items on this software. These settings may seem unnecessary if you just want to use a sequencer to produce a sound mix, but they are vital for proper metronome function and when the files are exported to notation programs or synchronized with audio data.

Metronome A metronome click is useful when recording, especially with the first few tracks so that you come close rhythmically to accurate performance. The closer you come to playing accurately, the more freedom you have in choosing options for quantizing (see below). The metronome is turned off and on in the same Transport panel. By clicking on the small graphic in the lower right of the metronome button in Figure 15.3a, the dialog box in Figure 15.3b appears. Here you can set where the sound of the click comes from (internal speaker of the computer or your MIDI device); the pitch, duration, and velocity (loudness) of the beat; and accents. If you choose Channel 10, you are likely to get a percussion sound set and if you choose to only hear the clicking in record mode, you can set this as well.

Filtering MIDI during recording Next, you might consider filtering certain MIDI data during recording. Figure 15.3c shows a dialog box that allows you to check off what you want. You can decide to filter out any MIDI data that are not desired, such as controller data or after-touch (special effect by a keyboard player after the key is struck). Here you can decide not to record audio and video as well.

Count-off, loop recording, overdub The dialog box to the left in Figure 15.3d provides a number of important options. Count-off controls the time clicked off before recording actually begins. You can set a "measure for nothing" to prepare yourself to begin accurately. You can also start recording anytime with the first note's performance.

Creating loops in sequencing software is always possible using features in this same dialog box. The loops created, however, are not specially "marked" for time and pitch change in the same way as those created in looping sequencers described in Module 12. The Record Mode in Metro is a nice way either to replace the material in a track completely or to place multiple lines of music in a single track.

Input quantization "Quantization" is a process that adjusts the onset of a MIDI note event so that it starts exactly on a beat division point, such as a quarter-, eighth-, or sixteenth-note. It is a powerful option for tightening up your rhythmic performance as you are recording, but it also can destroy the human feeling of the music if not used with care. Remember that no musician plays perfectly in time with the underlying "beat." To do so would be completely unmusical! The give-and-take of expression is a beautiful part of the musical experience. However, on many occasions real-time note entry will require some adjusting, and quantization is necessary for this. Nearly all packages offer some form of quantizing.

The dialog to the right in Figure 15.3d is shown by clicking on the Input Quantize button. Here, we set quantization for input. Sequencers offer post-production options for quantization as well (see below). The options presented include quantizing attacks and releases (ends of notes), resolution level of quantization (we chose the sixteenth-note), and special groove quantization that allows a performance style to be recognized and supported with different levels of strength.

LINK
The notion of quantizing was mentioned in Module 12 in reviewing multitrack audio sequencers.

LINK
You can find much more on MIDI timing in Module 18.

ASIDE
The notion of THRU described here is not the same as the function of a MIDI THRU port on a MIDI interface or sound device described in Modules 14 and 16 of this Viewport.

LINK
We will cover real-time and step-time entry with notation software as well in Module 20.

TIP
Percussion usually goes in Channel 10 with most sequencers using General MIDI as the bank for instrument sounds.

Sync clock   You can set your sequencer to listen to its inside clock to manage all event timing. If you choose external synchronization, the program will listen for a clock outside the computer. Set in the Transport panel in Figure 15.3a, this might be useful if at some point you want to sync to a video device or other hardware.

THRU   Most MIDI keyboards have an option in their hardware labeled Local Control on or off. Local Control Off prevents the keys from sounding notes; you may discover that your software and hardware work better together with this setting in the off position. This lets the computer take complete charge of the MIDI device during playback. The only problem is that you can't hear the sounds of the workstation while playing it! To remove this problem, most software includes a *THRU* option. You may want to have this selected so you can hear the workstation "thru" the computer. The software will simply send the MIDI data back to the keyboard so it can be heard.

Creating the Sequences

Now comes one of the most exciting parts of using sequencing software: recording the data. You have two approaches to consider: real-time and step-time. Real-time is by far the most common approach because sequencing software is optimized to work best using this approach. However, step-time can be helpful at times.

Real-Time Input

As we work through the following steps, refer to actual software, if you can, and practice some of this as you read.

STEP 1. Begin by thinking through your music. What line has the greatest continuity and would therefore be a good place to start? It might be good to put the drum line in first because that would set the proper feel for the rest of the work. However, if your music doesn't use a continuous drum line, you may want to choose something else. Remember: You can also record portions of a piece and add measures later.

STEP 2. Practice before recording. Sequencers are quite flexible, but they can't be expected to solve every performance problem. You need to practice until you feel quite comfortable with the music, knowing that you can fix some problems in the editing phase. Remember that sequencing software records all the nuances you perform, including rubatos, phrasing, articulations, and dynamics. Try to include as much of this as possible in your playing early in the recording; you can always "edit out" unwanted aspects of your performance but it's more difficult to "put in" missing elements! This is the major difference in approach between real-time entry in a sequencer versus a notation program. The emphasis here is on capturing as much of the performance data as possible.

STEP 3. Double-check all the settings. Decide if you are comfortable with how the metronome is set. Practice a little with the metronome to be sure.

STEP 4. Now, record your first track. Make sure that the track is "armed" by clicking into the column of the track that indicates recording.

STEP 5. Rewind and listen to the track, and perform it again if necessary. A wise safety procedure is to "deselect" the Record button to turn it off while listening.

STEP 6. Add a new track. If you want, you can now turn off the metronome while adding the second track. Make sure that the new track is in the record mode with the dot in its column for recording. Change the channel to a new number if

TIP

If you don't hear your MIDI device playing back different patches (timbres), your device may not be in "multi" or "poly" mode. You can change it to this mode either physically on the device itself or by a message from your sequencer software (see Module 14 for help with modes).

TIP

Step-time is great for musicians who don't play the piano well.

you're using a new timbre and be sure to choose the timbre you want ahead of time. You should hear the first track played back as you record the second.

Step-Time Entry

Sequencers accomplish step-time entry in different ways, but the basic concept is the same. You can draw in pitches and durations with a pencil tool or some other pointer device, or you can use the MIDI keyboard to determine a pitch level while you use your mouse or keyboard keys to choose a duration value. The latter approach is often called MIDI step entry.

Look at the two displays in Figure 15.4. The top view shows a track line with its data displayed in piano-roll fashion. The bottom view uses traditional notation. The tools at the top of each view allow you to pencil in a change and erase an event if you make a mistake. The vertical lines at the bottom of the top view are designed to control velocity (loudness) of each note—the higher the line, the louder. In the bottom view in traditional notation, dynamics are handled with dynamic markings.

Step-time entry in sequencing packages is often used to notate particularly difficult rhythmic sequences for which real-time performance is a problem. For instance, you might consider step entry for passages that require "tuplets." Tuplets are needed when a certain number of notes (usually an odd number) must be played in the space of a specified rhythmic division (usually even): for instance, three notes in the space of two eighth-notes. This would be a 3:2 designation or *three against two*. Another possibility might be 5:4 (five sixteenth-notes in the space of four).

There is actually a third way to enter music into a sequencer: by importing a standard MIDI file (SMF). Someone could send you an SMF on a CD or via the Internet. You may decide to import the file into a sequencer to build on to it or perhaps alter it for some purpose. Most sequencing programs offer this as a simple import option or allow you to open the SMF directly in the program.

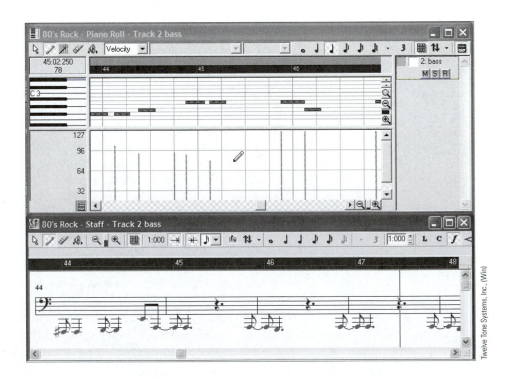

FIGURE 15.4 Piano-roll and traditional notation views from Cakewalk Home Studio

Editing and Saving Sequences

Careful performances will go a long way in creating your MIDI-based masterpieces, but editing is always necessary after the raw material is in. Here are a few of the most-often-used techniques.

Correcting Errors

Sequencing software offers a number of ways to correct errors. One approach is to use the tools shown in Figure 15.4. Here you can alter the pitch and duration of individual notes and also adjust the volume using the vertical lines. You can also drag the pencil tool across the vertical lines to help define a gradual crescendo and decrescendo.

Groups of notes can be highlighted for change. Cutting, copying, and pasting are all supported by sequencing software. Keep in mind that most packages treat cutting and deletion as two different concepts. If you want to eliminate the first two measures of a composition and have the sequence automatically shift to the left, for example, you probably need to use the delete option. Cutting may only remove the notes and leave the measures. Also, some sequencing software expects you to indicate whether to shift music backward in time following a deleted section. Many programs support Clear or Erase options. These differ from cutting because the material is not placed in clipboard memory for later retrieval but is simply eliminated from the score. Finally, if you copy and paste, be sure that the target track setup is similar to the one you are copying from; otherwise, the software may refuse to paste the material.

The Punch option is a great way to record a single measure or other small section in real time. Begin by identifying the spot you would like to change. Then start playing a few measures before it. When the section arrives, play the correct version in real time; the computer automatically knows to "punch in" the new material or insert it in the proper spot while overriding the offending data. The punch in-and-out button can be seen in Figure 15.3a in the Transport panel right next to the number displays under the Cue and Rec buttons.

Sometimes it's hard to pick out the offending errors in a complicated texture while listening. Most sequencing software provides an impressive *scrub* feature. For Home Studio, you can see the scrubbing feature in Figure 15.4 represented by the little speaker in the tools bar. Pulling this icon forward (or backward!) plays the notes underneath. This is an elegant option for "proofhearing" your music.

Editing with Event Lists

You've seen a number of ways in which sequencers provide views of the music. In addition to the track window, you've seen "piano roll" and traditional notation. These are, by far, the most common in sequencing programs, but at least one other view is worth your time—the event list.

Figure 15.5 displays an event list, which can be a very effective way to edit. An event list is just what it sounds like, a listing of each MIDI event as numbers in the order of their input to the computer in the MIDI data stream. Here, the list is open for a piano part in a composition using Cubase SE. Reading from left to right in the Event List window, you'll see values that define the position, length, and note name (if the event is a pitch).

Event lists offer an important window to the basic level of MIDI data, which is often necessary for precise control of performance data. You can look for the presence of controller data like pitch wheel or modulation information and use the editor to enter precise placement of program (patch or timbre) changes just where

LINK
Punching in and out in MIDI is similar to the same processes in recording digital audio in Module 12.

LINK
MIDI codes used in event lists are explained in Module 14.

LINK
See Module 19 in the next Viewport for information about controller data.

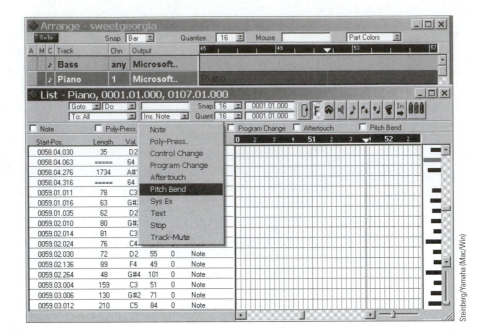

FIGURE 15.5 Event list in Cubase SE

you want them in the bit stream. The event list can also filter out certain kinds of MIDI events and only show others. Such detail can be very helpful in studying real-time music performance.

Menu-Driven Editing

Most sequencing software provides menus that allow for MIDI editing. Figure 15.6 displays this option in Home Studio. The graphic shows how controller data and velocity information can be changed in the piano-roll view with a pull-down menu right in the display.

Adjusting tempo and scaling time   Dialog boxes control tempo changes and scaling of MIDI data in this software. Gradual or less-gradual tempo changes can be accomplished with simply drawing changes over time. It is even possible to scale time much as you saw in Modules 9 and 12 with digital audio software. These edits can be performed quickly on a large chunk of MIDI data to offer a number of musical changes after the basic data has been captured.

Changing patches   Another example is the pop-up menu in Metro's Graphic Editor that allows you to change patches or programs much as you can with the event list. Figure 15.7 shows the menu, with options for seeing note values, controller data, and the like. We have chosen to show program change; you can see the little circles and horizontal lines that show the onset of a timbre. Clicking on the circle displays a Program Event Edit window that lets you specify exactly what you wish the program to change to.

Quantization (post-recording)   A final example is the ability to quantize a section of MIDI data after it has been entered, rather than as data are recorded. Figures 15.8a and b demonstrate how this is done and its effect. First choose the quantization resolution level, what is to be quantized, and any options for humanizing the changes. Figure 15.8a represents the timing of the pitches before and (b) shows how they have snapped into place in the grid after quantization.

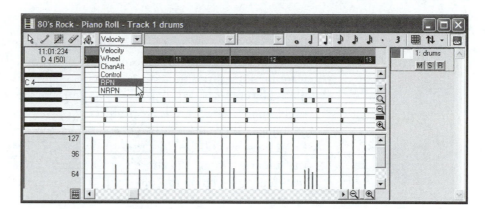

FIGURE 15.6 Menus for changing MIDI data in Home Studio

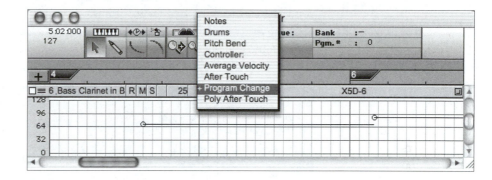

FIGURE 15.7 Menu to control views in Metro's Graphic Editor

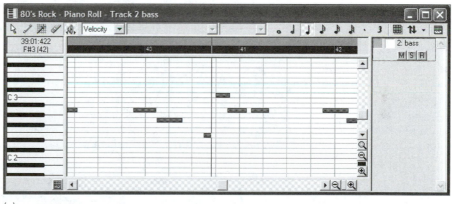

(a)

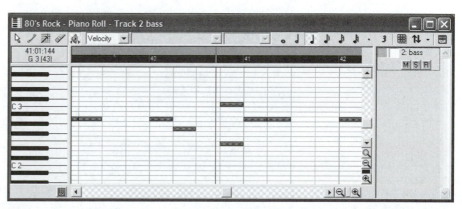

FIGURE 15.8 MIDI data (a) before quantization and (b) after quantization in Home Studio

(b)

Special Bank Selection

In the last module, you learned about the newer GM2 extensions for General MIDI and the possibilities for more than just the GM1 bank of sounds. Many software manufacturers include ways to change the bank of instruments that can be played by common MIDI devices. Figure 15.9a shows one way this is accomplished in Home Studio. We have right-clicked on the bass track (Track 2) in the example, which created the appearance of the Track Properties window. In Track Properties, we clicked on the "Instruments" button, which led to the Assign Instruments dialog. We chose the Yamaha XG instrument definition supported by this version of Home Studio, with the assumption that a Yamaha XG hardware instrument is connected to the computer. We then returned to the Track Properties window and chose the Bank 3 (Stereo) bank. Figure 15.9b shows how we then returned to Track 2's header information, which now shows the desired bank. By clicking on the "Pch" button in the header information, you can choose whatever instrument you want in the Yamaha XG's bank.

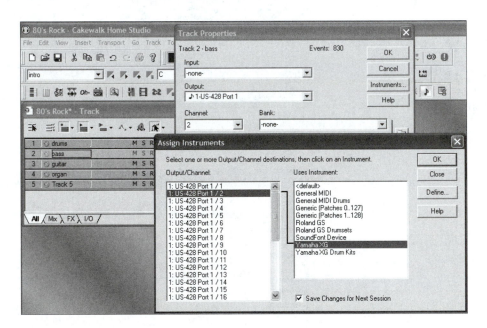

FIGURE 15.9A Track properties and assigning a different instrument bank in Home Studio

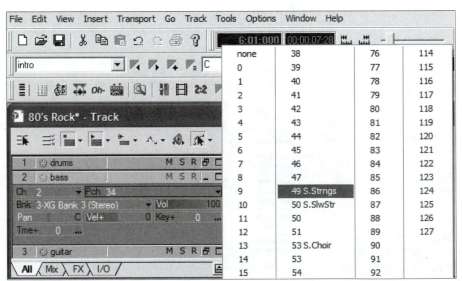

FIGURE 15.9B Changing a specific instrument in Home Studio

Plug-Ins: Applying MIDI Effects and Software-Based Instruments

In addition to the editing techniques we have just described, there are additional ways to alter and expand the sonic experience using MIDI data. As with digital audio, effects processing is possible with MIDI in the form of built-in effects and MIDI plug-ins. It is also possible to replace the hardware MIDI device with software instruments as either VST or DX plug-in extensions. We will revisit these ideas with the more advanced digital audio workstation (DAW) software in the next Viewport, but here are some examples of these enhancements with basic-level titles.

MIDI Effects

Figures 15.10a and b show the initial use of built-in MIDI effects in Home Studio and the actual dialog box for one of these effects: the Echo Delay. In this example, we applied the effect to a bass timbre. The effect list is displayed by right-clicking on the "Fx" area just below the track's name. Such effects only work for MIDI data tracks. A similar technique for audio tracks returns a list of all of the audio built-in effects that Home Studio has programmed, similar to the software in Module 12.

Notice in the Echo Delay dialog box the options for the units to be either Notes, MIDI Ticks, or Milliseconds. In order to hear the effect, you simply start the sequence going and manipulate the parameters. Another useful effect is the Arpeggiator.

Notice, too, in Figure 15.10a that another option was the MusicLab VeloMaster Lite plug-in. This particular plug-in, displayed in Figure 15.10c, is an example of a third-party MIDI plug-in that features sound compression, expansion, and other effects. We will explore more of these in the next Viewport.

Virtual Instruments

A recent development in MIDI sequencer technology is the use of virtual instruments. Rather than use the sounds from a MIDI device to play back the MIDI data, you can route the sounds internally to a software program designed to emulate a device or to create an instrument of its own. These are often referred to as "soft synths." Just as effects plug-ins must be written to a particular format, so too must these collections of virtual instruments. Both the VST and DirectX formats are common; these are often called VSTi (Mac/Win) and DXi (Win) plug-ins. Figure 15.11 provides a view of how these instruments work for Home Studio.

The first step is to create a spare audio track in a project. In that track, you right-click on the "Fx" area and choose the DX Instruments item in the pop-up box. This allows the instrument grouping to be made available in all the other MIDI tracks—in this case, five other tracks. In Figure 15.11, the VSC (Virtual Sound Canvas) from Edirol (Roland) has been accessed. We have chosen the "15488-GM2" bank in four of the five tracks and have used the "Pch" area to choose a particular timbre from that set of GM2 instruments. Notice the dialog box to the right, which contains a listing of the 16 tracks available and the options for effects such as volume, expression, reverb, chorus, and delay.

Once these sounds are chosen, pushing the play button routes the MIDI data through the virtual software so that you no longer need your outboard MIDI

ASIDE

The Audio Unit (AU) format for plug-ins on the Macintosh for music software is another format along with VST and DirectX.

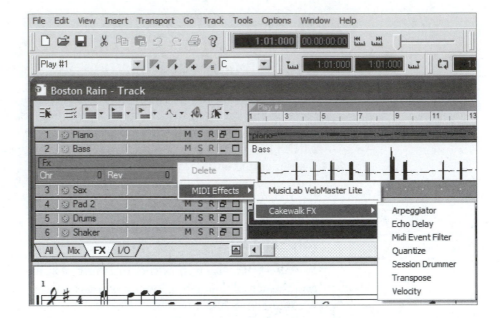

FIGURE 15.10A
Activating built-in effects in Home Studio

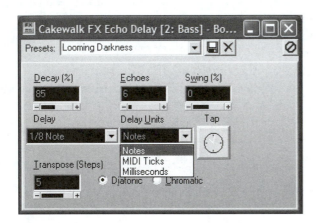

FIGURE 15.10B Echo delay effect in Home Studio

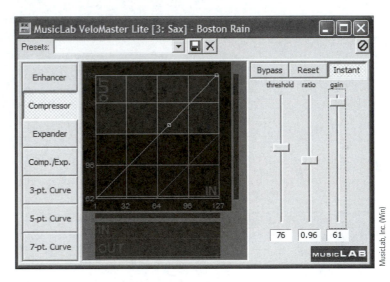

FIGURE 15.10C MIDI plug-in MusicLab Velomaster Lite

device. The VSC can also be played directly from the MIDI keyboard if you want. Software options such as these offer still more variety for your music.

DVD-ROM
Project 12 Working with Audio and MIDI Tracks

Adding Digital Audio

Up to this point, we have been concentrating on the MIDI side of sequencers. In this section, we will review some of the features that exist for entering and treating digital audio information, focusing on the entry, mixing and editing, and effects processing of sound in sequencing programs. Keep in mind that the entry and manipulation of digital sound has much in common with the multiple-track work in Module 12.

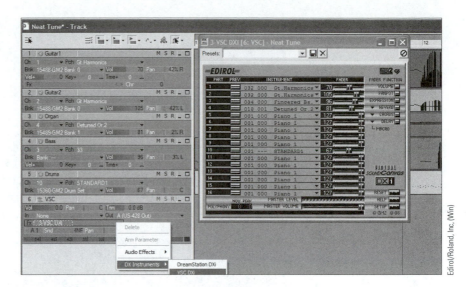

FIGURE 15.11   Using a virtual instrument in Home Studio, VSC

LINK
Reread the various options for microphones in Module 10.

Basic Entry and Data Representation

You can enter digital audio information into your sequencer by simply importing an already-created audio file or by recording sounds in real time, much like real time entry with MIDI data. By far the most common, this second approach is accomplished by using the microphone and sound-capturing hardware that is part of both Macintosh and PC machines. The microphones that come with computers work satisfactorily for low-stakes real-time recording, but you may want better-quality microphones as your needs become more demanding. For this reason, we recommend the digital audio interfaces reviewed in Module 13 and the multipurpose MIDI/digital audio interfaces highlighted in Module 16.

As you learned in Module 12, digital audio information is recorded directly to your hard disk. The number of tracks you can record for a project depends on the computer you're using and the limitations often imposed on cheaper versions of major software titles. Large amounts of hard-disk space are a must, especially if you're recording works that last longer than a few minutes.

Representation of digital audio by most sequencers is integrated right into the track window displays. Return to Figure 15.1, the Power Tracks Pro Audio program that opened this module. Notice there is an audio edit window that represents the audio in Track 3. In the Tracks window, the small icon in the "Ty" column represents MIDI and digital audio tracks. You also saw this mix of digital audio and MIDI in GarageBand in Module 12.

Figure 15.12a displays another example of MIDI and digital audio together in the software Tracktion. The top two tracks (drums and bass) are MIDI and the majority of the remaining tracks are digital audio. In this figure, we've highlighted the first guitar loop in the third track; its detailed information is displayed at the bottom of the graphic. Clicking on a MIDI track replaces the digital information with data about the MIDI track. In Figure 15.12b, we've done this to the bass line in track 2. Notice the display of MIDI notes in an expanded view. We've chosen the pencil tool to draw in volume changes, much as we did in Figure 15.4 in Home Studio.

Effects Processing

All of the digital audio built-in and plug-in effects presented in past modules are possible with the audio in sequencing software. In Figure 15.13, we've selected a short segment of audio and have called up several options in Home Studio for effects

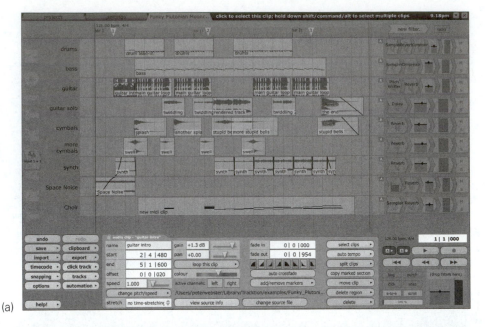

(a)

(b)

FIGURE 15.12 MIDI and digital audio together in Tracktion

Raw Material Software, Ltd. (Mac/Win)

processing. Many effects are built into the software, but others are plug-ins purchased especially for this purpose or found on the computer's hard drive, where other programs were installed. Notice the full set available in the Sonic Foundry folder installed with Sound Forge.

Another example can be seen with Tracktion in Figure 15.14. In the upper right-hand corner, the "new filter" graphic is dragged over the areas that require a new effect in the track lines below. The pop-up window appears with the catalog of effects available for Tracktion. Once chosen, the various effects controls are displayed in the bottom area of the main window. In Tracktion, effects can be chained, one after the other, depending on where they are dragged.

Mixing and Mastering

Can you mix and master in sequencing software as we described in Module 12 for multiple-track recorders? Yes, but perhaps not as effectively. Basic-level sequencing software that stresses MIDI tracks and companion digital audio tracks have

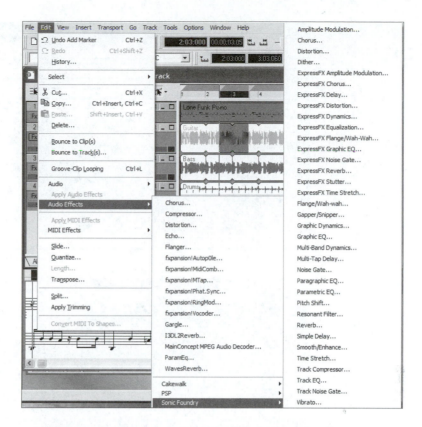

FIGURE 15.13 Effects-processing options in Home Studio

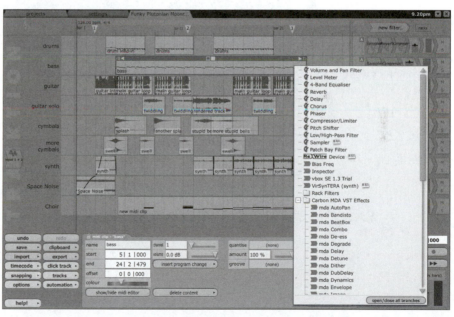

FIGURE 15.14 Effects-processing options in Tracktion

some mixing capabilities, but you will need to experiment with your software to see how easily the MIDI tracks can be controlled by the mixer. Direct control of the MIDI sound levels and properties may not be supported and you may need to consider a more advanced program.

Figures 15.15a and b show how you might be able to use virtual-instrument assignments to help mix with basic-level sequencers. Here, we've added the DXi instrument we used in Figure 15.11. In Figure 15.15a, we've assigned MIDI tracks 7 and 8 (Banjo and Shaker) to the Roland VSC instrument. Figure 15.15b shows the mixer that now controls not only all of the audio tracks but also the MIDI tracks.

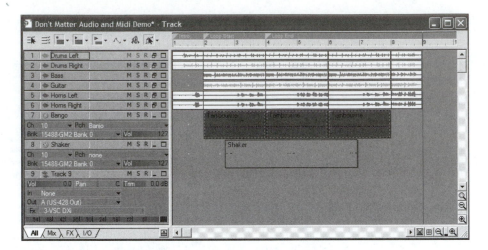

FIGURE 15.15A Tracks ready for mixing in Home Studio

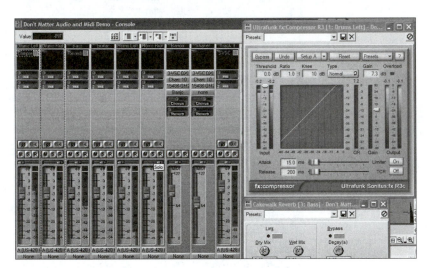

FIGURE 15.15B Mixer window and plug-in effects in Home Studio

You can also include some plug-in effects to help with mastering. Notice in the Drums Left and Bass tracks in Figure 15.15b that we've added these effects in the upper portion of the fader block. Adding these effects also prompts the dialogs on the right, which can be adjusted during playback.

Software-based automation of the built-in mixer settings is also possible. Home Studio allows you to "arm" a track fader for animation and then records your changes while the music is being played. Special bus routing is also a possibility in this software, much like what we described in Module 12. These capabilities are fine for most work. Should you need professional-level results for mastering, multiple-track recorders or DAW software are probably a better bet.

Saving Sequencing Files

After fine-tuning your music with or without digital audio, you'll want to save your work. You can save for live performance, production of a CD or DVD, or the Internet or other multimedia purposes. Sequencing files for performance can remain with mixed-data structures (MIDI and digital audio). This kind of mixed-data structure can be played directly from a sequencing software program to accompany instruments or voices in live performance. You can save these files in the file format of the particular sequencer. The computer keeps track of the digital audio segments and MIDI files in directories that you specify. Of course, this means that you need to have your computer with you for the performance venue.

If you want to use a mixed-media file for CD/DVD production or for creating files for Internet distribution, you'll need to convert the MIDI tracks to digital audio so that the entire work can be one data structure. Below, we will describe how to save sequencing files for all nonperformance purposes when you're dealing with only MIDI data or with both MIDI and digital audio.

MIDI Content Only

Most software sequencers allow you to save at least two kinds of standard MIDI Files (SMF). Type "0" puts all the data into one track and Type "1" saves data in multiple tracks. You will probably want to save your SMFs as Type-1 files so that individual tracks appear correctly in notation software and the files can be switched effectively between sequencing programs for track editing.

If you're planning to save files to be rendered on the Internet or in other multimedia programs, you'll want to assign instrument timbres (patches/programs) to the General MIDI bank set. This will ensure that the built-in instrument timbres within PCs and Macs play back the right sounds.

If you want to store sequencing files that have just MIDI data on CD- or DVD-ROM discs, simply save the information as data. If you have sequencing files that have only MIDI data and you want to distribute the files on CD- or DVD-Audio discs so you can play them back on CD or DVD players, you'll need to save your MIDI files as digital audio (see next section).

LINK
Study Module 11 for technical details on CD and DVD formats for data and for audio recording.

Mixed Data (MIDI/Digital Audio)

Saving mixed data for playback requires you to convert sequencing files into digital audio. You can't just ask your computer to convert MIDI files to audio, because MIDI files contain no direct information about the complex waveforms of digital audio. Another solution is necessary.

In the case of files whose MIDI codes rely on external MIDI hardware devices, you'll need to record the MIDI instrument's audio output back into the audio tracks of your sequencing software. This is actually quite easy to do. Connect the audio outputs of your device to the inputs of your digital audio interface (card or outboard box). Once the connections are made, you "arm" a new audio track on which you want to record and then record. The older MIDI track plays the device and the analog sound from the instrument is recorded digitally. You'll need to follow this procedure for each track of MIDI data.

When all this is done, your sequencing software will have tracks that have both the MIDI codes and the digital information representing the same sounds. You can then "mix down" all of the digital audio to a stereo or surround-sound mix and proceed to master and distribute on CD- or DVD-Audio discs.

Of course, if the sequencer files use software-based virtual instruments as described previously, it's a simple matter of mixing down to a stereo or surround-sound mix and proceeding as usual. This is another reason why virtual instruments appeal to musicians.

Module 16

MIDI Hardware: Interfaces, Keyboards, and Sound Modules

LINK
Module 18 presents more on MIDI controllers, SoundFonts, and MIDI and audio timing.

LINK
Be sure to integrate your study of the concepts here with the sections on MIDI concepts (Module 14) and sequencing software (Module 15).

In Module 16, we investigate the world of MIDI hardware. MIDI (Musical Instrument Digital Interface) hardware devices, which have been around for more than 20 years, are key to adding performance and control power to your computer music system. The performance options for MIDI controllers keep getting broader and the sophistication of MIDI sound-generation devices keeps getting richer. The hardware IPOS model for MIDI (Figure 16.1) introduces the topics to be covered in this module.

On the *input* side of the IPOS model is the most basic of controllers, the MIDI keyboard and keyboard workstation. For the *output* side of the IPOS model, music synthesis and digital sound production are packaged in a number of MIDI configurations, including MIDI workstations and sound and synthesizer modules.

MIDI *interfaces* are critical for communication among devices on a MIDI network. MIDI interface devices, including patchbays and thru-boxes, are all tools that can be used to build MIDI networks. With the use of USB and virtual-software MIDI devices, physical and virtual network issues need to be examined more closely. The module will be divided into two main sections:

- MIDI hardware basics with interfaces, networks, and patchbays
- MIDI keyboard controllers, sound modules, and keyboard workstations (the EMT-5 No-Frills MIDI System)

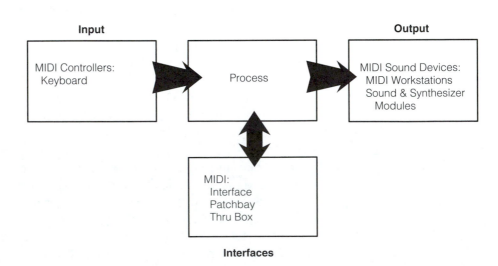

FIGURE 16.1 IPOS model showing MIDI devices for performing or composing

MIDI Hardware Basics

Understanding MIDI involves understanding how to build MIDI networks. MIDI is not just the codes used to program MIDI devices, but the engineering of the cabling and electrical signals that flow among these devices. The physical infrastructure of MIDI is very important and unique to MIDI alone. Having said that, it is also important to note that MIDI signals may be carried virtually over USB and Firewire cables and virtually routed among software applications within the computer.

MIDI Interfaces

Figure 16.2 shows a simple MIDI interface box and a MIDI cable with its distinctive connector. The MIDI interface is an electronic translator between a computer and MIDI devices like keyboards and sound modules. It translates the MIDI data sent from the computer into the standard electrical signals and timing recognized by other MIDI devices, or translates MIDI signals coming from other MIDI devices back into numeric data that the computer can understand. A simple MIDI interface typically has the following attributes:

- Serial device interfaced to a computer through a serial port or USB
- Standard 31.25-kHz data rate
- Broadcasts on 16 MIDI channels
- One MIDI IN and one or more MIDI OUT ports
- Optionally, one MIDI THRU port
- Powered by either the computer (e.g., through a USB connection) or its own power source
- MIDI standard five-pin DIN plugs, jacks, and cables for connections

The MIDI standard requires all devices to use the same type of cabling and connectors. To see what MIDI connectors look like, examine Figure 16.2. Notice that the connectors have five pins. This style of connector is known as a DIN connector, thus a five-pin DIN connector.

MIDI interfaces can be purchased as stand-alone boxes (like the one shown in Figure 16.2). They also come embedded in other audio and MIDI hardware. MIDI workstations, sound modules, control surfaces and mixers, portable studio recorders, and other hardware may have the minimum one MIDI IN and OUT port. Before purchasing a stand-alone MIDI interface, check to make sure one is not already available on the hardware in your music studio.

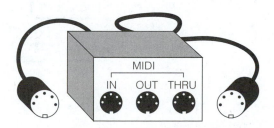

FIGURE 16.2   A simple MIDI interface box with a MIDI cable

MIDI Networks: Physical and Virtual

Physical

Figure 16.3 shows three simple configurations that would be appropriate for a simple MIDI network. The first (a) shows a computer and a sound module. This would be suitable for many music education applications in which only MIDI sound is required, for example, aural skills training or music accompaniments where no input is required. The software applications in Viewport VIII are excellent cases in point. Notice that only the MIDI OUT port of the interface is used.

The second setup (b) adds a MIDI controller to the network; for most music setups this would likely be a keyboard controller. The power of the MIDI standard makes it possible for someone to substitute almost any controller, be it wind, string, drum, or voice, for the keyboard device. Notice that the keyboard is connected to the MIDI IN port of the interface.

For the last setup (c), the computer is networked to a MIDI workstation that has a keyboard controller and a sound-generation module combined into a single unit. Notice the cabling. The IN of the interface is connected to the OUT of the workstation; the OUT of the interface is connected to the IN of the synthesizer.

The third setup (c) is probably the most common arrangement; the self-contained keyboard and sound generator is compact, portable, and cost-effective. However, if you were purchasing a new MIDI system, the second setup (b) would have advantages worth considering, especially for flexibility. Different keyboard, wind, or string controllers may be substituted or added, and sound modules can be selected with the best complement of digital sound banks and synthesizer capabilities.

Virtual MIDI Networks

The initial design of MIDI required that hardware and data codes depends on each other. To exchange MIDI between two or more devices, you needed MIDI connectors, interface boxes, and MIDI's unique cables. With the prevalence of USB and Firewire connectivity (e.g., the Yamaha mLAN noted in Module 18), and with the large number of music soft-synth applications, this is no longer the case. MIDI codes are sent among devices, over USB and Firewire cables, without need

TIP

One of the most common "gotchas" is to connect INs to INs and OUTs to OUTs. They must always be flip-flopped: IN to OUT and OUT to IN.

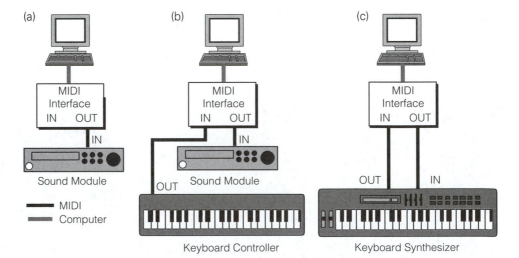

FIGURE 16.3 Three basic MIDI networks with a computer

for MIDI cables. Software synths and other software MIDI applications exchange MIDI data over virtual networks configured within a computer system.

The musician must now keep track of physical MIDI cable connections and virtual connections as part of the larger concept of a MIDI network. Software utilities for Mac and Windows assist in managing a MIDI network within this virtual space, and many software music sequencers provide management tools for physical and virtual MIDI connectivity.

Figure 16.4a is a Windows example of virtual MIDI network management with the utility MIDI-OX (James O'Connell shareware). A Korg Triton LE keyboard and a DrumKat controller are connected to a 2x2 MIDI interface; output devices are a Yamaha QY70 and a Creative Labs Extigy sound module, and the Microsoft GS software synth installed as part of Windows XP. The DrumKAT MIDI codes are routed out the QY70, and the Triton LE codes are routed out to the Extigy and the GS soft synth. The MIDI port activity among these devices is viewed in "MIDI Port Activity" window and the stream of MIDI codes is viewed in the "Monitor-Input" window.

Figure 16.4b illustrates a similar Mac OS X example with two software applications, MIDI Patchbay and SimpleSynth (Peter Yandell freeware). SimpleSynth is a software synth that uses QuickTime's MIDI capabilities as a sound module. The MIDI Patchbay application shows Port B (DrumKAT) routed on Channel 10 to the SimpleSynth and the Triton keyboard (Port A) routed to the SimpleSynth to three separate channels. This network arrangement uses *layering* of three different MIDI instruments (AnalogBrass 2, Violin, and Fantasia) for each key pressed on the Triton controller to create a new and unique timbre. Notice that the Patchbay software is used to transpose Channel 3 data up an octave (+12). This is a nice example of the flexibility of MIDI programming.

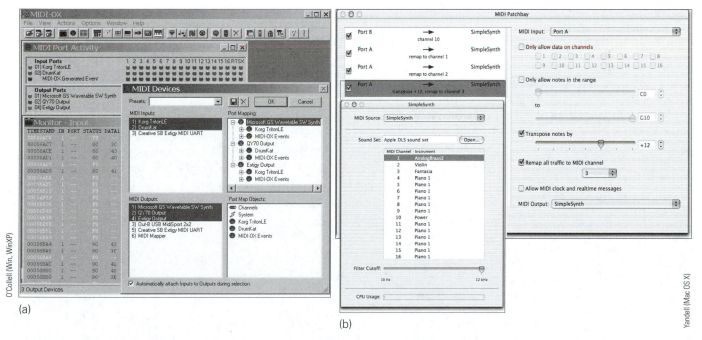

FIGURE 16.4   Two views of software MIDI network management: (a) MIDI-OX and GS Wavetable Software Synth; and (b) MIDI Patchbay and SimpleSynth

MIDI THRUs, Mergers, and Patchbays

As MIDI networks expand with more controller devices, additional MIDI hardware boxes are required to handle MIDI signal routing. Multiport MIDI devices with eight or more IN and OUT ports are readily and inexpensively available. At the heart of more complex network solutions are devices that offer network expansion: MIDI THRU, merger, and patchbay boxes. To help you understand the complex, we'll begin with the simple.

- *MIDI THRU boxes.* Take a situation where the network design needs several MIDI OUTs from the computer to connect to different sound modules and synthesizers. Figure 16.5a shows how to configure a MIDI network to increase the number of OUTs from a one-IN and one-OUT MIDI interface by using a MIDI "THRU box." This solution builds the network in a "star" configuration. The MIDI codes are transmitted across the three MIDI OUTs.
- *MIDI merger boxes.* Figure 16.5b shows how several MIDI INs may be added to a network. The MIDI "merger box" collects the MIDI data from the various controllers. It has a memory buffer to hold data from one device while it is processing data from another; when there is a lull in data transmission, the merger box then transmits the data in its memory buffer.
- *MIDI patchbays.* The MIDI patchbay, in its simplest form, is a bank of MIDI switches. Notice that the MIDI patchbay in Figure 16.5c has eight INs and eight OUTs. The patchbay offers the option of switching any of the eight INs to any of the eight OUTS. In the example, the three controllers—keyboard, guitar, or drum—are switched or routed to the first OUT port. Further advantages to patchbays include the fact that many of them let you store presets or snapshots, and some are MIDI programmable. With a MIDI-programmable patchbay, you can store the preset patch configuration as part of your MIDI sequencer data. Patchbay changes may be automated throughout a sequencer performance, and patchbay software can make it easy to manage the options in a virtual MIDI network.

Beyond 32 Channels

Professional-level software sequencers go far beyond the 16-channel limit to produce as many channels as the hardware will allow. To go beyond the initial 16 channels, you can use multiple 16-channel MIDI interfaces or more sophisticated hybrid MIDI interfaces. A "cable" in MIDI describes one set of 16 channels—matching a physical cable connecting any two MIDI ports, IN to OUT. A 2x2 MIDI interface, for example, would require four cables (two IN and two OUT) and provide 32 channels, in and out.

FIGURE 16.5 Three solutions for expanding MIDI OUTs and INs in a MIDI network: (a) MIDI THRU box, (b) MIDI merger box, and (c) MIDI patchbay

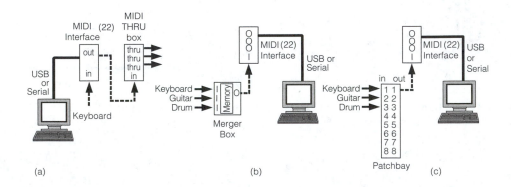

Edirol Corporation

FIGURE 16.6 Front and back views of the Roland UM-880 8x8 USB MIDI Interface

LINK

The more sophisticated MIDI interfaces with more than 32 channels or more are sometimes called "hybrid" MIDI interfaces because they combine many different features into one box, or "sync boxes" because they offer conversion of many different timing systems for synchronizing MIDI data. MIDI timing and synchronization are covered in Module 18.

MIDI interfaces by Mark of the Unicorn (MOTU), M-Audio, Digidesign, Steinberg/Yamaha, Roland, and others use advanced computer switching and control to provide 128–512 channels, or 8–32 cables of MIDI data. These high-end MIDI interfaces have eight independent MIDI IN/OUT ports and, most often, SMPTE-to-MTC-to-SMPTE synchronization. The interfaces can be daisy-chained to provide up to 512 channels (32 cables x 16 channels).

It is helpful to examine one of these 8x8 MIDI interfaces. The 8x8 matrix of IN/OUT ports represents 128x128 channels as a matrix of MIDI patches; each port has 16 MIDI channels. Figure 16.6 shows the front and back panel of the Roland UM-880 interface. Six of the eight IN/OUT ports can be seen on the back panel; two pairs of MIDI IN/OUT ports are on the front panel. Display lights on the front panel show MIDI activity for all eight IN/OUT ports, and the buttons allow you to manually patch directly from the UM-880. USB cable connectors are provided front and back. MIDI merge and patch were discussed earlier in this module. Buttons on the front panel of the UM-880 indicate "merge" and "patch" options, as well as the ability to load ("P.Load") and save ("P.Save") MIDI patch configurations. When not connected to a computer, the 8x8 interface can serve as a stand-alone MIDI patchbay.

Basic MIDI Keyboard Controllers and Sound Modules

Time to apply the study of MIDI networking to music hardware. Figure 16.7 returns to the familiar EMT workstation designs, this time for a "No-Frills MIDI" setup. The EMT-5 is appropriate for anyone beginning with MIDI equipment for music instruction, composing, or arranging. Three MIDI hardware devices are shown: a MIDI interface (22), a MIDI keyboard controller (21), and a MIDI GM2 sound module (26).

The first time you approach MIDI hardware, you may find the terminology confusing. Table 16.1 is a basic list of MIDI devices found in music systems, with a description of their function, and, in the case of controllers, the mechanisms by which they operate. These will each be discussed as we progress through the rest of this module, beginning with sound modules and keyboard controllers, and continue in Module 18 in the next Viewport.

MIDI Sound Modules

Returning to the No-Frills MIDI system in Figure 16.7, you should understand the role of the USB MIDI interface (22) in the diagram. In this configuration, MIDI IN data is being routed from the keyboard controller to the interface, and then MIDI

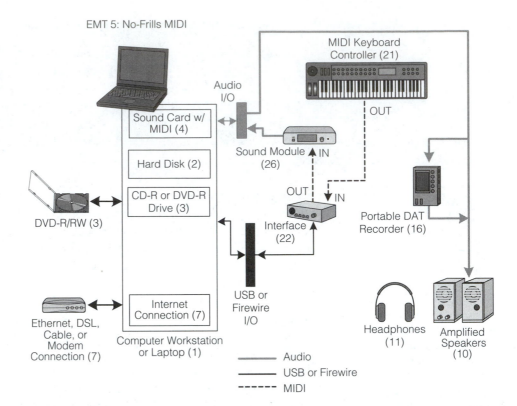

EMT 5: No-Frills MIDI

FIGURE 16.7 EMT-5 No-Frills MIDI Workstation

TABLE 16.1 Common Types of MIDI Instruments

MIDI Device	Function
Controller	Translate performance actions
Keyboard	Touch-sensitive switches
Drum	Trigger-to-MIDI converters
Voice	Pitch-to-voltage (PVC) and Pitch-to-MIDI (PMC) converters
Wind	PVC, PMC, and switches
String and Guitar	PVCs, audio pickups, and electronic switches
Synthesizer	Manipulate and create new analog and digital sounds
Sampler	Record and play back digital representations of sounds
Sample Player	Play back digital representations of sounds
Tone Generator	Generate sound with analog or digital oscillators
Effects Processor	Modify sound with effects like reverb, echo, flanging, pan, and so on
Drum Machine	Sequencing of percussion sounds
Sequencer (hardware)	Record and manipulate sequences of MIDI or digital performance data

signals are carried over the USB cable to computer software applications. MIDI OUT data from the computer is being routed to a MIDI GM2 sound module (26), likewise over USB to the MIDI interface, and then over MIDI to the sound module.

A *sound module* is a combination of a tone generator, a sample player, and possibly a synthesizer, depending on what techniques are included for sound genera-

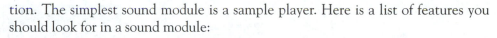

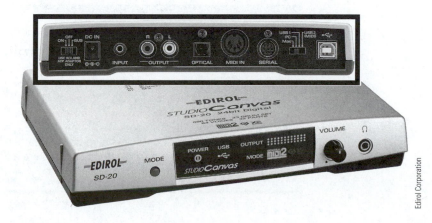

LINK

Soft-synth versions of
hardware sound modules also
exist. The Edirol Virtual Sound
Canvas is a case in point.
Check soft synths out in
Modules 15 and 17.

tion. The simplest sound module is a sample player. Here is a list of features you
should look for in a sound module:

- Number of timbres that can be played at once (multitimbral preferred)
- Number of voices that can be played at once (24-voice polyphony as a minimum)
- Number of instrument and percussion sounds in RAM or ROM (more is better,
  at least GM2)
- Sound-generation technique(s): basic sample player, digital wavetable synthe-
  sis, or physical modeling synthesis are among the many options
- General MIDI 2 standards
- Audio support and connections
- Packaging (device combined with controller, rack mounted, in stand-alone
  case, or as computer card)
- Power (battery for portable units, AC-adapter, or USB/Firewire cable)

The Edirol SD-20 shown in Figure 16.8 is typical of the sound module illustrated in the EMT-5 system. It exceeds the minimum specification list above, as
well as the GM2 requirements. The unit has 660 instruments, 23 drum sets, 64-
voice polyphony, and is 32-part multitimbral (four voices per part). Reverb and
Chorus effects are included (as required for GM2).

From the back panel shown in Figure 16.8, there is a MIDI, serial, or USB
port—note the switch on the far right for choosing the Mac or PC serial port, or
use of the USB1 or USB2 ports. It has both analog stereo output with two RCA
phono jacks and S/PDIF optical output; an analog audio device like a CD or Mini-
Disc player can be plugged into the system and audio will be passed through to the
output of the SD-20 to reduce the need for a mixer. On the front of the sound
module are a volume control, a headphone jack, and a mode button.

Note the MIDI IN port. With this option, the keyboard controller shown in
the EMT-5 could be connected directly to the SD-20 without the need for a separate MIDI interface. In fact, for portable MIDI needs or simple classroom MIDI
setups, Figure 16.9 illustrates a setup with laptop, controller, SD-20 sound module,
and headphone.

Most manufacturers of MIDI keyboard workstations also produce sound modules from their state-of-the-art sound-synthesis engines. The Edirol Studio Canvas
(SD-20 and SD-80) use much of the same hardware found in many Roland products based on the VX synthesis engine (e.g., the XV-2020 sound module) and offer
GM2, as well as GS and XGlite, compatibility. The Korg Triton-Rack module
is based on the Triton keyboard synthesizer series. The same applies to the Kurzweil ME1 sound module (KME-61) keyboard synth; and the Yamaha MU-50, -90,
and -100 sound modules (AWM2 sound-synthesis engine). All of these systems

FIGURE 16.8 Front- and
back-panel views of Edirol
SD-20 sound module

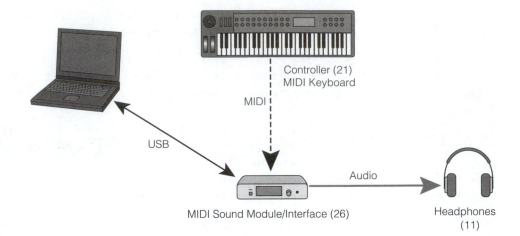

FIGURE 16.9 A minimal MIDI setup using the MIDI interface capabilities of the sound module, a keyboard controller, and a laptop computer

are significantly less expensive—some half the price—than the related MIDI keyboard workstation.

Keyboard Controllers

A MIDI controller is a device that translates music performance actions into MIDI data. Fingers pressing down keys; sticks hitting a drumhead; bowing, strumming, or plucking strings; air and lip pressure; a foot pressing a pedal; and possibilities not even thought of could be performance actions (see Table 16.1). All MIDI devices translate performance data into the unbiased MIDI code: The computer does not know whether the MIDI note data are from a drum pad or a violin. MIDI controllers can be flexibly interchanged among voice, wind, string, percussion, and keyboard instruments in any type of computer-based music environment.

Acoustic MIDI keyboard controllers are attached in some way to the action of a standard acoustic piano. Buchla MIDI Piano Bar, Gulbransen KS kits, and the Yamaha Disklaviers are examples. The Buchla and Gulbransen kits use optical or infrared sensors to convert a traditional piano into a MIDI keyboard controller. The Yamaha Disklavier is more than an acoustic controller. It is a true MIDI-ized, electronic player piano that still provides the action and feel of a traditional, acoustic piano keyboard.

Synthetic Keyboard controllers are the most common type of MIDI controller. MIDI keyboards come in sizes that range from 25 to 88 keys, using both

---

SIDEBAR
Acoustic and Synthetic MIDI Controllers

Traditional acoustic musical instruments can be equipped with sensors that translate analog actions or vibrations into digital MIDI data. Synthetic MIDI controllers are designed from scratch as electronic performance instruments. They may simulate acoustic instruments or offer new and unique instruments that optimize the electronic translation of performance actions to MIDI. Acoustic controllers give you the natural feel of a traditional instrument with a trade-off in electronic accuracy. Synthetic controllers give you the best electronic accuracy, with a trade-off in traditional performance realism.

miniature and full-size keys. The translation mechanism is some type of touch-sensitive switch. Note On and Note Off data are provided by the on-off state of the switch. Inexpensive keyboards provide only Note On/Off data. Others provide velocity and after-touch data representing the time it takes a key on the keyboard to transit from one position to another and the intensity with which the key was struck. The more expensive synthetic controllers simulate the key mechanism of an acoustic piano by using wooden, weighted keys. This type is preferred by pianists, but is more expensive.

Fatar/StudioLogic, Novation, M-Audio, Edirol, and Yamaha all offer keyboard-only controllers similar to the one illustrated in the EMT-5 No-Frills-MIDI System. Besides a keyboard, these controllers may also include pitchbend and modulation control wheels, sustain and hold pedal ports, a data slider, a MIDI interface, and USB computer connectivity.

TIP

Why MIDI workstations? These devices are designed to be all-in-one packages to meet the varied needs of a keyboard performer doing a gig; a composer/arranger without a computer; a music educator working with a class of students, possibly in a lab setting; and as a peripheral with a computer music system. When selecting a MIDI workstation, consider the features you need most. Buy smart! Don't pay for features you'll never use.

ASIDE

The presence of DSP synthesis and effects in entry-level workstations illustrates more power for less cost. As Table 16.2 demonstrates, high-end features like these have moved from professional down to low-cost solutions within just a few years.

MIDI Workstations

The EMT-5 system provides a starting point for using MIDI with a keyboard controller, an interface, and a sound module. We will now broaden the repertoire of MIDI devices with a study of MIDI workstations. The term *workstation* is used here to refer to any MIDI instrument where several of the sound-generating devices in Table 16.1 are combined with a keyboard controller into one package. A MIDI workstation has many of the following features (those features in italics are not critical for computer-based applications):

- Keyboard controller
- Alternative controllers such as pitch and modulation wheels, knobs and buttons, data sliders, and foot pedals for sustain, breath control, and other continuous controller applications
- Sample player with General MIDI/GM2 sound banks and user-defined samples
- *Real-time sampler*
- Synthesizer
- *Sequencer*
- Drum kit
- *DSP effects*
- Digital expansion for storage or connecting to other computers or digital devices

Some might call a MIDI instrument with various combinations of these features a MIDI keyboard, a MIDI keyboard synthesizer, or a MIDI music workstation. The presence of a sequencer, for some, is the determining factor for calling a MIDI device a "workstation."

Which features of a MIDI workstation can you do without when it is used as part of a computer music system (e.g., the EMT-1 through EMT-4 digital audio workstations)? The sequencer and effects processor are not critical. You can do real-time capture of digital audio with a computer, so a sampler is not necessary. Often, these features aren't needed when computers are available with lots of RAM, hard-drive space, digital audio and effects DSPs, and sequencing software such as described in Module 15. Real-time samplers are reserved for high-end workstations and typically sold as add-on modules.

LINK

Module 14 discussed channel and polyphonic after-touch, as well as a host of other terminology associated with MIDI. If you haven't done so yet, take some time to study this material.

Table 16.2 is a chart comparing MIDI workstation features from "entry level" ($500 or less), to "budget pro" ($1,000 range), to "mid-range pro" ($2,000 range). The features shown in each category are continuously changing. Advanced features on this chart may well move down into the lower-priced categories as additional hardware is provided for the same cost. Among the many companies making MIDI workstations are Alesis, Casio, Korg, Kurzweil, Roland, and Yamaha. A few instruments in each category are included as examples in the comparison chart.

Keyboard

All the workstation categories in Table 16.2 offer choices of 61-, 76-, or 88-key workstations with full-size, velocity-sensing keys. The more keys on the keyboard, the more expensive and the larger and heavier the instrument. Weighted or semi-

TABLE 16.2	A Comparison of Three Levels of MIDI Workstations		
Components	**Entry**	**Budget Pro**	**Mid-range Pro**
Keyboard	61 or 76 full-sized, unweighted keys; velocity sensing	61, 76 or 88 full-sized, weighted or semiweighted keys; velocity/aftertouch	61, 76 or 88 full-sized, weighted or semiweighted keys; velocity/aftertouch
Alternative Controllers	Pitch bend and mod wheel; drum pads; sustain-pedal jack	Pitchbend and mod wheels; joystick; programmable knobs, buttons, sliders; light-sensing beam	Multiple buttons, knobs, sliders; pitch-bend, mod, and breath-control wheels; various foot pedals and continuous-control pedals; pressure strips and ribbon controllers; and light-sensing beam
MIDI (notes/timbres)[1]	GM, GS, XG[4]; 24 or 32/16[1]	GM, GM2, GS, XG[4]; 64/16	GM and GM2[4]; 48–64/32
Sound Generation	Digital sampling	Digital sampling, wavetable synthesis, other digital solutions; typically better digital resolution than entry level (e.g., 24-bit/48-kHz or 128x oversampling)[5a]	Digital sampling with more sophisticated wavetable synthesis, shaping, and modeling[5b, 6]
Sample Player (ROM or RAM)	~4[2] MB (200–600 sounds) of sample ROM, including GM 128 patches	8–48 MB (600+ sounds) of sample ROM and RAM patches, including GM and GM2 (128 or 256 patches); user samples added to RAM	16–128 MB (1,024+ sounds) of sample ROM and RAM memory for preset or user patches, including GM and GM2 (128 or 256 patches)

[1]Notes/timbres refer to maximum polyphonic notes/maximum timbres played at one time.
[2]The tilde sign ~ indicates an approximate value.
[3a]Basic effects of reverb, harmony, chorus, phaser, flanger, enhancer, and Leslie; typically only one or two usable at a time, with few options.
[3b]Reverb, echo, chorus, flanging, phasing, pitch shifting, delay, distortion, enhancers, pan, and so on, with multiple effects that can be applied simultaneously and extensive programmable options.
[4]GM is General MIDI, GM2 is General MIDI 2, GS is Roland GM extended, XG is Yamaha GM extended MIDI.
[5a]Digital-synthesis examples include Korg Advanced Integrated and Hyper Integrated synthesis, Yamaha AWM2, Roland XV and JV2080 synthesis solutions, and Alesis QS Composite Synthesis.
[5b]Digital-synthesis examples include Korg Hyper Integrated synthesis, Kurzweil VAST (Variable Architecture Synthesis Technology), Yamaha AWM2, and Roland XV5080.
[6]Physical-modeling examples include Yamaha/Stanford VA synthesis/waveguides, Roland COSM, and Korg Prophesy.
[7]Pricing figures are intended to be relative benchmarks.

weighted key action and polyphonic after-touch are found in budget- and mid-range-pro workstations. The Casio WK-1630 in Figure 16.10 has 76 keys and velocity MIDI data; the Alesis QS8.2 has 88 keys fully weighted with velocity and release data (the Alesis QS6.2 has 61 keys); and the Korg Triton Pro has 76 keys with velocity and after-touch data.

Alternative Controllers

Expressive effects are critical to computer music activities. Controller wheels, sliders, and foot pedals generate many of the controller-change messages identified in Module 14. These messages can be used to create dynamic changes, tempo changes, timbral shifts, portamento effects, and the like.

TABLE 16.2   (continued)

Components	Entry	Budget Pro	Mid-range Pro
Drum Kits and Sounds	8–12 kits	8–30 kits, including GM/GM2 kits	64+ drum kits, including GM/GM2 kits
Real-Time Sampler	No	Yes, with add-on hardware	Yes, some add-on, some built-in; multiple channels of A/D input; 44- and 48-kHz/16-bit
Synthesis	Very basic layering and envelope shaping	Use of filters, envelope shaping, layering, LFO, effect controls, modeling, etc.	Most sophisticated digital shaping and modeling[5b,6]
Digital Effects	DSP for basic set, most have 1–2 effects at a time; 10–80 effect options[3b]	DSPs for multiple effects; 40–500 effect options[3a]	More DSPs for independent effects processing, up to eight or more simultaneously; enhanced modulation effects: pitch, filter, amp, LFO, etc.[3a]
Sequencer	Six tracks	0–16 tracks; arpeggiators, looping and groove patterns, and combinations assignable to keys	16–32 tracks; multiple arpeggiators, rhythm generators, looping and groove patterns, and phrase-shaping tools assignable to keys; many features unique to each instrument
Digital Expansion	MIDI, floppy disk for read/write SMF files	MIDI, PC-Card, SmartMedia or Compact Flash; read/write SMF Type 0 and 1 files.	MIDI, PC-Card, SmartMedia or Compact Flash; CD-ROM and CD-RW; read/write SMF Type 0 and 1 files.
Connections	Stereo line out, phones, MIDI IN/OUT, built-in speakers	Stereo line out, phones, MIDI IN/OUT/THRU, USB or serial computer interface, various expansion slots	Multiple stereo lines in/out, phones; MIDI IN/OUT/THRU; A/D inputs for sampling; USB, serial, or SCSI computer interface; various expansion slots; S/PDIF and AES/BEU
Representative Units	Yamaha PSR 550 and DGX300; Casio CTK-671 and WK1630	Roland RS-50 or -70; Korg X5D or Triton LE; Alesis QS6.2 or QS8.2; Yamaha S08	Roland Fantom; Korg Karma, Triton Pro or Studio; Kurzweil K2600; Yamaha Motif
Costs	Under $500[7]	Around $1,000	$2,000 or more

Look across the *Alternative Controllers* row in Table 16.2. As you move up in sophistication and cost, the workstations offer a greater variety of these controls and more flexibility in their programming. The mid-range-pro systems offer multiple continuous controller options (not just pedal switches), as well as pressure-sensitive strips, ribbon controllers, input for breath controllers, and even light-sensing control beams (called "D Beams") in the Roland RS-50/-70 (Budget Pro) and Fantom (Mid-range Pro).

A workstation needs to have at least one wheel and an input for a foot pedal; two wheels for pitch bend and modulation or vibrato control are desirable. The Casio workstation (shown in Figure 16.10a) has a pitchbend wheel, a modulation wheel, and a foot-switch control that can act as a sustain or damper pedal. The two controller wheels are visible in the lower, left-hand corner of the unit. Not all entry-level workstations are this generous, many only have a pedal switch and no controller wheels.

As you move up to the budget- and mid-range-pro workstations, you find more controller options. The Alesis QS8.2 (Figure 16.10b) has programmable pitch and mod wheels; two assignable pedal inputs, plus sustain pedal; and four slider controls. For the mid-range-pro workstation, the Korg Triton Pro (Figure 16.10c) comes loaded with pitchbend and modulation joystick; various real-time control knobs (also for controlling arpeggiators) and assignable switches for filters, amplitude, and portamento; a ribbon-touch controller; and inputs for up to two foot-pedal controllers.

MIDI Capabilities

You want a workstation with MIDI, preferably without General MIDI and GM2. The Casio WK-1630 has MIDI IN and OUT, as do all of the workstations in Table 16.2. All of the pro models compared have MIDI IN, OUT, and THRU. The entry-level workstations have General MIDI (none have GM2); most of the

ASIDE
General MIDI becomes less important the higher you get in the professional world of MIDI workstations and synthesizers. Review GM and GM2 specifications in Module 14.

(a)

(b)

(c)

FIGURE 16.10   Example of three levels of MIDI keyboard workstations: (a) Casio WK-1630 for entry level, (b) Alesis QS8.2 for Budget Pro, and (c) Korg Triton Pro for Mid-range Pro

budget-pro ones have GM and GM2, including the Yamaha and Roland units with extended XG and GS features, respectively.

Another issue in selecting a workstation is the number of notes it can play at one time (its *polyphony*, in MIDI terms) and the number of different sounds or timbres it can produce simultaneously (its *multitimbral* characteristic). Examining the *MIDI* row in Table 16.2, all the workstations can produce 16 timbres, and the number of polyphonic voices range between 24 and 64. Some workstations may have as many as 128 polyphonic voices. The General MIDI 2 standard is for 32-note polyphony, and the GM2 requirement is 16 unique timbres playing simultaneously. The 32/16 specification has influenced the design of entry-level MIDI workstations, even if they are not GM2 compliant. The Casio WK-1630 offers 32 polyphonic voices and 16 simultaneous timbres.

Be aware that, depending on the design of the MIDI instrument, the number of polyphonic voices can rapidly disappear! The polyphony of the instrument, remember, is essentially the number of notes or sounds of any kind that it can make simultaneously. To create complex timbres in a MIDI instrument, the manufacturers often use a concept known as *layering*. Layering means that more complex timbres are created by combining several of the instrument's preset timbres. If you have 32 polyphonic voices, 32 notes can sound at once. If the timbre you've chosen requires four layers (i.e., four timbres), then you have effectively reduced the number of notes you can play at once by a factor of four. This means that you can play eight simultaneous notes (8x4 layers or waveforms = 32 simultaneous sounds).

TIP
Layering sounds (such as in Figure 16.4) reduces the usable polyphony of a MIDI instrument. Each layer counts as a voice. For software sequencing, the more simultaneous timbres, the better.

Sound Generation and Drum Kits, Sample Playing, and Real-Time Sampling

Given the various MIDI devices listed in Table 16.1, most workstations can be classified by definition as *sample players*. This means that the workstations use some form of digital sound production with digital samples stored in ROM or RAM that retain the information even when the power is turned off. Should the workstation also provide the means for recording samples in real time, it would be classified as a *sampler* (see Table 16.1). Real-time sampling is usually a feature on the more expensive mid-range-pro workstations. The Triton LE, Pro, and Studio have an add-on module for sampling, as do the Kurzweil and Yamaha Motif.

LINK
Physical modeling, wavetable synthesis, and synthesis concepts are discussed in Module 8.

Sound Generation

Workstations typically offer some form of digital sound production through various combinations of waveforms, samples, and digital oscillators. At the entry level, sound generation is simple digital waveforms or PCM (Pulse Code Modulation). At the budget-pro and mid-range-pro levels, techniques like Korg's AI[2] (Advanced Integrated) and HI (Hyper Integrated) sample synthesis, Yamaha's AWM and AWM2 (Advanced Wave Memory), Kurzweil's VAST (Variable Architecture Synthesis Technology), and Alesis's QS Composite Synthesis offer more complex digital sound generation, where algorithms are used to *shape* the digital waveform through various combinations of digitally controlled amplifiers and filters. Sampling resolutions are usually 48-kHz/16-bit, with some using 1-bit, 128x oversampling. The more expensive the workstation, the greater flexibility you'll find in *shaping* sounds to create new or more realistic instruments.

TIP
Remember, once you leave the basic set of General MIDI sounds, your music sequence depends on the brand of MIDI workstation and the synthesis engine you used to create your sounds. If you synthesize some wonderful sounds with your Korg Triton, then that sequence will need to be played from the Korg Triton. The MIDI DLS file format for downloadable samples (discussed in Module 18) may help you export some, but not all, sound samples or SoundFonts with the standard MIDI file.

Sample Playing

Today, most workstations are sample players. Examine the *Sample Player* row in Table 16.2. Notice that the entry-level workstation has samples stored in ROM, usually the required 128 General MIDI instruments and drum kits, plus extra sounds provided. The entry-level Casio WK-1630 has 232 sample patches (128 GM + 64 Casio patches + 32 user patches + 8 drum sets). With the pro systems, the number of samples provided in ROM continues to expand, with some having more than 1,024 patches. The amount of memory expands as well, going from 4 MB for entry level up to 128 MB at the mid-range-pro level. The complexity of the sound samples also expands, consuming more memory per instrument patch. Consider the approximately 4 MB for Casio (Figure 16.10a) sounds, 16 MB for Alesis instrument sounds, and 32 MB for the Triton Pro, expandable to 64 MB. The Casio and Alesis sound sets are GM compliant; the Korg is GM2 compliant, with 256 sounds and nine drum kits.

The presence of RAM sample storage allows you to edit and create custom sounds directly through the workstation or computer software. All three workstations in Figure 16.10, even the Casio with 32 user patches, include this feature, a powerful and extremely useful one to look for when selecting a workstation.

Drum Kits and Sounds

Did you notice that we do not have a drum machine in the EMT-5 system? There's a good reason for that omission. Most workstations come with a full repertoire of drum sounds, eliminating the need for a separate drum machine (a drum controller perhaps, but not a drum machine). As the comparison table shows, all workstations come with a large number of drum kits or sets (see Table 16.2). GM requires one drum kit; GM2 nine drum kits. An entry-level workstation typically has 8–12 kits, and some entry-level workstations include small drum-pad controllers. As you move up to the pro level, workstations offer hundreds of different drum samples to work with. The challenge comes in keeping track of them all in sequencing software. The Casio (Figure 16.10a) has eight drum kits; the Alesis approximately 15 (their drum sounds are not organized in kits as such); and the Korg 64 (with nine GM2 drum kits).

Synthesis and Digital Effects

To be classed as a synthesizer, an electronic musical instrument must provide the means for creating new sounds by modifying and manipulating various sound parameters (refer to Table 16.1). The ability to simply play back sampled sounds does not make a synthesizer; that is the function of a sample player. In Table 16.2, the row labeled *Synthesizer* indicates that entry-level workstations are sample players with limited or no synthesis capability. To understand synthesis features in MIDI workstations (or sound modules for that matter), a few basic concepts are worth studying.

Shaping Instrument Sounds

In Module 8, three synthesis techniques were noted: additive; subtractive; and distortive (see Figure 8.18). Sample-based synthesizers can use any combination of these techniques. What this means is that complex waveforms (the samples) can be filtered (subtracting out sounds) to produce new sounds; several waveforms can be layered (adding sounds) to create new sounds; or waveforms can be enhanced through

TIP
Remember the effects discussion in Module 12? The effect power of a device is defined by the number of simultaneous effects that can be used in programming a sound and the number of master effects that can be applied to an overall track or tracks in a sound mix.

LINK
Physical-modeling synthesis shows up in soft synths like Yamaha's Sondius XG (XG combined with Yamaha's physical modeling SVA techniques). Check Module 8 for more on physical modeling and Modules 12 and 15 for software applications.

ASIDE
Just in case it shows up on a test: Roland's COSM stands for Composite Object Sound Modeling; Korg's MOSS stands for Multi-Oscillator Synthesis System; and CCRMA is the acronym for Stanford University's Center for Computer Research in Music and Acoustics. Yamaha's array of acronyms includes AWM for Advanced Wave Memory synthesis and SVA for Software Virtual Acoustic physical-modeling synthesis, including Virtual ("VL") acoustic synthesis.

various modulation controls or digital signal-processing effects (distorted). The primary components of the synthesis chain are the oscillator, the filter, the amplifier, and digital effect processors. Because we are dealing with digital synthesizers, all of these components are digital, designed to process sounds as streams of numbers.

Digital Effects

At the end of the synthesis chain comes some digital effect processing that can alter the sound by adding reverb, harmonizing, panning, distortion, pitch shifting, and a host of other effects (see the *Digital Effects* row in Table 16.2). The effects are typically generated by DSP chips optimized for processing large amounts of digital sound data. The greater the number of independent DSP chips, the greater the range of effects that can be imposed on the sound at one time.

Synthesis Controls

An additional level of control can be programmed to alter the pitch of the oscillator, the envelope of the filter, the envelope of the amplifier, or the effects processor. Control messages emanating from MIDI pitchbend or modulation wheels, foot pedals, sliders, breath controllers, and the like can all be programmed to alter the patterns of any of these functions.

The programming of this chain of synthesis events can also be defined through algorithms or patches either predefined in the instrument or programmed by the user. The number of algorithms available, and the number that can be used simultaneously, is a measure of the programming capabilities of the synthesizer. Each algorithm or patch will have a number of parameters that can be programmed either through manual controls on the workstation, programming controls in the workstation, or software patch editors on the computer.

Physical Modeling

Not all sound engines are sampling engines. The older FM synthesis made popular in the 1980s by Yamaha was not a sampling technique. Roland, Yamaha, and Korg, among others, use physical-modeling synthesis. This technique is especially useful when you are attempting to model in software the physical features of complex sounds from strings, drums, winds, and voice. Roland uses physical modeling with its COSM technology for its V-series guitar and drum-modeling synthesis; Korg uses modeling synthesis with its Triton synthesizer (included in the MOSS upgrade option); and Yamaha uses its SVA Physical Modeling Synthesis with its VL70 tone module (especially programmed for wind controllers) and other Yamaha VL synths and tone modules. The Yamaha modeling synthesis is licensed from Stanford University and the CCRMA research center, where the sound models were developed as "waveguides." This is the same research center where Yamaha licensed its FM synthesis some 20 years ago.

Bringing Synthesis Issues Together

To review, here are things to consider when evaluating the synthesis capability of a digital synthesizer:

- Layering and the number of layers per voice
- Filtering and the number of filters per voice
- Amplitude envelope per voice
- Digital effects-processing features, the number of preprogrammed effects, and the number of effects that can be used simultaneously

- Programmability of algorithms or patches, the number available, and the number that can be used simultaneously
- Alternative sound techniques like those for physical modeling

Primarily, basic layering and envelope shaping are available at the entry-workstation level. Basic digital effects like reverb and chorus, all DSP generated, are also common (see the *Synthesizer* and *Digital Effects* rows in Table 16.2). The Casio WK-1630 provides some synthesis functionality and 10 DSP-generated effects, such as reverb, phaser, flanger, chorus, and Leslie.

Budget and mid-range-pro workstations and their synthesis engines are often quite similar. The Alesis QS synthesis engine and the Korg AI² and HI engines, for example, are available on those companies' full range of workstations. What changes is the number of "programs" and "mixes" and the amount of waveform memory that comes with the workstation. The Korg Triton Pro (Figure 16.10c) provides five simultaneous insert effects, as well as master effects and a master three-band EQ for which the band frequencies can be adjusted. The Alesis QS8.2 has four independent stereo multieffect buses. Both the Korg and Alesis models provide many programmable variations of reverb, chorus, distortion, EQ, delay, Lesile speaker simulation, pan, and many more effects.

The more expensive MIDI workstations are often leading-edge systems developed to showcase the newest and most acoustically stunning sound-generation technology. The Korg AI² synthesis engine is used on many of its keyboards, including the budget-pro X5D. The HI synthesis system is an enhancement of the AI² and is used in the Korg Triton series. In addition, the Korg Triton and Triton Studio workstations (mid-range-pro and possibly higher) have an expansion option that uses the MOSS synthesis engine with an even wider array of algorithmic programming control and DSP synthesis options. Likewise, Yamaha has its leading-edge AWM2, Kurzweil its VAST, and Roland its JP and XV synthesis engines.

Sequencers

A built-in sequencer in a workstation is a nice feature if you use the instrument for solo performing, arranging, or composing away from a computer workstation. As Table 16.2 illustrates, you'd need to purchase a mid-range-pro workstation to get 32-track sequencing. The entry-level units, like the Casio WK-1630, have a simple, six-track sequencer. Budget-pro systems typically have 16-track sequencers, and some have no sequencer. The Alesis QS6.2 does not provide a sequencer. The Korg Triton Pro has a 16-track sequencer. Besides the number of tracks, a workstation's sequencing capacity is measured by the number of notes or the amount of memory available for sequencing and the number of songs it will store. The WK-1630 will store 4,900 notes and two songs, compared with the Triton Pro, which stores 200,000 notes and 200 songs. Remember: MIDI controllers can generate many MIDI event data that will very quickly fill up a sequencer's memory.

Pattern Generators

Groove boxes like the Boss JamStation, Roland PhraseLab, or Korg Electribe (EM-1) Music Production Station—to name but a few of the many available—are immensely popular for creating musical accompaniments from loops of rap

ASIDE
A few more acronyms defined: HI is Korg's term for Hyper Integrated synthesis, along with AI² for Advanced Integrated synthesis systems; Kurzweil's VAST stands for Variable Architecture Synthesis Technology.

beats, rhythm patterns, bass lines, digital audio samples, and melodic and harmonic patterns. It is possible to create complete compositions from "groove" boxes. Sequencing, looping, combinations, rhythm generators, and arpeggiators are used to create groove accompaniments.

Looking across the *Sequencer* row in Table 16.2, you will see that some of this same functionality is included in MIDI workstations. As you move up to mid-range-pro workstations, the repertoire of options expands, often with multiple arpeggiators, for example, that can be used simultaneously. For performance, patterns can be combined with instrument patches and assigned to specific keys on the keyboard so they can be played in real time. The entry-level Casio WK-1630 has a repertoire of 130 rhythm patterns with the capability of 10 user-pattern programs; the Korg Triton Pro has dual polyphonic arpeggiators with 180 preprogrammed patterns and the ability to add user-defined patterns. The Alesis QS8.2 provides no pattern generation, but many of the other budget-pro units do. Roland's RS-50 and RS-70, for example, include arpeggiators.

Digital Expansion and Connections

Given the large file sizes associated with samples and sequences, a method is required for moving files among MIDI workstations, or among a workstation and a computer. Initially, this was done over MIDI cables with bulk dumps of MIDI data files—a slow technique for exchanging large files. Then, floppy-disk drives were added to workstations for data transfer. As Table 16.2 indicates in the *Digital Expansion* row, floppy drives are being replaced with SmartMedia and Compact Flash cards, PC-Cards, and, most recently, CD-RW drive technology on the mid-range-pro workstations. Floppy drives are commonly found on the entry-level workstations (the Casio WK-1630 provides no media storage, depending on MIDI data transfers); the Alesis QS8.2 uses PC-Cards; and the Korgs use SmartMedia (with CD-RW on the high-end Triton Studio units).

The other solution along with media transfer is network connectivity between MIDI workstations and computers, something beyond MIDI file transfers, which are still viable but slow. Notice in Table 16.2 that a number of the budget- and mid-range-pro devices provide serial and USB computer interfaces, as well as the older SCSI connectivity.

Audio Connections

Examine the *Connections* row in Table 16.2. Standard fare across all units is stereo line out for audio and headphone jacks. The entry-level workstations may have built-in speakers, as well. Things get exciting if a MIDI workstation has digital audio ports with S/PDIF, ADAT, or AES/EBU. The feature is available on mid-range-pro workstations and continues to filter down to the budget-pro level. The Triton Pro, for example, has an installed option for adding digital audio for sampling. Digital audio input/output ports let you make direct digital connections between a MiniDisc, ADAT or DAT tape decks, computer digital audio cards, and a digital mixer with S/PDIF or AES/EBU connections.

More importantly, with digital audio I/O between a MIDI workstation and a computer, your MIDI performances can be mixed directly back into your computer sequencing software (e.g., SONAR or Logic Pro) through your digital audio sound card as a digital audio track, not an analog-audio track that requires digitizing first. Everything stays digital and clean!

LINK
Module 7 can help you with the various storage options, such as floppy disks, Smart-Media, Compact Flash, PC-Cards, and the like.

LINK
Firewire and the Yamaha mLAN network are discussed in Module 18. For future data exchange between MIDI workstations and other devices, the speed and convenience of Firewire networking through mLAN or a similar protocol looks very promising.

LINK
Digital I/O on a MIDI workstation is a boon to computer-based digital editing and production of music CD and DVD audio. If the terms digital I/O, Firewire, S/PDIF, and AES/EBU have left you baffled, you can look back to Module 13 for some help.

Workstations—In Conclusion

You can see that picking a workstation is not easy, as you need to take a lot of things into consideration. The philosophy behind your decision should be to find a workstation that has the critical components that meet your needs. You should first carefully consider an entry-level workstation under $500 that has good key action, good sampled sound, one or two controller wheels, and a foot-pedal input. If you find that the key action and sampled sounds are not up to your standards, then move up to the budget-pro level. Along with improved keyboards and sampled sounds, the budget-pro also offers more samples, synthesis, and digital effects processing. There's a good chance you won't need to go any higher unless you need the more powerful features of the mid-range-pro or even professional level. You should only consider putting the dollars down for a more sophisticated workstation if you truly feel your music creativity has outgrown the capabilities of your present system.

Doing More with MIDI and Beyond

"When I met Max Mathews at the Bell Labs when I was in New York in 1970 I thought: now here is the future. . . . When I put together IRCAM, of course I expected the computer to develop, but I had no idea it would be so dramatic. Even the top scientists who advised me at the time were not thinking in terms of what computers can do today."

—Pierre Boulez, interview after a rehearsal
with the Chicago Symphony Orchestra in December 1992

Overview

This Viewport builds on Viewport V by expanding your MIDI sequencing skills. First we look at integrating MIDI sequencing with more-advanced digital audio workstation (DAW) software. This includes software-based synthesizers and samplers that work as plug-ins or stand-alone applications, virtual studios, and programming environments for creating sounds and compositions. Second, we look much more closely at the variety of MIDI controller devices and important MIDI concepts to extend your knowledge of the creative possibilities for using MIDI, especially in performance venues.

Objectives

The DAW software described in Module 17 represents the newest and most complete sequencing applications available today. They do all the things that basic-level sequencing software does, plus much, much more. They work in tandem with third-party software like soft synthesizers and samplers. These "soft synths" and samplers represent an increasingly common trend for hardware devices that are realized in software. This trend is seen again in the virtual studios that contain simulated racks of hardware devices. We end the first module with a brief look at programming environments for creating music, sound, and full compositions. This software uses either object-oriented graphics or command line code to offer you great flexibility in designing music projects.

Module 18 examines MIDI controllers and more advanced options for combining MIDI with digital audio. Other MIDI topics include the SoundFont and DLS software additions and manufacturer-designed hardware schemes such as GX and XS. These are particularly important for understanding how the General MIDI specification has been improved in terms of sound quality. Finally, we review MIDI and audio timing, including the important SMPTE timecode. At the end of this Viewport you should understand:

- Interface, advanced editing, and mastering features of typical DAW software that integrates MIDI and digital audio
- How DAW software can be extended with software-based instruments, synthesizers, and samplers that act either as plug-ins or as stand-alone applications
- The virtual studio and its approach to including "all-in-one" components in a simulated-studio hardware rack
- Programming environments for sound synthesis and composition
- Hardware issues for expanding a studio or performance setup to include a wider array of MIDI controllers

MUSIC TECHNOLOGY IN PRACTICE

Henry Panion III

Distinguished University Professor at the University of Alabama—Birmingham, as well as a composer, conductor, and arranger for such well-known musicians as Stevie Wonder, The Winans, Dionne Warwick, Chaka Khan, The Lionel Hampton Orchestra, and Aretha Franklin. Dr. Panion's work has produced two Grammy Awards, two Dove Awards, and a host of other national music awards and nominations, including induction into the Alabama Jazz Hall of Fame.

Henry Panion in his studio at the University of Alabama—Birmingham

Applications

Henry Panion uses music technology for diverse tasks, from sound design, digital audio editing, multitrack sequencing and mixing, to music notation for his arrangements and compositions. Panion has been using notation and sequencing software since graduate school at The Ohio State University. Henry supplemented his income using the earliest version of MOTU's Professional Composer on a Mac to turn the oral tradition of gospel music into printed scores for music publishers. He quickly saw the potential that computer technology held for his own work as a composer, arranger, orchestrator, and music teacher.

When creating an orchestral arrangement for musicians like Aretha Franklin or Stevie Wonder, he relies on the ease with which Sibelius lets him audition the complete orchestral arrangement. As Henry points out, "Being able to allow my clients an opportunity to hear convincing representations of their arrangements before going into rehearsals is a great benefit of software like Sibelius or Finale." A second benefit, of course, is being assured that scores and parts will be formatted and printed accurately and just in time for the recording session. Time and time again he has been called on to create last-minute arrangements while on the road touring, even at 35,000 feet in the air flying to a concert with Stevie Wonder.

Dr. Panion shared the following experience of using his Mac and his DAW sequencing software:

"I have been using MOTU's Performer sequencers since their initial release in the 80s and feel that their interface, combined with their unmatched editing features, suits the way I work and think very well. On the last studio recording of the UAB Gospel Choir, *Lessons For Life,* we were able to use the sequencer to experiment with instrument combinations and song arrangements before committing them to disc. The 13 songs on the album ended up with an average of 60-plus audio tracks each. The power of Digital Performer enabled me to record MIDI arrangements and synchronize these arrangements to the live performance of the 100-voice choir captured on Tascam DA-88's digital tape recorders in the large UAB con-

DVD-ROM

As with all the software modules in this text, the accompanying DVD contains projects for you to use to practice your skills.

- New approaches to expanding the sounds created with MIDI, including hardware standards like GX and XG and software-based extensions like SoundFont and DLS
- MIDI timing and networking issues, especially SMPTE, Word Clock, mLAN, and others

DVD-ROM Software Projects

In terms of hands-on tasks, you should be able to:

- Work with DAW software to expand your sequencing skills (Project 13)
- Work with a virtual studio application to create a new composition (Project 14)

---

cert hall. The digital tapes were then brought back into the UAB recording studio—equipped with four Tascam Modular Digital Multitrack (32-track) recorders—where they were synchronized to the Pro Tools and Digital Performer materials.

One area where Digital Performer really shines is the ease with which device patches can be called up and assigned in tracks. Almost every instrument heard on this project is a result of layering two or three different patches from different keyboards, sound modules, or virtual synths. The large array of instruments is dispersed throughout the studio and control room, but all parameters are easily accessible from my master station (Star Trek's Mr. Sulu would be envious). Most importantly to a producer, when keyboardists were brought in to overdub parts, I was able to save on time and expense by preprogramming all the sophisticated combinations of sounds I wanted to use. Then, if we decided to experiment even further, we had the original sequences to tweak, in addition to the live recorded audio tracks from the choir."

Hardware and Software

Professor Panion frequently has to do his arranging and composing in airplanes, hotel rooms, or rehearsals. He prefers to use a mobile music workstation. For hardware, he has a 17" Mac G4 Titanium laptop (1 gHz CPU with 1 GB RAM) with a CD-RW/DVD-R built-in drive. In his home studio, he has a Kurzweil K2000 V3 keyboard synth and an M-Audio Radium 61 MIDI keyboard controller. His speaker power includes Harmon/Kardon Soundsticks and subwoofer and a pair of Yamaha NS-10s. Of course, he also has three Firewire hard drives for many gigabytes of storage space.

The photo shows Dr. Panion in his studio at the University of Alabama—Birmingham. His hardware options

get upscaled from his home studio to include the type of hardware he described above when preparing the UAB gospel recording. In addition to the digital tape decks, the studio houses two Yamaha 02R mixing consoles; Korg Triton and Trinity keyboards; Emu, Korg, and Yamaha sound modules; Akai and Roland drum modules; Digidesign 880 digital I/O and MOTU MIDI Timepiece; and lots of hard-disk storage added to the Mac OS X server.

Dr. Panion relies on four programs: Sibelius, Digital Performer, Reason, and Pro Tools. "The combination of these tools," he notes, "makes up a formidable arsenal for just about every type of project in which I am typically engaged, from works for symphony orchestra to pop and gospel productions for commercial recordings." Sibelius handles his music notation needs, and Digital Performer and Pro Tools provide multitrack mixing, editing, and effects processing for MIDI and digital audio tracks. Reason has a rather unique fit in his software repertoire; we'll let him explain:

First, I have used it to create self-contained instrumental works that were completely conceived, recorded, mixed, and exported in the Reason environment without using another sequencer, virtual synthesizer, effects plug-in, or mixer. Second, through ReWire, I use the instruments included in Reason as virtual synths for Digital Performer. Up to 64 Reason tracks (32 stereo) can be assigned as outputs in Digital Performer and digitally bounced to the assigned tracks, or simply played back in perfect synchronization. Finally, Reason has been a perfect tool for teaching the principles of recording engineering. The lifelike interface enables students to really get their "hands dirty" and virtually experience building and wiring racks of gear without blowing expensive circuits and fuses. Just press the Tab key while in Reason to see for yourself.

Module 17

Adventures in Sound Shaping and Synthesis

DVD-ROM
Projects 13–14 on the accompanying DVD are designed to give you hands-on experience with the tasks in Table 17.1.

LINK
Be sure to read Module 15 in the last Viewport before this module.

DVD-ROM
Project 13 Advanced Features of Digital Audio Workstation Software

We now turn our attention to the last major software section on digital audio and MIDI: digital audio workstation (DAW) software; software plug-in synthesizers, samplers, and virtual instruments; all-in-one virtual-studio software; and programming environments. This module is called "Adventures in Sound Shaping and Synthesis" because of this software's ability to create and combine sounds.

Keep in mind that this set of music technology topics could occupy hundreds of pages of information. We offer an overview of these programs and invite you to dig further on your own. We will assume that you understand basic design, data entry, editing, plug-in, and digital audio/MIDI features of sequencing software from Module 15. Table 17.1 will guide you in your exploration of software in this section.

Digital Audio Workstation (DAW) Software

Advanced software of this type typically offers all of the features of programs like Home Studio, Power Tracks Pro Audio, Metro SE, Tracktion, Logic Express, and Cubase SE, which we covered in Module 15. Typical DAW titles include Digital Performer (Mark of the Unicorn), Cubase SX (Steinberg/Yamaha), Logic Pro

TABLE 17.1	Tasks for Advanced Work with Sequencing	
Setting	**Task**	**Typical Software**
Studio with and without live performers	• Record, edit, and master using advanced features of digital audio workstation (DAW) software	Digital Performer, Cubase SX, SONAR, Logic Pro
Studio	• Add plug-in samplers, synthesizers, and virtual instruments in DAW software	Battery, Attack, EVP88, The Grand, B4, Pluggo, ES2, Tassman, Absynth, TERA, EXP24, Sampletank XL, HALion, Reaktor
Studio	• Create sounds with "all-in-one" virtual studios	Reason, Storm, Project5
Studio	• Work with programming approaches to sound creation	Max/MSP, Csound, SuperCollider

(Apple), and SONAR (Cakewalk/Twelve Tone Systems). In some cases, a title may have different versions based on included features. With these titles, you can expect:

- Support for much higher sample sizes and bit rates for audio files (24-bit, 192 kHz can be expected in some titles)
- Ability to use hardware "surfaces" such as those described in Module 16 for easier data entry and editing (examples are Mackie Control C4 or the Tascam US-428)
- More options for virtual tracks and channels
- Many more options for effects and plug-ins for altering MIDI and audio data and for expanding sound opportunities with virtual samplers and synthesizers (all titles come with an impressive collection of built-in effects and dozens of plug-ins)
- Project-management options that help you keep track of complicated project pieces involving samplers, synthesizers, and edit files
- Advanced automation options (Logic Pro offers the ability to automate groups of tracks as one unit)
- "Freeze" function that lets you take tracks that have been processed with plug-ins and effects that you like and freeze them as preprocessed tracks to reduce the load on the computer CPU for processing these functions again and again as you work on your mix
- More flexible visual representations for editing MIDI and digital audio data, including advanced menus, drum-mapping options, more flexible mixers, and custom interface designs (all titles offer extensive support for advanced mixing with sends, inserts, bus routing, and the like)
- Support for looping and time stretching (Cubase SX and SONAR include excellent tools for time stretching and hit-point creation)
- Integration with other programs, allowing a DAW software product to host a separate synthesis or sampler program (Digital Performer, Cubase SX, and SONAR support ReWire technology, which was developed collaboratively by the Steinberg/Yamaha and Propellerhead companies. ReWire is described in the Virtual Studios section of this module.)
- More options for saving and importing data (Digital Performer, SONAR, and Logic Pro support importing the OMF format commonly used in Digidesign's Pro Tools. This file format supports multiple tracks of digital audio, video, and additional support files.)
- New options for surround-sound mixing

We cannot cover each program in depth, but we do provide some highlights of each by first examining the overall interface features and then focusing on more advanced aspects of editing, plug-in support, and mixing/mastering. This will help you do the first task in Table 17.1, which includes recording, editing, and mastering with typical DAW software.

Interface Features

More advanced sequencers of the type described here include sets of windows that are much more complete than you have seen before. Plentiful menus and floating palettes are common.

Overview

To illustrate this, Figures 17.1a and b show an overview of two software titles, Digital Performer and Cubase SX. In the first figure, we see a collection of windows that not only refer to the MIDI and digital audio content but to the state of the

TIP

As you gain more experience with more advanced sequencing and music-notation software (Module 20), you will soon see the advantage of a large-screen display. At least a 17" if not a 20" monitor is highly recommended!

computer. Each DAW program has a sophisticated set of mixer windows where automation and mastering tasks can be executed. In addition, Digital Performer provides two kinds of track displays, an overview that displays the track information in the usual manner and a more detailed view of the content where edits can be made. At the top of the graphic are a number of controls that can be used for editing, along with the expected transport controls.

In Figure 17.1b, the Cubase SX software displays a similar set of detailed windows, including a "pool" window that accounts for all audio files associated with a project. In Cubase SX, a hierarchy of audio content similar to other DAW titles is supported. The original audio recording, called a "clip," remains in the pool of resources, unchanged from the editing that happens. However, when the clip is part of the track window, it becomes an "event" or "object" that *represents* the clip and can be manipulated without changing the original audio. Special regions of audio can be represented as well, including small "slices," or audio much like we described in Module 12 with looping sequencers. Detailed windows for controlling tempo and editing digital audio are displayed.

Project Management

To help manage the many options and parts of a project, software of this type provides many more interface options than are found in the software reviewed in Module 15. Customized screen layouts are possible (Figure 17.2). Here we have

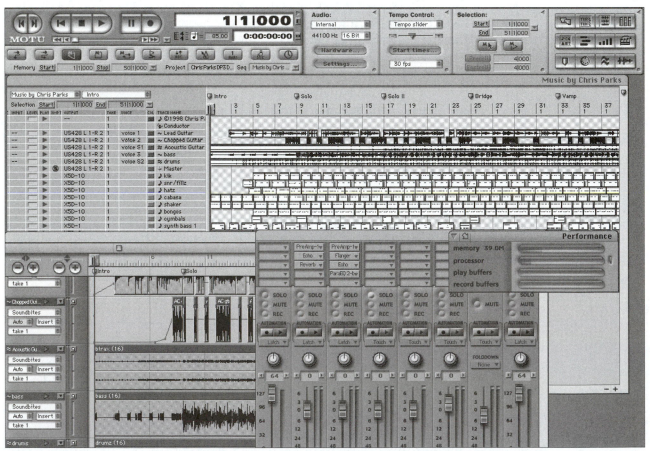

FIGURE 17.1A Overview of Digital Performer

Mark of the Unicorn, Inc. (Mac)

created four different layouts in SONAR according to the way we want to work with a project at any given time. These layouts are specific to a project or "song" in the language of SONAR. Cubase SX offers a "browser" window as a way to account for each project element.

Being able to work with both MIDI data and digital audio in an integrated environment is a real advantage. Software in this category offers displays of both types of data side by side, as seen in Figure 17.3. Notice that the top two tracks are MIDI displays and the third is digital audio. With the top MIDI track, we have added some automated volume adjustments; displayed to the right is an added echo MIDI effect. The audio display shows the relationship in time with the MIDI data and allows the usual editing for adjustments in time or timbre. Another feature of this software is that track displays can be independently sized so that digital audio views can be larger (for editing purposes) than MIDI data displays.

Digital Performer also features "mini menus" within many of its major editing windows. This increases ease of management because it places options in context with the window function. Figure 17.4 shows one of these menus and its extensions for the main track window. We have opted to add a track for a surround setup; note the surround-type options that Digital Performer provides. Other track options include creating Aux and Master Fader tracks that help with mastering and mixing.

A similar example of interface design can be seen in the use of the CTRL-click (Mac) or right mouse button (Win) in Cubase SX (Figure 17.5) to reveal more

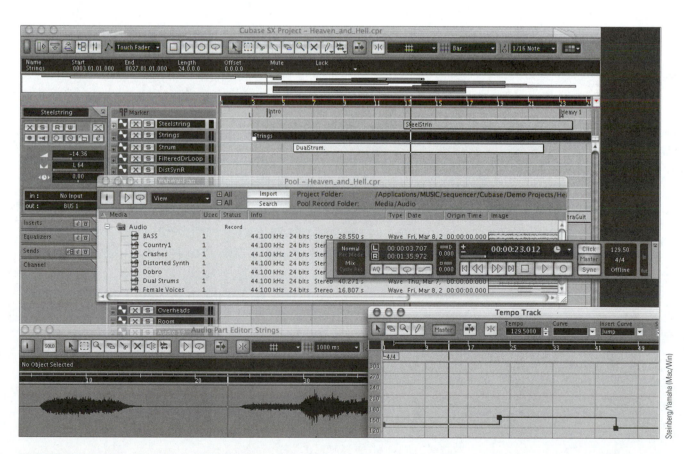

FIGURE 17.1B Overview of Cubase SX

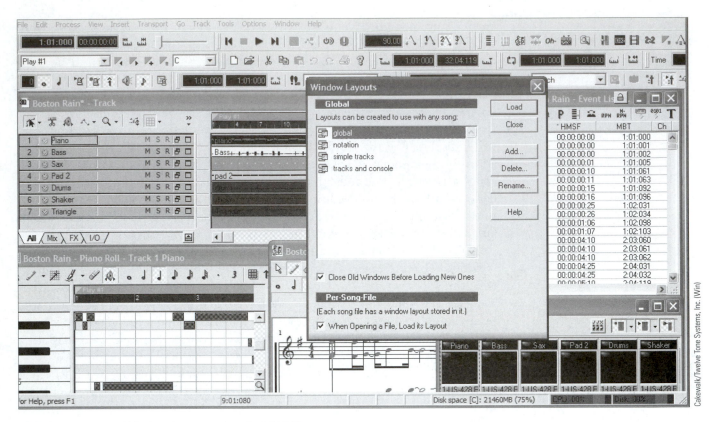

FIGURE 17.2 Window layout options in SONAR

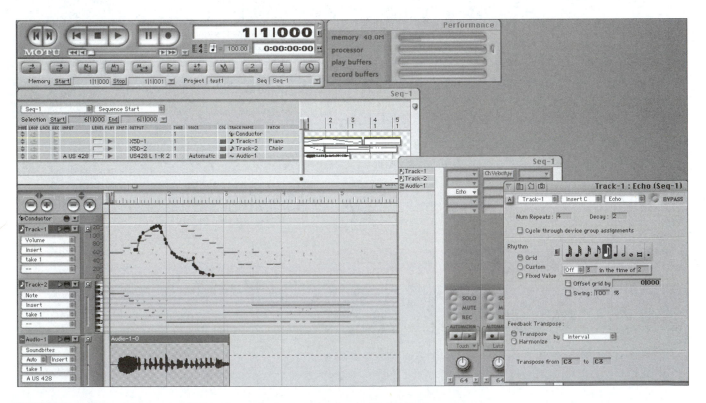

FIGURE 17.3 MIDI and digital audio tracks in combination in Digital Performer

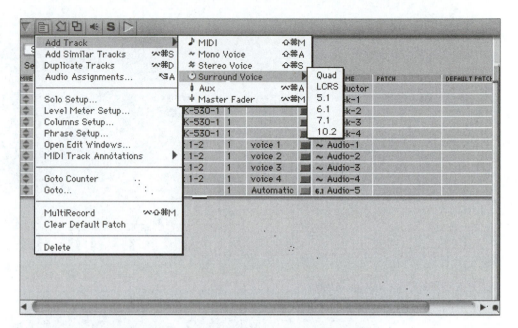

FIGURE 17.4 "Mini menu" in Digital Performer

FIGURE 17.5 Mouse-click options for tracks in Cubase SX

detailed options. By clicking on the track header, contextual menu items appear as options. Options include visual display choices, as well as specific track information editing.

A final management example includes the "environment" options in Logic Pro. All software reviewed in Module 15 and here provide choices for hardware connections designed to work with the operating system. Logic Pro, however, provides a more-detailed approach with its environment windows. Hardware and software interface details can be graphically represented and specialized routing of audio and MIDI data can be configured based on the kinds of hardware contained in a studio setup. Figure 17.6 shows how this is done. The top center window shows the "Click & Ports" option for a typical hardware setup that simply includes one MIDI device that is a controller. Notice that the routing includes a MIDI

FIGURE 17.6   Environment window in Logic Pro

LINK

See Module 18 for more on control surfaces like the Tascam.

metronome, an input view window that displays incoming data, and a link to the sequencer in Logic Pro. The windows below show other details about how the drums are mapped and the basic setup for digital audio.

Special Interface Options

Many control features of DAW software are enhanced. For example, options are offered for the transport palette in Logic Pro. A special menu for the transport palette can be revealed. You can customize the look of the palette, as well as the many options it contains.

Digital Performer allows for the custom creation of control graphics for MIDI controllers (Figure 17.7). For example, if you want to create a slider bar to control the modulation-wheel effect for MIDI data, you can do so in software with real-time automation. This is particularly useful if your MIDI device does not have such a modulation wheel (for instance, a rack-mounted MIDI module) or if you want to control a virtual synth as a plug-in.

Traditional notation views are now common in all levels of sequencing software, but in DAW titles, the notation capabilities are more like what you might expect in dedicated notation packages, which we will review in Viewport VII. Figure 17.8 provides a glimpse of this with Logic Pro. Notice the detailed options for screen displays. Even multiple music fonts are supported.

Digital video files such as QuickTime, Windows AVI, or MPEG can be imported into sequencing software in order to create and edit the audio track. DAW

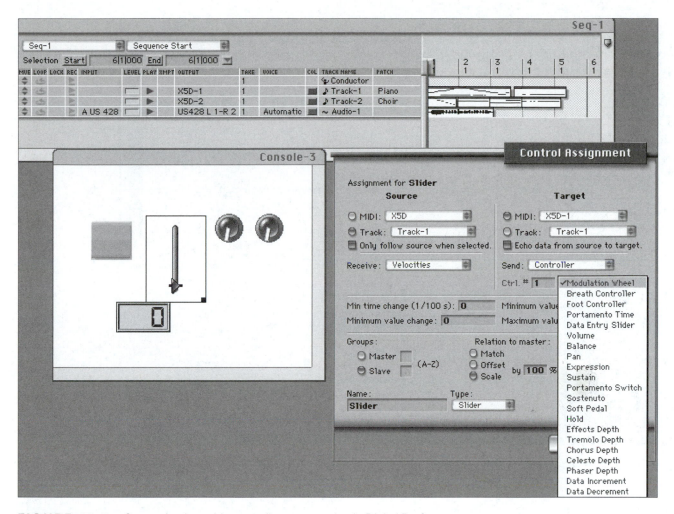

FIGURE 17.7   Customized graphic controller construction in Digital Performer

LINK
SMPTE, a timing code for working with video and sound, is described more fully in Module 18.

software allows considerably more options for this sort of work than can be found in basic-level programs. SMPTE control options are very common and the full range of sequencing-software processing can be applied to customize the movie's sound. In Figure 17.9, we display an example of how the reverb special effect in Digital Performer can be used to alter the sound track of a movie.

Finally, the interface in DAW software provides logical links among critical editing windows. A change in one window will automatically update elements in other windows when they are linked.

Editing and Input/Output

The usual editing and input/output features described for basic-level sequencers are all supported with DAW software. Here are a few examples of additional editing features found for both MIDI and audio data.

CD and DVD Audio Import

In addition to recording from live audio and MIDI sources, sounds can be imported from a CD or DVD into sound libraries for use in a project. Material can be auditioned and then imported (whole tracks or portions) and stored in a library of "soundbites" (Digital Performer) that can be used as a resource in the project.

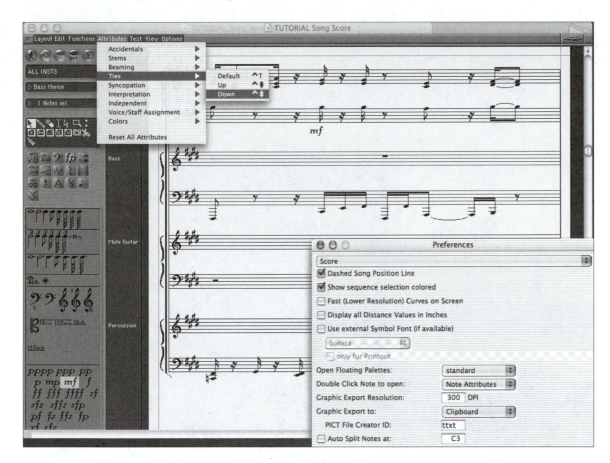

FIGURE 17.8   Notation control in Logic Pro

FIGURE 17.9   Movie sound editing in Digital Performer

"Take" Options

Digital Performer also offers a "take" option that allows you to create a series of digital audio "take" files (you saw this option in Module 12 when we discussed multiple-track programs like ProTools). Figure 17.10 shows the tracks window and the pop-up menu in the "take" column. You can create as many versions of a track as disc space allows and decide on which one you will use in the final mixing.

Edit History

Unlimited "undos" is a standard option in this software, allowing you to undo the last action and subsequent previous actions as many times as necessary. However, Cubase SX offers additional options for selectively changing past edits. You can select a group of changes and delete all of them without going through successive keystrokes.

MIDI Transformation, Quantization, and Loop Construction

Sections of MIDI can be altered in special ways in DAW software. For example, Logic Pro uses a "transform" window to alter MIDI data to form crescendos, change tempo, alter pitches, and make other changes. Once a range of events is selected that meets certain criteria, then the transformations can occur. Figure 17.11 shows this process. Transformations such as those displayed in the pop-up menu can have settings associated with them that can be saved as presets. Logic Pro also provides a pencil-editing option in the "HyperEditor" window.

MIDI data can be easily altered with various quantization schemes. Figure 17.12 shows the many options in Digital Performer for applying special quantization patterns and custom design parameters for each. "Humanize" adds a random element to straight quantization. With this option, you can choose to guide the randomization by setting parameters, as seen in the dialog box. This creates a sort of semiquantized result that is much closer to a real performance. "Groove" quantize creates a distinctive "feel" to the music by altering timing, accents, and note durations in a manner consistent with a popular style like swing, shuffle, or hip-hop.

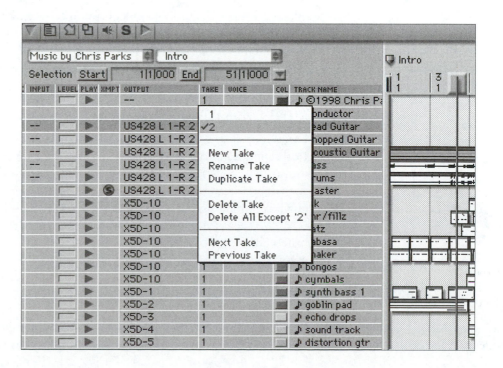

FIGURE 17.10   *"Take" options in Digital Performer*

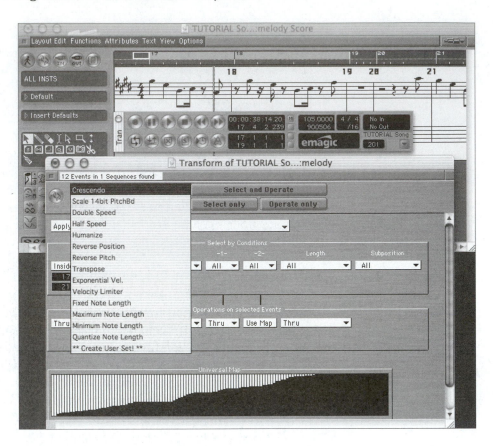

FIGURE 17.11
Transform window in Logic Pro

Digital Performer can use parameters from preset groove files and even use groove files from other programs like Cubase SX. "Smart" quantization is useful if the music is represented in traditional notation.

Subtle alterations in audio data are also possible. Sliced loops similar to the ones mentioned in Module 12 with software like ACID and Live can be created in DAW software. SONAR, for example, has a Loop Construction window that allows the creation of loops with hit points. The tempo and pitch of loops can be changed within a project, much as you would in a loop-based application. If your music largely comprises loops, however, you are better off using a multitrack program designed for this purpose or considering the virtual-studio software described later in this module.

MIDI Drum Editors

Drum loops using MIDI data can be uniquely constructed in software of this kind. Both Digital Performer (Figure 17.13) and SONAR contain special provisions for drum-track construction. For Digital Performer, a drum track was created using the timbres from the "GM Kit" or the standard General MIDI arrangement of percussion timbres as found on the Korg X5D keyboard. We entered a groove pattern in a two-measure sequence and are about to add a Groove Quantize option as noted above. Once created, this drum track can be saved and used as a basis for a composition in the project.

MIDI Extraction

One more editing feature that we will mention is the option to extract MIDI data from an audio-data source. SONAR does this, for example, by using peaks to analyze audio data's timing patterns and then creating a MIDI line of same-pitched

LINK
Be sure to check back to Module 15, where we described approaches to the opposite conversion: MIDI to digital audio.

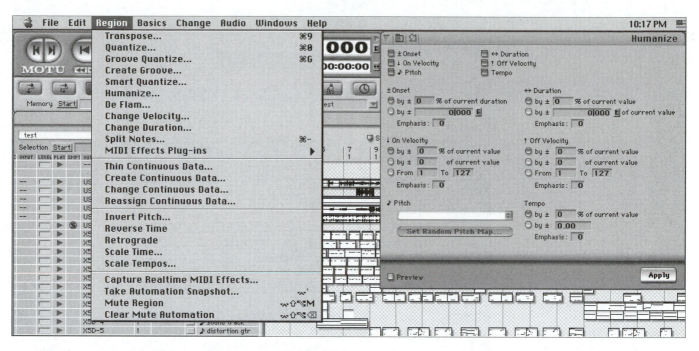

FIGURE 17.12   Quantization in Digital Performer

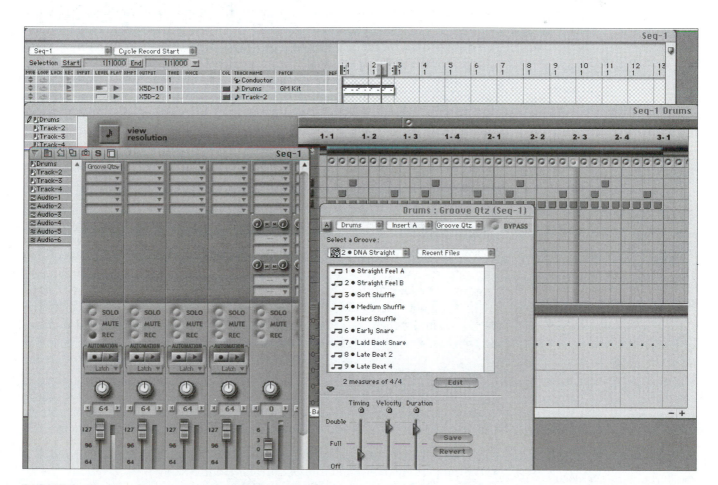

FIGURE 17.13   Drum track creation in Digital Performer

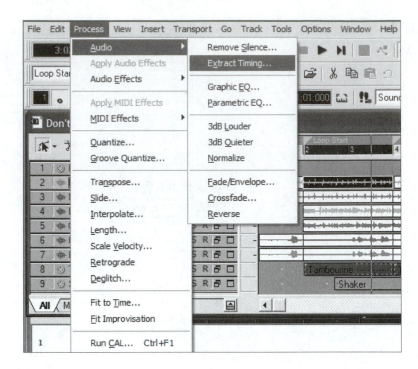

FIGURE 17.14 Extract timing command and parameter settings for MIDI extraction in SONAR

notes of different velocities that conform to the digital audio timing. This works best with single melodies in audio data and for more percussive delineated sounds. You need to assign pitches by hand after this is done, but you can easily accomplish this in any of the traditional editing windows. Figure 17.14 displays how this works. A region of digital audio is chosen and the "Extract Timing" command is issued. Next comes the dialog to set parameters and to audition the line to see how it worked. You can repeat the extraction after changing the parameters until you have the desired result. How can this be used? Imagine that you have an audio drum track that has a predominate snare drum and you want to reinforce it with an electric bass track. You could extract the timing from the drum track, assign pitches to create a MIDI track, and then create a base line.

Plug-In Effects

Each DAW program not only contains its own built-in audio and MIDI effects but also supports a number of plug-ins. In Module 12, we defined three groupings of plug-ins: (1) audio effects, (2) audio instruments, and (3) MIDI effects. We noted the use of audio-effects plug-ins in Modules 9 (audio editors) and 12 (multiple-track software). All three groups play a role in this module, as they did in Module 15 when we highlighted beginning-level sequencers.

Plug-In Formats

Recall that plug-ins are usually created by third-party companies and conform to certain standard formats. Each of our four advanced software titles use specific formats:

- SONAR: DirectX for audio effects, MFX for MIDI, and DXi for instruments
- Digital Performer: Audio Unit (AU), TDM, and MAS
- Cubase SX: VST, VSTi, and DirectX (PC version)
- Logic Pro: Audio Unit (AU)

ASIDE

Be cautious about overusing the plug-ins described here and elsewhere in this textbook. They often consume a large amount of processing power and, if expected to execute in real time, can affect performance. Be sure to use the "freeze" techniques described at the start of this module and the bus routing described in Module 12 to help ease the strain on your computer's processor.

Audio Effects

Figure 17.15 displays audio-effects plug-in options for SONAR. One way to apply these to a track is to use the FX (short for "effects") tab to reveal the FX line in the header. Right-clicking on the line produces a series of pop-up menus that we display here. Notice that on this particular computer there are various individual plug-ins and groups of plug-ins from Cakewalk, PSP, UltraFunk, and Waves. Here we have opened the Ultrafunk fx Compressor R3 for the audio data in Track 1. Multiple effects can be used for these tracks.

MIDI Plug-Ins Using Inserts

Figure 17.16 shows how MIDI effects are used in Cubase SX. The effects are called into action by using the "Inserts" bar in the Inspector on the left-hand side. The settings windows for two of the MIDI effects are open and can be worked in real time until the desired effect is reached. These effects are "chained" one to another so that the effect of one carries over in order to the next.

MIDI Plug-Ins Using Sends

One problem with the chained order described above is that you may not like the result of the sound. It may be ineffective to have the Arpache 5 effect come after the Chorder. You may also want the Quantizer effect to come from a completely different MIDI device. Many studio setups have multiple MIDI devices and you may want the flexibility to have the MIDI signal sounding in multiple ways from multiple devices. DAW software provides the flexibility to do this. Cubase SX uses the "Sends" bar in the track-Inspector window to the left of the track window. Figure 17.17 shows a track and two effects routed to two different devices. Notice that the Sends part of the Inspector is used; one effect is routed to the MIDI interface on Port 1 and the other one is on Port 2. With two MIDI devices connected to the respective ports, the result gives you much more independent control over sound

LINK

The concepts of "inserts" and "sends" were first introduced in Module 12.

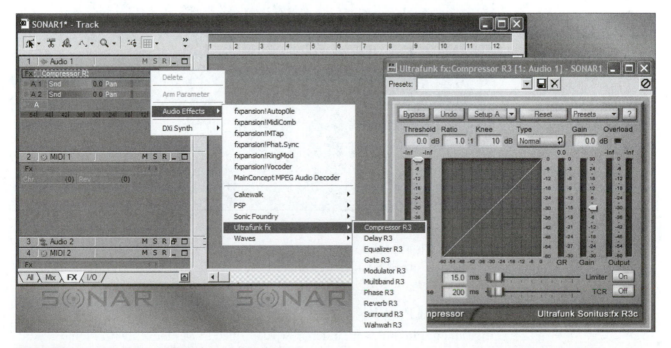

FIGURE 17.15   Audio effects plug-ins in SONAR

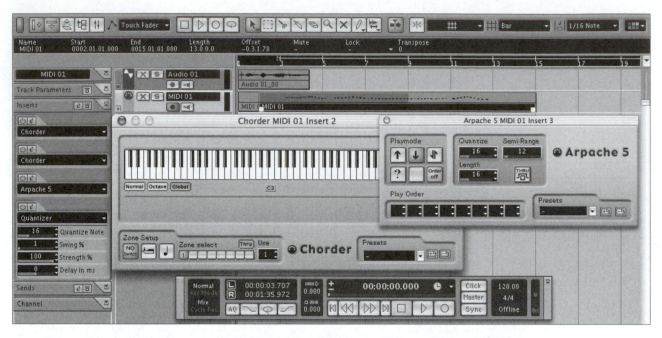

FIGURE 17.16 MIDI effects plug-ins using the "Inserts" option in Cubase SX

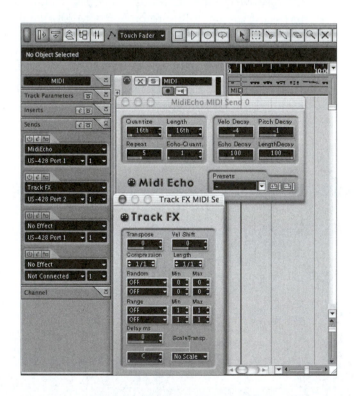

FIGURE 17.17 MIDI effects plug-ins using the "Sends" option in Cubase SX

subtleties. This same system of working with inserts and sends works for audio tracks, as well in Cubase SX. This example is an excellent reason why more-advanced studio designs use MIDI interfaces with multiple ports for "ins" and "outs."

Instrument Plug-Ins

Instrument plug-ins work much as we described in Module 15 with Home Studio, but with more options. Figure 17.18 shows how SONAR introduces instrument plug-ins. The DreamStation DXi polyphonic analog-synth plug-in comes pack-

TIP

Remember that the difference between audio effects and instrument plug-ins is that instruments actually create sounds that respond to the MIDI data in a track or directly from a MIDI controller; audio-effects plug-ins treat the digital audio data already in a track.

LINK

Mixing and mastering is also covered in some detail in Module 12. The techniques and software extensions described there all apply to working with DAW software.

aged with SONAR. The first track in the project is an audio track that uses DreamStation. The next track contains the MIDI data that drive the audio; the "Out" setting directs the track to sound the DreamStation. Sophisticated instrument plug-ins can accept multiple MIDI track inputs with many settings. Notice that SONAR keeps track of this sort of plug-ins in the "Synth Rack" palette at the bottom of the figure.

Logic Pro and Digital Performer provide very similar effect inserts and sends for audio, MIDI, and instrument sounds. Many plug-ins are shipped as part of DAW software and you may find that you do not need any others for your work. Additional plug-in software is available from a number of vendors. More-sophisticated plug-in samplers, synthesizers, and virtual instruments often used with DAW software are reviewed in the next major section of this module.

Mixing and Mastering with DAW Software

We arrive now at the last major topic for DAW software: working with mixers. All of our examples of plug-in applications have been geared toward options with tracks. Software in this category uses the mixer windows as places for similar work. In addition, the mixer supports adjustments in volume for channel output, real-time automation, sound routing, and final mastering—including surround-sound adjustments. The last step is final mix down before rendering to media in the form of AIF or WAV files.

Track and Mixer Layouts

A key to understanding mixers and their channel layout is to understand that the software creates mixers based on track organization. The mixer serves as a direct link between the track structures and their output of sound to the hardware. Mixer

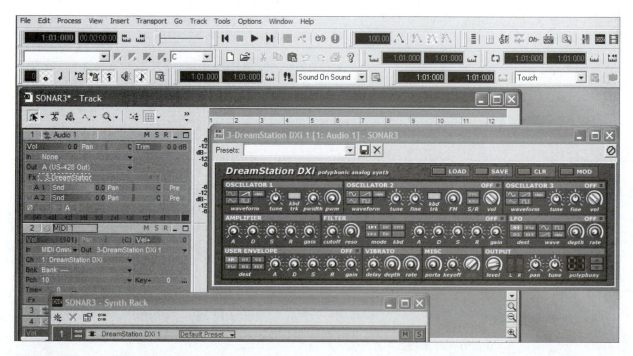

FIGURE 17.18 Instrument plug-in in SONAR

windows can reroute, combine, and split audio data apart, as well as add their own sets of effects before the sound is realized in its final form.

To understand this better, study Figures 17.19a and b, which represent a set of tracks and an associated mixer in Cubase SX. Compare the relationship between the two to see how the mixer (b) mirrors the track setup (a).

Much can also be learned by studying the mixer layout. The mixer in Figure 17.19b contains features very similar to other DAW software. The bottom portion contains the usual faders that control the sound level for each channel. Level meters run vertically next to the fader and support both mono and stereo signals. Each channel contains buttons that control options for soloing, muting, and reading and writing automation, as well as turning inserts and EQ settings off and on. Buttons on the far left of the bottom portion control appearance settings.

The top portion of the mixer contains the location for send effects and EQ settings for each channel. These options can be represented in several ways in this software, including virtual "dials" for the EQ settings. You can toggle back and forth between send slots and the EQ settings. Buttons on the extreme left control the appearance of the mixer, as do small "pull-down" menus along the center line that divides the top and bottom portions.

The mixer-channel layout is created automatically as the tracks (a) are created. Reading from left to right, the first two channels are related to the two audio tracks. The next four channels represent MIDI controls for the four MIDI tracks' data; since they are routed to a virtual instrument, the mixer includes the next four channels as audio channels that relate to the MIDI data. These central eight channels can support MIDI-effect sends for the MIDI channels and audio-effect sends for the audio tracks.

The next-to-last channel is created for the rhythm group (the combination of the "Bass" and Percs" channels). Finally, a "master" channel is created on the far right to control output to the sound card or external digital audio device (such as our Tascam US-428). We have added audio effects for these final two channels, including important mastering effects in the master channel. As you work with tracks in DAW software, you will quickly learn that moving among the track and mixer windows will provide a great deal of control and allow a number of options for mixing and mastering sounds.

Input/Output Routing

Routing in the Cubase mixer in Figure 17.19b is represented by the settings above and below the faders for each channel. For example, the first channel—the audio data in the "Bass" channel—is routed IN from the "IN 2" port on the Tascam. It is routed OUT to the "Rhythm Group" Channel to the far right of the mixer. In turn, the "Rhythm Group" channel is routed OUT to "Bus 1," which is the default setting for the Tascam audio interface. The third through sixth channels are MIDI-data channels and are served by the US-428 MIDI Port 1 for input. For output, they are routed out to the "A1" virtual synth and on to Bus 1 for auditing via the Tascam.

Similar routing patterns also exist for other software. Figure 17.20 displays how Digital Performer uses auxiliary channels. The channel to the extreme right accepts input from "bus 3–4 (Stereo)," and other channels, such as the guitar tracks, send their output to this bus. The Aux channel can add effects in the audio path and send them on to a specific device attached to the appropriate port on the audio interface.

One additional feature of these flexible mixer windows is the ability to send a channel either "pre" or "post" fader. This means that the audio controlled by the

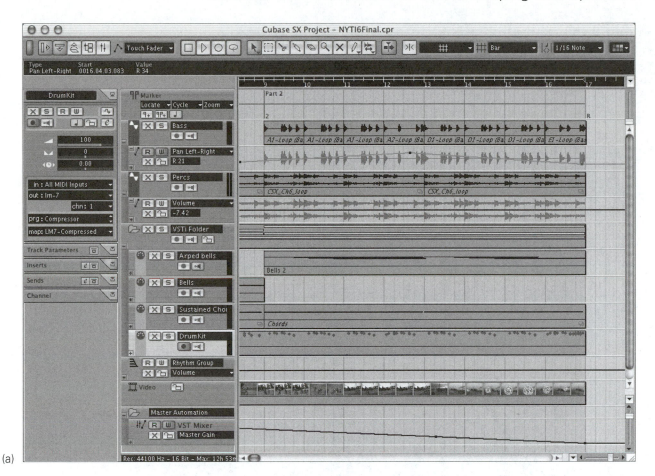

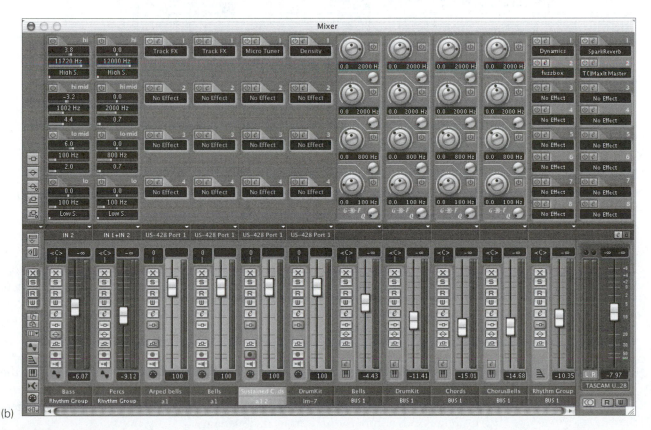

FIGURE 17.19   Track layout (a) and resulting mixer (b) in Cubase SX

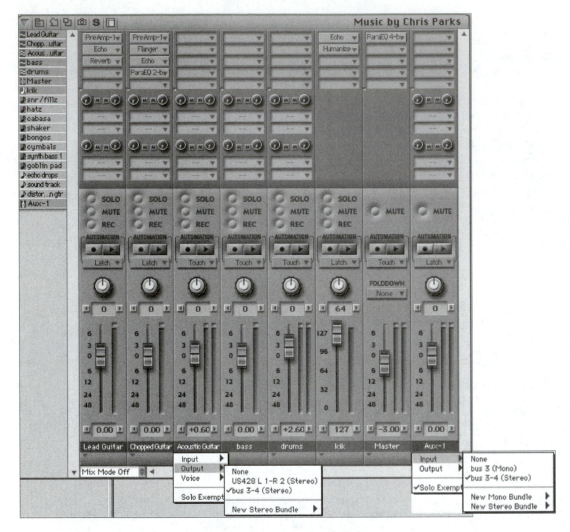

FIGURE 17.20   Mixer in Digital Performer

channel can be sent "before" its fader or "after"—thus allowing the fader to control only selected aspects of the signal.

Software-Mixer Automation

We have already noted how real-time changes in mixing levels can be added in tracks, but such changes can occur in mixers as well. Changes in volume and pan settings can easily be added in real time as you are listening to a mix. These changes can be recorded and become part of the data structure. When you play back your mix, you can watch the faders change in the software mixer as they respond to your mixing changes. Both MIDI and audio tracks can be automated this way; Figure 17.21 shows how this can be set up in Digital Performer. This matches the discussion in Module 10 on hardware mixers and automation that can be designed using software and hardware in combination. Here, everything is done in software.

DAW software offers different modes of automation, as seen in the pop-up menu on the left in the first channel. The "overwrite" mode replaces all of the parameters currently being automated in the track. This is useful if you want to simply start from scratch and remove all automated changes that might be there from previous automations or from track settings.

TIP

To move a virtual knob clockwise or counterclockwise, drag the cursor directly up and down.

LINK

We also covered surround sound in Viewport IV (Module 11 for data structures, Module 12 for multitrack-recording software, and Module 13 for hardware).

"Touch" allows you to overwrite and "touch up" only certain parameters as the track is being audited. For example, if you are only interested in adjusting the pan settings in a channel, you can choose the touch mode and adjust only the pan settings. All other automated-mixing settings will remain intact. In addition, the "touch" mode responds to your changes at that moment, but then returns to whatever settings already exist for the parameter.

"Trim" mode lets you scale an existing volume or send level in a track instead of replacing it completely. "Trim" is great for fine adjustments of already-present automation. "Latch" mode is like "trim," but stays in place after the changes and does not respond to any settings already there. For example, you can change a pan setting so that the sound is directed to the right rear speaker in a surround mix. In "latch mode," that channeled sound would remain in that setting throughout the composition unless you changed it.

Mixer automation graphically places automation results in the track window. Figure 17.22 shows how Logic Pro places envelope graphics in the tracks to the left, responding to the settings as they are changed in the mixer on the right. If you've invested in a hardware-control surface to work with your DAW software, this is an excellent place to use it, since moving controls in a software's virtual mixer is not always an exact procedure.

Surround Mixing and Mastering

Most DAW software titles support surround-sound mixing and mastering. The first step in using these titles for surround work is proper hardware. As noted in Module 13, your digital audio interface must support the number of physical ports for audio out that you need to match the desired format. For the commonly used Dolby Digital 5.1/AC-3 format, six outputs are necessary to support the six channels of sound that this format requires. In addition, you'll need reproduction hardware such as a proper decoder, amplifier, and speaker system that will allow you to monitor the mix-and-mastering work.

None of the DAW titles allow you to actually encode a CD or DVD with surround sound. As we explained in Viewport IV, this requires special software and a

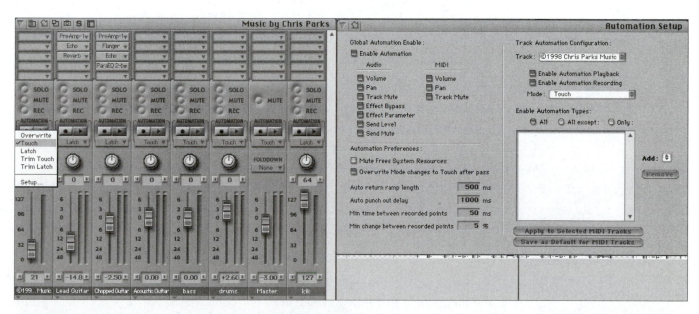

FIGURE 17.21 Mixer automation settings in Digital Performer

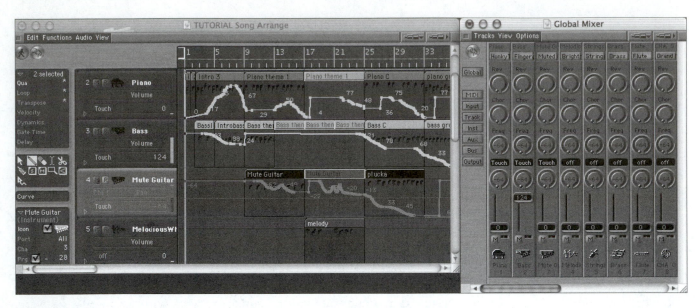

FIGURE 17.22 Graphic representation of Automated Editing in Logic Pro

ASIDE
SurCode or discWelder software (Minnetonka, Inc. [Mac/Win]), as examples, provide the capability to encode CD or DVD with surround sound.

LINK
See Modules 9, 12, and 15 for more information on plug-ins, especially the various formats that each host software program and computer platform supports.

CD or DVD drive capable of burning the encoded audio to laser disc. DAW software provides the capability of mixing and mastering the audio sound files and saves them to a hard disk. Each program has its own approach to surround-sound mastering and mixing that you can choose to support various formats.

For example, the approach for Cubase SX is displayed in Figure 17.23. The top left window is used to set up a project's output channels. Once created, you can assign channels in the mixer as noted in the middle graphic. The panner is shown in the upper right figure. In terms of how mastering effects can be used for each channel, the bottom graphic in Figure 17.23 shows how effects can be patched for each channel. Connecting the virtual patch cords through the effect will allow the channel to be changed by the effect.

Mixdown to Disk

Finally, all DAW titles allow you to save complex mixes to disk for distribution. A two-channel stereo file is probably the most common format; however, if more than stereo channel sound is desired, as with surround sound, multiple output files can be saved. Saving to disk is the final step in the mastering process. MIDI tracks will need to be either rerecorded into audio tracks or assigned to be played with virtual synths. All mixing levels, automation data for panning, muting, and other special effects are taken into account during the final mixdown. The channels' output settings are directed to the master channel, with stereo signals from each channel sent to the master with the stereo split in place.

"Bounce" is the term often used for combining multiple tracks into a single track. It is borrowed from the days when analog tape was used for mixing. Settings for start and end points, resolution, file format, file type, and dithering setting are common in "bounce" dialogs. If you are bouncing down to a stereo file for CD distribution, 16-bit sound is required and a dithering procedure is recommended to decrease noise if your resolution/original sampling rate for individual channels is greater than 16 bit/44mHz. Interleave file type is chosen here, resulting in one summed stereo file; however, separate but coordinated left and right mono files can be chosen if you intend to work further with the files in digital audio programs like Pro Tools.

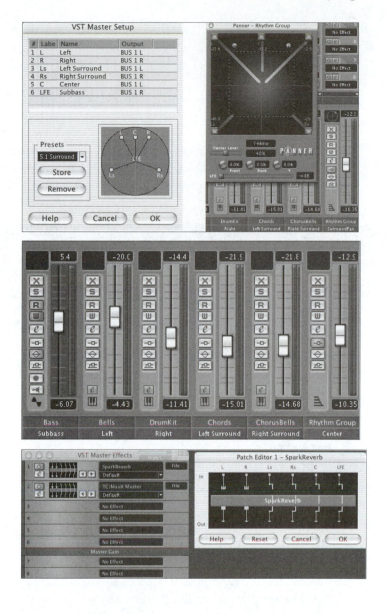

FIGURE 17.23
Surround-sound windows in Cubase SX

Specialized Plug-In Samplers, Synthesizers, and Virtual Instruments

The second task in Table 17.1 includes expanding DAW software with special plug-ins. In keeping with the title of this module, the plug-ins described here offer extraordinary resources for shaping and customizing sounds that can be used for creative work.

Plug-ins were explained in some depth in past viewports. In Modules 9, 12, and 15, we noted how plug-ins are used for sound effects, and in Module 15, we stressed the idea of "instrument" plug-ins in basic-level sequencers. In this module, we examine more-advanced instrument plug-ins that function as either dedicated instruments or software synthesizers and samplers. Many of these titles work as "stand-alone" programs as well.

Table 17.2 provides information for selected examples of this software. Hundreds of such programs are on the market; we have included a few of the more frequently cited titles. The type and content are noted, as well as the format and host platform. The groups are:

- Instruments (with little or no synthesis function)
- Synthesizers
- Sample players
- Combination synthesizers/samplers

In the past, hardware devices such as those described in Viewport V, Module 16, provided the musician with tools to synthesize sounds from scratch or to sample sounds for use in playback under MIDI control. Now, much of this work can be

---

TABLE 17.2   Examples of Virtual Instrument, Synthesizer, and Sampler Plug-Ins

Plug-In	Type and Content	Typical Format	Host Platform
Battery (Native Instruments)	**Instrument/Sampler:** percussion (drum kit) support for external samples	VST, DXi, AU, MAS, RTAS, stand-alone	Mac/Win
Attack (Waldorf)	**Instrument/Synthesizer:** percussion drum synth	VST	Mac/Win
EVP88 (Apple)	**Instrument:** electric pianos (sample sound: 12 vintage piano sounds)	Logic Series (AU), VST (VST version called EVP73)	Mac
The Grand (Steinberg/Yamaha)	**Instrument:** piano (sample sound: grand piano)	VST	Mac/Win
B4 (Native Instruments)	**Instrument:** organ (sample sound: Hammond B3 organ)	VST, AU, MAS, RTAS, DXi	Mac/Win
Pluggo (Cycling 74)	**Instrument:** many assorted sounds; some synthesizer/sampler functions as well	VST, MAS, AU, RTAS	Mac
ES2 (Apple)	**Synthesizer:** subtractive, vector, and FM	Logic Series (AU)	Mac
Tassman (Applied Acoustic Systems)	**Synthesizer:** physical modeling	DXi, VST, RTAS	Mac/Win
Absynth (Native Instruments)	**Synthesizer:** subtractive, FM, ring modulation	DXi, VST, MAS, AU, RTAS, stand-alone	Mac/Win
TERA (Virsyn)	**Synthesizer:** analog, waveshaping, physical modeling, FM, spectral	VST, SA	Mac/Win
EXP24 (Apple)	**Sample Player:** AIF, WAV, SDII, SoundFont2, Akai S1000/3000	AU, VST	Mac
Sampletank XL (IK Multimedia)	**Sample Player:** AIF, WAV, Akai S1000/S3000; many prepared sample sounds (sound-module approach)	VST, MAS, RTAS	Mac/Win
HALion (Steinberg/Yamaha)	**Sample Player:** Akai S1000/2000/3000; E-mu EIII/IIIX. ESI, Giga, SoundFont2, others	VST	Mac/Win
Reaktor (Native Instruments)	**Synthesizer/Sampler:** (flexible approach to sound construction); AIF, WAV. Akai S1000, SDII	VST, DXi, MAS, AU, RTAS, stand-alone	Mac/Win

done by the kind of software described here. Logically, these virtual synthesizers and samplers developed as partners with DAW software so that musicians can use the sounds as part of the creative process. To understand this software, read the Historical Perspective on Synthesizers. This will help you understand the heritage on which virtual instruments are built.

Historical Perspective on Synthesizers

We are all familiar with the sounds of traditional musical instruments, such as those in the brass, woodwind, string, and percussion families. These sounds are produced naturally by vibrating materials of one form or another and are most often played without any form of electricity or sound amplification. We have come to appreciate the wonderful sounds they produce. But what of sounds that come from electronic sources? It may be tempting to assume that such sounds are quite recent. After all, devices like computers, MIDI-equipped keyboards, and DVD players have come to us in just the last few decades. Actually, experiments with electronically produced sound and the use of such sounds for aesthetic purposes can be traced to the late nineteenth century.

Early Sound Synthesis

Building on the work of Joseph Saveu a century before, during the 1800s Jean Fourier and Hermann von Helmholtz studied overtones and complex waveforms. This pioneering investigation into the harmonic series and additive sound synthesis was at the heart of Thaddeus Cahill's construction of the Telharmonium in 1906. Cahill used electric dynamos that ran at different rates of speed, producing sine waves. These waves were synchronized and fed into telephone lines so people could hear complex waveforms produced at the other end of the line. He found that if he could vary these generators just right, he could produce reasonable representations of common complex waveforms. An organ keyboard and foot pedal were used to manage pitch and volume. For a monthly fee, subscribers could choose to hear music over their phone lines!

Although the experiment failed as a commercial venture, Cahill demonstrated effective electronic control over timbre. In fact, in 1929, Laurens Hammond used a similar but vastly more efficient system in his now famous Hammond organ. Other interesting experiments with electronic-performance instruments followed from 1930 to 1950 that used some form of either additive or subtractive synthesis to create sound by altering the amplitude of the harmonics.

Electronic Music Studios

In the early 1950s, more complex solutions were built in electronic-music studios such as the NWDR in Cologne, the RTF in Paris, and the RAI in Milan. Studios in the United States typically were universities, such as University of Illi-

From "New Music for an Old World" by R. Baker, *McClure's Magazine*, 1906

Dynamos and wires for Cahill's Telharmonium and a view of two performers at the keyboard in the upper right-hand corner

nois, Columbia, and Princeton. Important composers who worked in such studios included Babbitt, Davidovsky, Hiller, Luening, Maderna, Stockhausen, Ussachevsky, and Varèse. Edgar Varèse's *Poeme Electronique* (1958), Stockhausen's *Kontakte* (1959–60), and John Cage's *Fontana Mix* (1956–58) came out of these studios. Important new techniques were established that have now become standard fare for sound

(continued)

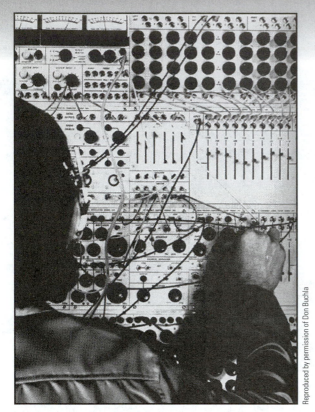

Reproduced by permission of Don Buchla

Modules and patch cords on a Buchla installation

synthesis. Instead of crude generators to produce sound, these studios used specially designed oscillators, filters, and ring modulators to create effects. To capture and further treat sounds, tape recorders were used and special techniques such as playing sounds backward or creating tape loops were developed.

The Voltage-Controlled Music Synthesizer

The voltage-controlled music synthesizer became the staple of analog-sound synthesis during the 1960s and 1970s. Most notable were the Moog and Buchla synthesizers. These devices were self-contained integrated systems designed to create synthesized sound. Most had music keyboards and could be programmed by using knobs, switches, and patch cords to connect internal components. Building on the concepts developed in the big electronic studios of the day, the voltage-controlled synthesizer became a popular instrument for smaller studios and school settings. These instruments were the forerunners of today's digital synthesizer. A typical voltage-controlled music synthesizer, like the Buchla pictured above, would have a voltage-controlled oscillator (VCO) as a sound source controlled by other voltage-

controlled devices like amplifiers (VCAs), filters (VCFs), and envelope generators. The sound could then be processed and mixed with effects like reverberation, filtering, and equalization. The final sound could be part of a live performance or, more typically, saved to analog tape for use in a composition. Morton Subotnick used the Buchla for his famous *Silver Apples of the Moon* (1967), and Wendy Carlos used the Moog to create the first popular electronic recording, *Switched-On Bach* (1968). These instruments were joined by ones produced by other companies such as Arp (with its classic Arp 2600 voltage-controlled system), Korg, Oberheim, Roland, and Sequential Circuits (with its classic Prophet-5 synthesizer). Some of these earlier electronic instruments have recently been reborn in "soft synth" recreations.

Digital Synthesis: A New Era

At the same time the famous electronic-music studios were being formed in the 1950s, others were working on an entirely different approach to creating and manipulating sound. Max Mathews, musician and engineer, was conducting experiments at Bell Labs using computers to convert analog speech to digital representation and back again in order to study telephone communications. He found this sound-sampling technology also worked well for generating music waveforms and composing music. The reasoning went something like this: Instead of using analog oscillators and envelope generators to produce sounds electronically and then manipulating them still further with filters and mixers, why not use a computer to sample or create basic ana-

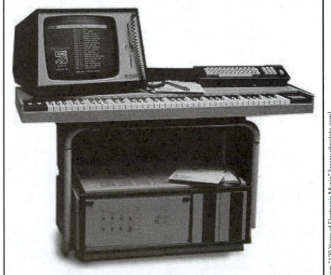

From "120 Years of Electronic Music" [www.obsolete.com]

The Fairlight CMI IIx Synthesizer/Sampler

log waveforms digitally, and then manipulate the numbers for the desired effect? Mathews and others created computer programs designed to do just this. Music software programs like Mathews's MUSIC IV and GROOVE are examples of this kind of computer-music application. Subroutines in this software replicated some of the basic analog processes like those used in Moog and Buchla synthesizers. Such an approach had an immediate appeal over analog synthesis. More control could be exercised over pitch materials, and sampling allowed a faithful representation of many complex waveforms. The immediate access to sounds and their editing was also seen as an improvement, eliminating some of the cumbersome physical problems of analog tape. Risset composed *Mutations I* (1969) using MUSIC V at Bell Labs. Vercoe composed *Synthesism* in the same year at the Princeton University lab using MUSIC 360, a programming language that ran much faster than older digital-composition programs. Throughout the 1960s and 1970s, digital electronic music was only possible at larger studios with ample resources. Digital encoding of high-quality sound placed huge demands on storage space and required large, expensive computers for processing. For this reason, both analog and digital systems coexisted until the technology improved.

Digital Synthesizers Come of Age

The technology did improve, and more modular instruments were built. During the 1970s and 1980s, storage became more affordable and chip design put more powerful electronic circuitry into smaller and cheaper packages. Two basic types of digital synthesizers emerged to carry on the tradition begun by the voltage-controlled devices. Digital samplers were designed to be used as major platforms for sound sampling. Once sampled, the sounds could then be used in many creative ways. The other type was manufactured with many preset waveforms digitally encoded and was designed to be used as the basis for sound synthesis. These instruments also added their own special techniques, such as FM and waveshaping synthesis. Today, we call these *synthesizers*. The Synclavier and Fairlight systems designed in the

The Yamaha DX7II FD mkII Synthesiser

Courtesy of Yamaha DX7 [www.thedx7.co.uk]

1970s were some of the first commercial sampler workstations. They contained powerful programmable digital technology, including sampling capabilities and waveform editing. These devices also broke new ground by having real-time capabilities. Musicians could experiment with changes in synthesis design and hear the results of these changes immediately. Certain models could be used in performance situations, as well as studios. Jon Appleton's *Georganna's Farewell* was written for an early version of the Synclavier; the Fairlight is still actively used in many major motion-picture and recording studios.

From "120 Years of Electronic Music" [www.obsolete.com]

E-MU Emax keyboard sampler

Both the Synclavier and the Fairlight were priced beyond the reach of most musicians. The early 1980s saw the development of two affordable keyboards that emphasized sound sampling: the E-MU Emulator and the Ensoniq Mirage. These devices did not have the computer-music capabilities of Synclaviers and Fairlights, but did have a MIDI sequencer and excellent sampling technology. To this day, the sampler keyboard offers the musician a very powerful device for sound creation. This type of keyboard sampler (like the Emax) is used by composers like Libby Larsen for concert music and by many artists performing and composing popular music. Digital synthesizers also continued to develop. The Yamaha DX7 was most popular in the mid-1980s, offering a digital approach to FM-sound synthesis; also very popular was the Casio CZ series, offering phase-distortion synthesis. As costs fell and MIDI became more pervasive, other digital synthesizers continued to be marketed. Most now use digital samples of instrumental timbres as the basis for sound synthesis. The designs and metaphors available in hardware and software today for music sampling and synthesis reflect the evolution from the electronic studios of the 1950s, the voltage-controlled techniques of the 1960s, the first computer-generated music and digital sampling in the 1950s and 1960s, and the first commercial workstations for music in the 1970s.

LINK
Hardware-based synthesizers and samplers are reviewed in Module 16 in Viewport V. Principles of sound synthesis (additive, subtractive, distortive, physical modeling, digital wave, and granular), together with envelope shaping, were covered in Module 8 in Viewport III.

How Specialized Plug-Ins Are Used

Before taking a tour of a few examples of the four groups, a word about practical use of plug-ins is necessary. Typically, these plug-ins are called into service by host software like Logic Pro, SONAR, Cubase SX, or Digital Performer. These advanced sequencing packages are designed to support a particular format such as VST, DXi, or AU, as we mentioned in Viewport III. You install the plug-in on your computer separately from the host software. When you start a program like Cubase or Logic Pro, it often searches for appropriate plug-ins that may already be installed on your computer.

The plug-in usually responds to the input from a MIDI track's data, but the digital audio that each plug-in creates is sent out by way of the mixer controls along with other digital audio. This means that the computer and its sound-card resources become the sole creator of sound and the MIDI device serves only as a convenient trigger for creating the musical gestures. Routing of the MIDI data is set either in the header of the tracks or in the software mixer and special-effects inserts can be added to the resulting sound, as you have seen before.

Each plug-in has its own editing window, as you will soon see. Settings in those windows can be extensive; their complex functionality is what helps to distinguish this category of software from others. Many programs reviewed here can produce as many as 32 separate timbres simultaneously in a single track and multiple tracks can use different plug-ins. Although we review only software-based plug-ins here, there are plug-in titles that work with dedicated, add-on hardware to help improve computer operation. A good example of this is Powercore from TC Works.

Virtual Instruments

We first encountered virtual instruments in Module 15 when dealing with beginning-level sequencers. These were instruments packaged with the sequencing software. Here, we present a number of products sold by third-party vendors; most are designed to work with a wide variety of host software. The first two titles listed in Table 17.2 are popular percussion-oriented programs that offer a great deal of flexibility.

Figure 17.24 displays a typical editing window from Battery. It runs as either a stand-alone program or as a plug-in, with many format options. Central to the program is a 56-cell or "pad" matrix; each cell can be assigned different pitches and supports one or multiple sampled percussion sounds, either from the program or from other sources. Battery supports sample formats such as SoundFont2, Akai, Reaktor, LM4, Loopazoid, and, MPC2000. Because each cell can contain multiple samples that exist in layers, you can program the cell to sound different samples depending on how hard you hit the controlling MIDI keyboard's keys.

In addition, each sample can be edited by Battery. You can define a volume or pitch envelope, along with other parameters; this means you can nondestructively alter the attack, decay, sustain, and release of any sample. Although you can't directly sample drum sounds, as with sampling plug-ins, and you can't apply filters, you can control for looping effects and assign outputs to multiple ports if your hardware and software support it. This means you can assign all your snare-drum sounds, for example, to a channel that has a reverb effect and keep the bass drum or cymbal separate.

Waldorf's Attack drum module does many of the same things, but is based on

LINK
For more information on SoundFont technology, see Module 18. You might also want to return to Module 8 in Viewport III to review the basics of digital audio.

FIGURE 17.24   Edit window for Battery

Native Instruments, Inc. (Mac, Win)

more of a sound-synthesis approach, using VCO and VCA concepts for creating sound. Basic waveforms use drum samples with many controls for shaping the envelope of sound. Many filter options are also provided, together with a host of special effects.

Logic Pro's EVP88 electronic piano modeling plug-in offers presets for 12 vintage pianos. Figure 17.25 shows how this plug-in is used in Logic Pro. In the background, we show the Arrange window with some MIDI data recorded into Track 9, an AutoInst track. On the extreme right, we show the mixer strip for that track and have called up the EVP88 from the I/O slot. The center window represents the editor window for the plug-in. Notice that the settings include adjustments for sound envelope, volume, and stereo intensity. EQ and phase can be adjusted and tremolo and chorusing effects can be added. The large dial at the top controls which of the 12 presets can be chosen. Up to 88 voices can be used within one track. The sounds are constructed from physical-modeling synthesis and reflect some of the physical properties of each instrument.

The Grand (Steinberg/Yamaha) provides a concert-grand-piano instrument. The software provides a full range of samples across the 88 keys of the traditional piano and does not use loops to recreate sustained sounds. The attack portion of the sound is loaded into RAM and the remainder of the sustained sound is streamed from the hard drive. Not only are samples mapped to different pitches but also different samples are supplied for different velocity settings for one pitch. This provides a much more accurate sound under performance conditions. Adjustments for sound character are provided (natural, soft, bright, and hard) and settings for nonweighted and weighted keyboards are provided. Up to 16-voice polyphony is provided. This software is an excellent example of sample technology used to replicate a single instrument.

FIGURE 17.25 EVP88 plug-in in context with Logic Pro

Our last example of instrument plug-ins, Pluggo 3 from Cycling '74, is actually a set of more than 100 separate programs that not only contain many dedicated instrument sounds but also include plug-ins for effects. Examples include bell sounds, drums, and bass lines. Instruments can be altered with filtering, LFOs, and envelope shaping. A bonus is that MIDI messages can be used to help control the editing.

Synthesizers

Figure 17.26 provides the editor view of the ES2 virtual synthesizer. Unlike the other plug-ins mentioned, this one has no instrument sound as a key feature. It provides a number of powerful options for creating sound from scratch that largely use the subtractive-synthesis technique. Other techniques are supported as well, including vector and FM. Each insertion of the ES2 into a DAW program track can support up to 32 voices in MIDI poly mode. Envelopes can be tied to changing sounds, so the timbre can begin with a bell sound and move, for instance, to a bass sound.

The controls for the waveforms of the three oscillators are in the upper left of the display, labeled 1 to 3. Proportions of each oscillator's sound can be controlled within the triangle graphic by moving the small dot in the center. Filtering takes place in the center with a multimode filter that can be blended in parallel or serially with a low-pass filter. The LFOs on the bottom left can be assigned to pitches and envelopes using the middle strip for routing. Still more special effects can be added by adding chorus, flanger, and phaser effects with the controls in the upper right. The possibilities for sound creation are extensive and this software represents a good example of the power of virtual synthesizers.

FIGURE 17.26   Editing window for ES2 Virtual Synthesizer

LINK

Lounge Lizard EP-1 featured in Figure 8.19 is another physical-modeling plug-in from Applied Acoustic Systems.

Tassman from Applied Acoustic Systems uses physical modeling as a technique for sound synthesis. First described in Module 8 of Viewport III, this technique uses the principles of physics to emulate the physical characteristics of an instrument or other vibrating source. The software comes with many presets for various instruments but also allows considerable freedom to create your own sounds.

Absynth from Native Instruments is more like the ES2 in design, but works as a stand-alone title as well as a plug-in. It uses a number of synthesis methods, including subtractive, FM, and ring modulation. Six oscillators are used, together with four filters and effects.

Sample Players

Technically, these resources are more like sample players than samplers in the true sense. Sample players use previously recorded sound and map that sound to pitch regions. Figure 17.27 shows the EXS24 editor window and one of its mapped zones. The timbre is a church choir, one of several preset timbres provided with the software. The top window hosts a small keyboard that serves as a reference for each sample's zones. Here, we've highlighted the right channel of the pitches just to the right of the #4 on the keyboard. Just below the keyboard is the zone data, including the name of the actual audio clip on the hard drive, its group, key note, range, and other data about the clip and its output.

Below this is the editor window for the sound itself. Most of the settings in this window allow for fine-tuning the sample. Filtering, LFOs, and envelope shaping are all possible, as with synthesizer software. Raw samples can be imported from a number of sources, including your own performances; this actually moves the EXS24 closer to a real sampler. EXS24 does not actually do the recording, however. You could use any of the programs in Viewport III or IV, of course, to capture your performances, save as a WAV or AIF file, and then import the sound into EXS24. The software does allow some looping possibilities, but you would be better advised to use a program like Sound Forge or Peak to make your sustained loops. Of course, the program also supports commercially acquired samples that conform to the sample formats listed for this software in Table 17.2.

Once an acceptable set of sounds have been imported, mapped, and tweaked in the editing window, the sampler is linked to a track in a program such as Logic Pro. A maximum of 64 notes is allowed per sampler used and you can use multiple instances of the sampler in a single composition. Since the samples are loaded into and performed out of RAM, physical memory can be a limiting factor with this software, especially if much filtering is used.

IK Multimedia's SampleTank offers a significant number of its own sampled sounds across a wide array of instruments. More than 450 instruments are included on a set of four CDs. The sound library can be installed on any available hard drive for quick use or remain on the CDs and loaded when needed for a project. A powerful search feature in the plug-in helps organize the library and a customized compression scheme (similar to how MP3 functions) allows the sample library to be especially manageable. The product features a 16-voice, multitimbral structure using 16 MIDI channel assignments internally. It can output to four different channels if your hardware and software host supports this. The software comes with some editing capability and the ability to use built-in effects as well as external ones, much like sequencing software. Using effects within the plug-in helps to lower the drain on the computer's CPU. Another nice feature is that samples are

FIGURE 17.27   Editing windows for ESX24

mapped not only to pitches but also to note velocities; this means that a different sample might be called into play for a pitch that is struck harder by the controlling MIDI input.

Another sampler instrument that offers many of the same features as Sample-Tank is HALion from Steinberg/Yamaha. HALion offers a multitimbral and multiple-channel output and can import a number of sampler file formats. What is different about HALion is its ability to stream samples from the hard drive and not require the full sample to be placed in RAM. This has decided advantages in processing speed and computer efficiency. Attack information is held in RAM, but as the sound is started, the remaining data is streamed from disc.

Synthesizer/Sampler Combinations

Our final example in this section is a program that has both synthesizer and sampler capability and much more. Reaktor is a construction kit for the creation of synthesizers, samplers, sequencers, and audio effects. The instruments created from the program can stand alone or be used as a plug-in. In addition to the building blocks for creating custom instruments, the software also comes with several prebuilt resources that can be tweaked for use in music projects.

Reaktor is designed hierarchically; Figure 17.28 demonstrates some of the levels. At the top level is the concept of an "ensemble." The window to the upper

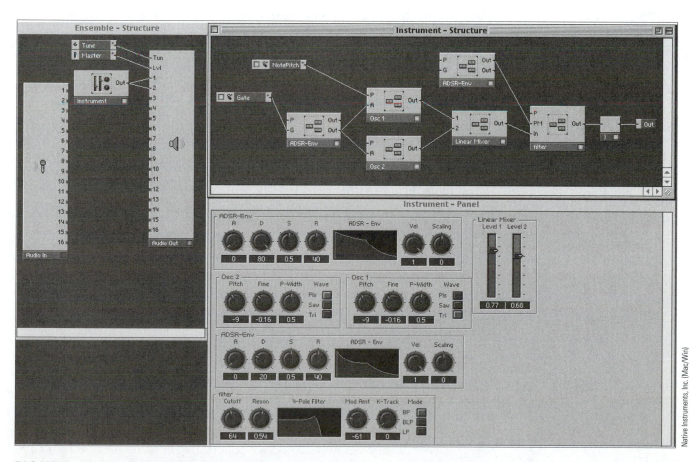

FIGURE 17.28 Building sounds in Reaktor

left is the ensemble structure of this simple example. The ensemble, the finished product, is what gets linked to a DAW program or stands alone. It displays the overall layout of the parts with graphics that represent input, output, and an "instrument."

The instrument is the next level down and is what you build in Reaktor to create sound. It can be a synthesizer, sample player, or effects generator. The window in the top right of our figure displays the structure of the instrument, which you can see is a simple synthesizer. A control panel for the instrument is displayed on the bottom right, with settings that can be manipulated in real time. Settings can be saved as "snapshots" for later use. The control panel itself can be created or altered in custom ways.

The parts of the instrument that appear in the instrument-structure window are "macros" and "modules." These are the building blocks at the lowest level of the hierarchy and can be grouped in infinite ways to produce the desired sound. The designer can "patch" together instruments made up of these building blocks. For example, synthesizers might be linked to sampler players that, in turn, are patched to effects units. Once built, the various parts can be saved as wholes and used in other projects, much like an object-oriented programming environment.

DVD-ROM
Project 14 Working with a
Virtual Studio

"All-in-One" Virtual Studios

We turn now to one of the latest categories of music software, the "all-in-one" virtual studio for music production. Software programs such as Home Studio, SONAR, Logic Pro, Cubase, and Digital Performer all began as MIDI sequencers. Digital audio was added in due course as computers became more capable. Effects and virtual instruments were added as both built-in and add-on resources with plug-in technology. Throughout this growth, the basic design of the software remained the same.

With "all-in-one" software, engineers have started from scratch to design these capabilities as inherent resources in one program. In software of this sort, sequencing, mixing, sampling, sound synthesis, and effects are built into one program. Table 17.1 lists the third task as working with these programs to create music; we will review two programs that fit this category.

Reason

Figures 17.29–31 display various views from Reason, a virtual-studio software program that uses a "rack" metaphor. The first three figures are software graphics representative of hardware modules. As you build a project in Reason, you create a rack of modules that function as if you were building a hardware studio. You begin with an interface module for your MIDI hardware and your digital audio interface. The top module in Figure 17.29 shows this; there are no controls for MIDI out, of course, since the program does not support MIDI equipment as sound-generation devices, only as input. Right below it is a 14x2 mixer board, complete with auxiliary ins and out for effects processing, EQ settings, pan, and level faders. If you need more mixing power for your project, just add another mixer and patch them together. All the modules in Reason can be duplicated as many times as your computer's CPU and RAM can handle.

FIGURE 17.29   Reason modules, front view

This figure also contains two effects processors, a delay, and a chorus/flanger unit. The Subtractor module at the bottom is a traditional synthesizer that supports both additive and substractive synthesis. The Subtractor is also continued in Figure 17.30. Note the settings for two oscillators (supports as many as 32 waveforms to choose from), LFOs, filters, and envelope control—all similar in design to other software synthesizers reviewed in this module. A set of presets that come with the program are loaded by the controls on the left. Notice the extraordinary attention to graphic detail, including the screens that hold the rack modules in place and the simulated tape placed on the channels for marking inputs and module names.

Continuing down the rack in Figure 17.30, we have a drum machine ("Re-Drum") and a loop player ("Dr. Rex"). The drum machine has 10 slots for drum-kit sounds and uses a 16–128th step resolution. There are special-effects settings

FIGURE 17.30 Reason modules, front view

for brightening the samples and the software gives you the ability to control the pitch of drum sounds and the onset of the envelope. The loop player allows you to introduce sliced loops in REX 2 format, similar to those discussed in Module 11 when we presented ACID and Live. Loops are transposable and can be treated with envelope controls. More than 300 loops come with the software and others can be imported from other programs.

Sampler-module options are also supported in Reason. The program comes with a complete set of orchestral instrument samples, as well as many other sampled sounds. SoundFont 2 format is also supported.

Figure 17.31 displays the back side of the modules in Figures 17.29 and 17.30. You get to this view by simply touching the tab key on the computer. Notice the cabling created by default to connect the various components. You can easily alter the cabling by using the mouse, if you so choose. Cables have different colors de-

FIGURE 17.31   Rear-panel displays in Reason

TIP
ReWire linkages are not supported by all DAW software, so check the documentation carefully if you want to use Reason as a partner with other software.

pending on what they connect and the ports are marked clearly for each module. The effects modules (Delay and Chorus/Flange) are routed as inserts, with the sends and returns routed into the auxiliary ports of the mixer.

Reason comes with a sequencer view similar to, but not as complete as, the sequencer windows in DAW software. The objects can be edited, however, and there are options for marking loops and doing quantization. There are no provisions for an event-list editor and you cannot program tempo or meter changes.

ReWire Connections

Reason does not natively support plug-ins, cannot burn CDs, and saves output only as either AIF or WAV files. However, many of these limitations can be overcome by linking Reason to other software using a technology called "ReWire."

ASIDE
Many other modules exist in Reason. Some of these include a granular synthesizer, a reverb unit, a compressor, and a matrix pattern sequencer that provides a step-time option for editing. The variety of modules helps the program support many styles of music.

ReWire is a system developed together by the Propellerhead and Steinberg companies to allow two programs to share software resources. It basically patches the outputs of one software program into the inputs of another. Rather than running inside a host program as with a VST-based virtual instrument, programs linked to each other with ReWire are separate programs that share the sound card, transport controls, and timing. It's like merging two separate programs together.

The Future of "All-in-One" Virtual Studios

Other programs using this approach include FL Studio (mentioned in Module 12, Viewport VI), Orion (Synapse Audio Software), Project5 (Steinberg/Yamaha), and Storm (Arturia). Each of these programs is designed primarily for the loop-based, pattern-generating market that supports more-popular music styles. We are guessing that more companies will produce such environments in the future and that there will be greater variety of audiences addressed. The integrated studio has great appeal for beginning and intermediate users who do not miss including MIDI tracks for hardware instruments.

LINK
The Pluggo software described earlier in this module was created with the aid of Max/MSP.

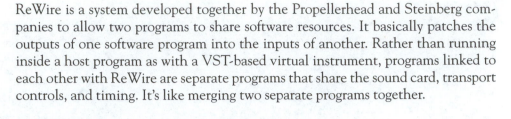

Programming Environments

We end this module with a brief section on the recent advances in programming environments for sound shaping and synthesis. This is the last task noted in Table 17.1 and is a category of software for those interested in building compositions, interactive controls, MIDI and audio utilities, and other creative projects in sound from either object-oriented languages or computing-language coding.

Max/MSP

Max/MSP is a real-time, object-oriented programming environment for MIDI and digital audio. Rather than presenting you with a track-based interface or a rack of soft synths or sample players, Max/MSP does not assume that the software will be used in any formal way and allows you to create environments for your own purpose. You can create systems that compose or improvise music, control external devices triggered by MIDI or audio, or accompany what you are playing on an acoustic or digital instrument. Electronic musicians have found Max/MSP a useful way to create interactive multimedia musical experiences. Because it is based on the C programming language, it also serves as a resource for creating programs such as plug-ins.

Max/MSP uses predefined "objects" that can be patched together. The Max portion of the program, which deals with MIDI data flow, has about 200 predefined objects. The MSP part deals with digital audio and includes its own set of 200 objects. Objects can be combined and saved as single objects on their own, sometimes called "abstractions." In some ways, Max/MSP is similar to the Reaktor program described earlier in this module. Reaktor's main thrust is the creation of sound-synthesis and sampler resources, whereas Max/MSP allows for many more uses. Max/MSP executes in real time, meaning that the object arrangements do not have to first be compiled by the environment in order to be tested; they work as soon as you create them. This also means that the programs created are interactive, which allows for applications in performance venues. A free runtime version of Max/MSP is available, so even if you don't own the programming environment, you can still use the programs created.

Figure 17.32 is an example of a simple set of programs ("patches") running in the Patch Window. Patch 1 responds to input by using the mouse on the keyboard object, returning information about pitch, velocity, and duration of the MIDI note. Patch 2 is designed to match each incoming MIDI note from a MIDI hardware device with a sounded pitch that is an inversion. If a scale is played, you hear sounds moving in the opposite direction to match each pitch of the scale.

In the first patch, notice the flow of the MIDI data controlled by the objects. The keyboard graphic sends MIDI data out of the bottom of the object and to the top of the next object. The pitch object box with the "E3" value has just responded to the user playing an E3 pitch on the keyboard. The patch chord sends the value out of the bottom of the pitch object box to the "makenote" object. That object gets velocity data from the keyboard, passes this on to the "noteout" object, and then passes the duration value on to the duration objects.

Figure 17.33 displays a simple audio construction using MSP objects. Here, a sample sound file is routed to objects that add reverberation. The window to the left is the patch window, where the action takes place. Sliders can be set using the mouse for reverb time, dry/wet balance, and other settings; buttons for presets are also provided. Windows to the right help manage both the sound and the audio interface drivers.

Much more complicated designs are possible. The documentation for Max/MSP is extensive and designed to be used by beginners, as well as seasoned programmers.

Other Programming Approaches

Csound and SuperCollider are two other programming environments to consider. Both use command-line programming with no graphic objects. Csound [Mac/Win] has been used by electronic-music composers since the late 1950s. Developed by

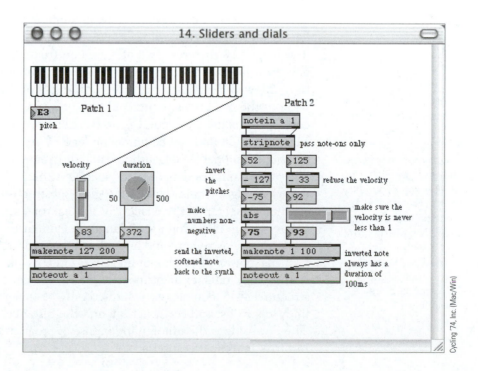

FIGURE 17.32 Simple MIDI flow patches in Max/MSP

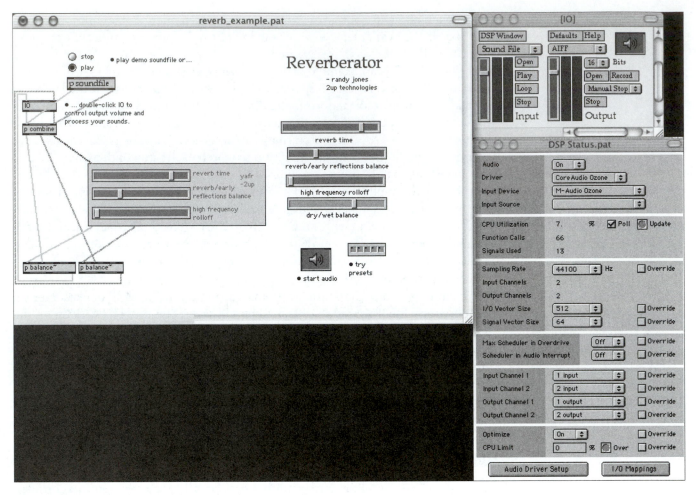

FIGURE 17.33 Simple audio-flow patches in Max/MSP

LINK

Csound, in its basic form, and many of its more-recent support programs are distributed on the Internet without cost. The most comprehensive site for Csound is run by Richard Boulanger at *www.csounds. com*. Csound is related in design to the initial work of Max Mathews and his Music I to V music coding system discussed in Module 19. Also related to this topic is the MPEG-4 SA standard presented in Module 11.

Berry Vercoe at MIT, Csound is a programming language optimized for sound rendering and signal processing. It uses building blocks called "opcodes" to help design sound structures. Two files are constructed, one that has the actual notes and the other that contains the instruments. A number of advances in recent years have allowed Csound to run more intuitively on Macintosh and PC computers, without the need to use command-line-programming code written in a word processor. For example, Csound is now available as an object running under Max/MSP. Also, Csound can be routed under ReWire to be used as a VST instrument.

SuperCollider [Mac], authored and distributed for free by James McCartney, is also a programming language for sound synthesis. It differs from Csound in that it is more algorithmic (based on logical substructures) and more object oriented (without the graphics of Mac/MSP or Reaktor), and renders in real time. It also behaves more like a high-level language (similar to SmallTalk and C++). It does not separate instrument and note files. The program integrates well with MIDI.

The power of programming environments like Csound and SuperCollider is that they offer extraordinary flexibility in constructing sophisticated sound structures. The complexity is limited only by imagination, skillful programming, knowledge of sound construction, and the resources of the computer being used. The downside is the unforgiving nature of programming code and the lack of an intuitive graphic user interface.

Module 18

Extending MIDI:
Controllers, SoundFonts, and Timing

LINK
"How MIDI Works" provides the basics of MIDI in Module 14 and MIDI sequencing software is reviewed in Module 15.

In Viewport V, we introduced the Music Instrument Digital Interface (MIDI) for coding music-performance data on computer and electronic music devices. In this module, we will extend these MIDI concepts through a variety of topics that enhance the MIDI experience. Those topics include:

- MIDI controllers: guitar, wind, voice, percussion, and experimental MIDI controllers
- Merging MIDI with digital audio (EMT-6 Digital Audio Workstation with MIDI)
- Subjective issues with MIDI controllers
- Enhancing the MIDI sound palette: GS, XS, SoundFonts, and DLS
- MIDI and Audio Timing: SMPTE, Word Clock, and others, including the mLAN music network specification.

Controller Cornucopia: Drums, Guitars, Winds, and More

The IPOS model in Figure 18.1 is an expansion of that presented in Figure 16.1. Beyond the basic MIDI keyboard and sound-module devices, a wide range of MIDI controllers is shown as alternatives to *input*. We will explore controllers that truly provide a "cornucopia" of performance instruments or "horns of plenty" for the musician: drums, guitar, strings, voice, winds, pitch-to-MIDI, custom controllers, and MIDI control surfaces. Some of these MIDI controllers have also been added to expand the EMT music workstation, as we will see in Figure 18.2.

A MIDI controller is any device that translates music-performance actions into MIDI data. As discussed in Module 16, there are two classes of MIDI controller design: acoustic and synthetic. Standard traditional music instruments can be turned into *acoustic* MIDI controllers by equipping them with sensors that translate analog actions or vibrations into digital MIDI data. *Synthetic* MIDI controllers are designed from scratch as electronic-performance instruments.

The quality of a controller's performance is affected by two functions: *tracking error* and *tracking delay*. *Tracking error* measures the accuracy with which a controller translates the performed pitch or action. *Tracking delay* measures the time it takes the controller to determine what note is being played. When you strum a guitar controller, generating sympathetic vibrations from other strings and incidental noises, tracking error is going to increase. When a controller is trying to

ASIDE
Synthetic MIDI instruments are not designed to be a substitute for their acoustic siblings. They are intended to be "new" instruments and "new" tools for creative expression in ways that their acoustic parallels could never accomplish.

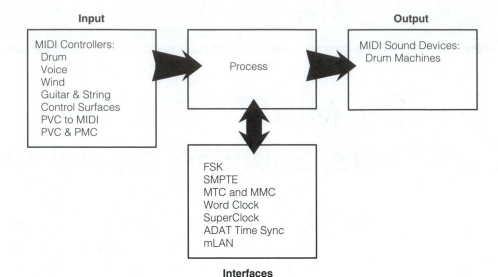

Input

MIDI Controllers:
  Drum
  Voice
  Wind
  Guitar & String
  Control Surfaces
  PVC to MIDI
  PVC & PMC

Process

Output

MIDI Sound Devices:
  Drum Machines

FSK
SMPTE
MTC and MMC
Word Clock
SuperClock
ADAT Time Sync
mLAN

Interfaces

FIGURE 18.1 IPOS model showing MIDI controllers beyond keyboards and sound modules

ASIDE
You might say that tracking delay is analogous to the latency issues with digital audio and software.

ASIDE
Drum machines (see Output in the IPOS Figure 18.1) are rhythm sequencers and synthesizers rolled into one stand-alone package and may or may not have controller options.

translate a flute sound or a human voice into MIDI data, tracking delay is going to occur. This means that the MIDI-note data will occur later than the human performance. The more complex the acoustic vibration that needs to be translated into MIDI data, the greater the likelihood of translation errors.

The enhanced MIDI with Digital Audio System (EMT-6) shown in Figure 18.2 has a keyboard workstation (20), a drum controller (23), a guitar controller (24), and a wind controller (25). The three controllers are routed to a 4x4 MIDI patchbay that is, in turn, routed to a MIDI control surface (17). Keyboard controllers and patchbays are discussed in Module 16, so we will pass over those and move on to the others, starting with drum controllers.

Drum Controllers

As with keyboards, there is a wide variety of MIDI drum controllers. The translation mechanism used in a drum controller is a *trigger-to-MIDI* converter. An electronic-trigger device picks up a vibration from the drum and creates a voltage that is converted into MIDI Note On/Off data. Usually, the drum controller detects only the Note On and sends an immediate Note Off to simulate the tap of a drumstick. Some drum controllers provide a control that will vary the time between the Note On and Off data. Velocity and after-touch data can be provided from the intensity or amplitude of the voltage created by the drumstick's impact.

Some acoustic drum controllers attach to the drum's head or shell, or are integrated into specially designed drum sets made for MIDI performance. Synthetic drum controllers may be called MIDI *drum pads*. They use a rubber pad much like any drum-practice pad; the trigger mechanism is placed under the rubber pad. More sophisticated pads have separate sensors for distinctive areas like the center, edge, and rim, each generating MIDI data.

Drum pads come in different shapes, with a varying number of pads in a set. The classic drumKAT, for example, shown in Figure 18.3, has 10 pads arranged to look like mouse ears. The KAT drums use force-sensing resistors (FSRs) covered by gum rubber instead of a trigger-to-MIDI solution. This technology provides a more comfortable and realistic drum-playing experience.

The Roland SPD-6 and SPD-20 drum controllers provide an arrangement of six or 10 velocity-sensing square pads. The SPD series integrates 113 or 700 on-

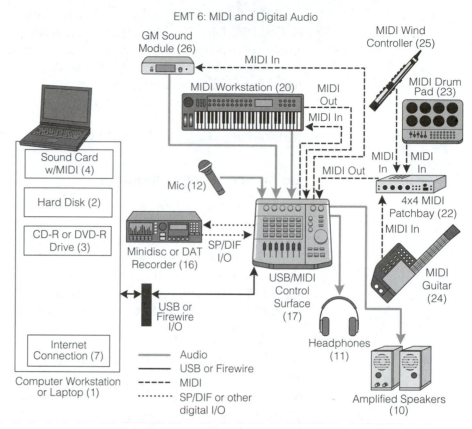

FIGURE 18.2 The EMT-6 workstation integrating MIDI and digital audio and adding a variety of MIDI controllers

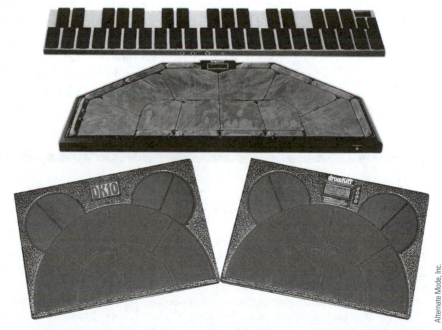

FIGURE 18.3 Alternate Mode's KAT line of MIDI percussion controllers: from the top down, the malletKAT, trapKAT, classic drum KAT (right), and DK10 (left)

Alternate Mode, Inc.

board sound samples and effects processing so that the device can be played with or without a connection to a MIDI sound module. Hands or a soft mallet can be used to perform on the SPD controller pads. Mallet drum controllers like the malletKAT (Figure 18.3) provide a keyboard-like arrangement of pads. Each pad, and locations within a pad, can be assigned to different notes or MIDI channels.

Roland's pro-level drum offering is the V-Drum series (V-Snare, V-Kicks, V-Cymbals, etc.). This series typifies the melding of traditional acoustic drums with MIDI trigger technology and high-end music synthesis. Physical modeling (COSM Variable Drum Modeling) is used to simulate drum instrument sounds, studio room sounds, and control-room mixing and effects. Yamaha's DTXtreme series is similar in design to the V-Drum series. The V-Drum and DTXtreme drums look like a traditional trap drum setup.

A 4x4 matrix of square MIDI drum pads (23) is installed as part of the EMT-6 computer music workstation in Figure 18.2. The unit is similar to the AKAI PD16 MIDI drum pad and the Roland SPD-6 and SPD–20 pads.

Guitar and String Controllers

Electric versions of most string instruments have been around since the 1930s: violins, basses, cellos, and, most notably, guitars. While there have been MIDI conversions of most electric and some acoustic string instruments, guitar conversion for MIDI is the most widely used. MIDI conversion from guitar performance is not a trivial engineering problem, and tracking error and delay, especially for fast playing, strumming, and articulation, can be problematic. The mechanisms for translating guitar performance into MIDI data apply to any of the other string instruments.

Synthetic or True MIDI Guitar Controllers

For a synthetic solution, finger movements need to be directly translated into MIDI codes, avoiding pitch-to-voltage conversion entirely. To do this, the guitar instrument needs to be built from scratch as a MIDI guitar. Switches or sensors are wired in some fashion into the fretboard and finger placement is electrically translated into MIDI note and controller codes. Synthetic guitar controllers, many of them no longer available commercially, include the SynthAxe, Casio MG-500, StarrLabs Ztar (still produced), Peavey Cyberbass, and, most recently, the Brian Moore MidiAxe guitars and Parker MIDIFly. The synthetic guitars have had difficulty being accepted professionally because of their nontraditional feel and lack of responsiveness—to many they are not a "real" guitar!

SIDE BAR

Pitch-to-MIDI and Pitch-to-Voltage Conversion

Pitch-to-voltage converters (PVCs), pitch trackers, pitch extractors, or, when applied to MIDI, pitch-to-MIDI converters (PMCs) are critical to acoustic wind, voice, guitar, and string controllers. If you want to sing into a computer and have it respond to the notes of your voice, you will need a PVC device. PVC devices are difficult to build and often suffer from tracking error and delay. Translating complex analog sounds from human voice, string, and wind instruments into a MIDI pitch value is not a trivial engineering task. The name PVC implies that it translates a pitch into a voltage; however, this is somewhat of a misnomer. What it really does is translate a complex acoustic sound vibration—like a tone from a singing voice or a vibrating string—into a voltage that represents its best guess as to pitch. The device mechanically attempts to make a human decision in a nonhuman way. How does a PVC make its best guess as to pitch? One technique is to electronically strip off or filter out all of the harmonics from the complex sound—typically from monophonic sound patterns—and find the fundamental frequency or a tone with as few harmonics as possible. The device can then decide what voltage to assign the frequency or, in the case of PMCs, which MIDI note to assign. Physical-modeling synthesis is then often used to virtually reconstruct the sonic nuances and articulation in digital form.

Acoustic MIDI Guitar Controllers

To continue to use a "real" acoustic or electric guitar for MIDI performance, a PVC or PMC interface is needed to take the complex vibrations of the many strings on an instrument and sort out the pitches being played. The technology for doing this continues to improve significantly.

There are two common solutions. For the first, much of the PVC conversion is built into the guitar itself (the Brian Moore iGuitar is an example) and a standard 13-pin RMC (Roland MIDI Control) jack is on the side of the guitar (see the illustration in the left-hand box of Figure 18.4). Piezoelectric sensors are built into the bridge of the guitar for each string; these translate the sonic patterns from string vibrations into voltage controls sent to a guitar synthesizer like the Roland GR-33 shown in Figure 18.4 (center) for the final MIDI-code assignments. Axon, Brian Moore Guitars, Yamaha, and Roland are examples of companies that make guitar synthesizers that accept the 13-pin RMC cables.

The second solution is to use a special hexaphonic divided pickup that can be mounted under the strings near the bridge to pick up the string vibrations. The Roland GK-2A shown in Figure 18.4 is such a device; the Yamaha G1D works comparably. This divided-pickup device has a 13-pin RMC jack that can be routed to a guitar synthesizer. This solution can be used on an acoustic, as well as an electric guitar, but some permanent modifications of the guitar are required.

For other string instruments the solutions are quite similar. The Zeta MIDI controller uses pitch-to-MIDI conversion from the Zeta electric violin, viola, or cello instrument or, with the Zeta RetroPak, from any acoustic violin, viola, or cello. The MIDI controller can then be connected to Zeta's Synthony synthesizer.

The EMT-6 computer music system (Figure 18.2) is configured for an acoustic guitar with a hexaphonic pickup installed, and interfaced with an RMC 13-pin connection to a guitar synthesizer. From the guitar synth, there is MIDI Out to the 4x4 MIDI patchbay.

ASIDE

Gibson Guitar has designed a new "digital guitar" that uses Ethernet networking to connect the specially designed guitar and a digital amplifier or laptop and a protocol called MaGIC for transmitting performance data.

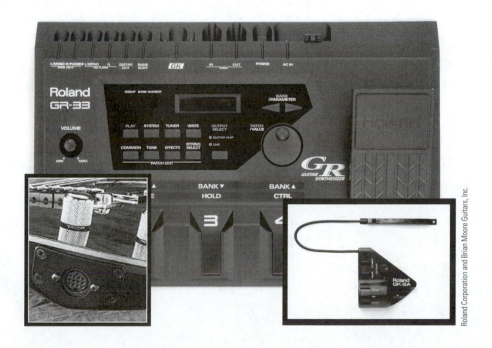

FIGURE 18.4 Components used for acoustic MIDI guitar control. In the center, a Roland GR-33 guitar synthesizer; to the right, a Roland GK-2A hexaphonic divided pickup; and, to the left, the characteristic RMC 13-pin connector (from a Brian Moore iGuitar) that routes PVC codes from the guitar to the guitar synthesizer for the final MIDI conversion

Roland Corporation and Brian Moore Guitars, Inc.

LINK
Finale 2005 uses pitch-to-MIDI conversion as an entry system for notation. More on this in Module 20.

LINK
Use of the SmartMusic application is covered in Module 22.

Voice Controllers

Using PVC devices to convert voice to MIDI has been a long-standing need in music technology. Setting aside the performance possibilities (perhaps you are thinking of karaoke?), just think of the music-instruction possibilities for computer-aided sight-singing and intonation training.

Developed in 1985, the IVL Pitchrider was one of the first commercial pitch-to-MIDI controllers. Originally designed as a training device for teaching sight-singing and intonation, the Pitchrider is no longer produced. The PMC technology developed by IVL Technologies, however, is still used in consumer karaoke machines, digital harmonizers, music-instruction devices, and a variety of MIDI devices.

Several PMC devices are being incorporated into music-education and music-performance systems. One of most exciting is the MakeMusic! SmartMusic system that uses PMC technology to track solo performance and synchronize prerecorded accompaniments to the soloist—what is called "intelligent accompaniment." "Amadeus al fine" is a hardware pitch-to-MIDI device being packaged by Pyware with its software for basic music skills, but it can be used with any software that accepts MIDI input.

These days, computers are fast enough that pitch-to-MIDI conversion can be done in software with just a microphone input to the computer. Digital Ear (Epinosis Software [Win]) is an example of software that converts real-time audio into MIDI codes. Sing or play your favorite instrument to input your music notation or sequence. Much of the PMC operation with MakeMusic!'s SmartMusic system is now done in software rather than the original hardware PMC device.

Wind Controllers

A MIDI wind controller, the Yamaha WX-5 (25), shown in the setup for the EMT-6 music workstation (Figure 18.2), is routed through the 4x4 MIDI patchbay to the MIDI-control surface.

Designers of wind controllers face the challenge of varying key and fingering layouts for acoustic wind instruments, both brass and woodwind. Acoustic wind controllers simply use PVC or PMC devices to convert these instruments into MIDI controllers. A PMC/PVC device is attached to the wind instrument so that it picks up its vibrations and then translates the acoustic sounds into MIDI data. The success of the PMC translation depends on the instrument; this approach inherits all of the tracking error and delay problems associated with pitch-to-voltage conversion.

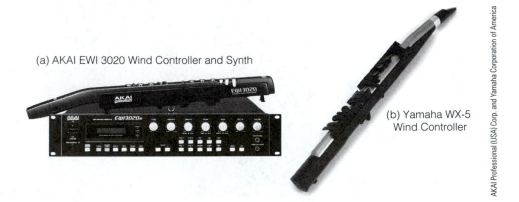

(a) AKAI EWI 3020 Wind Controller and Synth

(b) Yamaha WX-5 Wind Controller

AKAI Professional (USA) Corp. and Yamaha Corporation of America

FIGURE 18.5 Two MIDI wind controllers from AKAI and Yamaha

Synthetic wind controllers come in woodwind and brass varieties. Few of them have the feel of their acoustic counterparts. The pre-MIDI Lyricon (1972) was one of the first wind controllers for a synthesizer. It was based on a clarinet-key layout, and its signals came from a combination of electronic switches for the keys and transducers to pick up breath and lip-pressure changes.

The Yamaha WX-7 wind controller introduced in 1987 provided a MIDI Lyricon-like controller with lip- and breath-sensing control. The key layout, however, was modeled on the saxophone or, optionally, the recorder. It was replaced by the WX-11 and then the more-current WX-5 wind controller (Figure 18.5b). The WX-5 has a 16-key layout in a saxophone fashion with various switches for octave control and effects and a pitchbend wheel. The mouthpiece provides both wind and lip control through the MIDI breath and expression controllers. The fingering can be configured for three saxophone settings or flute fingering; and it can be pitched at C, B♭, or E♭. A recorder and a reed-based mouthpiece is included. The Yamaha physical-modeling sound module, VL70-m, is custom designed for the WX-5.

The EWI (Electronic Wind Instrument) and the EVI (Electronic Value Instrument) were developed from the Steiner Phone, a device created by Nyle Steiner in the late 1970s. AKAI markets MIDI versions of the instruments. Touch-sensitive plates or pads, rather than moving key switches, are used to simulate the fingering of a trumpet (EVI) and a clarinet or saxophone (EWI). The EWI 3020 controller, with its custom sound module, is shown in Figure 18.5a. It also uses a saxophone fingering system and provides wind and lip-pressure controls.

Mind-Expanding MIDI Controllers

All the controllers covered so far have conformed to traditional musical instruments, and, as you have seen, there is no limit to modifying these instruments for use as MIDI controllers. There are even MIDI accordions! However, don't let convention stand in your way. Almost anything that moves, including your body, can be converted through a MIDI controller to MIDI data for your computer to manipulate and transform with software.

The Pioneers Experimenting

The Theremin was invented by the Russian inventor Leon Theremin in the 1920s (see Figure 1.7 in Module 1). The Theremin uses the interaction of the performer's hands with two radio antennas to change frequency and amplitude. Its glissandi sounds became familiar as sound effects that accented many sci-fi movies: *The Day the Earth Stood Still* (1951) used a bass-and-violin Theremin. Robert Moog, who built Theremins to pay his way through school, produces a MIDI version called the "Ethervox MIDI Theremin" (Big Briar). Moog, of course, is one of the pioneers of the voltage-controlled synthesizers of the 1960s, along with Donald Buchla. Buchla's more recent experimentation has created the "Lightning II" MIDI controller. The Lightning uses two handheld wands with built-in infrared transmitters and an infrared monitoring device mounted on a stand in front of the performer. This device senses the movement of the wands in three-dimensional space and sends corresponding MIDI-controller data to a custom MIDI module. Max Mathews, the "father of digital music," designed a Radio Baton where the computer plays the notes and the performer (or conductor) uses the Radio Baton to control tempo, volume, articulation, and timbre.

LINK

Max/MSP (Cycling '74 [Win/Mac]) is a software tool of choice for musicians developing experimental MIDI controllers. Check it out in Module 17.

New Modes of Instrument Expression

Roy "Future Man" Wooten plays with Bela Fleck and the Flecktones using a custom-built MIDI controller, the "SynthAxe-Drumitar." The original casing for the instrument was the British MIDI SynthAxe, but the internal circuitry was completely redesigned by the engineer Chris deHaas. Richard Battaglia, the sound engineer for the Flecktones, added special sensors to the exterior. Battaglia mounted clusters of small discs with drum triggers and mounted additional clusters of small plastic discs with force-sensing resistors (FSRs) that look like bubbles on the body of the SynthAxe. The drum triggers can be tapped with the fingers like small drum pads. The FSRs replace the conventional wheel-type controllers on MIDI devices by creating voltages that match the pressure Future Man applies to the plastic bubbles with his finger. Chris deHaas's internal circuitry then converts the voltage into MIDI data. The instrument is designed to handle up to 127 pads, with each pad assigned to its own MIDI Note and MIDI Channel.

The result is a keyboard of miniature drum pads and FSR pads, all sending MIDI data to the samplers and synthesizers that Roy Wooten uses in performance. He sees his unique MIDI controller as using technology to create "sound clusters" that can be performed with the range and virtuosity possible on a piano keyboard. The commercial version of Future Man's SynthAxe Drumitar is the Zendrum.

Sweat, Body Movement, and Biofeedback Controllers   If the MIDI controllers so far sound a bit tame, then consider some more bizarre applications. The Amsterdam STEIM (Studio for Electro Instrumental Music) research center encourages performers and composers to create new MIDI instruments. Ray Edgar's Sweatstick is one such instrument developed from the STEIM SensorLab hardware and software toolkit. The stick bends in the middle, sending MIDI-controller data from the physical bending, as well as from sliding and twisting the two handgrips. The "sweat" term comes from the exercise necessary to physically play this MIDI controller. Another STEIM project is Michel Waisvisz's The Hand. These are MIDI gloves that translate finger patterns and hand gestures into sonic or light events.

Tod Machover (MIT) designed The Sensor Chair in the fall of 1994 for a new mini-opera entitled *Media/Medium,* and the device was later used in his *Brain Opera* performances at Lincoln Center. The Sensor Chair is an example of what Machover calls a "hyperinstrument." The person seated in the chair becomes an extension of numerous antennae placed in and around the chair. The strength of the signals picked up by the antennae is determined by the capacitance between the performer's body and any one of the antennae.

Figure 18.6 shows a custom MIDI instrument, the Beatbug, developed by Gil Weinberg (Georgia Institute of Technology) and Roberto Aimi (MIT) for performance with children and music novices. As the diagram indicates, the instrument processes audio as well as MIDI data. The player (see the hand position in the figure) can tap out rhythms on the back of the Beatbug, and then shape and transform sound patterns with pressure on the two antennae. Piezo sensors pick up the rhythmic tapping—more on piezo sensors in the next section.

There are many MIDI devices that provide MIDI sensing of body movement to choose from, all electronically working in different ways. The Yamaha "Miburi" MIDI suit provides sensors for shoulder and elbow movement, wrist movement, toe and heel impact, and grip units with various keys and controllers. The belt unit controls programming of the various sensors and the MIDI signals can either

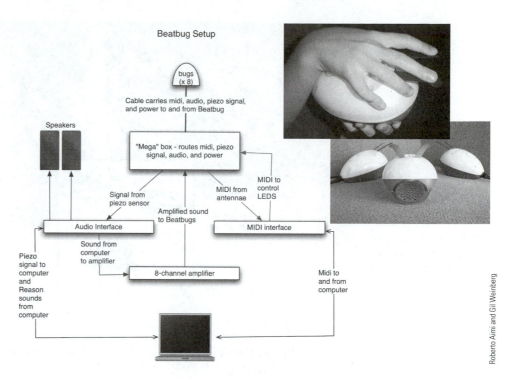

FIGURE 18.6 Gil Weinberg's Beatbugs, with a diagram illustrating the communication channels between the device and a computer and two views of the Beatbugs

be sent wireless or with a cable to the independent sound unit. The Danish Institute of Electroacoustic Music (DIEM) "Digital Dance System," as another example, uses a web of "bending sensors" that the dancer wears to measure the angle of his or her limbs. There's more:

- Mark Coniglio's "MidiDancer" translates body movements into MIDI data that control expressive music properties, stage lighting, and videodisc.
- Benjamin Knapp and Hugh Lusted's "Biomuse" is a "neural interface" that translates biofeedback data (galvanic skin response, muscle and eye movements, and brain waves) into MIDI data as a creative tool.
- The "Synth-A-Beam" or "OptiMusic" system converts physical body movements into MIDI data from interruptions to light beams projected across the movement field.
- The "SoundBeam," a British project, uses ultrasonic sensors to convert body movement into MIDI codes. Music educators like Kim McCord (Illinois State University) are successfully using the SoundBeam for music making with children and adults with severely impaired motor skills.

How to Build Your Own Controller So you want to build your own MIDI controller? Frank Clark (Georgia Institute of Technology) creates MIDI finger controllers with 75¢ piezo discs that can be wired to any trigger-to-MIDI converter (Figure 18.7a). Each button when pressed or struck provides a voltage that can be translated into MIDI-controller data. If just one of these isn't enough for your performing needs, you can do what James Bohn does and use hot glue and Velcro to attach a web of piezo discs to your clothing. His "Plaid Jacket Based MIDI Controller" (Figures 18.7b and c) provides the performer with a jacket that can be tapped, pressed, stroked, and massaged to trigger a phantasmagoria of sonic color for music performance.

To move a step up from piezo discs for the do-it-yourselfer, Infusion Systems' I-Cubex system offers a smorgasbord of possibilities programmable from Windows,

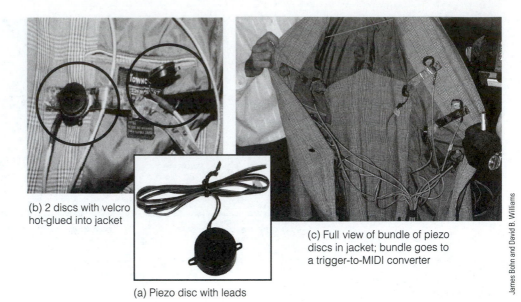

FIGURE 18.7 On the left (b), piezo discs; in the center (a), piezo disc with case removed and hot-glued into the "Plaid MIDI Jacket"; and, on the right (c), the inside web of piezo discs for the jacket

(b) 2 discs with velcro hot-glued into jacket

(a) Piezo disc with leads

(c) Full view of bundle of piezo discs in jacket; bundle goes to a trigger-to-MIDI converter

James Bohn and David B. Williams

Mac, or Linux OS. Some of the two dozen sensing modules that can be translated into MIDI signals by the I-Cubex digital-to-MIDI interface include light, temperature, humidity, touch, force and pressure, various sliding movements, and magnetic fields—and the list goes on.

With all these innovative ways to produce MIDI music, can't you see yourself putting on your Plaid MIDI Jacket, grabbing your Sweatstick, generating some sweat and tears, running a sequencing program like Cycling 74's Max, and putting your computer through a serious MIDI workout? MIDI exercise to the MAX!

Integrating MIDI and Digital Audio

Return to the EMT-6 workstation configuration shown in Figure 18.2. The digital audio components from previous EMT designs have been merged with the MIDI concepts and hardware presented in Module 16 and this Viewport. The 4x4 patchbay (22) has been added to accommodate the three additional MIDI controllers: wind (25), guitar (24), and drum (23). A GM2 sound module has been added to enrich the instrument-sound options (26).

A key new hardware component is the MIDI-control surface (17). Shown in the illustration is a Tascam US-428 (Figure 18.8 shows the top and back of the device), one of many options for MIDI-control surfaces. This hardware incorporates a MIDI interface (two IN/OUTs with 32 channels of MIDI); a digital audio interface (four-channel 24-bit ADCs, and two-channel 24-bit DACs); a mixer (four analog INs, two mic/guitar INs, stereo OUT); S/PDIF digital I/O; and a MIDI-control surface that can be synchronized with the software control panels in sequencing and digital audio software. The mixing features can be seen in the top view of the unit (Figure 18.8); the cabling options, on the back view of the 428.

Note in the EMT-6 diagram that audio from the MIDI workstation (20), the sound module (26), and the microphone (12) is routed to the audio inputs of the

FIGURE 18.8   The top and back of a Tascam US-428 Universal Serial Bus Digital Audio Workstation Controller with MIDI

Tascam/TEAC America, Inc.

TIP
Be sure to match the MIDI-control surface to the sequencing software! The Steinberg VST controller is specifically designed for their software, Cubase and Nuendo. For others, check the manual or the hardware specifications to see what driver support the manufacturer provides for various software sequencers.

Tascam. The Tascam's S/PDIF I/O is routed to a DAT recorder (16), and the analog out from the unit is routed to a pair of amplified speakers (10) and headphones (11). The entire unit is interfaced to the computer through the USB interface.

The Tascam MIDI-control surface has a 2x2 MIDI interface. For MIDI, the MIDI workstation's (20) MIDI IN and OUT are routed through the Tascam, as well as the MIDI OUT to the MIDI IN of the sound module (26). The MIDI OUT of the patchbay (22) is routed to the MIDI IN of the Tascam (17). The wind, guitar, and drum controllers MIDI OUTs all go to the MIDI INs of the patchbay (22).

As this MIDI setup demonstrates, the options in a device like the Tascam make it easy to integrate digital audio workstation and MIDI needs into an all-encompassing computer music setup. We will now examine other options beyond the Tascam 428 for MIDI-control surfaces.

MIDI Control Surfaces

After working with the sequencing software for an extended period of time, people discover that using a mouse to manipulate faders, buttons, jog wheels, and knobs while recording and editing can be tedious—especially the knobs. MIDI-control surfaces are designed to provide a hardware extension to the software controls by providing the tactile feel that a musician appreciates from conventional hardware mixers.

The Tascam was one of the first MIDI-control-surface devices that incorporated analog and digital audio into one unit. There are now a preponderance of these devices for a musician to choose from. The basic characteristics and optional features of the less-expensive units include the following:

- *Mixer controls.* An essential feature that makes the device a MIDI-control surface is traditional mixer controls. These include a bank of control faders (typically eight or more) and master faders; various knobs and buttons for pan, solo, mute, select, effects, and the like; data jog wheel for fast access to anyplace within the music sequence; and transport control for play, pause, record, rewind, and fast-forward. The JL Cooper FadeMaster, Mackie Baby HUI, and Steinberg Huston surface controllers are examples of units providing some combination of mixer controls that are designed to be a MIDI-control surface and nothing more. Foot-switch and pedal control is available on the FadeMaster unit. The Tascam 224 and 428 and the Event EZbus are examples of units that have the traditional array of mixer controls, but many additional audio I/O features as well. These are noted below.

- *Automated mixing.* With motorized faders and other controls, MIDI signals can be sent back from the computer software to automate mixing sessions. This feature adds to the complexity and expense of the hardware. Steinberg surface controllers, as well as the JL Cooper FadeMaster and Mackie Baby HUI units, are examples of units that provide automated mixing control from software. The Tascam 224 and 428 and the EZbus control surface do not offer this automated feature.

- *MIDI interface.* For the hardware controls of the mixer surface to communicate with the software sequencer, various MIDI-controller and system messages must pass between the device and the computer. At a minimum, MIDI OUT control is required. If the mixer hardware has motorized controllers, then MIDI IN would be needed for the software to automate the hardware mixing surface. Some devices go beyond this to offer a multichannel MIDI IN/OUT/THRU interface for other MIDI equipment. The Tascam 224 and 428 and EZbus provide 2x2 MIDI with 32 channels IN and OUT.

- *Digital ADCs and DACs (optional).* To go beyond simulating mixing controls in software with hardware, some units also function as real mixers and provide audio handling. The Tascam and EZbus MIDI controllers provide analog-to-digital and digital-to-analog conversion, typically with sampling resolutions of 24-bit/96-kHz. The Tascam 428 provides four ADCs IN and two DACs out. The EZbus handles AD/DC through the USB bus.

- *Digital I/O (optional).* For communication with other digital audio devices, S/PDIF and ADAT may be provided. The Tascam and EZbus models have S/PDIF; the EZbus also provides ADAT.

- *Analog audio (optional).* Again, to serve the same functionality as a mixer (not just the surface controls of a mixer), analog-audio capability is important. The Tascam 428 provides four IN and two OUT analog-audio lines (with two mic/guitar-line inputs) and the EZbus provides 18 IN and 8 OUT analog-audio lines with some balanced mic inputs.

- *USB interface (optional).* The Steinberg, Tascams, and EZbus are USB bus compatible for computer connectivity. The other units noted depend on MIDI for communication between the MIDI-surface controller and the computer. If available, USB 2.0 and Firewire 400 and 800 (refer to Module 7) are desirable alternatives when network speed is critical for more-intensive digital audio activities.

ASIDE
A keyboard can be added to a mixer controller+MIDI interface+digital audio+USB package to create units like the M-Audio Ozone or the Edirol PCR-A30.

Subjective Factors for MIDI Controllers

We have considered the important hardware features of MIDI-surface controllers, MIDI keyboards and workstations, and a wide variety of MIDI controllers for performance. You can read, measure, and count the details on specification sheets but, as every musician knows, ultimately the decision depends on the subjective factors of how it feels and sounds. Briefly, let's touch on a few of these:

- Instrument feel
- Controller feel (wheels, sliders, and pedals)
- Sound quality
- Layout and user interface for the workstation and mixing controls
- Aesthetic visual appeal of the device

To check out these factors, you need to play the instrument, working the keys, strings, sliders, or whatever hardware control techniques are provided on the instrument. Listen carefully to the sounds; flip through the instrument's presets and listen to the quality of the winds, strings, percussion, and so on. Your ear is the best test.

Are basic operations simple and intuitive? Ask to see a manual and the MIDI implementation chart. Try programming the workstation directly from its own panels and control buttons and sliders. Is it confusing or easy to program?

If students are going to be using this MIDI device in a music lab or MIDI ensemble, the user interface is a crucial feature. The easier it is to program, the less time an instructor will spend answering questions.

Finally, does it look "cool"? Is this a device that makes you want to experiment and perform with it? Do you want to show it off because it is aesthetically pleasing to you? Even this issue is important and may ultimately determine how much use you make of the device.

Should all these tests leave you feeling less than satisfied with a particular brand of workstation, keep looking. As you have seen in Module 16 and here, there are many options from which to choose.

LINK
Several concepts that come together under the topic of SoundFonts and DLS have been discussed earlier in the text. Wavetable synthesis is discussed in Module 8, MPEG-4 Audio SA in Module 11, General MIDI and Standard MIDI files in Module 14, and MIDI sequencers in Module 15.

Enhancing the MIDI Sound Palette: GS, XG, SoundFonts, and DLS

We've reviewed a wide array of MIDI instruments for your creative music activities. What tools help extend an instrument's repertoire of sounds beyond General MIDI? We look to GS, XS, SoundFonts, and DLS for possibilities. MIDI is the format of choice when it comes to file size, but the quality and diversity of the original General MIDI palette of timbres is limited, restricted to a basic bank of 128 instrument sounds. This is especially true when you wish to exchange MIDI files with other musicians across platforms and music applications.

The first extension to the GM standard was the GS format developed by Roland for its Sound Canvas MIDI technology. Following the same strategy as

TIP

Look at your MIDI equipment. See if logos are displayed for General MIDI, General MIDI 2, GS, or XG. These indicate the presence of additional capabilities provided by these extensions.

TIP

Some compatibility problems may exist between Sound-Font files for Mac and Windows. Not all SoundFonts work in the Mac OS without some conversion; uncompressed SoundFonts work best.

LINK

To review the various music-file extensions, revisit Table 8.2 in Module 8.

Roland, Yamaha developed its own proprietary XG extension to the GM format. Both GS and XG sound devices have a greatly extended range of instrument banks; the ability to alter instrument sounds for brightness, harmonic content, and attack-release times; and the ability to produce a wide range of sonic effects, from chorus and reverb to many others. The early efforts of Roland and Yamaha led the way to development of the MIDI Manufacturers Association (MMA) GM Level 2 specifications. Roland and Yamaha now provide GM2 compatibility while still expanding their GS and XG features as a superset of GM2.

MIDI SoundFonts

The MOD music-file format has been popular on electronic bulletin boards and the Internet since the first Amiga "tracker" software in 1986. MOD files are a combination of four tracks of non-MIDI codes for pitch and duration packaged with waveform samples for instrument tones to be used in playing back MOD music. All you need is a MOD music player to listen to the music.

SoundFonts, when packaged with a MIDI music file, offer the same concept, but for any GM MIDI music environment. The standard MIDI file provides the music codes (notes, rests, dynamic changes, etc.) and the SoundFonts provide custom musical-instrument patches for the music performance (the MIDI file can intermix SoundFonts and standard GM instrument patches).

The *SoundFont* format was developed by E-MU/Ensoniq for the Creative Labs Sound-Blaster sound-card series. SoundFonts use wavetable synthesis to create instrument sounds: Digital samples of various portions of a single instrument tone are combined with articulation parameters or instructions to shape the sound's envelope and apply effects processing.

SoundFonts are supported under both Mac (QuickTime) and Windows OS (QuickTime and DirectMusic) and across major music-software applications such as SONAR, ACID, Cubase, Reason, Live, and Finale. There are various freeware and shareware utilities for creating and editing SoundFonts and there are software-based music players for using SoundFonts that don't require Sound-Blaster-compatible hardware. The file extension for the original SoundFont 1.0 files was .sbk; the extension for the newer SoundFont 2.0 format is .sf2.

MIDI Down-Loadable Sounds (DLS)

The XG and GS extensions to MIDI were hardware-based solutions to enhancing the sound samples and their articulation within a General MIDI environment. In 1997, MMA endorsed a standard similar to SoundFonts in response to an industrywide need for such a software solution. The Down-Loadable Sounds, or DLS, standard provides the specifications for a package of digital sound samples and articulation parameters. The articulation parameters include features such as envelope and looping data that can be used by a digital oscillator and a digitally controlled amplifier in constructing a digital-instrument sound. In fact, one file of digital-sound data can be used with several sets of articulation parameters to generate several melodic instruments or drum kits. Using a unique set of coding through bank select, program changes, and SysEx MIDI codes, any DLS-compatible sound device, realized through either hardware or software, will be able to play GM music or sound sequences with DLS extensions, sound data, and effects attributes.

In a subsequent revision, DLS-2 standards encompassed greater compatibility with the Creative Lab SoundFonts, expanded the range of controls and options for waveform synthesis, and embraced both MPEG-4 Audio SA standards and Microsoft DirectX applications. Performance of DLS files (.dls) is integrated into Mac and Windows OS. QuickTime, for example, can load DLS files to provide different audio samples for use with its MIDI playback. Utilities are available to help with translation between SoundFont and DLS formats.

MIDI and Audio Timing: SMPTE, Word Clock, mLAN, and More

We have touched on many topics in expanding your understanding of MIDI and its applications. One more concept merits study before we end this module: timing as it applies not only to MIDI but also to audio. The IPOS model in Figure 18.1 shows the variety of timing standards that can be used in interfacing and synchronizing computer-music events.

The data structures studied so far in relation to MIDI have been, for the most part, static ones. The messages MIDI uses have been examined in terms of how performance data are exchanged among devices on a MIDI network. But music is sound events unfolding over time. Computers need to talk to synthesizers, drum machines, sound modules, wind controllers, tape recorders, mixers, and analog-to-digital and digital-to-analog devices. The flow of MIDI messages and audio data among all of these devices must be accurately synchronized.

Who's Conducting This Group?

Think of all the things a musician can do with a sequencer that require the software and hardware devices to always know where they are in time. The list would include multitrack recording; adding music to video productions; performing live with MIDI instruments; and producing multimedia presentations with audio, digital, and analog video; graphic stills; and MIDI-music events.

Have you ever seen a movie that shows how they put music to film in the old days? They would assemble the orchestra with a conductor. Behind the orchestra would be a large screen so the conductor could see the movie. Then the orchestra would perform the score as the conductor kept the music synchronized with the film using his or her eyes and ears as guides. In a computer music network, who is the conductor? How do all the components communicate and stay together?

Something must serve the role of the master-timing device from which all other devices (the slave devices, as they are called) keep time. Figure 18.9 shows three MIDI networks, each with a different "conductor." Figure 18.9a shows a MIDI network with a drum machine, a synthesizer, and a sound module. Note that the drum machine is the master, the external clock which generates the beat for the other two MIDI instruments; the synthesizer and sound module are set to receive the timing beat from the master drum machine (their internal clock is set to "slave" mode). This typical setup for any stand-alone MIDI configuration without a computer is commonly used for live performances.

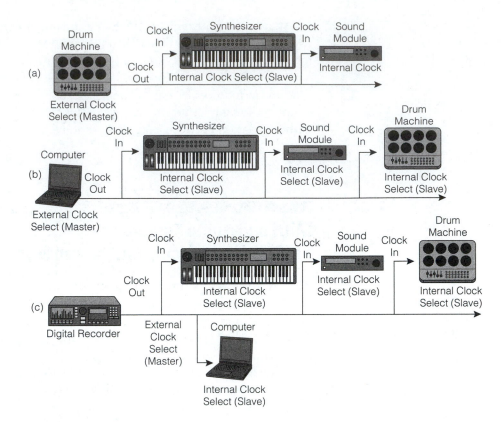

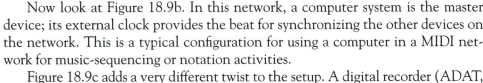

FIGURE 18.9 MIDI networks showing master-slave timing

ASIDE
Several different types of SMPTE timing are used in the video and audio recording industry. The discussion here is based on the most common format for MIDI environments, called either the "30 nondrop" or LTC (Longitudinal Time Code) format.

Now look at Figure 18.9b. In this network, a computer system is the master device; its external clock provides the beat for synchronizing the other devices on the network. This is a typical configuration for using a computer in a MIDI network for music-sequencing or notation activities.

Figure 18.9c adds a very different twist to the setup. A digital recorder (ADAT, DAT, MiniDisc, or hard-disk recorder) is included in the network. Notice that the tape recorder is the master device. The computer and all of the MIDI instruments are synchronized to the tape recorder in a very interesting configuration. This is one way to do multitrack recording with a MIDI setup.

More sophisticated MIDI interfaces can also be used to provide timing codes and translations. Now that you know how to pick a conductor (master) for a MIDI network, we turn our attention to the techniques used to keep everyone together in time.

Keeping the Tape Time

We can begin with the analog world of tape and video recording: non-MIDI devices. Two timing techniques will be described: FSK (frequency shift keying) code and SMPTE (Society for Motion Picture and Television Engineers, pronounced "simpty") code.

Frequency Shift Keying, or FSK, Coding

FSK timing is the simplest system for coding time on audio recordings. Understanding this system will help you understand more complex ones. An alternating pattern of two tones (e.g., 1 kHz and 3 kHz) is recorded on one of the tracks of a multitrack recording throughout the tape. This is like having someone record

"1 and 2 and 1 and 2 and 1 and 2 . . ." on a track of the tape. When music is added to the other tracks, a device listens to the FSK-coded track to keep the beat. There are electronic devices that can listen to the FSK-coded track and automatically synchronize events for recording and performing.

SMPTE (Society for Motion Picture and Television Engineers) Coding

The NASA space program in the 1960s developed a special coding system for recording telemetry data that was later adopted by the Society for Motion Picture and Television Engineers as the standard timing system for film, video, and television. This is known as SMPTE timecoding. It is much more sophisticated than FSK coding and much more accurate. Because film is structured as a series of still frames, the SMPTE timecode provides an absolute time address for each frame. In some cases, even timecodes within a frame, called *subframes* or *quarter-frames*, are available. Everything is measured in terms of number of frames per second (fps): American television and videotape use 30 fps and motion-picture film uses 24 fps (Figure 18.10).

Frames are coded as hours, minutes, seconds, and frames (hhmmssff) in eight-digit numeric values. For example, 01302015, would locate a frame that is 1 hour, 30 minutes, 20 seconds, and 15 frames into the film. Instead of the "1 and 2 and 1 and 2 . . . " pattern of FSK codes, SMPTE lays down a pattern of absolute references "00000000, 00000001, 00000002, . . . 01302015," and so on, one for each frame. SMPTE coding can also show a subframe with a 10-digit number; there are 80 subframes (b) per frame (hhmmssffbb). Another variation is the quarter-frame (q) system, where there are four units of time per frame (hhmmssffqq). This same concept will appear as part of the MIDI Time Code in a moment.

Because of the pervasiveness of the SMPTE timecode in the recording industry, it has become a common data structure for synchronizing audio, as well as video, recordings. Different kinds of SMPTE boxes are available for placing timecodes on video and audio recording. Special SMPTE generators create these timing patterns on tape with a technique known as *striping,* or prerecording SMPTE codes. SMPTE codes for video are directly coded into the video-signal data on each frame, and codes for audio are recorded onto an inaudible track of the tape. With technology such as that present in ADAT, DAT, hard-disk digital recorders, or synchronizer hardware, codes are automatically generated in the digital signals being sent between these devices, so striping an audio track is not necessary (essentially freeing up a track from timecodes).

ASIDE
Some MIDI devices generate more beats per quarter-note, like 48 or 96 pulses-per-quarter-note, or ppq, rates.

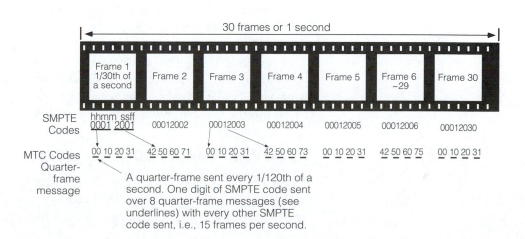

FIGURE 18.10 The data structure for SMPTE and MC codes mapped on 30 frames of a film

Keeping the MIDI Time: MIDI Time Codes

What about MIDI and timing? There are three systems within the current MIDI language for sequencing and synchronizing events over time:

MIDI Sync (Timing Clock)	System Real-Time Message
Song Position Pointers (SPP)	System Common Message
MIDI Time Code (MTC)	System Common Message

It's best to think of MIDI Sync and Song Position Pointers in a familiar music context. MIDI Sync is the musician's metronome beating away at 24 pulses per quarter-note, or 24 ppq. Tempo changes can speed up or slow down the rate, but the ppq remains constant. The 24-ppq timing clock keeps the MIDI instruments in sync with the same beat—their electronic "feet" tapping together, so to speak.

The next problem is getting the instruments to always start in the same place, or, if there is a need to jump around while rehearsing, having a way to communicate where the starting location is. The Song Position Pointer, or SPP, is the MIDI equivalent of the measure numbers in a musical score. Just as the conductor can say, "Start at measure 21," MIDI can say "Set the SPP to 500 beats from the beginning," or "Go set the SSP back to beat 201." The Start message sets the SPP to 0; the Stop message does not change the SPP but stays right where the beat stopped; and the Continue message resumes playing at the current SPP.

What about MIDI Time Code, or MTC? The MTC data structure is like the SMPTE code in that it provides an absolute reference; frames are coded with an absolute time value. MTC also captures the relative nature of MIDI sync or FSK coding by providing a constant pulse for maintaining synchrony among instruments.

The MTC quarter-time codes provide an absolute address in eight digits, just like the SMPTE code (hhmmssff); however, this address is provided every two frames. Within each frame there are four quarter-frame messages. The frame rate, as in SMPTE, is 30 frames per second. So an absolute frame address is provided every other frame, or 15 times per second. But, a pulse is also provided by the quarter-time messages, four times per frame or 120 times per second (4x30 fps).

One concern in a MIDI environment is the potential for overloading the MIDI network with too much data. Using SMPTE coding directly would use up about 10% of the traffic flow in a MIDI network. The MTC quarter-frame compromise coding, which distributes absolute addresses across two frames of data in eight quarter-frame messages, reduces the network load to about 8%.

You can now see that any MIDI device, including the computer, can be the "conductor" or master timing device on the network. This "conductor" can keep the beat through relative MIDI Sync and Song Pointers, or through absolute MIDI Time Codes that number frames 15 times per second. Should you want to work with audiotape or videotape, then that device becomes the "conductor" for your network. Using FSK or, more likely, SMPTE codes, both relative-beat and absolute-time references can be translated into MIDI SPP and MTC codes and back into SMPTE codes. Hardware synchronizers and the more sophisticated MIDI interfaces can perform SMPTE and MTC conversions automatically.

ADAT, Word Clock, and Digidesign Sync

Other timing systems have emerged from the need to keep audio hardware and MIDI devices synchronized: ADAT Clock, Word Clock, and SuperClock are common timing systems. Each time code evolved from the need to communicate

ASIDE

There are also MMC, or MIDI Machine Control, codes that can be used to send control signals between devices in a MIDI network to perform such functions as starting, stopping, and rewinding a MIDI-controlled recorder.

ASIDE

Just so you don't think all timing systems have been covered here, there are also MOTU's "direct time lock" (DTL) or "enhanced direct time lock" (DTLe); both work with SMTPE.

among unique audio, MIDI, or recording hardware. The *ADAT time sync* is designed for digital tape decks like the Alesis ADAT recorder, which is often the master synchronizer for a network of MIDI, computer, and recording devices. Most high-end MIDI workstations, effects processors, mixers, and the like can synchronize using ADAT time sync.

The *Word Clock timing code* is designed so that digital sampling or sampler devices can synchronize with each other; the timing is the sampling rate used to capture or generate the digital audio (e.g., 44.1 kHz, 96 kHz, etc.). Word Clock is a "handshaking" code that keeps everything timed together in synch; it does not provide location information, as MTC and SMPTE do. The master Word Clock device is often called the "house clock" to which other devices are slaved.

SuperClock is a timing system unique to Digidesign's Pro Tools and related digital audio hardware. It works in a similar fashion to Word Clock. SuperClock, however, runs at 256 times the sampling rate.

It is not uncommon, in a sophisticated computer-music studio, to deal with several of these timing systems. Various hardware devices can translate among these different timecodes and keep them all synchronized. Examples include Mark of the Unicorn's Universal Synchronizer, M-Audio Syncman, JL Cooper Synchronizer, and Digidesign SynchIO. Many sophisticated MIDI interfaces provide synchronization with MTC, MMC, or SMPTE, and many digital audio devices provide Word Clock and ADAT.

mLAN Music Network and Word Clock

As you have seen, the world of music technology is also a world of different cables and standards, as well as a world of many different events and event times. Yamaha's music network or mLAN is an attempt to simplify this world for professional music applications by integrating a network, timing base, and common cabling scheme into one standardized package. The mLAN network reduces all of this complexity down to one cable, a Firewire (1394 standard) cable that serves as a single 200-Mbps communications channel. mLAN-compatible MIDI devices, digital audio devices, mixers, video devices, DVD recorders, hard-disk and DAT recorders, and the like, are all connected with just one Firewire cable and a standard protocol between them.

Timing in the mLAN environment depends on Word Clock. Over the mLAN pathway, 100 channels of audio are provided, 256x16 channels of MIDI, as well as additional channels for video and applications. One common patchbay software application is available to route and synchronize music events within the network. For live-performance environments, a computer is not required for the network to function. Software applications such as Cubase, Logic Pro, and Digital Performer are mLAN aware. All this is done with one cable for each device, and the same cable and connector for every music device in the network!

VIEWPORT VII

Music Notation

"We need a way of getting music automatically for machine use rather than first translating into an input language. . . . It seems to be perfectly within the possibilities of today's techniques. . . . Such an optical reader would read the whole process. . . . You could have an entire repertoire stored in the memory of the machine."

—*Arthur Mendel at the first symposium*
on Musicology and the Computer (1965)

"Any music notation program that thinks it can tell what its users really want is going to do them a lot of favors they would have been better off without."

—*Donald Byrd (author of Nightingale),*
in Yavelow's Music and Sound Bible *(1992)*

Overview

We turn our attention next to an aspect of music technology that touches a very broad range of musicians: composers and arrangers, professional performers, K–12 music educators, church musicians, college music professors—in short, anyone who reads and produces written music with traditional notation. We begin by presenting information about data structures for representing music in a computer, making an important distinction between coding for performance and coding for display. An historical perspective of music-notation devices and computer-coding systems for music is included. We then present the features of MIDI-based notation programs using illustrations from a wide selection of software. The Viewport concludes with a glimpse at traditional and alternative hardware for entering music notation.

Objectives

Module 19 is all about coding systems for music notation. We explain why music-notation software is complex and challenging to write well. We demystify what a standard MIDI file is and review some of the more recent attempts to create a standardized notation format. In Module 20, we compare the features of seven notation programs that represent a wide range of cost and complexity. There is no one program appropriate for every need and this module should help in sorting out what is best for you. Finally, Module 21 helps with hardware choices for scanning and printing notation. We add music hardware to our EMT hardware model, stressing the fact that a music keyboard is not the only input device for notation software.

MUSIC TECHNOLOGY IN PRACTICE

Mike Wallace

Instrumental music educator for Bloomington Junior High School in Illinois, director of the Bloomington-Normal Community Band, private music teacher, and music director for various community theater productions.

Mike Wallace at his computer workstation at school working in PrintMusic!

Application

Mr. Wallace uses notation software in many practical ways. In his private studio, he often changes the key or clef of a piece to fit an instructional need. "I can quickly run the étude into Finale," he comments, "make the changes to a new clef or transposition, and print out a copy." For the community band, he often finds parts missing from an arrangement, especially some of the older tunes in the band library. Mike jokes that it is "usually flute parts for which the only alternative is a D-flat piccolo part." Again, he uses Finale to transpose an alternative for the missing parts. When he was directing a production of *42nd Street* with a community group, one of the leads couldn't make the range for the end of one song, so he used the notation software to transpose an entire section of the song down a minor third.

At school, Mike uses PrintMusic! to develop assessment materials that correlate with the curriculum the music teachers have developed. As he explains, "We use it to make lesson materials to publish on the Web for the students, scales that we require for each grade level." He uses Adobe Acrobat to transform the PrintMusic! files into PDF files for web publishing. The figure below shows the PrintMusic! screen on Mike's computer, the school's website with the scale exercises available for download, and the PDF version of the scales for students to use. Mr. Wallace lists a number of other ways he puts notation software to work for his junior-high-school musicians and ensembles: adjusting poorly written parts, creating parts as needed for students with special needs, rearranging an instrumental solo for a more accomplished young musician, creating more-meaningful French horn parts, and creating more-expanded percussion parts.

View of student exercise constructed with PrintMusic!, together with the PDF file and website

Hardware and Software

Mike's first foray into music technology was with an old Apple II, later stepping up to an Apple IIGS. He developed a software program to help students develop intonation skills. His first notation work was with an Apple GS program called Music Shop. As Mike says, "All it could do was a grand staff, but it was better than nothing."

Between work and home, Mike is bilingual, with an older PowerMac at school and an IBM laptop at home. He uses Finale extensively on the Mac and Finale PrintMusic! on his IBM laptop. Using the computer keyboard to enter music codes is still his preferred entry system. For printing music projects, he has his HP inkjet at home or the laser printers on the school network.

Jouni Koskimäki

Jouni Koskimäki is an internationally known composer, musician, and teacher from Finland. He studied musicology at the University of Jyväskylä, graduating in 2001. He has also studied classical guitar and contemporary and jazz composing and is well known as a mandolinist. Since 1982, his main work has been with the music department at the University of Jyväskylä, where he has been a lecturer teaching arranging/composing as a main topic since 1990. One of his key scholarly interests is the music of the Beatles.

Joona Jäntti (Jouni's younger son)

Jouni Koskimäki working at home in Jyväskylä, Finland, with Sibelius software.

Application

Jouni has used notation software in many different ways since the early 1990s, when the very early version of Encore was released. Notation software is the key medium for his artistic work: composing and arranging. The main difference between previous compositional methods that just used a pen and using a computer was actually hearing the score and making changes quickly: "... when I was composing for extended big band, I experimented with the length of sections and I was listening to different versions to see how it sounded and fit into the whole work. With pen and paper, that kind of thing would be very impractical and difficult to realize." He was also very impressed with part extraction and the enormous time this saved in the creative process. Since the release of Sibelius, the task of extracting parts has become quick and easy. "I could not imagine my work without notation software—I have now used it literally daily in my work for almost 15 years."

Jouni's main teaching topic in the music education department at the university is arranging/composing. He has been using Sibelius software and the Internet in his course in innovative ways. Students post their arrangements and compositions for all in the course to see and hear. Jouni gives feedback to the students by marking the score (using the highlighting features in Sibelius) and by making comments and suggestions. He then posts this feedback for all to study. It doesn't matter if students don't have Sibelius in their homes because they can use the Internet plug-in "Scorch" instead. With it, the documents are playable, printable, and transposable.

He also uses Sibelius to make really accurate transcriptions of the Beatles' music (or other music). The key method in making these solid transcriptions is the simultaneous use of transcribed MIDI information from the notation software and the original source—the recording itself. This allows him to make much more accurate adjustments in the notation to reflect the reality of the Beatles' music.

Hardware and Software

Jouni's computer career began at the university with an Apple Macintosh SE in the late 1980s, followed by an SE/30 in 1989. "This machine was a very fast computer in those days and reasonably easy to live with, but for some rather weird reason the most limiting feature was the very small display in all Macintosh machines in those days: the poor nine-inch screen! With notation software, THAT was the main problem!" Now the situation is far better for him: At home he has a 21-inch Apple Color display and at the university a thin and crystal-clear 20-inch Viewsonic display. At work, he uses a Macintosh G5 with OS X. For printing music, he uses an Epson Stylus Color 740 inkjet at home and at work a very high-end laser printer on the university's network.

Prior to 1996, Jouni used early products like Deluxe Music Construction Set, Notewriter, and Encore. The English notation software called "Sibelius" (actually Sibelius 7, which was the original name then) was launched in Finland in 1996. "That presentation was in Helsinki at the Sibelius Academy and about 100 Finnish composers and musicians were present. I had previously participated in about 10 presentations for different music software—but never like that particular Sibelius presentation. The audience was so enthusiastic about the new program that it applauded *seven* times during its presentation—a very memorable happening indeed and a true highlight moment for music technology," Jouni remembers. "Sibelius's key outstanding ability was its extraordinary speed—no task took more than about one second, no matter how big or complicated it was!"

At the end of this Viewport, you should understand:

- How notation is represented in a computer
- Differences between data representation for the printed images vs. the sound of these images
- The history of computer-music-coding systems over the last 50 years, including the recent development of intelligent, rule-based music codes
- Industry attempts to define an agreed-upon, standard file format for music notation
- How music notation can appear as part of web pages
- How music fonts work
- Basic operational features of selected notation programs
- Note entry and score design of selected notation programs
- Advanced editing in selected notation programs
- Play, print, and save features of selected notation programs
- Plug-ins for advanced music-notation programs
- Input devices for music notation, including computer keyboard, MIDI devices, analog voice, graphic palettes and mouse, and scanners
- Optical Music Recognition (OMR) and scanners
- Printing for music notation, including differences between laser and inkjet printers

DVD-ROM

As with all the software modules in this text, the accompanying DVD contains projects for you to use to practice your skills.

DVD-ROM Software Projects

In terms of hands-on tasks, you should be able to:

- Create a basic music score, using graphic note-entry methods, save, and print your music (Project 15)
- Use a MIDI keyboard for note entry, explore more advanced layout and formatting, and scanning music score (Project 16)

Module 19

Coding Systems for Music Notation and Performance

ASIDE
WYPWYP or "What You Play is What You Print" was coined by Christopher Yavelow, author of *Music & Sound Bible* (1992).

ASIDE
Common Music Notation (CMN) describes the general set of symbols used to represent printed music from the sixteenth century through to the present day of the Western music tradition.

Why can't all notation programs do all things? Why can't you just play some music patterns and have them appear on a printer all properly notated? Why don't we have "What You Play is What You Print" (WYPWYP) software? The answer to these questions lies in understanding the difference between how you represent music-performance data and how you represent music-printing or notation data in a computer. When you understand this distinction, you can more fully grasp the underlying conceptual issues for designing notation software and, at the same time, gain deeper insight into the design of music sequencers for performance.

How Is Notation Represented in a Computer?

To begin our discussion, we define the smallest music element you would want to store and manipulate in a computer. For the sake of discussion, we'll call this a music *object*. Such an *object* may represent any pattern of music, from a single note to a complex phrase. Our object needs to describe everything required to perform the music and to print or display its score. Figure 19.1 provides a simple model to illustrate.

To describe a music object's performance and notation requires a data structure with two sets of properties. The information or data needed for performing music are very different from the data needed for displaying or printing music.

Data Structures for Performing and Display

The discussion of MIDI in Modules 14 and 18 showed you that the data required for performing music is the same type of data you are able to represent with MIDI-control codes. With MIDI or any performance codes, the concern is with recording and playing events over time: pitch, duration, velocity or amplitude, control changes, and so on.

The data needed for displaying music on the printed page are different. Here, the concern is with locating symbols within the space of a printed page. Critical information for display includes:

- Page and staff layout
- Changes in key and meter signatures
- Enharmonic spellings
- Beaming, slurs, and spacing of notes
- Expressive markings and other performance directions
- Lyrics and text

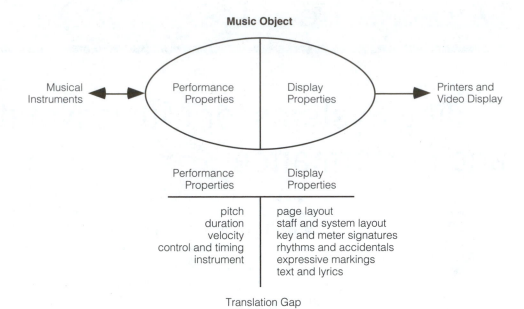

FIGURE 19.1 A model of a music object

Translating between Performance and Display Data

The elements needed to describe performance and notation are so different that translation between the two domains poses many problems. That is why the diagram of the "music object" has a line separating the two domains labeled the *translation gap*. As the operations move from performing to notating and back, critical elements that enable you to interpret the performance's expressive properties and render the printed page are lost in translation.

When software has to translate MIDI performance codes into notation codes, it must cross the translation gap. It can use the chromatic MIDI pitch information to decide what pitches (except for enharmonic spellings) to put on the page, but durations are more complex. What you play is not usually what you want to print. The performed durations have to be *quantized* or rounded off into rhythmic values or symbols: the traditional symbols for sixteenth-, eighth-, or quarter-notes, and so on. When duration is quantized, nuances in rhythmic performance data are lost.

SIDE BAR

Mockingbird Set the Standard

John Maxwell and Severo Ornstein set a standard for all future music-notation systems when they created the Mockingbird computer-notation system at the Xerox PARC research lab in the early 1980s. In designing Mockingbird, they defined three independent domains for representing music: logical, performance, and graphical. A fourth domain, analytical, was added later when the specifications for SMDL (Standard Music Description Language) were defined.

The logical domain describes the essential elements of the music: the pitches, rhythmic durations, key signatures, articulations, and the like. The graphical domain describes the placement and appearance of music symbols on the score page, including such elements as fonts, layout, and beaming. The performance domain describes the information required for recreating a live performance of the music: the MIDI codes, for example. The analytical domain represents symbols, for example, to describe Roman-numeral analysis, scale-degree numbers, or Schenkerian notation. An example to illustrate: A symbol is placed on the score page as a dotted quarter-note (logical); it has a diamond-shaped head (graphical); and it plays for 695 ticks, or 210 milliseconds (performance). For the discussion in this text, we deal with two domains: display and performance. Display incorporates the combined properties of the graphical and logical domains.

What about the key signature and accidentals, spacing on the page, beams, and stem direction? Either these notation elements must be added by human intervention, or the computer software needs rules to guide it in inferring these elements from the performance data.

What happens when the software needs to reconstruct a performance? When the software goes back across the gap to reconstruct a performance based solely on notation codes (without performance data), the performance sounds unmusical and sterile. Even if expressive markings like *rubato* and *andante* have been added to the printed score, the computer needs rules to translate those expressive markings into performance codes. *Rubato* would be extremely challenging to the software!

Having made this point, it needs to be emphasized that translating notation into MIDI is easier than translating MIDI into notation. Notation has much more explicit information that can be used in creating a performance. As Donald Byrd, the author of Nightingale music-notation software notes, the amount of programming code in notation software for translating MIDI or performance data into notation often matches the complexity of the task.

Table 19.1 helps summarize the key contrasts between structures for printing and for performing. Take particular note of how pitch is represented. With display codes, pitch is coded by graphic positions in relation to the staff and clef. With traditional Western music, this is a *MOD-7 system*, meaning that the staff positions are coded in seven numeric steps (0 to 6, or A to G) across octaves, with accidentals coded separately. With performance codes, accurate performance information is required. Here, pitch is traditionally coded in a *MOD-12 system*, where there are 12 chromatic steps to the octave (0 to 11, or C to B).

A Simple Music Coding

Figures 19.2 and 19.3 provide a comparison between notation and performance coding. A Beethoven theme is shown in traditional notation in Figure 19.2a. We've made up a "Simple Music Code" using alphanumeric characters found on any computer keyboard to illustrate how you might create such a coding system.

TABLE 19.1   Contrasts in Music Coding for Performance and Display

Performances	Display
Controlling instruments	Controlling symbols on a page
Time-based systems	Location- or space-based systems
Optimized for performance accuracy	Optimized for notational accuracy
Pitch coded as chromatic (MOD-12)	Pitch coded as display position (MOD-7)
Rhythm coded as temporal duration	Rhythm coded as shapes and horizontal positions
Interpretation embedded in pitch, duration, and velocity	Interpretation coded in signs and labels

FIGURE 19.2 Music example: (a) notation of theme from Beethoven's Symphony No. 5, 3rd Movement, and (b) theme coded in Simple Music Code

(b) !F !K3B !M34 !T120 G3Q / C4 E G / C5H EQ / DH F4#Q / GH. //

TABLE 19.2 Simple Music Code for Beethoven Excerpt	
Single-Line Code	
!F !K3B !M34 !T120 G3Q/ C4 E G / C5H EQ / DH F4#Q / GH. //	
Analysis	
!F !K3B !M34 !T120	Bass clef; key signature with 3 flats (3B); meter of 3/4; and Tempo 120
G3Q/	3rd octave G quarter-note and a barline
C4 E G / C5H EQ /	4th octave C, E, and G (continuing quarter-notes); barline; then 5th octave C half-note; E quarter-note; barline
DH F4#Q / GH. //	Half-note D (still 5th octave), 4th octave F-sharp quarter-note; barline; G dotted half-note with a double bar at the end

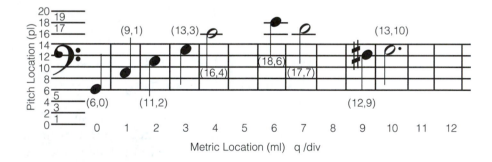

FIGURE 19.3 Matrix for deriving performance codes from Beethoven theme notation

LINK
Refer back to Figure 8.5 for translating keyboard notes to MIDI values and Figures 14.3 and 14.5 for MIDI codes for pitch and duration.

Table 19.2 provides an annotated analysis of this code's syntax. You should be able to get the gist of how the Simple Music Code works by studying the table and figures.

To get a flavor of how a computer might reverse the process and infer performance data from notation, examine Figure 19.3. Remember that pitch in music notation is MOD-7, A through G, and then repeats itself. This figure shows you how the chromatic MOD-12 pitch system can be mapped onto the MOD-7 notation system.

The series of notes may be viewed on an X-Y axis, with chromatic pitch vertical (MOD-12) on the X axis, and time horizontal on the Y axis. To compute the values necessary to play the notation as MIDI codes, for example, the information in parentheses (the XY coordinates) can be translated into MIDI values using a quarter-note as the metric pulse for duration (e.g., a value of 64 = quarter-note) and the chromatic pitch code to derive the MIDI pitch values (6 = MIDI 43, 9 = MIDI 48, etc.). Computer-programming code can easily be written to translate notation codes into performance codes.

ASIDE
Coda named its Finale music font Petrucci.

Tour of Computer Music-Coding Systems

One way to understand coding music-notation and performance data is by taking a brief look at some of the attempts that have been made, and continue to be made, to develop coding systems for representing music notation with computers. Musicians, engineers, and others have devised ingenious systems to mechanically code music events. In the following sections, we will blend an historical overview of music-notation systems with illustrations of different solutions to coding music notation. The objective is to show the evolution of data structures that underlie not only present-day notation software but sequencing software as well.

Pre-1950s: Mechanical Music Coding

As best we know, music notation has been around since the Chinese first used notation for their lute tablatures (100 AD or earlier). The emergence of the Western music-notation system we use today dates to around 1400 AD with the beginnings of mensural notation. Petrucci of Fossombrone, Breitkopf of Leipzig, and other early music typographers, including Pierre Attaignant and Tylman Susato,

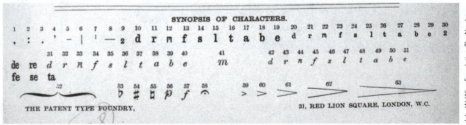

FIGURE 19.4A Two examples of Diamond music fonts used for piano and chant notation (note reversed bass-clef symbol)

FIGURE 19.4B A sample from mosaic music font with unique set of symbols used much as computer fonts are today, from Shanks & Co.'s *Specimens of Printing Types and Music Fonts*, 1873

developed the traditions and techniques of printing music from movable type. Music typography as it evolved from the 1400s on forms the basis for much current computer-generated notation. This lineage is present in the fonts, layout, rules, and techniques used to move music symbols around the computer screen and onto computer printers. A sample of these notation codes from an 1873 book of type-faces is shown in Figure 19.4; notice how each font piece has a corresponding numeric code. Computer fonts work the same way today.

Automated Processes

Until the middle of the nineteenth century, most music notation was done by hand. Early attempts at automating the process were proposed in theory by Johann Unger in 1745 with the design of his Machina ad Sonos et Concentus. The Machina was to print lines on paper with ink pens connected through rods and levers to the keys on a clavichord. Successful music typewriters appeared in the late 1800s: Angelo Tessaro's Tachigrafo Musicale (1887), and Noco-Blick's (1910) and J. Walton's (1920) music typewriters. Later, Armando Dal Molin (1948) and Cecil Effinger (1955) developed more-sophisticated music typewriters, with Dal Molin's system turning into his Music Reprographics printing business in New York City, and Effinger's Musicwriter becoming one of the most popular music typewriters for amateurs and professional musicians until personal-computer-notation software in the 1980s. The Musicwriter was even interfaced with the ILLIAC computer in order to print music. Effinger and Hiller are shown in Figure 19.5 with a version of the Musicwriter that could read and write five-holed paper punch tape for computer coding. Music-editing software for the ILLIAC and the Musicwriter could print music notation, change page margins, and extract parts.

(a) (b)

FIGURE 19.5 (a) 1950s model of Musicwriter, developed by Cecil Effinger and based on modified Olympia typewriter. Note music symbols embossed on the typewriter keys. Close-up view (upper left-hand corner) of typebars shows music-symbol typefaces that strike ink ribbon. (b) Cecil Effinger with Lejaren Hiller demonstrating Musicwriter interfaced to ILLIAC 1 computer at University of Illinois

Music Coding for Performance

Attempts at automating music performance in the late 1700s brought about the first mechanical music-coding systems. Music boxes, calliopes, mechanical orchestras, and the immensely popular player pianos coded their music with systems of pins on metal drums, punched holes in paper rolls, and holes in circular metal discs. Some consider Givelet and Coupleux's programmable organ (ca. 1929) to be one of the first programmable synthesizers; the organ's four oscillators were controlled by codes on punched-paper rolls.

The data structure for these devices consisted of pitch and duration coded over time on a revolving drum, paper roll, or disc; some of the more-advanced player pianos coded different dynamics through separate holes or tracks for pitch and velocity. The data structures have changed little over the years; just the delivery and storage technology are different. Today's music-sequencing software still uses the player-piano roll, now graphically portrayed on the computer screen.

1950s to 1960s: Notation to Feed the First Computer Music Synthesizers

In the 1950s, Mathews at Bell Labs, Olson and Belar at Columbia and Princeton, and Hiller and Isaacson at the University of Illinois programmed some of the earliest software for music synthesis on the ILLIAC and the RCA Mark I and II general-purpose computers. The only language available to program these machines was the native machine language, and input was through punched cards or punched-paper tape—not much different from coding on piano rolls. Expressing music codes in a readable form was the least of one's concerns; just being able to control a computer synthesizer with any notation system, no matter how cryptic and unfriendly, was sufficient reward.

Max Mathews developed a music-input language called MUSIC I (1957) that quickly went through several transformations, MUSIC III through MUSIC V (1968). Other versions of this code were developed at various universities: Princeton, Stanford, and Queens College.

Let's examine how Mathews's machine-friendly (music-unfriendly) system worked. In Table 19.3, you see the coding for our Beethoven excerpt from the Fifth Symphony (see the original notation in Figure 19.2).

The chart is self-explanatory. This is a performance-coding system much like MIDI is today. Pitch and loudness are coded in physical terms as frequency and amplitude, allowing considerable freedom in the intonation and intensity of each note. Duration is expressed in seconds (or fractions of a second), and the cumulative Start-time works similarly to the way MIDI timing does in most sequencing software.

There were two operations in the design of Mathews's music system: creating the instrument definitions or algorithms for generating sounds, and creating the score of codes for the music sequence, as shown in Table 19.3. You can see that composing an extensive composition by working directly with the numeric codes would be very tedious.

Mid-1960s to Mid-1970s: Friendlier Text-Based Music Coding

In 1963, the ASCII standard was defined for keyboard devices like computers and teletypes. The first generation of friendly notation systems for large mainframe computers appeared, with such names as DARMS (or Ford-Columbia Input

LINK
To check the frequencies against the notes for the Beethoven excerpt, use the keyboard diagram (Figure 8.5). MIDI timing is discussed in Module 18.

LINK
The ASCII standard for representing text in a computer was first discussed in Module 6.

TABLE 19.3   Mathews's MUSIC V Code for Beethoven Excerpt

Instrument	Start Time (secs)	Duration (secs)	Frequency	Amplitude
NOT 0	0	1	098	20,000
NOT 0	1	1	131	20,000
NOT 0	2	1	165	20,000
NOT 0	3	1	196	20,000
NOT 0	4	2	262	20,000
NOT 0	6	1	330	20,000
NOT 0	7	2	294	20,000
NOT 0	9	1	185	20,000
NOT 0	10	3	196	20,000

ASIDE

Smith's Score software began as a preprocessor to facilitate entering codes for music synthesis. In the 1970s, as we will see later, it was transformed into notation software for conventional music hard-copy output and engraving.

Language), MUSTRAN, Plaine and Easie Code, Score, and other derivations and inventions.

Stanford University enhanced Mathews's MUSIC V system for a PDP-10 computer (Music 10). Leland Smith developed one of several preprocessors that let musicians use a text- or ASCII-based coding system in place of the numeric codes shown in Table 19.3 for MUSIC V. Table 19.4 demonstrates Smith's preprocessor Score language for the Beethoven excerpt. Again, the example is self-explanatory. Notice that it is, indeed, a much friendlier notation language, permitting greater efficiency for entry and editing. You may notice some similarity to our Simple Music Code (Figure 19.2b), described earlier in this module, in the way pitch, rhythm, and octaves are coded.

In 1965, musicologists gathered for the first time to discuss computer applications at two symposia: Musicology and the Computer I and II. Several music-notation systems for music analysis, printing, and cataloging were presented. Most of them were single-line, text-based entry systems using alphanumeric codes that bore some resemblance to the music symbols. This was a landmark event in the history of computer-based notation systems; meetings continue to be held to discuss topic relevant to music notation and musicology.

TABLE 19.4   Smith's Preprocessor, SCORE, for Music 10 Coding for Beethoven Excerpt

Code	Comments
Tempo 13 120	120 beats per minute
il 0 13	Instrument 1 begins at time 0 and plays for 13 beats
p 3 Rhythm 4 / 4 / 4 / 4 / 2 / 4 / 2 / 4 / 2.;	Rhythm codes
p 4 notes g2 / c3/ e / g / c4 / e / d / fs3 / g;	Pitch codes
p 5 numbers 20000 * 13 ;	Amplitude for 13 notes
end;	

ASIDE

Bauer-Mengelberg also presented a musical application of the Photon in 1965, a device interfaced with the computer performing the DARMS translation. The Photon, an early photo-typesetter, was remarkably similar to present-day laser printers and digital photo-typesetters. It used a revolving glass disc with 1,440 symbols; the computer selected the symbol to be printed and then optically imaged that symbol onto film for printing.

In Table 19.5, you can see an illustration of the comprehensive DARMS (Digital Alternative Representation of Musical Scores) code developed by Stefan Bauer-Mengelberg. Its particular design was optimized for music printing. The coding system was centered around space or location codes graphically related to the printed staff. This system is very much like our Simple Music Code example presented earlier, where pitch codes were translated to display codes in much the same way. You will note other similarities as well. DARMS significantly influenced more recent notation-coding projects, as we will see later: GUIDO and NIFF are two examples.

Barry Brook's Plaine and Easie Code was designed for cataloging music scores. Its objective was to provide a human-readable code using standard keyboard characters on a single line. The Beethoven excerpt is coded with the Plaine and Easie Code in Table 19.6. This system contains many features of future text-based

---

TABLE 19.5   Bauer-Mengelberg's DARMS Code for Beethoven Excerpt

Single-Line Code

!F !K3- !M3:4 1Q/ 4 6 8 / 31H 33Q / 32H 7#Q / 8H. /

Analysis

Note: Display or space codes indicate unique location on the staff

!F !K3- !M3:4	Bass clef; key signature with 3 flats (3-); meter of 3/4
1Q/ 4 6 8 /	Staff display locations 1, 4, 6, and 8 with quarter-notes
31H 33Q /	Space codes 31 and 33; half- and quarter-note
32H 7#Q /	Space codes 32 and 7; half- and quarter-notes with a sharp sign
8H. /	Space code 8 with a dotted half-note

TABLE 19.6   Brook's "Plaine and Easie Code" for Beethoven Excerpt

Single-Line Code

(Allegro, bBEAminor, 3/4) „4G/ ‚C E G / '2C 4E / 2D ‚4#F / 2.G /

Analysis

Note: Octaves are designated ,, , ' "

(Allegro,	Tempo Marking
bBEAminor,	Key signature: 3 flats, which are B, E, and A, and A minor key
3/4)	Meter in 3/4
„4G/, C E G /	4 = quarter-note; pitches GCEG with octave markings
'2C 4E / 2D ‚4#F /	2 = half- and 4 = quarter-note; pitches are CED and an F #
2.G /	Dotted half-note G

computer-notation systems. Direct spin-off languages from Brook's code were Gould and Logemann's ALMA (ca. 1970) and Hofstetter's MUSICODE (1972).

The 1965 Musicology and the Computer symposia presented other notation systems besides Bauer-Mengelberg's and Brook's. Figure 19.6 illustrates Jerome Wenker's feature-laden notation language, MUSTRAN (called MUSAN at the symposium). It was unique in its ability to code music required for ethnomusicology research and cataloging. Notice how MUSTRAN codes micro-accidentals and subtle nuances of pitch change in documenting performed music.

1970s to Early 1980s: Experimentation and Graphic Display of Notation

Many different developments occurred during the 1970s. Musicians had mini-computers, graphic displays, early interactive operating systems, and voltage-controlled synthesizers to play with. Punch cards and tape were being replaced by magnetic tape and hard-disk storage. With minicomputers readily available, greater experimentation occurred with music-composing and notation systems. Just about any musician on a college campus with access to a computer could experiment with computer music analysis, composition, or cataloging using text-based coding systems like DARMS, Plaine and Easie, and MUSTRAN. The missing link for notation at this time was a low-cost, high-resolution music-printing device. History was waiting for the laser printer!

Graphic-display devices and interactive computer systems began to offer the opportunity for text-based notation systems to be augmented and enhanced with graphic display and editing of notation symbols. Mathews and Rosler at Bell Labs had started experimenting with graphic notation entry around 1965. They used one of the first remote graphic terminals, the Graphic 1, interfaced to an IBM 7090 computer. William Buxton, at the University of Toronto in the late 1970s, created one of the first entirely graphics-based music-score systems, the Structured Sound Synthesis Project (SSSP), using a digitizing tablet and custom slider box for music entry and editing.

The MusiComp system developed by Armando dal Molin (c. 1978) for his Music Reprographics music-printing firm was a custom computer system with a special music-symbol keyboard and graphic notation display. In addition, the CERL PLATO computer group at the University of Illinois, with their video displays and touch-sensitive panels, developed the LIME notation software.

The groundbreaking work that served as a template for personal-computer-notation systems to come was that of John Maxwell and Severo Ornstein at the Xerox Palo Alto Research Center (PARC). In the early 1980s, Maxwell and Ornstein designed the Mockingbird music-notation system (see Figure 19.7), perhaps the first screen-based, WYSIWIG (What You See Is What You Get), direct-user-manipulation interface for music notation. Mockingbird took full advantage of

(a)

FIGURE 19.6 Wenker's MUSTRAN code: (a) micro-accidental coding and (b) estimated pitch coding

GS,2E,4(+1)F,8\$(-3)G,8(+5)A,8N(+7)C,1D

(b)

GS,6=4,4D(++),4*F(+),8G(+),8C+(-),8C+(-),4G. JH+H(-),4G(-),//,END

Adapted from "A Computer Oriented Music Notation" by J. Wenker in *Musicology and the Computer*, B. Brook (ed.), The City University of New York Press (New York, 1970)

Charles Babbage Institute, University of Minnesota, Minneapolis

FIGURE 19.7 Xerox PARC Mockingbird music workstation

ASIDE
Douglas Engelbart designed the first computer "mouse" in the 1960s while working at the Stanford Research Institute (SRI).

many features emerging from PARC at that time, including a graphical user interface with a mouse and laser printing, to create a complete interactive environment with music keyboard for manipulating music symbols. Mockingbird also initiated the notion that music-information coding be represented as independent domains: logical, graphical, and performance.

Early 1980s: Personal Computers and Consumer Music Systems

With the introduction of the first personal computers in the late 1970s—the PET, Apple II, TRS-80, and others—the development of computer-music systems rapidly accelerated. Computer engineers and amateur experimenters alike, driven in part by a desire to create video games, designed impressive graphics features, as well as simple sound generation, into the first PCs. The sound capabilities were quickly enhanced by add-on cards and boxes that appeared in the late 1970s, like the ALF three-voice analog-music card and the Micro Music (MMI) four-voice digital-sampling card for the Apple II, and the MTU digital-music card for the Commodore PET. The next generation of sound systems for these early PCs included the Mountain Music System, the Wenger Sound-Chaser, the Alpha-Syntauri music system, and a wide variety of software for the Commodore 64's custom SID sound chip.

The music-coding systems and graphic display of music notation that had been reserved for mainframe and minicomputers quickly found their way to the early PCs. The MMI Music Composer software for the Apple II used a text-based, command-line notation system for entering up to four voices of polyphonic music. The notation appeared on screen and scrolled in time with the music. The command-line music code bore a resemblance to Brook's Plaine and Easie code. David Williams designed the Music Composer software, as well as the software that processed the music-sound and graphics coding used in the Music Composer

(Music Experimenters Package, or MEP) and in the large library of music CAI software produced by Micro Music in the early 1980s.

Other similar music software quickly appeared, and coding music for composing jumped from an esoteric pursuit of selected musicians in studios and colleges to an activity accessible to anyone. The software became more sophisticated, and true notation software appeared with such systems as Passport's Polywriter software and Jack Jarrett's MusicPrinter for the Apple II (published by Temporal Acuity Products). These systems used combinations of command-line input, custom music keyboards, and graphics display. A major limiting factor to computer music notation remained the lack of low-cost, high-resolution printing.

Mid-1980s: The Birth of Desktop Music Publishing

Several significant events surfaced from 1984 to 1986 that, when combined, changed music composing and notation and made high-quality music printing accessible to anyone:

- The Macintosh personal computer provided the ideal operating system, with its graphical user interface and mouse; music could now be manipulated directly without the need for intervening text or numeric codes, just as on Maxwell and Ornstein's Mockingbird system.
- The MIDI standard provided interchangeable input and output devices and a standardized data structure for music-performance codes.
- The HP and Apple laser printers provided low cost and high-resolution that were needed.
- Cleo Higgins of Adobe Systems created the first PostScript music font, Sonata, for the new laser-printer technology.
- Professional Composer (Mark of the Unicorn), Deluxe Music Construction Set, and Concertware provided graphics-based consumer and professional music-notation software on the Macintosh platform.

The IBM PC, with its traditional, command-line DOS operating system, was also rapidly gaining in popularity. Jim Miller's Personal Composer (Personal Composer Inc.), for the IBM platform, was the first widely used sequencer and notation program using graphic display and command-line notation input. Jarrett's Music Printer for the Apple II was given a major overhaul and emerged as Music Printer Plus for the IBM PC.

Leland Smith's Score notation software resurfaced as a professional-level, music-engraving program; however, its lineage dating back to the 1960s also gave it a very complex, text-based input language and no performance capability. Similarly, the LIME notation software was dusted off by the CERL group and adapted to the Macintosh and DOS/Windows PCs of the 1990s. And Keith Hamel's Notewriter and Frederick Noad's Speedscore provided music-printing software designed for free-form placement of music symbols on the page, with little concern for performance.

Music data structures go underground. There is a significant point to be made here in terms of the study of notation-coding systems for music. The musicians of the 1960s who developed DARMS and other programs were concerned with developing data structures for music that could be easily understood by musicians, especially for musicological and analytical research. With the proliferation of screen-based, GUI, direct-user-manipulation notation software on the computers of the 1980s, the data structure could now become transparent to the user: The user no longer needed to be aware of the complex codes that make computer notating or performance possible.

Late 1980s and 1990s: Intelligent Rule-Based Music-Coding Systems

Key developments in the design of music-coding systems in this period are fully graphic notation systems, rule-based integration of performance and notation activities, greater input and performance options, and machine independence. One of the premiere notation programs was Finale (published originally by Coda, now MakeMusic! [Win/Mac]), first released for the Macintosh in 1988 and subsequently for Windows computers. Finale is based on the ENIGMA notation software developed by Phil Farrand and Tim Strathlee of Opus Dei. Rule-based operations in the software enable accurate quantizing of performance data to notation data; transposition; error checking for meter and rhythm; and intelligent placement of notes, beams, and many other layout features. Donald Byrd's Nightingale (now Adept Music Notation Solutions [Mac]) rivaled Finale in its design sophistication and features, but was more sensitive to user interface and ease of use. Others to come on stage included Passport Design's Encore (now published by G-Vox), Concertware (Jump!), Mosaic (Mark of the Unicorn), and Opcode's Overture (now published by GenieSoft).

In Europe, Sibelius (Sibelius [Win/Mac]) was a professional-level notation program developed for the British Acorn computer. Developed by Jonathan Finn in machine language, it was first released in 1988. MIDI playback was added, as well as various extensions, in 1993. The code was completely restructured in C++ when it was converted to the Windows platform in 1997, and, subsequently, to the Macintosh platform.

According to Sibelius's founder and director, Ben Finn, Sibelius does not have a unique notation engine separate from the software program. One of its primary innovations is that the score layout is not stored in the Sibelius notation files. The layout is generated "on the fly" as the score is displayed. This results in small, efficient files, and makes it easy to reformat an entire score very quickly.

This period started the trend toward software that provided both performance and display in the same package, the concept introduced by Mockingbird. Notation software's increased sophistication depended on refinements in the intelligence of the software's rules to carry out the translations needed to cross between the display and performance domains.

Much of today's notation software depends heavily on rule-based structures for quantizing performance. If you are interested solely in music printing, this may be more of a hindrance than a gain. As Donald Byrd, author of Nightingale, noted, "Any notation program that thinks it can tell what its users *really* want is going to do them a lot of favors they would have been better off without." Notation software like Keith Hamel's Notewriter II (Opus 1 [Mac]) or Sion's Copyist ([Win]) represent a small number of notation applications that provide a free-form, space-oriented graphics environment (with no rules) for creating printed scores, where the musician is in complete control. The challenge for the next generation of software is to balance highly intelligent rule-based environments with a free-form graphic environment that gives musicians a choice over the degree of control needed for performing or printing music. One way this is being addressed is in the flexibility that software like Finale and Sibelius have built in for defeating or adjusting the rules. Most objects can be moved on the page.

LINK
Music-scanning software and scanners are addressed in the next two Modules, 20 and 21.

LINK
Standard MIDI files (SMF) are presented in Module 14; check there for a refresher if needed. Interestingly, SMF files have the ability to code key signatures, lyrics, and other display information as "metaevents," but few notation programs make use of these features.

ASIDE
Only a few of the industry participants in the NIFF project are still in business: Cakewalk, San Andreas Press, Musitek, and Mark of the Unicorn.

1990s: Seeking Interchangeable Notation-Coding Systems

The first few generations of notation software for personal computers did not give musicians the ability to interchange music files among software applications, notation-to-notation, and performance-to-notation applications. Few notation applications provided built-in translators, as word processors do: We are thinking here of translating Word to WordPerfect documents in word processing, compared with Finale to Sibelius files in music notation. This is a clue to the structural design underlying different notation software: How music display elements are coded may be radically different and proprietary to each application.

The challenge became finding a common music-file format that could transfer among as much music software as possible and exchange performance as well as display data. With the introduction of music-scanning software (optical music recognition, or OMR), the problem became more critical. The OMR software must be able to store the music codes in a form accessible to a number of notation applications. We will consider a few solutions to interchangeable notation solutions that emerged in applications during the 1990s, if not earlier: SMF, ETF, NIFF, MuseData, and Guido.

Standard MIDI Files (SMF)

The Standard MIDI File (SMF), approved by MMA in 1988, builds on the lineage of MIDI as the *lingua franca* of music software. MIDI files store performance events that happen over time: MIDI events such as note on, note off, velocity, control codes, and the like. None of the display information needed for notation is provided beyond these basic events. The translation gap remains when you try to move performance files into notation-display-code software environments and vice versa.

What use are SMF files for notation? SMF can be used in a notation environment similarly to ASCII text files in a word processor. SMF provides a way for importing and exporting the basic musical content: pitch and duration. Nearly all notation programs support the SMF standard, even given its glaring deficiencies, as it is the only "standard" between music software that presently exists.

Enigma Transportable File (ETF)

Finale's notation-file format originated with the first release of Finale for the Macintosh in 1988. Finale's proprietary file format offered an interchange format that other notation applications could read—but not necessarily write—simply because of the large installed base of Finale software. Finale is based on the Enigma notation engine, and Finale files can be saved in *Enigma Transportable File*, or *ETF*, format. Sibelius provides an option for importing ETF notation files. SmartScore OMR software will export to ETF, and an assortment of translators convert ETFs to other music-performance and display codes.

Notation Interchange File Format (NIFF)

NIFF was developed as a notation format apart from commercial music products. The idealized goal of the NIFF project was to create a standard notation-file system that could be used across a variety of music-notation applications, much as SMF is to sequencing applications. The specification for the *Notation Interchange File Format* was completed in 1995 through the collaboration of a large number of music-industry participants.

The data structure for NIFF was designed to be very flexible, allowing the simplest to the most complex of music notation to be stored within the data file: NIFF

```
Setup Section
Data Section LIST start

//////////////////////////////////////////////////////////////
Staff LIST start
Staff Header:
   (Anchor Override: Page Header)
   (Absolute Placement: 218,233)
   (Width: 4748)
   (Height: 233)
   (Number of Staff Lines: 5)

Time-Slice: MeasureStart 0/1 -------- pge 1 sys 1 stv 1 bar 0
--------
   (Absolute Placement: 0,233)

Time-Slice: Event 0/1
   (Absolute Placement: 833,233)
Clef: Fclef staffstep=6 NoNumber
   (Absolute Placement: -780,60)
Key Signature: 3b
   (Absolute Placement: -548,0)
Time Signature: 3/4
   (Absolute Placement: -270,0)
Stem:
   (Logical Placement: HDefault VAbove ProxDefault)
   (Absolute Placement: 0,-203)
   (Height: 203)
Notehead: Filled 0(G) 1/4
   (Part ID: 0)
   (Voice ID: 0)

Time-Slice: Event 1/4
   (Absolute Placement: 1028,233)
Barline: Thin ThruLastStaff 1

Time-Slice: MeasureStart 1/4 -------- pge 1 sys 1 stv 1 bar 1
--------
   (Absolute Placement: 1028,233)

Time-Slice: Event 0/1
   (Absolute Placement: 113,233)
Stem:
   (Logical Placement: HDefault VAbove ProxDefault)
   (Absolute Placement: 0,-289)
   (Height: 199)
Notehead: Filled 3(C) 1/4
   (Part ID: 0)
   (Voice ID: 0)
```

(a) Text display of NIFF binary codes for the first two notes of Figure 19.2.

```
<score-partwise>
      <identification></identification>
      <part-list></part-list>
      <part id="P1">
            <measure number = "1">
                  <attributes>
                        <divisions>1</divisions>
                        <key>
                              <fifths>-3</fifths>
                        </key>
                        <time symbol="normal">
                              <beats>3</beats>
                              <beat-type>4</beat-type>
                        </time>
                        <staves>1</staves>
                        <clef number = "1">
                              <sign>F</sign>
                              <line>4</line>
                              <clef-octave-change>0
                              </clef-octave-change>
                        </clef>
                  </attributes>
                  <note>
                        <pitch>
                              <step>G</step>
                              <octave>2</octave>
                        </pitch>
                        <duration>1</duration>
                        <voice>1</voice>
                        <type>quarter</type>
                        <stem>up</stem>
                        <notations>
                        </notations>
                  </note>
            </measure>
            <measure number = "2">
                  <note>
                        <pitch>
                              <step>C</step>
                              <octave>3</octave>
                        </pitch>
                        <duration>1</duration>
                        <voice>1</voice>
                        <type>quarter</type>
                        <stem>up</stem>
                        <notations>
                        </notations>
                  </note>
```

(b) musicXML codes for the first two notes of Figure 19.2.

SharpEyes NIFF to Text conversion utility (Win)

FIGURE 19.8   Text displays of first two notes of Beethoven theme in musicXML code

supports all three of the representational domains: logical, graphical, and MIDI performance. The NIFF data structure modeled its notation features on Smith's Score, added many useful functions from Bauer-Mengelberg's DARMS, and used the most-current format conventions for the computer industry at large, namely Microsoft's Resource Interchange File Format (RIFF), in its design.

NIFF files are coded as binary files and a software utility is necessary to create a text-readable display. Figure 19.8a shows a text display of NIFF codes for the staff setup and the first two notes of the Beethoven theme of Figure 19.2b. Notice both the "graphic" information codes (e.g., absolute placement, width, height, stem, barline, etc.) and the "logical" information codes (e.g., key and time signature, pitch with "0" for G and "3" for C, and duration "1/4" coded in the "notehead" attribute). By comparing this to the original notation, you can get a sense of NIFF's coding structure and the level of display detail for printing.

NIFF was designed as a wonderful cooperative venture that drew on the historical lineage of past computer-notation-coding systems. However, NIFF has not become a standard file format across music applications perhaps due to the complexities of its implementation and lack of support in Finale. Lime (CERL Sound Group [Win/Mac]), Igor (Noteheads [Win/Mac]) Personal Composer (Personal Composer, Inc. [Win]), and Sibelius notation software offer NIFF import and/or export features; SmartScore (Musitek [Win/Mac]) and SharpEyes (Visiv [Win]) music-scanning software provide NIFF export; and two Braille music-translation applications, Toccata (Optek Systems [Win]) and Goodfeel (Dancing Dots Braille Music Technology [Win]), use NIFF coding. Ararat's MIDIScorWrite [Win] provides score-to-NIFF translation.

MuseData and GUIDO

Numerous research ventures are exploring alternative music-notation-coding systems that may be used across applications and computer platforms. Hewlett's MuseData (1993) and GUIDO, developed by Hoos et al. (1996), are two examples. MuseData is the coding system behind the construction of full-text databases of numerous classical composers. The Center for Computer-Assisted Research in the Humanities (CCARH, directed by Hewlett) project has as its goal the representation of the "logical content of musical scores in a software-neutral fashion." The full-text databases are used for music printing, music analysis, and sound-file production.

We will briefly examine GUIDO, a music-representation system developed from the earlier SALIERI project of Holger Hoos and Kai Renz (University of British Columbia). GUIDO, like the DARMS code some 30 years earlier, was designed for a wide range of music applications in composition, notation, analysis, database retrieval, and performance. GUIDO has three levels of coding sophistication: Basic (the most common elements of music notation), Advanced (greater printing placement and control over notation and graphics; more sophisticated music coding for glissando, arpeggios, note clusters, different noteheads, etc.), and Extended (issues beyond conventional music notation, including user-defined tags).

Table 19.7 illustrates coding the Beethoven theme with GUIDO codes, along with an annotation of its syntax. GUIDO codes music in terms of events and tags;

TABLE 19.7 Hoos, et al.'s GUIDO Code for Beethoven Excerpt

Single-Line Code

```
[ \stemsauto \tempo<"1/4=120"> \clef< "bass"> \key<"c"> \meter< "3/4"> g-1*1/4
\bar c0*1/4 e& g \bar c1/2 e&/4 \bar d1/2 f#0*1/4 \bar g0/2. \doublebar ]
```

Analysis

[\stemsauto \tempo <"1/4=120">\clef< "bass">	Automatically set stem direction, display tempo marking of quarter-note = 120, bass clef
\key<"c"> \meter< "3/4">	Key of c-minor (lower case "c") and time signature of 3/4
g-1*1/4 \bar	Pickup measure with quarter-note g in −1 octave (middle C is 1, an octave lower is C0); the * separates the octave from the 1/4 code for a quarter-note; measure ends with a barline
c0*1/4 e& g \bar	2nd measure, note C0 is 1 octave below middle C, quarter-note ("1/4"), followed by a note E-flat (& = flat) and g in the same octave and same duration, then a barline
c1/2 e&/4 \bar	3rd measure, half-note middle C1, E-flat quarter-note, and barline ("c1*1/2 e&1*1/4" would also work, emphatically stating the octaves)
d1/2 f#0*1/4 \bar	4th measure, half-note D in the 1st octave, quarter-note F sharp in the 0 octave, barline
g0/2. \doublebar]	Last measure, dotted half-note g in the 0 octave and a double barline at the end

events describe notes and rests, tags describe various musical attributes such as clefs, key signatures, and the like. GUIDO is very extensible, including provisions for exact score-formatting information needed for printing, microtonality, and tuning systems. NoteAbility Pro (Opus 1 Music [Mac]) will read and write GUIDO notation codes. There are conversion tools for GUIDO to Sibelius, Finale, MIDI, XML, and others.

2000s: Web-Based Notation-Coding Systems

We come to the "now" of music-notation coding, publishing music notation in a format that is transportable to web and Internet publishing. There are several solutions, including direct coding in a web programming language, use of special plug-ins for notation display on the Web, and the use of graphic images of the notation.

SGML, HTML, and XML

To begin, a brief background sketch on web publishing, namely SGML, HTML, and XML web programming tools. The lineage for web-development tools can be traced back to the Generalized Markup Language (GML) developed by a team of IBM researchers led by Charles Goldfarb in the 1960s. It was formally recognized as Standard GML, or SGML, in 1986 by the International Standards Organization (ISO). SGML and its derivatives use a system of "tags" for the organization, structure, and layout of documents. The tags are uniquely recognized by the angle brackets (< and > signs) that surround them on pages of ASCII text (see Figure 19.8b for example). SGML-like tag codes are both device and operating-system independent, meaning they will work on just about any computer system. These tags are similar to those used in traditional printing and typesetting and in early word processors for PCs. The tags, in their simplest form, indicate placement and format of text, graphics, hypertext links, and the like. SGML was designed pre-Web and was used for a number of large-document projects in government and industry.

Tim Berners-Lee introduced his World Wide Web project for sharing documents over the Internet in 1991. This project embraced three key components now synonymous with what we know as the Web: URL, the Universal Resource Locator; HTTP, HyperText Transfer Protocol, which web servers use to function; and HTML, the HyperText Markup Language. HTML is a derivative of SGML (an SGML DTD, as we will see in a moment) and uses tags to control document layout for the World Wide Web and create web links or URLs between documents anywhere on the Internet.

XML, or the eXtensible Markup Language, entered the mix of web-document tools later, in 1998. XML is a simplified version of SGML; it extends HTML by providing the ability to create custom web "building blocks," so to speak, with a system of custom tags for structuring new types of data for web documents. A programmer defines the rules for the custom set of XML building blocks using "schemas" or "Document Type Definitions (DTDs)." Every set of XML tags—just as with sets of SGML tags—has a parallel schema or DTD that defines how those tags operate.

SMDL, HyTime, and Music XML Derivatives

It didn't take long for musicians to begin exploring the use of SGML and its derivatives for music notation. In 1986, Charles Goldfarb and Steven Newcomb headed a group working to define a music-markup language based on SGML. It was called the *Standard Music Description Language*, or *SMDL*. The HyTime (Hypermedia/Time-Based Structuring Language) standard for multimedia applications emerged from the efforts of SGML and was officially sanctioned by ISO in 1992. The SMDL markup language for music exists as a proposed subset of the HyTime standard.

A number of XML-based notation systems have been proposed or developed. We will note three of them: NIFFML, MEI, and MusicXML. The three distinct advantages to XML-notation solutions are that they provide a:

- text-readable format for notation coding
- web-based solution for sharing notation
- universal format for translating music notation among various coding systems.

NIFF, as previously noted, is a binary-coded representation for music notation. An XML representation for NIFF coding extends the usefulness of NIFF by providing a text-readable format for displaying NIFF codes. It also facilitates the interchange of NIFF notation data with other notation programs. Gerd Castan developed the NIFFML implementation.

In an attempt to develop a simpler, more-focused, online music-representation system, Perry Roland of the University of Virginia designed the Music Encoding Initiative (MEI). MEI, in contrast to SMDL's broadly defined music scope, concentrates on CMN (Common Music Notation). However, MEI is highly extensible and, therefore, useful for a wide variety of representational tasks. MEI is implemented as an XML DTD and thus has all the advantages of a platform-independent, open-standard, music-coding system for the Web. Roland draws on the work of the Text Encoding Initiative (for the display of literary and linguistic text), MIDI and HTML specifications, the Acoustical Society of America's system for recording pitch, and the Unicode standard set of 220 music symbols (another Roland project).

There is interest in using MEI for encoding traditional Korean music notation and for a digital library containing sheet-music images. As Roland comments, "By loosening the score-element model, you can indicate that the score contains no actual music markup at all, but rather a series of page images. The advantage of doing this in MEI is that later, when you want to add event-level information, it can be done very easily." Additional work is planned to transform MusicXML and other representations into MEI.

Probably the most extensive project is MusicXML, developed by Recordare under the leadership of Michael Good. Figure 19.8b shows the first two notes of the Beethoven theme coded as MusicXML. The XML tags are delineated by the familiar angle brackets (< >). The interpretation of these unique tags depends on MusicXML's schema or DTD. A rich number of options exist for translating music-notation coding in and out of MusicXML. On the import side, SharpEyes OMR, Finale, NIFF, and MuseData are but a few examples. On the export side, Finale, MIDI, Igor Engraver, and MuseData notation codings can be derived from MusicXML. A Finale viewer for MusicXML is distributed with Finale for Windows.

Plug-Ins for Web Music Notation

There are other alternatives for providing music notation from a web page. One is to provide a plug-in (much like Adobe Acrobat Reader or QuickTime) installed in a web browser so that it has unique programming code to display music notation. The Sibelius Scorch plug-in is an example of this. With Scorch installed, you

ASIDE
One of the first web-notation viewers was Nightingale's NoteView, provided as a helper application for web browsers, not a plug-in.

LINK
Many capabilities of the Scorch plug-in are reviewed in Module 20.

can download Sibelius proprietary music files and not only display them from a web page but also perform the music. This solution often provides high-quality display and performance over the Web, but it does not facilitate interchange with other notation programs as the XML solutions do.

Graphic Display of Web Music Notation

Music notation can be presented on the Web by using graphic images of the notation. This solution allows you to view the notation image only. Scanning music manuscript for web-page display is usually not very satisfactory due to the immense amount of detailed information on a score page. Scanning a score image at a high-enough resolution to show a satisfactory level of detail results in very large graphic files, impractical for online downloading.

Two solutions, however, seem to work reasonably well. The first is Adobe's PDF or Acrobat format. From any notation program that prints notation, with Adobe Acrobat installed, you can print the notation to an Acrobat file for subsequent display on the Web.

Another solution is the DjVu imaging format, originally developed by AT&T Labs and commercially distributed by LizardTech. The Variations2 project at Indiana University found that this imaging solution worked exceptionally well for music scores at a wide range of viewing magnifications. For both Adobe and LizardTech solutions, the author or musician creating the original file needs proprietary encoding software; the end user needs a proprietary reader to view the file. The readers are available free of change; Acrobat's PDF format is ubiquitous on the Internet.

Music Fonts for Notation

Parallel to music coding is the issue of structures for the files and fonts that support music-performing and -notation activities. Common problems occur when someone is trying to learn a new notation program: The notation generated by the printer is a curious jumble of alphanumeric characters instead of music symbols or an imported notation file is displayed without the beaming, spacing, slurs, page-layout, and other features. Both of these situations can produce a very frustrated musician! Figure 19.9 illustrates what happens when the proper music font is missing. These problems—and many others—can be explained by understanding music fonts.

FIGURE 19.9
Beethoven example displayed with and without proper music font installed; Courier font is shown in second example, instead of intended Sibelius Opus font

TIP
Remember that most music fonts are copyrighted and may require licensing fees for commercial use. However, most notation titles come with one or more fonts already licensed for your use.

Bitmapped Versus Outline Fonts

Music-notation fonts are a little different in design from other printer fonts. Keep in mind the difference between bitmapped fonts, which are created from patterns of digitized dots, and outline fonts (at first PostScript, and later TrueType and OpenType), which are created from mathematical outlines that describe the shape of each font symbol. On present-day computer systems, you don't have to worry about bitmapped fonts with jagged edges. Outline fonts are pretty much the order of the day with music-notation fonts; musicians can depend on the display and printing results being "always smooth" in most applications.

Coding Music-Font Symbols

The first PostScript music font was the Adobe Sonata font, designed by Cleo Huggins in 1986. It remains a venerable and commonly used music font. Figure 19.10 shows a sample from two music fonts: the Petrucci font (Finale) and the Fret font (freeware from Julian Plant) for notating guitar. Notice that the music symbols are matched to the ASCII alphanumeric set, with each character having a numeric code. The coding system is much like the nineteenth-century music typefaces noted earlier (Figure 19.4), with a number for every font symbol.

The keystroke for letter *e* (101), for example, gives you an eighth-note symbol, stem up in Petrucci; by adding the Shift key with the *e* (69), you get the same value with stem down. The letter *h* (104) gives you a half-note, *w* (119) a whole-note, and so on. Likewise, any guitar chord can be indicated by choosing the ASCII letter associated with the appropriate tablature. You could actually construct some music notation or provide guitar tablatures within any word-processor document by selecting a music font and looking up the corresponding ASCII characters or numeric values.

Solving music-font problems. With this background on music fonts, let's see if we can resolve the common problem with printing music that results in alphanumeric jumble on the printer page. If you do not have the PostScript, TrueType, or

ASCII	Petrucci	Frets	Numeric Code
U	⌢		85
?	𝄢	3fr.	63
&	𝄞		38
e	♪		101
h	𝅗𝅥		104
F	*mf*		70

FIGURE 19.10 Petrucci and Fret music symbols compared with ASCII characters

OpenType version of the font required by the notation program installed on your computer, the printout will be a string of alphanumeric characters. In the absence of the necessary music font, the printer substitutes its default font (which uses ASCII characters) for the music symbols. Remember, the music symbols are mapped onto the ASCII-character set used by all fonts.

If you have to purchase a music font, or if you try to use one from your other music programs, you need to be aware that many notation programs do not let you use music fonts other than the one for which the software was designed. If a program is designed for Sonata, then Sonata may be the only font you can use. Even though the music symbol may correspond to the same ASCII code, the form of each symbol in terms of height and width and other typographical factors may vary. Notation software is getting more flexible in this respect, but you still need to substitute music fonts with care.

Lots of Music Fonts

Many music fonts have been designed since Sonata in 1986, some created to add extra features and others to sidestep licensing. Finale's Petrucci and Maestro fonts and Sibelius's Opus font are examples. Others commonly used are Susato, Anastasia, Ghent, and Tamburo.

Music fonts that have the look of handwritten music charts for jazz and pop arrangements are popular. Sibelius's Inkpen font and the JazzFont designed by Richard Sigler (used in Finale) are but two examples.

Besides standard music-printing fonts, there are a host of specialty fonts. For shaped notes, there is Willard's Doremi font; Hindson's fonts for harp pedals, recorder fingerings, and saxophone fingerings; Clevenger's ChordSymbol font, which features a wide variety of analytical symbols, including Roman numerals and letter names, and figures and slashed figures in three tiers; Caltabiano's Sicilian Numerals font for Baroque figured-bass notation; the Seville font (Finale) and the Fret font (Julian Plant); and the Gregorian chant font, StMeinrad, from the Saint Meinrad Archabbey. Additionally, some notation programs let you create your own symbols. As an example, the Seville font for guitar frets is no longer provided with Finale; the Finale user can now design a custom fretboard and save the design in a library of fretboards.

ASIDE
The translation gap can be found in issues of musicianship in practice. Consider the amount of time an experienced musician spends interpretating a music performance in contrast to technique.

Is WYPWYP Music Software Possible?

You have completed the historical and analytical tour of a wide array of music-notation solutions. These notation solutions have been used in many contexts, from coding music for music analysis to publishing music on the World Wide Web. Additionally, you should now have some sense as to the nature of the fonts used to display and print music notation.

Are you beginning to get a sense of the difficulty of the "translation gap" noted at the beginning of this module? The data structures and rules for notation and translation between performance and notation are incredibly complex. Notation software designed solely for printing doesn't need any rules for translation; it is not "What You Play is What You Print" (WYPWYP) but strictly "What You See is What You Print" (WYSWYP).

On the other hand, notation software designed for composing relies heavily on rules programmed into the software for translating between the performance and notation domains. We need to see and hear what we are creating and would like to have a printed score when we are done. The more refined the rule structures, the better the translation.

Technologically, we keep getting closer, but we are not there yet. Some would say we are not even close! The rules are not refined enough to give us WYPWYP music software. Perhaps this is because the designer must make a decision about the program's bias, toward either composing or printing. If the notation software is composing biased, then it must rely heavily on rules for inferring the notation from the performance data. The notation will operate in a time-based rather than a space-based environment. When and if we do finally achieve the level of sophistication required for effective translation between notation and performance (WYPWYP software), we will probably no longer find it necessary to distinguish between sequencing software and notation software; they will have become one.

M o d u l e   2 0

Software for Music Notation

DVD-ROM
Projects 15–16 on the accompanying DVD are designed to give you hands-on experience with the features noted in Tables 20.1–4.

In Module 19, we explained important concepts about data structures for music notation, including issues of bitmapped and outlined fonts, the coding systems necessary to represent the complexity of music-notation software, and solutions for translating music-notation codes between applications and the Web. While reading that module, perhaps you were impressed with the complexity of notation software. Add to this the need for such programs to also represent the playing back of compositions that represent many different styles and you begin to sense the challenge that designers of such software face.

Although notation programs are still available that allow you to create the graphic representation only, without sound, the vast majority of all notation programs provide MIDI-based or even digital audio sound reproduction. Some even allow advanced features that do not use the literal notation but retain the performance "feel" of the live-performance input or provide intelligent reproductions of a certain performance style, such as jazz swing.

Content and Context: What Do You Need?

ASIDE
An example of a graphics-only notation program is NoteWriter [Mac] from Opus1 Music.

Many music-notation programs available today fit a number of needs. The two most popular and more-advanced products, Finale 2005 from MakeMusic! and Sibelius 3 from a company with the same name, provide the flexibility to meet the vast majority of notation tasks demanded by contemporary musicians. However, there are numerous products that cost less and may provide all the features you need.

Figure 20.1 provides examples of music notation from three very differently priced programs. Figure 20.1a was created by NotePad, a free program; Figure 20.1b came from PrintMusic!, a program that is budget priced; and Figure 20.1c was produced by Sibelius 3, a product at the higher end. Consider the following list of common uses for music-notation software, ranging from tasks that require basic features to requirements that must be supported by the most-expensive software.

- Single-line exercises for music teaching
- Short excerpts for demonstration in print or for the Internet
- Choral works for four or fewer voice parts or smaller-scale instrumental works that require basic text and notation
- Jazz charts or other applications that requires special music fonts

ASIDE
At the time of this writing, Sibelius 3 and Finale 2005 are the current software versions and are the versions referenced in Modules 19, 20, and 21.

- Arrangements or original compositions for larger ensembles with more-advanced technical capabilities
- Professionally prepared notation for large ensembles requiring "engraved" appearance
- Advanced contemporary notation requiring maximum flexibility for traditional notation and custom graphic layout

For the first two or three items on this list, notation programs that are free or cost only a few dollars might be all that you need. Figure 20.1a is a good example of this. For items further down on the list, more-expensive programs might be needed if you begin working with larger ensembles and if the music requires special notation. Figures 20.1b and c apply here.

Content is not the only set of considerations; other options related to context affect software choice. For example, how you want to distribute or purchase no-

FIGURE 20.1A Created by NotePad

FIGURE 20.1B Created by PrintMusic!

TIP

Many software companies offer a "family" of products that allow you to start with one level and move comfortably to the next without learning entirely new software. Examples include GenieSoft (ScoreWriter, Overture); Adept Music Notation Solutions (Night Light, Nightingale); goVivaldi (Vivaldi series); and Make-Music! (NotePad, Print-Music!, Finale 2005).

FIGURE 20.1C Created by Sibelius 3

tated scores is a consideration today. You may want to distribute your own scores for Internet purchase or for free with certain restrictions. You may also want to be able to print scores and parts on demand and not deal with ordering through the mail. If these options are important to you, companies like Sibelius, MakeMusic!, and goVivaldi might have the best options.

If scanning previously printed music into a notation program for further manipulation is important, you will need to determine which program does this to your satisfaction. Another input option noted in this module and Module 21 is audio input of music notation by microphone or with a pitch-to-voltage converter (see Module 18) in real time rather than a MIDI instrument. Only a few programs currently allow this. On the output side, you may want to produce intelligent accompaniment scores for solo performances—an option only provided by a limited number of titles. Finally, you may wish to invest in a notation program that offers a construction kit for designing your own plug-ins to expand the program's capability.

In the pages that follow, we will provide an overview of capabilities that will help you sort this all out. As with all other software categories in this text, we can't cover all the options and describe all the software available, but we do touch on many of the major topics and describe some of the most popular and powerful software titles available today.

Basic Operational Features

We begin with a few assumptions. You probably want a program that:

- offers traditional music notation and supports MIDI input and playback
- is based on rule structures that can be customized
- includes support for a full range of ensembles, from small chamber groups to symphony orchestras with voices
- can support a wide set of parameters, including text entry, part extraction, and excellent print quality

Many programs meet most of these basic needs; we will provide examples in the following pages. We begin by summarizing a set of operational features found in most music-notation software, followed by sections on basic note entry and advanced editing. Next comes a section on playing, printing, and saving features. We will end the module by examining some special features found in the most-advanced notation software. We will highlight Macintosh and Windows programs, providing comparison tables for seven representative products to help you compare features.

Table 20.1 compares operational features for our seven programs. Not all products include everything, especially in the lower-priced categories but each of these features help define how the programs are designed and function.

Help

The first set of items in Table 20.1 is support features to help you get started and to answer questions as you work with your notated scores. Most programs offer online help in the form of topic descriptions or the complete manual as a series of PDF files. Tutorials are offered as separate documents or as part of the manual. Many programs offer links to their support pages on the Internet. Finale 2005 offers video help in the form of animated movies that come as part of the installation CD.

When you first open a notation program, several options are presented to help you get started. Many programs offer templates of previously created scores, including Overture, as shown in Figure 20.2. Templates are designed to represent several standard score setups for instrumental and vocal compositions and, if you don't see one that meets your needs, most programs will let you customize your own.

Another approach to new score design is shown in Figure 20.3, Noteability Pro. Here the software provides a setup page with many options for score size, system and staff layout, and customization options. Still other programs, such as the MakeMusic! titles and Sibelius 3, use a step-by-step "wizard" that provides a series of options for creating new scores. If you open a previously saved score, these options are not offered. Any of these early decisions about score setup can be easily changed at any time you're working with the composition.

TIP
The subtleties of interface design for notation programs and their relative ease of use versus their range of capability have been debated endlessly in music-technology circles. Today's software represents some of the best solutions for users, so try out each program to see what fits your preferences.

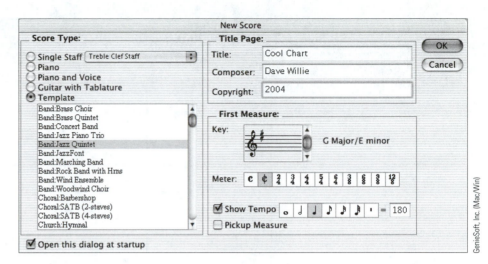

FIGURE 20.2 Template possibilities for Overture 3

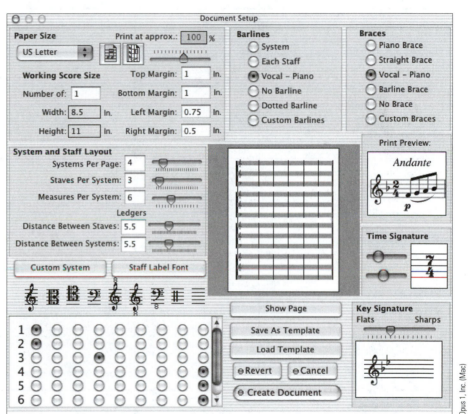

FIGURE 20.3 Score setup in NoteAbility Pro

Interface Design

The seven programs reviewed here all use three primary approaches for user interaction: menus, floating palettes, and dialog boxes. Computer-keyboard shortcuts are also offered by each program and most titles allow you to customize the shortcuts. However, the differences in how each program uses these interface properties require you to take some time to become used to how things work.

For example, the MakeMusic! family (NotePad, PrintMusic!, and Finale 2005) use an extensive number of floating palettes. Each of these palettes can be resized, hidden, and placed anywhere on the screen. Figure 20.4 displays a number of these palettes for Finale 2005. Using the Main and Advanced tool palettes is an important initial step in working with Finale 2005 and related programs. The type of

TABLE 20.1 Basic Operational Features of Selected Notation Programs

Feature	NotePad	PrintMusic!	Vivaldi Gold
Company	MakeMusic!	MakeMusic!	goVivaldi
Platform	Mac/PC	Mac/PC	Mac/PC
Pricing	Free	Entry	Mid-range
Help	✔	✔ (Manual)	✔
Tutorials	✔ (Online)		✔ (Online)
Video Tutorials		✔	
Setup Wizard	✔	✔	
Score Templates		✔	
Multiple Palettes, Boxes, and Menus	✔	✔	
Resizes Palettes	✔	✔	
Opens Multiple Scores	✔	✔	✔
Shifts Between Score/Parts		✔	✔
Variety of Note-Input Techniques	✔	✔	✔
Imports/Exports MIDI File		✔	✔
Imports MIDI-File Options			Limited
Rhythmic Values Supported	Whole to 32nd	Double Whole to 128th	Double Whole to 128th
Page Views	Full Page	Full Page and Scroll	Full Page
Reduces/Enlarges Scores	✔	✔	✔
Rulers		✔	
Colors for Elements		✔	✔
Fonts Included	✔	Multiple	✔
Third-Party Fonts Allowed			✔
MIDI-Based Playback	✔	✔	✔
Prints to Postscript Printers	✔	✔	✔
Extracts Parts		✔	✔

TABLE 20.1   *(continued)*

Feature	Overture 3	NoteAbility Pro	Finale 2005	Sibelius 3
Company	Genie-Soft	Opus 1 Music	MakeMusic!	Sibelius
Platform	Mac/PC	Mac	Mac/PC	Mac/PC
Pricing	Mid-range	Pro	Pro	Pro
Help		✔ (Manual)	✔ (Manual)	✔
Tutorials			✔ (Online and in Manual)	✔ (Printed Separately)
Video Tutorials	✔		✔	
Setup Wizard			✔	✔
Score Templates	✔	✔	✔	
Multiple Palettes, Boxes, and Menus	✔	✔	✔	✔
Resizes Palettes			✔	✔
Opens Multiple Scores	✔	✔	✔	✔
Shifts Between Score/Parts		✔	✔	✔
Variety of Note-Input Techniques	✔	✔	✔	✔
Imports/Exports MIDI File		✔	✔	✔
Imports MIDI-File Options	✔	✔	✔	✔
Rhythmic Values Supported	Triple Dotted Whole to 128th	Double Whole to 128th	Double Whole to 128th	Double Whole to 512th
Page Views	Full Page	Full Page	Full Page and Scroll	Full Page and Preview Selected Staff
Reduces/Enlarges Scores	✔	✔	✔	✔
Rulers	✔	✔	✔	✔
Colors for Elements		✔	✔	✔
Fonts Included	✔	✔	Multiple	Multiple
Third-Party Fonts Allowed	✔	✔	✔	
MIDI-Based Playback	✔	✔	✔	✔
Prints to Postscript Printers	✔	✔	✔	✔
Extracts Parts		✔	✔	✔

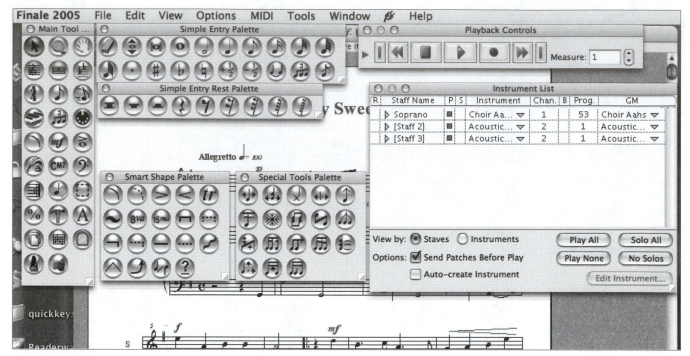

FIGURE 20.4 Overview of Finale 2005

tool chosen affects menu display and the way the program expects you to work with the score. Other palettes are used as the editing process continues. We have also displayed one important dialog box, the instrument list, which helps control the playback options. Typically, not all these palettes are displayed at one time, especially on smaller screens.

NoteAbility Pro takes a different approach (Figure 20.5). It has one major palette toolbar to the left and a vertical set of tools that form the header at the top of the screen. Two major dialog boxes, the Control and NoteAbility Inspector boxes, are the center of action. The Control box deals with formatting and playing back scores. The Inspector box contains two pull-down windows that link to attributes for accidentals, bar lines, measures, ties, symbols, tremolos, and 30 other categories. Choosing one of these attribute sets causes the dialog box to display specific options. NoteAbility Pro has 20 additional dialog boxes that control options for such functions as part extraction; lute, guitar, and dulcimer notation; and MIDI-playback settings.

Overture and Vivaldi Gold use palettes and boxes in similar ways and menus play a strong role in their interfaces. Overture features "tear-off" palettes from a vertical toolbar header and Vivaldi Gold uses movable palettes much like Finale 2005. Sibelius 3, on the other hand, combines a number of its options in the Keypad and Properties dialog boxes. Sibelius 3 also has a handy Navigator box for moving around the score and a Mixer for setting levels of either MIDI- or digital audio playback.

All of the user interfaces provide the ability to open multiple scores and to copy and paste between scores. Extracted parts can be opened at the same time as the full scores for most software, but intelligent linking between parts and scores (changes in a part or score automatically reflected in the respective score or part) is not yet supported for any of the seven software titles reviewed here.

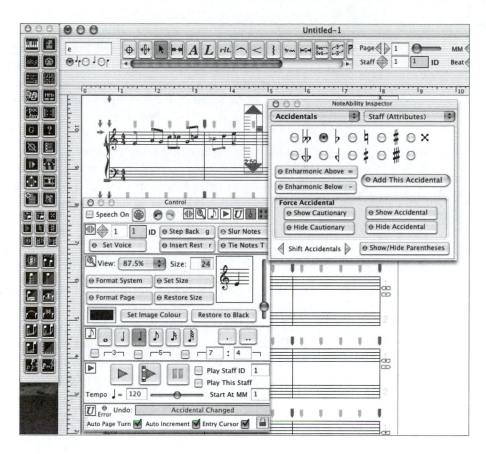

FIGURE 20.5   Overview of NoteAbility Pro

Getting Started

Today's notation software offers many note-entry options that most programs support; we will review these in more depth in the next section of this module. Simple note entry using the mouse, keypad, or other pointing device is the most basic approach and this process is aided by many computer-keyboard options such as shortcuts. A skilled user of music-notation software will develop a facile approach to using the mouse and computer keyboard to enter note data. MIDI devices can also be used by each program to help identify the actual pitches to enter and to enter music in real time.

All programs, with the exception of the free version of NotePad, can import and export MIDI files. (An upgrade—NotePad Plus—does allow MIDI capability and is available for a small additional cost.) Fewer of the programs reviewed, however, offer options for treating imported MIDI files.

Not all programs support exactly the same rhythmic values for notes and rests. The double whole-note value to the 128th note seems to be the norm for most of the seven programs reviewed here, but be aware of this limitation if your music is rhythmically demanding in terms of note values.

Score Display

Score display is an important consideration for software choice. The programs reviewed here offer a number of options for viewing your work. For example, Print Music! and Finale 2005 allow the entire score to be displayed in full-page view or in a "scroll" view that shows a system as a continuous stream. Sibelius 3 offers the same full-page view, plus a way to preview selected staves.

LINK

If you need to remember what terms such as "continuous data" or "quantization" mean, return to Viewport V and MIDI sequencing.

All of the software in our table comparison can resize a full score either larger or smaller, with the more advanced titles offering very precise percentages. This can be very important for working with very closely positioned score elements or for arranging views on smaller screens. Controlling precise placement of score elements can be aided by graphic rulers and other guideline grids. Figure 20.5 shows how this is done with NoteAbility Pro.

Most interfaces at least allow color coding for different lines of music on a staff and for text. Some of the more-advanced programs allow you to color a number of additional elements. Finally, music notation fonts are not limited to one installed version. Most titles support the installation of a third-party font as a substitute for what is provided, and three or more of the programs reviewed here provide at least a jazz font as an alternative.

Playback, Printing, and Distribution

Music-notation programs give you the ability to hear notation played back, allowing you to audit compositional decisions and check for errors. MIDI-based playback is the most common option and software allows you to assign staves either to MIDI devices connected to your computer or to soft synths installed on your computer. Figure 20.6 shows options for Vivaldi Gold. Using the mixer window in this software, you can assign tracks to an external device, resources in the sound card, or a soft synth. In this case, you see options for the Tascam US-428 interface, which is connected to an external MIDI device and the Microsoft GS Wavetable SW soft synth. The QuickTime Musical Instruments (referred to as the DLS Sound Set in Mac OS X) sound set might also be an option. For Sibelius 3, users can also choose the included soft synth, Kontakt Silver, from Native Instruments or elect to purchase the Gold version for additional sounds. Finale 2005 users may choose the SmartMusic SoftSynth.

All the programs reviewed here support printing to Postscript-based printers and work well with both inkjet and laser devices. Fonts used in notation programs are outline fonts (vector-based graphics) and can be scaled to different sizes

LINK

Be sure to read Modules 19 and 21 for more information about fonts and how printers work with notation programs.

TIP

How well you set the details for each instrument in your full score will pay off with more accurate notation when you extract the parts.

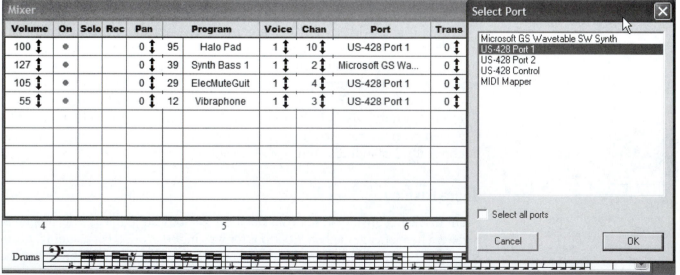

FIGURE 20.6 Mixer from Vivaldi Gold

without distortion. Just about any printer available today will produce excellent results.

All programs, except for NotePad, will extract parts. However, the more-expensive programs offer more control over this process. Figures 20.7a and b show options for part extraction and a resulting part using Sibelius 3. Notice the controls offered for layout, document size, spacing, transposition, and other functions. The resulting part contains compressed measures of rest and all the articulation and dynamics detail from the main score. The part itself is a file that can be edited for spacing and other details, if necessary.

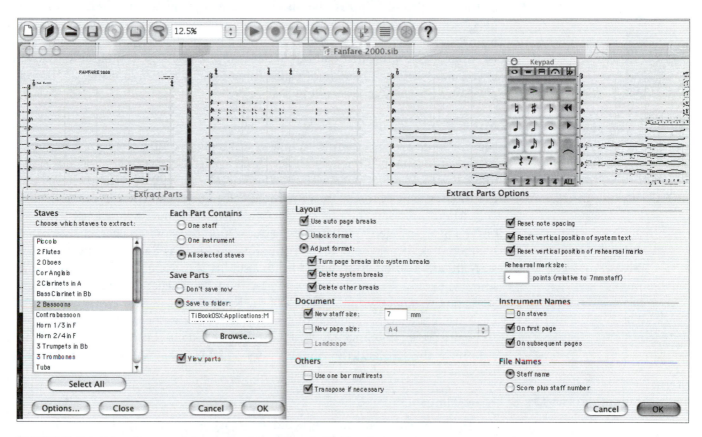

FIGURE 20.7A   Score and part-extraction options in Sibelius 3

FIGURE 20.7B   Part extracted using Sibelius 3

DVD-ROM
Project 15 Beginning Note-Entry Skills

ASIDE
You can use the computer keyboard to enter pitch information and the numeric keypad to enter rhythm and other notation information.

LINK
See hardware items noted in Module 21.

ASIDE
With each new version of Finale, Simple Entry becomes more like Speedy Entry (step-time); the MIDI keyboard can now be fully used in Simple Entry as well as many of the Speed Entry keyboard shortcuts.

Note Entry and Basic Score Design

Table 20.2, on page 370, lists features related to note entry and score design for our seven programs. We summarize these in this section and will expand your knowledge of how programs do more advanced editing in the next section.

Methods of Note Entry

In the last section, we noted that most music software programs will import MIDI files created by other programs. Certain titles will even allow you to import other formats. However, when it comes to entering music that does not previously exist, there are four distinct methods: mouse only, mouse with computer- or MIDI-keyboard assistance (sometimes called "step-time"), real time using a MIDI or acoustic instrument, and scanning.

Mouse Only

Simple note entry by pointing and clicking a mouse pointer, the most basic form of note entry, involves frequent choices from a palette or dialog box. Figures 20.8a and b show how this is done with Sibelius 3 and Finale 2005. With Sibelius 3, you use the Keypad box to choose a rhythmic value and then click the mouse on the staff where you want the note to go. As shown in Figure 20.8a, we are about to enter a quarter note to replace the quarter rest on the staff. You can choose other characteristics from the options in the Keypad, such as dotted rhythms, ties, or staccato articulation. Rests are added in a similar way using the rest button in the lower left of the Keypad. Sibelius 3 allows up to four separate voices on a single staff and the numbers on the button of the Keypad control this. As with any note entry using the mouse, computer-keyboard shortcuts can speed the process greatly. In Figure 20.8b, the Simple Entry tool in Finale 2005 is chosen in the Main Tool palette to the left, and the Simple Entry and Rest palettes are used to specify placement.

Step-Time

Mouse entry with computer-keyboard assistance is very precise, but also slow for those with some piano keyboard skill. You probably won't use this approach for most of your note entry, reserving it for more detailed work. Step-time entry is much faster because you can use a MIDI device or, in the case of Finale 2005, an acoustic instrument or human voice to specify pitch values. Figure 20.9 displays how this is done in Finale 2005 using "speedy entry." You choose the Speedy Entry Tool from the Main Tool palette and then click on a measure. The entry box appears, ready to accept a specific rhythmic value from the computer keyboard and a MIDI-note value from an attached instrument. As we have revealed in the menu, Finale 2005 provides a number of additional navigation shortcuts with this entry method.

Real Time

An even-faster method of note entry is real time. In Sibelius 3 (Figure 20.10 on page 372), this approach is called "Flexi-time." With this method, you simply set a metronome to provide a tempo, click on the desired measure in which you would like the recording to begin, wait for the one-bar count-in (or more if you want), and then start to play on a MIDI device. Sibelius 3 interprets your performance as

FIGURE 20.8A Sibelius
3 mouse entry

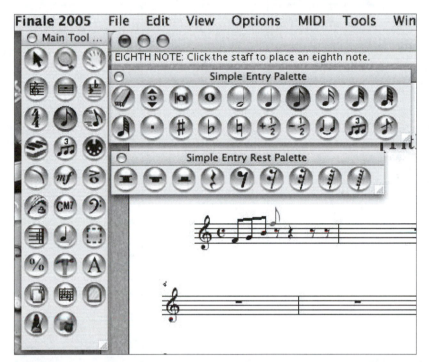

FIGURE 20.8B Finale
2005 mouse entry

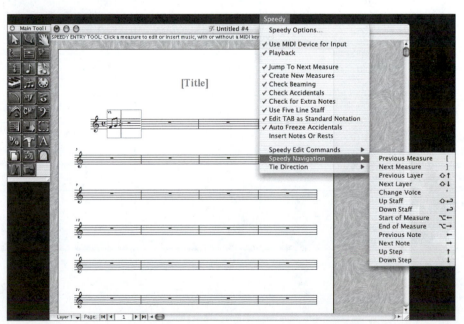

FIGURE 20.9 Step-time
note entry in Finale 2005

TABLE 20.2 Basic Note Entry and Score Design Features of Selected Notation Programs

Feature	NotePad	PrintMusic!	Vivaldi Gold
Company	MakeMusic!	MakeMusic!	goVivaldi
Platform	Mac/PC	Mac/PC	Mac/PC
Pricing	Free	Entry	Mid-range
Mouse: Point and Click	✔	✔	✔
Computer Keyboard	✔	✔	✔
MIDI Device		✔	✔
Step-Time Entry		✔	✔
Real-Time MIDI Entry with Computer Beat		HyperScribe	✔
Real-Time MIDI Entry with User-Defined Beat		HyperScribe	
Record Track/Hear Other		✔	
Acoustic Instrument			
Scanning Software Included		MIDIScan	Vivaldi Scan
Mass Editing	Cut, Copy, Paste	Cut, Copy, Insert, Paste	Cut, Copy, Paste, Clear
Number of Staves	8	24	Unlimited
Lines per Staff	5	1 or 5	Unlimited
Layers/Voices per Staff	4/2	4/2	8 voices
Standard/Nonstandard Key Signatures	Standard	Standard	Standard
Standard/Nonstandard Time Signatures	Standard	Standard	Both
Polytonality			✔
Clefs for Pitched Instruments and Percussion	4	8	11
Multiple Clefs in Measure			
Custom Noteheads			✔

TABLE 20.2 (continued)

Feature	Overture 3	NoteAbility Pro	Finale 2005	Sibelius 3
Company	Genie-Soft	Opus 1 Music	MakeMusic!	Sibelius
Platform	Mac/PC	Mac	Mac/PC	Mac/PC
Pricing	Mid-range	Pro	Pro	Pro
Mouse: Point and Click	✔	✔	✔	✔
Computer Keyboard	✔	✔	✔	✔
MIDI Device	✔	✔	✔	✔
Step-Time Entry	✔	✔	✔	✔
Real-Time MIDI Entry with Computer Beat	✔	✔	HyperScribe	Flexi-Time
Real-Time MIDI Entry with User-Defined Beat			HyperScribe	Flexi-Time
Record Track/Hear Other			✔	✔
Acoustic Instrument			MicNotator	
Scanning Software Included			SmartScore Lite	PhotoScore Lite
Mass Editing	Cut, Copy, Paste, Clear, Merge, Paste Special	Cut, Copy, Insert, Delete, Copy All Types, Paste Into, Paste Exact, Paste Over	Cut, Copy, Insert, Paste, Mirror	Cut, Copy, Paste, Delete
Number of Staves	64	Unlimited	Unlimited	Unlimited
Lines per Staff	0–16	1–6	0–100	Unlimited
Layers/Voices per Staff	8 voices	3	4/2	4
Standard/Nonstandard Key Signatures	Standard	Standard	Both	Standard
Standard/Nonstandard Time Signatures	Standard	Both	Both	Both
Polytonality	✔		✔	✔
Clefs for Pitched Instruments and Percussion	10	8	16, plus custom	25
Multiple Clefs in Measure			✔	✔
Custom Noteheads	✔	✔	✔	✔

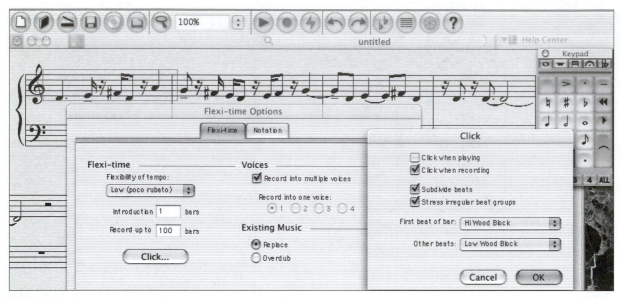

FIGURE 20.10   Flexi-time note entry in Sibelius 3

LINK
Entering music in real time with notation programs is similar to the process followed in sequencing programs reviewed in Viewport V. Some notation programs will even allow you to hear the other tracks as you record.

LINK
Read the description of optical music recognition (OMR) in Module 21.

best it can and notates the music. The program will follow your performance, adjusting to changes in tempo. After the music is recorded, you can return to the score and edit any errors using the methods previously described. Music can be recorded into multiple voices and staves as well.

Finale 2005 accomplishes a similar note-entry technique using its "Hyper-Scribe" tool. In Finale 2005, the user can specify a click track, or play music without such a track and add the beat points after the music is recorded. Finale 2005 also allows the player to add a click track interactively during performance, as well with a MIDI foot pedal or other defined MIDI value. For the Finale 2005 program, a microphone can also be used to capture pitch information acoustically for real-time entry of individual lines.

With both programs and with other software that supports real-time note entry, a quantized note value can be used to help accuracy during recording. The software does its best job capturing other performance data as well, such as articulation and dynamics. Obviously, the more accurate the playing, the better the results. Practice with all entry alternatives available in a notation program; you will find yourself using combinations of these to best fit the needs of the scoring task at hand.

Scanning

A surprising number of notation-software programs now support scanned input or optical music recognition (OMR). Improvements in the quality of scanners and in the software-recognition programs themselves have reached a point where scanning is a viable method for note entry when a printed score needs to be turned into a digital copy. Remember that scanning copyrighted music is illegal except under specific fair-use situations.

Sibelius 3 and Finale 2005 include "lite" versions of scanning software that work with their notation programs. For example, Sibelius 3 includes PhotoScore (Neuratron) Lite with its distribution. The program is designed to read up to 12 staves with single voices on each staff. The "lite" version is limited to note resolution of up to 16th-notes and does not recognize slurs, articulation marks, text, and other diacriticals. The professional version, which costs more, can read scores of up to 32 staves with multiple voices, can handle up to 128th-notes, and recognizes a number of notation marks, including guitar tabulature and chord symbols.

LINK
See Module 19 for a description of XML and NIFF formats.

Figure 20.11 displays PhotoScore Lite reading a scanned page of music. The program begins by linking to the scanner and scans in the music. It then "reads" the scan, creating a page of notation that represents the music. While still in PhotoScore Lite, you can correct any rhythm errors before asking the program to open the score in Sibelius 3 for further processing. The "lite" version supports up to 20 pages for a file, but the professional version can handle many more. The professional version can also save files in the MusicXML and NIFF formats, which can be read by programs other than Sibelius 3. Scanning software for the Finale 2005 family of products and Vivaldi Scan work in similar ways.

Mass Editing

Once a certain number of note values and other elements are in place, each of our seven software titles offers techniques for "selecting" these elements for further processing. Since we know that all styles of music use many repeated patterns rhythmically and melodically, looking for ways to copy and paste can save time. Also, cutting, moving, and transposing sections as your ideas develop is common. A review of our seven programs shows many common options, but certain programs offer additional special techniques. Here's an explanation of the techniques you can expect:

- *Cut.* This command removes the selected musical elements from a staff and places the material on the clipboard for possible pasting elsewhere. The measure structure is usually retained. In the case of the MakeMusic! family of software, the programs ask if the measures are also to be cut.
- *Delete/Clear.* This command removes the selected material, but does not copy to the clipboard.
- *Copy.* The copy command places a copy of the material on the clipboard for possible pasting elsewhere, but does not remove the original material.
- *Paste/Paste Into.* Material from the clipboard is pasted into a new location with the new location's context (time and key signature, staves, measure lengths, etc.) affecting the nature of the new material.
- *Paste Exact.* The exact nature of the original material is retained regardless of the new location context.

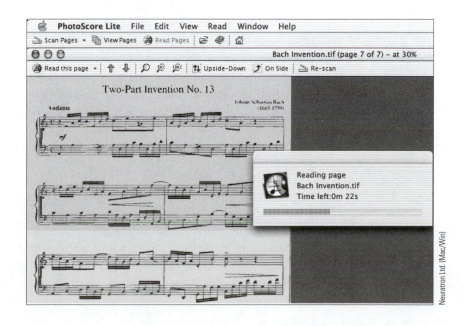

FIGURE 20.11
Scanned page from PhotoScore Lite

- *Paste Special*. Offers a dialog box that allows you to choose the kind of material (notes, chords, lyrics, meter, tempo changes, text) you wish to have pasted.
- *Paste Over*. Material is pasted over any existing material.
- *Merge*. Material is pasted into existing material without deleting the original material.
- *Insert*. Music is pasted into the new location, but existing music is shifted to the right.
- *Mirror*. Mirroring is a special tool in Finale 2005 (found in the Advanced Tool palette—see Figure 20.4) that allows you to identify measures and individual elements that are linked to each other. If an editing option is exercised with mirrored music, the change is made in all the mirrored material associated with it.

Keep in mind that the Edit menu for a certain program might not contain a technique in the list above, but there may be other ways that the software accomplishes the task. For example, NotePad and PrintMusic! do not have a "Clear" option in the Edit menu, but the program prompts users when using the Cut command about cutting only the music or the measures and the music. Finale embeds a number of these features within its Mass Mover tool. Sibelius 3 accomplishes many subtle cut, copy, and paste functions with special keyboard options.

Other Basic Features for Score Design

The remainder of Table 20.2 lists basic capabilities that can be used in the preliminary stages of score creation. Note values supported are usually double whole-notes to 128th-notes, but some exceptions are clearly shown.

Staves

The number of staves varies greatly from program to program and is a major difference that separates applications at different price points. The numbers of lines per staff can also be altered greatly in different programs and this is important for scores that demand elaborate percussion parts or that use guitar and lute tablature.

Figure 20.12 shows options for choosing voices for a single staff. This is an important option for those who want to write multiple lines of music with different rhythm patterns on a single staff and control the direction of note stems. Different voices can allow you to create complicated keyboard music and can be used effectively in writing large ensemble scores where a staff must contain, for example, a first- and second-flute part in order to save space. Voice creation is handled in different ways in our seven programs, using straight voices or layers with multiple voices. When it comes time to print, part-extraction techniques differ greatly for handling individual voices on a staff, with more expensive programs offering the best options. Usually, you can give each voice a separate instrument timbre for the purposes of playback, but this varies from program to program as well.

Time and Key Signatures

Standard options for time and key signatures can be expected for all notation programs and opening setup routines can handle their construction in a routine way. However, these signatures can be changed anywhere in the score. Standard key signatures include the usual range of up to seven sharps or seven flats in either major or minor keys; standard time signatures are basic duple and triple foreground and background signatures.

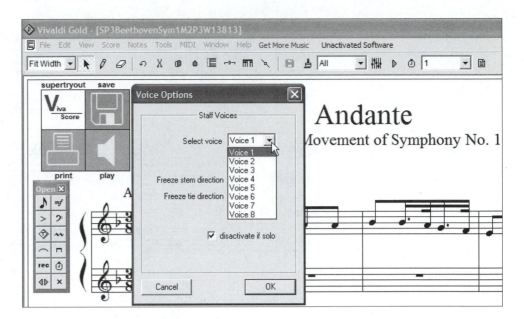

FIGURE 20.12 Voice assignment in Vivaldi Gold

Nonstandard time and key signatures are possible with more advanced programs. For example, Figure 20.13 shows dialog boxes for creating nonstandard time and key signatures in Finale 2005. In terms of unusual time signatures, the larger box in the background is in two parts: The top section is used to control the beaming pattern of the eighth notes and the bottom section is used to create the meter signature as it appears in the music. The smaller box to the lower right is used to specify the beat groups and durations. For unusual key signatures, the box to the lower left is used to specify nonstandard keys. Finale 2005 allows you to create nonlinear keys (keys that do not conform to the circle of fifths) that have scales with microtonal steps or a different order of half and whole steps than found in common scales. Such arrangements lead to nonstandard key signatures. Polytonality is

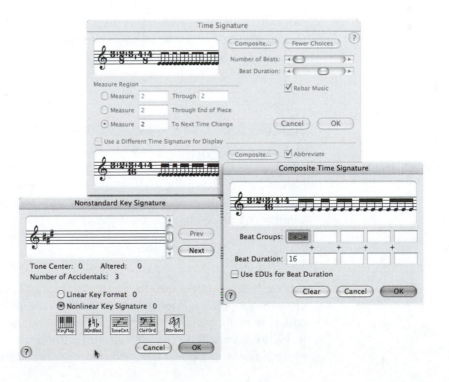

FIGURE 20.13 Setting nonstandard time and key signatures in Finale 2005

FIGURE 20.14
Notehead options in
Overture 3

also possible in notation software; this is not the same as having staves in different keys for transposing instruments, but means that some programs will support multiple keys occurring at the same time.

Clefs

A wide variety of clefs is possible with today's notation software, including the option for no clef at all. Having the option for no clef can make the notation of nonpitched or more-exotic instruments much more accurate. No clef might also be useful in contemporary writing with voices, where a choir might be doing special effects with no pitch content. Clefs may be used multiple times in a single measure, but, as Table 20.2 shows, the number of programs that support this is limited.

Noteheads

Noteheads can be customized for various styles of music and for specific functions. Multiple style noteheads are critical for writing percussion parts and for jazz and special notational needs. Figure 20.14 shows the Overture 3 options for a variety of different notehead shapes.

DVD-ROM
Project 16 More Notation
Skills and Music Scanning

Advanced Editing

Now that you have the basic notes in place and the score designed, it is quite likely that you'll want to apply some careful touches. This section will describe some of the more-important careful editing options.

Editing Aids

To begin, a few general tools are worth noting. Each program has a set of preferences or program options that are especially useful for editing. These options vary widely in scope across programs. Program preferences for Overture 3 are displayed in Figure 20.15. Note the options for defining where to save documents, whether to drag notes chromatically, and other general options that affect the interface.

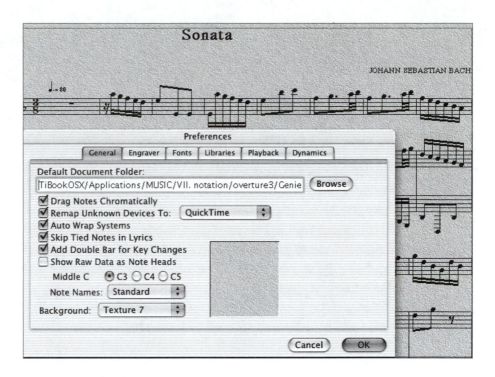

FIGURE 20.15
Preferences in Overture 3

TIP
Use the explode tool on small sections of music for best results; don't try to use it on an entire piece of music!

TIP
You may wonder why a "unison" transposition interval is included. The answer is that, to avoid certain awkward accidentals, choosing to transpose an augmented unison creates a nice movement of the notes up a half step. If you transpose to a very remote key (e.g., B flat to D sharp), it's recommended that you do so in intermediate stages.

Other tabs include engraver rules, font-choice library options, and playback and dynamics choices.

More-advanced software, such as Sibelius 3 and Finale 2005, offers global options for exact element placement. Engraver rules in Sibelius 3 specify the exact placement of spaces, dots, and many other settings that help to make the entire score uniform and acceptable for performers and publishers. Such adjustments, including preferences for music fonts, can be saved as "House Rules" and applied to other compositions created in the same style. Although it is possible to adjust all elements by hand in most programs, these global rules can be very helpful in preparing scores.

Other tools that help with careful editing include the Find options and support for multiple undos. The Find command works very much like similar commands in word processors and databases. You select a passage of music and the Find command executes a search of the musical score for similar music. Figure 20.16 displays options for the Find command in Sibelius 3. This option is a powerful way to locate similar patterns within a score, saving the composer time.

The option for multiple undos has been a very welcome addition to notation programs in the last few years. This feature allows you to retrace your actions, undoing at each step the actions you took using the program.

Transposition and Automatic Arrangements

Transposition of Notes, Passages, and Scores

Transposition commands can be applied to individual notes, selected passages of music, or an entire composition. The key can be changed or remain the same and transposition can be based on an exact number of half steps (often called "chromatic") or on an interval regardless of steps (often called "diatonic").

Each program accomplishes transposition somewhat differently. Sibelius 3 allows you to transpose up or down and specify an interval that ranges from a unison

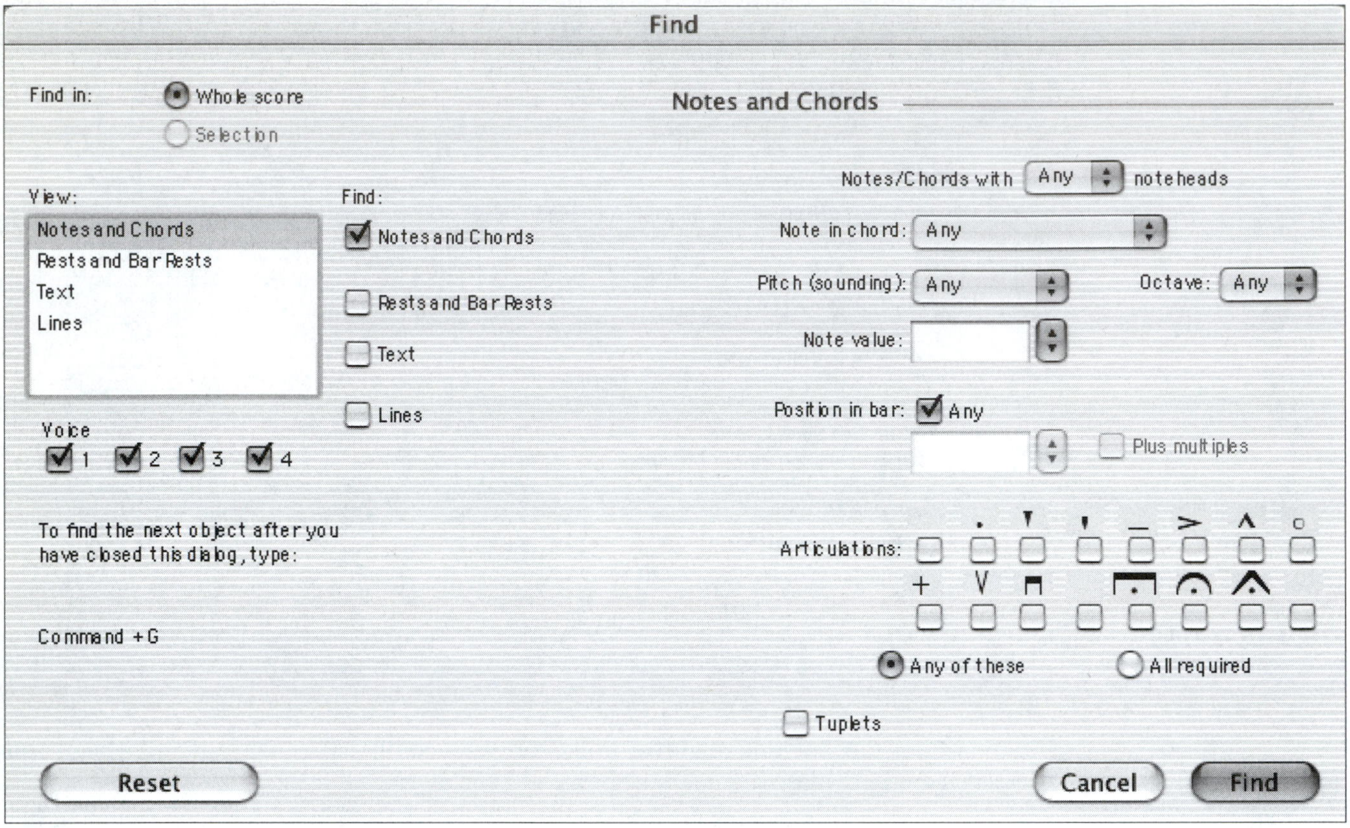

FIGURE 20.16   Find command in Sibelius 3

to two octaves. You can elect to transpose the key (recommended if you are transposing a multipart score from one key to another) and to use double sharps and flats. You can also specify half-step options by choosing major/perfect, diatonic, augmented, or diminished.

Figure 20.17 displays how these work in practice with an interval transposition of a semitone up. The original is changed diatonically in such a way that the notes retain the accidentals but move up a semitone. This results in different arrangements of half steps depending on the original note. The major/perfect solution (called "chromatic" by many programs) preserves the number of half steps. The augmented solution uses the major/perfect option, then raises the result by a half step. The diminished solution uses the major/perfect option and lowers the result by a half step. In practice, you're likely to use the latter three options, which preserve the exact relationship of half steps.

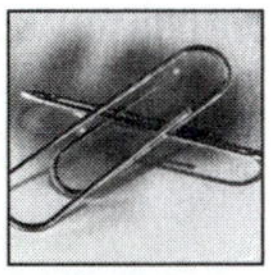

Transposing Instruments

Transposition is also necessary for scores that have instruments acoustically designed to play in certain keys other than concert "C" that traditionally read a transposed score (transposing instruments). Arrangers and composers must be conscious of how these transpositions work. You can quickly flip between concert and transposing pitch—the software is pretty smart about knowing what it needs to do with transposing instruments during entry, editing, and extracting parts. Fortunately, notation programs have built-in rules that account for these key changes for transposing instruments.

LINK

Finale 2005 features a plug-in for auto-harmonization based on the algorithms in the Band-in-a-Box software. See the plug-ins section at the end of this module and Module 23, Viewport VIII, on CAI.

FIGURE 20.17 Results of applying transposing options in Sibelius 3

Intelligent Arranging

A new feature in recent years for more-advanced programs is the explode or arrange capability and the ability to reduce larger scores to a piano score. Music from one system is selected and then automatically exploded or arranged into another more-expanded system. Usually this involves selecting piano music or other source material in a close and compact arrangement and then rescoring the music into a fuller score, such as an orchestra or band. The notation software either explodes the music line by line into the new score, as is the case with Finale 2005 (Figure 20.18), or more intelligently arranges the music using an internal formula, as in Sibelius 3 (Figures 20.19a and b).

The mass-mover tool in Finale 2005 is used to select the music to be exploded and then displays a dialog box that gives directions about how to split the music

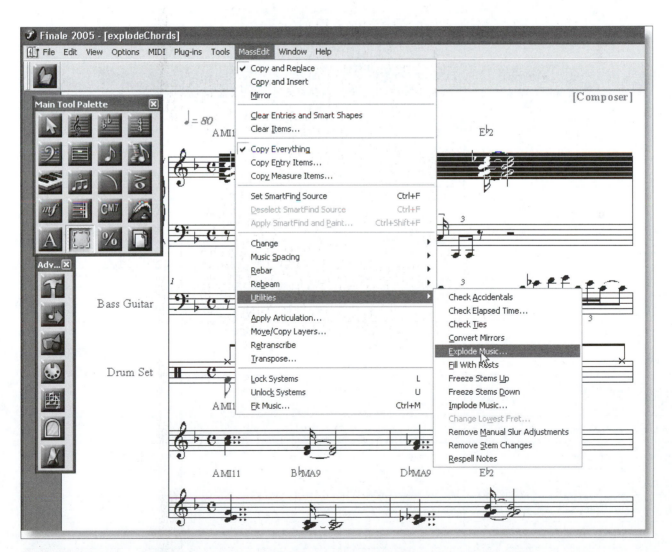

FIGURE 20.18 Using the mass-mover tool to select a passage for exploding in Finale 2005

into staves. The new music is then added where directed and you can edit from that point on.

The steps for this in Sibelius 3 are similar, except the program attempts to make intelligent decisions about where to place the music in the new score. In Figure 20.19a, on page 384, a piece of Chopin piano music is chosen and copied, a new score is created (in this case a piece for wind band), an arranging style is selected (Figure 20.19b on page 384), and then the result is created. The music is scored first in concert pitch and then parts will be automatically transposed before printing. Obviously, these options for exploding and arranging are only conveniences; composers and arrangers must then work with the parts to make it musical.

Still more-powerful tools for intelligent arranging are available. The opposite process can be accomplished by these same programs when a piano reduction is necessary. The music to be reduced is chosen and a command is given to reduce the music to a piano score.

Enhancing the Score

The next set of advanced editing features in Table 20.3 is designed to enhance both the musical expression of the score and its appearance. This is the core of "careful" editing.

TABLE 20.3   Advanced Editing Features of Selected Notation Programs

Feature	NotePad	PrintMusic!	Vivaldi Gold
Company	MakeMusic!	MakeMusic!	goVivaldi
Platform	Mac/PC	Mac/PC	Mac/PC
Pricing	Free	Entry	Mid-range
Program Preferences	✔	✔	✔
Find/Search			
Multiple Undos	✔	✔	✔
Transpose Options		✔	✔
Intelligent Arranging			
Time/Key Signature Change	✔	✔	✔
Expression, Articulation, and Line Markings	✔	✔	✔
Custom Graphic Creation			
Measures Attributes	Limited	Limited	Limited
Rehearsal/Measure Numbers		✔	
Brackets and Braces		✔	✔
Rebeam		✔	✔

ASIDE
Keep in mind that markings such as these are not recorded when you save your work as a MIDI file, but may be saved when using NIFF or musicXML file formats.

Time and Key-Signature Changes

After you make initial decisions about time and key signatures in setting up scores, you may change your mind about these settings or want to change meters or keys as the piece develops. Most of our seven programs in Table 20.3 can handle this, including adding alert accidentals for key changes.

Articulation, Expression, and Line Marking

Notation programs provide various ways to enter articulation, expression, and line markings of various kinds. Most software has custom-graphics capabilities, but represent the more conventional symbols in some way for easy entry. Figure 20.20, on page 384, shows a simple score being edited with expression markings and articulations. Notice the tools to the right for slurs, crescendos, decrescendos, trills, and the like. Articulations are added note by note or by choosing a passage and adding them for all the notes.

Standard expression markings, line types (arrows, glissandos, repeat markings), and fermata types are all supported by most programs; however, some do a more complete job than others. Generally, the notes are added first and these markings are then inserted during the careful-editing phase. Most programs also support playing back these markings with default MIDI values that are defined in a changeable database within the program. Additionally, these added markings are

TABLE 20.3   *(continued)*

Feature	Overture 3	NoteAbility Pro	Finale 2005	Sibelius 3
Company	Genie-Soft	Opus 1 Music	MakeMusic!	Sibelius
Platform	Mac/PC	Mac	Mac/PC	Mac/PC
Pricing	Mid-range	Pro	Pro	Pro
Program Preferences	✔	✔	✔	✔
Find/Search			✔	✔
Multiple Undos		✔	✔	✔
Transpose Options	✔	✔	✔	✔
Intelligent Arranging			✔	✔
Time/Key Signature Change	✔	✔	✔	✔
Expression, Articulation, and Line Markings	✔	✔	✔	✔
Custom Graphic Creation		✔	✔	✔
Measures Attributes	Extensive	Extensive	Extensive	Extensive
Rehearsal/Measure Numbers	✔	v	✔	✔
Brackets and Braces	✔	✔	✔	✔
Rebeam	✔	✔	✔	✔

(continued)

TABLE 20.3   Advanced Editing Features of Selected Notation Programs *(continued)*

Feature	NotePad	PrintMusic!	Vivaldi Gold
Cross-Staff Beaming			✔
Repositions/Adjusts Elements by Mouse (notes/slurs, etc.)	✔	✔	✔
Controls Stem Direction		✔	✔
Collision Avoidance			
Tuplets	Limited	Limited	Limited
Text Entry for Title, Credits	✔	✔	✔
Block Text		✔	✔
Alters Staff Name		✔	
Lyrics Lines Allowed	1	Unlimited	Unlimited
Types Lyrics in Score	✔	✔	
"Click In" Lyrics			✔
Shifts Lyrics Right/Left		✔	
Mixes Fonts, Sizes, and Styles in Lyrics		✔	
Places Chord Symbols		✔	
Creates Chords via MIDI		✔	
Automatically Creates Chord Symbols			
Guitar Fretboard Notation		✔	
Transposes Chord Symbols		✔	
Automatic Tablature			

"attached" to the note values, so if the music is reformatted and notes change position, the values remain connected.

Measure Attributes

Measures have a number of attributes that can be set, not the least of which are the right and left bar lines. Figure 20.21, on page 385, shows some of the options that can be controlled. Items within the measures can be controlled, such as the presence or absence of time and key signatures and cautionary elements. This dialog also controls multimeasure rests and note placement. Most programs can add measure numbers and rehearsal marks and carefully control their visual placement.

TABLE 20.3 *(continued)*

Feature	Overture 3	NoteAbility Pro	Finale 2005	Sibelius 3
Cross-Staff Beaming	✔		✔	✔
Repositions/Adjusts Elements by Mouse (notes/slurs, etc.)	✔	✔	✔	✔
Controls Stem Direction	✔	✔	✔	✔
Collision Avoidance		✔	✔	✔
Tuplets	Extensive	Extensive	Extensive	Extensive
Text Entry for Title, Credits	✔	✔	✔	✔
Block Text	✔	✔	✔	✔
Alters Staff Name		✔	✔	✔
Lyrics Lines Allowed	4	Unlimited	Unlimited	Unlimited
Types Lyrics in Score		✔	✔	✔
"Click In" Lyrics	✔		✔	✔
Shifts Lyrics Right/Left			✔	✔
Mixes Fonts, Sizes, and Styles in Lyrics	✔	✔	✔	✔
Places Chord Symbols	✔	Figured-bass only	✔	✔
Creates Chords via MIDI	✔		✔	
Automatically Creates Chord Symbols			✔	✔
Guitar Fretboard Notation	✔	✔	✔	✔
Transposes Chord Symbols			✔	✔
Automatic Tablature	Supports TAB manually		✔	✔

Brackets/Braces

Brackets and braces, which are used to organize staves visually, are used separately or together. To create these objects in most software, you create the staves, choose the appropriate button from the palettes, and then choose the staves to be unified with the bracket or brace.

Fine-Tuning Beams, Stems, and Other Elements

No matter how good a notation program is at creating notated symbols in combination, adjustments always need to be made. An important consideration for choosing a notation program is how easy it is to fine-tune beams, stems, and other elements on a complicated score where room is at a premium.

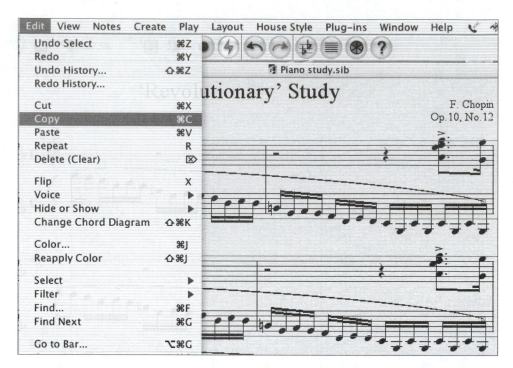

FIGURE 20.19A
Selecting music in Sibelius 3

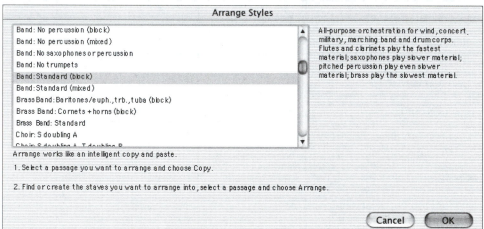

FIGURE 20.19B
Choosing an arrangement style

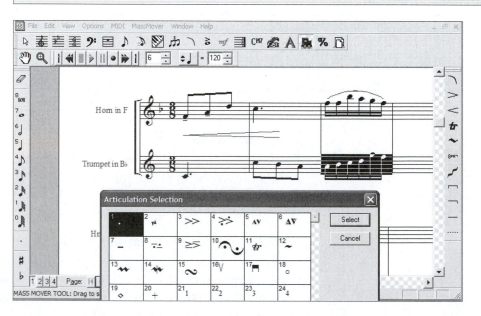

FIGURE 20.20
Expressions and articulations in PrintMusic!

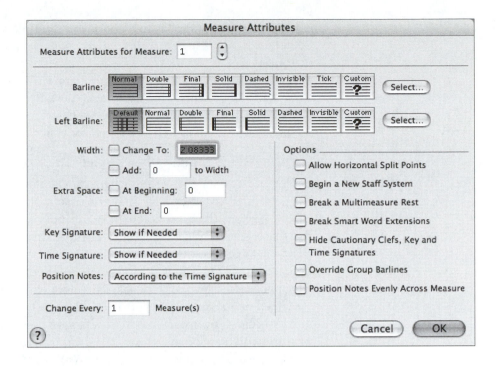

FIGURE 20.21
Measure attributes dialog in Finale 2005

Take a close look at Figure 20.22. We have revealed the special tool palette in Finale 2005 to the right. These tools allow for careful editing of beams, note and accidental placement, and note stems. In the graphic, we are using the beam-angle tool to change the angle of a beam in the second measure of the second system. The Special Tools menu is also being used to change the direction of a note stem. Fine adjustments like these are common in the latter stages of score preparation,

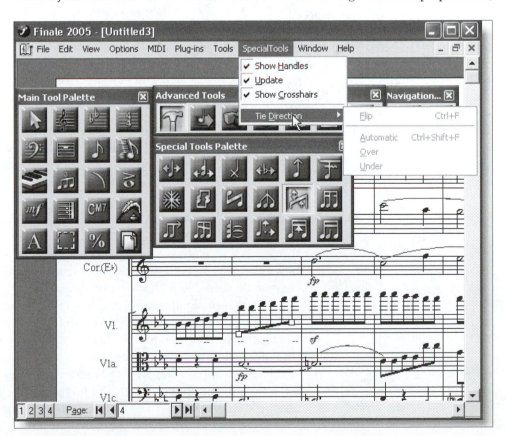

FIGURE 20.22 Fine editing of notational elements in Finale 2005

especially for very complicated scores with multiple voices on a single staff. Finale 2005 uses a sophisticated technique to avoid collisions of elements, but you still may need to alter some of its default placements. Other programs offer similar adjustment tools. An important consideration is the program's ability to allow cross-staff and cross-measure beaming, especially with complicated piano music. If your notation work requires this kind of careful editing, it is best to test each program carefully to see which one is best for you.

Creating Triplets and Other Tuplets

Tuplets are rhythmic structures where standard units of measure like quarter notes are performed together in a different time span than expected. For example, a triplet, perhaps the most common of all tuplets, could be three quarter notes in the space of two. Other examples of tuplets are five against four or 15 against eight. In some cases, two in the space of three, or four in the space of six, is possible; these may be thought of as duplets. The notation programs reviewed here all support some level of tuplets, some more extensively than others. The more-advanced programs also support nested tuplets (tuplets within tuplets) and allow tuplets notated over bar lines. The software usually requires the first note to be written (which establishes the unit of measure), then clicked on with a tuplet tool invoked, with a dialog box used to structure the notation. A bracket and the required number are often added on top of a tuplet.

Text and Lyrics

Text

Text entry for title, composer, copyright, or other standard text fields is often handled with the setup dialogs for each score. However, you can change any of these at any time during the scoring process or add them at the end. If you wanted to create a special text field on the score, usually double-clicking will create a "frame" or text block in which you can type freely or use the standard inserts that are shown on the menu. A wide variety of options are available for formatting and positioning.

Staff-instrument names are often established during the early stages of score creation during the setup period or when a new staff is added. Be aware that the name that appears in the score may not be changeable in some programs, which could pose a problem in certain cases.

Lyrics

If you intend to use your notation software for writing music for voice and you think you'll be adding a good deal of text, you should become very familiar with how text entry works for lyrics. Not all software does this easily and you need to become comfortable with the techniques.

The two predominate approaches include entering lyrics right on the score and adding them from a text box. A third possibility is adding lyrics from the clipboard after you have copied the text from a word processor or other program, but this approach is not widely supported.

The two approaches are demonstrated in Figures 20.23a and b. In each case, software programs have a particular method of separating syllables so they can be assigned to note values. In most cases, multiple lines of lyrics are supported, but be

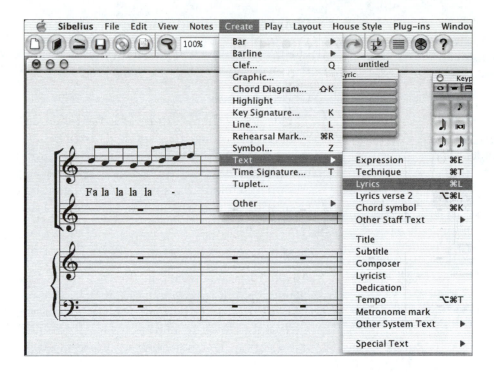

FIGURE 20.23A Lyric entry on the score in Sibelius 3

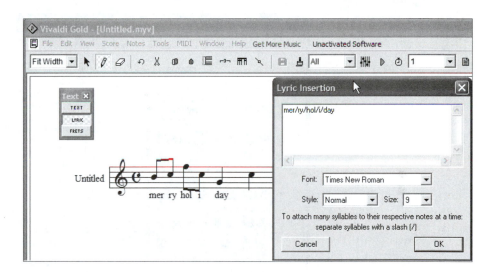

FIGURE 20.23B "Click-in" lyric entry in Vivaldi Gold

sure to experiment with how each software program handles this, especially line positioning.

The more-advanced programs include special features for lyrics. For example, Sibelius 3 allows several verses of lyrics to be positioned under the same melody line and supports elisions (two similar or identical syllables next to each other, often forming the end and the beginning of the next word). Both Finale 2005 and Sibelius 3 allow you to shift lyrics horizontally if necessary; these same programs support mixed fonts, font sizes, and styles in lyrics.

Most programs link lyrics to the notes so that if the location of the notes change, the lyrics move with the notes. Editing lyrics is similar to editing text in other contexts.

Chord Symbols and Tablature Notation

Finally, support for chord symbols and guitar and tablature notation complete this section on careful editing.

Chord Symbols

The names of chords can be added to scores either by hand, by MIDI-keyboard playing, or by automatic analysis of one or two staves of music. Figure 20.24 shows the choices for these and other options for chord-name entry in Finale 2005. Different styles of chord symbol are supported, as is location of the symbol itself. Another useful option is printing a fretboard based on the chord, which appears along with the chord name. Chord names and the fretboard syllables can be edited and transposed.

Tablature

Advanced programs support the creation of TAB staves for fretted instruments. Figure 20.25 displays standard notation on the top staff and the same music in TAB notation at the bottom. This was done by simply choosing the top line, copying it to the clipboard, and pasting it into the TAB staff. Sibelius 3 took care of the transcription. TAB notation can also be edited and customized.

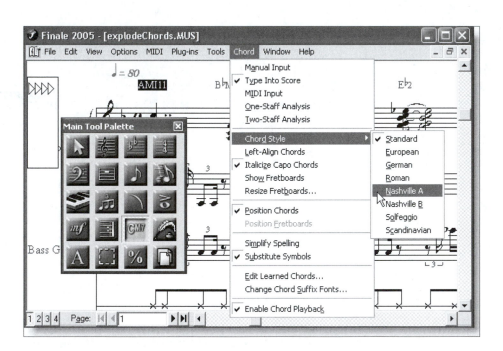

FIGURE 20.24   Chord insertion in Finale 2005

FIGURE 20.25   TAB notation in Sibelius 3

Play, Print, and Save

Table 20.4 provides our final cross-program analysis, this time for playing, printing, and saving. Many of these features come into the picture toward the end of development.

LINK
All the writing in past Viewports about MIDI, sound cards, and soft synths applies here to playback.

Playback Options

The basic option of playing back files with MIDI codes has been part of music-notation programs since the first program was written. Each program in our list supports MIDI-based playback. Usually, this playback is sent to a MIDI device connected to the computer (a keyboard with MIDI sounds or MIDI-sound module). However, other options are possible depending on the computer platform and the software's support design.

Finale 2005 for Windows uses the SmartMusic Softsynth, as well as the sound card. On the Mac side, Finale 2005 uses both the SmartMusic Softsynth and QuickTime. Sibelius 3 on both the Mac and Windows side uses both a sound card or a third-party soft synth from Native Instruments called Kontakt Silver, which is provided as part of the basic installation of the software. A more-advanced "Gold" version of this soft synth, which provides more instrument sounds, is available for additional cost. The soft synths respond to MIDI codes much as we described in Module 17. Additionally, these soft synths allow notation-software programs to also offer a "save as digital audio" feature that allows you to burn CDs!

To help control for these options in playback, most software provides a sequencing list or mixer. In these lists or mixers, you can assign a channel and a program (timbre) to each voice in a staff. With a multiport MIDI interface like the ones described in Module 16, it is possible to assign MIDI-based playback to a number of MIDI devices. Playback can also be controlled by soloing a particular line or muting others. Volume and panning can also be controlled. Sibelius 3 even provides a window for editing sound sets for a wide variety of popular hardware devices.

Regardless of where the MIDI codes are routed, programs provide editing capabilities for the nature of the MIDI code itself. The MIDI tool in Finale 2005 provides a menu with controls for key velocity, duration, and continuous data. The program offers very specific control over MIDI note values and even a database of MIDI values for articulations, expression markings, and other notation symbols. Both Sibelius 3 and Finale 2005 also offer control over the overall style of playback. An "as-performed" option allows you to play back the notation as it was performed before it was standardized for printing. Both programs also offer a "swing" style playback for jazz scores as well as other music style options.

Print Controls

Options for printing vary greatly by program. In the early days of music-notation software, perhaps the strongest complaints about practicality were directed to this aspect of software use. Today, many of the problems of margins, page breaks, and fine adjustments prior to printing have been solved. Figure 20.26 shows the document setup window in Sibelius 3, which is representative of some of the more-advanced programs. Notice the miniature view of the first page of a score that adjusts dynamically as you work with settings. The settings include options for

TABLE 20.4 Play, Print, and Save Features of Selected Notation Programs

Feature	NotePad	PrintMusic!	Vivaldi Gold
MIDI-Based Playback	✔	✔	✔
Digital-Audio Playback	Sound Card, QuickTime	Sound Card, QuickTime	Sound Card, QuickTime
Plays Markings		✔	
Defines Playback Markings		✔	
Edits MIDI events			
Plays as Performed		✔	
"Swing" Playback			
Maximum Page Size	11 x 17 inches	virtually unlimited	virtually unlimited
Placement Grid			
Distance Between Staves		✔	
Flexible Staff Size		✔	
Hides Elements			Limited
Page Breaks			
Layout Control of Parts		✔	✔
Server for Web Distribution	✔	✔	✔
Web Viewer Support	NotePad	NotePad	
Mac/Windows File Share	✔	✔	✔
Saves as Audio File			
Imports Formats for Individual Graphics			
Exports Graphic Formats			
Imports Notation-File Types Other Than Native and MIDI		Encore, Rhapsody, SmartScore, SharpEye, MidiScan	
Exports Notation-File Types Other Than Native		SmartMusic	

TABLE 20.4 *(continued)*

Feature	Overture 3	NoteAbility Pro	Finale 2005	Sibelius 3
MIDI-Based Playback	✔	✔	✔	✔
Digital-Audio Playback	Sound Card, QuickTime	QuickTime	Sound Card, QuickTime, SmartMusic SoftSynth	Sound Card/ QuickTime Kontakt Player
Plays Markings	✔	✔	✔	✔
Defines Playback Markings	✔	✔	✔	✔
Edits MIDI events			✔	✔
Plays as Performed	✔		✔	✔
"Swing" Playback	✔		✔	✔
Maximum Page Size	34 x 44 inches	virtually unlimited	virtually unlimited	virtually unlimited
Placement Grid		✔	✔	Guides
Distance Between Staves	✔	✔	✔	✔
Flexible Staff Size		✔	✔	✔
Hides Elements	✔	✔	✔	✔
Page Breaks			✔	✔
Layout Control of Parts	✔	✔	✔	✔
Server for Web Distribution			✔	✔
Web Viewer Support			NotePad	Scorch Plug-In
Mac/Windows File Share			✔	✔
Saves as Audio File			WAV, AIF, MP3, WMA	WAV, AIF
Imports Formats for Individual Graphics		TIFF, PDF	TIFF, EPS, PICT (Mac)	TIFF
Exports Graphic Formats	EPS, PICT (Mac)	Maxqlist/explode, EPS/PDF, JPG, GIF, PICT, XML (with nl2xml), GUIDO	EPS (Mac), TIFF, PICT (Mac)	PICT (Mac), BMP (Win), EMF (Win) EPS
Imports Notation-File Types Other Than Native and MIDI	Encore, MusicTime	SCORE, GUIDO	Encore, Rhapsody, SCORE, Enigma (ETF), Coda Template, musicXML (with Dolet)	Enigma (ETF), Allegro, Print Music!, SCORE, Acorn, NIFF (Win)
Exports Notation-File Types Other Than Native		SCORE, NoteWriter (Mac), GUIDO	SmartMusic, Enigma (ETF), Coda Template, musicXML (with Dolet)	Sibelius 2, ASCII Tab

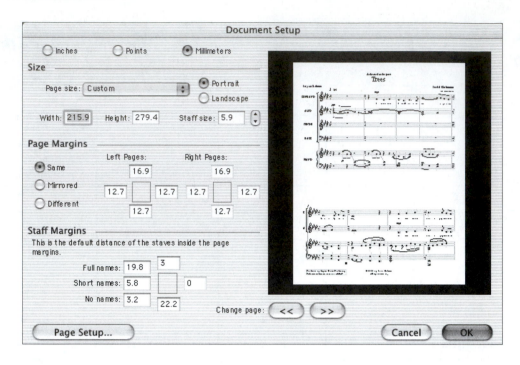

FIGURE 20.26
Document setup in Sibelius 3

overall size and margins for both right and left pages. Control over instrument-name placement is also offered.

This dialog box is not the end of the options for page layout in either Sibelius 3 or Finale 2005. The Layout menu in Sibelius offers additional options for page breaks in parts, adjustments for staff alignment, and hiding empty staves. Distance between staves is easily handled in advanced programs by moving the staff up and down with the mouse. The resize tool in Finale 2005 allows you to carefully adjust the physical size of a single staff in a larger score. In Figure 20.27, we display a hidden set of guides in Sibelius 3 that helps align all these elements of the score. Notice the attachment lines that help establish how expressive elements belong to certain notes. Other programs like NoteAbility Pro provide an extensive grid system to align elements.

Saving and Distribution

This final dimension of the notation software has changed dramatically in the last few years. No longer can music-notation programs only produce a hard copy product; web-based distribution is becoming more common, digital audio CDs can be created, and many formats are supported for importing and exporting.

Web Distribution

The companies that produce the MakeMusic! family of software (NotePad, Print-Music!, and Finale 2005), Vivaldi Gold, and Sibelius 3 all maintain web servers for file distribution. In the case of Vivaldi Gold, the server is designed to sell previously created scores that can be downloaded and hosted by the company's software. Other companies follow this model as well, using other notation products as hosts or simply selling PDF files.

MakeMusic! maintains a server for music rendered by its products, but allows anyone to upload music for free distribution. The NotePad application allows you to host any downloaded file from the MakeMusic! family. If you wish to embed

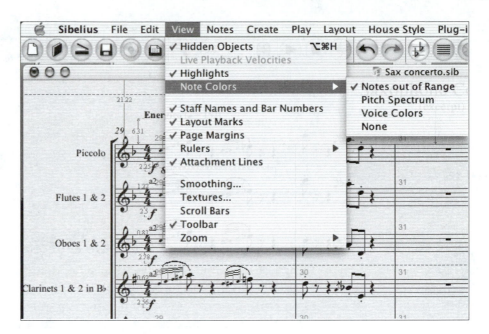

FIGURE 20.27 Guide markings in Sibelius 3

MakeMusic! scores in your personal web pages, the company suggests that you save the files as PDF files for visual display and as digital audio files for audio.

Sibelius 3, however, encourages a more-interactive approach. Its server is also open for anyone to upload works and gives users options for downloading free or for a fee. If for a fee, a portion of the amount is retained by Sibelius 3 and the composer or arranger receives payment for the work. Perhaps more importantly, Sibelius 3's technology for distribution is more integrated into the Internet than other companies. Scores are transformed by the Sibelius 3 user into interactive web pages that can be hosted on the Sibelius 3 site. Once the score is formatted in a manner appropriate for uploading, the "Publish on Sibeliusmusic.com" item is chosen under the File menu. This causes Sibelius 3 to launch browser software and link to the company's website. Here, you are presented with a set of questions that lead to your work being made available to others for free or for a fee. You can set the cost of your work and specify if others can transpose or change the solo instrument, if any. You may submit for distribution only those works to which you own the copyright.

You can also use the same technology to embed your Sibelius 3 files into your own personal web pages. To do this, choose "Save as Scorch Web Page" from the "Save As . . ." options in the File menu. Figure 20.28 shows the dialog box that results. Here, you specify the template look you like and dimensions and whether you want viewers of your page to be able to print and save your work. Clicking OK creates a file (or files) on your computer that can be used on your website. For users to view and/or hear your work on either your or Sibelius's site, a "scorch" software plug-in is required.

Save as Audio File

This option is possible in more-recent and -advanced software, in part because of the inclusion of soft synths as a playback resource and because of the high demand for a way to share audio on CDs and the Internet. Finale 2005 can save as straight WAV or compressed-audio files, such as MP3 or WMA. Saving in compressed format allows you to include your notation files in your digital music player's personal collection.

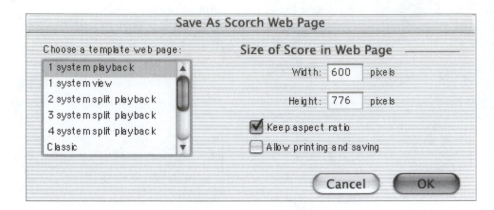

FIGURE 20.28 Dialog box for creating a Scorch web page in Sibelius 3

LINK
See Module 19 for extensive coverage of exportable notation options.

Importing and Exporting in Different Formats

The last section in Table 20.4 displays options for importing and exporting from music-notation programs in file formats other than native and MIDI. The first of these rows describes ways that notation software can import graphics as entities to include in the score. For example, you might want to create a logo or an instrument picture to help explain a technique. Also, you may need to add a playing instruction that uses graphics not contained in the notation program itself.

Exporting all or part of the score in a graphics format is very useful for preparing printed material. For example, Sibelius 3 includes different program formats for EPS, PICT, and TIFF on the Mac platform.

Finally, one notable option for the MakeMusic! family of software is its ability to save notated scores as SmartMusic scores for that program. For educators and performers interested in creating custom music for use with that program, these notation programs become especially useful.

Advanced Capabilities

We end this module by reviewing a few special tools or capabilities found in both Finale 2005 and Sibelius 3 that have not been mentioned previously. Also included is a short section on a few plug-ins available for both programs.

Additional Capabilities

- *Exercise templates.* These help create exercises for students based on scales, arpeggios, or other pedagogical constructs (Finale 2005/Sibelius 3)
- *Ossia support.* An ossia is a small measure above a regular measure of music that shows an alternative notation. Notation software offers an easy way to create such measures and handles spacing adjustments (Finale 2005/Sibelius 3)
- *Custom clefs.* This editor allows custom placement of traditional clefs or creation of new ones (Finale 2005)
- *Custom manuscript paper.* This provides options for creating different kinds of graphic backgrounds for music notation (Sibelius 3)
- *Add parallel interval.* A parallel line of music can be added to a selected region of notation without needing to enter each note one by one. (Sibelius 3)
- *Hide accidentals.* This permits you to hide an accidental without hiding the note to which the accidental refers (Sibelius 3/Finale 2005)

LINK
See Module 22 for a presentation on SmartMusic accompanying software.

- *Flow text.* This allows you to flow text around an irregular-shaped graphic (Finale 2005)
- *Timecode display.* This displays SMPTE timecode in either a fixed box or above measures (Sibelius 3)
- *Rhymer.* This resource helps find words that rhyme with a target word (Finale 2005)

Plug-Ins

Finale 2005 and Sibelius 3 both allow you to expand the core functionality of each program with plug-ins. Unlike the special features noted above, plug-ins are add-ons that are usually created by others. MakeMusic! provides a plug-in developer's kit and Sibelius 3 provides a language called ManuScript for developers to use for this purpose. With each new software version, a new set of plug-ins is provided.

Plug-ins are organized into categories in each program and are displayed as a menu on the program's main menu bar. As you consider the purchase of one of these programs, be sure to review the plug-ins available to see if any are especially useful for your particular work. Below are 10 plug-ins for each program, together with a short description.

Finale 2005

- *Band-in-a-Box Auto-Harmonizing.* Uses the intelligence for harmonization developed in the Band-in-a-Box program to create an orchestrated harmonization for any given melody, with or without chord symbols.
- *Composer's Assistant Collection.* A set of generative routines that aid the creative process, including chord morphing, reordering, splitting, and rhythm generation, among others.
- *MusicXML.* Imports and exports musicXML files (Dolet Lite for Windows only)
- *Smart Cue Notes.* Searches a score looking for opportunities to add cue notes and then helps add them.
- *Auto Dynamic Placement.* Places dynamics in a score based on MIDI-key velocities of notes played into the score.
- *Check Range.* Checks the written ranges of instruments in a score against a database for different levels of player experience
- *Drum Grooves.* Many drum grooves provided for your score, including percussion maps.
- *MiBAC Jazz Rhythm Section Generator.* Creates piano, bass, and drum accompaniments for melody with chord symbols (see Module 22 for more on MiBAC software).
- *Smart Page Turn.* Works with part scores to create smoother page turns when formatting parts.
- *Global Staff/Group Attributes.* Automatically applies the same staff or group attributes to any staff or group.

Sibelius 3

- *Add Accidentals to All Notes.* Places accidentals on all notes. Useful for creating atonal music that has no key signatures.
- *Add Note Names.* Places the letter names or notes in the score.
- *Find Motif.* Looks through the entire score for intervals, rhythm patterns, or both for a selected passage.

- *Convert Folders of Scores to Web Pages*. Creates web pages for Scorch with music notation in a batch-processing mode.
- *Add Drum Pattern*. Establishes a drum staff and writes a pattern in one of 24 styles.
- *Combine Tied Notes and Rests*. Merges tied notes and rests to create longer note values. Very useful in cleaning up Flex-Time input.
- *Add Harp Pedaling*. Automatically adds harp-pedal diagrams to hard parts.
- *Realize Figured Bass*. Aids in creating figured bass.
- *Align Lyrics*. Works to adjust the vertical spacing of multiple lyric verses.
- *Change Dynamics*. Changes all dynamic markings in a score one level up or down.

M o d u l e   2 1

Notation Hardware: Input Devices, Scanners, and OMR

We turn our attention to hardware needs for music notation. Figure 21.1 describes a No-Frills Notation Workstation (EMT 7). The two essential hardware elements for notation are a laser or inkjet printer (5) and a flatbed scanner (6). The music setup is very basic with a MIDI-keyboard controller (21) and a General MIDI 2 sound module with built-in MIDI interface (26/22). The following sections will review the input options for entering music notation and provide background information on scanners and Optical Music Recognition (OMR).

Input Devices for Music Notation

A variety of techniques are currently used with music-notation software for entering music codes. However, none of them reaches the goals of going flawlessly from printed music to music-notation codes, or directly from playing to the printed page (WYPWYP [What You Play is What You Print]). What we do have is a repertoire of entry techniques that can be used to suit the skill, needs, and preferences of the musician. That repertoire includes:

- Text codes or key codes entered from a computer keyboard and numeric keypad (see Module 19)
- Music performance entered from a MIDI-keyboard controller or wind, guitar, drum, or other controllers (see Module 16)
- Singing or playing traditional musical instruments and converting those analog vibration with pitch-to-voltage or pitch-to-MIDI (see Module 16)
- Gestures of selections from graphic palettes and menus with a mouse or other pointing device (see Module 4)
- Scanning from printed music using optical music recognition, or OMR (later in this module)

Text and Key Codes from the Computer Keyboard

Text-based music-coding systems have been around since the DARMS code was introduced in 1965. These coding systems are based on ASCII text commands and codes associated with the computer keyboard. Some notation programs still

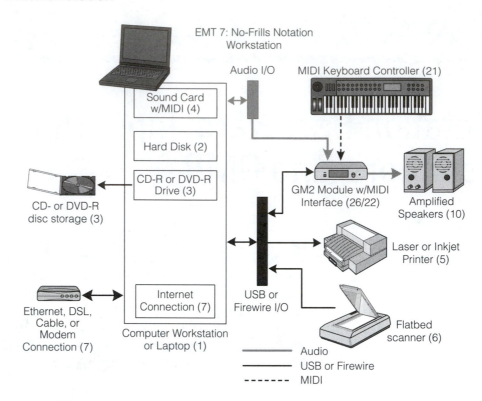

FIGURE 21.1 EMT 7: No-Frills Notation Workstation with printer and scanner

LINK
Be sure to check out Module 20, which covered entry-system options for music notation in much greater depth.

offer a text-based music code, at least as an alternative to graphic entry of notation. Some composers still find text codes a fast and desirable entry system. (See Tables 19.2 through 19.7 for examples of text-based codes.)

Music-notation applications also offer single keystrokes for entering pitch, rhythm, and other music symbols. Notation programs make effective use of numeric keypads, as well as the traditional QWERTY computer keyboard, for additional key-based options for coding music elements.

Pitch can be associated with key names, oftentimes either the corresponding letter of the alphabet or a physical relationship to the keyboard. Rhythms can be associated with numeric values on the keyboard. Figure 21.2, as an example, shows the Speedy Entry keys used from a numeric keypad in Finale for rhythm and other codes: one equated with the 64th note, to eight being associated with the double whole note. Keys on the main computer keyboard are also mapped to notes on a piano keyboard.

Key-coded systems like Finale's Speedy Entry can be used alone or in combination with a MIDI-music keyboard for quick notation input. Sibelius and other notation software offer similar associations between computer keys and music-entry functions. In fact, these keyboard "shortcuts" can become overwhelming when Shift, Option, Alt, Ctrl, and other such key combinations enter into the many key permutations.

It's possible to create your own custom key codes or macros within a program like Finale or Sibelius or with a separate software program. A macro is a recorded series of key and menu options. Keyboard macro-editor utilities like CE Software's QuickKeys X for Macintosh or Pitrinec's Perfect Keyboard for Windows let you create custom macros that can be executed with one keystroke from any given music application. For example, you might create a single macro that will save your current work, un-mute all voices, set the pointer to the beginning of the music, and then play the music from a single keystroke.

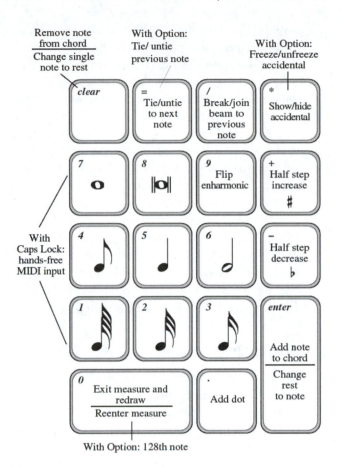

FIGURE 21.2 Speedy Entry codes mapped to a numeric keypad in Finale

LINK
MIDI-keyboard and other controllers, and pitch-to-MIDI and pitch-to-voltage converters, are discussed at length in Module 16.

Graphic Palettes and a Mouse

Most notation programs use the GUI interface and provide for the use of the mouse as a pointer device to select music symbols from an array of graphic palettes. Module 20 provided many examples of palettes from a variety of music-notation software. Mouse entry is suitable for novices who need visual representation of music symbols; mouse entry is also suitable for advanced scoring, where the notation pattern is very intricate and complex. Although the learning curve is steeper for step-time and key-entry systems, they can be a more direct means to encode music than point-and-click techniques with a mouse.

Several notation programs have devised clever systems for expanding on the basic mouse gestures of point-and-click, double-click, click-and-drag, and so on. The goal is to always reduce the number of actions required to enter a note. Nightingale especially has some unique mouse gestures. Shaking the mouse at a speed you specify toggles the cursor between the arrow pointer and the tool you previously selected. When you've clicked on the screen, hold down the Apple Command key and you can cycle through the duration values, or hold the Shift key down and cycle through the accidentals.

MIDI Controllers

The use of a MIDI keyboard is probably the most common entry option used with music-notation software. A MIDI keyboard (21) is shown in the setup for the No-Frills Notation Workstation (Figure 21.1). Don't overlook the obvious, however.

Any MIDI controller such as a guitar or wind controller can be used for music entry. Notation programs permit *real-time entry* of music through a built-in sequencer in the software. As Module 20 demonstrates, notation software is sophisticated enough to quantize or round off the rhythmic values as you perform the music to ensure clean rhythmic values for notation from variations in music performance.

Step-time entry with a MIDI keyboard is a simpler entry system than live performance and provides greater control and accuracy of rhythm. Step-time entry uses the MIDI keyboard for the pitch values, and keystrokes or mouse selections for the rhythm values. No rhythm or timing is required in entering notes. A numeric keypad can be helpful, either built into the computer keyboard or purchased separately; USB keypads are inexpensive.

Hit a key on the computer keypad to set the rhythm as you strike a key on the MIDI keyboard, blow the note on your wind controller, or pluck a string on your guitar controller. A foot-pedal control through the MIDI keyboard can also be used to trigger entry, with your foot tapping the beat with the pedal. Finale permits the use of a MIDI pedal, or any defined MIDI key for that matter, with its Hyper-Scribe entry system to establish the entry beat.

Singing in the Notes

If you are looking for even more alternatives, you can try singing in your notes. Finale's MicNotator feature encourages you to sing or play your own melodic instrument for music entry. Add-on solutions are also available. Software or hardware like Wildcat's Autoscore or Epinoisis Software's Digital Ear uses the microphone or microphone input built into your Mac or Windows PC computer and the computer's sound card. As you sing—or play—into the microphone, the software converts the sound into MIDI codes. You can then save your sequence as a standard MIDI file (SMF) and load it into any notation program for further editing. A hardware pitch-to-MIDI device is an even better alternative because it will let you directly use the hardware as a MIDI controller with the notation package. Pyware's Amadeus al fine [Win/Mac] is an example of a hardware solution.

No matter the entry options that notation software offers, in the end you should consider using a combination of entry systems for any notation task. Some notation sections demand the intricacy of graphic entry; others allow for the speed offered by playing in the music with real time entry from a keyboard or other MIDI device. The broader the repertoire of entry systems, the more facile you will become with computer notation.

Scanners and OMR

Optical Music Recognition (OMR)

Arthur Mendel commented at the 1965 Musicology and the Computer Symposium that "We need a way of getting music read automatically for machine use rather than first translating into an input language. . . . It seems to be perfectly within the possibilities of today's techniques." Nearly 40 years later, we are still working to perfect a solution for Optical Music Recognition (OMR). It is a very complex task for a computer to read the spatial layout of music notation on a score

LINK
If you need explanations for designations like NIFF, MusicXML, SMF, music-notation file formats were covered in depth in Module 19.

TIP
Scanners, as well as digital still and video cameras, use a standard driver software known as TWAIN. This makes them usable with a wide variety of software. Digital-imaging hardware that uses the TWAIN interface should be readable by your optical music scanning software, as well as your photo and video editing software, regardless of whether you have a Macintosh or a Windows computer system.

LINK
Information about these OMR packages can also be found in Module 20.

page, with all its nuances, and translate the graphic symbols it recognizes into accurate notation codes for further processing. It is not image-to-image, but image-to-computer, notation codes that can be flexibly manipulated.

Optical character recognition (OCR) for text on a personal computer has achieved a high degree of sophistication. Slip a document into a scanner and OCR software can translate the text into ASCII codes—including styles and tabs in some cases—and import it directly into your word processor.

Here is how music OMR works. You place a page of music on a flatbed scanner (usually TWAIN compatible) and scan it in at 200- to 300-dpi resolution. From the graphics or scanning software you are using, you save it as a graphic image (TIFF, JPEG, PICT, or other format). Then you use an OMR software package that attempts to translate the graphic image into standard MIDI codes (SMF), proprietary codes for specific notation software like Finale or Sibelius, or interchangeable NIFF or MusicXML codes. The OMR software may offer some editing capabilities for cleaning up the graphic image, and correct some recognizable errors in the translation. You then import the SMF, NIFF, MusicXML, or proprietary notation codes into the appropriate notation software and perform the final editing of the music.

Several OCR software packages are available, all of which require practice to get reliable translations from printed music to notation. Three major OMR products are Musitek's SmartScore, Neuratron's PhotoScore, and Visiv's SharpEyes. SmartScore is biased toward Finale and exports NIFF, SMF, and Finale ETF and MUS files. PhotoScore is biased toward Sibelius and exports to Sibelius files and SMF. SharpEye is not tied to anyone's notation application and will export SMF, NIFF, MusicXML, and its own format. Nightingale notation software has its own scanning solution, NoteScan.

The Mechanics of a Scanner

Scanners come in flatbed, sheetfeed, handheld, slide, overhead, and drum varieties. We will focus on the flatbed scanners. A flatbed scanner (6) is shown in the No-Frills Notation Workstation (Figure 21.1). The primary reason for including a scanner in a notation workstation is for optical music recognition (OMR).

To understand how scanners work, we visit the familiar photocopy machine. The first stage of the photocopy machine is the mechanism that captures the image from the original page, using light reflection. A scanner samples light frequencies using analog to digital conversion to produce bitmaps of graphic images.

Figure 21.3 reduces the operation of a scanning device to a very simple form. The diagram shows a light source illuminating the image. Have you noticed the

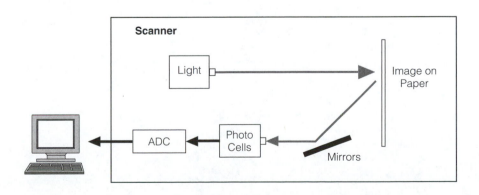

FIGURE 21.3   The basic mechanics of a computer scanner

light beam that scans the page any time you make a photocopy? That's the same type of light beam scanning the printed page. Using a system of mirrors, the light reflection is then magnified, focused, and aimed at a strip of photocells.

The resolution of the scanner is determined by how many photocells are along a strip as wide as the scanner's page size. Scanning density can range from 72 to 2,400 dpi, or 72 to 1,200 photocells per inch. If the photo cells can only detect the presence or absence of light, then the depth of the resolution is a one-bit image known as *line* art, in scanning nomenclature. A one-bit image is simply black and white (monochrome). If the photocell can detect multiple levels of light, then the depth of scanning resolution can be from four to 48 bits of gray or color. A 24-bit color scanner can capture millions of shades. For OMR work, a minimum of 16-bit grayscale or color is desirable.

With a *flatbed* scanner, the image lies on top of a plate of glass just as with a photocopy machine. This setup results in well-controlled and accurately aligned scanning. Flatbed scanners come in standard page sizes from 8.5x11 to 12x17 inches, with resolutions from 1,200 to 4,800 dpi. Interface connections to the computer are typically USB or Firewire. The Hewlett-Packard (HP) ScanJet was one of the first commercially successful low-cost scanners. Models from such firms as Canon, Epson, Hewlett Packard (HP), Microtek, Nikon, and Visioneer now populate the market with a variety of features. Almost any flatbed-scanner model will work for optical music recognition.

VIEWPORT VIII

Computer-Aided Instruction in Music

"If the computer is a universal control system, let's give kids universes to control."

—*Ted Nelson*, Dream Machines *(1974)*

"I think we have to have students writing music in whatever style they want. There is no way to teach a composer in the world how to compose. But there are plenty of wonderful ways to excite the creative logic that is part of the human brain. Music is about exploring the creative logic of the brain, and right now we aren't doing that in our schools in general. We don't value the creative logic. We need to have students just play more, building their own instruments, inventing their own notations—and not just in pockets of schools, but everywhere."

—*Composer Libby Larsen, from an interview in the* Washington Post *(2004)*

Overview

The role of music technology in today's educational settings continues to be a vital one. Professional standards are written to include technology expectations for teacher and student competencies. New software continues to emerge that meets the demand for knowledge, skills, and creative experiences.

This Viewport focuses on computer-aided instruction (CAI) in music and the variety of software that supports it. Many new products described in these last two modules make use of hardware, data structures, and software ideas presented earlier. In fact, we have placed this important topic at the conclusion of this text in large part because much of what has been presented thus far can be applied to music teaching and learning.

Objectives

We divide the many software approaches to music teaching into two modules, one focusing on knowledge and skills and the other on newer directions. A large part of these newer directions include creative and exploratory products, as well as Internet use. Module 22 presents examples of software that use the common drill-and-practice, flexible-practice, guided-instruction, and game-based approaches. Module 23 concludes with examples from creative/exploratory, Internet-based, and software designed for teacher use.

At the end of this Viewport, you should understand:

- The importance of CAI software
- Basic approaches to music-teaching software and examples of each approach
- How these examples fit into different content categories, such as software for beginning skills, aural skills/music theory, composition, improvisation, and music listening

MUSIC TECHNOLOGY IN PRACTICE

Susan Young

Music teacher at Northbrook Junior High School, District 28, Northbrook, Illinois. Teaches chorus and general music and offers innovative courses in music and the arts that use technology as a base. Active clinician, adjudicator, and guest conductor. Teaches courses in the use of technology in music education at area colleges.

Susan Young working with students

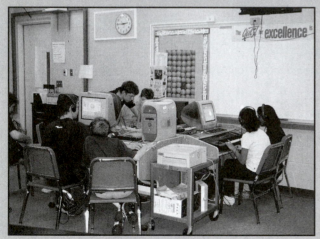
Susan Young's classroom, where middle-school students are working on class projects

Applications

An active music teacher for many years, Susan works with middle-school students to improve their understanding of music. She does this most often by designing creative projects for the students to complete. She believes in peer teaching and project-centered learning and encourages her students to create products that demonstrate their understanding.

She has created an entire curriculum based on teaching composition in the schools. One of her favorite projects is to create a sound track for a movie. In this assignment, students work in groups to review the movie's content and decide what kind of music might be best. The music must be original and the students use software of various types to complete their projects. Susan also engages the children in their own evaluation processes, using rubrics designed for this purpose. A large part of her style as an instructor is to first teach the skills necessary to complete projects and then allow the students to provide their own content.

Susan began working with music and technology in the 1970s, encouraging children to program microcomputers using BASIC. She continued her education with courses in music technology and continues to actively study the developments in the field.

Hardware and Software

Susan uses a variety of software in her teaching, including: iMovie, Movieworks, iDVD, Encore, Rock Rap'n Roll, Sibelius, Adobe Premiere, Musicshop, Band-in-a-Box, and Music Ace. She uses a Macintosh G4 tower computer with a large LCD screen at home. At school, she maintains a multistation laboratory in her chorus room with Macintosh iMacs and G3 machines with Korg M1 synthesizers. She uses simple USB MIDI interfaces and headphone amplifiers for each station. She also uses a Mackie 16-channel mixer and a laser printer.

- How to select appropriate software given your philosophical position, curriculum, and student characteristics
- How to use the software presented here and other titles described in this text in terms of the nine National Standards in Music Education

DVD-ROM Software Projects

In terms of hands-on tasks, you should be able to:

- Work with aural skills/music theory software (Project 17)
- Improve improvisation skills using software (Project 18)
- Evaluate CAI software for use in teaching (Project 19)

TIP
The National Standards publication is referred to at the end of the book.

DVD-ROM
As with all of the software modules in this text, the accompanying DVD contains projects for you to use to practice your skills.

Module 22

Music Software for Knowledge and Skill Development

DVD-ROM
Projects 17–19 on the accompanying DVD are designed to give you hands-on experience with selected titles in Tables 22.1 and 23.1.

Computer-aided instruction (CAI) is the major subject of this Viewport. In this module, we present descriptions of selected software designed to build knowledge and skills. Module 23 provides information about more-creative-based software, as well as Internet-based resources and materials designed just for teachers.

Most of the hardware and data structures from previous sections in this book apply to the software in this Viewport. For example, workstation designs EMT-1 and EMT-2 work well with music teaching and learning. MIDI and digital audio data are used extensively by CAI titles. In fact, we have put teaching software as the final topic in this book because it so nicely demonstrates how many of the major themes in music technology can be put into practice for genuine music experiences.

Although the software described here is designed specially for music teaching and learning, software described in other portions of this book can also be used in teaching settings. For example, teachers can use the features of digital audio, sequencing, and notation programs to teach a great deal about music. Software products described in these two modules, however, are designed exclusively for music learning.

Importance of CAI

CAI software is a vital resource for thousands of music teachers and soon-to-be music teachers who are in charge of instruction in studios, rehearsal halls, and classrooms. However, professional educators are not the only people concerned with good CAI. We all are students of music, no matter what our age, level of sophistication, or professional emphasis. Good musicians are always looking for ways to improve their understanding and ability, whether they are in formal classes or not. As the variety and quality of CAI technology grow, so does the importance of this technology to all of us interested in self-improvement.

In the early days of personal computers during the 1970s, authors primarily created drill-and-practice software that was quite basic in design. This pioneering work was impressive for the time, but by today's standards lacked individualization and technical sound quality. As will be demonstrated in the coming pages, contemporary CAI is intelligently designed, musically sensitive, flexible, and exciting. Just as modern computer and music-technology systems provide each of us with powerful ways to produce and notate music, so too have advances in hardware and software provided new ways to inform others about music.

Fred T. Hofstetter

A student studying music CAI on a PLATO terminal, with its distinctive touch-panel screen

There is a fascinating historical interplay among music instruction, automated teaching machines, electronic-music synthesizers, and the concepts of programmed instruction (PI) and computer-aided instruction (CAI). CAI and its paper-and-pencil predecessor, PI, evolved from the behaviorist theories of Skinner in the 1950s. The history of this interplay shows a quest among music educators to develop automated music training that provides instant access to realistic, high-quality sound production and intelligent sensitivity to individual learning needs. The devices that accompany automated music instruction can be divided into two types: audio playing and electronic music.

Audio-Playing Devices and Music Instruction. The early 1960s were marked by the use of the tape recorder and the large mainframe computer in music instruction. The PLATO system was invented at this time by Don Bitzer at the University of Illinois. PLATO, implemented on Control Data mainframe computers, was one of the most-extensive commercial CAI systems developed, and a large library of music-teaching materials was written for the system.

Experiments with programmed instruction and audio-recording devices included the extensive ear-training series developed by William Poland and Charles Spohn at Ohio State University, and James Carlsen's commercially successful melodic-dictation drills in the early 1960s. As computer-aided instruction replaced PI in the late 1960s, music PI migrated to mainframe computer systems and computer-controlled audio-tape recorders, both reel-to-reel and cassette. Tape recorders for automated music instruction met with mixed success, however, due to the slow, sequential nature of the medium.

Notable early experiments with computers and audio-recording devices for music CAI include the music-training materials developed by Ned Deihl, Robert Placek, G. David Peters, and John Eddins. Deihl used an IBM 1500 mainframe and computer-controlled prerecorded tapes. Placek, Peters, and Eddins used the PLATO system and a specially built computer-controlled magnetic-disc recording device.

Laser discs, first in the form of videodiscs in the 1970s and then compact audio discs in the early 1980s, provided a much-needed boon to automated music instruction. The Philips-Sony standards for commercial laser-disc production quickly changed music education's focus from tape to disc.

CD audio discs, videodiscs, and more recently, DVD discs, surpassed the capabilities of tape recording by providing fast, random access to music examples with audio and video fidelity that met the critical demands of the human ear and eye. Present-day music instruction now benefits from the combination of inexpensive and increasingly more-powerful personal computers and extremely accurate control over laser-disc recordings of exceptional quality.

Electronic Music Devices. One of the first uses of an electronic-music device interfaced to a computer for music teaching was in Wolfgang Kuhn's work at Stanford in the late 1960s. An electronic organ and a pitch extractor were interfaced to an IBM 1620 mainframe computer for automated aural-skill and sight-singing training.

In the early 1970s, using another CDC PLATO installation at the University of Delaware, Fred Hofstetter designed the GUIDO CAI music curriculum using a customized digital synthesizer interfaced to a computer. Many others used mini-computer systems (especially the popular DEC PDP systems) for music training in the 1970s by connecting just about any electronic-music device imaginable to a minicomputer.

The cost barrier to the mass application of music CAI to education was broken in the early 1980s with the introduction of the personal computer (Apple II, Commodore PET, and TRS-80), and the soon-to-come MIDI standardizing of electronic-music devices. The Apple II personal computer, with the addition of the Micro Music DAC card or the ALF three-voice analog synthesizer, provided a platform for developing hundreds of music CAI software programs. Through the pioneering efforts of Micro Music Inc. (MMI), Temporal Acuity Products (TAP), and Electronic Courseware Systems (ECS), schools and universities could now offer an expansive library of CAI applications for music training used on low-cost microcomputers with simple polyphonic synthesizers, both digital and analog.

With the entry of MIDI-music devices in the mid-1980s, the quality and control of music sound improved by leaps and bounds, as did the sophistication of input devices such as keyboard, wind, drum, and string controllers for training in music performance. While the Micro Music DAC card (1978) provided the first low-cost solution to digital audio technology and music CAI, digital-music synthesizers with astounding sophistication were developed over the next 10 years. Computers like the Apple IIGS, Macintosh, Amiga, and NeXT came with digital audio as part of the hardware, while companies like AlphaSyntauri, Creative Labs, Digidesign, Ensoniq, Korg, Mountain Music, and numerous others, using bus-extended music boards, matched the digital performance of CD audio by the 1990s.

Today, CAI systems depend less on hardware devices, since much of the instructional content and the sound generation is based in software. Music teachers are becoming more fluent in creating customized resources and are using the Internet as a major delivery system.

We are often asked about the best software for teaching. In Viewport I, we noted that software is one of the first things to consider in assembling a technology system. "What do I want the technology to do?" is the primary question, and it relates directly to a philosophy of music teaching and learning that should drive all curricular decisions. The question is: "As a music teacher, what kinds of music experiences do I want the software and hardware to support in order to make my teaching more effective?"

You need to ask yourself how the available technology will match your own philosophies about music teaching and learning, rather than just buying what seems to be the newest equipment or software. You also need to consider the individual student's personality, learning style, and motivation. This Viewport will help describe some of the software possibilities that match your needs as a teacher.

Categories of CAI Software: Approach and Content

As the sidebar illustrates, CAI has a long historical tradition. As important as the developments in sound and computer technology have been, perhaps the most important advances have been in the software design itself. Traditional drill-and-practice software continues to be produced today, taking full advantage of increased processing speed and vastly improved sound. However, additional types of software have emerged in recent years and changes in the delivery systems to include online resources are also evident.

Tables 22.1 here and 23.1 in the next module provide examples of software across categories arranged by approach and instructional content. Seven approaches are identified. Brief descriptions of all seven approaches are provided here and software examples will be given both in this module and Module 23. The seven approaches are:

- Drill-and-practice
- Flexible practice
- Guided instruction
- Game-based
- Exploratory/creative
- Teacher resource
- Internet-based

In each table, we consider six types of instructional content. Beginning skills are most appropriate for young children, while aural skills/music theory, extended listening/history, performance, improvisation, and composition are all possible for a wider age range. One way to use these tables to find appropriate software is to first consider what you want to teach (content) and then decide how you want to teach it (approach).

Not all approaches have content examples. For example, we have not seen game-based software for extended listening, performance, and improvisation or flexible-practice software for beginning skills or improvisation. Exploratory/creative software for aural skills and music theory is rare. This is to be expected since there are natural pairings of content and approach; however, missing categories might be of interest if you want to get involved in software design.

TABLE 22.1	Examples of Software for Knowledge and Skill Development			
	Drill and Practice	**Flexible Practice**	**Guided Instruction**	**Game-Based**
Beginning Skills	• Early Keyboard Skills (Mac/Win) • Clef Notes (Mac/Win)		• MiDisaurus Volumes 1–8; Focus Volumes 1–4 (Mac/Win)	• Musicus (Mac/Win)
Aural Skills/Music Theory	• Auralia (Mac/Win) • MiBAC Music Lessons I and II (Mac/Win)	• MacGamut (Mac/Win) • Practica Musica (Mac/Win)	• Music Ace and Music Ace 2 (Mac/Win) • Alfred Music Theory (Mac/Win)	• Hearing Music (Win)
Extended Listening/History		• Time Sketch Editor Pro (Mac/Win)		Pianist Performance Series (Mac/Win)
Performance	• Piano Suite (Win)	• SmartMusic (Mac/Win)	• eMedia Guitar Method 1 (Mac/Win)	
Improvisation			• Sheddin' the Basics: Jazz Piano; Latin Jazz (Mac/Win)	

Drill-and-Practice

Because a large part of music education focuses on skills in aural perception (listening) and theoretical knowledge, and because computer software can be written relatively easily to exercise these skills, traditional drill-and-practice remains a common approach for CAI. Software in this approach is largely "computer-determined," providing instruction in a manner dictated entirely by the software authors and the computer itself.

For example, software can be written that makes the computer display or sound a series of chords. The student is asked to respond by indicating the chord types or perhaps their function. If the student answers correctly, the software might provide a new set of chords that is more challenging. If the responses are incorrect, the software might branch off to an easier set. The music stimuli themselves are often quite short and are presented outside a musical context. For many, this software provides an efficient and direct means to improve specific skills.

Flexible Practice

Software that uses this approach also has the express purpose of developing skills, but adds features that allow flexibility of use for both instructors and musicians seeking self-improvement. Many of these features are a result of both the increased power of technology and more creative, and perhaps more musical, thinking by software authors. Software in this category is student- and teacher-centered in that choices allow people to have a hand in engineering their own music learning. For instance, students might use an understanding of their own chord-identification weaknesses to establish a special set of drills.

Flexible-practice software typically provides menus and dialog boxes that let students choose the settings for a series of exercises that best suit their needs. In a similar way, teachers can use these features to create a tailor-made curriculum for an individual or class. These flexible options allow musicians to work with more-realistic musical materials, while giving the software more depth of content.

Both drill-and-practice and flexible-practice software often feature both digital audio and MIDI. Because this software is often used for individualized instruction in large classes, it also provides some form of record keeping in a networking environment.

Guided Instruction

Instead of offering a series of strictly defined, isolated tasks for completion, guided-instruction software leads the student through a series of interconnected tasks designed to form units of instruction. An idea is presented through demonstration using text, audio, graphics, animation, movies, or some combination of all these. Often the software asks the student to interact with the tutorial in order to verify that the ideas are understood. Material is presented by level of complexity and may contain related games to test mastery. Guided-instruction software can be very imaginative and entertaining. As with drill-and-practice and flexible practice, music content is nearly always defined by the software author.

LINK
The following CAI approaches are covered in Module 23.

Game-Based

Some of the most motivational software for music teaching and learning, especially for younger children, is found in this approach. Here the emphasis is placed on basic-skill development and knowledge of musical elements such as melody and rhythm. This is done in a competitive way, sometimes allowing more than one user to have turns at the correct answers. Sometimes the games are more like adventures in which a single user is asked to solve a puzzle or arrive at some defined plateau. Such adventures often have music tasks to solve on the way to the final goal. Game software generally makes extensive use of graphics and animation to accompany its many uses of sound. It might also contain creative elements.

Exploratory/Creative

Software using this approach encourages students to explore and create music. The accent is less on mastering particular skills and more on gathering information about a topic through reading and listening or creating music through composition or improvisation. The user is not expected to work in a linear fashion from the beginning of the program to the end. To support listening, the software might offer a construction kit for creating images and words that demonstrate the organization of the music. Students are given a great deal of creative control. Many titles in this category use audio CDs, CD-ROMs, and DVDs. Digital audio and MIDI-based sound are often used, as are other multimedia resources.

Teacher Resource

One of the more recent approaches in CAI software development is to focus not on the students per se but on the teacher. These titles contain important information about music teaching and are designed to assist the teaching process. For example, sample lesson plans are provided, with multimedia resources like sound files and images to help explain a teaching approach. Work sheets may be provided that can be printed out and distributed to students. The focus of instruction might be on music itself or on music taught with the support of a particular software program. Often, the software refers to published teaching standards to help integrate technology into the curriculum. The format for such software is often a set of PDF files.

Internet-Based

This approach is unique in that it delivers content over the Internet. For example, resources might be devoted to interactive instruction in music theory and aural skills or possibly instrument identification. Other sites might feature music composition or music-listening support. Many of these resources are offered free of charge, while others require a small fee for instruction, especially if connected to an institution's course of study.

Many teachers develop online resources for formal courses taught at their schools. These materials are often available only to students enrolled in their classes by password access. Such course materials might be designed for students "in residence" or perhaps as part of a "distance-learning" program of study. Extensive use of multimedia resources such as sound files, graphics, and digital movies is common.

LINK
Be sure to link the descriptions here with those in Module 23 for a complete survey of CAI titles.

Examples of Knowledge and Skill-Development Software

We cannot describe all CAI music software available for personal computers, but the titles in Tables 22.1 and 23.1 represent typical products. Our inclusion of these programs does not necessarily constitute a listing of the "best" CAI software available, because this determination is always a very personal one based on individual circumstance. What we offer in this module and the following one are samples of titles we have seen being used by many music educators.

Software category placement is based on our judgment of the software's primary function; some titles contain content that relates to other categories. First, we describe the beginning-skills software for younger children across the four approaches. We then examine the remaining examples for older children organized by major approach.

Beginning-Skills Software for Knowledge and Skill Development

As educators and researchers have discovered the importance of music learning in the early years of life, software for this age group has become more common. In most software categories, examples of computer-aided instruction can be found that place less emphasis on word reading and use engaging graphics, animation, and speech. Most titles are appropriate for primary-school ages, but some can be used with even younger children.

The category, early keyboard skills, provides experiences with basic note identification and stresses relationships between notation and the music keyboard. The example in Figure 22.1 is a drill-and-practice routine that associates letter names with keys. The program supports both MIDI and digitized sound, as do others using this approach.

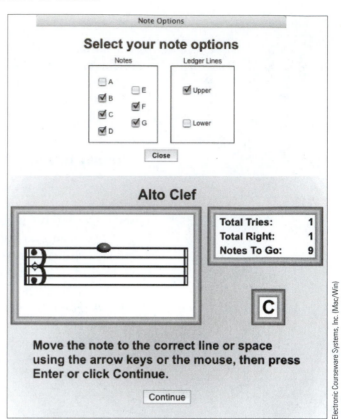

FIGURE 22.1 Early Keyboard Skills

FIGURE 22.2 Clef Notes

The same kind of skill building featured in Clef Notes (Figure 22.2) drills users in note names for tenor, alto, bass, and treble clefs. The program provides options for drills and an interactive game. Here, however, choices can be made for content by including certain pitches and ledger lines.

In the guided-instruction category, the titles in the MiDisaurus series are noteworthy. In eight volumes, the series features more than 500 activities that help teach basic music skills and knowledge. The approach makes heavy use of animation and a child's spoken voice, as well as music notation and digital audio. Figure 22.3 is taken from the first volume. Here, the task is to listen to two recorded examples and choose the notation that fits. Other volumes include work with music theory, aural skills, composition, and singing. Volume 5, for example, includes listening experiences for world instruments and Volume 8 introduces the blues.

The MiDisaurus series also includes four additional "focus" volumes that deal with notation, composers and their music, rhythm, and music instruments. In these and other volumes, the content is divided into chapters, with ample opportunity to complete short evaluation exercises to check for mastery.

Although many CAI titles have game elements, certain programs are especially game-based. Musicus and more advanced versions of the same program called Super Musicus and Challenge Musicus are similar in design to the "Tetris" computer games. As can be seen in Figure 22.4, falling blocks in the form of notation patterns must be moved to form levels. Points are awarded for successfully maneuvering the falling blocks into predetermined measures. The user must understand note values and their relationship to measures in order to place them correctly. Different difficulty levels are offered and notes with ties are placed across adjoining measures.

FIGURE 22.3   MiDisaurus, Volume 1

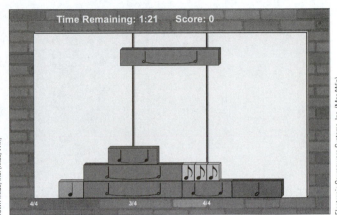

FIGURE 22.4   Musicus

DVD-ROM
Project 17 Practice Your Aural Skills with Auralia, MiBAC Music Lessons, and Practica Musica

Drill-and-Practice Software Examples

Aural Skills/Music Theory

Auralia and MiBAC Music Lessons I and II are examples of aural-skills and music-theory software that provide drill-and-practice routines for primary- and secondary-school students. Each support built-in instrument sounds and external MIDI instruments. Auralia also uses external microphone input for singing exercises.

Auralia offers 26 task sets of ear-training exercises organized in four categories: Intervals & Scales, Chords, Rhythm, and Pitch & Melody. Each set of drills offers multiple levels of complexity and some offer customization options. Figure 22.5a displays a screen from the Advanced Chord Progressions task set within the Chords category. Here the user is given an eight-chord sequence and is asked to identify the chord function from the choices in the rounded buttons in the screen's center. When you select a chord function, it is placed in the rectangular boxes above. The chord's position and type are also requested. The tasks become more difficult as you succeed with each drill.

In the Pitch & Melody category, singing drills are offered. The program records scale singing, for example, and evaluates pitch accuracy using microphone input. Perception of accurate tuning is also tested, as displayed in Figure 22.5b. Here the user is asked to adjust the tuning of interval's second note.

Auralia also offers information in the form of short tutorials on each of the 26 task sets. If the program is used in a class setting, administrative functions are included to track student progress. The software also supports the preparation of customized student tests.

MiBAC Music Lessons I and II offers sets of drill-and-practice routines for fundamentals (I) and chords and harmony (II). Music Lessons I covers note reading, the circle of fifths, key signatures, scales (including major, minor, modes, and jazz-based), scale degrees and intervals, and note and rest durations. Figure 22.6 shows a drill from the jazz-scales section. Input for answers can be supplied by typing or by using a MIDI device. Incorrect answers are identified and the program displays the correct answers for comparison.

Music Lessons II includes work on chord elements, triads, seventh chords, and

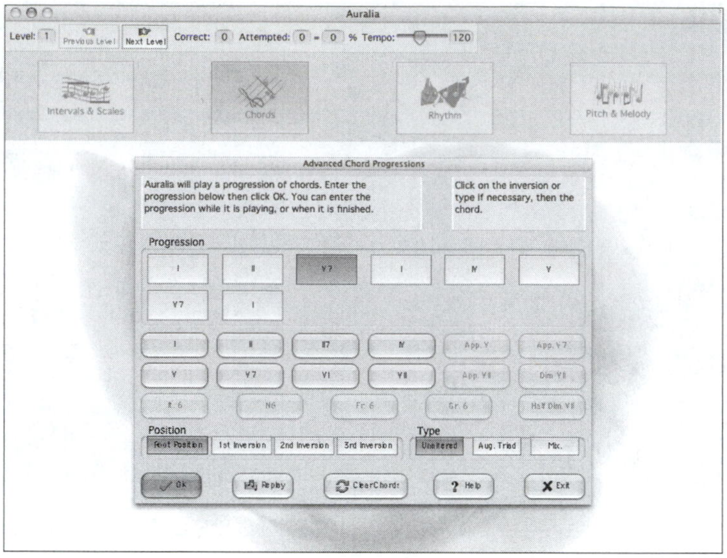

FIGURE 22.5A Auralia

Rising Software, Inc. (Distributed by Sibelius) (Mac/Win)

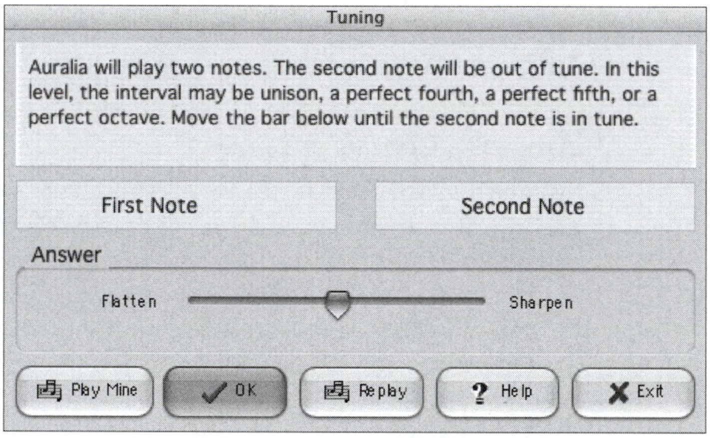

FIGURE 22.5B Auralia

chord functions. The theory of chords is covered, as well as ear-training identification. Each drill set has different levels of difficulty, and choices of clef are offered. Individual progress reports can be saved. As with Auralia, tutorials on music concepts are included. The user can choose several response options, including on-screen piano, guitar, and alphabet blocks, as well as attached MIDI devices and synthesized sounds. Music Lessons also provides many possibilities for custom level definitions for the lessons themselves. Options for choosing accidentals are supported, as are details for scoring.

Performance

Our last drill-and-practice example comes from performance study. Piano Suite is a set of activities that help you learn to play the piano keyboard with computer assistance. The software comes with a number of folk, jazz, popular, and standard piano works. The music is displayed on the screen, much like is shown in Figure 22.7. MIDI files of the pieces are controlled by the screen options for changing tempo, metronome, loudness, note size, and left or right hand only. Finger positions are included in the music and related to the keyboard below. The software monitors your playing and places a marking above notes that are played incorrectly. A short written summary is provided about your performance after you're

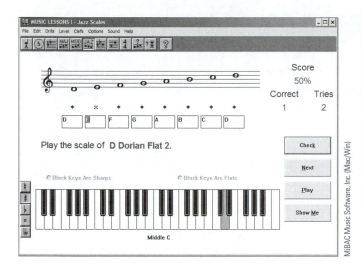

FIGURE 22.6   MiBAC Music Lessons I: Fundamentals

FIGURE 22.7   Piano Suite

done. You can ask the software to monitor just the accuracy of your rhythm, or just the note pitches, or both together in real-time performance. The software can keep records of your performance as well.

In addition to being able to monitor performance, the program offers a composition activity, a section on historical notes about the music, some guided instruction on music theory, and a few games. You must have a MIDI keyboard and the program uses the sound card of your computer to generate sound.

Flexible-Practice Software Examples

Aural Skills/Music Theory

We highlight two flexible-practice programs for aural skills and music theory that offer not only a number of prepared exercises but also powerful options for creating custom content. MacGAMUT offers drills for intervals, scales, chords, melodic, harmonic, and rhythmic dictation. Several levels are offered within each drill set. Scales are provided in both ascending and descending form, in both major and minor keys. Modes are also an option. Chord drills use both triads and seventh chords with different inversions. For dictation exercises, many levels are offered, ranging from very simple to quite complex. More than a thousand melodies and chord progressions are included across all levels.

In addition to all these choices, teachers using MacGAMUT can set mastery parameters for each level before the student can progress to the next level. If the teacher doesn't care for the melodies or harmonic progressions provided, the instructor's disk contains routines to create completely new examples.

Users can also choose to practice any level for any drill set without the pressure of showing mastery. Users can create their own drill examples for intervals, scales, and chords. There are options to practice notating and playing exercises similar to the ones in the program. MacGAMUT offers MIDI input and output, as well as digitized sounds.

Figure 22.8 offers an example from this software. Notice the feedback on the bottom left. Newer versions of MacGAMUT offer beaming options for the rhythmic and melodic dictation exercises and built-in stresses on the strong beats of each

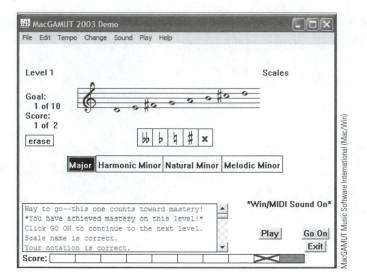

FIGURE 22.8
MacGAMUT

measure for a more natural feel to the music. Ties are used for more-sophisticated rhythmic work.

Practica Musica offers drills on more than 80 separate task sets, many of which are displayed in Figure 22.9a. Most of these have at least four levels of difficulty and each set has an information screen that helps the user with the tasks. Program content is tied to a theory textbook that is sold separately. Generally, the student responds to drills using a detailed on-screen piano keyboard graphic that offers options for displaying pitch symbols with enharmonic equivalents. MIDI input and output are recommended for this program, especially for the sight-reading exercises that help develop performance competency. Practica Musica also offers internal sound samples with options for piano, harpsichord, and organ timbres. A unique feature is the ability to choose internal tuning systems, such as just intonation and mean-tone tuning, as well as the standard equal-temperament system.

As with other CAI programs, Practica Musica provides feedback for pitch and rhythm drills. This is shown in Figure 22.9b. Incorrect notes are flagged with hints about rhythmic accuracy. The latest version of the program supports acoustic voice or instrument entry, with an added microphone for specific tasks like pitch reading and interval playing,

For dictation, Practica Musica supplies melodies in various styles and also allows for computer-generated tunes, and there is a useful editor for creating customized melodies. Additional options include a metronome sound and the ability to work on smaller sections of a long melodic series. Task sets that come with the program are all customizable.

Extended Listening/History

TimeSketch Editor Pro allows you to construct guided-listening maps to help students better understand form and learn more about the details of a composition. The editor works with CD audio, MP3, WAV, AIF, or MIDI sound files. Once the media have been referenced, the editor allows you to mark points in the sound file that, in turn, create "bubble charts" representing audio-file portions between markers.

Figure 22.10 provides a view of a map created this way. Note that the author of the chart has labeled certain sections and provided a text description in a box below the chart. Clicking on any part of the bubble chart will cause the computer

Ars Nova Software LLC (Mac/Win)

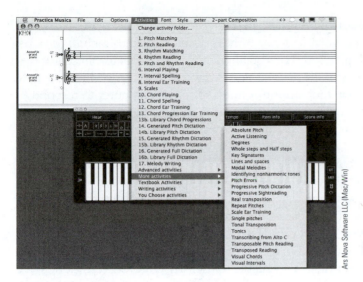

FIGURE 22.9A Practica Musica

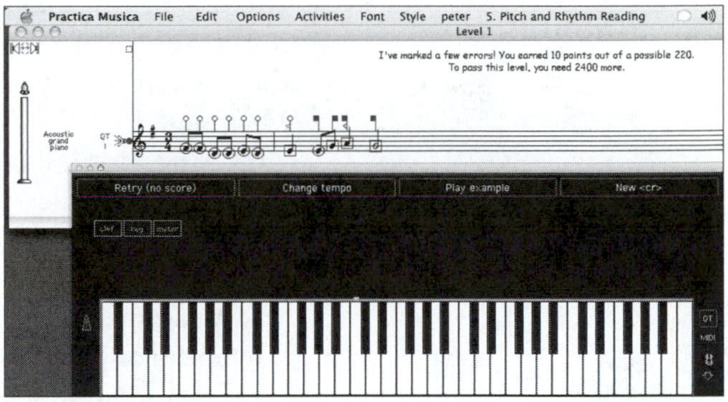

FIGURE 22.9B Practica Musica

Map supplied courtesy of Scott Lipscomb, Electronic Courseware Systems, Inc. (Mac/Win)

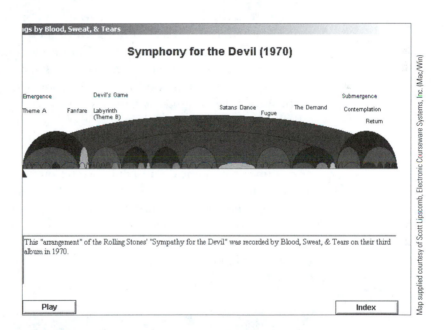

FIGURE 22.10
TimeSketch Editor Pro

to play that portion of the music. The media file must be on the computer for the music to sound. TimeSketch Editor Pro supports files distributed over the Internet. A free "player" application can be downloaded and used to support the playback. A cover page can be created to provide more detailed information and text can support hyperlinks to other locations. Text can be programmed to appear at key times as the music unfolds. TimeSketch is shown here as an author tool, but teachers can use it to encourage students to create charts as well.

Performance

Our final example of flexible-practice software is an accompaniment system for music performance. The SmartMusic system is designed to allow the computer to accompany instrumentalists and vocalists as they work on performance literature.

ASIDE
You can use the Yamaha Silent Brass, Silent Strings, and Silent Drums as input devices to SmartMusic with headphones for private music practice that doesn't disturb your neighbors!

LINK
See Module 20 for more about the MakeMusic! family of notation programs.

Unlike Piano Suite, SmartMusic is designed for a number of instruments (woodwinds, brass, strings) and voices. It not only uses standard music compositions, etudes, and lesson-book materials but also allows for importing custom scores created by the MakeMusic! family of notation software (e.g., PrintMusic!, Finale 2005). The software uses a microphone connected to the computer to respond to the acoustic instrument/voice and accompanies the player or singer. If requested, the software will also analyze your performance and save recorded performances as MP3 files.

Using synthesized sounds in the computer, the SmartMusic system intelligently accompanies the player or singer by following tempo variations. As the musician performs, the software "listens" to the solo line, identifies the pitch patterns, compares these with the data that represent the score, and produces the accompaniment. The system is sophisticated enough to "find" the soloists if they skip ahead or back in the score.

The literature supplied is made available to users by yearly subscription. More than 20,000 solo works, 50,000 exercises, and music from various band methods are available. Standard jazz solos are included, together with repertoires from many state solo and ensemble contest lists.

Figure 20.11 displays the main screen from SmartMusic. Notice that this main screen has controls for stopping, starting, and pausing. A foot pedal can also be added to the computer to help start and stop without a mouse. The software displays the measure and beat as the accompaniment is played. Here we have set the tempo to a quarter note = 80 and we can control the countoff and whether or not to hear the solo line and accompaniment. Sensitivity for following the soloist can also be set. To the right are buttons for additional services such as transposing and the setup of a practice loop to help work with difficult sections. Customization options are provided for special aspects, such as declaring breath points. A software tuner automatically responds to the pitch played and shows deviations in pitch. A metronome offers accented downbeats and subdivisions.

Some selections provide sheet music that can be printed, but most require the score to be supplied separately. Assessment options exist for certain scores. The computer evaluates the pitch and rhythm of your performance and marks the score accordingly.

FIGURE 22.11
SmartMusic

Guided Instruction

Mastery of specific skills has been the major goal of all of the software examples noted thus far. Guided instruction also has this as its mission, but it does so with ongoing guidance in the form of spoken tutorials. As software distribution moves to CDs, DVDs, and the Internet, more space is available for content. Speech, music, text, and graphics will be used more creatively, and there is likely to be growth in this category of software.

Aural Skills/Music Theory

A software series that demonstrates guided instruction for young and more-advanced students is Music Ace and Music Ace 2. Music Ace contains basic lessons on pitch identification, note reading, key signatures, scales, whole and half steps, and other knowledge. Music Ace 2 provides more advanced lessons, including standard notation, rhythm skills, melodic contour, syncopation, harmony, and much more.

Both programs offer a similar design approach. The opening screen allows the user to choose to work with a lesson and its representative game or with the "Doodle Pad." There is also an option for checking progress on the lessons. Figure 12.12a shows Lesson 12, devoted to the relationship between volume and pitch. The lesson begins with the Little Professor explaining how pitches heard at different loudness levels might confuse the hearing of pitch. The lesson provides the opportunity to match pitch at different loudness levels by using the slider bar to match the pitch. Each lesson has multiple levels. Other lessons include an introduction to the keyboard, staff, timbre, pitches, sharps and flats, key signatures, and major scales. The games provided for each lesson also have various levels.

The Doodle Pad is always available to allow users to experiment by creating their own compositions. Different timbres are possible, and notes can be dragged into place for each timbre. Speed and volume can be controlled. Figure 22.12b contains an example of a gigue by Buxtehude that has already been composed as an example from the "Jukebox" group of supplied tunes. Music Ace 2 follows the same approach, but uses more-advanced lesson content. Music Ace and Music

FIGURE 22.12A   Music Ace

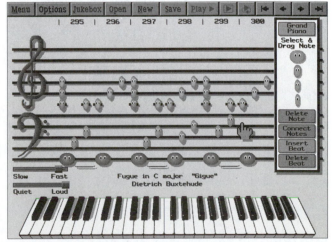

FIGURE 22.12B   Music Ace

Ace 2 both use MIDI sound and internal sounds. For both family and large-class use, multiple users are supported with progress charts maintained for each user.

Another example of a guided-instruction title in aural skills and music theory is the three volumes that comprise Alfred's Essentials of Music Theory. Topics covered in the 75 lessons range from basic note reading to basic forms of music. Music-theory knowledge is covered, as are basic ear-training and aural skills. Each lesson includes a spoken voice that guides you through the material presented. The voice narrates as parts of this window develop in time. When the dialog is finished, you might want to hear the blues scale or repeat the lesson. Figure 22.13a is an exercise window. Here you fill in the missing notes and, if you are successful, points are awarded to a cumulative score held in a database. Additional lesson parts might include larger musical examples, such as the music displayed in Figure 22.13b. The software contains many digital audio examples from a wide range of music styles.

Performance

Guided-instruction programs for instruments like guitar and piano are examples of this type of software applied to performance. eMedia Guitar Method 1 is an example. It contains 155 lessons covering topics such as strumming, melody playing, and other guitar techniques. Figure 22.14 shows a typical lesson in which you can see a discussion of 3/4 time and a digital movie clip that demonstrates a technique. Other software screens show an animated fretboard to assist with performance.

Extensive use is made of digital audio, movies, and variable-speed MIDI files. A tuner is included, along with a digital metronome and a 250-chord dictionary that provides visual and auditory examples. A special feature of the software is a set of more than 70 performances from famous guitarists in many different genres. You can record yourself and compare your performances with those of different artists.

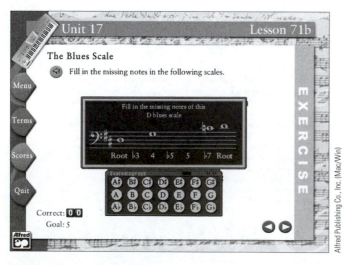

FIGURE 22.13A Alfred's Essentials of Music Theory

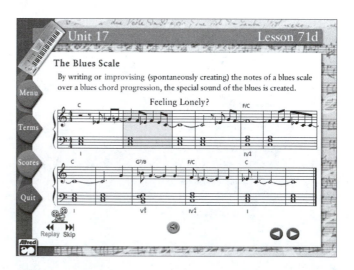

FIGURE 22.13B Alfred's Essentials of Music Theory

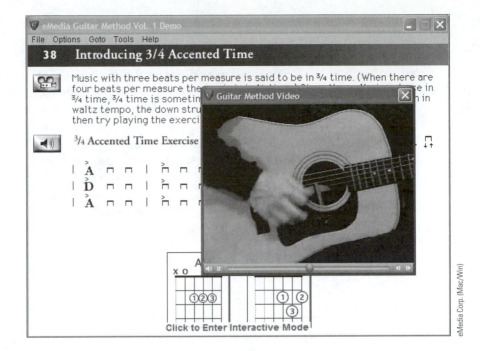

FIGURE 22.14   eMedia Guitar Method 1

Improvisation

The last examples in guided instruction deal with improvisation. Sheddin' the Basics: Jazz Piano is designed to help build skills in jazz-keyboard playing. Guided lessons are provided, including information on chord-voicing and voice-leading based on 21 tunes with standard progressions. The content is based on the teachings and playing of a master jazz artist, in this case Michael Kocour. The software provides exercises that you can play interactively with the computer. Figure 22.15 provides a view of this. Note the ability to turn on and off the accompanying instruments and to record your playing. The options are designed to allow Michael's playing to be heard, as well as that of the student using the software.

FIGURE 22.15
Sheddin' the Basics: Jazz Piano

The software includes printable lead sheets of the music, along with a fake book that contains songs and accompaniments. Professional recordings of the tunes are also included.

A second example from the same company is Sheddin' the Basics: Latin Jazz. Again, a professional performer is highlighted, in this case Ruben Alvarez. In this software, a similar approach is taken to allow students to hear typical Latin jazz music and to practice playing in that style. You can mute instrument lines, so that you can play that line together with the computer. A fake book is also included, with printable lead sheets that appear on the screen to guide improvisation. The software also contains sections on the history of Latin jazz and Latin jazz-band instruments, with digital video of musicians playing the instruments. These multimedia resources also make this product similar to the creative/exploratory software titles in Module 23.

Game-Based

Our last examples in this module use a gaming strategy to engage the user in music experiences. Game elements exist in other software as well, but the titles described here have gaming as a central feature.

Aural Skills/Music Theory

Hearing Music is the newest in a series of software products written by famed composer Morton Subotnick. This program centers on aural skills by providing four sets of tasks: comparing, ordering, matching, and reading. Figure 22.16a displays a view from the comparing task set. Notice that there are four levels. As you listen to two musical examples, you must compare the two and determine if the second one is somehow different from the first. We have gone right to level 4, where the task is more complex than at lower levels because the choices involve not only higher/lower or faster/slower but also backward and upside down. Figure 22.16b is an example from the reading task set. Here you have four levels, but also sets defined as beginning or advanced. The task is to listen to a target excerpt and

FIGUREFIGURE 22.16A Hearing Music

Viva Media, Inc. (Win)

FIGURE 22.16B Hearing Music

FIGURE 22.17   Pianist Performance Series (The Blues Pianist)

LINK

Return to Viewport V if you need to refresh your understanding of MIDI files.

compare it to the notation displayed in order to choose the right one. The music examples for all the task sets are digital audio, with many drawn from classical-music genres.

Extended Listening/History

Our last example in this module is the Piano Performance Series, which features the performances of major performers rendered in MIDI-file format. The software gives you access to these performances and lets you experiment with tempo and key. The series includes blues, Latin, modern jazz, and new age piano repertoire. Figure 22.17 shows a view of the blues program, with the music of Doc Fingers selected. The buttons on the left give you access to the total music list or to those selections included by certain artists. You can also sort by form and type. In this example, where we have chosen the "Cakewalk" selection, there is a brief description of the piece in the middle window. Also revealed is a notation window that scrolls along as the music is playing. The music can be stopped at any time and stepped through slowly for study or printed out. If the music includes other instruments, such as a bass or percussion, the notation for these can also be shown. The software allows you to assign MIDI patches to different instruments if you do not like the General MIDI patches chosen.

The reason we include this software under the games approach is because of the two game features that come with each piano series title. A "Guess!" option is provided. When you click on this, a random selection is made of all the blues pieces in the listing below and you are asked to identify which one is playing. In addition, you can play a trivia game at any time that tests your knowledge of blues music and the context in which it was composed and performed.

Module 23

New Directions in Music-Instruction Software

DVD-ROM
Projects 17–19 on the accompanying DVD are designed to give you hands-on experience with selected titles in Tables 22.1 and Table 23.1.

LINK
Be sure to read the last module for an overview of CAI software approaches and content.

LINK
The structure of this activity is similar to that of sequencing software, which we presented in Module 15.

We turn our attention now to newer directions in music-instruction software. In the last module, we reviewed many products that stress basic knowledge and skill development in music. In this module, we consider more-creative and exploratory software, as well as the new trend creating teacher resources in software. We also note the rise of Internet-based education efforts.

Examples of New Directions in Music-Instruction Software

Table 23.1 is our second table of software examples for music teaching. As we noted in Module 22, the exploratory/creative approach stresses music teaching from a generative perspective, encouraging the user to explore and construct understanding with creative experiences in music listening, composing, and improvising. The teacher-resource approach is emerging from companies anxious to help teachers construct better learning strategies. Although often tied to a particular product, this approach succeeds in stimulating teaching ideas and materials. The Internet-based approach is emerging as a multimedia resource for music teachers and has affected the number of multimedia products distributed in CD format.

Exploratory/Creative-Software Examples

Beginning Skills

Thinkin' Things is a series of three programs for young children designed to encourage exploration of arts and ideas. Music plays a major role in each set of programs.

Figure 23.1 shows "Oranga" and his band—an activity from the second set of programs. The Oranga character and his friends serve as performers for the sequence, which can be created in the three "tracks." This can be done by simply clicking on the cells in each track to have a sound occur and then by clicking on the Play button. The characters play what has been composed. The instruments the characters play can be changed to other timbres, and there is even an option for recording your own sound by using the computer's microphone. Two perception games are also included. One game asks the user to listen to a sequence and tell which character played a highlighted track; the second game reverses the task and asks which track was played by the highlighted character. A range of difficulty levels is offered.

TABLE 23.1   CAI Titles for New Directions in Music-Instruction Software

	Exploratory/Creative	Teacher Resource	Internet-Based
Beginning Skills	• Thinking Things 2 (Mac/Win) • Beethoven Lives Upstairs (Win)	• Sibelius Notes (Mac/Win)	• New York Philharmonic
Aural Skills/Music Theory		• Sibelius Instruments (Mac/Win)	• MusicTheory.net • MakingMusic
Extended Listening/History	• Oscar Peterson (Win) • Impromtu (Mac/Win)		• ArtsEdge Xploring Xtremes • ArtsAlive • Carnegie Hall Listening Adventures
Improvisation	• Rock Rap 'N Roll (Mac/Win) • Band-in-a-Box (Mac/Win)		• Berklee Shares
Composition	• Making Music and Making More Music (Mac/Win) • Dance eJay (Win) • SuperDuper Music Looper (Win)	• Teaching Music with Reason (Mac/Win) • Sibelius Compass (Mac/Win)	• Vermont MIDI Project

Beethoven Lives Upstairs, an interactive CD-ROM based in part on the film of the same name, provides the user with an exploratory set of music and art experiences. The CD uses digital video clips, as seen in Figure 23.2a in the upper right, and animated graphics. While reading the pages in the book that serves as the central focus of the CD, Beethoven pops up occasionally to offer special help and encouragement.

Rooms in Beethoven's upstairs apartment are featured, as noted in Figure 23.2b. In this case, the user is encouraged to choose a Beethoven music composition and

FIGURE 23.1   Thinkin' Things Collection 2

Edmark Corporation (Mac/Win)

March 8, 1824

Mr. Beethoven's room is such a mess. I am almost afraid to go inside. There are pianos on the floor, papers and food everywhere, and dirty clothes hanging from furniture.

...earing ...phony. ...uld make him ...py, but his temper just seems to get worse and worse...

FIGURE 23.2A
Beethoven Lives Upstairs

FIGURE 23.2B
Beethoven Lives Upstairs

decide which instruments each character will play. The animation continues by placing the instruments chosen in the characters' hands and then the software plays the composition with those instrument timbres. The software has interactive games, with composition as a focus, and a few drawing tasks. A journal can be kept of the various activities.

Extended Listening/History

The Oscar Peterson Multimedia CD-ROM is an example of extended listening in that it contains several performances of his music with digital audio commentary on that music by Peterson himself. Figure 23.3 displays listings of the CD's music and major chapters, as well as some music highlighted during performance. Audio

FIGURE 23.3
Oscar Peterson Multimedia
CD-ROM

files are generally MIDI files that can be altered for playback, including an option for "half speed" so the user can study the playing. The CD contains a number of photographs linked to audio interviews, an autobiography, a timeline of Peterson's life and achievements, and a song list.

Another example of extended-listening software that offers a creative approach is Impromtu (Oxford University Press [Mac/Win]), designed to accompany a music-listening textbook by the same name authored by the researcher and teacher Jeanne Bamberger. The software is a toolkit of sound objects representing melodies and rhythms that can be assembled in ways that let users construct their music understanding intuitively.

Improvisation

Rock Rap 'N Roll allows you to construct a composition from digitized sound excerpts and "improvise" with them in real time. Several styles of popular music are offered, including blues, techno-pop, rap, and soul. After picking a style, you are given a screen to construct the composition; Figure 23.4 shows a screen for the blues. The excerpts listed on the left can be dragged into the circles at the bottom to create a sequence. Once the sequence is chosen, clicking on the start button will play the excerpts in order. The excerpts are designed to sound reasonably good no matter what order is chosen; however, some choices are musically more likely than others. As the music is playing, you can add shorter sound licks with other buttons and keyboard options. We have revealed the key-map listing of what plays when individual keys are depressed. The "Bop-O-Rama" button can be assigned different sounds that are also displayed. The "Vibe-A-Tron" can be programmed the same way. The "Voc-A-Lizer" buttons control various vocal licks. You can even add your own custom sounds using your computer's microphone and add them to the "Bop-O-Rama" and "Vibe-A-Tron" options.

You can save your actions to form a session file. When you do this, you are not saving the sounds but rather the actions you made. Opening the file at a later time reconstructs the decisions and allows you to hear what you did. The program

FIGURE 23.4
Rock Rap 'N Roll

DVD-ROM
Project 18 Learning to
Improvise

allows teachers and students to study the choices and nature of the "improvisation" decisions made. Of course, you are not really playing the improvisations, but the planning for what elements sound where, opens the door to improvisational thinking.

Band-in-a-Box software gets much closer to simulating real improvisation. This program turns your computer and any MIDI sound device into a music ensemble devoted to supporting your solo improvisations. Chord changes are created in designated measures and built-in styles are provided that intelligently create a background for the changes given. Like many of the programs described in this module, you can run this program without external MIDI devices by software synthesis, but some kind of MIDI-input device like a keyboard controller is very valuable if you want to interact directly with the software for recording performances.

Figure 23.5a illustrates the improvisation screen with the main controls in the top half and the chord symbols on the bottom. Notice that the chord symbols are added in appropriate spots in measures 1–28, with measures 29–30 as the closing section. Band-in-a-Box accepts the names of a large variety of chord symbols by names typed on the computer keyboard. It also accepts chords as played on a music keyboard by analyzing the played chord and constructing the appropriate symbol. Once chord changes are entered, the program can be told how many verses to create and how to deal with repeats. Beginnings and endings can be created and you can also indicate which section is the "bridge" if the form dictates this. In addition to creating your own chord changes for a song, Band-in-a-Box comes with several compositions already created for you in many different styles. Tempo and key can be easily declared and the music can be transposed instantly to a given key if needed.

Clicking on the Play button causes the program to give a two-measure introduction and then to play an accompaniment that may use drum set, bass, piano,

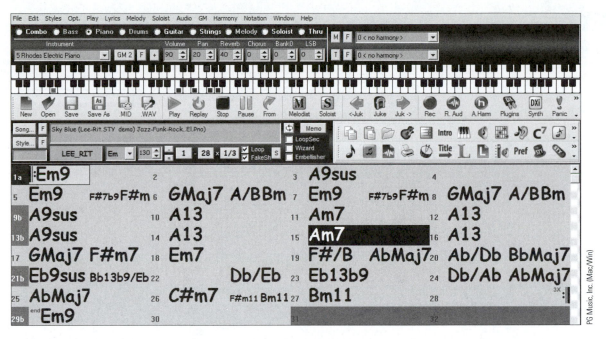

FIGURE 23.5A Band-in-a-Box main screen and chord entry

and guitar tracks or some other appropriate ensemble based on the style selected. If you have a MIDI controller attached to the computer, you can add a melody line or an improvised solo. The program allows you to change the accompaniment timbres instantly if you don't like what is given. Changing the style will create new rhythms and timbres that are appropriate for the style chosen.

Styles are selected from a list displayed in the window in Figure 23.5b. To the left are style categories supported. In the center are the specific styles for this software installation. We have highlighted a style named "60s Brit Rock Ballad." The algorithm that creates the style uses even 16th-note patterns and has an initial tempo of 77 beats per minute. Other styles that might fit your needs are shown with either an asterisk (*) or a carrot (^), indicating excellent or good fit to an imagined style. Clicking the preview button at the top plays the chord changes in the main window in that style. A demonstration song is available for all styles.

Notation is possible and can be viewed by instrument. Figure 23.5c demonstrates the notation view for the piano part of the "stride" style. Notation can be printed for further study. The software exports standard MIDI files for use in other music programs and can save the MIDI data into standard digital audio formats, including MP3. Digital audio can be recorded as the solo line by way of a microphone, thus allowing non-MIDI performers such as instrumentalists with acoustic instruments and vocalists to improvise with Band-in-a-Box and have their work saved with the accompaniment.

Composition

Morton Subotnick's Making Music and Making More Music allow students to actually draw music gestures on the screen and manipulate them much as composers do. Making Music is best suited for preschool and early elementary-aged children; Making More Music works best for older students who are beginning to learn traditional music notation and would like more advanced work.

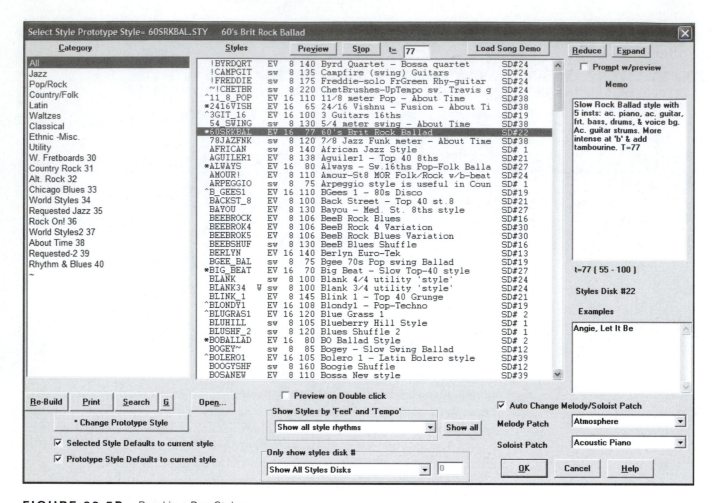

FIGURE 23.5B   Band-in-a-Box Styles

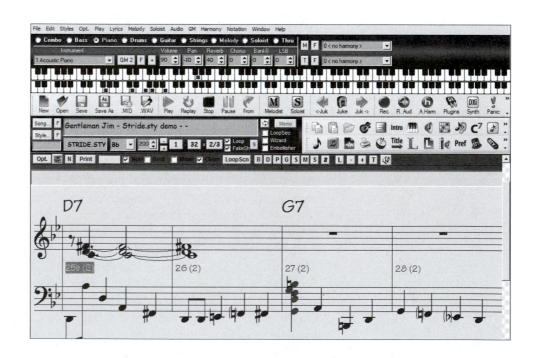

FIGURE 23.5C
Band-in-a-Box Notation

In Figure 23.6a, you can see the central screen for Making Music. We have drawn two musical lines using the paintbrush tool and assigned each to a different timbre by using the artist-palette tool. By using the mouse to sketch, a user can create a musical gesture. Other buttons allow a chosen portion of the gesture to be altered for dynamic change, pitch, or tempo. You can ask the program to make global changes such as inverting the intervals, playing the line backward (retrograde), or some combination of both. Smaller or larger sections of the musical gestures can be "picked up" and moved around to different pitch levels. You can even alter the underlying scale structures by electing to have minor, pentatonic, chromatic, or whole-tone scales. You can even create your own scales.

Other options exist for composition as part of the program. Making Music allows you to save multiple compositions into libraries of creative work and also offers a number of supportive games for aural-skills training similar in some ways to the Hearing Music games noted in Module 22.

Making More Music is similar in structure, but includes traditional notation. Instead of an open structure for drawing, the user works with a chamber-music metaphor of either four independent instruments, a solo instrument and piano, or two pianos. Drawing the music gestures is similar to Making Music except that you draw on a traditional staff. Figure 23.6b shows what happens in Making More Music when you ask the program to translate the drawings to traditional notation. Of course, you can also decide right from the start not to draw but to actually work with traditional notation. Making More Music also has a melody maker that allows you to choose the length of a melody, the complexity of the rhythm, and the general intervallic structure. You can make changes in tempo, dynamics, meter, and scale. The program comes with a Rhythm Band that uses percussion-instrument timbres and allows you to create rhythms for your compositions by tapping a pattern. There is a Theme and Variations maker and more advanced games that use full compositions in more sophisticated ways than Making Music. Both programs use external MIDI devices or built-in synthesized sounds.

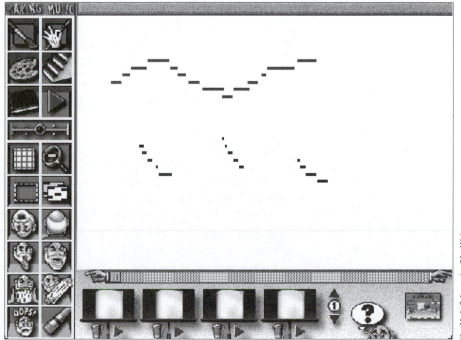

FIGURE 23.6A
Make Music

Viva-Media Software, Inc. (Mac/Win)

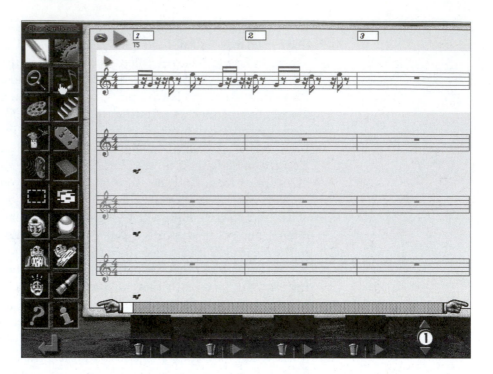

FIGURE 23.6B Making More Music

LINK

Review Module 12 on multiple tracks and looping software.

Super Duper Music Looper is produced by the same company that makes ACID and ACID Express. The program is really a simplified version of the ACID looping environment and takes on many of the same characteristics. Figure 23.7 displays a nine-track composition on which you can paint loops supplied by the software. In addition, you can record your own loops using the computer's microphone. Recorded loops get saved for future use.

Volume for each track can be edited in the track's header area. In addition, volume for the entire composition can be controlled at the top right, together with the key and tempo. Compositions can be saved as a small loop-project file with markers to the audio and an independent WAV file. You can also elect to e-mail the file to someone else. The program saves the file in WMA format and links to an appropriate e-mail program on the computer.

Teacher-Resource Software Examples

Beginning Skills

Sibelius Starclass software is a set of enhanced PDF files that contain a number of teaching lesson plans. Each lesson set contains several activities, for a total of 180 different lesson plans. Both British and American English spellings are supported.

Certain lessons are designed for teachers with limited music background. For example, Lesson Set 25 for teacher development and the element of form provides information on pattern and form design, together with teaching points and questions for learning that help guide teaching strategy. The blues form is explained. Other lessons deal with beginning and more-advanced general-music activities designed for children.

Other approaches are also designed as lessons for children and explore special topics like music and places, the natural world, and personal experiences. For ex-

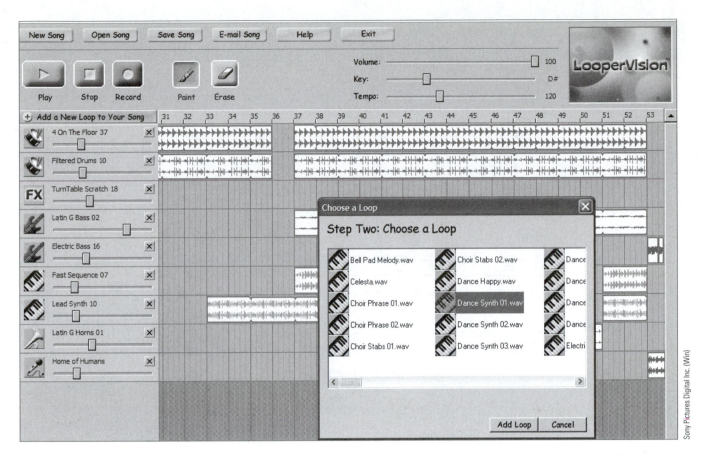

FIGURE 23.7 Super Duper Music Looper

LINK
The National Standards in Arts Education: Music are explained at the end of this Module.

ample, Lesson Set 29, "Magic Carpet," encourages children to imagine magic-carpet rides. Music activities are generated from these imaginary trips and the element of form is described in several different ways.

Figure 23.8 comes from Lesson Set 32, which combines tone color with the Introductory Activities dimension. In this second in a series of four short lesson activities, a folk tune played by different musical instruments is featured. The software supports graphics and digital audio clips. The page can be printed for children to see and the teacher can use the computer in class to play the examples.

Another software feature is the Pathway option in the top menu. Options here allow a teacher to seek content in the lesson plans based on the United Kingdom's Qualifications and Curriculum Authority (QCA) standards or the United States' National Association for Music Education National Standards for music. Other pathways are categorized by interests in dance, drama, literacy, numeracy, visual arts, and technology.

Aural Skills/Music Theory

Sibelius Instruments can be used both as a teaching resource and as a program to be explored by students. The software, an encyclopedia of instruments used in bands and orchestral ensembles, supplies detailed information about instruments and several recorded examples of how they sound. Figure 23.9 shows a detailed page for the violin that can be accessed by clicking on the instrument icons on the orchestra page. Notice the options for hearing different violin notes and timbres.

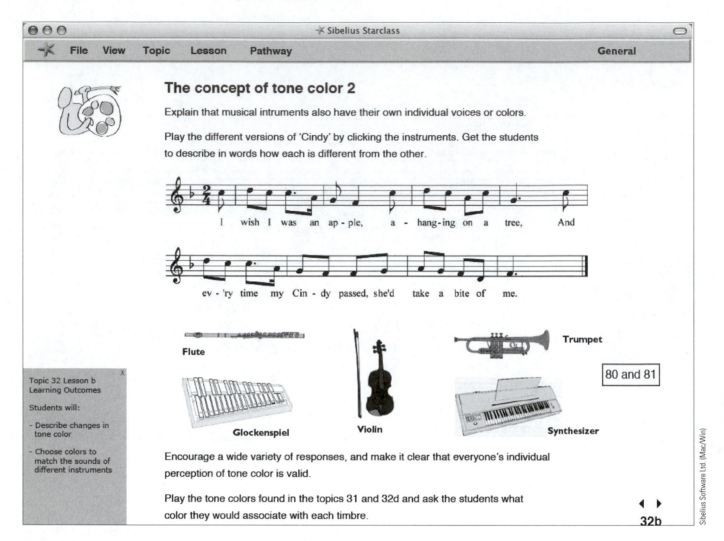

FIGURE 23.8 Sibelius Starclass

The software also provides many lesson plans, recommended listening lists, and written exercises and quizzes for teacher use.

Extended Listening/History

Sibelius Notes (Sibelius Software Ltd. [Mac/Win]) is a collection of digitally prepared work sheets and music scores (Sibelius format) to support instruction. The package's Teacher's Guide has notes and completed work sheets and a CD-ROM of PDF files and music scores. The material is graded and organized for quick access. We have included this in the extended listening/history content category because of the collection of scores that can be used for teaching.

Composition

Teacher resources for music composition can be found in many publications and software titles. Making Music, SuperDooper Music Looper, and many of the sequencing and notation programs covered in past modules are good programs for

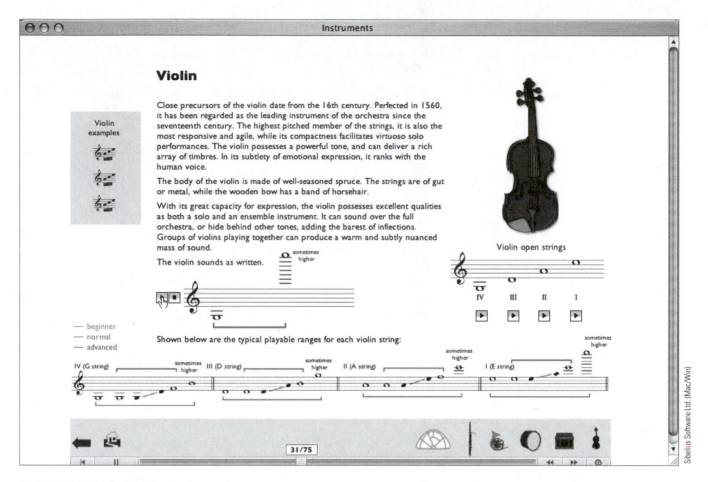

FIGURE 23.9   Sibelius Instruments

students to use. The two items described here add to this mix. Teaching Music with Reason, a text on music and music composition, is tied to the Reason software program presented in Module 17. The text includes lesson plans that use Reason as a way to learn more about music. The materials offer composition instruction while teaching about the software program. Teaching lessons, work sheets, and assessment tools are provided, along with group-project tips.

Sibelius Compass is similar in design to Sibelius Starclass, but concentrates almost entirely on composition. Seven sections deal with pitch shapes, chords and harmony, scales, melody, form, rhythm, and timbre and texture. Each section has subcategories that provide suggested strategies for learning about music through composition. Work sheets and quizzes are also provided. There are also learning pathways for approaching the material; a pathway for an experienced student composer would be different from one for a beginner. Figure 23.10 shows the tracker, a special feature of the software that students can use. This part of Compass provides a kind of programmed sequencer. Musical material from the upper set of defined elements can be dragged into place as objects in a chosen track. Each object can be opened and edited in a matrix editor so that the student can control note pitches and rhythms.

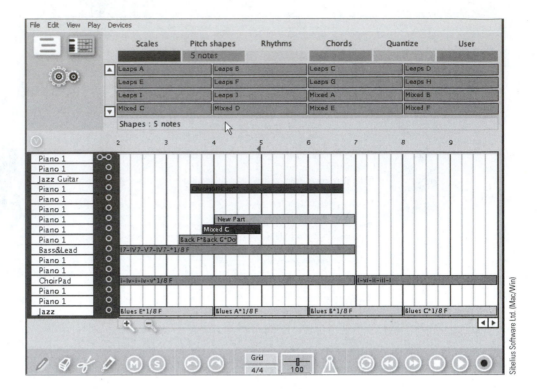

FIGURE 23.10
Sibelius Compass

LINK
Be sure to return to Modules 5, 6, and 7 to review the options and concepts for Internet use.

Internet-Based Software Examples

Our last category in this New Directions Module notes the remarkable growth of the Internet as a major source of music teaching and learning. Resources exist in all content areas and for learners of all ages. This approach is more about delivery than anything else, with an amalgam of approaches ranging from drill-and-practice to exploratory/creative. Many of these sites are available without cost.

Beginning Skills

Two sites from symphony orchestras are worth special mention. The New York Philharmonic KidsZone! provides a number of musical topics for young children. Hot links lead to a composer's gallery, featured musicians in the symphony, an instrument lab and storage area, and a game room. A conductor/soloist dressing area features a fascinating virtual walk to various rooms that feature past symphony conductors and soloists. Each artist's room includes a picture and some information about the person. There are even links to sound files that feature different orchestral excerpts.

Figure 23.11 shows the orchestration station, where you can first hear "The Old Castle" from *Pictures at an Exhibition* played as Musorgsky first wrote it for piano and then hear how Ravel orchestrated it. Next, you can drag different players into position to play the lines. Finally, you can click on the conductor to change the music style (legato, staccato, or special articulations).

The Dallas Symphony's DSOKids is a similar site, featuring a number of activities for music learning with younger children. Figure 23.12 displays the main page for children; clicking on the door labeled "Music Room" moves to a page for parents. The kid's room has links to an instrument encyclopedia, an orchestra seating chart, a practice room for tips on practicing, games, and more. One of the links on the file cabinet brings you to a project center for building your own instrument.

FIGURE 23.11 New York Philharmonic KidsZone!

FIGURE 23.12 Dallas Symphony Orchestra DSOKids

ASIDE
MakingMusic should not be confused with Subotnick's Making Music.

Aural Skills/Music Theory

Ricci Adams' http://www.musictheory.net is a site devoted entirely to music theory and aural-skills instruction. The accent is on music theory, with 34 different lessons on music-theory topics. We have chosen the lesson on common chord progressions in Figure 23.13. Each lesson is an animation authored for the Web using Macromedia's Flash software. There are 10 "trainers," which are interactive drills with sound support.

MakingMusic is a freely distributed program that uses the Web to achieve its desired effect. The program is an encyclopedia of music instruments, much like the Sibelius Instruments package. However MakingMusic includes a vast array of world-music instruments, as well as Western orchestral and band instruments. The program, which can be installed on your computer, uses the Internet to serve up the many instrument sounds. Figure 23.14 shows the simple interface. To the

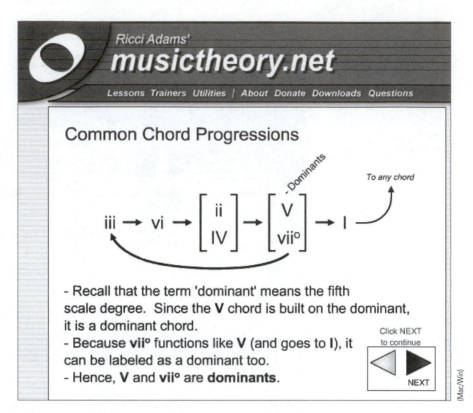

FIGURE 23.13
Ricci Adams' musictheory.net

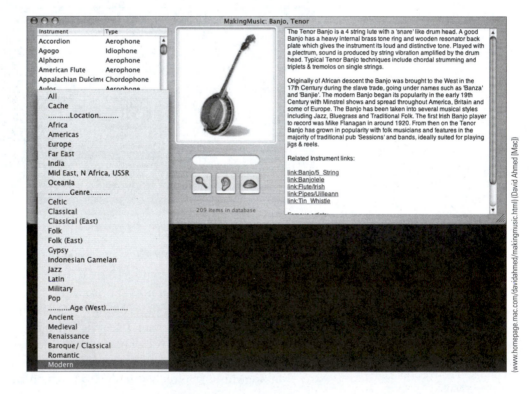

FIGURE 23.14
MakingMusic

right is a long passage of text about the instruments, including links to other sites. Clicking on the lips button actually reads the text box and is a handy way to help young students or those with visual disabilities. The ear button plays the instrument and a small music excerpt typical of the instrument. The magnifying glass searches for the chosen instrument on the left.

Extended Listening/History

Many sites supply links to MIDI and audio files of full pieces of music, but the sites described here offer educational information as well. The ArtsEdge Xploring Xtremes, sponsored by the Kennedy Center in Washington, DC (Figure 23.15), features the National Symphony Orchestra. Several links on this site provide information about music and play extended excerpts from the orchestra's concert season. The ArtsEdge main site also provides links to other music-based activities.

The National Arts Centre of Canada produces ArtsAlive.ca, its education and outreach website for the performing arts. This bilingual website (English and French) offers streaming audio and video, downloadable teacher resource kits, online games, masterclass archives, and other innovative multimedia content in support of the NAC Orchestra's education tours. Pictured in Figure 23.16 is a QuickTime movie of Pinchas Zukerman, violinist and conductor of the National Arts Centre Orchestra.

The Carnegie Hall Listening Adventures is yet another site. Produced by the Carnegie Hall Corporation and WNET/Thirteen New York, this site provides guided-listening experiences for selected masterworks.

Improvisation

Berklee Shares from the Berklee School of Music features some instructional content for the general public for no cost. Pictured here (Figure 23.17) is a lesson on using motives in improvisation featuring school faculty in the form of a Quick-Time movie. Other lessons provided on improvisation and other topics draw from school resources. Links to more-substantial course work are available, but may involve a fee.

Composition

Finally, the Vermont MIDI Project (Figure 23.18) offers opportunities for young composers to share their MIDI-based compositions for others to hear and critique. Older and more-experienced composers offer comment on the music, if desired,

ASIDE

Many sites on the Internet teach music for a fee, but more and more sites have emerged in recent years offering music instruction free of charge.

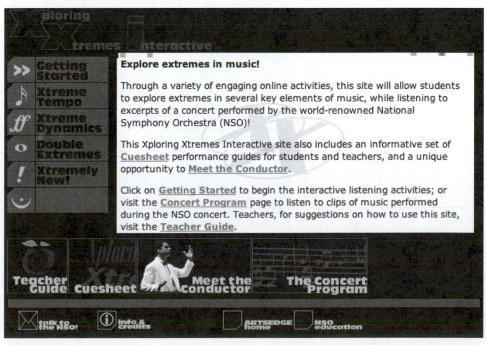

FIGURE 23.15
ArtsEdge Xploring Xtremes

(www.artsedge.kennedy-center.org/content/3062/) (Mac/Win)

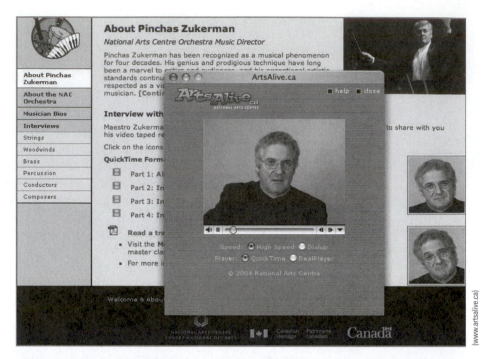

FIGURE 23.16
ArtsAlive

FIGURE 23.17
Berklee Shares

and teachers can direct their young composition students to these sites to listen to music. As programs like Apple's GarageBand become more commonly used and bandwidth and space restrictions lessen, more and more Internet-based sites will emerge for sharing creative thinking in music.

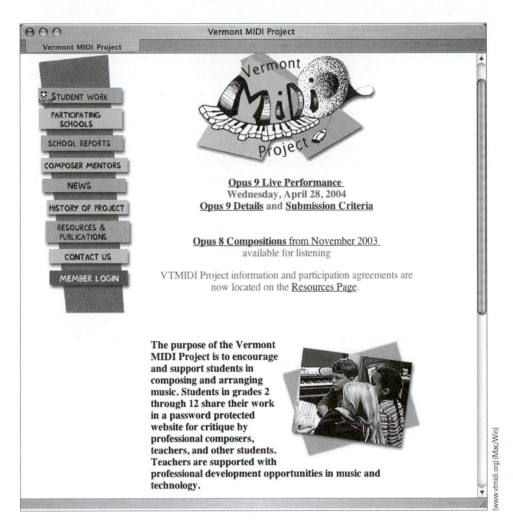

FIGURE 23.18
Vermont MIDI Project

DVD-ROM
Project 19 Evaluating CAI Music Programs

What to Choose: A Matter of Content and Need

It should now be clear that you have many choices for adding computer-aided instruction to your studio, rehearsal, or classroom. In the opening pages of this book, we pointed to the important first question that you need to ask: "What do I want the technology to do?" Choosing software is really an extension of your philosophy of music teaching and of what you want the music experience to be. Now that you have seen some examples of software using different approaches with different music content, consider these questions as a guide:

- What can the software best help to teach when I'm not around?
- Do I want the software to stress factual information, aural skills, or creative thinking?
- Am I only interested in software that reinforces performance ability?
- What is an acceptable balance between sound and visual information?
- Do I want the software to concentrate on shorter units of sound or longer ones?
- Do I want to control the content and the order of that content, or do I want to allow the student a good deal of freedom?

Here are some additional factors to consider as you attempt to answer these questions:

- **Age.** This is the most obvious factor, but often the most misunderstood. With the exception of software specifically designed for young children, no single program or program set should be considered appropriate for one age level alone. For example, drill-and-practice software should not be considered as appropriate only for adolescents and exploratory or creative titles as suitable only for adults. The reverse may actually be true for certain people. A decision to use a particular software title should not rest on age, but on readiness and internal motivation, which often comes from natural curiosity.
- **Learning style.** Research continues to demonstrate that individuals learn in different ways. Some learn best when sound is augmented by visual cues, others when sound is augmented with words, still others when it is augmented with physical movement. Choosing software to match learning-style preference is important.
- **Flexible choice.** Some individuals learn best when given choices about such things as drill criteria, time needed to use the software, music style, and aesthetic decision making. Others just want to be told what to do, and still others like a combination of these two methods.
- **Transfer.** We hope, and sometimes incorrectly assume, that students transfer understanding about one aspect of music to another (e.g., transferring rhythmic understanding to the ability to sing melodies). A good question to ask about music software is how well it helps transfer music learning between skills.
- **Technology itself.** Some students just don't like using computer technology to learn, period. If this is the case, you should not force the issue. Computer-aided music instruction is not for everyone.

Software from Past Viewports and CAI

Many software examples in this module stress music production, the very topic that has concerned us in previous Viewports. We need to stress how important all of the software in past Viewports is to music education. Although many products are written exclusively for music teaching and learning, which we are reviewing in this final section of the book, there are also many powerful ways that teachers can use the Internet and other software programs for digital audio, MIDI sequencing, sound design, and music notation within a music curriculum.

Table 23.2 provides a sample of the many tasks that can be planned for students using software described previously, as well as titles from this Viewport. In addition, we suggest how each Viewport might contribute to supporting the important National Standards in Music Education. These standards, published in 1994, have been an important part of curriculum design in the United States. Whether the goal is to involve students in knowledge and skill development or encourage creative thinking in music, software from this and all the other Viewports plays an important role in great music teaching.

TABLE 23.2 Software from Other Viewports Related to Typical Student Tasks and National Standards for Art Education (Music)*

Viewport	Topic	Student Task	National Standard*	Representative Software
II	Computer and Internet Concepts	• Browsing the Web for music information • Chatting with friends about music	6, 7, 8, 9	Internet Explorer, Safari, iChat
III	Capturing, Editing, and Storing Digital Audio	• Obtaining MP3 files from the Web for personal enjoyment and projects • Producing and editing digital audio for a website	6, 7	iTunes, QuickTime, Audacity, Winamp, Sound Forge Audio Studio
IV	Multiple Tracks and Channels of Digital Audio	• Recording and burning a CD for a school band, orchestra, or choir • Creating a dance loop for the school prom	1, 2	Audition, Deck, ACID Express, GarageBand, Toast
V	MIDI Sequencing and Digital Audio	• Forming a MIDI group and recording music • Combining MIDI and audio tracks for a personal web page	2	Logic Express, Cubase SE, Home Studio
VI	Sound Shaping and Synthesis	• Designing music for a play or dance recital • Producing digital-movie music for an integrated arts activity	8	Digital Performer, SONAR, Reason
VII	Music Notation	• Creating a music score for a composition contest • Arranging for a group and printing parts	4, 5	PrintMusic!, Finale, Sibelius
VIII	Computer-Aided Instruction	• Learning to sight-sing melodies • Learning to play with accompaniment • Learning to improvise and compose • Learning to listen	1, 2, 3, 4, 6	Practica Musica, SmartMusic, Band-in-a-Box, Making Music, Hearing Music

*National Standards for Arts Education (Music)

1. Singing, alone and with others, a varied repertoire of music.
2. Performing on instruments, alone and with others, a varied repertoire of music.
3. Improvising melodies, variations, and accompaniments.
4. Composing and arranging music within specified guidelines.
5. Reading and notating music.
6. Listening to, analyzing, and describing music.
7. Evaluating music and music performances.
8. Understanding relationships among music, the other arts, and disciplines outside the arts.
9. Understanding music in relation to history and culture.

Putting It All Together

DVD-ROM
All the tutorials described in this Viewport are available in Mac and PC versions on the accompanying DVD-ROM.

> ". . . and go on till you come to the end: then stop."
>
> —Alice in Wonderland, *Lewis Carroll*

Over the past eight Viewports, we have led you through many exciting experiences in the world of music technology. As you reach the end of your journey, we'd like to review the support materials provided on the DVD-ROM accompanying the textbook. It is time to "put it all together" and use your newly acquired skills and knowledge to do wonderful, creative things with music and music technology.

LINK
Consult our website: www.emtbook.net for more project tutorials and additional resources!

DVD-ROM Tutorial Materials and Selected Readings

Table 24.1 reviews the topics covered in the Viewports and provides a list of the tutorials available on the DVD-ROM. You may seek out any of these tutorials written for Mac or PC software to learn new techniques and acquaint yourself with a new software title. The various software applications relevant to each Viewport are noted in the last column of the table.

As another resource to help further your study of music technology, we have prepared a list of selected readings to parallel each Viewport of the textbook. You will find the Selected Readings list in the Appendix at the end of the book. Here is a wealth of titles that should help you pursue any topic of interest in more depth or just help satisfy your curiosity about music software, hardware, or data concepts discussed in these pages.

Expanding Your Skills and Creative Urge

Learning new skills is the first step. We encourage you, however, to go the extra mile and devise projects that help you assimilate these skills and produce creative experiences that showcase your understanding. Perhaps your instruction will require a large final project and you need ideas. To help you, Table 24.1 provides some suggestions to get the "creative juices" flowing, so to speak.

When you set out to do a project of this nature, it is helpful to do some pre-planning design work. Take a piece of paper or start up your word processor and ask yourself the following questions:

TABLE 24.1 Suggested Projects for Creative Experiences from the DVD-ROM Tutorials

Viewport	Topics	Tutorials	Creative Projects	Software
II	Computer and Internet Concepts	3. Setting Up and Understanding Your Computer 4. Surfing and Searching the Web for Music Resources	• Use the Web to study a new topic about music technology • Participate in a chat group to learn more about some topic in music • Set up your own web log, web page, or newsgroup on a music interest • Research the location of free WiFi wireless access in your community	Internet Explorer, Safari, iChat or AOL Instant Messenger, HTML/web-page editor of your choice
III	Capturing, Editing, and Storing Digital Audio	5. Using MP3 Jukebox Software 6. Basics of Digital Audio Editors 7. Applying Effects with Digital Audio Editors	• Obtain legal MP3 files from the Web to build a collection on one artist or group • Create a digital remix from an existing recording to share with others • Research the differences in audio quality between different MP3, WMA, and AAC digital-recording bit rates	iTunes, Audacity
IV	Multiple Tracks and Channels of Digital Audio	8. Recording and Basic Editing with Multitrack Recorders 9. Creating a Loop-Based Composition 10. Mixing, Mastering, and Burning a CD	• Record and burn a CD for a band, choir, or other musical group • Create a set of dance loops to share with others • Convert a stereo mix into a multi-channel audio recording • Study the differences in surround-sound formats among various commercial DVD-audio recordings • Research what surround-sound format was used for a set of your favorite movies	Deck LE, Audition, GarageBand, ACID Music Studio, Toast with Jam, and Easy Media Creator
V	MIDI Sequencing and Digital Audio	11. Editing MIDI Tracks with Basic Sequencing Software and Evaluating CAI Music Programs 12. Working with Audio and MIDI Tracks	• Form a MIDI group and record the performance • Combine MIDI and audio tracks for a recording and burn a CD • Compare the features of three popular MIDI-keyboard workstations and shop for pricing on the Web • Decode the MIDI implementation chart for a MIDI instrument	Cubase SE

• What is my *goal* for this project? What do I want to accomplish? What audience will it address?
• What will the final project look like? What is a *brief description* of what I hope to end up with when it is completed?
• What resources will I need? What software? Hardware? Will I need to do some research by surfing the Web, talking with people, or going to a bookstore or the library? What music do I need? Sound files? Graphics to scan or create on my own?
• What steps should I go through from beginning to completion? (Don't be too detailed here; just quickly draft out the steps. This process will help you think of things you hadn't thought about initially.)

Viewport	Topics	Tutorials	Creative Projects	Software
TABLE 24.1 *(continued)*				
VI	Sound Shaping and Synthesis	13. Advanced Features of Digital-Audio Workstation Software 14. Working with a Virtual Studio	• Design music for a play or dance • Take the video from an old silent-film clip and create a new music sound track • Experiment with different MIDI controllers other than keyboards • Build your own simple MIDI controller	Logic Express/Logic Pro, Home Studio, XL/SONAR 4, Reason
VII	Music Notation	15. Beginning Note-Entry Skills 16. More Notation Skills and Music Scanning	• Scan sheet music you like and recreate it in a notation program • Take a popular song, create an arrangement for a group, and print the parts • Find a way to publish some music on the Web	Finale, Sibelius, PhotoScore, Smartscore
VIII	Computer-Aided Instruction	17. Practicing Your Aural Skills 18. Learning to Improvise 19. Evaluating CAI Music Programs	• Learn some new music-theory concepts • Learn to play with accompaniment • Use software to generate a MIDI accompaniment for a song you like • Help someone else learn something new about music or create a music experience	Auralia, MiBAC, Practica Musica, Band-in-a-Box, and other CAI titles

DVD-ROM
The Creative Project Template is on the main home page of the DVD-ROM.

• How will I use the finished project? How will I share it with others? (This may well affect the format you use for the completed project.)

On the DVD-ROM, we have included a Creative Project Template you can print out or use with your word processor to help document your project-planning work. Look under the materials on the main home page of the DVD-ROM.

Closing Note

Reading each module within each Viewport and experimenting with some of the software and hardware described should provide you with an excellent foundation for understanding technology and its role in supporting the music experience.

One of our hopes in writing this book was to provide as complete an introduction to the topic of music technology as our space restrictions would allow. The large amount of technical information included is in a constant state of change and evolution. Despite our focus on the broad issues of music technology, some technical details will have undoubtedly changed by the time you read this. Although we have tried to anticipate important developments in software, hardware, and data structures, we probably will miss a few. This is to be expected and, quite honestly, is not that crucial. There are far more important, overarching issues to remember that do not change. We will leave you with these.

Music technology is as old as music itself. There is a long tradition of experimentation that began with the earliest curiosities about sound and extend today to computers, laser technology, MIDI devices, and extremely sophisticated software applications. This is part of music and always will be.

Technology is a tool. Historically, it has been used to support the music experience and it continues to fulfill that role today. No amount of technology can make poor music better. Beautiful music and the aesthetic experience that surrounds it can only be enhanced with technological assistance. Those who understand the potential in this principle stand to gain the most.

Finally, people are the most important component of any music-technology application. The magic happens when you use your creative abilities to make sounds expressive of feeling. Sophisticated hardware, software, and data provide nothing by themselves. The power of the human mind and spirit to use these resources for producing art is the essential point.

Good luck! Enjoy your adventures in putting it all together!

Appendix A

Selected Readings by Viewport

I. Books of Interest Organized by Viewport Topics

Viewport I: Musicians and Their Use of Technology

Braun, Hans-Joachim, and International Committee for the History of Technology. *Music and Technology in the Twentieth Century*. Baltimore: Johns Hopkins University Press, 2002.

Kettlewell, Ben. *Electronic Music Pioneers*. Vallejo, CA: www.artistpro.com, 2001.

Kurzweil, Ray. *The Age of Intelligent Machines*. Cambridge, MA: MIT Press, 1990.

———. *The Age of Spiritual Machines: When Computers Exceed Human Intelligence*. New York: Viking, 1999.

Naisbitt, John, Nana Naisbitt, and Douglas Philips. *High Tech, High Touch: Technology and Our Search for Meaning*. 1st ed. New York: Broadway Books, 1999.

Negroponte, Nicholas. *Being Digital*. 1st ed. New York: Knopf, 1995.

Pinch, T. J., and Frank Trocco. *Analog Days: The Invention and Impact of the Moog Synthesizer*. Cambridge, MA: Harvard University Press, 2002.

Tapscott, Don. *Growing up Digital: The Rise of the Net Generation*. New York: McGraw-Hill, 1998.

Turkle, Sherry. *The Second Self: Computers and the Human Spirit*. New York: Simon Schuster, 1984.

———. *Life on the Screen: Identity in the Age of the Internet*. New York: Simon & Schuster, 1995.

Viewport II: Computer and Internet Concepts for Musicians

Abrahams, Paul W., and Bruce R. Larson. *Unix for the Impatient*. 2nd ed. Reading, MA: Addison Wesley Pub. Co., 1996.

Ackermann, Ernest C., and Karen Hartman. *Searching and Researching on the Internet and the World Wide Web*. 3rd ed. Wilsonville, OR: Franklin, Beedle, 2003.

Coursey, David. *Mac OS X for Windows Users: A Switchers' Guide*. Berkeley, CA: Peachpit, 2003.

Engst, Adam C., and David Pogue. *Crossing Platforms: A Macintosh/Windows Phrasebook*. 1st ed. Sebastopol, CA: O'Reilly, 1999.

Fehily, Chris. *Windows XP, Visual Quickstart Guide*. Berkeley, CA: Peachpit, 2003.

Feiler, Jesse. *Mac OS X: The Complete Reference*. New York: McGraw-Hill/Osborne, 2003.

Fishman, Stephen. *The Public Domain: How to Find Copyright-Free Writings, Music, Art & More*. 1st ed. Berkeley, CA: www.nolo.com, 2001.

Gagnâe, Marcel. *Moving to Linux: Kiss the Blue Screen of Death Goodbye!* Boston: Addison Wesley, 2004.

Hafner, Katie, and Matthew Lyon. *Where Wizards Stay up Late: The Origins of the Internet*. New York: Simon & Schuster, 1996.

Lindsey, Marc. *Copyright Law on Campus*. Pullman: Washington State University Press, 2003.

Litman, Jessica. *Digital Copyright : Protecting Intellectual Property on the Internet*. Amherst, NY: Prometheus Books, 2001.

Maran, Ruth. *Teach Yourself Visually Mac OS X, Visual Read Less, Learn More*. Indianapolis: Wiley, 2003.

Mash, David. *Musicians and the Internet*. Miami, FL: Warner Bros., 1998.

Pfaffenberger, Bryan. *Webster's New World Computer Dictionary*. 9th ed. New York: Hungry Minds, 2001.

Phillips, Dave. *Linux Music & Sound: How to Install, Configure, and Use Linux Audio Software*. San Francisco: No Starch Press, 2000.

Pogue, David. *The Missing Manual. Mac OS X*. 2nd ed. Sebastopol, CA: Pogue Press/O'Reilly, 2002.

Ray, Deborah S., and Eric J. Ray. *Unix, Visual Quickstart Guide*. 2nd ed. Berkeley, CA: Peachpit, 2003.

Reid, Robert. *Architects of the Web: 1,000 Days that Built the Future of Business*. New York: John Wiley, 1997.

White, Ron, and Timothy Edward Downs. *How Computers Work*. 7th ed. Indianapolis: Que, 2004.

Viewport III: Digital Audio Basics

Apple Computer Inc. *Quicktime for the Web: A Hands-on Guide for Webmasters, Site Designers, and HTML Authors, QuickTime Developer Series*. San Diego; London: Morgan Kaufmann, 2000.

Appleton, Jon H. *21st-Century Musical Instruments: Hardware and Software, I.S.A.M. Monographs: No. 29*. Brooklyn: Institute for Studies in American Music, Conservatory of Music, Brooklyn College of the City University of New York, 1989.

Appleton, Jon H., and Ronald Perera. *The Development and Practice of Electronic Music.* Englewood Cliffs, NJ: Prentice-Hall, 1975.

Breen, Christopher. *Secrets of the iPod.* Berkeley, CA: Peachpit, 2002.

Dodge, Charles, and Thomas A. Jerse. *Computer Music: Synthesis, Composition, and Performance.* 2nd ed. New York: Schirmer Books, 1997.

Eargle, John. *Music, Sound, and Technology.* 2nd ed. New York: Van Nostrand Reinhold, 1995.

Ernst, David. *The Evolution of Electronic Music.* New York: Schirmer Books, 1977.

Franks, D. E. *Acid Power!* Cincinnati, OH: Muska & Lipman, 2001.

Garrigus, Scott R. *Sound Forge Power!* Cincinnati, OH: Muska & Lipman, 2001.

Hill, Brad. *The Digital Songstream: Mastering the World of Digital Music.* New York: Routledge, 2003.

Hill, Dave. *Ableton 2.0 Live Power!* Indianapolis: Muska & Lipman, 2003.

Keane, John. *A Musician's Guide to Pro Tools.* Paperback ed. Athens, GA: Supercat Press, 2002.

Keating, Carolyn, and Craig Anderton. *Digital Home Recording.* San Francisco/Emeryville, CA: Miller Freeman [distributor], 1998.

Pohlmann, Ken C. *Principles of Digital Audio. McGraw-Hill Video/Audio Professional.* 4th ed. New York: McGraw-Hill, 2000.

Rathbone, Andy. *MP3 for Dummies.* 2nd ed. New York: Hungry Minds, 2001.

Strong, Jeff. *Home Recording for Musicians for Dummies.* New York: Hungry Minds, 2002.

Viewport IV: Doing More with Digital Audio

Anderton, Craig. *Audio Mastering.* Bremen, Germany: Wizoo, 2002.

Bellingham, Dave. *Logic Audio Workshop.* New York: Amsco Music, 2003.

Chappell, Jon. *Build Your Own PC Recording Studio.* Paperback ed. Berkley, CA: McGraw-Hill/Osborne, 2003.

Eargle, John. *The Microphone Book.* Boston: Focal Press, 2001.

———. *Handbook of Recording Engineering.* 4th ed. Boston: Kluwer, 2003.

Edstrom, Brent. *Making Music with Your Computer.* Ann Arbor, MI: EMBooks, 2000.

Garrigus, Scott R. *Cakewalk Power!* Paperback ed. Cincinnati, OH: Muska & Lipman, 2000.

Katz, Bob. *Mastering Audio: The Art and the Science.* Paperback ed. Boston: Focal Press, 2002.

Pohlmann, Ken C. *Advanced Digital Audio.* 1st. ed. Carmel, IN: SAMS, 1991.

———. *The Compact Disc Handbook. The Computer Music and Digital Audio Series; V. 5.* 2nd ed. Madison, WI: A-R Editions, 1992.

Poyser, Debbie. *Users' Guide to Propellerhead Reason 2.* 1st ed. Cincinnati, OH: Muska & Lipman, 2002.

Rudolph, Thomas E., and Vincent A. Leonard. *Recording in the Digital World: Complete Guide to Studio Gear and Software, Berklee Guide.* Boston: Berklee Press, 2001.

Viewport V: Music Sequencing and MIDI Basics

Alexander, Peter. *How MIDI Works.* 6th ed. Milwaukee, WI: Hal Leonard, 2001.

Guerin, Robert. *Cubase SX Power!* Cincinnati, OH: Muska & Lipman, 2002.

———. *MIDI Power!* Cincinnati, OH: Muska & Lipman, 2002.

Huber, David Miles. *The MIDI Manual: A Practical Guide to MIDI in the Project Studio.* 2nd ed. Boston: Focal Press, 1999.

Jungleib, Stanley. *General MIDI, The Computer Music and Digital Audio Series; V. 11.* Madison, WI: A-R Editions, 1995.

Muro, Don. *Sequencing Basics.* Miami, FL: Warner Bros., 1998.

Rothstein, Joseph. *MIDI: A Comprehensive Introduction. The Computer Music and Digital Audio Series; V. 7.* 2nd ed. Madison, WI: A-R Editions, 1995.

White, Paul. *Basic MIDI.* Paperback ed. London: Sanctuary Publishing, 2000.

Whitmore, Lee. *MIDI Basics.* Miami, FL: Warner Bros., 1998.

Viewport VI: Doing More with Digital Audio

Aikin, Jim. *Software Synthesizers.* San Francisco: Backbeat Books, 2003.

Anderton, Craig. *Reason.* Bremen, Germany: Wizoo, 2001.

Cope, David. *Experiments in Musical Intelligence, The Computer Music and Digital Audio Series; Vol. 12.* Madison, WI: A-R Editions, 1996.

———. *The Algorithmic Composer, The Computer Music and Digital Audio Series; Vol. 16.* Madison, WI: A-R Editions, 2000.

Cope, David, and Douglas R. Hofstadter. *Virtual Music: Computer Synthesis of Musical Style.* Cambridge, MA: MIT Press, 2001.

Garrigus, Scott R. *Sonar 3 Power!* Paperback ed. Cincinnati, OH: Muska & Lipman, 2003.

Moylan, William. *The Art of Recording: Understanding and Crafting the Mix.* Boston: Focal Press, 2002.

Penfold, R. A. *Advanced MIDI User's Guide.* 2nd ed. Tonbridge, England: PC Publishing, 1995.

Sasso, Len. *Reaktor 3.* Bremen, Germany: Wizoo, 2002.

———. *Emagic Logic Tips and Tricks.* Indianapolis: Muska & Lipman, 2003.

Sitter, Martin. *Apple Pro Training Series: Logic 6.* Berkeley, CA: Peachpit, 2003.

Steiglitz, Kenneth. *A DSP Primer: With Applications to Digital Audio and Computer Music.* Menlo Park, CA: Addison Wesley, 1996.

Yonet, Henri. *Digital Performer 4 Power!* Paperback ed. Indianapolis: Muska & Lipman, 2004.

Viewport VII: Music Notation

Byrd, Donald Alvin. "Music Notation by Computer (Formatting)." In *DAI,* 46, No. 01B, (1984): 0230, 1984.

Finn, Ben, and Sibelius Software. *Sibelius 2, User Guide.* Ed. 2.0. Cambridge, UK: Sibelius Software, 2001.

Hewlett, Walter B., and Eleanor Selfridge-Field. *The Virtual Score: Representation, Retrieval, Restoration, Computing in Musicology, 12.* Cambridge, MA: MIT Press, 2001.

Krummel, Donald William, and Stanley Sadie. *Music Printing and Publishing. Norton/Grove Handbooks in Music.* 1st American ed. New York: W. W. Norton, 1990.

Purse, Bill. *The Finale Primer: Mastering the Art of Music Notation with Finale.* 2nd ed. San Francisco: Miller Freeman, 2000.

———. *The Finale Notepad Primer.* San Francisco: Backbeat Books, 2003.

Read, Gardner. *Music Notation: A Manual of Modern Practice.* 2nd ed. London: Gollancz, 1974.

———. *20th-Century Microtonal Notation, Contributions to the Study of Music and Dance,* No. 18. New York: Greenwood Press, 1990.

Rubin, David M. *The Desktop Musician.* Berkeley, CA: McGraw-Hill/Osborne, 1995.

Rudolph, Thomas E., and Vincent A. Leonard. *Finale: An Easy Guide to Music Notation.* Boston: Berklee Press, 2002.

Selfridge-Field, Eleanor. *Beyond MIDI: The Handbook of Musical Codes.* Cambridge, MA: MIT Press, 1997.

Viewport VIII: Computer-Aided Instruction in Music

Berz, William L., Judith Bowman, and Music Educators National Conference (MENC) (U.S.). *Applications of Research in Music Technology.* Reston, VA: MENC, 1994.

Consortium of National Arts Education Associations. *Dance, Music, Theatre, Visual Arts: What Every Young American Should Know and Be Able to Do in the Arts: National Standards for Arts Education.* Reston, VA: MENC, 1994.

Hickey, Maud. *Why and How to Teach Music Composition: A New Horizon for Music Education.* Reston, VA: MENC, 2003.

Reese, Sam, Kimberly McCord, Kimberly C. Walls, and MENC (U.S.). *Strategies for Teaching: Technology, MENC's Strategies for Teaching Series.* Reston, VA: MENC, 2001.

Rudolph, Thomas E. *Teaching Music with Technology.* Chicago: GIA, 1996.

———. *Technology Strategies.* Wyncote, PA: Technology Institute for Music Educators, 1997.

Webster, Peter R. "Computer-based Technology and Music Teaching and Learning." In R. Colwell and C. Richardson (eds.), *The New Handbook of Research on Music Teaching and Learning* (pp. 416–439). New York: Oxford University Press, 2002.

Wiggins, Jackie. *Synthesizers in the Elementary Music Classroom: An Integrated Approach.* Reston, VA: MENC, 1991.

II. Important Periodical Literature in Music Technology

Computer Music Journal
mitpress2.mit.edu/e-journals/computer-music-journal

Electronic Musician
www.emusician.com

Keyboard Magazine
www.keyboardmag.com/

Computer Music
www.computermusic.co.uk

Mix
www.mixonline.com

Appendix B

EMT Workstation Equipment Codes

1. Computer workstation
2. Hard disk
3. CD-R, DVD-R Drive
4. Printer
5. Multichannel digital I/O
6. Scanner
7. Internet connection
8. Receiver/amplifier
9. Zip, flash, or other removable media
10. Speakers
11. Headphones
12. Microphone
13. Mixer
14. Electric guitar
15. MP3 player
16. MiniDisc, DAT, tape recorder
17. USB/Mixer/DAW/MIDI controller
18. Multichannel integrated speakers
19. Surround-sound DA conversion
20. MIDI workstation
21. MIDI keyboard controller
22. MIDI interface/patchbay
23. Drum pad/controller
24. MIDI guitar
25. Wind controller
26. GM2 sound module

Guide to EMT Workstations

EMT Workstation	Description	Location in Text
1	Basic Computer Workstation	VP II, Mod 7, p. 58
2	No-Frills Digital Audio Workstation	VP III, Mod 10, p. 129
3	No-Frills Digital Audio Workstation with Mixer	VP III, Mod 10, p. 135
4	Multichannel Digital Audio Workstation with S/PDIF	VP IV, Mod 13, p. 200
4B	Multichannel Digital Audio Workstation with S/PDIF and Surround Sound	VP IV. Mod 13, p. 205
5	No-Frills MIDI Workstation	VP V, Mod 16, p. 256
6	MIDI and Digital Audio Workstation with Added MIDI Controllers	VP VI, Mod 18, p. 313
7	No-Frills Notation Workstation with Printer and Scanner	VP VII, Mod 21, p. 398

Index

A

AAC file format, 55, 98, 99
ABC computer, 7
Absynth, 301
Acid, 282
ACID Pro, 184–187, 192, 193
Acoustic controllers, 258, 311
Acoustic Mirror effect, 124–125
Acoustics, 81–90
    amplitude, 85–86
    envelopes, 86–87
    frequency, 84–85
    harmonic spectrum, 87–89
    and perceptual properties of sound,
      81–83
    vibrations, 84
Adams, Ricci, 437
Adaptive Difference Pulse Code
    Modulation (ADPCM)
    compression, 97
ADAT interface, 200
ADAT recorder, 207
ADAT time sync, 328–329
ADC See Analog-to-digital converter
    (ADC)
Additive synthesis, 99–100
Addresses, Internet
    e-mail internet addresses, 51
    server Internet addresses, 50–51
Adobe Acrobat, 353
Adobe Acrobat Reader, 54
ADPCM See Adaptive Difference
    Pulse Code Modulation
    (ADPCM) compression
ADSR See Attack/decay/sustain/release
    (ADSR)

AES/EBU See Audio Engineering
    Society/European Broadcast
    Union (AES/EBU) digital
    interface
Aesthetic dimension, 12
Affective dimension, 12
AIF file format, 55, 96
Aimi, Roberto, 318
Alfred's Essentials of Music Theory,
    420
Aliasing, 94
"All in one" virtual studio software,
    304–308
ALMA, 344
Altiverb, 182–183
Alvarez, Ruben, 422
Amadeus al fine, 400
Ames, Charles, 14
Amplifiers, 5
Amplitude, 85–86, 118–119
Analog audio, 28
Analog/digital conversions,
    46–47
    of sound, 90–95
Analog synthesis, 99–100
Analog-to-digital converter (ADC),
    128–129
Analytical Engine, 61
Anastasia font, 355
Andreeson, Marc, 11
Apple Computer, 29, 61
Appleton, John, 10, 297
Arithmometer, 4
ARP synthesizers, 100
Arranging, with music notation
    software, 379–380
Articulation, 83

Articulations, music notation software,
    381–382
ArtsAlive website, 439
ArtsEdge Xploring Xtremes website,
    439
ASCII file formats, 49, 53–54
ASIO, 115
Ask Jeeves, 40
Association for Technology in Music
    Instruction (ATMI), 22–23
Atanasoff, John, 9
ATMI See Association for Technology
    in Music Instruction (ATMI)
Attack, 299
Attack/decay/sustain/release (ADSR),
    86–87
Attaignant, Pierre, 339
Attitudes about music technology,
    12–13, 20
Audacity, 111, 112, 113
Audio, digital See Digital audio
Audio Engineering Society/European
    Broadcast Union (AES/EBU)
    digital interface, 200
Audition, 100, 111, 172, 174, 175,
    176–177, 178, 192
Auralia, 413
Autoscore, 400
AVI file format, 56

B

Babbage, Charles, 4, 9, 61
Babbage Difference Engine, 4
Babbitt, Milton, 9
Bach, Johannes Sebastian, 13
Backing up, 34